# New Pocket Hawaiian Dictionary

# New Pocket Hawaiian Dictionary

### with a Concise Grammar and Given Names in Hawaiian

MARY KAWENA PUKUI
SAMUEL H. ELBERT

WITH ESTHER T. MOOKINI AND YU MAPUANA NISHIZAWA

University of Hawaii Press
Honolulu

09  08  07  06  05  04    13  12  11  10  9  8

**Library of Congress Cataloging-in-Publication Data**

Pukui, Mary Kawena, 1895–
  [Pocket Hawaiian dictionary]
  New pocket Hawaiian dictionary : with a concise grammar and given
names in Hawaiian / Mary Kawena Pukui, Samuel H. Elbert ;
with Esther T. Mookini and Yu Mapuana Nishizawa.
        p.   cm.
  Originally published: The pocket Hawaiian dictionary. Honolulu :
University Press of Hawaii, [1975]
  Includes bibliographical references.
  ISBN 0-8248-1392-8
  1. Hawaiian language—Dictionaries—English.  2. English
language—Dictionaries—Hawaiian.   I. Elbert, Samuel H., 1907–
II. Title.
PL6446.P84        1992
899'.4—dc20                                          91-25854
                                                         CIP

University of Hawai'i Press books are printed on acid-free
paper and meet the guidelines for permanence and durability
of the Council on Library Resources.


Printed by Offset Paperback Mfrs., Inc.


www.uhpress.hawaii.edu

*E kuhikuhi pono i na au iki a me na au nui o ka 'ike.*
Instruct well in the little and the large currents of knowledge.

*'Ōlelo No'eau*, Pukui

# Contents

# Preface

The *New Pocket Hawaiian Dictionary* contains more than 10,800 entries from the approximately 41,500 entries in the *Hawaiian Dictionary: Hawaiian-English and English-Hawaiian,* Revised and Enlarged Edition, 1986, selected on the basis of frequency of usage and cultural importance. The scientific names of plants and animals have been updated.

The revision has benefited from the work of Yu Mapuana Nishizawa of Japan, who has recently published her translation of the *Hawaiian-English Pocket Dictionary.* A star hula dancer, she has added hula terms and has carefully checked the important *'okina* 'glottal stop' and the macron over long stressed vowels, as well as the entire manuscript.

Not all the Hawaiian equivalents of the English entries are included here. This would have doubled or tripled the number of entries on the Hawaiian side and it would no longer be a pocket dictionary. For these words the interested reader may consult the latest edition of the *Hawaiian Dictionary,* and incidentally be impressed with the richness of the Hawaiian language.

The concise grammar following the English-Hawaiian section is still concise and contains simple spelling rules.

The section on English given names used in Hawai'i includes names popular in the last few decades, such as Cheryl, Dawn, Darryl, Greg, Karen, Kevin, Kim, Jennifer, Sandra, and Toy.

Our thanks to Eileen D'Araujo, who copyedited the *New Pocket Hawaiian Dictionary.* Her experience as a scientific editor along with her knowledge of the Islands have enhanced the accuracy of this work. Iris Wiley's efforts, strongly seconded by University of Hawaii Press directors Robert W. Sparks and William Hamilton, have enabled the Pukui and Elbert publications to remain available for many decades for the people of Hawai'i and for Polynesianists everywhere.

SAMUEL H. ELBERT

# Pronunciation of Hawaiian

## Consonants

**p, k**   about as in English but with less aspiration.

**h, l, m, n**   about as in English.

**w**   after *i* and *e* usually like *v;* after *u* and *o* usually like *w;* initially and after *a* like *v* or *w*.

**'**   a glottal stop, similar to the sound between the *oh's* in English *oh-oh*.

## Vowels

*Unstressed*

|   |   |   |
|---|---|---|
| **a** | like *a* in above | |
| **e** | like *e* in bet | |
| **i** | like *y* in city | but without off-glides. |
| **o** | like *o* in sole | |
| **u** | like *oo* in moon | |

*Stressed*

|   |   |   |
|---|---|---|
| **a, ā** | like *a* in far | |
| **e** | like *e* in bet | |
| **ē** | like *ay* in play | but without off-glides; vowels |
| **i, ī** | like *ee* in see | marked with macrons are some- |
| **o, ō** | like *o* in sole | what longer than other vowels. |
| **u, ū** | like *oo* in moon | |

## Diphthongs

**ei, eu, oi, ou, ai, ae, ao, au**   these are always stressed on the first member, but the two members are not as closely joined as in English.

## Stress

On all diphthongs and vowels marked with macrons.

Otherwise on the next-to-last syllable and alternating preceding syllables of words, except that words containing five syllables without macrons or diphthongs are stressed on the first and fourth syllables. Final stress in a word (′) is usually louder than preceding stress or stresses (`): *hále, maká'u, hòlohólo, 'èlemakúle*. A few words are stressed: Kamèhaméha, *lùmalumá'i*.

For more details see section 2 of the Grammar.

# Abbreviations Used in the Dictionary

Cap.      beginning with a capital letter
Cf.       compare
Demon.    demonstrative
Eng.      of English origin
Fig.      figuratively
Lit.      literally
Redup.    reduplication
Syn.      synonym
Var.      variant

# Hawaiian-English

# A

**a.** Of.

**-a.** Passive/imperative suffix.

**ā.** 1. Jaw. 2. When, at the time when, until, to, and.

**'a.** Oh! Well! Ah!

**'a-.** Numeral prefix.

**'ā.** Fiery, burning. **ho'ā.** To set on fire, light.

**'ā-.** In the nature of. See *'āhina.*

**a'a.** Small root, vein, nerve, tendon.

**'a'a.** 1. To dare, challenge. 2. To gird, tie on. 3. Bag, pocket; fiber from coconut husk.

**'a'ā.** 1. To burn; glowing. **hō'a'ā.** To kindle, light. 2. *'A'ā* lava; stony, abounding with rough *'a'ā* lava.

**'ā'ā.** 1. Dumbness; to stutter, stammer. 2. Dwarf, small person. 3. Demented, panic-stricken. **hō'ā'ā.** To look about in confusion. 4. Male *'ō'ō* bird.

**'a'ahu.** Clothing in general; to put on or wear clothing. See *'ahu.*

**'a'ahuā.** To speak reproachfully; jealous challenge.

**'a'ai.** 1. Redup. of *'ai, 1;* eating, spreading, increasing (as a sore). 2. Bright, as of contrasting colors.

**'a'aiole.** Inferior, weak. *Fig.,* of persons dying before their time.

**'a'aka.** Surly, cranky, roiled.

**'a'aki.** Redup. of *'aki, 1;* to nip repeatedly. *Fig.,* thick, obscure, dark, penetrating.

**a'a koko.** Vein, blood vessel.

**a'a kūkūkū.** Varicose veins. *Lit.,* raised veins.

**'a'ala.** Fragrant, sweet-smelling. *Fig.,* of high rank, royal.

**'a'ala'ula.** A branching, velvety green, succulent-appearing seaweed *(Codium edule).*

**a'alele.** Pulse. *Lit.,* leaping vein.

**'a'ali.** Redup. of *'ali, 1;* scarred, marked, grooved.

**'a'ali'i.** Native hardwood shrubs or trees *(Dodonaea,* all species).

**'a'alina.** 1. Scarred. 2. Large, fat, weak.

**'a'alo.** Redup. of *'alo, 1, 2.*

**'a'a lole.** Coconut cloth, European cloth.

**a'alolo.** Nerve. *Lit.,* brain vein.

**'a'alu.** Ravine, small stream, valley.

**'a'ama.** 1. A large, black, edible crab *(Grapsus grapsus tenuicrustatus)* that runs over shore rocks. 2. To spread and relax, as the fingers.

**'a'ā maka.** To stare with wide-open eyes, as in desire, fear, or intent to frighten. **hō'a'ā maka.** To stare.

**'a'amo'o.** Young coconut cloth; gauze. *Lit.,* lizard coconut cloth.

**'a'ana.** To use abusive language, revile.

**'a'anema.** To criticize maliciously.

**'a'a niu.** Coconut cloth.

**'a'ano.** Overbearing, arrogant, daring. **hō'a'ano.** To act the bully, boast of courage that is lacking; to challenge, dare.

**'a'api.** Warped, curved.

**'a'apo.** To learn quickly.

**'a'apu.** Coconut-shell cup; cup-like. **hō'a'apu.** To form a cup of the hollow of the hand; to fold a leaf into a cup.

**a'apūhaka.** Girdle, belt. *Lit.,* loin belt.

**'a'ā pu'upu'u.** Sharp or water-worn, coarse gravel or rock.

**'a'au.** To move here and there, rove.

**'ā'aua.** Coarse, as wrinkled or blotched skin.

**'a'awa.** Wrasse fishes, including hogfish *(Bodianus bilunulatus).*

**a'e.** 1. Several native trees, soap-berry *(Sapindus saponaria).* 2. *(Cap.)* Northeast trade wind. Cf. *Moa'e.* 3. To, upward, obliquely, sideways; next; then (directional particle). 4. Sign of the comparative degree.

3

**'ae.** 1. Yes; to say yes, consent, agree, approve. 2. Sap wrung from seaweed or leaves of plants such as taro; saliva, drooling of the mouth. 3. Fine, smooth. **hō'ae.** To make fine, soft, etc. 4. To rise (of the tide).

**'a'e.** To step over, get on top of, tread upon, trespass. *Fig.*, oppressed.

**aea.** To rise up; to raise the head; to come up from under water.

**'ae'a.** Wandering, shiftless, unstable; to wander. **hō'ae'a.** To cause to wander; to wander.

**aeae.** A prolonged sound, wail. **ho'āeae.** A style of chanting with prolonged vowels and fairly short phrases.

**a'ea'e.** Mixing of a dark or brilliant color with a lighter one, as feathers in a lei.

**'ae'ae.** Redup. of *'ae, 3.*

**'a'e'a'e.** Redup. of *'a'e.*

**'ae'a hauka'e.** Vagrant person, trespasser; to trespass.

**'ae kai.** Place where sea and land meet; water's edge.

**'aeko, aeto.** 1. Eagle. 2. Alto. *Eng.*

**'aeko kula.** Golden eagle.

**'aelike.** Agreement, contract, truce.

**āelo.** Rotten (of eggs that do not hatch due to infertility). *Fig.*, spoiled, worthless.

**a'e nei.** Just now, lately; nearby, not far; ordinary.

**ae'o.** 1. Stilts. 2. Hawaiian stilt (bird).

**āewa.** 1. Thin, spindly; to weave to and fro, as seaweed. 2. Possessing a family or lineage.

**aha.** Why? What? For what reason? To do what? *He aha kēlā?* What's that? *No ke aha?* Why?

**āhā.** Aha (exclamation of surprise).

**'aha.** 1. Meeting, assembly, gathering, court. 2. Sennit; cord braided of coconut husk or human hair; string for a musical instrument; measurement of an edge or border. **hō'aha.** To make or braid *'aha.*

**'ahā.** Four (usually in counting in a series); four times. *Pō'ahā,* Thursday.

**ahaaha.** To pant, to breathe hard with heat, as a dog.

**'aha'aha.** 1. Cordage. 2. To sit with back stiff and upright, arms akimbo, head up, as with haughty air of superiority.

**'aha'aina.** Feast, banquet; to feast. *Lit.*, meal gathering.

**'Aha'aina a ka Haku.** Holy Communion; feast of the Lord.

**'aha'aina ho'ola'a.** Feast of consecration or dedication, as of a house, church, canoe, or fish net.

**'aha'aina ho'omana'o.** Commemorative or anniversary feast.

**'aha'aina komo.** Initiation feast.

**'aha'aina laulima.** Feast held after completion of a joint project or cooperative undertaking, especially harvest.

**'aha'aina make.** Funeral feast, intended to comfort the mourners.

**'aha'aina male (mare).** Wedding feast or reception.

**'aha'aina māwaewae.** Feast given shortly after the birth of the first child, intended to clear the way *(māwaewae)* of misfortune for that child and for all others to follow.

**'Aha'aina Mōliaola.** Feast of the Passover.

**'Aha'aina Pelena (Berena).** Holy Communion. *Lit.*, feast of bread.

**'aha'aina piha makahiki.** Feast on the first birthday of a child, or to celebrate any anniversary. *Lit.*, feast for completion of the year.

**'aha'aina puka.** Graduation feast.

**'aha'aina. 'ūniki.** Graduation feast, as for hula dancing.

**'aha 'āpana.** District court.

**'aha 'elele.** Convention of delegates; name for American presidential conventions.

**ahahana.** Syllables repeated in chants; a taunting singsong teasing phrase, used especially by children.

**'aha hāwele.** Cord support for gourd water bottles.

**'aha hīmeni.** Song festival, concert.

**'aha hō'ike makahiki.** Annual meeting of Sunday schools, as of Congregationalists.

**'aha ho'okolokolo.** General name for court assembly.

**'aha ho'okolokolo 'āpana.** District court.

**'aha ho'okolokolo ho'omalu.** Police court.

**'aha ho'okolokolo ka'apuni.** Circuit court.

**'Aha Ho'okolokolo Ki'eki'e.** Supreme Court.

**'aha ho'okolokolo koa.** Military court.

**'aha ho'okolokolo ko'iko'i.** Superior court.

**'aha ho'omalu.** Administrative body, assembly.

**'aha ho'oponopono i ka nohona.** Court of domestic relations.

**'ahahui.** Society, club, association.

**'Ahahui Hō'ikaika Kalikiano.** Christian Endeavor Society.

**'ahahui hō'ole wai 'ona.** Temperance union.

**'Ahahui Kanu Kō Hawai'i.** Hawaiian Sugar Planters' Association.

**'ahahui kula Kāpaki (Sabati).** Sunday school association.

**'Ahahui Māmakakaua.** Sons and Daughters of Hawaiian Warriors. *Lit.,* warriors' society.

**'Ahahui Mo'olelo Hawai'i.** Hawaiian Historical Society.

**'āha'i.** To carry off, chase, rout; to flee, run away.

**'āha'iha'i.** Redup. of *'āha'i.*

**'aha iki.** Small gathering for private conversation; small or secret council.

**'aha'ilono.** Reporter, messenger, bringer of news; to tell the news.

**'aha inu.** Drinking party.

**'āha'i 'ōlelo.** Messenger; to carry word.

**'aha ka'apuni.** Circuit court.

**'aha kākau.** Court of records.

**'aha kau kānāwai.** Session of the legislature.

**'Aha Ki'eki'e.** Supreme Court.

**'ahakū.** Cord used for measuring.

**'aha kuhina.** Cabinet, assembly of ministers.

**'aha kūkā.** Council meeting, discussion meeting, conference.

**'ahalualike.** Rectangle. *Lit.,* two equal sides.

**'aha lunakahiko.** Meeting of elders.

**'aha lunakānāwai.** Judiciary session, meeting of judges.

**'aha maha.** Place or assembly for practice of athletic games. *Lit.,* assembly for relaxation.

**'aha mele.** Concert, song concert, song festival.

**'aha mokupuni.** Island conference, with representatives from a single island, especially of Congregationalists.

**ahana.** Same as *ahahana.*

**'aha'ōlelo.** Legislature, assembly; to hold such meetings.

**'aha'ōlelo kau kānāwai.** Legislature, law-making body.

**'aha'ōlelo lāhui.** Congress of the United States; national assembly.

**'aha'ōlelo nui.** Congress.

**'aha o nā lunakānāwai 'āpana.** District court.

**'aha pae'āina.** Convention of delegates from all the islands, especially one held by the Hawaiian Evangelical Association of Congregational Christian Churches.

**'aha pule.** Congregation, prayer assembly.

**ahe.** Breeze; to blow or breathe gently.

**ʻahē.** A hacking cough; to cough.

**ʻāhē.** Timid, shy.

**āhea.** When (interrogative, future).

**aheahe.** Redup. of *ahe;* soft, gentle in sound.

**ʻāheahea.** To wilt, as a plant; warm, insipid.

**ʻāhewa.** To condemn, blame. **hoʻāhewa.** To find guilty.

**ahi.** Fire, match; to burn in a fire, destroy by fire.

**ʻahi.** Hawaiian tuna fishes, especially the yellow-fin tuna *(Thunnus albacares).*

**ʻahia.** How many (interrogative).

**ahiahi.** Evening; to become evening.

**Ahiahi Kalikimaka.** Christmas Eve.

**Ahiahi Makahiki Hou.** New Year's Eve.

**ʻāhihi.** Any plant with long runners or creepers.

**ʻahiku.** Seven (especially in counting in a series); seven times.

**ʻāhina.** Gray, gray- or white-haired. See *hina,* 2.

**ʻāhinahina.** 1. Same as *ʻāhina.* 2. The silversword *(Argyroxiphium sandwicense),* a native plant found only at altitudes of 6,000 feet or more on Maui and Hawaiʻi.

**ahipele.** Match.

**ʻāhiu.** Wild, untamed, as animals or plants.

**ʻāhiwa.** Dark, somber, dusky.

**aho.** 1. Line, cord, lashing, fishing line. 2. Breath; to breathe. *Fig.,* patience. **hoʻāho.** A narrow escape. 3. It is better (always used after *e). E aho ia,* that's better.

**ʻaho.** Thatch purlin and rafter.

**āhole.** A fish *(Kuhlia sandvicensis).*

**āholehole.** Young stage of the *āhole* fish.

**ahona.** Better, well, improved.

**ahonui.** Patience; patient, enduring. *Lit.,* great breath.

**ahu.** Heap, pile; altar, shrine. **hoʻāhu.** To pile or heap up; to lay away.

**ʻahu.** Garment or covering for the upper part of the body and shoulders, as a cape, shirt, coat; to put on or wear such.

**ʻāhua.** To swell, as a wave; heap, mound. **hoʻāhua.** To pile up.

**ahuahu.** Healthy, vigorous; strength and vigor; to grow rapidly.

**ahu ʻai.** To overeat, waste food.

**ʻāhui.** Bunch or cluster, as of bananas.

**ʻāhui hala.** Pandanus fruit.

**ahu lāʻī.** Ti-leaf raincoat or cape.

**ahulau.** Pestilence, epidemic.

**ahuliʻu.** Overheated; white-hot.

**ahulu.** Overdone, overcooked.

**ʻāhuluhulu.** Young of the *kūmū* fish.

**ahupuaʻa.** Land division usually extending from the uplands to the sea.

**ʻahu ʻula.** Feather cloak or cape.

**ahu waiwai.** Storehouse, heap of goods.

**ai.** 1. Who. 2. Short for *aia,* there. Cf. *ai hea, ai lalo, ai loa.* 3. To have sexual relations. 4. Anaphoric particle.

**aī.** Interjection of surprise.

**-aʻi.** Transitive suffix. See *luaʻi, lumaʻi.* Cf. *Kauaʻi, kaulaʻi.*

**ʻai.** 1. Food or food plant, especially vegetable food; to eat; to rule *(Fig.).* **hōʻai.** To feed, give food to. 2. Score, points in a game; stake, wager.

**ʻāʻī.** Neck.

**aia.** 1. There, there it is. 2. Depending on, only if. *Aia nō ia iāʻoe,* depending on you; it's up to you.

**ʻaiā.** Ungodly, wicked.

**aia hoʻi.** Behold!

**aʻiaʻi.** Bright, as moonlight; fair, shining.

**aia kā.** There now!

**aia lā.** There!

**'aialo.** Attendant or intimate of a chief.

**'aiana.** Clothes iron; to iron, press, as clothes. *Eng.*

**aia na'e.** But, furthermore.

**'ai'ē.** Debt: to owe. **hō'ai'ē.** To loan; to borrow.

**'aiea.** All species of the genus *Nothocestrum,* soft-wooded shrubs and trees.

**ai hea, aia i hea.** Where?

**'aihue.** To steal, rob; thief.

**'aihue kanaka.** To kidnap; kidnapper.

**'ā'īkala.** Collar. *Lit.,* neck collar *(Eng.).*

**'aikalima.** Ice cream. *Eng.*

**'ai kanaka.** Cannibal; maneater.

**aikāne.** Friend; friendly.

**'ai kapu.** To eat under taboo; to observe eating taboos.

**'ai kepa.** To cut or tear obliquely, as with teeth or edged instrument.

**'ai kepakepa.** Redup. of *'ai kepa;* to snap the jaws; to speak rapidly.

**'aikola.** Interjection of scorn or derision. **hō'aikola.** To treat contemptuously.

**ai lā.** Short for *aia lā.*

**'aila.** Any oil, grease; to oil, grease. *Eng.*

**'ai lā.** Scorched by the sun.

**'ailahonua.** Kerosene. *Lit.,* earth oil.

**'aila ho'omalo'o pena.** Turpentine. *Lit.,* oil for drying paint.

**'aila ho'onahā.** Castor oil. *Lit.,* purge oil.

**ai laila, aia i laila.** There, to be there.

**'aila koka (koda).** Cod-liver oil.

**'aila kolī.** Castor oil. *Lit.,* castorbean oil.

**ai lalo, aia i lalo.** Down there.

**'aila māhu.** Kerosene. *Lit.,* steam oil.

**'ailana.** Island. *Eng.*

**'aila palai.** Frying oil. *Eng.*

**'aila pua'a.** Lard, pork grease.

**'ailea.** Gasoline (contraction of *'aila,* oil, and *ea,* air).

**ai loa, aia i loa.** Away off in the distance.

**'ailolo.** Ceremony marking the end of training.

**-'ailona. hō'ailona.** Sign, symbol, emblem, mark; trophy, emblem of victory. *Hua hō'ailona.* Abbreviation.

**ai luna, aia i luna.** Up there.

**'ai māmā.** Light meal, snack.

**'ai moku.** Ruler of a *moku* (district or island).

**'āina.** Meal.

**'āina.** Land, earth.

**'āina ahiahi.** Evening meal, supper, dinner.

**'āina awakea.** Noon meal, lunch.

**'āina 'ē.** Foreign land.

**'āina hānau.** Land of one's birth, native land, homeland.

**'āina kakahiaka.** Morning meal, breakfast.

**'āinakini.** Navy blue cotton cloth.

**'āina kō.** Cane trash, bagasse.

**'āina kū'ai.** Land purchased or for sale; land in fee simple.

**'āina lei ali'i.** Crown lands.

**'āina makua.** Fatherland.

**'ai noa.** To eat without observance of taboos.

**a i 'ole.** Or.

**'ai pa'a.** Cooked taro pounded into a hard mass not mixed with water, sometimes preserved in ti-leaf bundles. *Fig.,* a difficult problem. *Lit.,* hard *poi.*

**'ā'īpahāha.** Mumps. *Lit.,* swollen neck.

**aipuni.** To encircle, go around.

**'ā'īpu'upu'u.** Steward.

**āiwa.** Same as *āiwaiwa. Kapuāiwa* (name of Kamehameha V), mysterious thing.

**'aiwa.** Nine (usually in counting in a series); nine times.

**'ai waiū.** To suckle, nurse. *Lit.,* to eat milk.

**āiwaiwa.** Inexplicable, mysterious. **ho'āiwaiwa.** Mystifying, causing wonder.

**aka.** Shadow, reflection, image. **hoʻoaka.** To cast a shadow or reflection.

**aka-.** Carefully, slowly.

**akā.** But, however, nevertheless, on the other hand.

**ʻaka.** To laugh; laughter.

**akaaka, akaka.** Clear, luminous; distinct. **hoʻākaaka.** To clarify, explain.

**ʻakaʻaka.** To laugh, ridicule; laughter, merriment. **hōʻakaʻaka.** To cause laughter, create mirth.

**ʻakaʻakai.** 1. The great bulrush *(Scirpus validus)*. 2. Onion.

**ʻakaʻakai pilau.** Garlic.

**ʻakaʻakai pūpū.** Garlic. *Lit.,* bunched onion.

**akahai.** Modest, gentle, meek.

**akahele.** Slow in doing anything; cautious, careful.

**ʻakahi.** 1. One (especially in counting in a series). 2. For the first time, never before.

**akahoe.** To paddle carefully, silently.

**akaholo.** To sail or run cautiously.

**a kai.** By the sea.

**ʻakakē.** Spry, quick, especially about getting into people's way.

**akakū.** Vision; reflection, as in a mirror.

**akakuʻu.** Lessened; grow calm; quieted.

**ʻākala.** 1. Pink. 2. Two endemic raspberries *(Rubus hawaiiensis* and *R. macraei)* and the thimbleberry *(R. rosaefolius)*.

**akamai.** Smart, clever.

**ʻAkamu, Adamu.** Adam. *Eng.*

**ʻākau.** 1. Right (not left). 2. North.

**akaʻula.** Red sunset. *Lit.,* red shadow.

**ake.** 1. Liver. 2. To desire, yearn.

**ākea.** Broad, wide, public, at large. *Fig.,* liberal.

**ʻākea.** Starboard or outer hull of a double canoe.

**ʻākeʻakeʻa.** To block, hinder; obstruction.

**ake maka.** Raw liver, as eaten after cleaning and salting.

**akemāmā.** Lung. *Lit.,* light liver.

**akena.** To boast, brag.

**ākepakepa.** Unkempt, as hair; oblique.

**ʻakeu.** Active, lively; pleasant.

**ʻaki.** 1. To take a nip and let go; to nibble; to bite off the bark of sugarcane; to heal, as a wound; sharp recurring pain. *Fig.,* to attack, snap at. 2. Height, tip, top (preceded by *ke*). 3. Pillow.

**ʻakiʻaki.** Redup. of *ʻaki, 1;* to nibble, as a fish.

**ʻakiʻaki haole.** Buffalo grass *(Stenotaphrum secundatum).*

**ʻakiki.** Dwarfed; dwarf.

**ʻakilolo.** A wrasse fish of the *hīnālea* type *(Gomphosus varius).*

**ʻakimalala, adimarala.** Admiral. *Eng.*

**ʻakiu.** To search, seek, probe.

**ako.** Thatching; to thatch.

**ʻako.** 1. To cut, shear, clip, trim, as hair. 2. Itch, throat irritation. *Fig.,* lust.

**ʻakoʻako.** 1. Redup. of *ʻako, 1, 2.* 2. Crest of a wave; to break or swell, as waves.

**ʻākoakoa.** To assemble; assembled, collected. **hoʻākoakoa.** To assemble, congregate.

**ʻākoʻakoʻa.** Coral in general.

**ʻakolo.** To creep; to put out small roots, as potatoes.

**ʻakolu.** Three (as in counting in a series); three times.

**aku.** 1. Skipjack *(Katsuwonus pelamis);* to run, of *aku* fish. 2. Particle expressing direction away from the speaker, and time either past (with *nei*) or future.

**akua.** God, goddess, spirit, image, idol; divine, supernatural, godly. **hoʻākua.** To deify, make a god of; godlike.

**Akua Kahikolu.** Holy Trinity.

**akua lapu.** Ghost, apparition.

**akua loa.** A tall image, especially an image of Lono carried on a circuit of the island during the *makahiki,* harvest festival.

**akua pā'ani.** Image representing the god of sports that accompanied the *akua loa* on its circuit, to preside at the sport festivals.

**akua poko.** God of the *makahiki* that went only as far as the border of a district.

**'āku'iku'i. 1.** To pound. See *ku'i, 1.* **2.** A long fish net; to drive fish into the net by striking the water with sticks.

**'akūkū.** Tossing; jolting, as a vehicle on a rough road.

**akule.** Bigeye or goggle-eyed scad fish *(Trachurops crumenophthalmus).*

**'ākulikuli.** General name for succulent plants.

**'ākulikuli lei.** The ice plant *(Lampranthus glomeratus),* from Africa, a low succulent with thick, narrow leaves and pink, rose, or orange flowers (used for leis).

**'akumu.** Broken or cut off; blunt, stumpy.

**aku nei.** A while ago. See *aku, 2.*

**ala. 1.** Path, road, trail. **2.** To waken; awake. **ho'āla.** To awaken someone. **3.** To rise up, come forward. *Ala hou,* resurrection. **ho'āla.** To arouse, stir up.

**'ala.** Fragrant, perfumed; fragrance (preceded by *ke*). *Fig.,* esteemed, chiefly. **hō'ala.** To perfume.

**'alā.** Dense waterworn volcanic stone, as used for *poi* pounders, adzes, hula stones.

**'āla'a.** A large endemic tree *(Planchonella* spp.).

**'ala'ala wai nui.** All species of *Peperomia,* small native succulent forest herbs, related to *'awa.*

**'alae.** Mud hen or Hawaiian gallinule *(Gallinula chloropus sandvicensis);* a cry of this bird, believed a bad omen.

**'alaea.** Water-soluble colloidal ocherous earth, used for coloring salt, for medicine, and dye.

**'alae kea.** Hawaiian coot *(Fulica americana alai),* a marsh and pond bird.

**'alae 'ula.** Hawaiian gallinule or mud hen *(Gallinula chloropus sandvicensis).*

**alahaka.** Plank bridge; rough road over ravines or chasms.

**alahaki.** Mountain ladder or steps cut into a cliff.

**alahao.** Railway, railroad track. *Lit.,* iron road.

**alahe'e haole.** Mock orange *(Murraya paniculata).*

**ala hele.** Pathway, route, road, way to go, means of transportation.

**ala hele wāwae.** Pedestrian's road, sidewalk.

**alahia.** Passive/imperative of *ala, 2.*

**ala hou.** Resurrection; to rise again.

**alahula.** A frequented and well-known path.

**ālai.** Obstruction; to hinder, oppose.

**'ala'ihi.** Various species of squirrelfishes of the family Holocentridae.

**ā laila.** See *laila.*

**ala kai.** Sea course, as of canoe or ship; path where one must swim around a projecting cliff or bluff.

**alaka'i.** To lead, direct; leader, conductor.

**alakō.** To drag.

**'alalā. 1.** To bawl, cry, caw, scream. **2.** Hawaiian crow *(Corvus tropicus).*

**alaloa.** Highway, main road, belt road around an island.

**'alamihi.** A common black crab *(Metopograpsus thukuhar).*

**alamimo.** Quick.

**ala muku.** Cut-off or unfinished road, dead-end road.

**alana.** Awakening, rising. See *ala, 2, 3.*

'ālana. 1. Offering, especially a free-will offering. 2. Light, buoyant.

alani. Brown seaweeds (*Dictyota* spp.), regularly divided into narrow segments, and very bitter to the taste.

'alani. Any kind of orange, both fruit and tree.

'alani Pākē. Tangerine *(Citrus reticulata* cv. 'deliciosa'). *Lit.,* Chinese orange.

alanui. Street, road, highway. *Lit.,* large path.

alanui hele wāwae. Sidewalk.

ala 'ololī. Narrow path, lane.

'ālapa. Athletic, active; athlete.

'alapahi. Slander, falsehood; to defame.

alapi'i. Stairs, steps, ladder.

alapi'i kū. Steep road or path.

alapi'i mele. Musical scale.

alapine. 1. Quick. 2. Frequent, often.

alaula. Light of early dawn, sunset glow. *Lit.,* flaming road.

ala'ula. Red dust in a road.

ala'ume. To draw, pull, attract.

'alawa. To glance.

alawai. Channel, canal.

alawī. To shriek; shrill.

alawiki. To hurry; quick.

ale. To swallow, gulp.

'ale. Wave, crest of a wave; to form waves; to well, as tears in the eyes.

'ale'ale. Redup. of *'ale;* stirring, moving, rippling.

alelo. 1. Tongue, language. 2. Concave curve of the lower portion of the *lei palaoa,* whaletooth pendant, suggestive of a tongue.

'alemanaka. Almanac, calendar. *Eng.*

'ale'o. Tower, high lookout; towering.

'alepapeka, alepabeta. Alphabet. *Eng.*

'āleuleu. Old, worn out, as tapa, mats, clothing.

'ālewa. Same as *'ālewalewa.*

'ālewalewa. Buoyant, floating.

'ali. 1. Scar, depression, groove. 2. To dig.

alia. To wait, stop; usually as a command: Stop!

ālia. Salt bed, salt-encrusted area; salty.

aliali. Crystal clear, white. hoāliali. To whiten, shine.

'alihi. 1. Cords or fine ropes threaded through marginal meshes of upper and lower edges of nets, to which were attached floats and sinkers. 2. Horizon.

'alihikaua. General, commander in battle.

ali'i. Chief, chiefess, king, queen, noble; royal, kingly; to rule or act as a chief. *Fig.,* kind.

ali'i 'ai moku. Chief who rules a *moku* (district).

ali'i koa. Military officer, officer of army or navy.

'ālikalika. Clammy, sticky, tenacious. *Fig.,* stingy.

'ālike. Alike.

'alima. Five (especially in counting in a series); five times.

'alimakika, arimatika. Arithmetic. *Eng.*

'ālina. Scar, blemish; maimed. *Fig.,* low, disgraced.

alo. Front, face, presence; upper surface.

'alo. 1. To dodge, evade, avoid. 2. To be with, go with, attend.

aloali'i. In the presence of chiefs; royal court.

aloalo. All kinds of hibiscus.

'aloe. Aloe, any plant of the genus *Aloe.*

aloha. Aloha, love, mercy, compassion, pity; greeting; loved one; to love; to greet, hail. Greetings! Good-by! Common greetings follow: *Aloha 'oe,* may you be loved, or greetings (to one person). *Aloha kāua,* may there be friendship between us, greetings (to one person). *Aloha kākou,* same as above, but to more than one person. *Ke aloha nō! Aloha!* Greetings! *Aloha ali'i,* royalist. *Aloha 'āina,* love of the land. *Aloha 'ino!* What a pity! *Aloha akua,* love of god. *Me ke aloha o Kawena,* with the love (or greeting) of Kawena. *'O wau iho nō me ke aloha,* I remain, with very best regards. The following greetings were introduced by the missionaries: *Aloha ahiahi,* good evening. *Aloha kakahiaka,* good morning.

**aloha kakahiaka.** See *aloha.*

**ālohaloha.** Redup. of *aloha.* **hō-'ālohaloha.** To make love; to give thanks.

**aloha 'oe.** See *aloha.*

**aloha 'ole.** Pitiless, without love.

**'alohi.** To shine, sparkle; bright, brilliant.

**'ālohilohi.** Redup. of *'alohi.*

**alolua.** Two-sided, two-faced; facing one another, as cliffs on opposite sides of a valley.

**alu.** Combined, acting together; to cooperate, act together.

**'alu.** Depression, ravine; descent, as of trail or road; to bend, stoop. **hō'alu.** To slacken; depression.

**'alua.** Two, twice.

**alualu.** To follow, pursue; to run, as for political office.

**'alu'alu.** Loose, flabby; wrinkled, uneven. **hō'alu'alu.** To slacken; to make gathers, as in a skirt.

**ālualua.** Rough, bumpy, pitted with holes.

**'āluna.** Descent, loosening. See *'alu.*

**'āluna ahiahi.** Late afternoon or early evening.

**'āluna awakea.** Early afternoon.

**'ālunu.** Greedy.

**ama.** Outrigger float.

**'ama.** 1. Light, bright. 2. Talkative.

**'ama'ama.** Mullet *(Mugil cephalus),* a very choice fish.

**'āma'amau.** In rapid succession.

**'amakihi.** Small Hawaiian honeycreepers *(Loxops virens).*

**'āmama.** Finished, of a pre-Christian prayer.

**'āmana.** Y-shaped crosspiece at the end of a pole; branches of a tree in the form of a Y; gallows; T-shaped.

**'ama'u.** All species of an endemic genus of ferns *(Sadleria).*

**'ama'uma'u.** Plural of *'ama'u;* many *'ama'u* ferns, ferny.

**ā me.** And. Cf. *me.*

**'Amelika, America.** America; American. *Eng.*

**'Amelika 'Ākau.** North America.

**'Amelika Hema.** South America.

**'Amelika Huipū.** United States of America.

**'amene.** Amen.

**'ami.** 1. Hinge. 2. A hula step with hip revolutions; to do this step.

**'ami'ami.** Redup. of *'ami, 1, 2.*

**āmio.** Narrow channel, as to a sea pool; to pass in and out. *Fig.,* to die. Cf. *mio.*

**amo.** To carry a burden on the shoulders; a burden. *Fig.,* responsibility. Cf. *'auamo.*

**'amo.** Wink, sparkle; to wink.

**amu.** To curse, revile. Cf. *kūamuamu.*

**amuamu.** Redup. of *amu.*

**'āmuku.** To cut off.

**ana.** 1. To measure; pattern. **ho-'oana.** To make measurements. 2. To have enough or too much, satisfied. 3. Cave, grotto. 4. Larynx. 5. Particle after *e* (verb). See *e* (verb) *ana.* 6. Particle after words with meaning "there," or "then," and often used as indicative of the future. 7. Demon. following verbs indicating a single event, whether a command or a statement, wnether completed or incompleted.

**āna.** His, her, hers, its (zero-class, *a*-class).

**'ana.** 1. Nominalizing particle. 2. Pumice, used for rubbing.

**ana 'āina.** Land surveying.

**'anā'anā.** Black magic, evil sorcery.

**'anae.** Full-sized *'ama'ama* mullet fish.

**anahonua.** Geometry.

**ana honua.** Surveying; to measure the surface of the earth.

**anahulu.** Period of ten days; for ten days.

**anaina.** Congregation, audience; to assemble.

**anaina ho'olewa.** Funeral wake or gathering.

**anaina ho'omana.** Congregation for worship.

**'anakā.** Anchor. *Eng.*

**'anakala.** Uncle. *Eng.*

**'anakē, anate.** Aunt, auntie. *Eng.*

**'anali'i.** 1. Wee, stunted. 2. A native fern *(Asplenium lobulatum).*

**ana loa.** Measurement of length.

**anana.** Fathom.

**ananū.** Turnip.

**ana 'ole.** Without equal.

**'anapa.** To shine, gleam, glitter.

**'anapau.** To leap, frisk, frolic; frisky.

**ana piwa.** Thermometer. *Lit.,* fever *(Eng.)* measure.

**anapuni.** Boundary, perimeter; to go around.

**anawaena.** Diameter. *Lit.,* middle measure.

**ana wai.** Water meter.

**ana waina.** Liquid measure.

**ana wela.** Thermometer; to measure heat.

**ane.** A dermestid beetle; to be insect eaten.

**ānea.** 1. Insipid, tasteless. 2. Vibration caused by heat. 3. Passive/imperative of *ane;* moth-eaten. 4. Bare, leafless.

**'ane'ane.** Nearly, almost, scarcely.

**'āne'e.** To move along by jerks.

**'āne'e ali'i.** Parasite or sponger on a chief.

**ānehe.** To come upon quietly, move stealthily.

**anei.** Particle, following a word, indicating that a question may be answered by yes or no.

**'ane'i.** 1. Here (usually after *ma-, i,* or *kō*). 2. Doubtful (used idiomatically).

**'ānela.** Angel.

**'anemoku.** Peninsula. *Lit.,* near island.

**ani.** To beckon, wave. **ho'āni.** To beckon, wave; to blow softly; to let wind.

**aniani.** 1. Mirror, glass; clear, transparent. 2. Cool; to blow softly. 3. To travel swiftly.

**aniani ho'onui 'ike.** Magnifying glass. *Lit.,* glass to enlarge vision.

**aniani kilohi.** Mirror, looking glass.

**aniani kū.** Standing mirror.

**aniani kukui uila.** Electric-light bulb. *Lit.,* electric-light glass.

**aniani pa'a lima.** Hand mirror.

**ani pe'ahi.** To wave or beckon, as with the hand.

**ano.** Awe, reverence; weird solitude; awestruck. **hō'ano.** Holy, hallowed.

**'ano.** 1. Kind, nature, character (preceded by *ke*). 2. Somewhat, rather; to show signs of.

**'ānō.** Now; present.

**'ano'ai.** 1. Greeting. 2. Unexpected. 3. Perhaps.

**anoano.** Redup. of *ano.*

**'ano'ano.** Seed, kernel.

**'ano 'ē.** Strange, odd, unusual.

**'ano hou.** New variety or kind; new.

**'ano'i.** Desire; desired one; beloved.

**'ano like.** Resembling; of similar nature or type.

**'ano nui.** Important.

**'ano 'ole.** Insignificant, trivial.

**anu.** 1. Cool, cold. **ho'ānu.** To cool. 2. Cold; to have a cold.

**anuanu.** Redup. of *anu,* cold.

**ānuenue.** Rainbow.

'**anuhe.** Caterpillar. See *'enuhe.*

**anuhea.** Cool, soft fragrance.

'**anu'u. 1.** Stairs, terrace. **2.** Tower in ancient *heiau.*

**ao. 1.** Light, daylight; to dawn. **ho'āo.** To marry. **2.** Any kind of cloud. **3.** World, earth.

**a'o.** Instruction, learning; to teach, advise. **ho'ā'o.** To test, try, taste.

'**ao. 1.** A new shoot, leaf or bud, especially of taro. **2.** Dried baked taro or sweet potato.

'**aoa.** To bark, as a dog; to howl.

'**ao'ao. 1.** Side, boundary. **2.** Group; party, as a political party. **3.** Page. **4.** Way, mode of living.

'**ao'ao kālai'āina.** Political party.

'**ao'ao kū'ē.** Opposition, opponent, as in a trial.

'**ao'ao kūpale.** Defense, as in a trial.

'**a'ohe.** None; no, not; to have none.

**a'o heluhelu.** Reader, primer; to learn or teach to read.

**a'o hōkū.** Astronomy; to teach or learn astronomy.

**aokanaka.** To think or behave reasonably.

**a'o kepela (sepela).** Spelling book.

**a'o kiko.** Manual of punctuation.

**a'ole.** No, not; to have none. *'A'ole loa!* Certainly not! Not at all! Never!

'**aono.** Six (especially in counting in a series); six times.

**a'o palapala.** Instruction, education; to teach or learn writing.

**a'o pili'ōlelo.** Grammar, instruction in grammar.

**aouli.** Firmament, sky.

'**apa.** To delay, waste time, keep others waiting.

'**āpala.** Apple. *Eng.*

'**āpana.** Piece, portion, section, land division.

'**āpani.** To block, shut.

'**apapane.** A Hawaiian honeycreeper *(Himatione sanguinea).*

**āpau.** All, entirely.

'**ape.** Large taro-like plants *(Alocasia macrorrhiza, Xanthosoma robustum).*

'**ā pele.** Volcanic rock of any kind.

'**Apelika, Aferika.** Africa; African. *Eng.*

'**Apelila, Aperila.** April. *Eng.*

'**api. 1.** Soft spot in the temples. **2.** To palpitate, throb. **3.** Fish gills. **4.** A surgeonfish *(Acanthurus guttatus).*

'**api'api.** Redup. of *'api, 2, 3;* elastic, springy; short of breath.

'**āpi'i.** Curly.

'**āpi'ipi'i.** Wavy, kinky, very curly.

'**āpiki.** Crafty, mischievous; trickery, treachery.

'**āpikipiki. 1.** Troubled, agitated, as the sea. **2.** Fold, pleat; to fold.

**apo.** Circle, hoop, belt, ring; embrace.

'**apo.** To catch, grasp; acceptance.

'**āpo'ipo'i.** To pounce.

**apo kula (gula).** Gold bracelet.

**apo lima.** Bracelet.

'**āpona.** Embracing.

'**āpono.** To approve, accept. **ho'āpono.** To approve, find not guilty in a trial.

'**apōpō.** Tomorrow.

'**apu.** Coconut shell cup.

'**āpu'epu'e.** Difficulty; to struggle.

'**āpuka.** To swindle, cheat; forgery.

'**āpulu.** Worn out, as a garment; to show wear and tear.

**au. 1.** Period of time, age, era; the passing of time. **2.** Current (of water). **3.** Movement, eddy, tide. **4.** Gall, bile. **5.** Also **wau.** I.

**āu.** Your, yours (singular, zero-class, *a*-class).

**a'u. 1.** Swordfish, sailfish, marlin. **2.** Me (used after *e* and *me* and fusing with *iā* to form *ia'u*). *'Ai 'ia e a'u,* eaten by me. *Hā'awi mai ia'u,* give to me. **3.** My, mine (zero-class, *a*-class).

**-a‘u.** Me (see *ia‘u*).

**‘au. 1.** To swim, travel by sea. **hō‘au.** To teach to swim, learn to swim. **2.** Handle, staff, stem. **3.** Group.

**‘au‘a.** Stingy; to withhold, detain, refuse to part with.

**‘auamo.** Pole or stick used for carrying burdens across the shoulders; yoke, palanquin. *Lit.,* carrying handle.

**‘auana.** To wander, drift, go from place to place.

**auane‘i. 1.** Soon, by and by; probably, merely. **2.** Probably not, possibly, doubtful.

**‘au‘au.** To bathe. **hō‘au‘au.** To give a bath.

**auē, auwē.** Oh! O dear! Alas! Too bad! (much used to express wonder, fear, scorn, pity, affection); to groan, moan, grieve. *Auē noho‘i ē!* Goodness! Alas! Oh!

**‘auhau.** Tax, assessment, levy; to levy a tax, tax.

**‘auhea. 1.** Where (in questions). **2.** Listen (usually in commands).

**‘auhea ho‘i.** Where indeed (with implication of neglect or indifference)?

**‘auhe‘e.** To flee from danger.

**auhele.** To go looking from place to place without any definite course, to drift or sail aimlessly.

**‘auhuhu.** A slender, shrubby legume *(Tephrosia purpurea),* formerly used for poisoning fish.

**‘aui. 1.** To turn aside, pass by. **2.** To swell and roll, as the sea. **3.** A hula step.

**auī.** Ouch (expression of pain)!

**‘auina, auwina.** Bending, sloping; descent.

**‘auinalā.** Afternoon. *Lit.,* declining sun.

**‘aukā.** Bar, as of soap or gold.

**‘aukai.** To travel or swim by sea; seafaring; sailor.

**‘Aukake.** August. *Eng.*

**‘aukā kopa.** Bar of soap.

**‘au ko‘i.** Axe handle.

**‘au kolo.** Crawl (swimming); to swim thus.

**‘auku‘u.** Black-crowned night heron *(Nycticorax nycticorax hoactli).*

**‘aulama.** To light with a torch.

**aulau.** To gather leaves to wrap fish in for cooking.

**‘aulau.** Leaves strung on lines at ends of seines, as ti leaves.

**aulele.** To fly, as a frightened flock of birds.

**aulike. 1.** Even, smooth, as timber. **2.** To treat kindly.

**‘au lima. 1.** Bone of arm below elbow. **2.** Fire-plow. See *‘aunaki.*

**‘aumakua.** Family or personal god.

**‘aumākua.** Plural of *‘aumakua.*

**‘aumoana.** To travel on the open sea; sailor.

**aumoe.** Late at night, as about midnight. *Lit.,* time to sleep. **hō‘aumoe.** To pass the night.

**‘au moku.** Fleet of ships.

**‘aunaki. 1.** Stick in which the *‘au lima* is rubbed in obtaining fire by friction. **2.** Also **‘aunake, auneki.** Ounce. *Eng.*

**aupuni.** Government, kingdom, nation; national.

**‘au umauma.** Breast stroke (swimming); to swim thus.

**‘au wa‘a.** Canoe fleet.

**‘auwae.** Chin. *Fig.,* indifferent, scornful. **hō‘auwae.** To show no interest.

**‘auwaepa‘a.** Firmly opposed, set against. *Lit.,* firm chin.

**‘auwaepahāha.** Mumps. *Lit.,* puffed chin.

**‘auwai.** Ditch.

**‘auwai papa.** Flume.

**‘auwana.** Var. spelling of *‘auana,* to wander.

**‘auwina.** Var. spelling of *‘auina.*

**awa. 1.** Port, harbor; channel or passage, as through a reef. **2.** Milkfish *(Chanos chanos).*

**‘awa. 1.** The kava *(Piper methysticum).* **2.** Sour, bitter. **hō‘awa.**

To make bitter. **3.** Cold mountain rain; to rain or mist. *Fig.*, tragic misfortune.

**'awa'awa. 1.** Redup. of *'awa, 2;* bitter, sour. **hō'awa'awa.** To embitter; bitter tasting. **2.** Redup. of *'awa, 3.*

**awakea.** Noon; to be at noon; to become noon.

**awa kū moku.** Ship harbor or anchorage.

**'ā wale.** To burn for no particular reason; spontaneous combustion; overcooked.

**'awalu.** Eight (usually in counting in a series).

**'awapuhi.** Wild ginger *(Zingiber zerumbet).*

**'awapuhi 'ai.** Same as *'awapuhi Pākē. Lit.,* edible ginger.

**'awapuhi ke'oke'o.** White ginger *(Hedychium coronarium).*

**'awapuhi ko'oko'o.** Torch ginger *(Phaeomeria speciosa). Lit.,* walking-stick ginger.

**'awapuhi luheluhe.** Shell ginger *(Alpinia speciosa). Lit.,* drooping ginger.

**'awapuhi melemele.** Yellow ginger *(Hedychium flavescens).*

**'awapuhi Pākē.** Ginger *(Zingiber officinale). Lit.,* Chinese ginger. Also called *'awapuhi 'ai.*

**'awapuhi 'ula'ula.** Red ginger *(Alpinia purpurata).*

**awāwa.** Valley, gulch. **ho'āwāwa.** To make a groove.

**awe. 1.** Strand, thread, tentacle. **2.** Wake of a ship.

**'awe 1.** Pack, knapsack carried on the back. Cf. *'auamo, hā'awe.* **2.** Tentacle.

**'awe'awe.** Redup. of *'awe, 1.*

**'āwe'awe'a.** Faint trace, glimpse; faint, faded, dim.

**'āweoweo.** Various Hawaiian species of *Priacanthus,* red fishes, sometimes called bigeye.

**'āwihi.** To wink, ogle.

**'āwiki.** To hurry, be quick.

**'āwikiwiki.** Redup. of *'āwiki.*

**'āwili.** To mix, interweave, entwine.

**'āwini.** Sharp, bold, forward.

**'āwīwī.** To hurry; quick, fast.

# B

Loan words from English sometimes spelled with initial *b* are entered under *p-*. For example, for *ballot,* see *pāloka.*

# D

Loan words from English with initial *d* are entered under *k-*. For example, for *driver,* see *kalaiwa.*

# E

**e. 1.** Particle marking imperative/intentive mood. **E hele!** Go! **2.** By, by means of. *'Ai 'ia ka poi e a'u,* the poi was eaten by me.

**ē.** Vocative particle. *Ē Pua,* oh Pua.

**'e-.** Prefix to numbers.

**'ē. 1.** Different, foreign, strange. **2.** Away, off. *Hele ma kahi 'ē!* Go away! **3.** Beforehand, already. **4.** Yes. **5.** The letter *e.*

**ea. 1.** Sovereignty, rule, independence. **2.** Life, breath, vapor, air, spirit. **3.** To rise, go up.

**'ea. 1.** Coated tongue; the thrush disease of children, infectious disease. **2.** Hawkbill turtle.

**'eā.** Isn't that so? Isn't it?

**'ē a'e.** Different, other.

**'eā'eā.** Particle at end of verses in some songs and chants that maintain rhythm and afford pleasure in repetition.

**e** (verb) **ai.** Particles indicating imperative/intentive mood or future tense, and accompanying subordinate verbs.

**e** (verb) **ala.** Same as *e* (verb) *lā.*

**e** (verb) **ana.** Particle indicating incompleted action and future tense.

**e'e.** To climb on, mount, go aboard; one who mounts, boards. **ho'ē'e.** To rise or swell, as surf; to mount, as a surfer mounts a wave.

**'ē'ē.** 1. Redup. of *'ē, 1.* 2. Armpit.

**'e'ehi.** Same as *hehi,* to step on.

**'e'ehia.** Overcome with fearful reverence; awe-inspiring; fear.

**e'e kuahiwi.** To climb mountains; mountain climber.

**e'e moku.** To board a ship; ship passenger; immigrant.

**'e'epa.** Extraordinary, incomprehensible, as persons with miraculous powers; such persons.

**'eha.** Hurt, in pain, aching, pained; injury, suffering; to cause suffering. **hō'eha.** To inflict pain or punishment.

**'ehā.** Four; four times.

**'eha'eha.** Redup. of *'eha;* great pain.

**'ēheu.** Wing, as of bird, kite, or airplane; winged.

**'ehia.** How many (usually in questions); how much, what price.

**'ehiku.** Seven; seven times.

**'eho.** Stone pile, especially as used to mark land boundaries; stone image; heap of stones under water.

**'ehu.** 1. Spray, foam (formerly *ehu*). 2. Reddish tinge in hair, of Polynesians and not of Caucasians; one with *'ehu* hair.

**'ehu kai.** Sea spray, foam. Formerly, *ehu kai.*

**'ehu pua.** Flower pollen.

**eia.** 1. Here, here is, here are, present (as response to roll call). 2. This place.

**eia a'e.** Here close by, here approaching.

**eia aku.** Approaching, nearby, soon.

**eia ala.** Here, here it is; you over there, you.

**eia ho'i.** And, finally, behold.

**eia iho.** Wait a moment.

**eia kā.** So at last, then.

**e ia nei.** You, you there; the one here (sometimes affectionate).

**eia (nō) na'e.** But, furthermore.

**ei nei.** Same as *e ia nei.*

**'eiwa.** Nine; nine times.

**'eka.** 1. Dirty; filth. 2. Acre. *Eng.*

**'ekā.** Hand, as of bananas.

**'ēkaha.** Birds-nest fern *(Asplenium nidus).*

**'ekahi.** One; once.

**'ekalekia, ekalesia.** Church (the organization, not the building).

**'eke.** Sack, pocket, bag; scrotum.

**'eke huluhulu.** Gunny sack. *Lit.,* hairy sack.

**'ekeke'i.** Short, as a dress.

**'eke leka (leta).** Mail pouch, mailbag.

**'ekemu.** To answer briefly.

**'eke pa'a lima, 'eke'eke pa'a lima.** Handbag, brief case.

**'eki.** Ace. *Eng.*

**'ekolu.** Three; three times.

**'eku.** To root, as a pig. *Fig.,* prow of a canoe.

**e** (verb) **lā.** Similar to *e* (verb) *nei,* except that *lā* indicates action away.

**'ēlau.** 1. Tip, point, end. 2. Bayonet, spear point, short spear.

**'ēlau alelo.** Tongue tip.

**'ele.** Black.

**'ele'ele.** 1. Black, dark; the black color of Hawaiian eyes. **hō-'ele'ele.** To blacken, darken; to become dark. 2. Long, green, edible seaweeds *(Enteromorpha* spp.).

'elekū. 1. Coarse vesicular basalt. 2. Entirely black, said jokingly of dark people, including Negroes.

'elele. Messenger, delegate; any diplomatic representative.

elelo. Same as *alelo*, tongue.

'elelū. Cockroaches (Blattidae).

'elemakule. Old man; to become an old man; old (of males).

'elepaio. A species of flycatcher with subspecies on Hawai'i *(Chasiempis sandwichensis sandwichensis)*, Kaua'i *(C. sandwichensis sclateri)*, and O'ahu *(C. sandwichensis gayi)*.

'elepani, elepani. Elephant. *Eng.*

'eleu. Active, alert, lively. hō-'eleu. To animate, stir into action.

'eli. To dig, excavate.

'elima. Five; five times.

'elua. Two; twice.

emi. 1. To diminish, reduce; to droop, lower. ho'ēmi. To reduce, lessen. 2. Cheap. ho'ēmi. To lower the price.

'emo. A waiting, delay.

'emo 'ole. Without delay, immediately, suddenly.

'ena. Red-hot, glowing. *Fig.*, raging, angry.

'ena'ena. Redup. of *'ena;* glowing, red-hot, raging.

e (verb) nei. Particles indicating incompleted aspect and future tense and accompanying subordinate verbs. The *nei* indicates action here or now.

'enemi. Enemy; to feel enmity; to be an enemy. *Eng.*

'enuhe. Caterpillar, as of hawk or sphinx moths (Sphingidae). Also, *nuhe, 'anuhe.*

eo. To win; winning.

eō. 1. Yes, I am here (in answer to a call by name). 2. Call; to call, answer.

'eono. Six; six times.

'epa. Tricky, mischievous.

'eu. Mischievous, naughty. hō'eu. To stir up, incite, encourage.

'euanelio. Evangelical; gospel.

'eu'eu. Exciting, rousing; alert, aroused. hō'eu'eu. To encourage, stir; spirited.

'Eulopa, Europa. Europe; European. *Eng.*

ewa. Unstable, wandering.

'ewa. 1. Crooked, out of shape, imperfect. 2. *(Cap.)* Place name for area west of Honolulu, used as a direction term.

'ewalu. Eight; eight times.

ēwe. 1. Sprout; lineage, kin; birthplace; family trait. 2. Navel string. 3. Same as *'iēwe*, afterbirth.

# F

Loan words from English sometimes spelled with initial *f* are entered under *p-*. For example: *falu,* see *palū,* flu; *fea,* see *pea,* fair; *fiku,* see *piku,* fig; *fila,* see *pila,* fiddle; *fiwa,* see *piwa,* fever.

# G

Loan words from English sometimes spelled with initial *g* are entered under *k-*. For example: *gita,* see *kīkā,* guitar; *gula,* see *kula,* gold.

# H

**hā.** 1. Four, fourth. 2. To breathe, exhale. 3. Hoarse. 4. Stalk. 5. Trough, ditch, sluice.

**hā-.** Same as *ha'a-*.

**ha'a.** 1. Low; dwarf. 2. A dance with bent knees.

**ha'a-.** Prefix similar to *ho'o-*.

**hā'ae.** Saliva, spittle; to slobber, drool.

**ha'aha'a.** Redup of *ha'a, 1;* low, lowly, humble, meek, modest. **ho'oha'aha'a.** To lower, debase, humiliate.

**ha'aheo.** Proud, haughty; to strut; to cherish with pride. **ho-'oha'aheo.** To act haughty.

**ha'alele.** To leave, desert, abandon, quit, give up, reject.

**ha'alele loa.** To abandon permanently or completely; extremely.

**ha'alulu.** To shake, quake, tremble.

**ha'anui.** To boast, brag, exaggerate, gloat.

**hā'awe.** To carry a burden on the back; a bundle or burden so carried.

**hā'awi.** To give, grant; to offer.

**ha'awina.** Lesson, task, portion, appropriation.

**ha'awina ho'i hope.** Review lesson. *Lit.,* lesson going backward.

**ha'awina hō'ike.** Examination, test. *Lit.,* showing lesson.

**hae.** 1. Wild, furious, ferocious. **ho'ohae.** To make wild or savage; to provoke, tease. 2. To bark, growl, of a dog; to chirp noisily or scold, as a mynah bird. **ho'ohae.** To cause to bark, growl. 3. To tear. 4. Flag, banner.

**hae Hawai'i.** 1. Hibiscus. *Lit.,* Hawaiian flag, from having red petals striped with white. 2. Carnation *(Dianthus caryophyllus)* having petals red with white stripes. 3. A variety of plumeria.

**haele.** To go, come (dual or plural).

**haha.** 1. Redup. of *hā, 2;* to breathe hard. 2. Same as *haha kā 'upena,* net gauge or spacer.

**hāhā.** To grope, feel.

**-hāhā. ho'ohāhā.** To beat, pound.

**hahae.** To strip, as pandanus leaves for plaiting; to tear.

**hahai.** To follow, pursue, hunt; to go with.

**haha'i.** To break into pieces; to break off.

**hahaki.** Redup. of *haki,* to break.

**hāhālua.** Manta ray.

**hahana.** Warm, hot. **ho'ohahana.** To create heat; to rouse to fury.

**hahao.** To insert, put in.

**hāhāpa'akai.** Salt bed or pool; to gather salt. **ho'ohāhāpa'akai.** To gather salt.

**hahau.** To strike, thrash; to throw down a playing card with force; to play, as a card or *kōnane* pebble.

**hahu.** To clear; to purge.

**hai.** 1. Offering, sacrifice; to sacrifice. 2. To follow.

**ha'i.** 1. To break, as a stick; fracture. 2. To say, tell. 3. Another person or place, someone else (not used with the articles).

**hāiki** (in fast speech, *haiki*). Narrow, pinched; restriction.

**ha'ikū.** *Kāhili* flower *(Grevillea banksii).*

**hailepo.** Sting ray.

**haili.** Same as *hali'a.*

**ha'ilono.** To tell the news, to spread a report.

**hailuku.** To stone.

**ha'i mana'o.** To state an opinion, testify.

**ha'i manawa.** To tell of the times.

**haina.** Offering, sacrifice.

**hainā.** Cruel.

**ha'ina.** Saying, statement, song refrain, riddle answer. *Ha'ina 'ia mai ana ka puana,* tell the refrain.

**ha‘ina hou.** Repeat the *ha‘ina* of a song.

**hainakā.** Handkerchief. *Eng.*

**ha‘i‘ōlelo.** Speech, address; to preach; speaker.

**haipule.** Religious.

**ha‘i waha.** Word-of-mouth, verbal; to tell verbally.

**haka.** 1. Shelf, perch, platform; roost as for chickens. 2. Medium, one possessed. 3. Vacancy; empty, full of holes or spaces.

**hakahaka.** Redup. of *haka, 3;* vacant space; blanks, as in a questionnaire; thin, emaciated.

**hakakā.** To fight, quarrel; a fight.

**hakakā-a-moa.** Cockfight.

**haki.** Same as *ha‘i, 1.*

**hāki‘i.** To tie, bind.

**hākikili.** Peal of thunder.

**hākilo.** To observe closely, spy on, eavesdrop.

**hakina.** Broken piece, remnant, portion; fraction, as in arithmetic.

**hakina maoli.** Common fraction.

**hakina ‘ōlelo.** Portion of a word, syllable.

**hākōkō.** Wrestling; to wrestle.

**haku.** 1. Lord, master, employer, owner. **ho‘ohaku.** To act as *haku;* to rule others. 2. To compose, arrange. 3. Stone.

**haku ‘āina.** Landowner; landlord.

**hakuhaku.** To fold.

**haku hale.** Landlord, house owner, host, hostess.

**haku hana.** Overseer, superintendent, employer.

**hākuma.** Pockmarked, as by smallpox; ravaged, as by leprosy.

**haku mele.** Poet, composer; to compose song or chant.

**haku mo‘olelo.** Author, story writer.

**haku nui.** Manager, as of a plantation or firm.

**hala.** 1. Sin, error, offense; to sin. **ho‘ohala.** To cause to sin, lead astray. 2. To pass, as time; to pass by; to die. **ho‘ohala.** To pass, as time. *Ho‘ohala manawa,* to pass the time. 3. The pandanus or screw pine *(Pandanus odoratissimus).*

**halahala.** Redup. of *hala, 1;* correction, criticism, complaint. **ho‘ohalahala.** To criticize, complain, find fault.

**hala kahiki.** Pineapple *(Ananas comosus). Lit.,* foreign *hala.*

**hālala.** To bend low.

**hala loa.** Gone a long distance or time; far.

**halalū.** 1. Young of the *akule,* a fish. 2. To rumble.

**hālau.** Long house, as for canoes or hula instruction.

**hālawa.** Same as *kālawa.*

**hālāwai.** Meeting; to meet. **ho‘ohālāwai.** To arrange a meeting.

**hale.** House, building; to have a house. **ho‘ohale.** To lodge in a house; to receive in a house.

**hale ‘aina.** Restaurant, cafe, eating house.

**hale ali‘i.** Chief's house, royal residence, palace.

**hale ‘au‘au.** Bathhouse.

**hale ‘auhau.** House where taxes are paid; tax building.

**hale aupuni.** Capitol building, government building.

**hale hālāwai.** Meetinghouse, synagogue.

**hale hō‘ike‘ike.** Exhibition hall, museum, art academy. *Hale Hō-‘ike‘ike o Ka-mehameha,* Bishop Museum.

**hale hō‘ike‘ike i‘a.** Aquarium.

**hale ho‘okipa.** Guesthouse, lodging house.

**hale ho‘okolokolo.** Courthouse.

**hale ho‘olewa.** Funeral parlor, undertaker's establishment.

**hale ho‘omaha.** Rest house.

**hale ho‘omalu.** Quarantine house or station.

**hale ho‘oponopono.** Administrative building.

**hale inu pia.** Beer parlor.

**hale ipukukui.** Lighthouse.

**hale ka‘a.** Garage.

**hale keaka.** Theater.

**hale kinai ahi.** Fire station.

**hale kipa. 1.** Guesthouse, inn, house of hospitality. **2.** Hospitable friend.

**hale koa.** Armory, barracks.

**hale kū‘ai.** Store, shop.

**hale kū‘ai lā‘au.** Drugstore, pharmacy.

**hale kū‘ai lole.** Clothing store, dry goods store.

**hale kū‘ai mea ‘ai.** Grocery store.

**hale kū‘ai palaoa.** Bakery.

**hale kuke (dute).** Customhouse.

**hale kula.** Schoolhouse.

**hale leka.** Post office. *Lit.*, letter *(Eng.)* house.

**halelū.** Psalm, in the Bible; to sing psalms. Hebrew, hallelu-yah?

**hale ma‘i.** Hospital.

**hale māka‘i.** Police station.

**hale noho.** Dwelling house, residence.

**halepā.** Cupboard, safe. *Lit.*, dish house.

**hale pa‘ahana.** Workshop, tool house.

**hale pa‘ahao.** Jail, prison.

**hale pa‘i.** Publishing house, printing establishment.

**hale pe‘a. 1.** Tent. **2.** Menstrual house.

**hale pili.** House thatched with *pili* grass.

**hale puhi kō.** Sugar mill; boiling house of a sugar mill. *Lit.*, cane cooking house.

**hale pule.** Church, chapel. *Lit.*, prayer house.

**hāleu.** Toilet paper; to wipe, as with toilet paper.

**hale wili kō.** Sugar mill.

**hali‘a.** Sudden remembrance.

**hāli‘i.** A covering, spread; to spread, as a sheet.

**hāli‘i moe.** Bedspread or sheet.

**hālike.** Alike, similar. **ho‘ohālike.** To compare, make alike.

**hālikelike.** Redup. of *hālike*. **ho‘ohālikelike.** Redup. of *ho‘ohālike*.

**hālili.** Sundial shell (*Architectonica* sp. or *Philippia* sp.). Also called *pūlewa*.

**haliu.** To turn, look, hearken.

**halo.** Motion of the fins or hands in swimming; motion of rubbing.

**hālō.** To peer, as with the hands shading the eyes.

**hāloa.** Far-reaching, long.

**hālo‘i.** To well with tears.

**haluku.** To clatter, bang, rattle.

**halulu.** To roar, thunder; loud noise, racket.

**hāmale, hamare.** Hammer; to hammer. *Eng.*

**hāmama.** Open, as a door or obstruction; to open, gape. **ho‘ohāmama.** To open, expose.

**hāmau.** Silent; silence. **ho‘ohāmau.** To silence, hush.

**hame.** Ham. *Eng.*

**hamo. 1.** Anointed, smeared; to rub, as with oil; to fondle, caress. **2.** To spread, as butter.

**hamo puna.** Plasterer; plaster; to plaster, whitewash.

**hamu.** To eat scraps.

**hana. 1.** Work, labor, job, duty, office; activity of any kind, act, deed; to develop, as a picture. **ho‘ohana.** To use, employ, cause to work, carry out; use, employment, management, administration. **2.** Same as *hahana*, warm. **3.** Notch.

**Hana-.** Bay, valley, as in *Hanalei, Hanauma*.

**-hana.** Nominalizing suffix similar to *‘ana*.

**hana aloha.** Love magic; to make such.

**hana ho‘ohiwahiwa.** Celebration, as to honor an individual.

**hana ho‘onanea.** Pleasant pastime, hobby, avocation.

**hana hou.** To do again, repeat; encore.

**hānai. 1.** Foster child, adopted child; foster, adopted. **2.** To raise, feed, nourish, sustain; provider.

**hana ʻino.** To mistreat, abuse, treat cruelly; cruel.

**hana kīwila.** Civil service.

**hana kolohe.** Mischief; to do mischief.

**hana lepo.** Dirty work; excrement; to excrete.

**hana lima.** Handmade, manual; to work with the hands.

**hana maʻi.** Sexual intercourse. *Lit.*, genital activity.

**hana make.** Thing of destruction, as a weapon; to kill, destroy.

**hana paʻa.** 1. To make secure, fasten. 2. Steady employment.

**hanapēpē.** To bruise, crush.

**hana pipi.** To work with cattle, especially as a cowboy.

**hana punahele.** Favorite pastime, hobby.

**hānau.** 1. To give birth; to lay (an egg); born; offspring, childbirth. **hoʻohānau.** To act as midwife, deliver a baby. 2. Happy birthday (as in toasts).

**hānau hope.** Younger brother or sister; the last-born.

**hānau hou.** Reborn; baptism.

**hānau mua.** First-born child.

**hanauna.** Generation; ancestry, birth.

**hanawai.** 1. Irrigation; to irrigate. 2. Menstruation; to menstruate. 3. Urine; to urinate.

**hanele, haneri.** Hundred. *Eng.*

**hani.** To step or move lightly or softly; to touch.

**hanini.** To overflow, pour out; to pour down, as rain.

**hano.** 1. Hoarse. 2. Nose flute.

**hānō.** Asthma; to wheeze.

**hanohano.** Glorious, honored, dignified; pomp, glory. **hoʻo-hanohano.** To honor, exalt, glorify.

**hanu.** To breathe, smell; respiration. **hoʻohanu.** To cause to breathe, resuscitate.

**hānuna.** Nasalized; snoring.

**hanu pau.** Last breath or gasp.

**hao.** 1. Iron; brand, as on a horse. 2. All native species of a genus of small trees *(Rauvolfia)*. 3. To come with force, as wind or rain; to do with force and energy.

**hao hakahaka.** Grill, as for broiling. *Lit.*, iron with spaces.

**haʻohaʻo.** Strange, puzzling; astonished, puzzled; to wonder. **hoʻohaʻohaʻo.** To arouse wonder, surprise, puzzlement.

**haole.** White person; formerly any foreigner; foreign, introduced, of foreign origin. **hoʻo-haole.** To act like a white person, to ape the white people, or assume airs of superiority (often said disparagingly, especially of half-whites). *Hoʻohaole ʻia,* Europeanized, Americanized; to have become like a white man, to have adopted the ways of a white man.

**hao mākēneki (mageneti).** Magnet.

**hao waha.** Bit of a bridle. *Lit.*, mouth iron.

**hapa.** 1. Portion, fragment, part; to be a portion, less. (*Eng.,* half.) 2. Of mixed blood; person of mixed blood.

**hapahā.** One fourth, one quarter; quarter, twenty-five cents; quarterly. *Lit.*, fourth part.

**hapa haole.** Part-white person; of part-white blood; part white and part Hawaiian, as an individual or phenomenon.

**hāpai.** 1. To carry, lift, raise. 2. Pregnant. **hoʻohāpai.** To cause conception.

**hapaipū.** Heavy breathing, as of one with asthma; to breathe heavily; to carry or raise in unison.

**hapakolu.** Third; one third.

**hapakuʻe.** Crooked, deformed, crippled; to speak with an impediment, as one who has had a stroke; crippling.

**hāpala.** To daub, blot, besmear, spread, as butter on bread.

**hapalima.** Fifth; one fifth.

**hapalua.** Half; half dollar; in two portions.

**hapa makahiki.** Semiannual.

**hapa nui.** Majority, most; greatest or largest portion.

**hapa'umi.** Tenth part; five cents.

**hapa 'u'uku.** Minority, small portion; less.

**hapawalu.** One eighth; eighth part.

**hape.** Incorrect, faulty.

**Hapenuia.** Happy New Year. *Eng.*

**hāpuna. 1.** Spring, pool. **2.** Harpoon. *Eng.*

**hāpu'u. 1.** An endemic tree fern *(Cibotium splendens)* common in many forests of Hawai'i, as at Kīlauea Volcano, and now frequently cultivated. **2.** Grouper, a fish *(Epinephelus quernus).*

**hāpu'upu'u.** Young *hāpu'u* ferns that have not yet developed trunks.

**hau. 1.** A lowland tree *(Hibiscus tiliaceus).* **2.** Cool, iced; ice, dew, snow; to blow, of a cool breeze. **3.** Same as *hahau;* to hit, smite.

**hau-. 1.** Intensifying prefix. See examples below. **2.** *(Cap.)* Prefix to names of goddesses and in the common feminine names *Haulani, Haunani.*

**hau'eka.** Defiled, filthy, smutty.

**hauhana.** Lashing.

**hauhia.** To hit.

**hauka'e.** Stained, smeared, smudged; to stain; defiled, as taboo food. **ho'ohauka'e.** To spoil, as a ballot.

**haukalima.** Ice cream. *Lit.,* creamed *(Eng.)* ice.

**haukapila.** Hospital. *Eng.*

**hā'uke.** To search for lice.

**hau kea.** White snow, snow.

**hā'uke'uke.** An edible variety of sea urchin *(Colobocentrotus atrata).*

**hā'ule.** To fall, drop; dropped. **ho'ohā'ule.** To cause to fall.

**hā'ule lau.** Fall, autumn. *Lit.,* leaf falling.

**haumana, haumāna.** Student, pupil, apprentice. Perhaps *lit.,* to lay before one a ball of masticated food *(māna);* to feed masticated food. **ho'ohaumana.** To act as a pupil, become a pupil.

**haumia.** Uncleanliness, defilement; contaminated. **ho'ohaumia.** To pollute, defile.

**hauna.** Unpleasant odor, as of spoiling fish or meat. **ho'ohauna.** To cause an offensive odor.

**haunaele.** Panic, commotion, riot. **ho'ohaunaele.** To provoke panic, riot.

**hau'oli.** Happy, glad, joyful; happiness, joy. *Hau'oli Makahiki Hou,* Happy New Year. *Hau'oli lā hānau,* happy birthday. **ho'ohau'oli.** To cause happiness, gaiety, joy.

**haupia.** Pudding made from coconut cream, formerly thickened with arrowroot, now usually with cornstarch.

**hā'upu.** To recall, recollect, remember.

**hauwala'au.** To gossip, chatter.

**hawa.** Defiled, filthy.

**hāwa'e.** A sea urchin *(Tripneustes gratilla).*

**Hawai'i.** Hawai'i (both the island and the group of islands); Hawaiian person; Hawaiian.

**hāwanawana.** To whisper; whispering.

**hāwāwā.** Unskilled, awkward; blunder, incompetence.

**he.** Indefinite article, usually at the beginning of a phrase: a, to be a, have (with a possessive). *He Hawai'i au,* I am a Hawaiian.

**hē. 1.** General name for caterpillar. **2.** To rub. **3.** The letter *h.*

**hea. 1.** To call, name; to sing or recite a name chant; to give a name to. **2.** Which (in questions and after other words). *Ka mea hea?* Which thing? **3.** Where (in questions, and after *ai, 'au-, i, ma-, mai, no, 'o).*

**he aha, heaha.** See *aha*.

**heahea.** To call frequently; to call hospitably.

**hea inoa.** To give a name; to chant a name chant; to call the roll.

**heana.** Corpse, victim.

**he'e.** 1. Octopus (*Polypus* spp.). 2. To slide, surf, flee. **ho'ohe'e.** To cause to slide; to put to flight. 3. To hang down, sag, as fruit.

**he'ehe'e.** Breast disease with caking during lactation and great pain.

**he'e nalu.** To ride a surfboard; surfing; surf rider. *Lit.*, wave sliding.

**he'e pū loa.** Ornated octopus (*Polypus ornatus*). *Lit.*, long-headed *he'e*.

**he'e umauma.** Body surfing.

**heha.** Lazy, indolent, drowsy.

**hehena.** Insane, raving, mad, crazy, possessed; insanity, lunatic.

**hehi.** To stamp, tread, step on.

**hei.** 1. Net, snare; to ensnare, catch in a net. **ho'ohei.** To snare, tangle. 2. String figure, cat's cradle; to make string figures.

**hē'ī.** 1. Same as *mīkana,* papaya. 2. Wild banana.

**heiau.** Pre-Christian place of worship.

**heiau ho'ōla.** *Heiau* for treating the sick.

**heiau ho'oulu 'ai.** *Heiau* where first fruits were offered to ensure further growth. *Lit.*, *heiau* for the increase of food.

**heiau ho'oulu i'a.** *Heiau* where fish were offered to ensure good fishing.

**heiau ho'oulu ua.** *Heiau* where offerings were made to ensure rain.

**heiau po'o kanaka.** *Heiau* where human sacrifices were offered.

**heihei.** Race, as foot race, canoe race; to race. **ho'oheihei.** To run swiftly, take part in a race.

**hekau.** Anchor, stone anchor, towline; to anchor, make fast.

**heke.** 1. Best. 2. Top gourd in a gourd hula drum.

**hekili.** Thunder; to thunder.

**hela.** 1. To spread, as the arms. 2. Red, raw.

**hele.** 1. To go, come, walk; to move, as in a game; going, moving. *Hele mai,* come. **ho'ohele.** To cause to move. 2. Everywhere, here and there, continuously. *Holo hele,* run here and there. 3. To tie, bind, snare. 4. To cut.

**helehelena.** Features, face.

**hele hewa.** To go wrong, take the wrong path, to go astray.

**helei.** Pulled down, as an eyelid.

**helele'i, helelei.** Falling; scattered, as rain, tears; crumbling, as the earth. **ho'ohelele'i.** To scatter, sow.

**hele loa.** To go or come far; to go permanently.

**hele malihini.** To go to a place for the first time or as a stranger.

**hele mauna.** To travel in the mountains; mountain climber.

**hele pēlā.** Get out! Go away!

**heleuma.** Anchor, stone anchor.

**hele wale.** To go naked; to go without fixed purpose, or far and wide; to go empty-handed.

**hele wāwae.** To walk, go on foot; pedestrian.

**helo.** Red, as *'ōhelo* berries.

**helu.** 1. To count, number, list; to assess, as taxes; to chant a list of names, as of genealogy; census, figure, inventory. 2. Arithmetic, score; serial, numbered. 3. To scratch the earth, as a hen.

**heluhelu.** To read, count.

**heluna.** Number, count, total sum; grade (evaluation).

**heluna papa.** Grade or mark, as given in school; number of a school grade (class).

**helu nui.** Large number; plural number.

**helu pāloka (balota).** To count ballots; election teller.

**helu papa.** To count in order or consecutively.

**helu waiwai.** Inventory.

**hema. 1.** Left; left side. **2.** South.

**hemahema.** Awkward, clumsy, unskilled, inexpert; to not know well.

**hemo.** Loose, separated; discharged, divorced, opened; taken off, as clothes. **hoʻohemo.** To loosen, undo, unfasten, free.

**hemolele.** Perfect, faultless, holy; perfection, virtue, holiness; angel, person without fault.

**henehene.** To laugh at, ridicule, giggle. **hoʻohenehene.** To tease, laugh at.

**heno.** Same as *henoheno*. **hoʻoheno.** To cherish, love, caress; expression of affection.

**henoheno.** Lovable, sweet.

**hepa.** Imbecilic; idiot.

**hepekoma, hebedoma.** Week; seven years. *Greek.*

**Hepekoma Hemolele.** Holy Week.

**heu.** Down or fine hair, fuzz, loose fibers on certain fruits or leaves.

**hewa.** Mistake, fault, error, sin, guilt; wrong, incorrect, wicked, sinful; to err. **hoʻohewa.** To cause one to do wrong, cause or feign a mistake; to blame, condemn.

**hī. 1.** To cast or troll, as for bonito. **2.** Dysentery, diarrhea; to flow, hiss.

**hia.** Desire.

**-hia. 1.** How many? How much? (follows ʻa-, ʻe-, or pā-.) **2.** Pas./imp.

**hiʻa. 1.** To make fire with the fireplow. **2.** Needle for making nets.

**hiaʻaiʻono.** Pleased with, delighted with; appetite.

**hiamoe.** Sleep; to sleep, fall asleep. **hoʻohiamoe.** To put to sleep, lull to sleep.

**hiamoe iki.** A little sleep, nap; to take a nap.

**hiamoe loa.** To oversleep, sleep deeply; death, eternal sleep.

**hiapo.** First-born child; first born.

**hie.** Attractive, distinguished. **hoʻohie.** Stately, delightful.

**hiehie.** Redup. of *hie*. **hoʻohiehie.** To beautify, make distinctive, beautiful.

**hihi.** To entangle, intertwine; entanglement. **hoʻohihi.** To cause entanglement; to entwine.

**hīhī.** Redup. of *hī, 2;* to hiss.

**hihia. 1.** Entangled, interwoven; snarl, problem, trouble. **hoʻohihia.** To get into difficulties, entangle. **2.** A lawsuit or case before the court.

**hihia kalaima.** Criminal case.

**hīhīmanu. 1.** Various sting rays (Dasyatidae) and eagle rays *(Actobatus marinari).* **2.** Lavish, magnificent, elegant.

**hihiu.** Wild, untamed.

**hiʻi.** To hold or carry in the arms, as a child.

**hiʻikua.** To carry on the back, as children.

**hiʻilawe.** To lift, carry.

**hiʻimoʻopuna.** To bear a grandchild in the arms; to be a grandparent (a term of pride and affection).

**hiʻipoi.** To tend, feed, cherish, as a child.

**hiki. 1.** Can, to be able. **2.** All right, O.K. (in sense of "able to do"). **3.** To get to or reach a place, arrive. **4.** Next.

**-hiki. hoʻohiki.** To vow, swear, take an oath.

**hikiʻe.** Large immovable Hawaiian couch. See *pūneʻe.*

**hīkiʻi.** Binding; to tie, make fast.

**hīkiʻikiʻi.** Redup. of *hīkiʻi.*

**hikilele.** To jump or start from shock; shock.

**hikina. 1.** East. **2.** Coming.

**hikina ʻākau.** Northeast.

**hikina hema.** Southeast.

**hiki nō.** All right, O.K.

**hiki ʻole.** Impossible.

**hikiwale.** Easy.

**hiki wale.** To come accidentally.

**hikiwawe.** Quickly; possible to do quickly. **ho'ohikiwawe.** To accelerate, hurry.

**hiku.** Seven; seventh (usually preceded by the numeral prefix 'e).

**hila. 1.** Same as *hilahila*. **2.** Heel. *Eng. Hila 'auli'i,* high heels.

**hilahila.** Bashful, shy, embarrassed. **ho'ohilahila.** To make ashamed, humiliate; shameful, bashful.

**hili. 1.** To braid, plait, string, as flowers for a lei or candlenuts for a torch. **2.** To turn, wander, stray. **3.** To whip, bat; batter, as in baseball.

**hilina'i.** To believe, trust; to rely on.

**hilo. 1.** To twist, braid; threadlike; faint streak of light. **2.** *(Cap.)* First night of the new moon. **3.** *(Cap.)* Name of a famous Polynesian navigator.

**hilu.** Various species of reef fishes of the genus *Coris.*

**hiluhilu.** Elegant, beautiful.

**hīmeni.** Hymn, any song not used for hulas; to sing a *hīmeni. Eng.*

**hina. 1.** To fall over, tumble, or topple from an upright position; to throw down. **2.** Gray- or white-haired; gray. **3.** *(Cap.)* Name of a goddess.

**hinahina. 1.** The silversword *(Argyroxiphium sandwicense).* See *'āhinahina, 2.* **2.** Spanish or Florida moss *(Tillandsia usneoides),* an air plant, growing on tree branches and hanging baskets.

**hīna'i.** A kind of basket fish trap.

**hinakā.** Handkerchief. *Eng.*

**hīnālea.** Small- to moderate-sized, brightly colored wrasses. Varieties include *hīnālea lauwili (Thalassoma duperreyi), hīnālea luahine (T. ballieui),* and *hīnālea nuku'i'iwi (Gomphosus varius).*

**hīnano.** Male pandanus blossom.

**-hine.** Female, feminine.

**hinihini.** Indistinct.

**hinu.** Oil, grease; oily; smooth and polished, lustrous.

**hinuhinu.** Intensification of *hinu;* bright, glittering, as of polished stones or shells. **ho'ohinuhinu.** To shine, polish.

**hio.** To blow in gusts.

**hiohio. 1.** To whistle softly; to blow softly. **2.** Gibberish.

**hiolo.** To tumble down, collapse; overthrown; landslide. **ho'ohiolo.** To overthrow, demolish.

**hi'ona.** General appearance, as of a person.

**hipa.** Sheep. *Eng.*

**hipahipa.** Hip, hip, hurrah! Cheers! *(Eng.,* hip.) *'Ekolu hipahipa no ka mō'ī,* three cheers for the king!

**hipa kāne.** Ram. *Lit.,* male sheep.

**hipa keiki.** Lamb.

**hiu.** To fling.

**hi'u. 1.** Hind part or tail section of a fish. **2.** Caudal fin.

**hiwa. 1.** Entirely black, as of pigs offered to the gods. **2.** Choice. See *hiwahiwa.*

**hiwahiwa.** Precious, beloved, esteemed; favorite. **ho'ohiwahiwa.** To honor, adorn; to display, as the flag; to treat as a favorite.

**hiwi.** Ridge.

**hō. 1.** To give, transfer, go (followed by directionals). **2.** Hoe; to hoe. *Eng.*

**hō, ho'-, hō'-.** Same as *ho'o-.*

**hoa. 1.** Companion, friend, associate, partner. **ho'ohoa.** To make friends. **2.** To tie, lash. **3.** To strike.

**-hoa. ho'ohoa.** To challenge, dare; defiant.

**hō'ā. 1.** To set on fire, burn, ignite. See *'ā.* **2.** To drive, as cattle.

**hō'ā ahi.** To kindle fire.

**hoa hana.** Fellow worker, colleague, partner.

**hoahānau.** Cousin; brother or sister, as a church member.

**hoa hele.** Traveling companion, fellow traveler.

**ho'āhewa.** To blame, condemn. See *'āhewa.*

**hō'ai.** To feed. See *'ai,* food.

**hō'ailona.** See - *'ailona.*

**hoaka. 1.** Crescent, arch; crest, as on a helmet. **2.** *(Cap.)* Second day of the month. **3.** Brightness; to glitter, shine.

**hō'aka'aka.** See *'aka'aka,* to laugh.

**hoa kamali'i.** Childhood playmate.

**hoa kanaka.** Fellow man.

**ho'ākoakoa.** See *'ākoakoa.*

**hoa kūkā, hoa kūkākūkā.** Consultant, adviser, one with whom one confers and deliberates.

**hoa kula.** Schoolmate.

**ho'āla.** See *ala,* to waken, rise up.

**hō'ala.** See *'ala,* fragrant.

**hoalauna.** Neighbor, close associate or friend.

**hoa lawehana.** Fellow laborer or workers, helper.

**hoa like.** Companion or contemporary of equal status.

**hoaloha.** Friend. *Lit.,* beloved companion. Cf. *aloha.* **ho'ohoaloha.** To make friends, be friendly.

**hō'alu.** See *'alu,* depression.

**hō'alu'alu.** See *'alu'alu,* loose.

**hoa lumi.** Roommate.

**hoa moe.** Sleeping companion, bedfellow.

**hoana.** Hone, whetstone, grindstone; to rub, grind.

**ho'āna.** See *ana,* to measure.

**hoana ka'a.** Grindstone, rolling grindstone.

**ho'āni.** See *ani,* to beckon.

**hoa noho.** Neighbor, one who lives with or near another.

**ho'ānu.** See *anu,* cool.

**ho'āo.** Marriage. See *ao, 1,* light.

**ho'ā'o.** To try, taste. See *a'o,* instruction.

**hoa pa'ahana.** Fellow worker.

**hoa paio.** Opponent, antagonist, enemy.

**hoa pili.** Close, intimate, or personal friend.

**ho'āpono.** To approve. See *'āpono.*

**hō'au.** See *'au,* to swim.

**hō'auana, ho'o'auana.** See *'auana,* to wander.

**hō'au'au.** See *'au'au,* to bathe.

**hoe. 1.** Paddle, oar; to paddle, row. *Fig.,* to travel, get to work, continue working. *Hoe aku i ka wa'a,* paddle ahead the canoe (do your share; continue; keep going). **2.** To draw in the breath and expel it with a whistling sound, as when tired.

**hō'ea.** To arrive.

**hō'ele'ele.** To blacken. See *'ele'ele.*

**ho'ēmi.** To reduce, diminish, cheapen. See *emi, 1, 2.*

**hoene.** A soft sweet sound, as of song; to sound softly.

**hō'ewa.** See *'ewa,* crooked.

**hoe wa'a.** Oarsman, paddler; to paddle a canoe.

**hohola.** To spread out, unfold.

**hohono.** Unpleasant acrid odor, body odor; to smell thus.

**hohonu.** Deep, profound.

**hoi.** Bitter yam *(Dioscorea bulbifera).*

**ho'i. 1.** To leave, go or come back; to cause to come back. **2.** Intensifying particle. *Maika'i ho'i,* fairly good. See *noho'i.* **3.** Also, besides. *'A'ole ho'i,* neither. **4.** Particle expressing doubt, uncertainty. *Pehea ho'i,* how indeed, I don't know.

**ho'ihā.** Intensive of *ho'i, 2. E hele ho'ihā kāua,* well, let's go then.

**hoihoi.** Pleased, happy, joyful, entertaining, interesting; pleasure, interest. **ho'ohoihoi.** To entertain, charm, please.

**ho'iho'i.** To return, send back, restore.

**ho'i hope.** To go back, return, revert, backslide.

**ho'i hou.** To go or come back, return.

**hō'ikaika.** See *ikaika,* strong.

**hō'ike.** To show, exhibit. See *'ike.*

**Hōʻike ʻAna.** Revelation (Biblical).

**hōʻikeʻike.** Display. See *ʻikeʻike.*

**hoʻīli.** See *ili, 1, 2.*

**hoʻīlo.** See *hoʻoilo.*

**hoka. 1.** Disappointed, baffled; frustration. **hoʻohoka.** To cause disappointment, to thwart. **2.** To squeeze.

**hōkā.** Same as *hoʻokā.* See *kā, 1.*

**hokahokai.** Redup. of *hōkai.*

**hōkai.** To confuse; to blunder along; bother, disorder.

**hōkake.** To interfere, as would a child. See *kake, 1.*

**hōkana, hosana.** Hosanna.

**hōkele, hotele.** Hotel. *Eng.*

**hōkeo.** Large gourd calabash.

**hoki. 1.** Mule, ass. (*Eng.,* horse.) **2.** Barren, as of a woman. *Modern.*

**hōkio.** A small gourd whistle, musical pipe; to whistle.

**hōkiokio.** Gourd whistle, musical pipe; to whistle.

**Hoku.** Night of the full moon.

**hōkū.** Star.

**hōkū ʻaeʻa.** Planet. *Lit.,* wandering star.

**Hōkūao.** Morning Star, Venus when seen in the morning.

**Hōkū keʻa.** Southern Cross. *Lit.,* cross star.

**hōkū lele.** Shooting star, meteor, any moving star.

**hōkū lewa.** Moving star, planet.

**Hōkū paʻa.** North Star. *Lit.,* immovable star.

**hōkū welowelo.** Shooting star, comet. *Lit.,* streaming star.

**hola. 1.** Hour, time, o'clock, *Eng. Hola ʻehia kēia?* What time is it? **2.** Same as *hohola,* to spread.

**holahia.** Passive/imperative of *hola, 2.*

**Hōlani. 1.** Name of a mythical place. **2.** Holland; Dutch. *Eng.*

**hole.** To skin, peel; to strip, as sugarcane leaves from the stalk.

**holi.** To sprout, as plants or a youth's beard.

**holina.** Immature and inferior, as breadfruit falling prematurely.

**hōlina.** Haul in! Help! *Eng.*

**holo. 1.** To run, sail, ride, go; to flow, as water; to run, as for political office; to slide, as an avalanche; fleet, fast. **hoʻoholo.** To sail, run; to cause to run, sail, run free, as a horse; to add water, as to *poi;* to flush, as a toilet. **2.** Decided, agreed upon, passed, enacted. **hoʻoholo.** To decide, determine, settle, conclude; decision. **3.** Hall. *Eng.*

**holoāiʻa.** To swim like a fish; to get the bends; to drown.

**holoʻanai.** To gallop.

**holohau.** To ice skate, ski. *Lit.,* ice run.

**holo hele.** To run to and fro; bustle.

**holohiʻa.** To dart this way and that, as children at play.

**holoholo. 1.** To go for a walk, ride, or sail; to go out for pleasure. **hoʻoholoholo.** To take someone out for a drive; to escort. **2.** Basting; to baste, sew. **hoʻoholoholo.** To make large running stiches.

**holoholo kaʻa.** To go for a drive, ride.

**holoholona.** Animal, beast.

**holoholoʻōlelo.** To gossip, slander; tattler, spreader of gossip.

**holo hōlua.** Course for *hōlua,* sledding.

**holoi.** To wash, clean; washing, erasure. **hoʻoholoi.** To have washed, cleaned.

**holo i mua, holoimua.** To progress, advance; successful. Also *holomua.*

**holo kaʻa.** To ride in a car or carriage.

**holokahiki.** Sailor; to sail to foreign lands.

**holokai.** Seaman, seafarer; to sail on the sea.

**holokē.** To run here and there; helter-skelter.

**holokikī.** To run or sail swiftly; headlong.

**holokū.** A long, one-piece dress, usually fitted and with a train and a yoke, patterned after the Mother Hubbards of the missionaries.

**holo kūkū.** To trot, as a horse.

**holo lio.** To ride horseback; horseman, rider.

**holomakani.** Breezy, airy. *Lit.,* wind running.

**holo manaʻo.** To decide, determine.

**holomoku.** Sailor, passenger, anyone who sails; to take a sail or ocean trip.

**holomū.** A long, fitted dress, a combination of *holokū* (without a train) and *muʻumuʻu. Modern.*

**holomua.** Same as *holo i mua;* improvement, progress.

**holoʻokoʻa.** Whole, entire, all; entirely; paramount.

**holo paheʻe.** To skate, skid.

**holopeki.** To trot. *Lit.,* pace *(Eng.)* run.

**holopono.** To pass off successfully, succeed; success.

**holopuni.** To sail or travel around, circumnavigate.

**holo pupule.** Reckless, mad running; to speed recklessly, as an auto.

**holowai.** Water ditch; to run in such courses; watery.

**holu.** Springy, pliable, resilient, as a mattress; to sway, as palm fronds; to ripple, as waves; bumpy, as an airplane ride.

**hōlua.** Sled, especially the ancient sled used on grassy slopes; the sled course.

**holu nape.** To sway.

**home.** Home. *Eng.*

**home hoʻopaʻa.** Detention home.

**hone. 1.** Sweet and soft, as music; sweetly appealing, as perfume or a memory of love; to tease, mischievous. **2.** Honey. *Eng.*

**honekakala.** Honeysuckle.

**hōnēnē.** To attract.

**honi. 1.** To kiss; formerly to touch noses on the side in greeting. **2.** To smell, sniff; a scent.

**honi lima.** To throw a kiss; such a kiss.

**hono. 1.** To stitch, sew, mend; a joining, as of mountains. **2.** Back of the neck. **3.** Rite at the end of *kapu loulu* rituals during which chiefs sat without shifting positions while a *kahuna* prayed for as long as an hour.

**Hono-.** Bay, gulch, valley (as a part of place names such as Honolulu, Honokōhau, Honoliʻi, Honomanu). See *Hana-.*

**honohono.** Short for *honohono kukui.* See also *ʻokika honohono.*

**honohono kukui.** Basket grass *(Oplismenus hirtellus).*

**Honolulu.** Name of the capital city in the Hawaiian Islands. *Lit.,* sheltered bay.

**honu.** General name for turtle and tortoise.

**honua.** Land, earth; background, as of quilt designs; basic, at the foundation, fundamental.

**honuaʻula.** A variety of sugarcane, a dark brown-red mutant of *manulele,* with purple leaf sheaths and leaves.

**honuʻea.** Hawkbill turtle *(Chelonia);* the shell of this turtle was used as medicine for the disease called *ʻea,* and was also used for combs and fans.

**hoʻo-.** A very active former of causative/simulative derivatives. *Hoʻo-* usually precedes stems beginning with the vowels *i-* and *u-* and all the consonants except the glottal stop. Important meanings are: **(1)** Causation and transitivization, as *pono,* correct; *hoʻoponopono,* to correct. **(2)** Pretense, as *kuli,* deaf; *hoʻokuli,* to feign deafness. **(3)** Similarity, as *kamaliʻi,* children; *hoʻokamaliʻi,* childish. **(4)** No meaning, as *kāholoholo,* to hurry; *hoʻokāholoholo,* to hurry. The meanings of some *ho‘o-* derivatives are quite different from the meanings of the stems, as *maika‘i,* good; *ho‘omaika‘i,* to congratulate. *Ho‘o-* derivatives are defined under the stems. Delete *ho‘o-* and see the stems.

**ho‘oha‘aha‘a.** See *ha‘aha‘a,* low, humble.

**ho‘oha‘aheo.** See *ha‘aheo,* proud.

**ho‘ohae.** See *hae,* wild, and *hae,* to bark.

**ho‘ohahana.** See *hahana,* warm.

**ho‘ohaku.** See *haku,* lord.

**ho‘ohala.** See *hala,* to sin, and *hala,* to pass.

**ho‘ohalahala.** See *halahala.*

**ho‘ohala manawa.** To pass the time.

**ho‘ohālike. See** *hālike,* alike.

**ho‘ohāmama.** See *hāmama,* open.

**ho‘ohanohano.** See *hanohano,* glorious.

**ho‘oha‘oha‘o.** See *ha‘oha‘o,* puzzling.

**ho‘ohauka‘e.** See *hauka‘e,* stained.

**ho‘ohā‘ule.** See *hā‘ule,* to fall.

**ho‘ohaumia.** See *haumia,* defilement.

**ho‘ohaunaele.** See *haunaele,* panic.

**ho‘ohe‘e.** See *he‘e,* to slide.

**ho‘ohei.** See *hei,* snare.

**ho‘oheihei.** See *heihei,* race.

**ho‘ohele.** See *hele, 1.*

**ho‘ohelele‘i.** See *helele‘i,* falling.

**ho‘ohemo.** See *hemo,* loose.

**ho‘ohenehene.** See *henehene.*

**ho‘oheno.** To cherish. See *heno.*

**ho‘ohewa.** See *hewa,* mistake.

**ho‘ohiamoe.** See *hiamoe,* sleep.

**ho‘ohie.** See *hie,* attractive.

**ho‘ohihia.** See *hihia,* entangled.

**ho‘ohiki.** See *-hiki.*

**ho‘ohilahila.** See *hilahila,* bashful.

**ho‘ohinuhinu.** See *hinuhinu.*

**ho‘ohiwahiwa.** See *hiwahiwa,* precious.

**ho‘ōho.** See *oho,* to call.

**ho‘ohoa.** See *hoa,* companion, and *-hoa.*

**ho‘ohoihoi.** See *hoihoi,* pleased.

**ho‘ohoka.** See *hoka,* disappointed.

**ho‘oholo.** See *holo,* to run, and *holo,* decided.

**ho‘ohopohopo.** See *hopohopo,* anxiety.

**ho‘ohū.** See *hū,* to swell.

**ho‘ohua.** See *hua,* fruit.

**ho‘ohu‘a.** See *hu‘a,* foam.

**ho‘ohuhū.** See *huhū,* angry.

**ho‘ohuhuki.** See *huhuki,* to pull.

**ho‘ohui.** See *hui,* club, and *hui,* to join.

**ho‘ohu‘ihu‘i.** See *hu‘ihu‘i,* cold.

**ho‘ohuikau.** See *huikau,* mixed.

**ho‘ohuki.** See *huki,* to pull.

**ho‘ohuli.** See *huli,* to turn, and *huli,* to look for.

**ho‘ohulu.** See *hulu,* esteemed.

**ho‘ohūnā.** See *hūnā,* to hide.

**hō‘oia.** See *‘oia,* truth.

**hō‘oia‘i‘o.** See *‘oia‘i‘o,* true.

**ho‘oiki.** See *iki,* small.

**ho‘oili.** See *ili,* stranded, and *ili,* inheritance.

**ho‘oilina.** See *ilina,* recipient.

**ho‘oilo.** Winter, rainy season.

**ho‘oinu.** See *inu,* to drink.

**ho‘okā.** See *kā, 1.*

**ho‘oka‘a.** See *ka‘a, 1, 3.*

**ho‘oka‘awale.** See *ka‘awale.*

**ho‘okae.** See *kae.*

**ho‘okahe.** See *kahe,* to flow.

**ho‘okahi.** See *kahi, 1.*

**ho‘okahua.** See *kahua.*

**ho‘okahuli.** See *kahuli,* overthrow.

**ho‘okala.** See *kala, 1, 3.*

**ho‘okali.** See *kali,* to wait.

**ho‘okamakama.** See *-kamakama.*

**ho‘okamani.** See *kamani, 2.*

**ho‘okani.** See *kani,* sound.

**ho‘okano.** See *-kano.*

**ho‘okaulike.** See *kaulike,* equality.

**ho‘okē.** See *kē, 1.*

**ho‘okele.** See *kele,* watery, and *kele,* to sail.

ho‘ōki. See *oki,* to stop.
hō‘oki. See *‘oki,* to cut.
ho‘oki‘eki‘e. See *ki‘eki‘e,* height.
ho‘okīnā. See *kīnā,* blemish.
ho‘okino. See *kino,* body.
ho‘okipa. See *kipa.*
ho‘okipi. See *kipi,* rebellion.
ho‘okō. See *kō,* to fulfill.
ho‘okoe. See *koe,* to remain.
ho‘okohu. See *kohu,* resemblance, and *-kohu.*
ho‘oko‘iko‘i. See *ko‘iko‘i,* weight.
ho‘okokoke. See *kokoke,* near.
ho‘okolokolo. See *kolokolo.*
ho‘okomo. See *komo,* to enter, and *komo,* to dress.
ho‘okū. See *kū,* to stand, and *kū,* in a state of.
ho‘okū‘ē. See *kū‘ē,* to oppose.
ho‘oku‘i. See *ku‘i,* to pound.
ho‘okūkū. See *kūkū,* to shake, and *-kūkū.*
ho‘okuli. See *kuli,* deaf.
ho‘okumu. See *kumu,* beginning.
ho‘okū‘ono‘ono. See *kū‘ono‘ono,* well-off.
ho‘okupa. See *kupa,* citizen.
ho‘okupu. See *kupu,* sprout, and *-kupu.*
ho‘oku‘u. See *ku‘u,* to release.
ho‘olā. See *lā,* sun.
ho‘ōla. See *ola,* life.
ho‘ola‘a. See *la‘a, 1.*
ho‘olaha. See *laha,* extended.
ho‘olaka. To tame. See *laka.*
ho‘olako. See *lako.*
ho‘olalau. See *lalau,* mistake.
ho‘olana. See *lana,* floating, and *-lana.*
ho‘olapa. See *lapa,* ridge, and *lapa,* energetic.
ho‘ōla pāna‘i. See *ola pāna‘i.*
ho‘olapu. See *lapu,* ghost.
ho‘olau. See *lau,* leaf; *lau,* dragnet; and *lau,* much.
ho‘olaulā. See *laulā,* broad.
ho‘olaule‘a. See *laule‘a.*
ho‘olauna. See *launa,* friendly.
ho‘olawa. See *lawa, 1.*
ho‘olawe. See *lawe.*
ho‘olawehala. See *lawehala,* sin.

hō‘ole. See *‘ole.*
ho‘olei. See *lei, 2.*
ho‘olele. See *lele, 1.*
Hō‘ole Pope. Protestant. *Lit.,* Denier of Pope.
ho‘olewa. See *lewa,* to float, and *-lewa.*
ho‘olilo. See *lilo, 1, 3.*
ho‘olimalima. See *limalima.*
ho‘olohe. See *lohe,* to hear, obey.
ho‘ololi. See *loli,* to change.
ho‘olono. See *lono, 1.*
hō‘olu. See *‘olu,* cool.
ho‘olua. See *lua, 1, 3.*
ho‘oluhi. See *luhi.*
ho‘oluli. See *luli,* to shake.
hō‘olu‘olu. See *‘olu‘olu.*
ho‘olu‘u. See *lu‘u,* to dive.
ho‘oma‘ama‘a. See *ma‘ama‘a.*
ho‘oma‘ema‘e. See *ma‘ema‘e.*
ho‘omaha. See *maha,* rest.
ho‘omahana. See *mahana, 1.*
ho‘omāhua. See *māhua.*
ho‘omaika‘i. See *maika‘i,* good.
ho‘omaka. See *maka, 3.*
ho‘omāka‘ika‘i. See *māka‘ika‘i,* to visit.
ho‘omaka‘u. See *maka‘u.*
ho‘omākaukau. See *mākaukau.*
ho‘omake. See *make,* to die.
ho‘omāke‘aka. See *-māke‘aka.*
ho‘omālamalama. See *mālamalama.*
ho‘omalimali. See *malimali.*
ho‘omalolo. See *malolo,* to rest.
ho‘omalu. See *malu,* shade.
ho‘omāluhiluhi. See *māluhiluhi.*
ho‘omana. See *mana,* power.
ho‘omānalo. See *mānalo,* sweet.
ho‘omanamana. See *manamana.*
ho‘omana‘o. See *mana‘o.*
ho‘omanawanui. See *-manawanui,* patience.
ho‘omaopopo. See *maopopo.*
ho‘omau. See *mau, 1, 2.*
ho‘omo‘a. See *mo‘a,* cooked.
ho‘omoana. See *moana,* campground, and *moana,* broad.
ho‘omoe. See *moe,* to sleep, and *moe,* to marry.
ho‘omū. See *mū, 2, 3.*
ho‘onā. See *nā,* calmed.

ho‘ona‘auao. See *na‘auao*.

ho‘onanea. See *nanea*.

ho‘onanenane. See *nanenane*.

ho‘onani. See *nani*.

ho‘ōne. See *one*, sand.

ho‘one‘e. See *ne‘e*, to move along.

hō‘oni. See *‘oni*, to move.

ho‘onipo. See *nipo*, *1, 2*.

hŏ‘ono. See *‘ono*, delicious.

ho‘onui. See *nui*.

hō‘o‘opa. See *‘o‘opa*, lame.

ho‘opā. See *pā*, to touch.

ho‘opa‘a. See *pa‘a*.

ho‘opa‘apa‘a. See *pa‘apa‘a*.

ho‘opae. See *pae*, cluster, and *pae*, to land.

ho‘opahe‘e. See *pahe‘e*, slippery.

ho‘opai. See *pai*.

ho‘opa‘i. See *pa‘i*, to slap.

ho‘opailua. See *pailua*, nausea.

ho‘opakele. See *pakele*, to escape.

ho‘opala. See *pala*, ripe, and *pala*, dab.

ho‘opale. See *pale*, *1*.

ho‘opāna‘i. See *pāna‘i*, revenge.

ho‘opāpā. See *pāpā*, to touch.

ho‘opau. See *pau*, finished.

ho‘opaumanawa. See *-paumanawa*.

ho‘opē. See *pē*, crushed; *pē*, perfumed; and *pē*, drenched.

hŏ‘ope. See *‘ope*, bundle.

ho‘opiha. See *piha*, full.

ho‘opi‘i. See *pi‘i*, *1, 2*, and *-pi‘i*.

ho‘opili. See *pili*, to cling, and *pili*, to refer.

ho‘oponopono. See *ponopono*, *1*.

ho‘opū‘iwa. See *pū‘iwa*, surprised.

ho‘opuka. See *puka*, *1, 2, 3*.

ho‘opulapula. See *pulapula*, seedling.

ho‘opulu. See *pulu*, wet, and *pulu*, mulch.

ho‘opuni. See *puni*, *1, 2, 3*.

ho‘ou‘i. See *u‘i*.

ho‘ouka. See *-uka*.

ho‘ouku. See *uku*, pay.

ho‘ouli. See *uli*, *1*, dark.

ho‘oulu. See *ulu*, *1, 2*.

ho‘ouna. See *-una*.

ho‘owā. See *wā*, roar.

ho‘owahāwahā. See *wahāwahā*.

ho‘owalewale. See *walewale*.

ho‘oweliweli. See *weli*.

ho‘owili. See *wili*, to turn.

hope. **1.** After, behind; last, rear; afterwards. (This common word occurs without a preceding *k*-demonstrative or *k*-possessive; it frequently follows *ma-*.) *Mahope*, afterwards, by-and-by. *I hope*, in back, behind. **2.** Result, conclusion, end. **3.** Deputy, assistant, acting officer. **4.** Posterior, buttocks.

hopena. Result, conclusion, ending.

hope‘ō. Wasp, yellow jacket. *Lit.*, spearing rear.

hope pelekikena (peresidena). Vice-president.

hope po‘o. Acting or deputy head, director.

hōpoe. **1.** Fully developed. **2.** *(Cap.)* A legendary woman in the Pele and Hi‘iaka legend cycle.

hopohopo. Anxiety, uncertainty, doubt; in doubt, fearful. ho‘ohopohopo. To produce anxiety.

hopu. To seize, grasp, arrest; taking, seizure.

hopuna. **1.** Grasping, taking; arrest. **2.** Pronunciation.

hopuna ‘ōlelo. **1.** Pronunciation. **2.** Paragraph. **3.** Syllable.

hou. **1.** New, fresh, recent. **2.** Again, more. *Hana hou*, to do again, encore. **3.** To push, stab, inject. **4.** Perspiration, sweat; to perspire, sweat.

hō‘ulu‘ulu. See *‘ulu‘ulu*, collection.

houpo. Diaphragm, chest.

houpo ‘ume pau. Heart attack.

hū. **1.** To rise or swell, as yeast or souring *poi*; to ferment, boil over; to surge or rise to the surface, as emotion; rising, swelling; overflow. **ho'ohū. (a)** To leaven, cause to rise. **(b)** Yeast, baking powder, leaven. **2.** To roar, grunt, hum.

**hua. 1.** Fruit, egg, ovum, seed; to bear fruit, seed; to bear a child; fruitful. **ho'ohua.** To bear fruit, reproduce, give birth; to swell high, as a wave. **2.** Result, effect; credit, as for a university course. **3.** Testicles. **4.** Word, letter.

**huā.** Envy, jealousy; to stir up trouble.

**hu'a.** Foam, bubble, suds.

**hua 'ai.** Edible fruit or seed.

**hua'ala.** Nutmeg. *Lit.*, fragrant fruit.

**huaaale.** Pill. *Lit.*, seed to swallow.

**huaaale ho'omoe.** Sleeping tablet.

**hua 'ē.** Child born out of wedlock, that is accepted by the husband or wife of the parent and treated as his own. *Lit.*, strange fruit.

**hua hapa.** Half note, as in music.

**hua hapahā.** Quarter note, as in music.

**hua hā'ule.** Fallen fruit or seed. *Fig.*, friendless, illegitimate child (modern); fetus lost through miscarriage.

**huahekili.** Hail. *Lit.*, thunder fruit.

**hua helu.** Figure, number (the character).

**huahua. 1.** Fruitful, productive; to bear many fruits; to lay many eggs. **2.** Testicles.

**huahua'i.** Redup. of *hua'i;* to boil up, as water in a spring; to gush forth.

**hu'ahu'a kai.** Sea foam; crest of a wave breaking into foam.

**hu'ahu'a kopa (sopa).** Soapsuds.

**hua'i.** To disclose, reveal, uncover, as an oven; to pour forth; to churn water, as the propeller of a ship.

**hua iki.** Small letter; small fruit.

**hua kahi.** An only child or offspring.

**hua kai.** Scrambled eggs.

**huaka'i.** Trip, voyage; procession, parade; to travel.

**huaka'i hele.** Travels, a long trip; to keep traveling.

**huaka'i pō.** Night procession or parade, especially the night procession of ghosts that is sometimes called *'oi'o.*

**hua kanu.** Seed, as of mango; bulb.

**huakē.** Full and plump, as a healthy person.

**hu'a kopa.** Soap bubble.

**hua kukui.** *Kukui* (candlenut) nuts.

**hu'alepo.** To scatter dust; to hit an underhanded blow.

**huali.** Bright, polished clean, pure, white, gleaming; morally pure.

**hua loa'a.** Product, answer, as in arithmetic.

**hu'a lole.** Trimmings or borders of a garment; hem of a dress.

**hū'alu.** Loose skin over the eyeball.

**hua mele.** Notes in music; words of a song.

**hua moa.** Chicken egg.

**hua mua.** Offering to a Congregational church of the first earnings in a new job or undertaking; offerings in gratitude for a particular success, as a big fish catch. *Lit.*, first fruit.

**hua nui. 1.** Large fruit, egg. **2.** Capital letter.

**hua 'oko'a.** Whole note in music.

**hua 'ole.** Fruitless, unproductive, worthless.

**hua 'ōlelo.** Word.

**hua pākā.** Scrambled eggs, omelet.

**huapalaoa.** Wheat. *Lit.*, flour *(Eng.)* seed.

**hua palapala.** Letter of the alphabet. *Lit.*, writing letter.

**hua pāma.** Date (the fruit).

**hua pōpolo.** *Pōpolo* berry.

**hua waina.** Grape, grapes. *Lit.*, wine *(Eng.)* fruit.

**hua waina malo‘o.** Raisins. *Lit.*, dry grapes.

**hue.** Gourd, water calabash, any narrow-necked vessel for holding water.

**hu‘e.** To remove, lift off, uncover; to open, as an oven; to wash out, as flood waters.

**huehue.** Pimples, acne; to have pimples.

**huelo.** Tail, as of dog, cat, pig; train of a dress.

**hū‘ena.** Very angry.

**hue wai.** Gourd water container, bottle.

**hue wai pū‘ali.** Gourd water container with constriction around the middle.

**hue wai pueo.** Water gourd shaped like an hourglass. *Lit.*, owl water gourd.

**hūhā.** Chat, talk; to chat.

**huhu.** A wood-boring insect; worm-eaten, rotten.

**huhū.** Angry, offended; anger, wrath; to scold, become angry. **ho‘ohuhū.** To provoke anger.

**huhui.** Cluster.

**huhui waina.** Cluster of grapes.

**huhuki.** Redup. of *huki;* to pull hard or frequently. **ho‘ohuhuki.** To pull, cause to pull.

**huhū wale.** Short-tempered; angry without cause.

**hui.** **1.** Club, association, firm, partnership, union; to form a society or organization; to meet. **ho‘ohui.** To form a society. **2.** To join, unite, combine. **ho‘ohui.** To join, as two words; to add on, annex, append; to introduce one person to another; meeting of persons. **3.** A plus sign. **4.** Cluster, as of grapes or coconuts; bunch, as of bananas. **5.** Chorus of a song.

**hūi.** Halloo. *Modern.*

**hu‘i.** Aching; ache. *Niho hu‘i,* toothache.

**hui hō‘ai‘ē kālā (dālā).** Credit union. *Lit.*, society for loaning money.

**hui ho‘opa‘a.** Insurance company.

**huihui.** **1.** Mixed, mingled, joined; to pool together, as to buy cooperatively. **2.** Cluster, collection, bunch. **3.** Constellation.

**hu‘ihu‘i.** Cold, cool, chilly; numbing, tingling, as love. **ho‘ohu‘ihu‘i.** To make cold, chill, as by refrigeration.

**huihui ā kōlea.** To gather together like a flock of *kōlea* birds.

**hui ‘ia.** Incorporated, united, joined.

**huika, huita.** Wheat. *Eng.*

**hui kahi.** United in one.

**huikala.** To absolve entirely, forgive all faults.

**hui kālepa.** Trading company, mercantile firm.

**huikau.** Mixed, confused; mixup. **ho‘ohuikau.** To mix, confuse.

**Hui Ke‘a ‘Ula‘ula.** Red Cross.

**hui kinai ahi.** Fire department.

**huila.** Wheel. *Eng.*

**huila kaulike.** Disc wheel of a sewing machine.

**huila nui.** Large wheel; fly-wheel, as of a sewing machine.

**huila wai.** Water wheel, windmill.

**hui malū.** Any secret society or fraternity, as the Masons; Masonic; to meet secretly.

**huina.** **1.** Sum, total. **2.** Angle; corner, as of a house or street; crossroads, intersection.

**huina-.** Geometric figure. See *huinahā, huinakolu,* and others.

**huina alanui.** Crossroads, street corner.

**huinahā.** Quadrangle, quadrilateral.

**huinahā kaulike.** Square.

**huina helu.** **1.** Sum of several numbers, total. **2.** General arithmetic.

**huinakolu.** Triangle.

**huina kūpono.** Right angle.

**huinalima.** **1.** Pentagon. **2.** Joining of two hands, especially in hand wrestling *(uma).*

**huini. 1.** Needle-pointed, sharp-pointed. **hoʻohuini.** To carve or sharpen into a point. **2.** Sharp, shrill sounds.

**hui pū.** To mix, unite, combine. *ʻAmelika Huipū,* United States of America.

**hui puhi ʻohe.** Band (musical).

**huka.** Hook, as on a door; to hook. *Eng.*

**huki. 1.** To pull, as on a rope; to draw, stretch, reach. **hoʻohuki.** To pull gently; headstrong, willful. **2.** A fit of any kind, convulsion, stroke, epileptic fit; cramp, as in the leg; to have a fit or cramp.

**hukihuki. 1.** To pull or draw frequently, or by many persons; to pull by jerks, as in the tug-of-war game. **2.** To disagree, quarrel; not cooperative, headstrong. **3.** Tug-of-war game; to play the game.

**hukilau.** A seine; to fish with the seine. *Lit.,* pull ropes *(lau).*

**huki like.** To pull together, cooperate.

**huki wai.** To draw water; one who draws water.

**hula. 1.** The hula, a hula dancer; to dance the hula. **2.** Song or chant used for the hula; to sing or chant for a hula.

**hula ʻauana.** Modern hula.

**hulahula.** Ballroom dancing with partners, American dancing, massed hula dancing; to dance thus.

**hula ʻiliʻili.** Hula in which smooth water-worn stones are used as clappers or castanets; the pebble hula.

**hula kahiko.** Traditional hula.

**hula kōlea.** A kneeling hula imitative of the *kōlea,* plover.

**hula kuʻi Molokaʻi.** An ancient fast dance of Molokaʻi.

**hulali.** Shining, glittering, glossy; to shine, reflect light.

**hūlalilali.** Redup. and intensification of *hulali.*

**hula ʻulīʻulī.** Hula with *ʻulīʻulī,* gourd rattles.

**huli. 1.** To turn; to curl over, as a breaker. *Fig.,* to change, as an opinion or manner of living. **hoʻohuli.** To turn, change, convert. **2.** To look for, search. **hoʻohuli.** To look for. **3.** Section, as of a town or place. **4.** Taro top.

**huli ʻaoʻao.** To lean over to one side, turn to the side.

**huliau. 1.** Turning point, time of change. **2.** To think of the past, recall the past.

**huli hele.** To search here and there.

**hulihia.** Passive/imperative of *huli 1,2;* overturned; a complete change, overthrow; turned upside down.

**hulihuli.** Redup. of *huli 1, 2;* to search repeatedly or long.

**huli kanaka.** Profound studies, moral philosophy, science; to engage in such.

**huli kua.** To turn one's back, refuse to help, ignore.

**hulili.** Dazzling light, vibration; to dazzle, swell.

**huli manaʻo.** To seek an opinion; to change an opinion. **hoʻohuli manaʻo.** To induce change of opinon.

**huli pau.** To overturn completely; to search everywhere.

**huli pū.** To overturn, turn upside down, overthrow.

**hulu. 1.** Feather. **2.** Esteemed, choice; esteemed older relative, as of parents' or grandparents' generations. **hoʻohulu.** To esteem, prize. **3.** Fur, wool, fleece, human body hair (contrasting with *lauoho,* head hair).

**huluʻānai.** Scrubbing or painting brush, formerly made of a coconut husk.

**hulu hipa.** Sheep wool, fleece; woolen cloth.

**huluhulu. 1.** Body hair, hair of eyelashes, fleece, fur; hairy. **2.**

Frayed, rough, not smooth. **3.** Feathers. **4.** Down or fuzz on plant stems. **5.** Flannel. **6.** Blanket.

**hulu kuʻemaka.** Eyebrow.

**hulu manu.** Bird feather.

**hulumanu.** Tick used for mattresses and pillow covers, so called because they were stuffed with bird feathers.

**hulumoa.** The Hawaiian mistletoes (*Korthalsella* spp.), evergreen, cylindrical- or flat-stemmed shrubs with tiny, inconspicuous leaves and flowers.

**hulu pena.** Paintbrush.

**hume.** To bind about the loins, as a *malo;* to put on a *malo;* to wear a sanitary napkin.

**humehume.** Redup. of *hume*.

**humu.** To sew, stitch; seam, stitch; to bind, as a book.

**humu hoʻi.** Back stitching; to sew with back stitching.

**humu (humuhumu) hoʻoholoholo.** Running stitch, basting.

**humuhumu. 1.** Redup. of *humu;* to sew. **2.** Triggerfish.

**humuhumu-nukunuku-ā-puaʻa.** Varieties of *humuhumu (Rhinecanthus aculeatus, R. rectangulus). Lit.,* humuhumu with a snout like a pig.

**humuhumu puke.** Bookbinding.

**humuhumu puke ʻili lole.** Cloth bookbinding.

**humuhumu puke ʻili pepa.** Paper bookbinding.

**humuhumu ulana.** To darn, as socks.

**humuhumu umauma lei.** Triggerfish *(Balistes bursa). Lit.,* lei [on] chest *humuhumu*.

**humukā.** Cross-stitching; to do cross-stitching.

**humu kaulahao.** Chain stitch; to make chain stitches.

**humulau.** To embroider.

**humu peʻa.** Sail making; to sew sails.

**humu puka pihi.** Buttonhole stitch.

**huna. 1.** Minute particle; small, little. **2.** Hidden secret.

**hūnā.** To hide, conceal. **hoʻohūnā.** To hide.

**hunahuna.** Fragments.

**hunahuna ʻōlelo.** Particle, as Hawaiian *ua, i, e.*

**hunakai. 1.** White-flowered beach morning glory *(Ipomea stolonifera).* **2.** Sanderling *(Calidris alba),* a winter migrant to Hawaii. *Lit.,* sea foam, so called from the bird's habit of following close behind receding waves.

**huna kai.** Sea spray, sea foam.

**huna wai.** Drop of water, spray, mist.

**huna wailele.** Spray from a waterfall.

**hune. 1.** Poor, destitute; a poor person. **2.** Fine, tiny.

**-hune. hoʻohune.** To nag, tease, persist with avidity.

**hunehune.** Redup. and intensification of *hune, 2;* very fine, delicate.

**hune kai.** Sea spray, sea foam.

**hune one.** Fine-grained sand, sand particles.

**-hūnōai.** Father- or mother-in-law, usually after *makua* and followed by *kāne* or *wahine* for specific designation of sex.

**hūnōna.** Son- or daughter-in-law, followed by *kāne* or *wahine* for specific designation of sex.

**huoi.** Suspicion. **hoʻohuoi.** To suspect.

**hupa.** Hoop. *Eng.*

**hūpē.** Nasal mucus.

**hūpēkole.** Running nose; to sniffle.

**hūpō.** Ignorant, unintelligent; fool. *Lit.,* swelling darkness.

# I

**i. 1.** Particle and clitic preceding nouns and marking direct and indirect objects, with additional meanings: to, at, in, on, by, because of, due to, by means of. **2.** Particle and clitic preceding subordinate verbs and marking completed or past action and state or condition. **3.** If. **4.** While, when, no sooner than.

**'ī.** To say.

**ia.** He, she, it, this, that, aforementioned.

**iā. 1.** Yard (unit of measure). *Eng.* **2.** Yard (spar on a sailing vessel). *Eng.* **3.** Particle replacing *i, I,* before pronouns and names of people, and, optionally, before place names.

**'ia.** Particle marking passive/imperative.

**i'a. 1.** Fish or any marine animal, as eel, oyster, crab. **2.** Meat or any flesh food. **3.** *(Cap.)* Milky Way.

**i** (verb) **ai.** Particles indicating completed aspect or state or condition and accompanying subordinate verbs.

**iāia. 1.** Him, her; to him, to her; because of or due to him or her. **2.** While he or she, as soon as he or she.

**'iako. 1.** Outrigger boom. **2.** Forty, as in counting tapas.

**i'a maka.** Raw fish.

**i'a makika.** Mosquito fish *(Gambusia affinis).*

**ia nei.** This person, he, she (after *'o,* subject marker).

**'Ianuali, Ianuari.** January. *Eng.*

**'Iao.** Jupiter appearing as the morning star; valley and peak, West Maui.

**Iāpana.** Japan. *Eng.*

**ia'u. 1.** Me, to me; because of or due to me. See *-a'u.* **2.** While I, at the time that I, as soon as I.

**i'e.** Tapa beater.

**'ie.** Aerial root of the *'ie'ie* vine; the vine itself.

**'ie'ie.** An endemic, woody, branching climber *(Freycinetia arborea).*

**Ielukalema, Ierusalema.** Jerusalem. *Eng.*

**'iewe. 1.** Afterbirth, placenta. Also *ēwe.* **2.** Relatives of a common ancestry.

**ihe. 1.** Spear, javelin, dart. **2.** Halfbeak fish.

**i hea.** See *hea,* where.

**ihe laumeki, ihe laumaki.** Barbed spear.

**ihe 'ō.** Dart; piercing spear.

**ihe pahe'e.** Short spear.

**ihe pakelo.** Lance.

**ihi.** To strip, peel.

**'ihi. 1.** Sacred, diginified; treated with reverence or respect. **hō'ihi.** To treat thus. **2.** Wood sorrels *(Oxalis).*

**ihihī.** To neigh.

**'ihi lani.** Heavenly splendor; reverence due a chief.

**iho. 1.** To go down; to go south or before the wind. **2.** Core, as of apple; pith. **3.** Down, below (directional particle following words). *Hele iho,* to go down, descend. **4.** Same particle and reference as above but with reflexive meaning, often following words describing activities of the body, as eating, drinking, thinking. *'Ai iho,* to eat. **5.** Same particle and reference as above with meaning "self." *E hana ana 'oia nona iho,* he will work for himself. **6.** Same particle and reference as *iho, 3, 4, 5,* but used with words of time. *'Ānō iho nei,* just now, recently. *Mahope iho,* afterwards.

**ihola.** Directional and reflexive particle *iho,* plus clitic demonstrative *-la.*

**iholena.** A favorite and common native variety of banana.

**ihona.** Descent, incline.

**i hope.** See *hope.*

**ihu. 1.** Nose, snout; toe of a shoe; a kiss. **2.** Prow or bow of a canoe or ship.

**ihu ʻeʻeke.** To wrinkle up the nose, as to show scorn.

**ihu ʻeka.** Dirty nose, a disparaging epithet.

**ihu hānuna.** To snore or speak with nasalized sounds.

**ihuihu.** Rising upward, as the prow of a canoe. *Fig.,* scornful.

**ihu kāmaʻa.** Toe of shoes.

**ihu kū.** Tilted nose, pug nose. *Fig.,* haughty.

**ihu pī.** To breathe with difficulty due to partial obstruction of the nostrils, as of one with a cold. See *pī, 2.*

**ihu piʻi.** Elevated nose. *Fig.,* scornful, haughty.

**ihu waʻa.** Bow of a canoe, bowsprit.

**ʻiʻi.** Small, stunted, undersized; dwarf.

**ʻiʻike.** To see well; observant; to recognize and accost in a friendly way.

**ʻiʻimi.** To seʼ again and again; one seeking everywhere, as for knowledge.

**i** (verb phrase) **inā.** Same as *inā* (phrase) *inā.*

**ʻiʻini.** To desire, crave; liking.

**ʻiʻiwi.** Scarlet Hawaiian honeycreeper *(Vestiaria coccinea)* found on all the main islands; its feathers were used extensively in featherwork. Also called *ʻiwi.*

**ʻiʻiwi haole.** Cape honeysuckle *(Tecomaria capensis).*

**īkā.** To drift upon; to turn aside from a straight course; flotsam and jetsam. **hoʻoīkā.** To put or throw ashore.

**ikaika.** Strong, powerful; strength, force, energy. **hoʻoikaika, hōʻikaika.** To make a great effort, encourage.

*Hoʻoikaika kino,* body-building exercise.

**ikaika lio.** Horsepower.

**Ikalia, Italia.** Italy; Italian. *Eng.*

**ikamu, itamu.** Item. *Eng.*

**ʻike.** To see, know, feel, greet, recognize, understand; to know sexually; knowledge; sense, as of hearing or sight; vision. **hōʻike. (a)** To show, make known, display, exhibit, reveal, explain; proof, guide, exhibition. *Haʻawina hōʻike,* examination. **(b)** Witness, as in court. **(c)** School commencement. **(d)** Congregational convention of various Sunday Schools with singing and recitation.

**ʻike hānau.** Instinct. *Lit.,* birth knowledge.

**ʻikeʻike.** Rare redup. of *ʻike.* **hō-ʻikeʻike.** To display, exhibit, as in a museum or show. *Hale hōʻikeʻike,* museum.

**ʻike kumu.** Basic or fundamental knowledge.

**ʻike maka.** Eyewitness; visible.

**ʻikena.** View, seeing, knowing.

**ʻikeoma.** Idiom; idiomatic. *Eng.*

**ʻike pāpālua.** To see double; to have the gift of second sight and commune with spirits.

**ʻike pono.** To see clearly; certain knowledge.

**iki.** Small, little, slightly, a little. **hoʻoiki.** To lessen.

**ikiiki. 1.** Stifling heat and humidity; acute discomfort. **2.** *(Cap.)* Name of a month in the summer season.

**ʻikuwā. 1.** Noisy, clamorous, loud-voiced; to make a din. **2.** *(Cap.)* Month near the end of the Hawaiian year, named for the roar of surf, thunder, and cloudbursts of this month.

**ila.** Dark birthmark.

**i laila.** See *laila.*

**i lalo.** See *lalo.*

**ilāmuku.** Executive officer, marshall, sheriff.

**ili. 1.** Stranded, aground, as a ship

on the reef; to run over, as with a car. **ho'ili, ho'oili.** To land upon, load, as freight on a ship; to transfer, transmit. **2.** Inheritance; to inherit. **ho'ili, ho'oili.** To bequeath or leave in a will; to save. **3.** To fall upon, as sorrow, responsibility, blessings, curses.

**'ili. 1.** Skin, hide, scalp, bark. **2.** Leather. **3.** Surface, area. **4.** Binding, cover. **5.** Land section. **6.** Strap of any kind, as reins, fan belt, hose.

**-'ili.** (With *hō-*) **hō'ili.** To collect; to bunch together as fish in a net.

**'iliahi.** All Hawaiian kinds of sandalwood (*Santalum* spp.).

**'ili 'āina. 1.** Land area. **2.** An *'ili* land division.

**'ili hau.** Bark of the *hau* tree, as used for rope and for modern grass skirts.

**ilihia.** Stricken with awe.

**ili hinuhinu.** Patent leather. *Lit.*, shiny leather.

**'ili holoholona.** Leather; fur, as about the neck.

**'ili honua.** Surface of the earth.

**'ilihune.** Poor, destitute; poverty, poor person. *Lit.*, tiny skin.

**'ili'ili. 1.** Pebble, small stone, as used in dances or *kōnane. Hula 'ili'ili,* pebble dance. **2.** To pile, overlap. **hō'ili'ili.** To gather, collect, save, store away.

**'ilikai. 1.** Surface of the sea. **2.** Horizontal.

**'ili kala.** Skin of *kala,* a fish, sometimes stretched over a coconut shell to form the top of the small *pūniu,* knee drum.

**'ili kani. 1.** A skin that sounds, as used in drums. **2.** Tough skin.

**'ili kea.** Fair skin, of Hawaiians.

**'ili ke'ehi.** Stirrup.

**'iliki. 1.** To strike suddenly, pour down, as rain; downpour. **2.** A varnish, as made of candlenut *(kukui)* bark, ti root, or banana stump.

**'ilikini.** Indian (of America). *Eng.* Also, **'Inikini.**

**'ilikole. 1.** Poverty-stricken, very poor; pauper (stronger than *'ilihune*). *Lit.*, bare skin. **hō'ilikole.** To cause poverty. **2.** Flesh of half-ripe coconut.

**'ilikona.** Wart. *Lit.*, hard skin.

**'ili kou.** Dark-skinned, as dark Hawaiians. *Lit., kou*-wood skin.

**'ili kūpono.** A nearly independent *'ili* land division within an *ahupua'a.*

**'ili lā'au.** Tree bark.

**'ili lele.** Portion of an *'ili* land division separated from the main part of the *'ili* but considered a part of it. Also called *lele.*

**'ili luna.** Epidermis; outer bark.

**'ilima.** Small to large native shrubs (all species of *Sida,* especially *S. fallax*). The *'ilima* is the flower of O'ahu.

**'ili mānoanoa.** Callus; calloused skin.

**ilina. 1.** Grave, tomb, cemetery, mausoleum, plot in a cemetery. **2.** Recipient. **ho'oilina, ho'ilina.** Heir, inheritance; successor.

**'īlio.** Dog.

**'īlio 'aukai. 1.** Sea dog, experienced sailor. **2.** Warship.

**'īlio hae.** Fierce or vicious dog; wolf, jackal.

**'īlio hahai holoholona.** Hunting dog.

**'īlio hahai manu.** Bird dog.

**'īlio hanu kanaka.** Bloodhound. *Lit.*, dog that smells man.

**'īlio hipa.** Sheep dog, shepherd dog.

**'īlio hohono.** Skunk; bad-smelling dog.

**'īlio 'i'i.** Small curly haired native dog.

**ili 'ōlelo.** A tattletale, talebearer; to gossip.

**'ili 'ōmaka.** Foreskin.

**'īlio māku'e.** Native dog, brown dog.

**'īlio pulu.** Bulldog. *Lit.*, bull *(Eng.)* dog.

**'ili pa'a.** An *'ili* land division complete in one section, as distinguished from an *'ili lele.*

**'ili palapala.** Parchment.

**'ili pala uli.** Dark-complexioned.

**'ili pale o kāma'a.** Sole of a shoe.

**'ili pāpa'a.** Sunburned or tanned skin.

**'ili pipi.** Leather, cowhide.

**'ili po'o.** Scalp.

**'ilipuakea.** White person.

**'iliwai. 1.** Surface, as of water; level. **hō'iliwai.** To grade or level, as a road. **2.** Carpenter's or surveyor's level. **3.** Water hose.

**ilo. 1.** Maggot, grub; to creep, as worms. **2.** Young shoot; to germinate, sprout. **ho'oilo.** To cause germination.

**-ilo. ho'oilo, ho'īlo.** Rainy, winterlike months, winter.

**iloilo.** Redup. of *ilo, 1, 2;* wormy; sprouting.

**-iloilo. ho'oiloilo.** To predict disaster.

**i loko.** See *loko.*

**'īloli.** Unpleasant sensations of pregnancy; emotional disturbances; intense yearning, longing. **ho'īloli.** To feel the discomforts of pregnancy; to suffer emotional disturbance.

**i luna.** See *luna.*

**'imi.** To look, hunt, search.

**'imi ā loa'a.** Discoverer; to discover.

**'imi hala.** To find fault with, blame.

**'imi hana. 1.** To seek work. **2.** To stir up trouble.

**'imi 'ike.** To seek knowledge; a seeker of knowledge.

**'imi kālā.** To seek money, to earn a livelihood; commercial.

**'imi loa.** To seek far; distant traveler. *Fig.,* one with great knowledge.

**'imina.** Looking, seeking; search.

**'imi na'auao.** To seek knowledge or education; ambitious to learn; one seeking education or learning.

**'imi 'ōlelo.** To lie, slander, stir up trouble by gossip.

**'imi pono.** To seek or strive for righteousness; endeavor.

**'imo.** To wink, twinkle; winking, twinkling.

**'imo'imo.** Redup. of *'imo. Hōkū 'imo'imo,* twinkling star.

**imu.** Underground oven; food cooked in an *imu.* Also *umu.*

**i mua.** See *mua.*

**inā.** If, would that.

**'ina.** Small sea urchin *(wana),* *Echinometra* spp., especially *E. diadema.*

**ināhea.** When (in questions in the past).

**'īna'i.** Accompaniment to *poi,* usually meat, fish, or vegetable.

**inaina.** Anger, hatred, malice; to hate; moved with hatred, angry. **ho'oinaina.** To stir up anger, rouse hate.

**inā** (phrase) **inā.** If . . . would. *Inā he nui ke kālā, inā ua holomua ka hana,* if there were much money, the work would progress.

**'inamona.** Relish made of the cooked kernel of candlenut *(kukui)* mashed with salt.

**'īnana.** To come to life or activity, as of a sick person; animated; stirring of life. **ho'īnana.** To animate; give life to.

**'īnea.** Hardship, suffering, distress.

**i nehinei.** See *nehinei.*

**i ne'i.** See *ne'i,* here.

**'Inia.** India; East Indian. *Eng.*

**'Iniana.** Indian, as Indian Ocean. *Eng.*

**'īniha.** Inch. *Eng.*

**'ini'iniki.** To pinch or nip repeatedly; tingling, as with cold.

**'īnika.** Ink. *Eng.*

**iniki.** To pinch; sharp and piercing, as wind or pangs of love.

**'Inikini.** Same as *'Ilikini,* Indian. *Eng.*

**'inikiniki** (sometimes pronounced *'inisinisi* in songs). Same as *'ini'iniki.*

'inikua. Insurance. *Eng.*

'inikua ka'a. Automobile insurance.

'inikua ola. Life insurance.

'inikua pau ahi. Fire insurance.

'inikua ulia. Accident insurance.

'ino. 1. Wicked, sinful; sin. **hō-'ino, ho'o'ino.** To insult, dishonor. 2. Spoiled, contaminated. 3. To injure, harm. **ho'o'ino.** To harm, damage. 4. Storm; stormy. 5. Very, very much, intensely. *Aloha 'ino,* too bad, what a shame.

inoa (in fast speech often preceded by *ke*). 1. Name. 2. Name chant.

inoa kapakapa. See *kapakapa, 2.*

inoa pō. Dream name.

'ino'ino. 1. Spoiled, contaminated; damaged. **hō'ino'ino.** To mar, disfigure, damage, speak evil of. 2. Stormy; storm. 3. Wicked, sinful; sin.

inu. To drink; a drink, drinking. **ho'īnu, ho'oinu.** To give to drink.

inu lama. To drink rum or other alcoholic drink; one who drinks.

inu li'ili'i. To drink but a little, sip.

inumia. Passive of *inu.*

inu 'ona. To drink until intoxicated.

io. Paddle rib.

i'ō. See *'ō,* yonder.

'io. 1. Hawaiian hawk *(Buteo solitarius),* an endemic hawk found only on the island of Hawai'i. 2. To twitter, chirp.

'i'o. 1. Flesh, meat, flesh and blood. 2. True, genuine, significant, real; really, truly; true worth.

'i'o hipa. Mutton, flesh of sheep.

i'o holoholona. Meat.

'i'o huki. Muscle.

ioio. Rounded grooves in carving, as made in *kukui* nuts used in necklaces; depression made by stitches in quilting.

'io'io. Redup. of *'io;* cheeping, peeping.

'i'o'i'o. Clitoris.

'iolana. To soar; soaring hawk.

'io lani. Royal hawk.

'Io-lani. Name of the Palace and of a school in Honolulu.

i'ole. So that not, in order not.

'iole. Hawaiian rat *(Rattus exulans);* introduced rat.

'iole lāpaki (rabati). Rabbit.

'iole li'ili'i. Little rat; mouse.

'iole manakuke. Mongoose.

'iole nui. Introduced large rat.

'iole pua'a. Guinea pig.

i ona. To him, her; him, her. *Lit.,* to his, hers.

'i'o nīoi. Condiment of boiled pulp of chili peppers *(nīoi),* often mixed with relish such as *'inamona.*

'i'o niu. Flesh of coconut.

'i'o pale niho. Gums. *Lit.,* tooth-protecting flesh.

'i'o pipi i wili 'ia. Hamburger, ground round steak. *Lit.,* ground beef flesh.

'i'o pua'a uahi. Bacon. *Lit.,* smoked pork flesh.

i o'u. To me, me. *Lit.,* to my.

ipo. Sweetheart, lover. **ho'oipo.** To make love, court.

ipoipo, ho'oipoipo. To make love.

ipu. 1. Bottle gourd *(Lagenaria siceraria).* See *pōhue.* 2. Watermelon *(Citrullus lanatus).* 3. General name for vessel or container, as dish, mug, calabash, pot, cup, pipe. 4. Drum consisting of a single gourd or made of two large gourds of unequal size joined together.

ipu 'ai maka. Watermelon, melon. *Lit.,* melon to eat raw.

ipu 'aina. Scrap bowl, refuse container.

ipu 'ala. 1. Cantaloupe melon *(Cucumis melo* var. *cantalupensis).* 2. Container for perfume or other fragrant matter. *Lit.,* fragrant gourd.

ipu 'au'au. Washbasin; container of water for a bath.

**ipu hao.** Iron pot; kettle or saucepan of any sort, whether glass, aluminum, or enamel. *Lit.*, iron container.

**ipu haole.** Watermelon. *Lit.*, foreign gourd. See *ipu, 2.*

**ipu heke 'ole.** Gourd drum consisting of a single gourd without a top section.

**ipu hōkiokio.** Same as *hōkiokio,* gourd whistle.

**ipu holoi.** Washbasin.

**ipu holoi lima.** Finger bowl. *Lit.*, container wash hand.

**ipu hula.** Dance drum made of two gourds sewed together.

**ipu i'a.** Meat dish.

**'īpuka.** Door, entrance, exit, gate, opening in the wall for the admission of light or air.

**ipu kai.** A dish for meat or any dish deep enough to hold gravy *(kai);* gravy boat.

**ipu kālua.** Baked pumpkin or squash.

**ipu kī.** Teapot.

**ipu kuha.** Spittoon.

**ipu kukui.** Lamp, candlestick. *Hale ipu kukui,* lighthouse.

**ipu kukui hele pō.** Lantern. *Lit.*, light for going at night.

**ipu kula.** The cup-of-gold *(Solandra hartwegii). Lit.*, golden *(Eng.)* container.

**ipu lepo.** Earthenware pot, clay pot. *Lit.*, dirt container.

**ipu mimi.** Chamber pot, container for urine.

**ipu pa'i.** Gourd drum. *Lit.*, gourd to beat.

**ipu paka (baka).** Tobacco pipe.

**ipu pū.** Same as *pū,* a general name for pumpkin and squashes.

**ipu pueo.** Gourd with hourglass shape.

**ipu wai.** Water container, water bottle.

**ipu wai 'au'au.** Washbasin.

**'iu.** Lofty, sacred, revered, consecrated.

**'iu'iu.** Intensification of *'iu;* majestic, very high; distant, far away.

**i uka.** See *uka.*

**Iukaio, Iudaio.** Jew; Jewish.

**Iulai.** July. *Eng.*

**Iune.** June. *Eng.*

**Iupika, Iupita.** The planet Jupiter. *Eng.*

**iwa.** Ninth, nine.

**'iwa. 1.** Frigate or man-of-war bird *(Fregata minor palmerstoni). Fig.*, thief. **2.** A fern *(Asplenium horridum).*

**i waena.** See *waena.*

**i waho.** See *waho.*

**'iwa'iwa.** All maidenhair ferns *(Adiantum* spp.).

**iwakālua.** Twenty.

**iwi 1.** Bone. **2.** Shell, as of coconut, candlenut *(kukui),* gourd, egg, shellfish.

**'iwi. 1.** Same as *'i'iwi.* **2.** Eyetwitching.

**iwi ā.** Jawbone.

**iwi 'ao'ao. 1.** Rib, rib bone. **2.** Assistant leader in a hula troupe.

**iwi hilo.** Thighbone.

**iwi hoehoe.** Shoulder blade.

**iwi hope.** Bone forming the posterior segment of the skull.

**iwi hua.** Hipbone; round bone fitting into a socket.

**iwiiwi.** High cheekbone; bony; skinny.

**iwi kamumu.** Cartilage.

**iwi kanaka.** Human bone or skeleton.

**iwi kānana.** Bone of the anterior part of the skull, forming the skeleton of the forehead.

**iwikuamo'o. 1.** Spine, backbone. **2.** Near and trusted relative of a chief who attended to his personal needs and possessions and executed private orders; family.

**iwi lā'ī.** Stem and midrib of a ti leaf.

**iwilei. 1.** Collarbone. **2.** Measure of length from the collarbone to the tip of the middle finger with the arm extended; yard (measure).

**iwi loa.** A tall bone. *Fig.,* a tall person.

**iwi 'ō.** Wishbone.

**iwi po'i.** Kneecap.

**iwi po'o.** Skull, head bone.

**iwi pūhaka.** Pelvic bone.

**iwi pūniu.** Coconut shell. *Fig.,* skull.

**iwi umauma.** Breastbone, sternum.

# J

For loanwords from English beginning with *j-*, substitute *i-* or *k-*. For example: for June, July, see *Iune, Iulai;* for Japanese, jury, see *Kepanī, kiule.*

# K

**ka. 1.** The one, the person in question (usually followed by *i* and a verb). **2.** Definite article; *ka* is replaced by *ke* before words beginning with *a-, e-, o-,* and *k-,* and before some words beginning with the glottal stop and *p-*. *Ka* is usually translated "the," except that it is not translated before English mass nouns or status titles.

**kā. 1.** To hit, strike, hack, hurl, dash, especially with a quick hard stroke; to bail water, as from a canoe; to turn a rope for children to jump; to snare, as birds. **ho'okā.** To dash down, shatter, break, strike. **2.** Canoe bailer. **3.** Exclamation of mild disapproval or surprise. Oh! So! (If spoken alone it is frequently pronounced Chā! or Sah!). *'O 'oe kā!,* So it's you! **4.** Of, belonging to (*a*-class possessive). **5.** Container.

**kā-. 1.** A prefix with meaning similar to that of the causative/simulative *ho'o-,* but used with only a few bases. Cf. *kāhinu, kāko'o, kāwili,* etc. **2.** Inclusiveness, in pronouns *kāua, kākou* and possessives *kā kāua, kō kāua, kā kākou, kō kākou.*

**ka'a. 1.** To roll, turn, twist, revolve; rolling, twisting. *Ka'a pa'akai,* to roll in salt. **ho'o-oka'a.** To cause a rolling, turning. **2.** Vehicle, carriage, automobile, car. **3.** To pay; paid. **ho'oka'a.** To pay a debt. *Ho'o-ka'a hapa,* partial payment.

**ka'aahi.** Train; locomotive engine. *Lit.,* fire wagon.

**ka'a hale.** Trailer, house on wheels.

**ka'a hehi wāwae.** Bicycle, tricycle. *Lit.,* vehicle press feet.

**ka'ahele.** To make a tour, travel about; a tour.

**ka'a holo hau.** Sled. *Lit.,* vehicle running [on] snow.

**ka'a huila kahi.** Wheelbarrow. *Lit.,* single-wheel vehicle.

**ka'a huila lua.** Any two-wheeled vehicle, as cart or buggy.

**ka'a huki.** Handcart. *Lit.,* pull vehicle.

**kā'ai.** Sash, belt.

**ka'akepa.** Diagonal, cut at an angle; to avoid, shy away from.

**ka'a kinai ahi.** Fire engine. *Lit.,* vehicle extinguish fire.

**ka'ā kolu.** Three-stranded; threefold.

**ka'akūmākena.** Period of mourning, especially wailing in grief.

**ka'akupapa'u.** Hearse.

**kā'ala'ala.** Vigorous, sturdy, as of an infant or young animal.

**ka'a lā'au.** To wield a war club.

**ka'a lau niu.** Coconut-leaf thatching.

**ka'a lawe ma'i.** Ambulance.

**ka'alele.** To sway, reel; to fly or soar, as birds.

**ka'alina.** To bruise; to pelt, as rain. Cf. *'ālina.*

**ka'a lio.** Horse-drawn vehicle, wagon, carriage.

**kā'alo.** To pass by, go by. Cf. *mā'alo.* **ho'okā'alo.** To pass to and fro, to cause to pass.

**kā'alo'alo.** Redup. of *kā'alo.*

**ka'alolohi.** Slow-moving, slow to anger.

**ka'ā lua.** Two-ply, two stranded.

**ka'a ma'i.** Siege of sickness; a long or chronic illness.

**ka'a malo'o.** To wipe dry, as dishes with a cloth.

**ka'a mola.** To turn around loosely, as a screw or peg that does not fit; loose, unsteady.

**ka'ana.** To divide, share, apportion. **ho'oka'ana.** To divide equally among, share.

**ka'anini.** To writhe, squirm, as a fidgety child or one in a tantrum. Cf. *niniu,* spin.

**ka'ao.** Legend, tale, usually fanciful; fiction.

**ka'a 'ōhua.** Vehicle carrying passengers for hire, as a bus or taxi.

**ka'aoki.** To finish or complete, as a canoe; to put on the last touches.

**ka'apā.** To toss from side to side, as a restless child in bed; in spasms.

**ka'āpahu.** To cut off squarely or crosswise.

**ka'a paikikala.** Bicycle. *Lit.,* bicycle *(Eng.)* vehicle.

**ka'a pau ahi.** Fire engine. Also *ka'a wai.*

**ka'apuni 1.** To make a tour, go around, travel. *'Aha ka'apuni,* circuit court. **2.** The hula step now called "around the island." **3.** Revolution, revolving.

**ka'au.** Forty.

**ka'a uila.** Streetcar, electric bus.

**ka'a wai. 1.** Vehicle carrying water. **2.** Fire engine.

**ka'awale.** Separate, free, empty; to separate; free time; distance separating places or objects. *Manawa ka'awale,* spare or free time. **ho'oka'awale.** To separate, distinguish; to set aside; to establish as a separate entity.

**ka'a wale.** To turn or roll freely, independently, or without control.

**kā'awe.** To tie anything tightly around the neck, to choke, strangle, hang.

**ka'awili.** To turn, twist, writhe as in pain; to knead, as bread.

**kae. 1.** Refuse, rubbish. **2.** Treated with contempt, scorn. **ho-'okae.** To despise, treat with contempt or scorn; destroy. *Ho'okae 'ili,* race prejudice.

**ka'e. 1.** Brink, border, edge; toothless gums; projecting brow of a hill. *He ka'e wale nō,* only gums and no teeth. **2.** To sulk, fuss. **3.** To smudge, dab. **hō-ka'e, ho'oka'e.** To daub, smudge, soil.

**ka'e'e.** Hard, stiff, not soft or pliable; dried up, withered as by heat.

**kā'ei pāpale.** Hatband.

**kā'ekā.** Entangled, confused, twisted.

**kaekae.** Smooth, polished, perfect; young, attractive, desirable, as of a woman; tasty, mellow, soft, as of sweet potatoes; to rub smooth, polish, finish.

**kā'eke'eke.** Bamboo pipes varying in length from one to several feet, usually with one end open; to play bamboo pipes.

**ka'ele.** Empty and hollow, as of a bowl, poi board, canoe hull; inside bottom, as of a calabash or poi board.

**Kā'elo.** Name of a wet month.

**kaena.** To boast, brag, praise; boastful, conceited.

**kā'eo. 1.** Full, as a food calabash.

*Fig.,* full of knowledge. **2.** Strong, zealous.

**ka'e pa'a.** Selvage of cloth. *Lit.,* solid edge.

**kā'eu'eu.** Helpful, cooperative; joyous, active; larger. Cf. *'eu.* **ho'okā'eu'eu, hōkā'eu'eu.** To encourage and rouse to action.

**kaha. 1.** To scratch, mark, draw, cut, cut open or slice lengthwise, as fish or animals; to operate, as on the sick; to give a grade or mark to; to engrave; a line in mathematics; punctuation mark; stripe, as in the flag or on uniforms of enlisted men in the armed forces; a grade, as earned in school; long striped cloth. See *kaha ki'i. He aha ko'u kaha?,* What was my grade? **2.** Place (today usually followed by a qualifier, as *kahakai, kahaone, kahawai;* often used without *ke,* as *hele i kahakai,* go to the beach). **3.** To swoop, as a kite; to go by, pass by; to turn and go on; to surf, body surf.

**kahaapo.** Circumference, parentheses, brackets. *Lit.,* mark embrace.

**kaha'ea.** Cumulus clouds, often colored, thought to be a sign of rain.

**kāhāhā.** Interjection of surprise, wonder, displeasure; to wonder or be surprised; astonished. **ho-'okāhāhā.** Surprising; to cause astonishment.

**kahahui.** Plus sign in arithmetic. *Lit.,* joining mark.

**Kaha'i.** A culture hero.

**kahakaha. 1.** Redup. of *kaha, 1;* to mark frequently, to draw lines; to scarify, engrave. *Pepa kahakaha,* scratch paper. **2.** Redup. of *kaha, 3.* **ho'okahakaha.** To parade back and forth, to make a display; to show off; to drill; parade.

**kahakai.** Beach, seashore.

**kaha ki'i.** To draw or paint a picture or draw plans; artist.

**kaha ki'i hale.** Architect; to draw building plans.

**kaha kuhi.** Reference mark in writing or printing to direct attention, as asterisk, dagger, arrow.

**kāhala.** Amberjack or yellowtail *(Seriola dumerilii).*

**kaha loa.** To turn and then go straight for a long distance.

**kahana.** Cutting, drawing of a line; turning point.

**kaha nalu.** Body surfing. Cf. *kaha, 3.*

**kahaone.** Sandy beach.

**kahawai.** Stream, river, ravine whether wet or dry; valley.

**kahe. 1.** To flow, trickle, menstruate; in heat (of a bitch). *Kahe ka hā'ae,* to drool at the mouth. **ho'okahe.** To water or irrigate, to drain. **2.** To cut or slit longitudinally; to circumcise.

**kāhea.** To call, cry out; to name; recital of the first lines of a stanza by the dancer as a cue to the chanter; to greet; to give a military command; a call, alarm.

**kāhea pau ahi.** Fire alarm.

**kāheka.** Pool, especially a rock basin where the sea washes in through an opening and salt forms.

**kahe koko.** Flow of blood; hemorrhage. **ho'okahe koko.** To shed blood; bloodshed.

**kāhela.** To lie spread out; to sweep back and forth, as billows.

**kahe ule.** To circumcise. *Lit.,* cut penis.

**kāhewa.** To miss, not succeed; foiled in an attempt.

**kahi. 1.** One, only one, alone, some (usually following the numeral classifiers *'a-* and *'e-,* or *ho'o-*); also, besides; someone else. *Na'u kahi,* give me some. **ho'okahi.** One, alone; oneness; together as a unit; to make one; same; similar; a. *Noho ho'oka-hi,* to live alone. **2.** To cut longitudinally, shave, comb. **3.** Place (contraction of *ka wahi;* never used with *ke*); duty; where; in case of. *Kahi ʻē,* elsewhere.

**kahiki. 1.** Any foreign country. **2.** *(Cap.)* Tahiti. *Holo i Kahiki,* sail to Tahiti.

**kahiko.** Old, ancient; old person. (Usually in the singular; cf. *kāhiko, 2.*) *Wā kahiko,* old times. See *hula kahiko.* **hoʻokahiko.** To think, act, speak in the old way; to speak of old times; to cling to old customs; old-fashioned.

**kāhiko. 1.** Finery; to wear finery. **hoʻokāhiko.** To wear fine clothes. **2.** Plural of *kahiko.*

**Kahikolu.** Trinity; three in one.

**kāhili. 1.** Feather standard, symbolic of royalty. **2.** *Kāhili* ginger *(Hedychium gardnerianum).*

**kahi moe.** Place to sleep, bed, cot.

**kāhinu.** To rub with oil, grease, petroleum jelly. Cf. *hinuhinu.*

**kahi ʻō.** High-backed comb with long prongs (ʻō) such as worn by Spanish women.

**kahi ʻumiʻumi.** To shave the whiskers; barber.

**kāholo. 1.** Hasty, nimble, swift, quick; to move fast. **hoʻokāholo.** To cause to hurry; to speed, hurry. **2.** To sew with long stitches; basting. *Lopi kāholo,* basting thread. **3.** The "vamp" hula step.

**kāhonua.** Globe of the earth.

**kahu. 1.** Honored attendant, guardian, keeper, administrator; pastor of a church; one who has a dog, cat, or any pet. *Kona kahu,* his attendant. *ʻO ka ʻīlio kahu,* the dog's master. **hoʻokahu.** To act as a *kahu.* **2.** To tend or cook at an oven; to build an oven fire; one who tends an oven, a cook. **hoʻokahu.** To make a fire for cooking in the oven.

**kahua. 1.** Foundation, base, site, grounds, platform, as of a house; an open place, as for camping or for sports; playground, camp. *Fig.,* declaration of principles, doctrine. *Ka Monroe kahua kālai ʻāina,* Monroe doctrine about land division. **hoʻokahua.** To lay a foundation; to camp, as soldiers; to settle down, as homesteaders. **2.** Base of a quilt on which the pattern *(lau)* is appliquéd.

**kahua hale.** House foundation or site.

**kahua hana.** Subject, as of a discussion; foundation principles, as a political platform.

**kahua hōʻikeʻike holoholona.** Zoo.

**kahua hōlua.** Sledding course.

**kahua hoʻolele leo.** Radio-broadcasting station. *Lit.,* site for making voice fly.

**kahua hoʻolulu mokulele.** Airport.

**kahua hoʻouka.** Battleground; place used for competitive sports or contests. *Lit.,* site for attack.

**kahua kaua lewa.** Air base.

**kahua kinai ahi.** Fire station. *Lit.,* place quench fire.

**kahua leʻa, kahua leʻaleʻa.** Playground.

**kahu aliʻi.** Royal guardian in the family of a high chief.

**kahua paʻa.** Terra firma, the solid earth. *Fig.,* security.

**kahua pāʻani.** Stadium; playground of any kind. *Lit.,* site for play.

**kahu ʻekalekia (ekalesia).** Pastor of a church.

**kahu hānai.** Foster parent (of adopted children).

**kahu hipa.** Shepherd; to tend sheep.

**kahu hoʻoponopono.** Administrator.

**kāhūhū.** Interjection of surprise or anger.

**kahu kula.** Schoolmaster, school supervisor.

**kahu kula nui.** School superintendent.

**kahuli.** To overthrow, overturn, upset. **ho'okahuli.** To overthrow.

**kāhuli.** 1. To change. 2. Land shells (*Philonesia* spp.).

**kāhulihuli.** Unsteady, shaky; to sway; tossed about, as a ship.

**kahuli pū.** Turned completely over, upside down.

**kahu ma'i.** Nurse.

**kahu mālama.** Custodian, caretaker.

**kahu mālama hale.** Housekeeper. *Lit.*, guardian to care for house.

**kahuna.** Priest, minister, sorcerer, expert in any profession; to act as priest or expert. **ho'okahuna.** To ordain or train as a *kahuna*.

**kāhuna.** Plural of *kahuna*.

**kahuna 'anā'anā.** Sorcerer who practices black magic.

**kahuna a'o.** Teaching preacher, minister.

**kahuna ha'i'ōlelo.** Preacher, especially an itinerant preacher.

**kahuna ho'ouli 'ai.** Agricultural expert.

**kahuna kālai.** Carving expert; sculptor.

**kahuna kālai wa'a.** Canoe builder.

**kahuna kilokilo.** Priest or expert who observed the skies for omens.

**kahuna lapa'au.** Medical doctor, medical practitioner. *Lit.*, curing expert.

**kahuna pule.** Preacher, pastor, priest. *Lit.*, prayer expert.

**kahu pipi.** Herdsman, keeper of cattle, rancher.

**kahu puke (buke).** Librarian.

**kahu wai.** One in charge of water rights and division.

**kahu waiwai.** Trustee, executor. *Lit.*, custodian of wealth or property.

**kai.** 1. Sea, sea water. *I kai*, toward the sea. *Makai*, on the sea-side, toward the sea, in the direction of the sea. 2. Gravy, dressing. 3. Interjection. My, how much! How very! *Kai ke kolohe!* Oh, how mischievous!

**ka i, kai.** Contraction of *ka mea i*, the one who did.

**kai-.** Person (used as term of reference for sibling terms).

**kaī, kaīī.** Interjection of displeasure, annoyance, prolonged to indicate greater force.

**ka'i.** To lead, direct; to walk in a row; to walk deliberately, as in a procession, or as a child learning to walk. Cf. *alaka'i, huaka'i*.

**kai a malō, kai a malo'o.** An extreme low tide with reef exposed. *Lit.*, dry sea.

**kaiāmū.** To sit in silence, as at a meeting.

**kai a Pele.** Tidal wave. *Lit.*, sea of Pele.

**kai apo.** Rising or high tide. *Lit.*, encircling sea.

**kai au.** Sea where a moving current is visible. *Lit.*, current sea.

**kaiāulu.** Community, neighborhood, village.

**kai ea.** Rising tide; sea washing higher on land than usual. *Lit.*, rising sea.

**kai e'e.** Tidal wave. Also *kai ho'ē'e. Lit.*, mounting sea.

**kaiehu.** To scatter or stir up, as dust or dirt; tossed, as spray.

**kai emi.** Ebbing sea. *Lit.*, decreasing sea.

**kai he'e.** Receding sea or wave.

**ka'i hele.** To walk, move, proceed; to walk holding on to something or with uncertainty, as a child learning to walk; to move, as in checkers.

**kai ho'ē'e.** Var. of *kai e'e*.

**kai hohonu.** Deep sea; high tide.

**kai ho'i.** Ebbing sea. *Lit.*, returning sea.

**kai holo.** Running sea or current.

**kai ho'olulu.** Calm sea water.

**ka'i huaka'i.** Parade; to march in a parade.

kā'i'ī. Hard, rigid; stingy; to refuse to help.

kaikaina. Younger sibling or cousin of the same sex, as younger brother or male cousin of a male, or younger sister or female cousin of a female.

kaikamahine. Girl, daughter, niece.

kaikamāhine. Plural of *kaikamahine.*

kaikea. White sea foam, especially as washed up on a beach.

ka'i ke'a. Station of the cross (Catholic); procession of the cross.

kai kō. Sea with a strong current.

kaiko'eke. Brother-in-law or male cousin-in-law of a male; sister-in-law or female cousin-in-law of a female.

kaikua'ana, kaiku'ana. Older sibling or cousin of the same sex; sibling or cousin of the same sex of the senior line, whether older or younger.

kaikuahine. Sister or female cousin of a male.

kaikunāne. Brother or male cousin of a female.

kai lawai'a. Fishing grounds.

kāili. Runner on sweet potato vine; string of fish.

kā'ili. To snatch, grab, take by force; to gasp.

kai make. Low tide.

kai malo'o. Low tide, as when much of the reef is exposed. *Lit.,* dry sea.

kaimana, daimana. Diamond. *Eng.*

Kaimana-Hila. Diamond Head. *Lit.,* Diamond Hill *(Eng.).*

kai miki, kai mimiki. Receding sea, especially immediately before a tidal wave. *Lit.,* shrinking sea.

kaimoku. Receding of the tide. *Lit.,* cut sea.

kaina. 1. Same as *kaikaina,* most used as term of address. 2. Kind. *Eng.*

kainō, kainoa. Why not; I thought (but it was not so). *Kainō ua hele 'oe,* I thought you had gone.

kai nui. High tide, big sea.

kaiolohia. Calm, tranquil sea. *Fig.,* peace of mind.

kaio'o. Strong sea; to be such.

kai piha. High sea, high tide, full sea.

kai pi'i. High or rising tide.

kai po'i. Breaking waves or surf.

kai pupule. Crazy, restless, wild sea.

kai ulu. Sea at full tide; mounting sea.

Kai Waena Honua. Mediterranean Sea. *Lit.,* sea middle earth.

kai wahine. Calm, gentle sea. *Lit.,* feminine sea.

kaka. To rinse.

kākā. 1. To strike, dash, beat, chop; to thrash or beat out, as grain; to strike, as flint and steel; to fence. 2. To excrete; excreta (a euphemism, taught to children).

kaka'a. To roll, turn over; to revolve as a wheel; rolling, turning, etc. ho'okaka'a. To cause to turn, roll, etc.; to turn somersaults or cartwheels.

kakahiaka. Morning. *Kakahiaka nui,* early morning.

kākai. Handle, as of a bucket, pot, basket; strings by which a netted *(kōkō)* calabash is hung.

kaka'i. To walk along with a group; to follow in line, as chickens after a hen; procession.

kaka'ikahi. Scarce, sparse, rare, few; seldom, rarely.

kā kākou. Our, ours (*a*-class possessive, plural, inclusive).

kākā lā'au. Spear fencing; to fence.

kakale. Redup. of *kale.*

kakalina. Gasoline. *Eng.*

kākāmaka. Raw salted meat; to cut raw meat into large pieces and salt it. *Lit.,* chop raw.

Kākana, Satana. Satan. *Eng.*

**kakani.** Noisy; to make repeated noises; pealing, ringing. **ho‘o-kakani.** To make noises.

**kākā ‘ōlelo.** Orator, person skilled in use of language; advisor; storyteller; to orate. *Lit.,* to fence [with] words.

**kākau. 1.** To write; to print on tapa; writing. *Mea kākau,* writer, author. **2.** To tattoo; tattooing.

**kā kāua.** Our, ours (*a*-class possessive, dual, inclusive).

**kākau ho‘opa‘a.** To register.

**kākau inoa.** To sign a name, register; sign, signature.

**kākau kaha.** To make lines, print, mark, tattoo.

**kākau lima.** Handwriting; written by hand.

**kākau mo‘olelo.** Author; secretary or recorder.

**kākau ‘ōlelo.** Secretary, clerk.

**kākau ‘ōlelo pōkole.** Stenographer; shorthand.

**kake. 1.** Chants with mixed or garbled words, for and by chiefs. **ho‘okane.** To speak *kake;* to speak unclearly. **2.** To slip back and forth; to mix. **ho‘okake, hōkake.** To disturb.

**kakekimo.** Catechism.

**kākela. 1.** To perform well. **2.** Castle. *Eng.*

**kākele. 1.** To rub with oil; to mix or stew with sauce or gravy. **2.** To slide; to go rambling at will and hence to do as one pleases.

**kāki.** Khaki. *Eng.*

**kakiana.** Sergeant. *Eng.*

**kāki‘i.** To strike at, aim at; to brandish threateningly, as a war club.

**kākini.** Dozen; stocking, sock. *Eng.*

**kāki‘o.** Mange, impetigo, itch, itching pustules of the skin.

**Kakōlika, Katolika.** Catholic. *Eng.*

**kāko‘o.** To uphold, support, assist, prop up; girdle. Cf. *ko‘o,* support.

**kākou.** We (plural, inclusive). *Kō kākou,* our, ours.

**kākū.** Barracuda *(Sphyraena barracuda).*

**kākua.** To bind or fasten on, as a sarong.

**kala. 1.** To loosen, untie, free; to forgive, pardon, excuse; proclaim. *E kala mai ia‘u,* excuse me. **ho‘okala.** To release. **2.** Screwdriver. **3.** Several species of surgeonfish (genus *Naso*). **4.** Rough, as sharkskin. **ho‘okala.** To sharpen, grind. **5.** Gable, as of a house. **6.** A tern. **7.** Thorn.

**kālā, dala.** Dollar, silver, money. *Eng.*

**kāla‘au.** Stick dancing; to stick dance.

**kāla‘e.** Clear, calm. **ho‘okāla‘e.** To cause to clear.

**kalahala.** Atonement; to pardon, absolve from sin. *Lit.,* forgive sin.

**kālai.** To carve, cut, hew; to divide, as land.

**kālai‘āina.** Political; politics; political economy. *Lit.,* land carving. *Kuhina Kālai‘āina,* Minister of Interior.

**kalaima, karaima.** Crime; criminal. *Eng. Hana kalaima,* criminal act.

**kālaimoku.** Counselor, prime minister; to hold such office. *Lit.,* manage island.

**kālai pōhaku.** Stone cutter; to carve or hew stone.

**kalaiwa.** To drive, as a car; driver. *Eng. Kalaiwa ka‘a,* to drive a car; car driver.

**kālai wa‘a.** Canoe carver; to build a canoe.

**kālā ke‘oke‘o.** Silver money.

**kalakoa.** Calico; variegated in color, as croton leaves; printed cotton cloth (modern). *Eng.*

**ka lākou.** Their, theirs (*a*-class possessive, plural).

**kalakupua.** Magic; magical, mysterious. **ho‘okalakupua.** Magician, enchanter; to do wondrous acts.

**kalalī.** To go quickly, briskly, without noticing anyone; to walk or talk in a brisk, haughty way; proud.

**kalana.** Division of land smaller than a *moku* or district; county.

**kālana. 1.** Stationery. **2.** Same as *kānana, 1, 2.*

**kālana kākau.** Notebook, tablet.

**kālani, galani.** Gallon. *Eng.*

**kālā pepa.** Paper money.

**kalapu. 1.** Club, society; club in a deck of cards. *Eng.* **2.** To strap, tie; a strap. *Eng.*

**kā lāua.** Their, theirs (*a*-class possessive, dual).

**kalaunu (karauna).** Crown, corona. *Eng.* Cf. also *pua kalaunu.*

**kālawa.** Curve, as in the road or along a beach. Also *hālawa.*

**kālawe.** To hold and carry, as a pail.

**Kalawina.** Calvinistic, Congregational. *Eng.*

**kale.** Watery, nearly liquid, as thin poi. *Waha kale,* to talk excessively.

**kalekale.** Same as *kakale;* to gossip. **hoʻokalekale.** To make watery; to lie, deceive; soft, spongy.

**kālele.** Support, railing; to lean upon, as a support; to have faith in. **hoʻokālele.** To cause to support; stress.

**kalelē.** Celery *(Apium graveolens). Eng.*

**kaleiei.** To turn toward, listen to.

**kālele leo.** Stress mark; emphasis.

**kālele manaʻo.** To stress, emphasize.

**kāleo.** Saying, expression.

**kālepa.** Trader, merchant; to trade, sell as merchandise. *Lit.,* strike flag, so called because a salesman hoisted a small flag to show that poi or another article was for sale. *Moku kālepa,* trading ship.

**Kaleponi.** California. *Eng.*

**kālewa.** To move from place to place; to float or move with the wind, as clouds; to peddle (formerly of goods carried suspended and swinging on a carrying pole); to lie off, as a ship.

**kali.** To wait, loiter, hesitate; slow. **hoʻokali.** To cause to wait; lingering.

**kālī.** Spine; string, as used to thread things upon, as flowers for a lei, or candlenuts for a torch.

**kalia.** A native tree *(Elaeocarpus bifidus).*

**kalika.** Silk. *Eng.*

**kālika, galika.** Garlic. *Eng.* See more common *ʻakaʻakai pūpū.*

**Kalikamaka.** Same as *Kalikimaka.*

**kāliki.** Corset, girdle, tight waist binder, suspenders; to tie as a corset.

**Kalikiano, Kristiano.** Christian. *Eng.*

**Kalikimaka.** Christmas. *Eng.*

**kāliki waiū.** Brassiere, corset cover. *Lit.,* breast corset.

**kalima.** Cream. *Eng.*

**kalima hamo.** Face cream.

**kalima waiū.** Cream.

**kalo.** Taro *(Colocasia esculenta).*

**kāloa. 1.** Oval wooden dish or platter. **2.** *(Cap.)* Names of three nights of the month; see below.

**Kāloa Kū Kahi.** Twenty-fourth day of the Hawaiian month. *Lit., Kāloa* standing first.

**Kāloa Kū Lua.** Twenty-fifth day of the Hawaiian month. *Lit., Kāloa* standing second.

**Kāloa Pau.** Twenty-sixth day of the Hawaiian month. *Lit.,* last *Kāloa.*

**kalokalo.** Conversational prayer to the gods.

**kālole.** Straight, as hair.

**kalo paʻa.** Cooked unpounded taro.

**kālua. 1.** To bake in the ground oven; baked. **2.** Double, two-stranded.

**kālua pa'a.** To bake whole, as a pig.

**kaluhā.** Papyrus (*Cyperus papyrus*), a large sedge.

**kāluhe.** To droop, bend, vibrate as a leaf in the wind; to act the coquette.

**kama.** Child, person. *Kama'ole*, childless, barren. **ho'okama.** To adopt a child or adult one loves, but for whom one might not have the exclusive care.

**kāma'a.** Shoe, sandal, slipper; ti-leaf or tapa sandal. *Cf. ma'a*, to bind. **ho'okāma'a.** To put on shoes, to furnish shoes.

**kāma'a hakahaka.** Openwork shoes, sandals. *Lit.*, shoes [with] spaces.

**kāma'a hao.** Horseshoe. *Lit.*, iron shoe.

**kāma'a 'ili.** Leather shoes.

**kama'āina.** Native-born; host; native plant; acquainted, familiar. *Lit.*, land child. **ho'okama-'āina.** To become acquainted with.

**kāma'a lō'ihi.** Boot, boots, hip boots. *Lit.*, tall shoes.

**kāma'a pale wāwae.** Slippers. *Lit.*, shoes protecting feet.

**Ka-māhana.** The constellation Gemini. *Lit.*, the twins.

**kamaha'o.** Wonderful, astonishing, surprising, remarkable. **ho-'okamaha'o.** To be or do something wonderful.

**kama hele.** Traveler.

**kamahine.** Girl. See *kaikamahine*.

**kama'ilio.** To talk, converse; conversational. *Kama'ilio 'ana*, conversation.

**kama kahi.** Only child, single child.

**-kamakama. ho'okamakama.** To prostitute; prostitution. *Lit.*, to cause children.

**kāmakamaka. 1.** Fresh, as of leaves or fresh fish; to lay green leaves on an oven. **2.** Prayer asking forgiveness. **ho'okāma-**

**kamaka.** To ask forgiveness, to seek restoration of friendship.

**kā mākoi.** To fish with a pole.

**kā mākou.** Our, ours (*a*-class possessive, plural, exclusive).

**kamalani.** Child of a chief; a petted child. **ho'okamalani.** To make a favorite of a person; to treat with indulgence; to be finicky.

**kama lei.** Beloved child.

**kamali'i.** Children (used only in the plural; sometimes used without the particle *nā*). *Lit.*, small child. **ho'okamali'i.** Childish.

**kamali'i wāhine.** Girls, a group of girls.

**kamāli'i wahine.** Princess (short for *kama ali'i wahine*, female chiefly child).

**kamanā.** Carpenter. *Eng.*

**kamanā kāpili moku.** Shipwright. *Lit.*, carpenter joining ships.

**kamani. 1.** A large tree (*Calophyllum inophyllum*). **2.** Smooth, polished, as *kamani* wood. **ho-'okamani.** To act the hypocrite; to deal falsely.

**kamani haole.** The false *kamani* (tropical almond, *Terminalia catappa*).

**kāmano.** Salmon. *Eng.*

**kāmano kini.** Canned salmon.

**kāmano lomi.** Salted salmon, cut and mashed with onions and tomatoes and a little water.

**Kama-pua'a.** Name of the pig demigod famous in legend.

**kāmau. 1.** To keep on, continue, persevere. **2.** To drink, especially intoxicants; a toast, somewhat like "to your health." **3.** Card game; trumps; to trump.

**kā māua.** Our, ours (*a*-class possessive, dual, exclusive).

**kamawae.** Selective, difficult to please, finicky. *Lit.*, person [who] chooses.

**kāmeha'i. 1.** Unusual, surprising, astonishing. **2.** Illegitimate child, since the identity of the father may be unknown.

3

**kameki.** Cement. *Eng.*

**kāmelo.** Camel. *Greek.*

**kamepiula.** Computer. *Eng.*

**Kāmoa.** Samoa; Samoan (old name was *Haʻamoa*).

**kāmoe. 1.** To go straight ahead; to recline; flattened. **2.** Recumbent weft of mat, so called because the strands lie horizontally *(moe);* overcasting stitches that lie neatly in the same direction.

**kamu.** Gum. *Eng.*

**kana.** Tens (usually compounded with numbers from three to nine to indicate 30 to 90). *Kanaiwa,* ninety.

**kāna. 1.** His, hers, its (*a*-class possessive). **2.** Also **Sana.** *(Cap.)* Saint (used in proper names). *Kāna Lui,* Saint Louis.

**kānaenae.** Chanted supplicating prayer; chant of eulogy.

**kanahā.** Forty.

**kanahiku.** Seventy.

**kanaiwa.** Ninety.

**kanaka.** Human being, man, human, mankind, person, individual; subject, as of a chief; human; inhabited; Hawaiian.

**kānaka.** Plural of *kanaka.*

**kanaka ʻē.** Foreigner.

**kanaka hana.** Worker, servant.

**Kanakaloka.** Santa Claus. *Eng.*

**kanaka makua.** Adult, mature person.

**kanakē.** Candy. *Eng.*

**kanakolu.** Thirty.

**kanalima.** Fifty.

**Kanaloa.** Name of one of the great Hawaiian gods.

**kānalua.** Doubtful; to doubt, hesitate.

**kānana. 1.** Sieve, strainer; to strain; to sift, as flour. **2.** Writing paper. Also *kālana.*

**kānana palaoa.** Flour sifter; to sift flour.

**-kananeʻo. hoʻokananeʻo.** To disregard, as instruction, warning, danger; careless of danger.

**kanaono.** Sixty.

**kānāwai.** Law, code, rule, statute; legal; to obey a law. *ʻAha kau kānāwai,* legislature, law-making body. **hoʻokānāwai.** To impose a law.

**kānāwai koa.** Military law.

**kānāwai maʻamau.** Common law, customary law.

**kānāwai mele.** Musical notes.

**kanawalu.** Eighty.

**kane.** Tinea, a fungus skin disease.

**kāne. 1.** Male, husband, male sweetheart, man; brother-in-law of a woman; male, masculine; to be a husband or brother-in-law of a woman. *Pipi kāne,* bull. **2.** *(Cap.)* Name of one of the four leading Hawaiian gods. **3.** *(Cap.)* Name of the twenty-seventh night of the lunar month.

**Kaneka, Saneta.** Saint; holy.

**kāne make.** Widowed; dead husband. *Wahine kāne make,* widow.

**kāne makua.** Elder brother or elder male cousin in the senior line of a woman's husband.

**kāne male (mare).** Married man, bridegroom, husband to whom a woman is legally married.

**kāne manuahi.** Common-law husband, lover.

**kāne ʻole.** Spinster, one without a husband.

**kāne ʻōpio.** Younger brother or younger cousin in the junior line of a woman's husband.

**kāne wahine make.** Widower. *Lit.,* man [with] dead wife.

**kani.** Sound of any kind; pitch in music; to sound, cry out, ring, peal, crow; to strike, of a clock; voiced. Cf. *leokani. Kani ka moa,* the rooster crows. **hoʻokani.** To play a musical instrument; to cause to sound; to ring up on the telephone.

**kaniʻāʻī.** Adam's apple, larynx, trachea, neck, throat. *Lit.,* hard neck.

**kanikau.** Dirge, lamentation, chant of mourning; to chant, wail. *Lit.,* sound chant.

**kanikē.** Tolling of a bell, ding-dong; sound of clashing objects.

**kanikela, kanikele.** Consul. *Eng.*

**kani koʻo.** Aged person; aged, so old that one walks with a cane. *Lit.,* sounding cane.

**Kani-lehua.** Name of a mistlike rain famous at Hilo. *Lit.,* [rain that] *lehua* flowers drink.

**kaniwāwae.** Infantryman, infantry. *Lit.,* sound [of] feet.

**kano.** Large, hard stem, as on a banana bunch; tool handle; bones of the lower arm or lower leg; male erection; stiffening; hard. **hoʻokano.** To harden.

**-kano. hoʻokano.** Haughty, proud, conceited, disdainful of others.

**kānoa.** Bowl.

**kanu.** To plant, bury; planting, burial. *Mea kanu,* crops, plants.

**kānuku.** Funnel.

**kao.** 1. Dart, javelin; spike as on tail of a stingray; skyrocket; to throw a spear, javelin, etc. 2. Goat.

**kāohi.** To hold back, restrain, try to hold back, control.

**kao hihiu.** Wild goat.

**kao keiki.** Kid, young goat.

**kao lele.** Dart, javelin, fireworks.

**kaʻolo.** Jowl, sagging chin, double chin.

**kā ʻolua.** Your, yours (*a*-class possessive, dual).

**kaomi.** To press down, squeeze with downward pressure; to suppress, as a thought.

**kaomi waina.** Wine press.

**kaona.** 1. Hidden meaning in Hawaiian poetry. 2. Town. *Eng.*

**kā ʻoukou.** Your, yours (*a*-class possessive, plural).

**kapa.** 1. Tapa, as made from *wauke* or *māmaki* bark; formerly quilt or clothes of any kind, or bedclothes. 2. To call, term, give a name to. *Kapa ʻia,* called, named. 3. Edge, border, boundary; side, as of a road (often not preceded by *ke*). 4. Labia.

**kapa ʻāpana.** Quilt with appliquéd designs. Also called *kapa lau. Lit.,* piece tapa.

**kāpae.** To set aside, turn aside, lay aside, spare, stow away. **hoʻokāpae.** To push aside, parry.

**kapakahi.** One-sided, crooked, lopsided; baised; to show favoritism. *Lit.,* one side.

**kapakapa.** 1. Plural of *kapa, 3;* human crotch. 2. Redup. of *kapa, 2;* to invoke, summon. *Inoa kapakapa,* nickname, fictitious name, pet name, pen name.

**Kāpaki, Sabati.** Sabbath. *Eng.*

**kapakū.** Overwhelmed, destroyed.

**kāpala.** Printing, blot, daub; to smear, smudge.

**Kapalakiko.** San Francisco. *Eng.*

**kapa lau.** Quilt with appliquéd designs. Also called *kapa ʻāpana.*

**kapalili.** Palpitating, as in fear or joy; trembling; quivering, as a leaf in the wind.

**kapalulu.** Whirring, as of quail taking flight; roaring, as of an airplane.

**kapa moe.** Blanket, quilt, bedspread (general name); sleeping tapa.

**kapa poho, kapa pohopoho.** Patchwork quilt of varied color or design. *Lit.,* patch quilt.

**kapa pulu.** Padded quilt, comforter. *Lit.,* pad covering.

**kāpehi.** To throw at, pelt, strike.

**kāpeku.** To splash the feet in the water, as in scaring fish. *Fig.,* blustering, harsh.

**kāpena.** 1. Captain. *Eng.* 2. Cabin. *Eng.*

**kāpī.** To sprinkle, as with salt; to salt; to scatter, as sand or salt.

**kapikala.** Capital, capitol (city, building). *Eng.*

**kāpiki.** Cabbage. *Eng.*

**kāpiki pua.** Cauliflower. *Lit.,* flowering cabbage.

**kāpili.** To build, put together, put on (as glasses), fit together, mend, repair, unite; to shoe, as a horse.

**kāpili manu.** To catch birds with lime.

**kāpili moku.** Shipbuilding; shipbuilder.

**kapolena.** Tarpaulin, canvas. *Eng.*

**kapu.** Taboo, prohibition; special privilege or exemption from ordinary taboo; sacredness; forbidden; sacred, holy, consecrated. **hoʻokapu.** To make taboo, prohibit, sanctify.

**kapuahi.** Fireplace, stove, furnace, heater, hearth; censer for sacrifice.

**kapuahi ea.** Gas stove.

**kapuahi hoʻomahana hale.** House heater, furnace.

**kapuahi uila.** Electric stove.

**kapuaʻi.** Sole of the foot, footprint, track; foot measure; paw of an animal.

**kapuaʻihao lio.** Horseshoe. *Lit.,* horse iron tread.

**kapu ʻauʻau.** Bathtub.

**kapu holoi.** Washtub.

**kapukapu.** Dignity, regal appearance; entitled to respect and reverence, difficult of access because of rank, dignity, and station. **hoʻokapukapu.** To impose a taboo, especially on something not previously taboo; to praise, glorify.

**kāpulu.** Careless, slovenly, unclean, gross, untidy.

**kapu moe, kapu ā moe.** Prostration taboo.

**kapu noho.** Taboo requiring everyone to sit in the presence of the chief, or when his food container, bath water, and other articles were carried by.

**kapuō.** Var. spelling of *kapuwō.*

**kapu wai.** Washtub; water tub.

**kapuwaʻi.** Var. spelling of *kapuaʻi.*

**kapuwō.** A cry proclaiming a taboo on the approach of a sacred personage or as part of a ceremony.

**kau. 1.** To place, put, hang, suspend; to set, rest; to enact, impose, or pass, as a law; to levy, as a tax; to ride, as on a horse or in a car; to board, mount; to rise up, appear, as the moon; to come to rest, as the setting sun; to come to pass; to hang up, as a telephone receiver. **hoʻokau.** To put on, place on, lay on, as responsibility; to happen, come to pass. *Hoʻokau hiamoe,* to fall asleep. **2.** Period of time; any season, especially summer; session of a legislature; term, semester. **3.** A sacred chant. **4.** Particle indicating plural, much less commonly used than *nā* and *mau* except in the compounds *kauhale, kauwahi.* **5.** Particle expressing superlative, preceded by *hoʻi* or *mai hoʻi. He nani mai hoʻi kau!* Oh, so beautiful!

**kāu.** Your, yours (singular, *a*-class possessive).

**kaʻu.** My, mine (*a*-class possessive).

**-kaʻu.** Hesitation, fear. See *kaʻukaʻu, kaʻunē, makaʻu.*

**kaua.** War, battle; army; to make war.

**kāua.** We (dual, inclusive).

**kauā, kauwā.** Untouchable, outcast, pariah; a caste that lived apart and was drawn on for sacrificial victims; slave.

**Kauaʻi.** Kauaʻi (name of one of the Hawaiian islands).

**kaua kūloko.** Civil war, internal war.

**kaua lio.** Cavalry; cavalry war. *Lit.,* horse war.

**ka ua mea.** Cause. See *mea,* 5.

**kau anu.** Winter, cold season.

**kaua paio.** Combat, debate.

**kauʻeliʻeli.** To dig up the past, to review the past.

**kauhale.** Group of houses composing a Hawaiian home. *Lit.,* plural house.

**kauhola.** To open, unfold, as a tapa; to expand, as a flower in bloom.

**kauhua.** State of pregnancy. **hoʻo-kauhua.** To cause pregnancy; pregnancy sickness.

**kau hua.** Fruit season.

**kauhuhu.** Ridgepole.

**kauila, kauwila.** A native tree in the buckthorn family (*Alphitonia ponderosa*).

**kauʻīpuka.** To loiter about the door of a house as though desiring food gifts; one who does so. *Lit.*, placed {at the} door.

**kauka.** Doctor, physician; medical. *Eng.*

**kauka haʻihaʻi iwi.** Chiropractor. *Lit.*, bone-breaking doctor.

**kaukahi.** 1. Standing alone, solitary; singleness of purpose. 2. Single canoe. Cf. *kaulua*.

**kauka holoholona.** Veterinarian. *Lit.*, animal doctor.

**kauka hoʻohānau.** Obstetrician.

**kauka kaha.** Surgeon. *Lit.*, cutting doctor.

**kauka lapaʻau.** Medical doctor.

**kauka lomilomi.** Osteopath. *Lit.*, massage doctor.

**kaʻukama.** Cucumber, introduced. *Eng.*

**kaukani, tausani.** Thousand. *Eng.*

**kauka niho.** Dentist. *Lit.*, tooth doctor.

**kaukau.** Chant of lamentation, asaddressing the dead directly; to advise, admonish, especially in a kindly or affectionate manner.

**kaʻukaʻu.** To slow down, hesitate; reluctance.

**kaukaualiʻi.** Class of chiefs of lesser rank than the high chief.

**kau koho pāloka.** Election season, election.

**kaula.** Rope, cord, string, line; arc of a circle in geometry; chain, as used by surveyors and engineers.

**kāula.** Prophet, seer.

**Kaʻula.** Name of an islet off Niʻihau.

**kaula ahi.** Wick.

**kaula hao.** Chain. Lit., iron rope.

**kaula hoʻohei.** Rope for lassoing or ensnaring.

**kaula hope.** Line from mast to stern.

**kaula huki.** Drawstring, rope or cord to pull on.

**kaula huki peʻa.** Halyard.

**kaulaʻi.** To hang up, as to dry in the sun.

**kaula ihu.** Line from mast to bow (*ihu*).

**kaulaʻi iwi.** To talk too much of one's ancestry and to reveal the secrets of the ancestors. *Lit.*, expose bones.

**kaulaʻi lā.** To sun; to bleach in the sun; sun bath.

**kaula ʻili,** Leather rope, lassoing rope, lariat.

**kaula kaulaʻi lole.** Clothesline. *Lit.*, line to dry clothes.

**kaula lei.** Cord on which flowers are strung into a lei; streamer.

**kaula lī.** Lacing, as for shoes or corset.

**kaula lī kāmaʻa.** Shoelace.

**kaula lio.** Halter. *Lit.*, horse rope.

**kaula moku.** 1. Ship line of any kind. 2. Broken rope, string.

**kaulana.** 1. Famous, celebrated, renowned; fame; to become famous. **hoʻokaulana.** To make famous. 2. Resting place; restful, quiet.

**kaula paʻa lima.** Leash. *Lit.*, rope held hand.

**kaula uaki.** Watch chain.

**kaula waha.** Bridle, reins; to bridle. *Lit.*, mouth chain.

**kāula wahine.** Prophetess, priestess.

**kau lei.** To sell leis; to hang leis.

**kaulele.** 1. To take flight; soaring, on the wing. 2. Stress; to accent in music. 3. Extraordinary, over and above the ordinary.

**kauleo.** To urge, exhort, command. *Lit.*, to place the voice.

**kaʻulī.** To creep along with a hissing sound, as fire.

**kaulike.** Equality, justice; equal, impartial; to balance evenly, make alike, treat fairly and impartially; dispense justice. **hoʻo-kaulike.** To equalize.

**kau lio.** To ride horseback.

**kaulua. 1.** Double canoe, pair, yoke, two of a kind; to put together, to yoke or harness together; to double in quantity. Cf. *kaukahi*. **2.** *(Cap.)* One of the many names for the star Sirius.

**kaumaha. 1.** Heavy; weight, heaviness; sad, depressed. **hoʻo-kaumaha.** To burden, load down, oppress, cause sadness or grief. **2.** Offering.

**kaumaha lua.** Very heavily laden; bearing a heavy load; extremely sad.

**kaumahana.** Native mistletoes. Also called *hulumoa*.

**kau maʻi.** Period or time of sickness.

**kau mau.** Regular session, as of legislature.

**kāuna.** Four. *ʻEkolu kāuna*, twelve.

**kaunaʻoa.** A native dodder *(Cuscuta sandwichiana)*, parasitic on other plants. **2.** A gastropod mollusk with a wormlike shell, family Vermetidae.

**kaʻunē.** Slow, lagging, delaying.

**kaunu.** Love-making.

**kauō. 1.** To drag, haul, draw along. *Pipi kauō*, oxen. **hoʻokauō.** To cause to be dragged. **2.** Yolk or white of an egg.

**kauoha.** Order, command, decree; to order, command, commit into the hands of.

**Kauoha Hou.** New Testament.

**Kauoha Kahiko.** Old Testament.

**kauō keʻokeʻo.** White of an egg.

**kau ʻokoʻa.** Placed apart; to separate.

**kauō melemele.** Yolk of egg.

**kaupale.** Boundary, barrier; to thrust aside, parry; to cover an earth oven, especially with rocks on its edge to keep earth out. *Lit.*, place ward off.

**hoʻokaupale.** To cause a separation.

**kaupalena.** To limit, mark a border, set a deadline; limitation.

**kaupaona.** Scales, weight; to weigh. *Lit.*, place pound *(Eng.)*.

**kaupeʻa.** Crisscross, interwoven.

**kaupoku.** Ridgepole, highest point, roof. (Often used with out *ke.*) *Fig.*, greatest.

**kaʻupu.** A bird, probably albatross.

**kauwahi.** Some, a little, a few; something; some place.

**kau wale.** To put or place for no reason; to ride free of charge; to ride bareback.

**kau wela.** Summer, hot season.

**kauwila.** Var. spelling of *kauila*.

**kawa.** Leaping place, as a precipice above a pool.

**kā waʻa.** Canoe bailer; to bail a canoe.

**kawakawa.** Bonito, little tunny *(Euthynnus yaito)*.

**kāwele. 1.** Kind of chant with clear, distinct pronunciation. **2.** A hula step. **3.** Towel, napkin, dishcloth; to wipe or dry with a cloth. *(Eng.,* towel.)

**kāwele ʻauʻau.** Bath towel.

**kāwele holoi.** Washcloth.

**kāwele wai.** To mop or wipe with wet cloth or water.

**kāwelowelo.** To flutter, whip, as a flag in the wind.

**kawewe.** To clatter, as dishes; to roar, as a sudden downpour; to snap or crackle.

**kāwili.** To mix ingredients; to ensnare birds, as with lime; entwined, interwoven.

**kāwili lāʻau.** To mix ingredients, drugs; pharmacist.

**kāwili palaoa.** Flour mill; to grind flour.

**kāwiliwili humuhumu.** Sewing machine worked by hand rather than by a foot treadle.

**-kāwōwō. hoʻokāwōwō.** To roar, as a wind or waterfall.

**ke.** 1. Var. of *ka, 2,* often translated "the." *Ke* replaces *ka* before all words beginning with *k-, a-, e-,* and *o-,* and before some words beginning with *p-* or the glottal stop. 2. Contraction of *ka mea e,* the one who will, should, or is; the thing that is, will, should. 3. A particle meaning "when, if" in the future. *Ke hele ‘oe, hele au,* if you go, I'll go. 4. A particle connecting certain forms, as *hiki* and *pono,* with following verbs. *Hiki ia‘u ke hele,* I can go. 5. See *ke* (verb) *nei.*

**kē.** 1. Protest, complaint, criticism; critic, especially a hula critic; to criticize; to push, shove, struggle against, avoid, abstain from, refuse. *Kē ‘ai,* to fast. **ho‘okē.** To crowd, elbow, push aside, oppress, shun. 2. To clang, as a bell or gong; to dingdong, strike, as a clock.

**kea.** White, clear; fair-complexioned person.

**ke‘a.** 1. Cross, crucifix, any crossed piece; main house purlin. *Fig.,* to hinder, obstruct, intercept. **ho‘oke‘a.** To cross, block. 2. Bow, dart; to shoot with bow and arrow.

**ke‘ahakahaka.** Abdomen.

**keaka.** 1. Theater; theatrical *Eng. Hale keaka,* theater building. 2. Jack (in a deck of cards). *Eng.* 3. To chat, speak. *Eng.*

**keakea.** Semen. *Fig.,* child, seed.

**Ke‘a ‘Ula‘ula.** Red Cross.

**ke‘e.** Crookedness; fault, flaw; full of faults. *Nānā ke‘e,* to look at with disfavor. **ho‘oke‘e.** To make a turn, as in walking or cutting paper or cloth; to form an angle.

**ke‘ehana.** Any footrest, footprint; ground or floor stamped on or trodden on.

**ke‘ehi.** To stamp, step, tread; to strike against; to put foot into stirrup in mounting a horse; to

"put the foot down" in ending a situation.

**ke‘eke‘e.** 1. Redup. of *ke‘e.* **ho‘oke‘eke‘e.** Redup. of *ho‘oke‘e* (see *ke‘e*); zigzag, angular. 2. Same as *kekē,* surly, cranky.

**ke‘ena.** Office, room; department, board, bureau.

**ke‘ena hana.** Place to work, office, laboratory.

**ke‘ena kapu.** Taboo room; tabernacle, sanctuary.

**ke‘ena koho pāloka.** Voting booth.

**kēhau.** Dew, mist, dewdrop.

**kēhau anu.** Cold dew, frost.

**kēia.** This, this person, this thing; the latter. Also, *keia.*

**keiki.** Child, offspring, descendant, boy, son; calf, colt, kid; to have or obtain a child; to be or become a child. Cf. *keiki kāne.*

**keiki ali‘i.** Prince, child of a chief.

**keiki hele kula.** School child.

**keiki hipa.** Lamb. *Lit.,* sheep *(Eng.)* offspring.

**keiki kameha‘i.** Illegitimate child whose father is not definitely known. *Lit.,* wonder child.

**keiki kāne.** Boy, son.

**keiki makua ‘ole.** Orphan. *Lit.,* child without parent.

**keiki manuahi.** Illegitimate child. *Lit.,* gratis child.

**keiki po‘o ‘ole.** Illegitimate child. *Lit.,* headless child.

**kekahi.** A, some, one, other, another; besides, too, also, including; moreover; someone, anyone. *Kekahi lā,* another day, some other day, a certain day.

**kēkake.** Donkey, jackass. *Eng.*

**kekē.** 1. Scolding, shrieking angrily; exposure of the teeth, as in derision, anger; surly, sharp-tongued. **ho‘okekē, ha‘akekē.** To scold, expose the teeth, etc. 2. Indecent exposure by a woman or girl; admonition to a female to sit properly.

**keke‘e.** Redup. of *ke‘e* but more common; crooked, twisted.

**ho'okeke'e.** To crook, bend, twist out of shape.

**kekele, degere.** Degree. *Eng.*

**Kēkēmapa, Dekemaba.** December. *Eng.*

**kekē niho.** Surly, cross, violently rude, snarling, often in the sense of making threats that may not be carried out.

**kekē nuku.** About the same as *kekē niho,* but with more verbalization and scolding.

**keko.** Monkey, ape.

**kekona, sekona.** Second (the time unit). *Eng.*

**kela.** Excelling, exceeding, projecting beyond, reaching high above; to excel. **ho'okela.** To outdo, surpass; to show off, to show preference.

**ke** (verb) **lā.** Particle denoting present tense at a distance from the speaker. Cf. *ke* (verb) *nei.*

**kēlā.** That, that one, he, she, it, that person or thing; the former.

**kēlā . . . kēia.** This and that, all, every, everything, here and there; miscellaneous. *I kēlā me kēia lā,* daily.

**kelakela.** Redup. of *kela.* **ho'oke-lakela.** To brag, show off; overbearing.

**kela (tela) lole.** Tailor, dressmaker. *Lit.,* clothes tailor *(Eng.).*

**kelamoku. 1.** Sailor. *Lit.,* ship sailor *(Eng.).* **2.** Checkered jacket and the material from which it is made.

**kelawini.** Gale. *Lit.,* wind gale *(Eng.)*

**kele. 1.** Watery, muddy, swampy, greasy. *Fig.,* impurity. *Wao kele,* forested uplands. **ho'okele.** Same as *ho'okelekele* (see *kelekele, 1*). **2.** To sail; reached by sailing. *Awa kele,* harbor that may be reached by sailing. **ho'okele.** Steersman, helmsman; to sail or navigate, as the master of a ship; to steer; to drive, as a car.

**keleawe.** Brass, copper, tin.

**kelekalama, teregarama.** Telegram. *Eng.*

**kelekalapa, telegarapa.** Telegraph. *Eng.*

**kelekele. 1.** Redup. of *kele, 1;* mud, mire, slush, fat; muddy, oily, rich, greasy. **ho'okelekele.** To make muddy; to soak material, as pandanus leaves in water to make pliable for plaiting; to fatten. **2.** Redup. of *kele, 2.* **ho'okelekele.** Redup. of *ho'o-kele* (see *kele, 2*); to steer, navigate or sail frequently.

**Kelemānia.** Germany; German. *Eng.*

**kelepona, telepona.** Telephone; to telephone. *Eng.*

**kelikoli, teritori.** Territory; territorial. *Eng.*

**kemokalaka, demokarata.** Democrat; democratic. *Eng.*

**kemu. 1.** To absorb, consume. **2.** Game. *Eng.*

**kena. 1.** Quenched; satisfied, of thirst. **2.** Weary, as from heavy toil; grieved and distressed.

**kēnā. 1.** To command, order, give orders, send on business. **2.** That (near the person addressed).

**ke** (verb) **nei.** Particle denoting present tense near the speaker. Cf. *ke* (verb) *lā.*

**keneka.** Cent, penny. *Eng.*

**kenekoa.** Senator. *Eng.*

**kenelala, generala.** General. *Eng.*

**keni.** Change (money), small change. *Eng. He keni nō kāu?* Have you change?

**kenika.** Tennis. *Eng.*

**kenikeni.** Dime, ten cents, small change. *(Eng.,* ten.)

**ke'o. 1.** White, clear. **ho'oke'o.** To whiten, bleach. **2.** Clitoris. **3.** Proud.

**ke'oke'o. 1.** White, clear. *Kālā ke'oke'o,* silver money. **2.** White muslin (usually followed by *maoli, pia,* or *wai*). **3.** Proud.

**ke'oke'o maoli.** Bleached muslin

of good quality. *Lit.,* genuine whiteness.

**ke'oke'o pia.** Bleached muslin of inferior quality.

**ke'oke'o wai.** Bleached muslin.

**keonimana.** Gentleman. *Eng.*
**ho'okeonimana.** Gentlemanly conduct; to act as a gentleman.

**kepa.** Notched; cut or trimmed obliquely; to turn to one side.

**Kepakemapa.** September. *Eng.*

**Kepanī.** Japanese. *Eng.*

**Kepania, Sepania.** Spain; Spanish. *Eng.*

**kēpau.** Lead, pitch, tar, resin; gum, as on ripe breadfruit.

**kēpau kāpili palapala.** Sealing wax. *Lit.,* gum-stick document.

**kepela, sepela. 1.** Spelling. *Eng. Puke a'o kepela,* spelling book. **2.** Also **zebara.** Zebra. *Eng.*

**keu.** Remaining, excessive, additional, extra, more, too much (often accompanied by *ā*). *Kanahā ā keu,* forty and more. *He keu ā ke kolohe!* Very, very mischievous!

**kewe. 1.** Convex, concave; crescent-shaped, as the moon. **2.** Boom, crane.

**-ki.** Transitivizer.

**kī. 1.** Ti, a woody plant *(Cordyline terminalis)* in the lily family. **2.** To shoot or aim, as with a gun; to squirt water, as with a syringe; to spit, as an angry cat. **3.** Bundle of 40 pandanus leaves, sorted for size and length and set aside for plaiting. **4.** Key, latch; key, pitch, and clef in music; to lock, as a door; to wind or set, as a clock. *Eng.* **5.** Trigger of a gun. **6.** Tea. *Eng.*

**kia. 1.** Pillar, prop, post; mast of a ship; nail; rod used in snaring birds with gum; one who so snares birds. **2.** Also **dia.** Deer. *Eng.*

**kia-.** Prefix to types of canoe. See *kialoa, kiapā.*

**kia'āina.** Governor; governorship. *Lit.,* prop [of the] land.

**kī'aha. 1.** Cup, pitcher, tumbler, mug. **2.** *(Cap.)* The Big Dipper (modern).

**kī'aha aniani.** Glass (for drinking). *Lit.,* glass cup.

**kī'aha inu waina.** Wineglass.

**kia hō'ailona.** Signpost.

**kia ho'omana'o.** Monument, gravestone.

**kia'i.** Guard, watchman; to watch; to overlook, as a bluff. **ho'o-kia'i.** To post a watch.

**kia'i kai.** Coast guard. *Lit.,* sea guard.

**kia'i kino.** Bodyguard.

**kia'i ola.** Lifeguard.

**kia'i pō.** Night watchman, night watch.

**kia kahi.** Sloop; one-masted vessel.

**kia kolu.** Three-masted vessel.

**kialoa.** Long, light, and swift canoe used for display and racing.

**kia lua.** Brig, two-masted vessel, two-masted schooner.

**kia manu.** Bird catcher, bird catching by gumming.

**kī'amo.** Plug, stopper; sanitary napkin.

**kianapauka.** Dynamite. *Lit.,* giant powder *(Eng.).*

**kiapā.** Swift-sailing canoe.

**kiapolō, diabolo.** Devil; devilish. *Greek.*

**kī'apu.** Ti leaf folded into a cup and used for dipping water; the two hands rounded to form a cup for drinking water.

**kiawe.** Algaroba tree *(Prosopis pallida).*

**ki'ei.** To peer, peep, as through a door or crevice.

**ki'eki'e.** Height, tallness; high, lofty, exalted, majestic, superior. **ho'oki'eki'e.** To elevate, promote; overbearing in conduct; conceit.

**kiele.** Gardenia *(Gardenia augusta).*

**kiha.** Supernatural lizard.

**kīhā. 1.** Belch, burp; to belch or

burp. **2.** To rise and pitch, as a canoe in a heavy sea.

**kīhae.** To tear or strip, as leaves; to remove thorns from pandanus leaves; to shred, as ti leaves for dance skirts.

**kīhāpai.** Small land division, smaller than a *paukū;* cultivated patch, small farm; parish of a church; department of a business or office.

**kihe.** Sneeze.

**kīhei.** Shawl, cape; rectangular tapa cloak tied in a knot on one shoulder; bed covering; to wear a *kīhei.*

**kīhei moe.** Light bedspread.

**kihi.** Outside corner, edge, tip; apex of an angle; to turn aside. *Maka kihi,* looking out of the corners of the eyes. *Kihi alanui,* street corner. **hoʻokihi.** To make a corner by overlapping, as in plaiting.

**kihikihi. 1.** Corners; angular, full of corners. **2.** A small fish *(Zanclus cornutus),* also called the Moorish idol.

**kihi poʻohiwi.** Points or edges of the shoulders; shoulder; shoulder of a mountain.

**kī hōʻalu.** Slack key.

**kiʻi. 1.** Image, statue, picture, doll, petroglyph; plans, as for a house. **2.** To fetch, procure, send for, go after. **hoʻokiʻi.** To send; to have sent for.

**-kiʻi.** See *hākiʻi, hīkiʻi, mūkiʻi, nākiʻi, nīkiʻi,* all meaning to tie, bind.

**kiʻi akua.** Idol, image.

**kiʻihele.** To gad about, wander; such a person.

**kiʻi hoʻākaaka.** Illustration, picture. *Lit.,* clarifying picture.

**kiʻi hoʻolele.** Enlargement of a picture.

**kiʻi kālai ʻia.** Carved image, graven image.

**kiʻi ʻoniʻoni.** Moving picture, movie.

**kiʻi palapala.** Printed picture, as in a newspaper.

**kiʻi pena.** Painting. *Lit.,* painted picture *(Eng.).*

**kiʻi pōhaku.** Stone statue; petroglyph.

**kika. 1.** Slippery, slimy, as with mud. **2.** Also **tita.** Sister. *Eng.* **3.** Also **sida.** Cider. *Eng.* **4.** Also **tiga.** Tiger. *Eng.*

**kīkā. 1.** Guitar. *Eng.* **2.** Cigar. *Eng.* **3.** The cigar flower *(Cuphea ignea).*

**kīkaha.** To soar, glide, poise; to turn aside; to maneuver, as fighting cocks.

**Kikako.** Chicago. *Eng.*

**kīkala.** Hip, coccyx; posterior; stern as of a canoe.

**kīkānia. 1.** Cockleburs *(Xanthium* spp.). **2.** Zizania, tares *(Greek).*

**kīkā Pukikī.** Mandolin. *Lit.,* Portuguese guitar *(Eng.).*

**kīkē.** To rap, knock; to break open, as with a hammer; to click glasses, as in drinking a toast.

**-kīkē.** Back and forth. See *ʻōlelokīkē, walakīkē, pākīkē, kīkēʻōlelo.* **hoʻokīkē.** Ready with a rude retort.

**kīkeʻe.** To bend, crook; zigzag. *Alanui kīkeʻe,* zigzag road.

**kīkeʻekeʻe.** Redup. of *kīkeʻe. Alanui kīkeʻekeʻe,* road with many turns.

**kīkēʻōlelo.** To argue, talk back.

**kīkepa.** Tapa or sarong worn by women, the upper edge passing under one arm and over the shoulder of the opposite arm.

**kiki. 1.** To sting, as a bee; to peck, leap at, as a hen. **2.** Plug.

**kikī.** To flow swiftly; to spurt, as water from a hose; to do swiftly.

**kīkī.** Redup. of *kī, 2;* to shoot, as a gun. *Wai-kīkī* (name), spouting water.

**kīkīao.** Sudden gust of wind, squall.

**kikili.** Redup. of *kili, 1, 2.*

**kīkīpani.** Conclusion, last, end.

**kikī wai.** To shoot water with a hose or water pistol, to hose.

**kiko.** Dot, point, speck of any

kind; punctuation mark; punctuation; section of a story; dot in music indicating time added to a note, also to repeat; dotted; to dot, mark; to pick up food, as chickens; to injure fruit, as by a fruit fly; tattooed with dots on the forehead.

**kiko hoʻomaha.** Punctuation mark, indicative of a pause, as comma, colon, semicolon, period. *Lit.,* resting punctuation.

**kīkoi.** 1. Rude, sarcastic. 2. To do in irregular, haphazard fashion, as skipping about while reading; irregular.

**kiko kahi.** Period mark in punctuation. *Lit.,* single dot.

**kikokiko.** 1. Dotted, spotted; to dot frequently; to peck repeatedly, as a feeding hen. 2. To type.

**kikokiko hua.** To typewrite; typist. Cf. *mīkini kikokiko hua.*

**kiko koma.** Semicolon. *Lit.,* dot comma. *Eng.*

**kiko moe.** Hyphen. *Lit.,* supine mark.

**kiko nīnau.** Question mark.

**kīkoʻo.** Span; extent; to stretch, extend, as the hands, or as a bird its wings; to shoot, as from a bow; to pay out money, draw money from the bank.

**kīkoʻolā.** 1. Sarcastic, rude, impertinent. 2. Haphazard; here, there, and everywhere; entangled; of awkward shape, as a package.

**kīkoʻo pānaʻi.** Bill of exchange. *Lit.,* exchange disbursement.

**kīkoʻo panakō.** Bank check.

**kiko pūʻiwa.** Exclamation mark.

**kikowaena.** Center of a circle; central, telephone operator, headquarters; bull's eye.

**kila.** 1. Also **sila.** Seal, deed, patent; sealed; to fix a seal. *Eng.* 2. Steel, chisel, knife blade. *Eng.*

**kilakila.** Majestic, tall, strong.

**kili.** 1. Raindrops; fine rain; to

rain gently. See *kili hau, kilihune, kili nahe.* 2. Peal of thunder; to thunder.

**kili hau.** Ice-cold shower; to rain thus.

**kilihē.** Drenched, as by sea spray.

**kilihune.** Fine, light rain; wind-blown spray.

**kilika.** 1. Silk. *Eng.* 2. The black mulberry *(Morus nigra).*

**kilika lau.** Brocaded silk.

**kilika nehe.** Taffeta. *Lit.,* rustling silk.

**Kilikiano, Kiritiano.** Var. of *Kalikiano,* Christian.

**kili nahe.** Light, soft, gentle rain.

**kili noe.** Fine, misty rain, somewhat heavier mist than the *kili ʻohu.*

**kili ʻohu.** Fine rain and light mist.

**Kilipaki, Gilibati.** Gilbert Islands; Gilbertese. *Eng.*

**kilo.** Stargazer, reader of omens, seer, astrologer; to watch closely.

**kilohana.** The outside, decorated sheet of tapa in the *kuʻinakapa,* bed coverings; the four inner layers were white, contrasting with the decorated *kilohana.* Hence extended meanings: best, superior, excellent.

**kilo heʻe.** One who fishes for octopus by looking through a glass-bottomed box; to fish thus.

**kilohia.** Passive/imperative of *kilo.*

**kilo hōkū.** Astrologer, astronomer; to observe and study the stars.

**kiloi.** To throw away.

**kilo iʻa.** A man who observes fish movements from a high place and directs fishermen.

**kilo lani.** Soothsayer who predicts the future by observing the sky.

**kilo makani.** One who observes the winds for purposes of navigation.

**kilo moana.** Oceanography, oceanographer; to observe and study the open seas.

**kilo nānā lima, kilokilo nānā
lima.** Palmistry, palmist.

**kilu.** A small gourd or coconut
shell, usually cut lengthwise,
used for storing small, choice
objects, or to feed favorite children from. Used also as a quoit
in the *kilu* sexual game; to play
*kilu.*

**kimo. 1.** A game similar to jacks.
**2.** *(Cap.)* James. *Eng.*

**Kina.** China; Chinese. *Eng.*

**-kina, hoʻokina.** To persist; inces-
sant.

**kīnā.** Blemish, blotch, disfigure-
ment or physical defect of any
sort; disfigured, maimed, etc.
**hoʻokīnā.** To cause defect,
disaster, etc.

**kinai.** To quench, as fire; to put
out, as a light.

**kinai ahi.** Fireman, fire extin-
guisher; to put out fires.

**kinamu.** Gingham. *Eng. Pua
kinamu,* flower appliquéd, as on
quilt or cushion cover.

**kīnana.** Mother hen or bird and
her brood.

**kīnaʻu.** Stain, blemish, defect,
minor flaw.

**kini. 1.** Multitude, many; forty
thousand. **2.** King. *Eng.* **3.** Also
**tini.** Tin, pail, can. *Eng. Kini
ʻai,* pail for carrying poi or other
food. *Lit.,* food [or poi] pail. **4.**
Also **gini.** Gin. *Eng.*

**kini akua.** The thousands of spirits and gods, the multitudinous
spirits.

**kinikini. 1.** Redup. of *kini, 1;*
numerous. **2.** Marble, game of
marbles; to play marbles.

**kini lau.** Numerous, very many.

**kini ʻōpala.** Garbage or rubbish
can.

**kinipōpō.** Ball, baseball; to play
ball.

**kinipōpō hīnaʻi.** Basketball.

**kinipōpō paʻi.** Tennis. *Lit.,* ball to
strike.

**kinipōpō peku.** Football. *Lit.,*
kick ball.

**kino. 1.** Body, person, individual,
self; bodily, physical. **hoʻokino.**
To take shape; to develop, as a
puny infant; to take form, as a
spirit. **2.** Person in grammar;
personal. *Kino mua, kino kahi,*
first person.

**kinohi.** Beginning, origin, gene-
sis.

**kīnohi.** Decorated, ornamented;
decoration.

**kīnohinohi.** Redup. of *kīnohi;*
printed, as calico.

**kino kanaka.** Human form.

**kino lau.** Many forms taken by a
supernatural, as Pele.

**Kino o ka Haku.** Corpus Christi.

**kinoʻole.** Frail and thin.

**kino wailua.** Spirit of the dead;
dead person, corpse.

**kio. 1.** To cheep. **2.** A mollusk.

**kiʻo.** Pool, cistern; to settle, as
dregs; to excrete. Cf. *kiʻo lepo.*

**kiʻo ahi.** Fiery pit, hell.

**kīʻoʻe.** Ladle, dipper, cup; scoop
or spoon made of coconut shell;
arm or wrist motion in paddling
or dipping; to dip, ladle, scoop.

**kioea. 1.** An extinct honeyeater
*(Chaetoptila angustipluma).* **2.**
Bristle-thighed curlew *(Nume-
nius tahitiensis).*

**kiola.** To throw away.

**kiʻo lepo.** Swamp, mire; mud
puddle.

**Kio-paʻa.** North Star. *Lit.,* fixed
projection.

**kīʻope.** A bundle; to make a bundle.

**kiʻo wai.** Pool of water, water
hydrant, fountain.

**kipa. 1.** To visit, call. **hoʻokipa.**
To entertain; hospitality. **2.** To
turn aside.

**kīpā.** Chinese gambling game
*chee-fah;* to play this game.

**kīpaʻi.** To shoo away, as by clapping *(paʻi).*

**kipaku.** To send away, drive away,
expel, banish.

**kīpalalē.** Disorder, jumble; rapid
flow, as of a swollen stream;

unsystematic; to extend in a disorderly fashion.

**kīpapa.** Pavement, level terrace; to pave.

**kipa wale.** To pay a visit without being asked; to intrude.

**kīpehi.** To pelt, throw at.

**kīpi. 1.** Rebellion, revolt; to resist lawful authority; to conspire against. **hoʻokīpi.** To foment or act in revolt. **2.** To dig.

**kipikua.** Pickaxe.

**kīpou.** To drive down, as a stake into the ground; to lean, as a post.

**kīpū.** To hold back or brace, as a canoe on a wave with a paddle; to rein in, as a horse; to fold tightly about one, as a blanket.

**kī pū.** To shoot, fire a gun. Cf. *laikini kī pū.*

**kīpuka. 1.** Variation or change of form *(puka,* hole), as an opening in a forest; especially an "island," often vegetated, of older lava land completely surrounded by a more recent lava flow. **2.** Short shoulder cape; cloak, poncho.

**kīpūkai.** Seaside heliotrope *(Heliotropium curassavicum).*

**kīpuka ʻili.** Leather lasso.

**kiu. 1.** Spy; to spy, observe secretly. Cf. *mākaʻikiu,* detective. **2.** *(Cap.)* Northwest wind.

**kiule, kiure.** Jury. *Eng.*

**kiwi.** Horn of an animal; curved object such as a sickle; curved, bent.

**kīwila.** Civil, civic; civilian. *Eng. Hana kīwila,* civil service.

**kīwini.** Brazen, bold.

**kō. 1.** Sugar cane *(Saccharum officinarum).* **2.** Dragged; long, as a vowel sound; to drag; pull, tug. **3.** To fulfill, come to pass; fulfilled. **hoʻokō.** Executive; to fulfill; to carry out, as a contract. **4.** Of *(o-*class possessive). *Kō kākou,* our (plural, inclusive). **5.** Your (of one person; singular possessed object; replacing both *kou* and *kāu).*

**koa. 1.** Brave, fearless; bravery. **2.** Soldier; martial. *Kānāwai koa,* martial law. **3.** An endemic forest tree *(Acacia koa),* the largest and most valued of the native trees; its fine wood was used for canoes, surfboards, calabashes.

**koʻa. 1.** Coral, coral head. **2.** Fishing grounds. **3.** Shrine used in certain ceremonies, as to make fish multiply.

**kōʻā.** Arid, barren.

**koaʻe.** The tropicbird or boatswain bird, particularly the white-tailed tropicbird *(Phaethon lepturus dorotheae).*

**koa haole.** A common roadside shrub or small tree *(Leucaena leucocephala). Lit.,* foreign *koa.*

**koa hele wāwae.** Infantry soldier. *Lit.,* soldier goes afoot.

**kōʻai.** To stir with a circular motion of the hand; to creep around, as a vine.

**koaiʻe.** A native tree *(Acacia koaia).*

**koa kahiko.** Veteran, old soldier.

**kō ā kai.** Shore dweller.

**koʻa kea.** White coral.

**koa kiaʻi.** Military sentry, guarding soldier.

**kōʻala.** To broil (of meat, fowl, fish). Cf. *kunu, pūlehu.*

**koali, kowali. 1.** Morning-glory *(Ipomoea* spp.). **2.** Swing; to swing, twirl about. *Lele koali,* to jump rope, ride in a swing.

**koana.** Spacing, space, as between rows of stitching in a quilt.

**koʻana.** Dregs, sediment; to settle, as dregs.

**kō ā uka.** Upland dweller.

**koe. 1.** To remain; remaining, excessive; remainder; except; soon, about to; only thing remaining, not yet. *Koe aku ia,* except for this; this is not known or included; I don't know. **hoʻokoe.** To save, reserve for later use. **2.** To scratch, scrape; to strip pandanus leaves; garden rake.

**ko'e.** Worm.

**koehonua.** A large remainder, a balance.

**ko'eke.** Same as *kaiko'eke,* most used as a term of address.

**ko'ele.** Tapping sound.

**kō'ele.** Small land unit farmed by a tenant for the chief.

**koena.** Remainder, surplus, bal-·ance (in accounts), remains. Cf. *koe, l.*

**kohā.** Crack of a whip, report of a pistol; to resound thus.

**kohana.** Nude, naked; alone, by itself. *Kū kohana,* to stand naked.

**kohe. 1.** Mortise; crease, as in the center of the crown of a hat; corner in a pandanus mat. **ho'o-kohe.** To fold pandanus matting to form a corner. **2.** Vagina.

**kōhi.** To gather, as fruit; to split, as breadfruit.

**koho.** Guess, election, choice, selection; to choose, vote, elect. *Lā koho,* election day.

**kohola.** Reef flats, bare reef. *Kai kohola,* lagoon.

**koholā.** Humpback whale.

**koho mua.** First choice, first guess; hypothesis.

**koho pāloka.** To cast a ballot, vote; voting.

**koho pololei.** Right choice; to vote a straight ticket.

**koho wae moho.** Primary election. *Lit.,* candidate-selection election.

**kohu. 1.** Resemblance, appearance, likeness; suitable, in good taste, attractive, resembling, alike. **ho'okohu.** To assume a likeness to; to presume to. **2.** Sap, stain; stained.

**-kohu. ho'okohu.** To appoint, authorize.

**kohu like.** Similar, alike, uniform. See *kohu.*

**kohu 'ole.** Not matching, ill-suited; poor taste.

**kohu pono.** Decent, upright.

**koi.** To urge, implore, require, claim; requirement.

**ko'i.** Axe, adze.

**kō ia ala.** His, hers.

**ko'ihonua.** Genealogical chant; to sing such chants.

**koikoi.** Redup. of *koi.*

**ko'iko'i.** Weight, responsibility; stress, accent; heavy, weighty, prominent, emphatic; harsh. **ho'oko'iko'i.** To stress or emphasize in speech; to burden, oppress.

**ko'iko'ina.** Stressing, accent.

**koi pohō.** To sue for damages.

**kō kākou.** Our, ours (o-class possessive, plural, inclusive).

**kō kāua.** Our, ours (o-class possessive, dual, inclusive).

**koke.** Quick, near; quickly, soon, immediately. Cf. *kokoke.*

**kōkeano.** Silent, deserted.

**kōkī.** Extremity, tiptop, topmost; upper limit.

**koki'o.** Native hibiscus *(Hibiscus kokio)* with red flowers.

**koki'o kea, koki'o ke'oke'o.** A native hibiscus *(Hibiscus arnottianus)* with white flowers.

**koki'o 'ula'ula.** Native hibiscus *(Hibiscus kokio)* with red flowers.

**koko.** Blood; rainbow-hued. *Ho-'okomo koko,* blood transfusion.

**kōkō.** Carrying net, usually made of sennit, as used for hanging calabashes.

**kokoke.** Near, close; to draw near. Cf. *koke,* fast. **ho'okokoke.** To draw near, approach.

**kokoko.** Bloody.

**kokoleka.** Chocolate. *Eng.*

**kokolo.** Redup. of *kolo,* to creep.

**kokololio.** Wind gust; to blow in gusts.

**kōko'o.** Partnership, partner, companion (nearly always followed by a number designating the number of associated persons, as *kōko'olua, kōko'o-kolu).*

**kōko'okolu.** Partnership of three, one of three associates.

**kōko'olua.** Companion, partner, union (always of two).

**koko pi'i.** High blood pressure. *Lit.,* mounting blood.

**kōkō 'ula.** Network of red color, as of a spreading rainbow.

**kōkua.** Help, assistant, helper; Comforter (Biblical); cooperation; to help, assist, support, second a motion.

**kōkua kauka.** Doctor's aide, intern.

**kōkua kumu.** Assistant teacher, substitute teacher.

**kokuli.** Ear wax.

**kola.** Hard, rigid, sexually excited.

**kō laila.** Those of that place.

**kō lākou.** Their, theirs (*o*-class possessive, plural).

**kolamu.** Column. *Eng.*

**kō lāua.** Their, theirs (*o*-class possessive, dual).

**kole.** 1. Raw, as meat; inflamed; red, as a raw wound or as red earth. *Kole ka ihu,* nose inflamed with cold. 2. Surgeonfish *(Ctenochaetus strigosus).*

**kōlea.** 1. Pacific golden plover *(Pluvialis dominica). Fig.,* to repeat, boast. 2. Stepparent, as *makuahine kōlea, makua kāne kōlea.* 3. *(Cap.)* Korea; Korean. *Eng.*

**kolekole.** Redup. of *kole. Pipi mo'a kolekole,* beef cooked rare.

**kolekolea.** To cry or chirp, said of the *kōlea* bird, and of the *kāhuli* (land shell) in Hawaiian belief.

**koli.** To whittle, pare; to trim, as a lamp or the raveled edges of a dress.

**kolī.** Same as *pā'aila,* castor bean or castor oil plant.

**kolo.** 1. To creep, crawl; to move along, as a gentle breeze or shower; to walk bent over as in respect to a chief or as indicative of humility. **ho'okolo.** To cause to creep, crawl; to follow a trail, track. 2. To pull, tow, drag; to pull a seine. See *moku kolo.*

**koloa.** Hawaiian duck *(Anas wyvilliana).*

**kolohala.** Ring-necked pheasant *(Phasianus colchicus torquatus). Lit.,* creep go on.

**kolohe.** Mischievous, naughty; unethical or unprincipled in any way; rascal, prankster, vandal; to act in this fashion (very common use). **ho'okolohe.** To do mischief, play pranks, etc.; to disturb, annoy; to do amusing things to create laughter.

**koloka.** Cloak, cape. *Eng.*

**kolokolo.** 1. Redup. of *kolo, 1;* to track down, investigate. **ho'o-kolokolo.** To try in court; trial. See *hale ho'okolokolo.* 2. Any creeping vine.

**kololani.** To go away silently.

**kolomoku.** Tugboat; to tow a ship.

**kolona.** 1. Colon. *Eng.* 2. Also **korona.** Crown, rosary. *Eng.* Cf. *lei kolona.*

**kolonahe.** Gentle, pleasant breeze. *Lit.,* gentle creeping.

**kolopā.** Crowbar. *Eng.*

**kolu.** Three.

**kolū.** 1. Glue. *Eng.* 2. Bluing, used in washing clothes. *Eng.* 3. Screw. *Eng.*

**Kolukahi Hemolele.** Holy Trinity.

**koma.** Comma. *Eng.*

**kō mākou.** Our, ours (*o*-class possessive, plural, exclusive).

**kō māua.** Our, ours (*o*-class possessive, dual, exclusive).

**kōmike, komite.** Committee. *Eng.*

**komikina, komisina.** Commissioner; commission. *Eng.*

**komo.** 1. To enter, go into; to join, as a class or organization; entered, filled. **ho'okomo.** To insert, put in, enter, deposit. 2. To dress, put on, wear. **ho'okomo.** To dress another person. 3. Ring, thimble.

**komohana.** West, western, so called because the sun "enters" *(komo)* the sea in the west.

**komohana hema.** Southwest, southwestern.

**komohewa.** To trespass, enter by mistake or illegally; to put on in a wrong way, as clothes wrong side out.

**komo humuhumu.** Thimble. *Lit.,* sewing ring.

**komo lole.** To dress, put on clothes.

**komo wale.** To enter without permission or ceremony; to trespass, intrude.

**komunio.** Communion. *Latin.*

**Kona.** 1. Leeward sides of the Hawaiian Islands. 2. Name of a leeward wind; to blow, of this wind. **kōna.** His, her, hers, its (*o*-class possessive).

**konā.** Hard, unyielding, haughty. Cf. *mākonā.*

**konakona.** Strong, bulging with muscles; rough and uneven, as a surface; hard. Cf. *pūkonakona.*

**kōnane.** 1. Bright moonlight; to shine, as the moon; clear, bright. 2. Ancient game resembling checkers; to play *kōnane.* 3. Tapa-beater design.

**konela.** 1. Colonel. *Eng.* 2. Tunnel (also called *konela puka*). *Eng.*

**koni.** To throb, tingle, beat; to flutter, as the heart; to tug, as a fish on a hook. *'Eha koni,* throbbing ache; *fig.,* pangs of love.

**kono.** 1. To invite, ask in, entice. *Palapala kono,* (written) invitation. **ho'okono.** To invite. 2. See *kono manu.*

**konohiki.** Headman of an *ahupua'a* land division under the chief; land or fishing rights under control of the *konohiki;* such rights are sometimes called *konohiki* rights.

**kono manu.** To entice a bird, as by imitating its call, and then to snare it; a bird catcher.

**-konu.** See *waenakonu,* center.

**konuwaena.** Same as *waenakonu.*

**ko'o.** Brace, support, prop; to uphold. Cf. *kāko'o.* **ho'oko'o.** Prop with a pole.

**ko'o-.** Partner. See *ko'olua.*

**ko'oko'o.** Cane, staff, rod; support, means of livelihood; staff in music. **ho'oko'oko'o.** To push, brace, resist, lean back and brace oneself.

**ko'oko'olau.** All kinds of beggar ticks (*Bidens* spp.); the leaves are used medicinally by Hawaiians, as a tonic in tea; sometimes used in preference to commercial tea.

**ko'oko'ona.** To reach far for; to rest one hand for support *(ko'o-ko'o)* and reach out with the other.

**Ko'olau.** Windward districts, Kaua'i, Maui, Moloka'i; windward range, O'ahu. *Lit.,* windward.

**ko'olua.** Var. of *kōko'olua.*

**kō 'olua.** Your, yours (*o*-class possessive, dual).

**kō 'oukou.** Your, yours (*o*-class possessive, plural).

**kopa, sopa.** Soap; to cover with soap. *Eng.*

**kōpa'a.** Sugar. *Lit.,* hard sugarcane.

**kopalā.** Shovel. *Eng.*

**kope.** 1. Rake, shovel; to rake, scratch. 2. Coffee, coffee beans. *Eng.* 3. Copy; to copy. *Eng.*

**kope ahi.** Fire shovel, rake for ashes.

**kōpī.** To sprinkle, as salt, sand; to salt, as fish or meat.

**kopiana.** Scorpion. *Eng.*

**kou.** 1. A tree *(Cordia subcordata)* widely distributed from East Africa to Polynesia; its soft, beautiful wood was used for cups, dishes, and calabashes. 2. *(Cap.)* Old name for Honolulu harbor and vicinity. 3. Your, yours (*o*-class possessive, singular).

**-kou.** Indicator of plurality in the plural pronouns and possessives only *(kākou, mākou, 'oukou, lākou)*.

**ko'u.** My, mine, of me (o-class possessive).

**kōwā.** Intervening space or time; channel, strait; separated, as by a passage or channel.

**kowali.** Var. spelling of *koali*.

**kōwelo, koelo.** To stream, flutter; to trail behind, as the train of a gown.

**Kristiano.** Var. spelling of *Kalikiano*.

**kū.** **1.** To stand, stop, halt, anchor; to rise, as dust; to hit; to park, as a car; to stay, remain; to reach, extend; upright, standing, parked. **ho'okū.** To set up, make stand, establish, as a society; to brace a canoe with a paddle while sailing or coasting over waves in order to steer and steady the canoe; to carry on, as a family name. **2.** Stand, pedestal. **3.** In a state of; resembling, like; due to, because of (often followed by *i* or *ā*). **ho'okū.** To produce a likeness. **4.** To appear, show, reveal; to change into; beginning, appearance, arrival. **5.** To run in schools, as fish. **6.** Suitable, proper, O.K.; ready, prepared. Cf. *kūpono*. **7.** *(Cap.)* Name for the third, fourth, fifth, and sixth days of the month. **8.** *(Cap.)* Name of a major god.

**kua.** **1.** Back; burden. **2.** Yoke of a dress; back of a garment. **3.** Poles used in quilt making. **4.** Var. of *akua*, god. **5.** To cut, chop, hew. **6.** Tapa-beating anvil.

**kua-.** Generations back, two (or sometimes today, one) more than the suffixed number; see *kuakahi, kualua, kuakolu, kuahā.*

**kū ā.** To turn into. *Kū ā pōhaku,* to turn to stone. See *kū, 4.*

**kua'āina.** Country (as distinct from the city); person from the country, rustic. *Lit.,* back land. **ho'okua'āina.** To act like one from the country; countrified.

**kua'ana.** Term of address for older sibling or cousin of the same sex, or cousin of the same sex of the senior line of a family; also sometimes used to replace the much more common *kaikua'ana* or *kaiku'ana.*

**kuaehu.** Silent, still, lonely.

**kuahā.** Six generations removed. Cf. *kua-.*

**kua hao.** Anvil, as used by blacksmiths.

**kuahaua.** Proclamation, declaration; to proclaim.

**kuahine.** **1.** Term of address for a male's sister or female cousin, sometimes replacing the more common *kaikuahine.* **2.** *(Cap.)* Name of a rain in Mānoa Valley, O'ahu. Often called *ua Tuahine.*

**kuahiwi.** Mountain, high hill.

**kuahu.** Altar.

**kūāhua.** Heap, pile; heaped, piled up; hunchback. *Lit.,* back heap *(āhua).*

**kuai.** To scour, scrape.

**kua'i.** To remove internal organs of animals; to clean, as chickens.

**kū'ai.** To buy, barter. *Lit.,* to stand up food. *Kū'ai mai,* to buy. *Kū'ai aku,* to sell. *Kū'ai hele,* to go shopping.

**kuaka.** Quart. *Eng.*

**kuakahi.** **1.** Once, singly; first; single. **2.** Three generations removed, as great-grandparent *(kupuna kuakahi)* and great-grandchild *(mo'opuna kuakahi).* Sometimes today *kuakahi* denotes two generations removed.

**kuakea.** Faded, bleached; white and encrusted, as salt deposits left by evaporated sea water; to bleach white; foam. **ho'okuakea.** To bleach or whiten.

**kū ākea.** To stand openly or in public; to take a public stand.

**kuakini.** Innumerable.
**kuakolu.** 1. Five generations removed; for some speakers, four generations removed. 2. Thrice, three times.
**kua lā'au.** Hewer of wood, axman.
**kualana.** Lazy, indolent, bored.
**kualapa.** Ridge.
**kualima.** 1. Seven generations removed. Cf. *kua-.* 2. Five times; by fives.
**kualono.** Area near mountain tops.
**kualua.** 1. Four generations removed. 2. Twice, second.
**kuamo'o.** Backbone, spine; road, path. Cf. *iwikuamo'o.*
**kūamuamu.** To revile, blaspheme, curse.
**kua nalu.** Surf just before it breaks; place where the surf breaks.
**kuano'o.** Thoughtful, meditative, comprehending.
**kū'ao'ao.** Attendant or witness at a wedding. *Lit.,* standing [at the] side. *Kū'ao'ao o ke kāne,* best man. *Kū'ao'ao o ka wahine,* bridesmaid, maid of honor.
**kuapā.** 1. Dashing, slashing, as waves on a shore. 2. Wall of a fish pond.
**kuapapa.** 1. Heap, pile; to heap or pile up; heaped up. 2. Peace, quiet, tranquility.
**kuapo.** Belt; to put on a belt.
**kuapo'i.** Weatherboard covering a canoe top fore and aft.
**kuapo'imaka.** Eyelid.
**kuapo 'ōpū.** Belt.
**kuapu'u.** Hunchback; hunchbacked; hump, as of a camel.
**kū'auhau.** Genealogy, pedigree; genealogist; to recite genealogy.
**kua'ula.** Ribbed or grooved tapa cloth, as made with a grooved board.
**kuauli.** Verdant countryside. *Lit.,* green back.
**kū'au lima.** Arm below the elbow.
**kū'au wāwae.** Leg; shinbone.

**kū'au wili.** Crank. *Lit.,* turning handle.
**kuawa.** Guava *(Psidium guajava). Eng.*
**ku'āwa'awa'a.** Hilly, gullied.
**kū'ē.** To oppose, resist; objection; opposite. *Lit.,* stand different. **ho'okū'ē.** To cause opposition; to stir up resistance.
**kuea.** 1. Square. *Eng. Kamaki Kuea,* Thomas Square. 2. To swear. *Eng. 'Olelo kuea,* oath.
**kū'ē'ē.** Redup. of *kū'ē;* disagreement, opposition; to quarrel, disagree. **ho'okū'ē'ē.** To stir up opposition or disagreement.
**kuehu.** To shake, stir up, as dust; to toss up, as spray.
**kueka.** Sweater. *Eng.*
**ku'eku'e.** Elbow, wristbone, joint, knuckle. **ho'oku'eku'e.** To elbow, push with the elbows.
**ku'eku'e lima.** Elbow.
**ku'eku'emaka.** Eyebrow. **ho'o-ku'eku'emaka.** To frown.
**ku'eku'e pipi.** Beef joint or knuckle; soupbone.
**ku'eku'e wāwae.** Ankle joint, heel.
**ku'emaka.** Eyebrow. **ho'oku'e-maka.** To frown.
**kuene.** Waiter, steward; to wait on table; to supervise. *Kuene wahine,* waitress.
**kuewa.** Vagabond, wanderer; wandering, homeless.
**kuha.** Saliva, spittle; to spit.
**kūhalahala.** To find fault with, criticize.
**kūha'o.** Standing alone, independent.
**kū hele.** To get up and go. *Kū hele pēlā!* Get out!
**kūhewa.** Sudden attack, stroke, as of heart failure; sudden wind gust; suddenly attacked by a stroke.
**kuhi.** 1. To point, gesture, as in speaking, directing an orchestra, or dancing the hula; gesture, pointing. 2. To suppose, infer.
**kuhi hewa.** To suppose wrongly;

to err in judgment; to mistake a person for someone else.

**kuhikuhi.** Redup. of *kuhi, 1, 2;* to show, designate, teach, point out.

**kuhikuhipuʻuone.** Seer, soothsayer.

**kuhina.** Minister, premier, regent, ambassador; cabinet member.

**kuhina nui.** Powerful officer in the days of the monarchy.

**kuhina o nā ʻāina ʻē.** Minister of foreign affairs.

**kuhina waiwai.** Minister of finances.

**kui.** 1. To string pierced objects, as flowers in a lei, or fish; to thread, as beads. 2. Needle, pin, spike, nail, screw.

**kuʻi.** 1. To pound, punch; to beat out, as metals; to boom, as thunder. **hoʻokuʻi.** To hit, pound. 2. To join, stitch, sew; joined; seam. **hoʻokuʻi. (a)** To join, connect; to spell; to dovetail; to add up, as numbers. **(b)** Zenith. 3. Artificial. *Lauoho kuʻi,* wig. 4. To disseminate news.

**kuʻia.** Passive/imperative of *kuʻi, 1;* to meet an obstacle, stumble; to waver or be unsettled mentally.

**kui hao.** Nail, iron spike.

**kuʻi hao.** To pound and shape iron; to forge; blacksmith.

**kui humuhumu.** Needle.

**kui iwi.** Bone awl.

**kuʻikahi.** Treaty, covenant, agreement; united. *Kuʻikahi like,* agreement. **hoʻokuʻikahi.** To unite, reconcile, make a peace treaty or armistice.

**Kuʻikahi Pānaʻi Like.** Reciprocity Treaty.

**kui kaiapa.** Safety pin. *Lit.,* diaper pin.

**kui kala.** Screwdriver. Commonly called *kala.*

**kuʻi kālā (dala).** Silversmith; to weld silver.

**kūikawā.** Temporary, for the time

being, special, free and independent. *Lit.,* standing at the time.

**kūʻike.** 1. To know by sight; to understand or know in advance. 2. Cash. *Uku kūʻike,* cash payment.

**kui kele.** Large needle, as for darning or on a sewing machine. *Lit.,* steering instrument.

**kuiki.** Quilting; to quilt. *Eng.*

**kuikui.** Same as *kukui,* candlenut. *Niʻihau.*

**kuʻikuʻi.** 1. Redup. of *kuʻi, 1;* boxing; to box. 2. Redup. of *kuʻi, 2.* 3. Redup. of *kuʻi, 4.*

**kui lāʻau.** Wooden peg.

**kui lauoho.** Hairpin.

**kui lei.** To string flowers, beads, seeds, shells into leis; a lei stringer.

**kui lihilihi.** Crochet hook.

**kui lima, kuikui lima.** To go arm in arm, to hold hands; arm in arm.

**kuʻi lima.** Boxer, pugilist; to strike with the fist.

**kuina.** A stringing together, as of leis.

**kuʻina.** 1. Blow, punch; peal, as of thunder. 2. Joint, joining, seam. *Fig.,* center, key.

**kui nao.** Screw, large nail.

**kuʻinehe.** Quiet and still, without rustling.

**kuʻineki.** Crowded, as a street.

**kuini.** Queen. *Eng.*

**kui ʻōmou.** Stickpin, common pin. *Lit.,* pin to attach.

**kuʻi ʻopihi.** To pry *ʻopihi* (limpets) loose, done formerly with stones.

**kuʻipaʻa.** Lockjaw. *Lit.,* tight molar.

**kui pahu.** Thumbtack. *Lit.,* pushing nail.

**kuipapa.** Method of making a hat lei by sewing leaves and flowers to a pandanus strip; to make such a lei. *Lit.,* string on a base.

**kuʻi pehi.** To pummel, pound, abuse horribly. *Lit.,* pound pelt.

**kui ulana.** Knitting needle.

**kuka.** Coat. *Eng.*

**kūkā.** Same as *kūkākūkā, ʻAha kūkā,* council, conference.

**kūkaʻa.** 1. Roll, bolt of cloth; rolled pack, as of pandanus leaves ready for plaiting; to roll up, as a bundle of cloth or tapa. 2. Wholesale.

**kuka ʻaila.** Raincoat.

**kūkae.** Excreta.

**kūkaehao.** Rust; rusty. *Lit.,* iron excrement.

**kūkaelio.** Toadstool, mushroom. *Lit.,* horse dung.

**kūkaeloli.** Mildew; mildewed. *Lit.,* sea cucumber dung.

**kūkae manu.** Bird dung, guano.

**kūkaenalo.** 1. Mole on the body, believed to be deposits of flies during infancy. *Lit.,* fly dung. 2. Beeswax.

**kūkaepaʻa.** Constipation. *Lit.,* hard excreta.

**kūkaepele.** Sulphur, brimstone, match. *Lit.,* Pele's dung.

**kūkaepuaʻa.** A small weedy, creeping grass *(Digitaria pruriens).*

**kūkaeuli.** Ink squirted by octopus to discolor water.

**kūkaha.** To stand sideways, as in making room for another to pass.

**kūkahekahe.** To while the time away in pleasant conversation; chatting. *Lit.,* stand flowing.

**kū kahi.** Standing alone, outstanding, unique, first.

**kūkaʻi.** To exchange, as greeting *(aloha),* conversation *(kamaʻilio),* letters *(leka).*

**kūkaʻi leka.** To correspond back and forth; to exchange letters.

**kūkaʻi ʻōlelo.** To converse.

**kūkā kamaʻilio.** Interview, conference. *Lit.,* confer chat.

**kūkākūkā.** Consultation, discussion; to consult, confer.

**kūkala.** To proclaim publicly, tell abroad, announce.

**kūkālā, kudala.** Auction; to sell at auction. *Lit.,* stand dollar *(Eng.).*

**kuka ua.** Raincoat.

**kukaweke.** Raincoat. (Perhaps *Eng.,* coat and [souʻ]wester.)

**kuke.** 1. To nudge, push, jostle. **hoʻokuke.** To shoo, banish. 2. Cook; to cook. *Eng.* 3. Customs, duty. *Eng.* 4. Also **duke.** Duke. *Eng.*

**kuke awa.** Harbor duty or tax.

**kuke kū.** To push with elbows and shoulders, as forcing a way through a crowd.

**kūkele.** 1. Muddy, slippery; to slip, slide, as in mud. 2. To sail, as a boat.

**kuki.** See *mea ʻono kuki,* cookie.

**kūkini.** 1. Runner, swift messenger, as employed by chiefs, with a premium on their speed. 2. Close together, in great numbers, as plants. 3. Cushion. *Eng.*

**kūkiʻo.** Small pool of water. *Lit.,* standing pool.

**kuko.** Lust. *Kuko hewa, kuko ʻino,* lecherous, lewd, randy.

**kuku.** 1. To beat, as tapa. 2. Stick, as used to support a net.

**kukū.** 1. Thorn, spine, burr; barbed, thorny; hurt by a thorn. 2. Redup. of *kū, 1;* crowded.

**kūkū.** 1. (Usually pronounced *tūtū.*) Granny, grandma, grandpa; any relative or close friend of grandparent's generation. 2. To shake in jerks, bounce, trot, as on a horse. *Holo kūkū,* to trot. **hoʻokūkū.** To cause to shake; uncomfortably full, as after overeating. 3. Gourd beat, as used for hula dancing.

**-kūkū. hoʻokūkū.** 1. Contest, game, match; to hold a contest. *Hoʻokūkū hīmeni,* song contest. 2. To fit, as a garment; a fitting.

**kukuʻe.** Clubfoot; one with a twisted or deformed foot.

**kukui.** 1. Candlenut tree *(Aleurites moluccana),* the state tree. 2. Lamp, light, torch. *Fig.,* guide, leader.

**kukui haole.** General name for any nut not native to Hawai'i.

**kukui hele pō.** Lantern. *Lit.*, light [for] going [at] night.

**kuku'i 'ōlelo.** Storyteller; to recite, narrate. *Lit.*, joining speech.

**kukui pa'a lima.** Flashlight. *Lit.*, light hold hand.

**kukui uila.** Electric light.

**Kukui Wana'ao.** Morning Star. *Lit.*, early morning light.

**kukuli.** Redup. of *kuli, 1;* to kneel; to crouch or lie as an animal, with feet under the body. *Noho kukuli*, to sit on bended knees, with the feet stretched backwards, and with the front of the toes down.

**kukulu.** Same as *kulu, 1*.

**kūkulu. 1.** Pillar, post; horizon. *Nā kūkulu 'ehā*, four cardinal points. **2.** To build, as a house; to establish, set up; to put up, as a tent; to found, as a society; to establish, as a name or dynasty. **3.** To tie, tether; to park.

**kukuluae'o. 1.** Stilts; to walk on stilts. **2.** Hawaiian stilt (the bird; *Himantopus himantopus*).

**kukuna.** Ray, as of the sun; radius of a circle; spoke of a wheel. *Kukuna X*, x-ray.

**kukuna-o-ka-lā.** Mangrove *(Bruguiera gymnorhiza);* calyx of a mangrove flower, as used in leis. *Lit.*, ray of the sun.

**kula. 1.** Plain, field, open country, pasture. **2.** *(Cap.)* Land areas and forest reserve, upper East Maui. **3.** Source; container. **4.** School; to teach school, go to school; to hold school or class sessions. *Eng.* **5.** Also **gula.** Gold; golden. *Eng.*

**kula aupuni.** Public school, government school.

**kula hānai.** Boarding school. *Lit.*, feeding school. Also called *kula noho pa'a*.

**kula'i.** To push over, knock down, overthrow.

**kulāiwi.** Native land; native. *Ku'u home kulāiwi*, my own homeland.

**kula kahuna pule.** Theological seminary. *Lit.*, minister school.

**kula kakalina.** Gasoline drum.

**kula kamali'i.** Primary school, kindergarten. *Lit.*, children's school.

**kula Kāpaki (Sabati).** Sunday school.

**kula ki'eki'e.** High school.

**kula koa.** Military academy.

**kula kumu.** Teachers' training school, normal school.

**kula manu.** Gathering place of birds.

**kulana.** To tilt, rock, reel, sway.

**kūlana.** Station, rank, position, place, situation; outstanding, prominent.

**kūlanakauhale.** Village, town, city. *Lit.*, place plural households.

**kūlana nalu.** Place where the waves swell up and the surfrider starts paddling and racing the wave, usually at the most distant line of breakers. Also called *kūlana he'enalu*.

**kūlana pa'a.** Standard, as weight or money.

**kūlana pule.** Prayer meeting or other religious service.

**kulanui.** University, college; formerly high school. *Lit.*, big school.

**kulapepeiao. 1.** Earring. *Lit.*, gold [for] ears. **2.** Fuchsia *(Fuchsia magellanica)*.

**kula pō.** Night school.

**kula uku.** Private school. *Lit.*, paying school.

**kula wai.** Watering trough, water source.

**kula waiwai.** Source of income or livelihood.

**kuleana.** Right, title, property, responsibility, jurisdiction, authority, claim, ownership; reason, cause, justification; small piece of property; tenure.

**hoʻokuleana.** To entitle, give right to possess. See *palapala hoʻokuleana.*

**kūlepe. 1.** Split open from head to tail, as fish prepared for drying and salting; to split thus. **2.** To flap, flutter; strong, of wind. **3.** Same as *ʻūlepe.*

**kūlewa.** Moving slowly through space, as clouds.

**kuli. 1.** Knee. **2.** Deafness, deaf person; deaf; noisy. **hoʻokuli.** Deaf; to feign deafness.

**kūlia. 1.** Passive/imperative of *kū, 1;* to stand. **2.** To try, strive.

**kūlike.** Alike, identical; standing in similar fashion or in even rows. **hoʻokūlike.** To conform, make alike.

**kulikuli.** Noise, din; noisy, deafening. Be quiet! Keep still! Shut up!

**kūlina, kurina.** Corn, maize *(Zea mays). Eng.*

**kūlina ʻono.** Sweet corn. *Lit.,* delicious corn.

**kūlina pohāpohā.** Popcorn.

**kulipeʻe.** To creep along, as a sick person; to walk as though weak-kneed.

**kūlipo.** Dark, deep, as a cave. *Fig.,* extremely, intense.

**kūliʻu.** Deep, as a voice; penetrating, profound, as thoughts.

**kūloko.** Local, domestic. *Lit.,* state of being inside. *Kaua kūloko,* civil war.

**kūloku.** Falling, flowing, as rain or stream; flattened, as plants by rain.

**kūlolo.** Pudding made of baked or steamed grated taro and coconut cream.

**kūlono.** Sheer, precipitous.

**kūlou.** To bow the head, bend. Also *kūnou.* **hoʻokūlou.** To bow down, humiliate; to subdue, as an enemy.

**kūlou poʻo.** To bow the head; to dive headfirst.

**kulu. 1.** To drip, leak, trickle; to flow, as tears; a drop; general

name for distilled liquor. **2.** Timber used in houses, as sticks, posts.

**kulu aumoe.** Latenight, midnight.

**kulukulu.** Redup. of *kulu, 1;* to drip, leak, drop.

**kuluma.** Accustomed to; acquainted with; customary.

**kūmā-.** Prefix to numbers, as *ʻumi kūmākahi, ʻumi kūmālua,* etc.

**kūmaka.** Seen by the eye, visible; to see for oneself.

**kūmakahiki.** Annual, yearly.

**kūmakani.** Windbreak; wind resisting.

**kūmākena.** To lament, bewail, mourn loudly for the dead.

**kumamā-.** Same as *kūmā-* (rarely used in conversation, Biblical).

**kūmau.** Customary, usual, regular. *Uku kūmau,* usual fees, taxes, dues.

**kūmimi.** Small inedible crabs, as *Lophozozymus intonsus.*

**kūmoe.** Bedstead. *Lit.,* standing bed.

**kūmoena. 1.** Longitudinal mat commencement. **2.** Pile of mats; spread out as a mat.

**kumu. 1.** Bottom, base, foundation, basis, main stalk of a tree; basic, hereditary. **2.** Teacher, manual, primer. **3.** Beginning, source, origin. **hoʻokumu.** To make a beginning, establish, start. **4.** Reason, cause. **5.** An article bought, sold, or exchanged; price. Cf. *kumu kūʻai.*

**kūmū. 1.** Goatfish *(Parupeneus porphyreus).* **2.** Good-looking, handsome, especially of a sweetheart. *Modern slang.*

**kumu aʻo.** Teaching; teacher.

**kumuhana.** Topic, subject (as topic of discourse or as grammatical subject). *Lit.,* work source.

**kumu hele.** Crotch. *Lit.,* source of going.

**kumu hipa.** Flock of sheep.

**kumu honua.** Beginning of the world, origin of the earth.

**kumu hoʻolaha.** Means of propagation, source of progeny.

**kumuipukukui.** Lamp, not including the chimney; candlestick. *Lit.,* base light bowl.

**kumu kahi.** Origin, beginning.

**kumukānāwai.** Constitution, law code. *Lit.,* source of laws.

**kumu kūʻai.** Price. *Kumu kūʻai nui,* high-priced, expensive.

**kumu kula.** Schoolteacher.

**kumulāʻau.** Tree.

**kumulani.** Base of the sky; horizon.

**kumulipo.** Origin, source of life; name of the Hawaiian creation chant.

**kumumanaʻo.** Topic, subject; text, as of a sermon.

**kumu niu.** Trunk of the coconut tree.

**kumupaʻa.** 1. Principal, capital (contrasting with interest). 2. Firm foundation, ancient times; firmly established.

**kumu ʻūhā.** Groin, joining of leg and torso. *Lit.,* source of thigh.

**kumu wai.** Source of a stream, spring.

**kumu waiwai.** Source of wealth; resources; capital.

**kuna.** 1. A freshwater eel. 2. Schooner. *Eng.*

**kūnaʻe.** To stand firmly against opposition; unyielding.

**kūnāhihi.** Weak, as from shock; dismayed, horrified.

**kūnānā.** 1. Puzzled, stumped, at wit's end. *Lit.,* stand look. 2. Goat.

**kunāne.** Brother or male cousin of a female, usually used only as term of address or as an affectionate variation of *kaikunāne.*

**kūneki.** Filled to overflowing; to flow away.

**kuni.** 1. To burn, blaze, kindle, scorch, brand; to etch, in leather. *Hao kuni,* branding iron. 2. Postmark, seal; to

stamp. 3. Type of black magic that results in the death of a sorcerer.

**kuni ahi.** Fire kindler; to kindle or light a fire.

**kūnihi.** Steep.

**kūnou.** Var. of *kūlou.*

**kunu.** 1. To broil on coals, as of meat, fish. 2. To cough.

**kunukunu.** 1. To grumble, complain. 2. Redup. of *kunu, 1, 2.*

**kūʻokoʻa.** Independence, liberty, freedom; independent. **hoʻokūʻokoʻa.** To establish independence.

**kuolo.** 1. To rub, scrub, polish. 2. To tremble, as the voice; to shake, as with palsy; to vibrate, resonate, as a chanting voice. *Kai kuolo,* sea with an undertow.

**kūʻolo.** Sagging, baggy, as of clothes; old, as of a person with sagging cheeks.

**kūʻono.** 1. Nook, cranny, gulf, bay; inside corner. **hoʻokūʻono.** To indent, form a bay. 2. Deep, as a cave; profound.

**kūʻonoʻono.** 1. Well-off, comfortably situated, wealthy. **hoʻokūʻonoʻono.** To prosper. 2. Redup. of *kūʻono, 2.*

**kupa.** Citizen, native; well-acquainted. **hoʻokupa.** To naturalize, make a citizen.

**kūpaʻa.** Steadfast, firm, immovable; loyal, faithful; constant; loyalty, firmness. **hoʻokūpaʻa.** To remain loyal; to strengthen, establish.

**kupaianaha.** Surprising, strange, wonderful, extraordinary, marvelous. Also *kupanaha.*

**kūpale.** Defense; to defend, ward off.

**kupanaha.** Same as *kupaianaha.*

**kūpaoa.** 1. Strong permeating fragrance, as of jasmine. **hoʻokūpaoa.** To emit fragrance; fragrant. 2. Night cestrum *(Cestrum nocturnum)* and the endemic Hawaiian *Railliardia* spp., both having very fragrant flowers.

**kūpāpā. 1.** To grope, feel, as when looking for flaws in a wooden bowl. **2.** Hand-to-hand fight, struggle; to fight.

**kūpapakū.** Bedrock; to stand on bedrock; depths of the earth.

**kupapaʻu.** Corpse, dead body.

**kūpau.** Entirely finished.

**kūpeʻe.** Bracelet, anklet; fetters, manacles, handcuffs; to put on or tie on bracelets, anklets, fetters.

**kūpeʻe niho ʻīlio.** Dog-tooth anklets.

**kūpeʻe pipi.** To bind feet of cattle, especially with the lasso.

**kūpehi.** To pelt, throw at. Cf. *pehi,* to throw.

**kūpele.** To knead, as bread dough or very hard fresh *poi.*

**kūpihipihi.** Tiny, small, insignificant; to become insignificant.

**kūpikiʻō.** Agitated, raging, as wind or storm. *Fig.,* mentally disturbed.

**kūpola.** To roll, wrap up, as a package; to wither and curl up, as a banana leaf.

**kūpono.** Upright, perpendicular, honest, proper, right, just, fair; worth, merit. **hoʻokūpono.** To behave uprightly, honestly; to conform to.

**kūpono ʻole.** Unsuitable, improper.

**kūpou.** To go down, walk downhill fast, stagger; to bend far forward, as one reeling drunk.

**kūpouli.** Befuddled, mentally clouded, stricken.

**kūpoupou.** Redup. of *kūpou.*

**kupu.** Sprout, growth; offspring; upstart, as one rising suddenly and conspicuously to high position; to sprout, increase. **hoʻokupu.** To cause growth, sprouting; to sprout.

**-kupu. hoʻokupu.** Tribute, tax, ceremonial gift-giving to a chief as a sign of honor and respect;

to pay such tribute; church offering.

**kupua.** Demigod, especially a supernatural being possessing several forms.

**kupuʻeu. 1.** Rascal, scamp. **2.** Hero, wondrous one.

**kūpuku.** Clustered, thick, rank.

**kupukupu. 1.** Redup. of *kupu.* **2.** General name for ferns on a single stem, such as *3.* **3.** Sword fern *(Nephrolepis exaltata).*

**kupukupu ʻala.** Rose geranium *(Pelargonium graveolens).* Also called *kupukupu haole.*

**kupulau.** Spring season. *Lit.,* leaf sprouting.

**kūpule.** Days set aside for prayer; to set aside time for prayer.

**kupuna.** Grandparent, ancestor, relative or close friend of the grandparent's generation, grandaunt, granduncle. **hoʻokupuna.** To take an unrelated person as a grandparent or grandaunt or granduncle because of affection; to act as a grandparent.

**kūpuna.** Plural of *kupuna.*

**kupuna kāne.** Grandfather, granduncle, male ancestor.

**kupuna wahine.** Grandmother, grandaunt, female ancestor.

**kūpuni.** To stand around, surround.

**kupupuʻu.** Redup. of *kūpuʻu.*

**kūpuʻu.** To eat taro not pounded to *poi;* to take potluck.

**kuʻu. 1.** To release; to free, give up; to pay out, as a line or cable; to lower, as a net; to settle, as earth. *Fig.,* at peace. **hoʻokuʻu.** To release, let go, send away; to expel, as from school; to discharge, as from work; to free, liberate. **2..** My, mine (this form may replace either *kaʻu* or *koʻu*).

**kū uaki.** To stand a watch; watchman, sentinel, guard.

**kūʻula.** Any stone god used to attract fish; open altar near the sea for worship of fish gods. *Lit.,* red *Kū.*

kū'ululū. To shiver and be numb with cold.

ku'upau. To do with all one's might or strength, to go the limit; to release all checks, restraints.

ku'uwelu. To hang loose; to float in the wind; to fall, as ripened fruit; fringed; tassel.

kūwaho. Outside, outer, foreign.

kuwala, kuala. 1. Somersault; to fall backwards; to turn somersaults. 2. Interest, usury.

kūwili. To move restlessly, embrace; to spin in a dance. *Lit.*, interwoven state.

kūwiliwili. Redup. of *kūwili*.

kūwō, kūō. To cry loudly, as with joy or pain; to howl, as a dog; to roar, as a lion.

# L

lā. 1. Sun, sun heat; sunny. ho'olā. To sun, put out in the sunlight. 2. Day. *Kēia lā*, today. 3. Fin. *Kua lā*, dorsal fin. 4. Sail. 5. Clitic demonstrative following directionals, nouns, verbs: there, that, then. 6. Particle expressing doubt. *Pehea lā!* How, I don't know! 7. The letter *l*.

lā-. 1. Short for *lau, 1*, with *k-* of the following word omitted: *lā'alo* for *lau kalo*, taro leaf. 2. Third person, in the dual and plural pronouns only, *lāua* and *lākou*.

la'a. 1. Sacred, holy, consecrated, dedicated. ho'ola'a. To consecrate, dedicate, hallow. 2. Time, season. Cf. *la'a make*. 3. Also, together with, besides. *E la'a me kēia*, besides this, like this.

lā 'aha'aina. Feast day.

la'a kea. Sacred light, sacred things of day, as sunshine, knowledge, happiness. *Lit.*, light sacredness.

la'alā'au. Small sticks, twigs, shrubs, bush. *Pā la'alā'au*, hedge.

la'a make. Season when plants die or grow slowly. *Lit.*, dead season.

lā'au. 1. Tree, plant, wood, timber, forest, stick, club; blow of a club; wooden, woody. 2. Medicine; medical.

la'a ua. Rainy season.

lā'au 'aila. Castor-oil plant. *Lit.*, oil plant.

lā'au 'ala. Fragrant wood, especially sandalwood.

lā'au ana. Yardstick, ruler, surveying rod, measuring stick.

lā'au ho'ohiamoe. Drug, narcotic, anesthetic, medicine to cause sleep, chloroform.

lāu'au ho'oka'a. Rolling pin, any wooden roller.

lā'au kāhea. A type of faith healing of broken or crushed bones or sprains. *Lit.*, calling medicine.

lā'au Kalikimaka. Christmas tree.

lā'au ke'a. Wooden cross or crucifix; bar to hold a gate shut, brace.

lā'au kia. Stick for snaring birds.

lā'au ku'i. Ladder, tree with crosspieces used as a ladder. *Lit.*, joined wood.

la'a 'ula. Autumn. *Lit.*, red time [of leaves].

lā'au lalo. Boom of a vessel. *Lit.*, down stick.

lā'au lapa'au. Medicine. *Lit.*, curing medicine.

la'a ulu. Spring, time of growth.

lā'au māka'i. Policeman's club.

lā'au make. Poison.

lā'au 'ōhikihiki niho. Toothpick. *Lit.*, stick to pick teeth.

lā'au pa'i kinipōpō. Ball bat, tennis racket, ping-pong paddle; any kind of paddle for hitting a ball. *Lit.*, stick for beating ball.

**lā'au pālau.** Fighting club.

**-la'a wa'a. ho'ola'a wa'a.** Blessing of a canoe launching; to dedicate a canoe.

**lae. 1.** Cape, point, promontory. **2.** Forehead, brow. **3.** Wisdom; mental or emotional qualities. Cf. *lae o'o, lae pa'a, lae 'ula.*

**la'e.** Same as *la'ela'e.* **ho'ola'e.** To clear up, brighten.

**la'ela'e.** Bright, shiny, clear, serene, calm, pleasant. **ho'ola'ela'e.** Redup. of *ho'ola'e.*

**lae la lae.** Syllables repeated in songs at ends of verses to mark time and for gay effect.

**laenihi.** Various high-headed labroid fishes of the genera *Hemipteronotus* and *Iniistius.*

**lae o'o.** An expert. *Lit.,* mature brow. Cf. *lae 'ula.*

**lae pa'a.** Hard-headed, obstinate, closed in mind and hostile to new ideas. *Lit.,* hard brow.

**lae 'ula.** A well-trained, clever person; expert. *Lit.,* red brow [red being the sacred color]. Cf. *lae o'o.*

**laha.** Extended, spread out, broad, published, circulated, distributed, broadcast; increased, numerous. **ho'olaha.** To spread abroad, publish, broadcast, advertise.

**lahalaha.** Redup. of *laha.*

**lā hana.** Workday.

**lā hānau.** Birthday. *Hau'oli lā hānau,* happy birthday.

**laha 'ole.** Rare, choice, unique.

**lahi.** Thin, frail, delicate.

**lā hiki.** Eastern sun, rising sun; eastern. *Mai ka lā hiki a ka lā kau,* from sunrise to sunset [a whole day or whole life span].

**lahilahi.** Redup. of *lahi. Kou pāpālina lahilahi* (song), your dainty cheeks.

**laho. 1.** Scrotum. **2.** Male, as *pipi laho,* bull.

**Lā Ho'ālohaloha.** Thanksgiving Day. *Lit.,* day for expression of affection.

**lā ho'āno.** Holy day, day of worship.

**laholio.** Rubber, automobile tire. *Lit.,* horse scrotum.

**Lā Ho'omaika'i.** Thanksgiving Day. *Lit.,* day to bless.

**lā ho'omana'o.** Day of commemoration, anniversary day.

**lāhui.** Nation, race, tribe, people, nationality; species, as of animal or fish; national, racial. **ho'olāhui.** To form a nation, race, etc.

**lāhui hui pū.** United nation. *Nā Lāhui Huipū,* United Nations.

**lāhui kanaka.** Nation, people, tribe, multitude.

**lai.** A fish of the genus *Scomberoides.*

**la'i.** Calm, stillness, quiet, as of sea, sky, wind; peace, contentment; quiet, silent, peaceful. *Pō la'i, 'ihi'ihi ē,* silent night, holy. **ho'ola'i.** To cause to be still; to quiet, as a mob; calm, peaceful, quiet.

**-la'i.** A transitivizer occurring in *kaula'i, kula'i.*

**lā'ī.** Ti leaf (contraction of *lau kī*).

**lā'ie.** Short for *lau 'ie, 'ie* vine leaf.

**laiki, raisi.** Rice. *Eng.*

**laikī.** Litchi. *Eng.*

**lā'iki.** Tight, as a dress; painfully stuffed, as the stomach after overeating; narrow, as a gate opening (contraction of *lā'ā,* wide, and *iki,* small). *Lima lā'iki,* long, narrow sleeve.

**laikini.** License. *Eng.*

**laikini ka'a.** Auto or vehicle license.

**laikini kī pū.** Firearms license.

**laila.** There, then. (Follows particles with varying meanings: *Ā laila,* then. *I laila,* there, at that place. *Kō laila,* of that place, local. *Malaila,* there. *Mai laila,* from there, thence. *No laila,* therefore, for that reason, hence; belonging to that place. *O laila,* of that place.)

**laina. 1.** Line. *Eng.* **2.** Cane trash (*Eng.,* rind), bagasse.

**laina mokuahi.** Steamship line.
**laipela, raifela.** Rifle. *Eng.*
**laipila.** Libel; to libel. *Eng.*
**laka. 1.** Tame, domesticated, gentle; attracted to, fond of; to tame, domesticate. **hoʻolaka.** To tame; to treat with kindness. **2.** *(Cap.)* Goddess of the hula. **3.** *(Cap.)* A god of canoe makers. **4.** *(Cap.)* Name of a legendary hero. **5.** Lock; to lock. *Eng.*
**lākana. 1.** Lantana *(Lantana camara)*. *Eng.* **2.** *(Cap.)* Also **Ladana.** London. *Eng.*
**Lā Kāpaki.** Sabbath Day.
**lā kau.** Setting sun. See *lā hiki.*
**Lā Kau Pua.** Decoration Day. *Lit.,* day [to] place flowers.
**laki.** Luck; lucky. *Eng.* **hoʻolaki.** To bring luck; lucky.
**lākī.** Ti leaf (short for *lau kī*).
**lākike, latike.** Lattice. *Eng.*
**lakikū, latitu.** Latitude. *Eng.*
**Lākina, Latina.** Latin. *Eng.*
**lako.** Supply, provisions; wealth; well-supplied, well-furnished, well-equipped; rich, prosperous. **hoʻolako.** To supply, provide, furnish, enrich.
**lākō.** Sugarcane leaf (same as *lāʻō,* contraction of *lau kō*).
**lako hale.** Furniture and fixtures for a house. Same as *pono hale.*
**lako kākau.** Stationery supplies.
**lako keʻena.** Office supplies.
**lako kula. 1.** School supplies. **2.** Also **lako gula.** Jewelry, especially gold.
**lākou.** They, them (more than two). *Kā lākou,* their *(a-class). Kō lākou,* their *(o-class).*
**lala. 1.** Diagonal, slanting, oblique; diagonal surfing or surf. **hoʻolala.** To turn aside. **2.** To warm, as over a fire; to bask in the sun; to cook over a fire. **hoʻolala.** To heat, as by holding over a fire; to warm.
**lālā. 1.** Branch, limb, bough; timber as of outrigger boom or float; to branch out, form branches. **hoʻolālā.** To cause to

branch out, as by topping a tree; to branch out. **2.** Member, as of a society. **3.** Slip, as of a plant.
**lālā kanu.** A cutting (to plant).
**lalana. 1.** Spider. Also called *lanalana, nananana.* **2.** Warming, as at a fire. Cf. *lala,* warm.
**lālani.** Row, rank, line; verse of poetry.
**lalau.** Mistake, blunder, going astray; to wander, err. **hoʻolalau.** To cause to wander, to lead astray; to dillydally, kill time.
**lālau.** To seize, take hold of, reach out for.
**lalau hewa.** To wander in error; to sin.
**lale.** To hasten, hurry, push on; to encourage, urge on. **hoʻolale.** To hasten, hurry; to urge.
**lali.** Greasy, as pork fat; slippery and shiny, glittering; sticky. **hoʻolali.** To cause greasiness, glitter.
**lalo. 1.** Down, downward, under, beneath; depths (frequently preceded by *i* or *ma,* sometimes joined as one word). *I lalo, malalo,* below, underneath. **2.** Leeward, southern.
**lama. 1.** Native Hawaiian trees of the genus *Diospyros* (ebony family). **2.** Torch, light, lamp. *Lama* wood was used in medicine, and a piece of it was placed on altars of the goddess Laka because its name suggested enlightenment. **3.** Also **rama.** Rum; any intoxicating drink. *Eng.*
**lamalama.** Torch fishing; to go torch fishing.
**lama paʻipaʻi ʻia.** Mixed alcoholic drink, cocktail, highball.
**lana. 1.** Floating, buoyant; to lie at anchor, as a fishing canoe; calm, still, as water. **hoʻolana.** To cause to float; to right a canoe. **2.** Also **rana.** Frog.
**-lana. hoʻolana.** Cheerful, hopeful; to cheer up.
**-lana.** Nominalizing suffix corresponding to *ʻana.*

**lana hele.** To drift, as a ship.

**lānahu.** Charcoal, coal. See *nānahu.*

**lānai.** Porch, veranda; temporary open-sided roofed structure near a house.

**Lānaʻi.** Lānaʻi Island.

**lanakila.** Victory; to triumph, win.

**lanalana. 1.** Redup. of *lana, 1.* **hoʻolanalana.** Redup. of *hoʻolana.* **2.** Lashings, as of ornamental sennit binding the float *(ama)* to outrigger booms *(ʻiako).* **3.** Spider. Also, *lalana, nananana.*

**lani. 1.** Sky, heaven; heavenly, spiritual. **2.** Very high chief, majesty, high born, aristocratic.

**lani paʻa.** Firmament. *Lit.,* solid heaven.

**lanipō.** Dense, dark, as of plants, rain; said of luxuriant growth.

**lānui.** Holiday, important or big day.

**Lānui o nā Limahana.** Labor Day. *Lit.,* holiday of the laborers.

**lāʻō. 1.** Same as *lau kō,* sugarcane leaf. **2.** Ornated wrasse *(Halichores ornatissimus).*

**lapa. 1.** Ridge, steep side of a ravine; ridged. **hoʻolapa.** To form a ridge; ridge. **2.** Overactive, energetic, mischievous. **hoʻolapa.** To rise up; to boil; to swell, as a blister; to excite, animate. **3.** Clot, as of blood.

**lapaʻau.** Medical practice; to treat with medicine, heal, cure; medical, medicinal. *Kauka lapaʻau,* medical doctor.

**lāpaki.** Rabbit. *Eng.*

**lapalapa. 1.** Redup. of *lapa, 1;* steep-ridged; many-ridged. **2.** Redup. of *lapa, 2;* to bubble, boil; to cavort. **3.** Clotted.

**lapa uila.** Lightning flash; to flash, as lightning.

**lapawāwae.** Shin. *Lit.,* leg ridge.

**lapu.** Ghost, apparition; haunted; to haunt. **hoʻolapu.** To pretend

to be a ghost, as children on Halloweʻen.

**Lāpule.** Sunday. *Lit.,* prayer day.

**lapuwale.** Vanity, worthlessness; of no value.

**lau. 1.** Leaf; to leaf out. *Lau* is sometimes contracted to *lā-,* as *lā ʻī, lā ʻie.* **hoʻolau.** To grow leaves. **2.** Dragnet, seine. **hoʻolau.** To use a *lau.* **3.** To be much, many; very many, numerous; four hundred. **hoʻolau.** To make numerous; to assemble, as of numerous persons or animals. **4.** Tip, as of the tongue.

**lāua.** They, them (dual).

**lauaʻe. 1.** A fragrant fern *(Phymatosorus scolopendria,* syn. *Microsorium scolopendria).* **2.** Beloved, sweet, of a lover. **hoʻolauaʻe.** To cherish, as a beloved memory.

**lauahi.** To destroy, as by fire or lava flow.

**lau ʻai.** Salad. *Lit.,* edible leaves.

**lau alelo.** Tongue tip.

**lau hala.** Pandanus leaf, especially as used in plaiting.

**lauhulu.** Dry banana leaf.

**lauʻī.** Ti leaf. Also *lā ʻī, lau kī.*

**lauʻīpala.** A tang fish *(Zebrasoma flavescens).*

**laukahi.** Broad-leafed plantain *(Plantago major),* a cosmopolitan weed. *Lit.,* single leaf.

**laukanaka.** Densely populated, having many people; many people. **hoʻolaukanaka.** To have many people about one; to dispel loneliness with people.

**lau kī. 1.** Ti leaf. **2.** Tea leaf.

**laukō.** Dragnet.

**laulā.** Broad, wide; liberal; widely known; publicly. *Hele laulā,* to act with freedom or liberty.

**laulau.** Wrapping, wrapped package; individual servings of pork or beef, salted fish, and taro tops, wrapped in ti leaves or banana leaves, and baked in the ground oven, steamed, or broiled; any cloth, net, or leaves used as a wrapper or carrier; to wrap or carry in such bundles.

**laule'a.** Peace, happiness, friendship; happy, peaceful. **ho'olaule'a.** Celebration, gathering for a celebration, large party; satisfaction; to hold a celebration; to preserve friendship and good will.

**lau li'i.** Small-leafed; qualifying term for some plants, as *maile*.

**laulima.** Cooperation; group of people working together; community food patch; to work together. **ho'olaulima.** To cause to cooperate.

**lauloa.** Long wave or surf, as extending the entire length of the beach.

**lau loa. 1.** A long leaf. **2.** Length; lengthwise.

**lau mau'u.** Blade of grass.

**laumeki. 1.** A kind of barbed spear. **2.** To recede, ebb, as the tide or flood waters. **3.** To wilt, as plants without water.

**launa.** Friendly, sociable; to associate with, meet with. Used idiomatically with *'a'ohe, 'a'ole, 'ole: 'A'ohe launa ka maka'u,* terrible fear; there's no limit to the fear; *lit.,* no meeting the fear. **ho'olauna.** To introduce one person to another; to be friendly.

**lau nahele.** Plants, forest growth, or leaves.

**lau niu.** Coconut leaf, frond.

**lau'ō. 1.** Sugarcane leaf (same as *lau kō*). **2.** Young white coconut leaves near the heart.

**lauoho.** Hair of the head. *Lit.,* head leaf.

**lauoho o Pele.** Pele's hair: fine, glassy filaments of lava.

**lau pala.** Fading leaf turning yellow, red, or brown. *Fig.,* person failing in health.

**laupapa. 1.** A broad flat area, as of coral, lava, reef. **2.** Board, lumber. *Pā laupapa,* wooden fence.

**lawa. 1.** Enough, sufficient, ample; to have enough. **ho'olawa.** To supply, apportion sufficiently. **2.** Possessed of enough or ample knowledge, hence wise, capable. **3.** As soon as. *I lawa nō ā pau ka hana, ho'i kāua,* as soon as the work is finished, we'll leave. **4.** To tie.

**lawai'a.** Fisherman; fishing technique; to fish, to catch fish.

**-lawalawa. ho'olawalawa.** Redup. of *ho'olawa,* to supply.

**lāwalu.** Fish or meat bound in ti leaves and broiled on coals; to cook thus.

**lawa puni.** Enough for all, well-supplied.

**lawe.** To take, accept, carry, bring; portable; bearer. **ho'olawe.** To cause to take, deduct, subtract.

**lawehala.** Sin, sinner, delinquency; evil, sinful; to sin. *Keiki lawehala,* delinquent child. **ho'olawehala.** Accusation; to accuse; to grow worse, of a sickness.

**lawehana.** Workman, laborer; industrious; to do labor. *Hoa lawehana,* fellow worker.

**lawe hānai.** To adopt, as a child.

**lawe kāhili.** Bearer of the feather standard of royalty *(kāhili).*

**lawelawe. 1.** To serve, work for, minister to, attend to, do; to treat, as the sick; to wait, as on tables; to handle. **2.** To pilfer, make off with. *Lima lawelawe,* pilfering hand.

**lawelawe hana.** Function, administration.

**lawelawe lima.** To pitch in and lend a hand; to assault, beat, tackle.

**lawe leka.** Mail carrier, postman; to carry mail or letters.

**lawe lima.** To carry by hand. *Puke lawe lima,* handbook.

**lawe 'ōhua.** Passenger carrier; to carry passengers.

**lawe 'ōlelo.** Talebearer; gossip; to gossip, bear tales.

**lawe wale.** Extortion, seizure of property with the owner's knowledge; to take without right.

**le'a. 1.** Joy, pleasure, happiness; pleasing, delightful, merry; delighted, pleased. *Hā'awi manawale'a,* to give gladly; *lit.,* to give [with] happy heart. **ho'ole'a.** To cause pleasure, joy; to praise, please, delight. **2.** Clearly, perfectly, thoroughly, successfully.

**le'ale'a. 1.** Redup. of *le'a, 1.* **ho'ole'ale'a.** Redup. of *ho'o-le'a;* to amuse oneself, have fun.

**lehe.** Lip. See *lehe luhe, lehe 'oi.*

**lehelehe.** Lips; labia of vagina.

**lehelehe nui.** Thick lips. **ho'olehelehe nui.** Sullen, sulky, pouting.

**lehe luhe.** Pouting lip.

**lehe 'oi.** Sharp-lipped; sharp-tongued, of one who makes cutting remarks.

**leho. 1.** General name for cowrie shell, as *Cypraea tigris.* **2.** Callus, as on shoulders from carrying heavy loads. **3.** Covetous. Cf. *maka leho.*

**lehu. 1.** Ashes; ash-colored, as a chicken. *Lā Hāpala Lehu,* Ash Wednesday. **ho'olehu.** To reduce to ashes. **2.** The number 400,000; numerous, very many. Cf. *lehulehu.*

**lehua. 1.** The flower of the *'ōhi'a* tree *(Metrosideros macropus, M. collina,* subsp. *polymorpha);* also the tree itself, a favorite native tree; the *lehua* is the flower of the island of Hawai'i, famous in song and tale. *Fig.,* warrior, beloved friend, sweetheart. **2.** *(Cap.)* Small island just beyond Ni'ihau. **3.** Expert, as in fishing. **ho'olehua.** Swift, expert, strong.

**lehulehu.** Multitude, crowd, great number, the public; numerous.

**lehu pele.** Volcanic ash.

**lei. 1.** Lei, garland, wreath; necklace of flowers, leaves, shells, ivory, feathers, or paper; beads; any ornament worn around the head or about the neck; to wear a lei; crown. *Fig.,* a beloved child, wife, husband, sweetheart, younger sibling. **ho'olei.** To put a lei on oneself or on someone else; to crown. **2.** To leap, fling, toss. Usually used with *ho'o-.* **ho'olei.** To cast, throw, toss, pitch; to stretch.

**lei 'ā'ī.** Lei for the neck; necktie; scarf, neckerchief. *Fig.,* beloved person, especially mate or child. *Lit.,* neck lei.

**lei ali'i.** Royal lei, chief's lei, crown, diadem.

**lei hala.** Lei made principally or solely of pandanus keys.

**lei hulu.** Feather lei. *Fig.,* dearly beloved child or favorite person.

**lei kolona (korona).** Rosary, prayer beads. *Lit.,* crown *(Eng.)* lei.

**lei kukui.** Lei of candlenut *(kukui)* nuts.

**leina.** Spring, leap, bound; place to leap from.

**lei niho 'īlio.** Dog-tooth necklace.

**lei niho palaoa.** Same as *lei palaoa.*

**lei palaoa.** Ivory pendant, originally probably whale's tooth suspended by two coils of braided human hair; necklace of beads of whale's teeth; today, any pendant shaped like the old whale-tooth pendant. *Lit.,* ivory lei.

**lei po'o.** Lei worn on the head *(po'o).*

**lei pūpū.** Shell lei.

**leke.** Also **lede.** Lady. *Eng.*

**lēkō.** Watercress.

**lele. 1.** To fly, jump, leap, hop, burst forth; to sail through the air, as a meteor; to get out of, as from a car; to land, disembark, as from a canoe; to move, as stars in the sky; a jump, leap, attack. **ho'olele.** To cause to fly; to fly, as a kite; to embark, as on a project. **2.** Windblown, of the rain. **3.** A detached part or plot of land belonging to one *'ili,* but located in another *'ili.*

**lelea.** A kind of prayer to send kava essence to the gods.

**lele 'ao'ao.** To leap sideways; to shy, as a horse.

**lele 'ē.** To speak prematurely or before one is spoken to; to jump to conclusions.

**lelehuna, lelehune.** Fine windblown rain.

**lele'ino.** To spring or leap violently, as in an attack or fright; to rush violently. *Lit.,* to fly evil.

**lele kawa.** To leap feet first from a cliff into water without splashing, or (at Ka'ū) into soft earth. *Papa lele kawa,* diving board.

**lele koa'e.** Flight of tropic birds; to fly like a tropic bird. *Fig.,* sheer, steep.

**lele koali.** To swing; to jump rope; swinging on a *koali* vine rope, an ancient sport.

**lele koke.** To leap suddenly, immediately. *Fig.,* short-tempered, excitable, quick to fight.

**lele lā'au.** Pole vaulting; to pole vault.

**-lele leo. ho'olele leo.** To broadcast; radio broadcast.

**-lele lupe. ho'olele lupe.** To fly kites.

**leleo.** Redup. of *leo.*

**lele'oi.** Excessive, very great. *Lit.,* excessive leap.

**lele pali.** To leap or fall from a cliff; to practice the ancient sport of leaping from a precipice into water.

**lelepau.** To trust completely.

**lele pi'o.** To fly or jump in a curve; to fly as a comet through the sky.

**lelepo'o.** To dive headfirst.

**lele ua.** Windblown rain.

**lelewa. 1.** Redup. of *lewa, 2.* **2.**

Hangers-on about a chief; parasitic persons.

**lele wale.** To fly, jump, move of one's own accord or for no reason.

**lelo.** Tongue (short for *alelo, elelo*).

**lemi.** Lemon, lime. *Eng. Wai lemi,* lemonade, limeade.

**lemu.** Buttocks.

**lena. 1.** Yellow, yellowish; jaundice; bile. **2.** Variant name for the *'ōlena* or turmeric plant. **3.** To stretch out, as to dry; to sight or aim; to bend, as a bow.

**lenalena.** Redup. of *lena, 1.*

**leo.** Voice, tone, tune, sound, command, advice, syllable; to speak, make a sound. Cf. *leoleo, leo 'ole.*

**leo ho'onani.** Song of praise, hymn.

**leo kāne.** Male voice, bass.

**leokani.** Vowel. *Lit.,* voiced sound.

**leokanipū.** Consonant. *Lit.,* sound said together.

**leokū pāhā.** Quartet.

**leokū pākahi.** Solo. *Lit.,* single standing speech.

**leokū pākolu, leokū pāpākolu.** Trio. *Lit.,* triple standing speech.

**leokū pālua.** Duet. *Lit.,* double standing speech.

**leoleo.** To speak loudly, angrily; to wail, as for the dead.

**leo mele.** Song tune; notes on the scale.

**leo nui.** Loud voice; to speak loudly.

**leo 'ole.** Uncomplaining, agreeable; considerate of feelings of others; giving generously. *Lit.,* no voice.

**leo pa'a.** Deaf-mute, dumb person. *Lit.,* held voice.

**leo wahine.** Soprano, soprano voice, feminine voice.

**lepa.** Flag, tapa cloth on end of a stick, as used to mark a taboo area. Cf. *kālepa.*

lepe. 1. Hem or fringe, as of a garment; any loose attachment, as of torn cloth or torn flesh. ho‘olepe. To cut, tear; to stir, as water. 2. Rooster's comb; turkey wattles.

lēpela, lepera. Leprosy, leper; leprous. *Eng.*

lepelepe. 1. Redup. of *lepe, 1;* fringed. 2. Wattles.

lepelepe-o-Hina. Monarch butterfly; Kamehameha butterfly.

lepo. Dirt, earth, ground, filth, excrement (euphemism); dirty, soiled.

lepolepo. Dirty, turbid; contaminated, as water.

lepo lo‘i. Taro-patch mud.

lepopele. Match, sulphur (euphemism for *kūkaepele*). *Lit.,* volcanic dirt.

Lepupalika, Repubalika. 1. Republican. *Eng.* 2. *(Not cap.)* Republic.

lewa. 1. Sky, atmosphere, upper heavens. 2. To float, dangle, swing, hang; swinging, pendulous, unstable. *Hōkū lewa,* moving star, planet. ho‘olewa. (a) To float, as a cloud; to lift up and carry, as on a stretcher. (b) To rotate the hips in dancing.

-lewa. ho‘olewa. Funeral.

lewa lani. Highest level of the heavens.

lewalewa. Redup. of *lewa, 2.*

lewa luna lilo. Highest atmosphere, outer space.

lī. 1. Chills; to have chills; to tremble with cold; shuddery feeling of horror. *Lī ka ‘ili, lī ka ‘i‘o,* to have goose flesh. 2. Lace, as of shoes; to lace or tie.

lī-. A prefix to many kinds of seaweeds, short for *limu.*

lia. Same as *liha, 1.*

-lia. Suffix corresponding to ‘*ia* but inseparably bound to a base.

li‘a. Strong desire, yearning; to wish for ardently.

liha. 1. Nit, louse egg. Also *lia.* 2. Same as *liliha;* dreadful, fearful.

lihaliha. 1. Same as *liliha.* 2. Redup. of *liha, 1;* many nits.

līhau. Gentle cool rain that was considered lucky for fishermen; moist and fresh, as plants in the dew or rain; cool, fresh, as dew-laden air.

lihi. 1. Edge, rim, border, boundary. Also *nihi.* 2. Small quantity, particle, a little bit; slight. ‘*Ike lihi,* to glimpse.

lihilihi. 1. Same as *lihi, 1, 2.* 2. Eyelashes, eyelid. 3. Lace.

lihilihi hana lima. Handmade lace; crocheting; any handmade trimming, as of knitting, tatting.

li‘i. 1. Small, tiny. 2. Short for *ali‘i,* chief, being especially common after *nā: nā li‘i,* the chiefs.

li‘ili‘i. Here and there, piecemeal, a little at a time; small, little, in bits, diminutive, infantile. *Kū‘ai li‘ili‘i,* retail buying or selling. ho‘oli‘ili‘i. To decrease, lessen, make small.

lī kāma‘a. Shoelace; to lace shoes.

like. Alike, like, similar, resembling, equal. Cf. *‘ālike, hālike.* ‘*Ālike ‘ālike,* midway, equally. *Like pū,* just the same, exactly alike.

likelike. Redup. of *like.*

like ‘ole. Various, all, different, not alike.

like pū. See *like.*

likiki. Ticket, receipt. *Eng.*

liko. 1. Leaf bud; newly opened leaf; to bud; to put forth leaves. *Fig.,* a child; youth. 2. Shining, glistening, as with dew; sparkling.

līlā. Spindly.

lili. Jealous; highly sensitive to criticism; jealousy; anger and mental anguish felt if one's loved ones are criticized. ho‘olili. To provoke jealousy; jealous.

lilia. Any kind of lily. *Eng.*

liliha. Nauseated, nauseating, of rich or fatty foods only; very rich, of fatty, oily food. *Fig.*, revolting; dreadful.

**lilikoʻi.** The purple water lemon or purple granadilla (*Passiflora edulis*, one of many passionflower or passion fruit vines). The yellow *lilikoʻi*, which has better-tasting fruit, is grown commercially in Hawaiʻi and widely used for desserts and beverages.

**lilinoe.** Fine mist, rain.

**liliʻu.** Scorching, burning, smarting, as salt in a raw wound or pain in the eyes.

**lilo. 1.** To accrue, be lost, pass into the possession of, be gone; to become, turn into; to overcome; taken. **hoʻolilo.** To transfer, change. **2.** Busy, absorbed, engrossed, devoted, dedicated. **3.** Expense, expenditure. **hoʻolilo.** Expense; to spend; to lose; to buy or sell. **4.** Far, distant, out of sight, completely. *I luna lilo,* way up.

**lilo loa.** Completely engrossed, dedicated, absorbed; permanently lost, taken, or given.

**lima. 1.** Arm, hand; sleeve; finger. **2.** Five; fifth.

**lima ʻākau.** Right hand; right-handed; dependable helper, right-hand man.

**limahana.** Labor, laborer, worker; busy.

**lima hema.** Left hand; left-handed.

**lima ikaika.** Strong hand or arm; power, strength; strong-arm.

**lima iki.** Small hand; little finger.

**lima kākau.** Handwriting; hand to write with.

**lima kuhi.** Index finger. *Lit.,* pointing hand.

**lima kuhikuhi.** Hands of a clock. *Lit.,* pointing hands.

**limalima. 1.** To handle, use the hands; to pilfer. **2.** To hire. **hoʻolimalima.** To rent, hire, employ, lease, charter; a lease, rental.

**lima nui.** Big hand, thumb.

**limu.** A general name for all kinds of plants living under water, both fresh and salt; also algae growing in any damp place, as on the ground, on rocks, and on other plants; also mosses, liverworts, lichens.

**limu kala.** Common long brown seaweeds (*Sargassum echinocarpum*).

**limu kele.** Moss growing on trees in rain forests.

**limu kohu.** A soft, succulent, small red seaweed (*Asparagopsis taxiformis*), one of the best-known and best-liked of edible seaweeds. Also called *limu koko.*

**lina. 1.** Soft; adhesive, sticky; glutinous, as taro of poor quality. Cf. *papālina.* **2.** Scar. Cf. *ʻālina.* **hoʻolina.** To scar. **3.** Ring (*Eng.*), hoop, racetrack.

**lino. 1.** Bright, shiny, dazzling, brilliant. **2.** To weave, twist, braid, tie. **3.** Same as *linolino, 2.*

**linolino. 1.** Redup. of *lino, 1, 2.* **2.** Calm, unruffled. Cf. *malino.*

**lio.** Horse. *Holo lio,* to ride horse-back.

**līʻō.** To act wild, as a frightened animal; to open the eyes wide in terror. **hoʻolīʻō.** To frighten, cause to shy, leap.

**lio heihei.** Racehorse.

**lio lāʻau.** Merry-go-round; horse on a merry-go-round; sawhorse; wooden horse, as used in quilting. *Holo lio lāʻau,* to ride on a merry-go-round.

**lio lawe ukana.** Packhorse. *Lit.,* horse carry gear.

**liʻoliʻo.** Bright, dazzling; dazzled.

**liona.** Lion. *Eng. Hui Liona,* Lions Club.

**liona kai.** Sea lion.

**lio wahine.** Mare.

**līpahapaha.** All kinds of sea lettuce (*Ulva fasciata* and *Monostroma oxyspermum*), edible but not well liked.

**lipaki, libati.** Liberty. *Eng.*

**lipe'e, lipe'epe'e.** Some native species of edible red seaweeds *(Laurencia parvipapillata, L. dotyi, L. succisa).*

**lipelala, liberala.** Liberal. *Eng.*

**lipi.** Adze, chisel; any sharp edge; sharp mountain ridge; sharp, tapering.

**lipilipi.** Redup. of *lipi.*

**lipina, ribina.** Var. of *lipine.*

**lipine, ribine.** Ribbon; tape, of a tape recorder. *Eng.*

**lipine kikokiko.** Typewriter ribbon.

**lipo.** Deep blue-black, as a cavern, the sea, or dense forest; dim, distant. *Kumulipo,* the origin in the deep, blue-black past [a Hawaiian creation poem].

**lipoa.** Two popular edible brown seaweeds *(Dictyopteris australis, D. plagiogramma).*

**lipu'upu'u.** An edible green seaweed.

**liu.** Bilge water, leakage; to leak.

**li'u. 1.** Slow, tardy, taking a long time; a long time. **2.** Well-salted, salty; seasoned. *Fig.,* deep, profound, as of skill or knowledge.

**li'ulā.** Twilight; mirage.

**liuliu.** Prepared, ready; to make ready. **ho'oliuliu.** To prepare.

**li'uli'u.** Redup. of *li'u, 1;* to pass much time; to spend much time. **ho'oli'uli'u.** To cause a delay, prolong.

**lō.** Earwig.

**loa. 1.** Distance, length, height; distant, long, far, permanent. Cf. *loloa.* **ho'oloa.** To stretch, extend, prolong, lengthen. **2.** Very, very much, too, most. *Maika'i loa,* very good. *Aloha nui loa,* very much *aloha.*

**loa'a.** To find, get, obtain, acquire, have, gain, receive; gain, earnings, profit, wealth, success; to have a child, beget a child; to be born; unequaled, incomparable. (This extremely common word takes an agent preceded by *i* or *iā*). *Loa'a ka hale i ke ali'i,* the chief has a house.

**loea.** Skill, ingenuity, cleverness; expert, clever, skillful; skilled person.

**loha.** Drooping, wilting; hanging low, as a branch; beaten down, as by rain. *Fig.,* sullen, spiritless.

**lohe.** To hear; to mind, obey; to feel, as the tug of a fishing line; obedient. **ho'olohe.** To obey.

**lohelohe. 1.** Redup. of *lohe;* to listen carefully, eavesdrop. **2.** Dragonfly larva, cocoon.

**lohe 'ōlelo.** Hearsay, gossip.

**lohe pepeiao.** Hearsay; to hear of.

**lohi. 1.** Slow, tardy, late. *'Ōlelo lohi,* speak slowly. **ho'olohi.** To delay, make slow, detain; to go slowly. **2.** Short for *'alohi,* sparkle.

**loi.** To look over critically.

**lo'i.** Irrigated terrace, especially for taro, but also for rice.

**lō'ihi. 1.** Length, height, distance. *Lō'ihi ke ala,* the road is long. **ho'olō'ihi.** To lengthen, extend, prolong. **2.** *(Cap.)* A young, growing submarine volcano 30 kilometers southeast of the island of Hawai'i.

**loina.** Rule, custom; principle, as of a political party.

**loio. 1.** Thin, spindly. **2.** Lawyer *(Eng.),* attorney; to act the lawyer; to judge. **ho'oloio.** To act the lawyer; to show off knowledge.

**loio ho'okolokolo.** Prosecutor.

**loio kuhina.** Attorney general.

**lōkahi.** Unity, agreement, accord; agreed, in unity. *Mana'o lōkahi,* unanimous. **ho'olōkahi.** To bring about unity; to make peace and unity.

**loke. 1.** Rose; rosy. *Eng.* **2.** Also **roke.** Roast. *Eng. Pipi loke,* roast beef.

**loke lani, roselani.** The common small red rose.

**loke lau.** Green rose *(Rosa chinensis* var. *viridiflora).*

**loko.** 1. In, inside, within; interior, inside; internal organs, as tripe. **ho'oloko.** To insinuate, suggest, implant a thought, either good or bad. 2. Character, disposition, heart. Cf. *loko hāiki, loko 'ino, lokomaika'i.* 3. Pond, lake, pool. 4. Mainland of the United States. *I loko aku nei au,* I've been to the mainland. 5. In spite of. *I loko nō o ka waiwai, hana nō,* in spite of wealth, working anyway. 6. By means of.

**loko hāiki.** Hard-hearted; narrowminded; tight-fisted.

**loko 'ino.** Merciless, evil, cruel; such a person.

**loko kai.** Lagoon.

**lokomaika'i.** Generosity, kindness, good will; benevolent.

**loko pa'akai.** Salt pond or lake.

**loku.** Downpour of rain; blowing of wind; to pour, of rain. *Fig.,* to feel deep emotion, pain, sorrow. **ho'oloku.** To pour, as rain; to disturb.

**lola.** 1. Drooping, hanging downward; lazy, idle. 2. Roller, rolling pin; to roll. *Eng.*

**lole.** 1. Cloth, clothes, dress; to wear clothes. 2. To unfold, turn inside out, reverse.

**lole holoi.** Laundry; soiled clothes ready to be washed.

**lole komo.** Clothes. *Lit.,* clothes to put on.

**lole moe pō.** Nightgown. *Lit.,* night-sleeping clothes.

**lole wāwae.** Trousers, pants, panties, slacks. *Lit.,* leg clothes.

**loli.** 1. To turn, change, alter, turn over. **ho'ololi.** To change, take a new form, amend. 2. Sea slug, bêche-de-mer, sea cucumber, trepang *(Holothuria* spp.).

**loliloli.** Redup. of *loli, 1;* changing, turning, changeable.

**lolo.** 1. Brains, bone marrow. 2. Religious ceremony at which the brain of the sacrificed animal was eaten (such ceremonies occurred at a canoe launching, the start of a journey, completion of instruction); to have completed the *lolo* ceremony, hence expert, skilled. 3. A strikingly colored species of wrasse fish. Also, *'akilolo.*

**lōlō.** Paralyzed, numb, feebleminded.

**loloa.** Redup. of *loa, 1. Lima loloa,* long sleeve.

**lolohe.** Redup. of *lohe;* to listen carefully, attentively. **ho'ololohe.** To listen carefully; to strain the ear to hear.

**lolo iwi.** Bone marrow.

**loloka'a.** Dizziness, with spinning head.

**lolo po'o.** Brain. *Lit.,* head brain.

**lolo uila.** Computer. *Lit.,* electric brain.

**lolo wa'a.** Canoe-launching ceremony; to perform the ceremony.

**loma.** Idle.

**lomi.** To rub, press, crush, massage, rub out; to work in and out, as claws of a contented cat.

**lōmilo.** To spin with fingers; to twist, as thread in making rope or cord. Cf. *milo,* to twist.

**lomilomi.** Redup. of *lomi;* masseur, masseuse.

**lonikū, lonitu.** Longitude. *Eng.*

**lono.** 1. News, report, remembrance, rumor (sometimes formerly preceded by *ke*). **ho'olono.** To listen, hear, obey; obedient. 2. *(Cap.)* One of the four major gods brought from Tahiti, the god of the *makahiki* harvest festivities and of agriculture. 3. *(Cap.)* The twenty-eighth day of the lunar month. 4. *(Cap.)* Hawaiian name for Captain Cook.

**lo'ohia.** Possessed, overwhelmed, overcome; to befall, happen.

**lōpā.** Shiftless; poor tenant farmer.

**lopi, ropi.** Thread. (*Eng.,* rope.)

**lopi hoʻoholoholo.** Basting thread.

**lopi kāholo.** Basting thread.

**lou.** Hook; to hook, to fasten with a hook. **hoʻolou.** To hook; to put on a hook, as bait. **2.** Fruit-plucking pole; to pluck with a *lou*.

**loʻu.** To overhang, as a cliff; to bend over, as with grief or laughter; bent over, as a laden branch.

**loulu.** All species of native fan palms *(Pritchardia)*.

**lū.** To scatter, throw, as ashes; to sow; to shed, as a chicken its feathers or a tree its leaves; to shake; to cast off, as grief; to squander. See *lūlū*.

**lua. 1.** Hole, pit, grave, den, cave, mine, crater. **hoʻolua.** To bake in the oven. Cf. *kālua*. **2.** Toilet, outhouse. **3.** Two, second, secondary, twice; doubly, much, a great deal. **hoʻolua.** To do twice, repeat, do over and over. **4.** Equal, likeness, duplicate, copy, match. Cf. *lua ʻole*. **5.** Companion, mate. Cf. *kōkoʻo*.

**-lua. 1. hoʻolua.** *(Cap.)* Name of a strong north wind. **2.** Dual number, only in pronoun and possessive, as *ʻolua koʻolua, kā ʻolua*.

**luʻa.** Old and wrinkled; worn and shabby with use.

**-luʻa. hoʻoluʻa. (a)** To bear many children. **(b)** To lay an egg.

**lua ahi.** Pit of fire; hell.

**lua ʻeli pōhaku.** Quarry. *Lit.,* pit [for] digging stones.

**luahine, luwahine.** Old woman, old lady; to be an old woman. **hoʻoluahine.** To act or dress like an old lady.

**luaʻi.** Vomit; volcanic eruptions; to vomit, erupt. Cf. *luaʻi koko*. **hoʻoluaʻi.** Emetic; causing vomiting; to cause a vomiting.

**luaʻi koko.** Any kind of sickness with vomiting of blood; to vomit blood.

**luaʻi pele.** Volcanic eruption, lava, sulphur, brimstone.

**luakaha.** Enjoyable, pleasant, as a place to which one is attached; to while away the time enjoyably.

**luakini.** Temple, church, cathedral, tabernacle; large *heiau* where ruling chiefs prayed and human sacrifices were offered.

**lua kupapaʻu.** Tomb, grave. *Lit.,* corpse pit.

**lua liʻiliʻi.** Outhouse, toilet.

**luana.** To be at leisure, enjoy pleasant surroundings and associates; to live in comfort and ease. **hoʻoluana.** To be at leisure.

**luana iki.** To pause a moment; to enjoy oneself a little.

**lua ʻole.** Superior, incomparable, unequalled, second to none.

**lua ʻōpala.** Rubbish pit.

**lua pele.** Volcano, crater. *Lit.,* volcanic pit.

**lua puhi.** Blowhole, eel hole.

**lūʻau. 1.** Young taro tops, especially as baked with coconut cream and chicken or octopus. **2.** Hawaiian feast.

**luawai.** Well, pool, pond, reservoir.

**luea.** Seasickness, nausea, dizziness.

**luhe.** To droop.

**lūheʻe.** Fishing for octopus with line and cowrie lure; the octopus lure; to fish thus.

**lū heleleʻi.** To scatter, strew; to let hair hang loose and unbound.

**luhi.** Weary, tired, fatigued; wearisome, tiresome, tedious; burden; labor, work, pains. **hoʻoluhi.** To bother, disturb, trouble, overburden.

**luhia.** A species of shark.

**luhiluhi.** Redup. of *luhi*. **hoʻoluhiluhi.** To make tired, disturbed.

**luina.** Sailor.

**lukānela, lutanela.** Lieutenant. *Eng.*

**Lukia, Rusia.** Russia; Russian. *Eng.*

**Lūkini.** Russian. *Eng.*

**luku.** Massacre, slaughter, destruction; to destroy, massacre, lay waste, exterminate.

**luku wale.** Vandalism, useless slaughter or destruction; to destroy thus.

**lula, rula.** Ruler, tape measure; rules, manners, regulations. *Eng.*

**lula kumu.** Fundamental or basic rule.

**luli.** To shake, as the head in approval or disapproval; to roll, as a ship; to sway to and fro. **ho'oluli.** To rock, as a child; to sway.

**lulu.** Calm, peace, shelter, lee, protection, shield; to lie at anchor. **ho'olulu.** To lie quietly in calm water, as a ship in port; to be calm.

**lūlū.** 1. Redup. of *lū;* to scatter, sow, as seeds; to shake, as an earthquake. 2. Donation, offering, as in church; raffle; to make an offering.

**lūlū lima.** To shake hands; handshake.

**luma, luma'i.** To douse, duck; to upset, tumble, as in the surf.

**lumakika, rumatika.** Rheumatism. *Eng.*

**lumi, rumi.** Room. *Eng.*

**lumi 'aina.** Dining room.

**lumi 'au'au.** Bathroom. *Lit.,* washing room.

**lumi ho'okipa.** Parlor, living room. *Lit.,* entertaining room.

**lumi kuke.** Kitchen. *Lit.,* cooking room.

**lumi moe.** Bedroom. *Lit.,* sleeping room.

**lumi waiho pā.** Pantry. *Lit.,* room [for] leaving plates.

**luna.** 1. High, upper, above, over, up; on, in, into. *Luna* follows particles expressing place, as *ā, i, kō, ma-, mai, no, o. Kau i luna o ke ka'a,* get into the car.

2. Foreman, boss, overseer, supervisor. **ho'oluna.** To appoint as foreman, officer, etc.

**luna 'auhau.** Tax collector.

**luna aupuni.** Government official.

**luna hana.** Overseer, foreman, anyone in charge of work.

**luna helu.** Census taker. *Lit.,* counting supervisor.

**luna helu kālā.** Teller, as of a bank. *Lit.,* officer who counts money.

**luna ho'ohana.** Manager, administrative head, overseer. *Lit.,* supervisor to cause work to be done.

**luna ho'omalu.** Chairman; speaker, as of the House of Representatives.

**luna ho'oponopono.** Editor.

**luna ho'opuka.** Publisher. *Lit.,* officer who makes appear.

**luna'ikehala.** Conscience. *Lit.,* officer who knows wrong.

**lunakahiko.** Elder; elderly leader.

**luna kānāwai.** Judge, magistrate; Book of Judges in the Old Testament; judicial. *Lit.,* law officer.

**luna kānāwai ki'eki'e.** Chief justice.

**luna kia'i.** Supervisor.

**luna kula.** School superintendent, schoolmaster.

**luna leka.** Postmaster. *Lit.,* letter officer.

**lunamaka'āinana.** Representative in the legislature. *Lit.,* people's officer.

**luna māka'i.** District sheriff, chief of police.

**luna nui.** Chief officer or foreman, especially head overseer of a sugar plantation; supervisor.

**lupe.** 1. Kite. *Ho'olele lupe,* to fly a kite. 2. Same as *hīhīmanu,* sting ray.

**lupo.** 1. A fish, perhaps *pāpiopio.* 2. Wolf.

**lūpō.** Same as *pāpiopio.*

**lu'u.** To dive, plunge into water, immerse; to dip in, as a shrimp net. **ho'olu'u.** To dip, immerse, etc.

**lu'ulu'u.** Bent or bowed down, as with weight, sorrow, or trouble; painful, sorrowful. **ho'olu'u-lu'u.** To cause sorrow, grief; to oppress.

# M

**ma.** At, in, on, beside, through, by means of, because of, according to (mā frequently before primary stress). *Makai*, at the sea, seaward. *Mauka*, inland.

**mā. 1.** Faded, wilted, stained, discolored, blushing. **2.** Particle following names of persons: and company, and others, and associates, and wife. *Ke ali'i mā*, the chief and his retinue. *Mea mā*, they. **3.** Variant of *ma-*.

**mā-. 1.** Stative derivative former, as in *'alo, mā'alo*. **2.** Exclusiveness, in pronouns and possessives.

**ma'a. 1.** Accustomed, used to, knowing thoroughly, experienced. Cf. *ma'ama'a, ma'amau*. **ho'oma'a.** To practice, gain experience or skill, become accustomed (less used than *ho'oma'ama'a*). **2.** To tie. Cf. *kāma'a*. **3.** Sling.

**ma'alahi.** Easy, simple.

**ma'alea.** Cunning, craft, trickery; crafty, deceitful, shrewd, skillful.

**ma'alili.** Cooled, of what has been hot, as food; abated, calmed, of anger, love, passion. **ho'oma'a-lili.** To cause to cool; soothe.

**mā'alo.** To pass along, by, or alongside, as to overtake and pass a car; to pass through, as land.

**mā'alo'alo.** Redup. of *mā'alo;* to pass to and fro, back and forth; to pass frequently.

**ma'ama'a.** Redup. of *ma'a, 1;* accustomed, experienced, used. **ho'oma'ama'a.** Same as *ho'oma'a;* to practice, become accustomed.

**ma'amau.** Usual, customary, regular, habitual, ordinary. *Uku ma'amau*, customary fee. **ho'oma'amau.** To become accustomed, familiar.

**ma'ane'i.** See *'ane'i*.

**ma'awe.** Fiber, thread, strand, as of a spider web; to tread, track, follow, as a trail; weak, sickly. **ho'oma'awe.** To make a tracing; footprint, track; to make small fibers or threads.

**mā'awe'awe.** Redup. of *ma'awe;* streaked, as with different colors.

**mae.** To fade, wilt, wither; partially dry, as clothes; to fade away; to waste away, as with illness. **ho'omae.** To cause to wilt, fade; to fade.

**maea.** Malodorous.

**mā'e'ele.** Numb, as a foot that has "gone to sleep"; numb with cold or deeply moved by love; shocked; stricken with fear, horror, grief. **ho'omā'e'ele.** To cause numbness, shock, great love.

**mā'ele.** Same as *mā'e'ele*.

**ma'ema'e.** Clean, pure, attractive, chaste; cleanliness, purity. **ho'oma'ema'e.** To clean, cleanse.

**māewa.** Swaying, swinging, as something with an anchored base, as seaweed, hair, or leaves; fluttering; unstable.

**ma'ewa.** Reproachful, scornful, mocking, sneering; scorned, abused. **ho'oma'ewa.** To reproach, sneer at, mimic.

**mā'ewa'ewa.** Redup. of *ma'ewa*.

**maha. 1.** Temple, side of the head. **2.** Rest, repose; freedom from

pain; at ease. See *mahamaha.*
**ho‘omaha.** Vacation; rest in
music; to take a rest or vacation;
to retire, stop work; to obtain
relief.

**mahae.** To tear, split, separate.
*Mahae lua,* to split in two. Also
*nahae.*

**mahaehae.** Redup. of *mahae;* to
tear to shreds.

**mahalo. 1.** Thanks, gratitude; to
thank. *Mahalo nui loa,* thank
[you] very much. **2.** Admiration, praise; to admire, praise.

**mahamaha.** Redup. of *maha, 2;*
to rest, stop.

**mahana. 1.** Warmth; warm. Cf.
*hahana, pumehana.* **ho‘omahana.** To warm, create warmth,
heat. **2.** Rest. Cf. *maha, 2.*
**ho‘omahana.** Vacation, rest.

**māhana.** Twins; double; having
two branches or forks.

**maha‘oi.** Bold, impertinent, ner-
vy, brazen. *Lit.,* sharp temple.

**mahea.** See *hea, 3,* where.

**Māhea-lani.** Sixteenth night of the
lunar month, night of the full
moon.

**māhelahela.** Clearly shown, as
wood grain.

**mahele.** Portion, division, bureau, department; share, as
of stocks; installment; measure
in music; land division of 1848;
the Great Mahele; part, as
of the body; to divide, apportion, cut into parts. **ho‘oma-
hele.** To have a division made,
etc.

**mahele lā‘au.** Portion of medicine, dose.

**mahele manawa.** Division of
time, as of a fiscal period.

**mahele ‘ōlelo.** Interpreter, translator; to translate, interpret.

**mahi. 1.** To cultivate, farm; a
farm, plantation. Cf. *mahi ‘ai,
mahina mahina ‘ai.* Mahi *kō,*
sugar plantation. **2.** Strong, energetic, as a worker. *Moa mahi,*
fighting cock.

**mahi ‘ai.** Farmer; to farm, cultivate; agricultural.

**māhie.** Delightful, charming,
pleasant. **ho‘omāhie.** Delightful, charming.

**māhiehie.** Redup. of *māhie.*

**mahiki. 1.** To jump, leap, hop,
move up and down; to teeter,
seesaw. **ho‘omahiki.** To cause
to leap, jump, etc. **2.** To pry;
peel off, as a scab; to appear.

**māhikihiki.** Redup. of *mahiki, 1,
2.*

**mahimahi.** Dolphin fish *(Cory-
phaena hippurus).*

**mahina. 1.** Moon, month; moonlight. *Mahina meli,* honeymoon.
**2.** Farm, plantation, patch.

**mahina ‘ai.** Same as *mahi ‘ai;*
farm; to farm.

**māhinahina.** Pale moonlight.

**mahina hou. 1.** New moon, new
month. **2.** Church offering on
the first Sunday of the month, in
Congregational churches.

**mahina piha.** Full moon.

**mahina poepoe.** Full moon. *Lit.,*
round moon.

**mahiole.** Feather helmet; helmet;
to wear a helmet.

**mahi pua.** Flower garden or
patch; horticulture.

**mahi waina.** Vineyard; one who
raises grapes; to cultivate grapes.

**mahoe.** Twins.

**māhola.** To spread out, extend.

**mahole.** To bruise, skin, scrape,
as a flesh wound; to injure, as
the feelings. Cf. *hole,* peeled.

**mahope.** See *hope,* after.

**māhu.** Steam, vapor; to steam,
exude vapor.

**mahū.** Weak, flat, as stale beer;
insipid.

**māhū.** Homosexual, of either sex;
hermaphrodite. **ho‘omāhū.** To
behave like a homosexual or hermaphrodite.

**māhua.** Increase, growth; to increase, thrive, multiply. **ho‘o-
māhua.** To increase, expand,
enlarge, multiply.

**māhuahua.** Redup. of *māhua;* to grow strong, as a ruler.

**mahu'i.** To guess, surmise.

**mahuka.** To run away, escape. **ho'omahuka.** To assist or help escape.

**mai.** 1. Direction toward the speaker. Come, come here; say, give (used without particles). *Hele mai,* come. 2. Also **mai . . . mai.** From. *Mai Hilo mai ka lei,* the lei is from Hilo. 3. Particle of negative command. Don't. 4. Almost, nearly.

**ma'i.** 1. Patient, sick person, sickness, disease; sick, ill. 2. Genitals. *Mele ma'i,* song in honor of genitals, as of a chief, as composed on his or her birth.

**mai'a.** All kinds of bananas.

**mai'a Pākē.** Chinese banana *(Musa xnana,* syn. *M. cavendishii).*

**maiau.** Neat and careful in work; skillful, expert; correct, careful, as in speech.

**ma'i Hepela (Hebera).** Smallpox. *Lit.,* Hebrew disease.

**maika.** Ancient Hawaiian game suggesting bowling; the stone used in the game; shot-put. Also, *'ulu maika.*

**maika'i.** Good, well, fine, excellent; handsome; goodness, well-being; good health. **ho'omaika'i.** To thank, bless, congratulate, praise, improve. *Ho'omaika'i'i!* Congratulations!

**ma'i keiki.** Pregnancy sickness; child's disease.

**maiko, maikoiko.** A surgeon fish *(Acanthurus nigroris).*

**Maikonekia, Maikonikia.** Micronesia; Micronesian. *Eng.*

**maila.** The directional *mai* plus *lā,* there, then.

**mailani.** To extol, praise. **ho'omailani.** To praise.

**maile.** A native twining shrub *(Alyxia olivaeformis),* with shiny fragrant leaves, a favorite for decoration and leis.

**maile lau li'i.** A kind of *maile* with narrow, pointed leaves. *Lit.,* small-leaved *maile.*

**maile lau nui.** A kind of *maile* with large leaves. *Lit.,* big-leaved *maile.*

**ma'i lele.** Contagious disease. *Lit.,* jumping disease.

**maile pilau.** Stink vine *(Paederia foetida). Lit.,* stinking *maile.*

**mā'ili.** Pebble, as used for making sinkers for squid fishing; pebbly, full of pebbles.

**mai . . . mai.** See *mai, 2.*

**māino.** Cruelty, misery, harm; cruel, miserable. **ho'omāino.** To treat cruelly, abuse, persecute; to cause misery and suffering.

**mā'ino'ino.** To deface, mar, spoil; defamed, defaced. **ho'omā'ino'ino.** To defame, slander, deface.

**ma'i ola.** To cure sickness; curable disease.

**ma'i Pākē.** Leprosy. *Lit.,* Chinese disease.

**ma'i pu'upu'u li'ili'i.** Smallpox. *Lit.,* disease with many little pimples.

**ma'i pu'uwai.** Heart disease, heart attack.

**māi'u'u.** Toe or finger nail; hoof, claw.

**maka.** 1. Eye, eye of a needle, face, countenance; presence, sight, view. 2. Beloved one, favorite person. Cf. *makamaka* (very common). 3. Point, bud; nipple, teat; sharp edge or blade of an instrument; point of a fishhook; land point; beginning, source. **ho'omaka.** To begin, start; to appear, of a child's first tooth; to put forth buds; to come to a head, as a boil. 4. Mesh of a net; mesh in plaiting; stitch, in sewing. 5. Raw, as fish; uncooked; green, unripe, as fruit; fresh as distinct from salted provisions.

**māka.** Mark, target; to mark. *Eng.*

**maka ʻāhewa.** Walleyed; cross-eyed. *Lit.*, eyes that err.

**makaʻāinana.** Commoner, populace, people in general; citizen. Cf. *lunamakaʻāinana. Lit.*, people that attend the land.

**makaʻala.** Alert, vigilant, watchful, wide awake.

**makaaniani.** Eyeglasses, spectacles. *Lit.*, crystal eye.

**makaʻē.** To look at with disfavor; to look askance.

**makaʻeleʻele.** Chilled, frozen.

**mākaha.** Fierce, savage, ferocious.

**mākahakaha.** Clearing, as rain. **hoʻomākahakaha.** To show signs of clearing.

**makahehi.** Admiration, desire for, wonder, amazement; attractive; to admire.

**makahekili.** Hailstone. *Lit.*, thunder eye.

**maka hiamoe.** Sleepy eyes; sleepy, drowsy.

**makahiapo.** First-born child, oldest child. *Lit.*, first-born person.

**makahiki.** 1. Year, age, annual, yearly (sometimes written *MH*). 2. Ancient festival beginning about the middle of October and lasting about four months, with sports and religious festivities and taboo on war.

**Makahiki Hou.** New Year. *Hauʻoli Makahiki Hou*, Happy New Year.

**makahiki lele ʻoi.** Leap year. *Lit.*, year jump ahead.

**maka hilahila.** Bashful eyes; bashful, timidly averting one's gaze.

**maka hou.** Beginning, new start. **hoʻomaka hou.** To begin again.

**mākaʻi.** Policeman, guard; to police, inspect, spy. Cf. *luna mākaʻi*. **hoʻomākaʻi.** To act as a policeman; to appoint or invest as a policeman.

**maka ihe.** Spear point.

**mākaʻi hoʻomalu pō.** Patrolling night police. *Lit.*, police making night peaceful.

**maka ihu.** Bowsprit of a canoe; sharp point at the bow. *Lit.*, bow point.

**mākaʻikaʻi.** To visit, see the sights; to stroll, take a walk. *Mākaʻikaʻi hele*, to stroll here and there. **hoʻomākaʻikaʻi.** To take others on a visit; to show the sights; to escort.

**mākaʻikiu.** Detective. *Lit.*, spying police.

**mākaʻi koa.** Military police. *Lit.*, soldier police.

**mākaʻi nui.** Sheriff.

**mākaʻi pō.** Night watchman, night police.

**makaiwa.** Mother-of-pearl eyes, as in an image, especially of the god Lono.

**mākaʻi wahine.** Police matron.

**maka kiʻekiʻe.** Proud look; haughty air.

**maka kilo.** Observant, watchful eyes; to watch with great attention.

**makākiu.** Spy, detective, spying eye; watchful, spying; to spy. **hoʻomakākiu.** To spy, watch, reconnoiter.

**maka koa.** Bold, unafraid, fierce. *Lit.*, brave eye.

**maka koʻa.** Landmark for a fishing ground. *Lit.*, fishing-ground point.

**maka kui.** Needle or nail point; stitch.

**makala.** To loosen, undo, untie, open a little, set at liberty; to remit, as a debt; to open, as a flower.

**mākala.** 1. Myrtle. *Eng.* 2. Marshal. *Eng.* 3. *(Cap.)* Marshall (Islands). *Eng.*

**makalapua.** Handsome, beautiful; to blossom forth.

**makalē.** Mackerel, canned sardines. *Eng.*

**maka leʻa.** Twinkle-eyed, happy-eyed, mischievous.

**maka leho.** Covetous, lustful,

wanton, lascivious. *Lit.*, cowrie eyes, perhaps so-called because octopus cling to cowries.

**makali.** To bait a hook.

**makaliʻi. 1.** Tiny, very small, fine, wee, small-meshed. **2.** *(Cap.)* Pleiades; Castor and Pollux. **3.** *(Cap.)* Name of a Hawaiian month; the six summer months collectively.

**makalika.** Marguerite, daisy. *Eng.*

**maka loa.** Very green, as a fruit; barely cooked, very raw.

**maka lokomaikaʻi.** Bountiful eye; one who looks kindly, charitably, and with good will. *Lit.*, good-hearted face.

**maka luhi.** Tired eyes, tired people, especially those who have been working hard on a community project.

**makamae.** Precious, of great value, highly prized, darling.

**makamaka.** Intimate friend with whom one is on terms of receiving and giving freely; host. Cf. *maka,* beloved. **hoʻomakamaka.** To befriend, be a friend to, make a friend, cause to be friends.

**maka mua.** First, beginning, commencement, first time; first child of a family. *Lit.*, first end.

**makana.** Gift, present, reward; prize; to give a gift. Cf. *maka, 2.*

**makana aloha.** Gift of friendship or love; free-will offering.

**makana hele.** Parting gift. *Lit.*, going gift.

**makani.** Wind, breeze; gas in the stomach; to blow. Cf. *ani.*

**maka ʻoi.** Piercing, penetrating, sharp eyes.

**maka piapia.** Eyes sticky with viscous matter; watery eyes.

**makapō.** Blindness, blind person; blind. *Lit.*, night eye. **hoʻomakapō.** To cause blindness, to feign blindness, to blindfold.

**makapōuli.** Dizziness; dizzy, faint. *Lit.*, black-night eyes.

**makau.** Fishhook.

**makaʻu.** Fear; frightened, afraid. **hoʻomakaʻu.** To frighten, scare, terrify; to pretend to fear; to fear.

**makaʻuhia.** Passive/imperative of *makaʻu.*

**mākaukau.** Able, competent, capable, efficient, skilled; prepared, ready; competence, efficiency, preparation; to know how, to know well. Cf. *ʻākau,* right. **hoʻomākaukau.** To prepare, make ready.

**maka ʻulaʻula.** Pinkeye; inflamed eye. *Lit.*, red eye.

**maka uli.** Black eye, as from a bruise.

**maka ʻupena.** Net mesh.

**makaʻu wale.** Coward, cowardice; afraid for no reason, easily frightened.

**maka wai.** Watery-eyed; eyes welling with tears; tender-eyed.

**makawalu.** Numerous, many, much. *Lit.*, eight eyes.

**makawela.** Glowing, burning; full of hate.

**make. 1.** To die; defeated, killed, unfortunate; to faint; death, peril, destruction; to kill (when used transitively, the subject is preceded by *i* or *iā*); deathly, deadly. **hoʻomake.** To kill; to let die; to let diminish, grow faint. **2.** Desire, want; to want. Cf. *make ʻai.*

**make ʻai.** Hungry. *Lit.*, want food.

**-mākeʻaka. hoʻomākeʻaka.** Witty, comic, funny; to cause laughter, exercise wit.

**makeʻe.** Covetous, greedy, desirous to have; to have affection for.

**makehewa.** Bad bargain, vain undertaking; in vain, useless, without profit. Cf. *makepono.*

**mākeke.** Market. *Eng.*

**mākeke nui.** Large market, supermarket.

**make loa.** To die (in contrast to *make,* which may mean "defeated, faint").

**makemake.** Desire, want, wish; to want, like, wish (often replaced colloquially by *mamake*).

**makemakika.** Mathematics. *Eng.*

**makepono.** Bargain, profitable, reasonable in price. Cf. *makehewa*.

**make wai.** Thirst; thirsty.

**make wale.** To die of itself, to die without cause.

**mākia. 1.** Aim, motto, purpose; to aim or strive for. **2.** Pin, nail, bolt; to nail, bolt, crucify, pin; to establish, as a kingdom; to drive stakes, as in surveying.

**makika.** Mosquito. *Eng.*

**mākō.** Rough, rocky; large.

**mākole.** Inflamed eye; red-eyed; red-hot; red or yellow, as dying leaves. **ho'omākole.** To cause redness or soreness of the eyes.

**mākolu.** Thick, heavy, deep, as clouds; thick-coated, as dust; laden, as a high chief with taboo.

**mākonā.** Hard, mean, hardhearted. **ho'omākonā.** To act mean, hard, etc.

**mākou.** We, us (plural, exclusive).

**makua.** Parent, any relative of the parents' generation, as uncle, aunt, cousin; Father (God, in Christian prayers); Catholic father; main stalk of a plant; adult; full-grown, mature, older, senior. **ho'omakua.** To grow into maturity, mature; to act the part of a parent; to adopt, as a child; to call or treat as a parent.

**mākua.** Plural of *makua*.

**makua ali'i, makuali'i.** Progenitor, patriarch, head of a tribe.

**makuahine.** Mother, aunt, female cousin or relative of parents' generation. *Lit.,* female parent. *'Ōlelo makuahine,* mother tongue.

**mākuahine.** Plural of *makuahine*.

**makuahine kōlea.** Stepmother.

**makuahine papakema.** Godmother.

**makuahūnōai.** Parent-in-law; uncle- or aunt-in-law; cousin of parent-in-law (sex may be designated by addition of *kāne,* male, or *wahine,* female).

**makua kāne.** Father, uncle, male cousin of parents' generation.

**mākua kāne.** Plural of *makua kāne*.

**makua kāne kōlea.** Stepfather.

**makua kāne papakema.** Godfather.

**māku'e. 1.** Dark brown, any dark color. **2.** Frown, scowl; to frown, scowl.

**makule.** Aged, old, of people. Cf. *'elemakule,* old man.

**mala. 1.** Aching, as after unaccustomed exercise; stiff and sore; bruised. **ho'omala.** To cause such an aching. **2.** Sour, as fermented sweet potato.

**māla.** Garden, plantation, cultivated field, as *māla 'ai.*

**māla 'ai.** Taro patch, food garden, or plantation.

**māla'e.** Clear, calm; clear of weeds, as a field; serene, as a cloudless sky. **ho'omāla'e.** To clear, explain clearly; to calm, cheer, dispel gloom; to clear away, as brush or weeds.

**malahia.** Passive/imperative of *mala, 1.*

**malaila.** See *laila.*

**malakeke.** Molasses. *Eng.*

**Malaki.** March (the month). *Eng.*

**malalo.** See *lalo.*

**malama.** Light; month, moon. Cf. *lama,* torch.

**mālama.** To take care of, care for, preserve; to keep or observe, as a taboo; to conduct, as a service; to serve, honor, as God; care, preservation, support, fidelity, loyalty; custodian, caretaker. Cf. *mālama hale, mālama moku.*

**mālama hale.** Custodian of a house, janitor, housekeeper.

**mālamalama.** Redup. of *malama;* light of knowledge, clarity of thinking or explanation; shining, clear. **hoʻomālamalama.** To cause light, brighten, illuminate, enlighten, inform.

**mālama moku.** Mate of a ship.

**mālama waihona puke.** Librarian.

**māla pua.** Flower garden.

**male.** Phlegm, mucus from lungs or throat.

**malia.** Perhaps, maybe (usually followed by *o* or *paha*).

**mālie.** Calm, quiet, still, gentle; calmly, slowly, quietly. *Noho mālie,* keep still, sit still. **hoʻomālie.** To calm, quiet, hush, soothe.

**malihini.** Stranger, newcomer, guest; one unfamiliar with a place or custom; new, unusual, rare, or of foreign origin; for the first time. **hoʻomalihini.** To be or act as a stranger, guest.

**māliko.** To bud, as leaves.

**malimali.** To flatter, soothe, persuade with soft words, cajole. **hoʻomalimali.** To flatter; to mollify with soft words or a gift; to soothe, quiet.

**malino.** Calm, quiet, as the sea. *Malino ke kai,* the sea is calm.

**maliʻo.** Dawn light, twilight, especially as it pierces the shadows of night.

**maliu.** To heed, give attention, listen, look upon with favor, turn toward. **hoʻomaliu.** To cause to heed, heed.

**malo.** Male's loincloth; chant in praise of chief's loincloth.

**mālō.** Taut, firm, straight. *Kino mālō,* straight body. **hoʻomālō.** To make straight, firm, as a cord; to tighten.

**maloka, hoʻomaloka.** Skeptical, unbelieving.

**maloko.** Inside. See *loko.*

**malolo.** To rest, pause, adjourn. **hoʻomalolo.** To cease work for a time, recess; adjourn temporarily.

**mālolo.** General term for Hawaiian flying fishes.

**maloʻo.** Dry, dried up, evaporated; drought, dryness. **hoʻomaloʻo.** To dry out; to season, as lumber; tracing, as of genealogy.

**malu.** Shade, shelter, protection, peace; shaded, peaceful; reserved; taboo; the stillness and awe of taboo. **hoʻomalu.** To bring under the care and protection of, to protect; to keep quiet, still; to restrict; to make peace between warring parties; to preside, as at a meeting; probation. Cf. *hale hoʻomalu, luna hoʻomalu.*

**malū.** Secretly, clandestinely, illegally. *Lawe malū,* to take secretly.

**maluhia.** Peace, quiet, serenity; safety; peaceful, restful. **hoʻomaluhia.** To cause or give peace, protect; to arbitrate between warring parties.

**māluhiluhi.** Tired, weary; tiresome, wearisome, fatiguing. **hoʻomāluhiluhi.** To cause fatigue, exhaust, tire; tiresome, exhausting.

**malule.** Limp, weak, flexible; soft and fragile, as some eggshells. **hoʻomalule.** To make lax, limp, weak; to relax, weaken; to change from a caterpillar into a butterfly.

**maluna.** See *luna.*

**mama.** To chew, masticate (but not swallow; cf. *nau*).

**māmā.** 1. Fast, nimble, speedy of movement. 2. Light, of weight. *Fig.,* eased of pain, ache, of distress. *Eamāmā,* oxygen. **hoʻomāmā.** To lighten, as a load; to ease pain; to cheer. 3. Mama, mother. *Eng.*

**mamae.** Redup. of *mae;* sickly, listless; weakening or withering effect of pain; wan or pale, as after illness.

**mamake.** 1. Redup. of *make, 1;* to die, of several; to wilt, of plants. **2.** Colloquial for *make-make*, to want, like.

**māmaki.** A small native tree (*Pipturus* spp.) whose bark yielded a coarse tapa.

**māmala. 1.** Fragment, splinter, piece. **2.** *(Cap.)* Bay outside Honolulu Harbor, from about Pearl Harbor to Kewalo Basin.

**Māmala hoa.** Var. of *Māmala hoe.*

**Māmala hoe.** Name of Kamehameha I's famous law of the splintered paddle (*lit.,* paddle fragment), which guaranteed the safety of the highways to all—as women, children, sick, and aged.

**māmalaʻōlelo.** Sentence, clause, phrase. *Lit.,* speech fragment.

**māmalu. 1.** Redup. of *malu;* protection, shade; shaded. **hoʻo-māmalu.** To protect; to make shady; to cast gloom. **2.** Umbrella, parasol.

**māmane.** A native leguminous tree *(Sophora chrysophylla).*

**mamao.** Far, distant; high in rank. **hoʻomamao.** To keep away; to keep one's distance; to go far.

**mamo. 1.** A mostly black Hawaiian honeycreeper *(Drepanis pacifica);* its few yellow feathers above and below the tail were used in choicest featherwork. **2.** Descendant, posterity. **3.** Var. of *maomao.*

**mamua.** See *mua.*

**mamuli.** See *muli.*

**mana. 1.** Supernatural or divine power, mana, miraculous power; a powerful nation, authority; to give mana to; to have mana, power; possessed of mana, power. *Mana makua,* parental authority. **hoʻomana. (a)** To place in authority, empower. **(b)** To worship; religion, sect. *Hoʻomana Kepanī,* Buddhist; Buddhism. **2.** Branch, limb; crosspiece, as of the cross; a line

projecting from another line; stream branch; road branch; variant, version, as of a tale; to branch out, spread out.

**māna.** A chewed mass, as of kava for drinking, coconut flakes, or *kukui* nut for medicine. *Māna ʻai,* food chewed by adult for child; any mouthful of food.

**mānā.** Arid; desert.

**mānai.** Needle for stringing leis; to string leis.

**manakā.** Boresome, tiresome, dull, monotonous; bored, uninterested. **hoʻomanakā.** Same as *manakā;* to cause boredom.

**manakō.** Mango *(Mangifera indica).*

**manakō kāne.** Mango chutney.

**manakuke.** Mongoose. *Eng.*

**mānalo.** Sweet, potable, of water that may be drunk but is not deliciously cool *(huʻihuʻi).* **hoʻo-mānalo.** To remove bitterness or saltiness, as of overly salty salmon.

**mana lua.** Two branches, fork, as in a road.

**manamana. 1.** Redup. of *mana, 1.* **hoʻomanamana.** To impart mana or deify, as idols or objects; superstitious. **2.** Redup. of *mana, 2;* appendages, branches, rays, forks; to branch out. **3.** Finger.

**manamana kuhi.** Index finger; hand of a watch or clock.

**manamana lima.** Finger.

**manamana lima nui.** Thumb. *Lit.,* big finger.

**manamana nui.** Big branch; big toe, thumb.

**manamana wāwae.** Toe.

**manaʻo.** Thought, idea, opinion, theory, meaning, mind; desire; to think, consider. **hoʻoma-naʻo.** To remember, recall, commemorate.

**mahaʻohaʻi.** Something to say, thought to express.

**manaʻo hoʻohālikelike.** Comparison.

**mana'o ho'onalonalo.** Hidden meaning.

**mana'o 'ino.** Evil thought or idea, hatred.

**mana'o'i'o.** Faith, confidence; to have faith, confidence; to believe. *Kumu mana'o'i'o*, creed.

**mana'olana.** Hope, confidence; to hope. *Lit.*, floating thought.

**mana'o maoli.** Literal meaning; a real or true opinion.

**māna'ona'o.** Horrible, dreadful, horrifying, gruesome; shocked, horrified; heartsick. **ho'omāna'ona'o.** To cause a sensation of horror, grief.

**mana'o nui.** Important matter or idea, meaning.

**mana'opa'a.** Conviction, determination; convinced.

**mana'o ulu wale.** Whim, fancy, impulse.

**manauea, manauwea.** A kind of small red seaweed *(Gracilaria cornopifolia),* today often called *ogo* (Japanese, dialectal).

**manawa. 1.** Time, turn, season, chronology. Cf. *ha'i manawa.* **2.** Anterior fontanel in the heads of infants; top of the head of adults at position of the fontanel.

**manawahua.** Discomfort of the stomach, with gas and often diarrhea; to grieve. *Lit.*, swollen stomach.

**mana wai.** Stream branch.

**manawa 'ino.** Evil disposition, hard feelings; time of storm.

**manawakolu.** Eternal.

**manawa kūpono.** Opportune time, appropriate time, opportunity.

**manawale'a.** A generous heart; charity; to give freely; gratis, free.

**-manawanui, ho'omanawanui.** Patience, steadfastness, fortitude; to have patience; patient, steadfast; courageous and persevering; to try one's patience. *Lit.*, large disposition.

**mānele.** Sedan chair, palanquin, litter, stretcher; to carry on a stretcher, bier, sedan chair.

**manene.** Shuddery sensation of fear, as on looking over a precipice or if confronted by sudden danger; sensation of disgust or repugnance; to shudder, quake.

**mane'o.** Itch; itchy; smarting, as the throat; prickly; sexually titillated; ticklish; tickling. **ho'omane'o.** To cause to itch; to tickle.

**mānewanewa.** Grief, sorrow, mourning; exaggerated expression of grief. **ho'omānewanewa.** To display violent grief.

**mania. 1.** Shuddering sensation as on looking down from a great height, or on hearing a saw filed; dizziness; dizzy; to shudder. **2.** Inactive, drowsy, sleepy. **ho'omania.** To cause sleepiness, drowsiness.

**mānienie.** Bermuda grass *(Cynodon dactylon).*

**manini. 1.** Small striped surgeonfish *(Acanthurus triostegus),* very common on Hawaiian reefs. **2.** Stingy. *Modern slang.*

**manino.** Var. of *malino,* calm.

**manioka.** Cassava or manioc *(Manihot esculenta). Eng.*

**mano.** Many, numerous; four thousand; thick. Cf. *kini, lau.* **ho'omano.** To increase; to do repeatedly or persistently.

**manō.** Shark, general name.

**mānoa.** Thick, solid, vast; depth, thickness. **ho'omānoa.** To thicken.

**manō kihikihi.** Hammerhead shark *(Sphyrna zygaena). Lit.*, angular shark.

**manomano.** Redup. of *mano;* great; greatness; four thousand times four thousand.

**manu. 1.** Bird; any winged creature; wing of a kite. **2.** Canoe end-piece part.

**manuā.** Warship, man-of-war. *Eng.*

**manuahi.** Gratis, free of charge; adulterous. *Keiki manuahi,* illegitimate child.

**manu-'ai'mīkana, manu-'ai-papaia.** Linnet, house finch, or papaya bird *(Carpodacus mexicanus frontalis).* Lit., papaya-eating bird.

**manu aloha.** Lovebird, parakeet; parrot.

**manu kapalulu.** Quail. *Lit.,* whirr bird.

**manu kū.** Dove, pigeon. *Lit.,* coo bird *(Eng.)*

**manu mele.** Songbird, especially canary.

**manu 'ula'ula.** Cardinal, redbird. *Lit.,* red bird.

**mao.** Cleared as rain; alleviated, as grief; to clear up, as rain; to pass, as sadness.

**ma o.** Because of, due to, by means of, through. Cf. *ma,* at.

**ma'o. 1.** Green. Cf. *'ōma'oma'o.* **2.** Native cotton *(Gossypium sandvicense).* **3.** Same as *'ōma'o,* Hawaiian thrush.

**ma'ō.** See *'ō,* there.

**mā'oi.** Same as *maha'oi,* bold. **ho'omā'oi.** To act bold, impertinent.

**maoli.** Native, indigenous, genuine, true, real; very, really, truly. *Maika'i maoli,* very good indeed.

**maomao.** A sergeant fish *(Abudefduf abdominalis).*

**ma'oma'o.** Green, greenness. **ho'oma'oma'o.** To paint green, make green.

**mā'ona** (usually pronounced but not written *mā'ana*). Satisfied after eating, full, satisfying; to have eaten, to eat one's fill. **ho'omā'ona.** To eat all one wants, to feed all that is wanted.

**maopopo.** To understand, recognize; clear; plainly, clearly. **ho'omaopopo.** To understand; to make plain or clear, tell clearly; to pay attention in order to understand.

**māpala.** Marble *(Eng.),* granite.

**māpela, mabela.** Var. of *māpala.*

**māpu.** Fragrance, especially windblown fragrance; wafted; dipping, swooping.

**māpuana.** Same as *māpu.*

**māpuna.** Bubbling spring.

**mau. 1.** Always; steady; constant; to continue; continuation. **ho'omau.** To continue, keep on, persist, renew. **2.** Stopped, as menstruation; snagged, caught, as a fish or hook; grounded, as a canoe; stuck, stalled, as a car. **ho'omau.** To make fast, as an anchor in sand; to cause to be grounded, stopped. **3.** Particle marking plural used principally after the *k*-class possessives and demonstratives, numerals, and *he.*

**ma'ū.** Damp, wet, moist, cool, refreshing. **ho'oma'ū.** To dampen, moisten, irrigate, soak; to shade, cool.

**māua.** We, us (dual, exclusive).

**Maui.** Name of one of the Hawaiian islands. Cf. *Māui,* the demigod.

**Māui.** Name of the famous demigod and trickster who snared the sun and discovered fire.

**mauka.** See *uka,* inland.

**ma'ukele.** Rain forest.

**ma'ule.** Faint, fainthearted, dispirited. **ho'oma'ule.** To cause fainting; to faint; to feign fainting.

**mauli.** Life, heart, seat of life; ghost, spirit.

**mauli'awa.** Hiccough; dying gasp; to hiccough, gasp in dying.

**ma'uma'u.** Same as *'āma'uma'u,* ferns.

**mauna.** Moutain, mountainous region; mountainous.

**maunaloa.** Vines *(Dioclea wilsonii,* a sea bean, and *Canavalia cathartica).* Both, and especially the latter, have flowers used in intricate and beautiful leis; the beans are used for medicine.

**Mauna Loa.** Names of mountains on Hawai‘i and Moloka‘i and of a Moloka‘i village. *Lit.,* long mountain.

**maunu.** Bait; objects used in sorcery, as hair, spittle, nail parings, excreta, clothing, food leavings.

**māunu.** To moult; to change skin, as of snakes.

**mau‘u.** General name for grasses, sedges, rushes, herbs.

**mau‘u Kepanī.** Velvet grass *(Zoysia tenuifolia). Lit.,* Japanese grass.

**mau‘u malo‘o.** Hay, straw, any dry grass.

**māwae.** 1. Cleft, fissure, crack, as in rocks; to crack, split. 2. To separate, sort, select; to cleanse, as from defilement. Cf. *wae,* to select.

**mawaena.** See *waena.*

**mawaho.** See *waho.*

**me.** 1. With. *A me,* and. 2. Like, as. *Like me ‘oe,* like you. Cf. *mehe.*

**mea.** 1. Thing, person. Cf. *mea ‘ole.* 2. Possessor of. Cf. *mea ‘āina, mea hale.* 3. One who does, did, is, was (in compounds; see *mea hula, mea kia‘i, mea oli).* 4. What-d’you-call-it, so-and-so (said when one is at a loss for a word or name); such and such. *‘O mea mā,* so-and-so and the others. 5. Cause, reason; means of; because. *No ka mea,* because. 6. Reddish-brown, yellowish-white.

**mea ‘ai.** Food.

**mea ‘ai māmā.** Light refreshment.

**mea ‘ai momona.** Dessert.

**mea ‘āina.** Landowner.

**mea ‘ē.** Extraordinary, unusual, strange, wonderful; unusual person; stranger, alien.

**mea hale.** House owner; something belonging to a house.

**mea hou.** News; new. *He aha ka mea hou?* What’s new?

**mea hula.** Hula dancer.

**mea iki.** Trifle, inconsequential thing. *He mea iki,* just a trifle, you’re welcome [sometimes said in reply to “thank you”].

**mea inu.** Beverage, drink.

**mea kākau.** Writer, author.

**mea kanu.** A plant.

**mea kia‘i.** Guard, preserver, protection.

**mea koho.** Voter.

**mea nui.** Beloved person or thing; important person; thing of importance.

**mea ‘ole.** Inconsequential, trifling, insignificant; null and void; a mere nothing.

**mea oli.** Chanter of *oli;* one with an *oli* chant in his honor; *oli* chanter.

**mea ‘ono.** Cake of any kind, pastry, cookie. *Lit.,* delicious thing.

**mea ‘ono kuki.** Cookie.

**mea ‘ono pua‘a.** Chinese pork cake (today called *manapua).*

**mea ulu.** Vegetable, growing plant.

**me‘e.** Hero.

**mehameha.** Loneliness, solitariness, hushed silence; lonely, solitary; silent, as during the hush of taboo. **ho‘omehameha.** To cause silence, loneliness; to hush.

**mehe.** Like, as though.

**meheu.** Track, footprint, tracing; trodden, beaten, as a path; walked on. **ho‘omeheu.** To make a track.

**Mei.** May. *Eng.*

**meia.** Mayor. *Eng.*

**me ia.** With him, her.

**meka, mesa.** Mass. *Pule meka,* mass.

**mekala.** 1. Also **medala.** Medal. *Eng.* 2. Also **metala.** Metal *(Eng.);* tag, as a dog license.

**mekanika.** Mechanic. *Eng.*

**mekia.** 1. Major (the military title). *Eng.* 2. Also **Mesia.** *(Cap.)* Messiah. *Biblical.*

**Mekiko.** Mexico; Mexican. *Eng.*

**Melanikia.** Melanesia; Melanesian. *Eng.*

**mele. 1.** Song, chant of any kind, poem; to sing, chant (preceded by both *ke* and *ka*). **ho'omele.** To cause and sing or chant. **2.** Yellow. **3.** Merry. *Eng. Mele Kalikimaka,* Merry Christmas. **4.** *(Cap.)* Mary. *Eng.*

**mele aupuni.** National anthem.

**mele hai pule.** Hymn, religious song.

**mele ho'ohiamoe keiki.** Lullaby. *Lit.,* song to put children to sleep.

**mele ho'oipoipo.** Love song. *Lit.,* wooing song.

**mele ho'onānā keiki.** Lullaby, song to soothe children.

**mele inoa.** Name chant, i.e., chant composed in honor of a person, as a chief. Also called *inoa.*

**mele kāhea.** Chant for admittance to an old-time hula school. *Lit.,* calling song.

**Mele Kalikimaka.** Merry Christmas. *Eng.*

**mele kanikau.** Dirge, mourning song.

**melekule.** Pot marigold *(Calendula officinalis).*

**mele ma'i.** See *ma'i, 2.*

**melemele. 1.** Yellow, blond. **ho'omelemele.** To color or paint yellow. **2.** *(Cap.)* Name of a star.

**meli.** Bee, honey. *Nalo meli,* bee. *Wai meli,* honey.

**melia.** All species and varieties of *Plumeria;* plumeria, frangipangi.

**mene. 1.** Dullness, bluntness; dull, blunt, as a knife. **ho'omene.** To make dull; dull. **2.** To move back, step back, shrink.

**Menehune.** Legendary race of small people who worked at night building fishponds, roads, temples; if the work was not finished in one night, it remained unfinished.

**me'o.** To nag and tease, usually indirectly; to drool at the mouth while watching, as food being prepared; to linger about with greedy eyes.

**me'ome'o.** Redup. of *me'o.*

**mī. 1.** Urine; to urinate (less used than *mimi*). **2.** Seventh note in musical scale, ti. **3.** Mister. *Eng. Mī Laiana,* Mr. Lyons.

**-mia.** Suffix corresponding to *'ia,* but closely bound to a base. See *inumia.*

**mihi.** Repentance; to repent, apologize, be sorry, regret; to confess, as to a priest.

**mika.** Mister. *Eng.*

**mīkana.** Papaya *(Carica papaya).*

**mikanele.** Missionary. *Eng.* Also *mikinele, mikionali.* **ho'omikanele.** To act as a missionary; to be a goody-goody.

**miki. 1.** Quick, active, nimble, prompt, alert, fast and efficient in work; speed, alertness. **2.** To suck in, dip in; to shrink, as clothes or as salt beef in boiling; to spring together, as sides of a steel trap; to draw in, as an octopus; to recede, as an undertow; evaporated, as water by boiling.

**miki'ala.** Alert, prompt; early on hand.

**miki'ao.** Claw, nail, as of finger or toe.

**mikilana, misilana.** Chinese rice flower *(Aglaia odorata),* a shrub with dark, shiny leaves and fragrant flowers. *(Chinese, mei-sui-lan).*

**mikimiki.** Redup. of *miki, 1, 2.*

**mikinele.** Same as *mikanele,* missionary.

**mīkini.** Machine *(Eng.),* motor, engine.

**mīkini e ho'āhu 'ikena, hana makemekena, ho'okō kauoha.** Computer. *Lit.,* machine to store knowledge, do mathematics, execute orders.

**mīkini helu.** Adding machine, comptometer.

**mīkini holoi.** Washing machine.

**mīkini humuhumu.** Sewing machine.

**mīkini kikokiko hua.** Typewriter.

**mīkini ʻoki mauʻu.** Lawn mower. *Lit.,* grass-cutting machine.

**mīkini paʻi nūpepa.** Printing press. *Lit.,* machine to print newspapers.

**mikinolia.** Magnolia.

**mikioi.** Dainty and neat in craftsmanship, or in doing anything; excellently made, as result of workmanship. **hoʻomikioi.** To do neatly and skillfully.

**mikiona, misiona.** Mission. *Eng.*

**mikionali, misionari.** Missionary. *Eng.* Also, *mikanele, mikinele.*

**miko.** 1. Seasoned with salt; salted. **hoʻomiko.** To season with salt. 2. To kink, snarl, become ensnared; kink.

**mile.** Mile. *Eng.*

**mili.** To handle, feel of, fondle, caress, as a beloved child; fondled, beloved.

**mili ʻapa.** Slow, dilatory.

**mililani.** To praise, exalt; to give thanks; to treat as a favorite.

**milimili.** Redup. of *mili;* toy, plaything; favorite, beloved.

**miliona.** Million. *Eng.*

**milo.** 1. A shade tree *(Thespesia populnea)* growing usually near the beach; its beautiful wood is made into calabashes. 2. Curl; to curl, twist, as sennit strands; to whirl, as water; abortion.

**milu.** 1. Soft, rotten. 2. *(Cap.)* Underworld, ruler of underworld.

**mimi.** Urine; to urinate. **hoʻomimi.** To cause urination; to help to urinate, as a child.

**mina.** Same as *minamina, 1, 2, 3.*

**minamina.** 1. To regret, be sorry; to grieve for something that is lost; regret, sorrow. 2. To prize greatly, value greatly, especially something in danger of being lost; value, worth. 3. Saving, economical, miserly; covetous of things that one values; economy, thrift.

**mino.** Dimple, depression, dent; dimpled, wrinkled.

**minoʻaka.** Smile; to smile. *Lit.,* laughing dimple. **hoʻominoʻaka.** To cause to smile; to smile a little.

**minuke, minute.** Minute. *Eng.*

**mio.** 1. To disappear swiftly; to move swiftly, as a stream of water; to make off with quickly; to steal; to depart quickly. 2. Narrow, pointed, tapering.

**miona.** 1. Swift disappearance or movement. 2. Crease, as in the buttocks.

**miula.** Mule, ass. *Eng.*

**miulana.** Orange or white champak or mulang *(Michelia champaca* and *M. longifolia),* tall trees from the Himalayas related to the magnolia; they bear very fragrant orange or yellow flowers. The white-flowered species is the Chinese *pak-lan,* also called *pakalana* by Hawaiians.

**mō.** Short for *moku, 1, 2. Mōkapu* (place name), taboo district.

**mō-.** 1. Short for *moʻo,* succession. Cf. *moʻolelo,* story. 2. Short for *moʻo,* lizard. *Mōʻiliʻili* (place name), pebble lizard.

**moa.** Chicken.

**moʻa.** Cooked; burned, as by sun; cooking. **hoʻomoʻa.** To cook.

**Moaʻe.** Trade wind. See *aʻe, 2.*

**mōakaaka, moakaka.** Clear, plain, intelligible; clarity. Cf. *akaaka.* **hoʻomōakaaka.** Explanation, definition; to explain clearly, clarify, define.

**moa kāne.** Rooster, cock. *Lit.,* male chicken.

**moamoa.** To act the part of a cock; to care for, attend to; to supply with food, as a child or ward. **hoʻomoamoa.** To accompany, as a cock with hens; to care for, protect, cherish. 2. Same as *pahu, 5,* boxfishes.

**moana.** 1. Ocean, open sea. 2. Campground, consultation place for chiefs. **hoʻomoana.** To camp. 3. Broad, wide, extended, expansive, spread out. **hoʻomoana.** To spread down, as mats.

**moani.** Light or gentle breeze, usually associated with fragrance; wafted fragrance; to blow perfume.

**moano.** Two species of goatfish *(Parupeneus multifasciatus* and *P. chryserydros).*

**moa wahine.** Hen. *Lit.,* female chicken.

**moe.** 1. To sleep, lie down; to lie in wait, ambush; to prostrate oneself, as before a chief; to lay down, as cards; to sit on eggs. **hoʻomoe.** To put to sleep, to lay down, to set, as a hen or fish net; to "drop" a matter; to defer, postpone; to table, as a motion. 2. To marry, mate with, sleep with; marriage. **hoʻomoe.** To arrange a match. 3. Bed, sleeping place. 4. Dream.

**moe ʻino.** Nightmare; bad dream; to toss, turn while sleeping.

**moe ipo.** To have an affair; to sleep with a lover; to commit adultery.

**moekolohe.** Adultery; to commit adultery, fornicate; adulterous. *Lit.,* illegal mating. **hoʻomoe-kolohe.** To lead into adultery.

**moe lepo.** Earth sleeper; to sleep in the earth. *Fig.,* the dead; dirty, shiftless individual.

**moemoe.** Ambush; to lie in ambush; to lurk. **hoʻomoemoe.** To cause to lie down; to hush or put to sleep; to arrange a match.

**moena.** Mat. Cf. *moe,* to lie down.

**moena weleweka.** Soft carpet of any kind. *Lit.,* velvet *(Eng.)* mat.

**moe paipai.** Cradle. *Lit.,* rocking bed.

**moeʻuhane.** Dream; to dream. *Lit.,* soul sleep.

**mōhā.** Fully developed, as a flower; of fine physique, as a person.

**mōhai.** Sacrifice, offering; to offer a sacrifice. Cf. *hai.*

**mōhai aloha.** Free-will offering; love offering.

**mōhai hoʻomalu.** Peace offering.

**mohala.** Unfolded, as flower petals; blossoming, opening up; blooming, as a youth just past adolescence; shining forth, as a light; appearing clear, as a thought; evolved, developed. **hoʻomohala.** To open, unfold, spread, recover; development, etc.

**mōhalu.** 1. Loose, slack; at ease, unrestrained, at liberty; comfortable. *Hale mōhalu,* house of relaxation. **hoʻomōhalu.** To slacken, relax; to cause relaxation, ease. 2. To open, unfold, as flowers. Also *mohala.*

**moho.** 1. Candidate, as in politics; representative selected to participate in a race, or wrestling or betting contest. 2. Hawaiian rail *(Pennula sandwichensis),* an extinct flightless bird. 3. To unfold, of leaves.

**moi.** Threadfin fish *(Polydactylus sexfilis).*

**mōʻī.** King, sovereign, ruler, queen.

**mōʻī wahine.** Queen.

**mōkākī.** Scattered, littered; disorder.

**mokihana.** A native tree *(Pelea anisata),* found only on Kauaʻi; its small, leathery, anise-scented fruits are strung in leis.

**mōkio.** 1. To pucker or contract, as the lips for whistling, or the nostrils after diving. 2. Also **motio.** Motion. *Eng.*

**moko.** Same as *mokomoko.*

**mokomoko.** Rough, hand-to-hand fighting of any kind, whether boxing *(kuʻi)* or free-for-all wrestling; a fighter, boxer; to box, fight.

**moku.** 1. To be cut, severed, amputated, broken in two, as a rope; broken loose, as a stream after heavy rains, or as a bound person. *Moku ka pawa,* dawn has broken. **hoʻomoku.** To cut and divide; a cutting, division, separation. 2. District, island, section; forest, grove; severed portion, fragment, cut. Cf. *mokupuni, momoku.* **hoʻomoku.** To place an individual in charge of a *moku,* district. 3. Ship.

**mokuahi.** Steamship. *Lit.,* fire ship.

**mokuʻāina.** State, as of the United States; district, island.

**mokuhia.** Passive/imperative of *moku, 1.*

**moku kaua.** Battleship, warship.

**moku kia kahi.** One-masted ship, sloop.

**moku kia kolu.** Three-masted ship, bark.

**moku kia lua.** Two-masted ship, as a schooner; brig.

**moku kolo.** Tugboat.

**moku lawe ʻōhua.** Passenger ship.

**moku lawe ukana.** Freighter.

**mokulele.** Airplane.

**mokumāhu.** Steamship.

**mokuna.** Division, boundary, as of land; severed portion, cut piece, part; chapter, section, as of a book.

**moku ʻō koholā.** Whaling ship. *Lit.,* ship for piercing whales.

**moku pāpapa.** Low reef island.

**moku peʻa.** Sailing vessel.

**mokupuni.** Island.

**mole.** 1. Tap root, main root; bottom, as of a pit or of a glass; ancestral root; foundation, source, cause. 2. Smooth, round, bald. **hoʻomole.** To smooth.

**mōlehu.** Twilight, dusk; tipsy. Cf. *lehu,* ashes.

**molemole.** Redup. of *mole, 2.* **hoʻomolemole.** To smooth.

**Molemona, Moremona.** Mormon. *Eng.*

**mōlia.** To set apart for the gods; to sacrifice or offer to the gods; to bless; to curse.

**Molokaʻi.** Name of a Hawaiian island.

**molowā.** Lazy.

**momi.** Pearl.

**momoe.** Redup. and plural of *moe, 1, 2.*

**momoku.** Redup. of *moku, 1;* broken fragments, severed pieces; breaking forth, as of water from a dam.

**momona.** 1. Fat; fertile, rich, as soil; fruitful. **hoʻomomona.** To fatten, fertilize. *Hoʻomomona lepo,* fertilizer; to fertilize the soil. 2. Sweet. **hoʻomomona.** To sweeten; candy.

**moni.** To swallow, gulp down, absorb. *Moni ka hāʻae,* to water at the mouth; *lit.,* swallow the saliva.

**moʻo.** 1. Lizard, reptile of any kind, dragon, serpent; water supernatural (extremely common in legends). 2. Succession, series, especially a genealogical line. Cf. *moʻo aliʻi, moʻo ʻōlelo.* **hoʻomoʻo.** To follow a course, continue a procedure. 3. Story, tradition (less common than *moʻolelo*). 4. Narrow strip of land, smaller than an *ʻili.* Also called *moʻo ʻāina.*

**moʻo aliʻi.** Genealogy of chiefs, history of chiefs; chiefly line of succession.

**moʻo kūʻauhau.** Genealogical succession.

**moʻolelo.** Story, tale, history, tradition, legend, journal, record, article; minutes, as of a meeting (from *moʻo ʻōlelo,* succession of talk).

**moʻolelo ʻahaʻōlelo lāhui.** Congressional record. *Lit.,* national legislative journal.

**mo'olelo haku wale.** Fiction; an invented story.

**mo'olelo pōkole.** Short story, anecdote.

**mo'o lio.** Sea horse. *Lit.,* horse reptile.

**mo'o'ōlelo.** Same as *mo'olelo.*

**mo'opuna.** Grandchild; grand-niece or grandnephew; relatives two generations later, whether blood or adopted; descendant; posterity. *Kāna mo'opuna,* his grandchild. **ho'omo'opuna.** To claim a *mo'opuna* relationship; to address and treat as a *mo'opuna,* as from affection.

**mo'opuna kāne.** Grandson.

**mo'opuna wahine.** Granddaughter.

**mouo.** Buoy; float, as on a fishing net; board or anything to float on; to lie at anchor.

**mū.** 1. General name for destructive insects that eat wood, cloth, or plants; cane borer; caterpillar in the cocoon stage. 2. Silent; to shut the lips and make no sound. **ho'omū.** To sit in silence; to refuse to answer; speechless. 3. Gathered together, of crowds of people. Cf. *mumulu.* **ho'omū.** Same as above; multitude; to cause a gathering. 4. *(Cap.)* Legendary people, Kaua'i. 5. Bigeye emperor fish *(Monotaxis grandoculis).*

**mua.** Before; front; first, foremost; previously, beforehand; oldest, older brother or sister; senior branch of a family; leader, senior partner, senior; more than. *I mua! Mamua!* Forward! **ho'omua.** To push forward, to do something first; to claim to be senior.

**mūhe'e.** 1. Cuttlefish. 2. Mother-of-pearl lure.

**mui.** Assembled, gathered together; an assembly.

**mūkā.** Sound of lips popped open; clicking sound, as in urging a horse to speed up; smack, as in eating.

**mūkī.** Sucking noise made by pursing the lips and expelling or drawing in the air, as in kissing; to suck into the mouth, as when lighting a pipe; to sip, as birds sip honey.

**mūki'i.** To tie; tether. Also *nāki'i, hīki'i.*

**muku.** Cut short, shortened, amputated; at an end, ceased; anything cut off short.

**mukumuku.** Redup. of *muku.*

**muli.** After, behind, afterward; last, following behind; younger; youngest; stern of a canoe. *Mamuli o kona akamai,* because of his cleverness.

**muli hope.** Youngest child; very last.

**muliwai.** River, river mouth; pool near mouth of a stream, as behind a sand bar, enlarged by ocean water left there by high tide; estuary.

**mumuhu.** Buzzing, humming sound, as of flies; to swarm.

**mumuku.** Redup. of *muku;* amputated, maimed; premature, as a baby.

**mumule.** Speechless, silent, taciturn, mute, sullen, sulky.

**mumulu.** To swarm, as flies, bees, mosquitoes.

**mu'o.** Leaf bud; to bud, of a leaf; younger branch of a family.

**mu'umu'u.** 1. Cut off, shortened, amputated, maimed; person with arms or legs missing, amputee. *Hula mu'umu'u,* a sitting dance. 2. A woman's underslip or chemise; a loose gown, so called because formerly the yoke was omitted (cf. *mu'umu'u, 1),* and sometimes the sleeves were short. Cf. *holokū.*

# N

**na.** By, for, belonging to (a-class).

**-na. 1.** Nominalizer. **2.** Passive/imperative suffix. **3.** Third person singular possessive.

**nā. 1.** Calmed, quieted; settled, as a claim. **ho'onā.** To relieve pain, soothe, quiet; to settle a claim. **2.** To moan, groan, wail. **3.** Plural definite article preceding nouns. **4.** Demonstrative particle indicating the addressee.

**na'ana'au.** Small intestine.

**na'au.** Intestines, bowels; mind, heart; of the heart or mind.

**na'auao.** Learned, intelligent; learning, science. Cf. *'imi na'auao. Lit.,* daylight mind. **ho'ona'auao.** To educate, instruct; educational.

**na'au ho'oki'eki'e.** Conceited, proud; proud heart.

**na'au 'ino'ino.** Malicious; evil heart.

**na'aukake.** Sausage, wiener. *Lit.,* sausage *(Eng.)* intestines.

**na'aumoa.** Appendix. *Lit.,* chicken intestines.

**na'aupō.** Ignorant, unenlightened; ignorance. *Lit.,* night mind. Cf. *na'auao.* **ho'ona-'aupō.** To cause or feign ignorance; ignorant.

**na'au pono.** Upright, just; rightminded.

**nae.** Shortness of breath; to puff.

**na'e.** But, yet, furthermore, still.

**naha. 1.** Bent, curved, bowlegged. **2.** Union of a chief with his half-sister; their offspring was entitled to the *kapu noho.*

**nahā.** Cracked, broken, as a dish; smashed to bits, as masonry; to act as a purgative; to split. *Lā'au nahā,* purgative. **ho'onahā.** To smash, crack, split; to take a purgative.

**nahae.** Torn, rent; tear; to tear. See *mahae.*

**naheka, nahesa.** Snake.

**nahele.** Forest, grove, wilderness; trees, shrubs, vegetation, weeds.

**nāhelehele.** Redup. of *nahele;* weeds.

**nahenahe.** Soft, sweet, as music or a gentle voice; soft, as fine cloth; soft-spoken.

**nāhi. 1.** Some, few, the little (contraction of *nā,* the, and *wahi,* little). **2.** The fires (contraction of *nā ahi*).

**naho.** Hollow; deep-set, as eyes of a starving person; eye sockets.

**naholo.** To flee, of several; to run away; gone away. **ho'onaholo.** To cause to run, to chase.

**nāholoholo.** Redup. of *naholo.*

**nahu.** To bite; to sting, as beating rain; pain, as of stomach ache or of childbirth. **ho'onahu.** To bite; cause a stomach ache.

**nahunahu.** Redup. of *nahu;* to suffer pangs of childbirth.

**na'i. 1.** To conquer, take by force; conqueror. **2.** To strive to obtain, endeavor to examine or understand.

**nai'a.** Porpoise.

**naio. 1.** Pinworm, as in the rectum; larvae, as of mosquitoes. **2.** The bastard sandalwood *(Myoporum sandwicense),* a native tree.

**naka. 1.** To quiver, shake, as jello or as with cold or fear; shaky, unsteady, shivering. **2.** To crack open, as earth from the heat. **3.** A sea creature.

**nakeke.** Rattling, as of a window; rustling, as of paper. **ho'ona-keke.** To make a rattling or rustling noise.

**nakele.** Soft, boggy, slippery; yielding, sinking in.

**naki.** Same as *nāki'i.*

**nāki'i.** To tie. Cf. *nīki'i.*

**nāki'iki'i.** Redup. of *nāki'i.*

**-nakoa. ho'onakoa.** Brave, daring.

**nākolo.** Rumbling, roaring, as of surf or thunder; reverberating.

**nākolokolo.** Redup. of *nākolo.*

**naku.** To root, wallow, as a hog; to tread, trample, push, as through mud or grass; to struggle; to roil, as water.

**nāku'i.** To rumble, roar, thrum; rumbling; beating, as of the heart.

**nakulu.** Dripping, as water; patter, clatter, echo; rumbling, as the stomach; grumbling; to spread or circulate, as rumor.

**nali.** To nibble, gnaw.

**nalinali.** Redup. of *nali.*

**nalo. 1.** Lost, vanished, concealed, forgotten; to pass away, disappear. **ho'onalo.** To cause to be lost. **2.** The common housefly and other similar insects.

**nalohia.** Passive/imperative of *nalo, 1.*

**nalo hope 'eha.** Hornet and other Hymenoptera. *Lit.,* fly with stinging posterior.

**nalo meli.** Honey bee. *Lit.,* honey fly.

**nalo meli mō'ī wahine.** Queen bee.

**nalonalo.** Redup. of *nalo, 1.* **ho-'onalonalo.** Hidden; to cause to disapear. Cf. *'ōlelo ho'onalonalo, mana'o ho'onalonalo.*

**nalowale.** Lost, gone, forgotten, vanished; disappeared.

**nalu. 1.** Wave, surf; full of waves; to form waves. **ho'onalu.** To form waves. **2.** To ponder. **3.** Amnion, amniotic fluid.

**nalulu.** Dull headache; dull pain in the abdomen. **ho'onalulu.** To cause a pain in head or stomach.

**namu. 1.** Unintelligible muttering, gibberish; any foreign language, especially English; to speak gibberish or a foreign language. *Namu haole,* English. **ho'onamu.** To pretend to speak in a foreign language, to mutter, speak gibberish. **2.** To nibble; to chew with closed mouth.

**namunamu.** Redup. of *namu, 1, 2;* to grumble, complain.

**namu pa'i 'ai, namu pa'i kalo.** Pidgin English. *Lit.,* hard-poi gibberish, hard-taro gibberish.

**nāna.** For him, her, it; by him, her, it (*a*-class).

**nanā.** Snarling; to strut, as one looking for a gight. **ho'onanā.** Aggressive, looking for a fight, threatening.

**nānā.** To look at, observe, see; to care for, pay attention to, take care of. **ho'onānā.** To cause to look, show.

**nānahu.** Var. of *lānahu.* **ho'onānahu.** To turn into charcoal, as burnt wood.

**nānaina.** General appearance, view.

**nānālā.** Sunflower. *Lit.,* sungazer.

**nānā maka.** To look at without helping; indifference to one in trouble.

**nananana. 1.** Spider. **2.** Var. of *lanalana, 1, 2.*

**nānā 'ole.** Disregard, heedless disregard; to pay no attention to.

**nānā pono.** To watch carefully, pay particular attention to, note carefully.

**nane.** Riddle, puzzle; parable, allegory; to riddle, speak in parables. **ho'onane.** To make riddles, speak in parables.

**nanea.** Of absorbing interest; fascinating, enjoyable; repose, leisure; relaxed; engaged, busy with. **ho'onanea.** To pass the time in ease, peace, and pleasure.

**naneha'i.** Problem, riddle to be solved. *Lit.,* telling riddle.

**nane huna.** Hidden riddle, conundrum.

**nanenane.** Redup. of *nane.* **ho'o-nanenane.** Same as *ho'onane;* puzzling, riddling; figurative.

**nani.** Beauty, glory, splendor; beautiful, pretty, splendid. **ho-'onani.** To beautify, adorn, decorate; to glorify, honor, exalt; decorative, glorifying.

**nani ahiahi.** The four o'clock

*(Mirabilis jalapa). Lit.,* evening beauty.

**nani ali‘i.** Allamandas with large yellow flowers *(Allamanda cathartica* and some varieties). *Lit.,* chiefly beauty.

**nani mau loa.** An everlasting or strawflower *(Helichrysum bracteatum);* also called *pua pepa.*

**nanue.** Var. of *nenue.*

**nao. 1.** Ripple; ridge, as of twilled cloth or a tapa beater; groove; thread of a screw; grooved. *Kui nao,* screw; *lit.,* nail with thread. **2.** To thrust the hands into an opening, as in fishing; to probe.

**na‘o.** Spittle, phlegm, mucus; slimy.

**naoano. 1.** Ants. Also called *nonanona.* **2.** Redup. of *nao, 1, 2.*

**na‘ona‘o.** Redup. of *na‘o.*

**naonao lele.** Termite. *Lit.,* flying ant.

**naowili.** A bit for a drill. *Lit.,* twisting thread.

**napa. 1.** Uneven, bent, crooked, out of shape; warped. **2.** Flexible, springy, elastic. **3.** Delay. **ho‘onapa.** To cause delay.

**napanapa.** Redup. of *napa, 1, 2;* to writhe and twist, as an eel.

**nape.** Bending and swaying, as coconut fronds; surging, as the sea; to rise and fall, as the chest in breathing; yielding, springy.

**napenape.** Redup. of *nape;* fluttering, flickering.

**napo‘o.** Cavity, hollow, depression; armpit; to sink, go down, set (of the sun), to enter or sink out of sight.

**nāpo‘opo‘o.** Redup. of *napo‘o.*

**nau.** To chew, munch, masticate, gnash the teeth; grinder, as of a sugar mill. *Nau kamu,* to chew gum.

**nāu.** Yours, belonging to you, for you, by you (singular, *a*-class).

**na‘u.** Mine, belonging to me, for me, by me (singular, *a*-class).

**naue, nauwe.** To move, shake, tremble; to quake, as the earth; to vibrate; to march; loose and insecure, as a tooth. **ho‘onaue.** To cause to shake, revolve, sway, rock, etc.

**nāueue.** Redup. of *naue.*

**nauki.** Impatient, irritable, cross. **ho‘onauki.** Causing irritation; aggravating, annoying.

**nāuki.** Intensive of *nauki;* vexation, anger.

**nāukiuki.** Redup. of *nauki.* **ho‘o-nāukiuki.** Redup. of *ho‘o-nauki.*

**nāulu.** Sudden shower; showery; to shower.

**naupaka.** Native species of mountain or seashore shrubs *(Scaevola);* the small, whitish flowers look like half flowers.

**naupaka kahakai.** The beach *naupaka.*

**naupaka kuahiwi.** All mountain species of *naupaka.*

**nāwali.** Weak, feeble, infirm, limp; weakness. **ho‘onāwali.** To cause weakness; to enfeeble; to feign weakness. See *wali.*

**nāwaliwali.** Redup. of *nāwali,* weak.

**ne‘e.** Moving along little by little or by fits and starts; to step, hitch along; to push along, as work; to squirm. **ho‘one‘e.** To cause to move, hitch along, push ahead.

**ne‘e hope.** To retreat, move backward; to back up, as a car. **ho‘o-ne‘ehope.** To back up, as a car. *Ho‘one‘ehope i ke ka‘a,* back up the car.

**ne‘emua.** To advance, go forward, progress. **ho‘one‘emua.** To cause progress.

**ne‘ene‘e.** Redup. of *ne‘e;* to edge along. *Ne‘ene‘e ā pili,* move close by, snuggle.

**nehe. 1.** To rustle, as leaves or the sea; rumbling; groping with the hands, as in searching. **2.** Taffeta, so called because it rustles *(nehe).*

**nehinei.** Yesterday (usually preceded by particle *i*).

**nehu.** Anchovy *(Stolephorus purpureus)*, similar to the herring; the most important tuna-bait fish in Hawaii.

**nei.** **1.** To rumble, as an earthquake; sighing, as of the wind. **2.** This here. Cf. *e ia nei, ke* (verb) *nei. Hawaiʻi nei,* this [beloved] Hawaiʻi. **3.** Last. *I ka pō nei,* last night.

**neʻi.** Here, this place (often preceded by *i, ma, o*). Cf. *ʻaneʻi, ʻoneʻi.*

**neia.** This. Similar to *kēia* (mostly Biblical).

**nele.** Lacking, destitute, deprived of, needy, wanting, without. **hoʻonele.** To deprive, make destitute; to deny, impeach.

**nema.** Criticizing; critical; to criticize, find fault, censure.

**nemanema.** Redup. of *nema.*

**nemo.** Smooth, smoothly polished; rounded smooth, bare. **hoʻonemo.** To polish, smooth.

**nemonemo.** Redup. of *nemo.*

**nene.** Var. of *manene.*

**nēnē.** **1.** To chirp, as a cricket; to croak, as a mudhen; crying, as in distress; rumor, gossip; to be attracted to; to cherish. **hoʻonēnē.** Same as above. **2.** Hawaiian goose *(Branta sandvicensis).*

**nenue.** Rudder or pilot fish *(Kyphosus bigibbus* and *K. vaigiensis);* also *nanue.*

**neo.** Empty, bare, desolated; nothing, naught; getting nowhere. **hoʻoneo.** To lay waste, make destitute; desolation.

**newa.** **1.** Fighting club; policeman's club. **2.** To reel, stagger; dizziness, vertigo; dizzy. **3.** *(Cap.)* A constellation, probably the Southern Cross.

**newanewa.** Redup. of *newa,* 2.

**newe.** Plump; filled out, full, as a pregnant woman.

**newenewewe.** Redup. of *newe.*

**nia.** Smooth, round, bald; calm, as a smooth sea. **hoʻonia.** To make smooth and even, as in carving.

**nīao.** Mewing, purring.

**nīʻau.** **1.** Coconut-leaf midrib; rib of an umbrella. **2.** Ramrod.

**nīʻau kāhili.** Broom made of coconut-leaf midribs tied together at one end.

**nīʻau kani.** A true Jew's harp. *Lit.,* sounding coconut midrib.

**nīʻaupiʻo.** Offspring of the marriage of a high-born brother and sister. *Lit.,* bent coconut midrib, i.e., of the same stalk.

**nīʻau pūlumi.** Broom straw. *Lit.,* broom *(Eng.)* coconut-leaf midrib.

**nīele.** To keep asking questions; inquisitive; to quiz, pump. As an exclamation of annoyance: you are too inquisitive! **hoʻonīele.** Questioning, especially by leading up indirectly rather than directly; curious.

**nieniele.** Redup. of *nīele;* to investigate.

**nihi.** **1.** Edge, brink, rim, border; sideways, on edge, standing on edge. Also *lihi.* **2.** Stealthily, quietly; creeping silently and softly, as on tiptoe; circumspect; with discrimination.

**nihinihi.** Redup. of *nihi, 1, 2;* fastidious.

**niho.** Tooth; toothed; nipper, as of an insect; claw, as of a crab; tusk; stones set interlocking, as in a wall; biting, of the teeth. **hoʻoniho.** To lay stones interlocking; to set stones, as in a fence.

**nihoa.** **1.** Passive/imperative of *niho;* toothed, notched, jagged; firmly imbedded and interlocked, as stones in a fence. **2.** *(Cap.)* Name of an island between Kauaʻi and Midway.

**niho ʻelepani.** Elephant tusk, ivory.

**niho hoʻokomo.** False tooth.

**niho hu‘i.** Toothache; having a toothache.

**nihoniho.** Set with teeth, as a saw; toothed, notched; scalloped, as lace; scalloped, as potatoes. **ho‘onihoniho.** To make into a toothed, scalloped, notched design; to make teeth.

**niho ‘oki.** Shark's-tooth knife, used formerly for wood carving and cutting hair. *Lit.*, cutting tooth.

**niho palaoa.** Whale tooth, whale-tooth pendant, a symbol of royalty.

**niho pua‘a.** Pig tusk, especially that worn as an ornament.

**niki.** Same as *nīki‘i*.

**nīki‘i.** To tie, as a rope or knot. Also *hīki‘i, hīki‘iki‘i, mūki‘i, nāki‘i, nāki‘iki‘i, niki, nikiniki*.

**nikiniki.** Redup. of *niki*.

**ninaninau.** Redup. of *nīnau*.

**nīnau.** Question; to ask a question; interrogation; interrogating. Cf. *noi*, to ask for something. **ho‘onīnau.** To ask a question; to have questions asked.

**nīnau hō‘ike.** Interrogation, usually oral; quiz, examination; catechism. *Lit.*, revealing questions.

**nini. 1.** Ointment, balm; to apply ointment; to pour; spill. **2.** Fence, line of stones; pavement. Cf. *pānini*.

**ninini.** To pour.

**niniu.** Redup. of *niu, 2;* to spin; worried, sad; dizzy; dizziness; blurred, indistinct. **ho‘oniniu.** To cause dizziness; to spin, as a top.

**ni‘o.** Highest point; to reach the summit.

**nīoi.** Any kind of red pepper.

**nīoi pepa.** Chili pepper.

**nīoi pūha‘uha‘u.** Bell pepper or sweet pepper.

**nipo. 1.** To yearn for; to be in love with; to love, long for. **ho‘onipo.** To make love, court. **2.** Drowsy, languid, sleepy. **ho‘onipo.** To cause sleepiness.

**niponipo.** Redup. of *nipo, 1, 2.*

**niu. 1.** The coconut. *Wai niu,* coconut water. *Wai o ka niu,* coconut cream. **2.** Spinning, whirling. Cf. *niniu.*

**niuhi.** A large, gray, man-eating shark.

**niu kahiki.** Date palm. *Lit.*, foreign coconut.

**niu malo‘o.** Copra, dry coconut meat.

**no.** Of, for, because of; resulting from, concerning, about, from (*o*-class). *No laila lākou?* They are from there?

**nō.** Intensifying particle. Very, quite. *Maika‘i nō,* quite good, very good. *‘O au noho‘i,* really me.

**noa.** Freed of taboo, released from restrictions; to adjourn, as a meeting. **ho‘onoa.** To cause to cease, of a taboo; to free from taboo.

**noe.** Mist, rain spray; to form a mist. *Ua noe,* misty rain. **ho‘onoe.** To form mist, vapor, fog.

**no‘eau.** Clever, skillful, wise. *‘Ōlelo no‘eau,* wise or entertaining proverb, saying.

**nohea.** Handsome, lovely, of fine appearance.

**no hea.** From where, whence.

**noho. 1.** Seat, chair, stool, bench, saddle; to sit. **2.** To live, dwell, stay, marry, be in session. **ho‘onoho.** To take up residence; to install, establish, locate, rule; to set, as type. **3.** To be, act as (followed by a complement). See *noho ali‘i.*

**noho ali‘i.** Throne; reign, chieftainship; to reign, to act as chief.

**noho aloha.** Dwelling at peace; friendly relationship.

**noho ‘ana.** Conduct, bearing, way of life, term of office.

**noho aupuni.** To rule; a reign.

**noho hale.** House occupant.

**noho huila.** Wheel chair.

**noho'i.** Intensifying particle *(nō + ho'i).*

**noho'ie.** Wicker chair.

**noho kai.** Dweller on the seashore; to live by the sea.

**noho kālele.** Armchair.

**noho kāne.** To marry, of a woman; to live with a man.

**noho lio.** Saddle.

**noho loa.** To remain long, permanently, for life.

**nohomālie.** The yellow oleander or be-still tree *(Thevetia peruviana). Lit.,* be still.

**nohona.** Dwelling, residence, seat, mode of life, relationship.

**nohonoho.** Redup. of *noho.* **ho-'onohonoho.** Redup. of *ho'onoho;* to arrange, classify.

**noho paipai.** Rocking chair.

**noho papa.** Arranged in order, as feathers in a hatband, shingles on a roof. **ho'onoho papa.** To arrange, put in order.

**noho pono.** Sitting properly, behaving well.

**noho uka.** Upland dweller; to live inland.

**noho wahine.** To marry, of a man; to live with a woman.

**noho wale.** To do nothing; to stay without working or payment.

**nohu.** Scorpionfish *(Scorpaenopsis cacopsis* and other scorpaenids), which resemble the tropical Pacific stonefish and have poisonous spines.

**noi.** To ask for something, make a request, make a motion; petition. Cf. *nīnau,* to ask a question. Cf. *noinoi, nonoi.*

**no'iau.** Var. of *no'eau.*

**noi'i.** To seek information or knowledge in great detail.

**noinoi.** Redup. of *noi.*

**noio.** The white-capped noddy or Hawaiian tern *(Anous tenuirostris).*

**nōkali, notari.** Notary. *Eng.*

**no ka mea.** Because, whereas (in legal documents). *Lit.,* because of the thing.

**noke.** To persist, continue, persevere.

**no ke aha?** Why? See *aha.*

**nokenoke.** Redup. of *noke.*

**no laila.** See *laila.*

**nolu.** Soft, yielding.

**nona.** His, hers, its; for him, her, it.

**nonanona. 1.** Ant (same as more common *naonao).* **2.** Gnat.

**noni.** Indian mulberry *(Morinda citrifolia),* a small tree or shrub, formerly useful to Hawaiians as a source of dyes, food, and medicines.

**nono. 1.** Red, redness; rosy-cheeked; red-faced, as from sunburn; sunburned, bronzed. **2.** Full of holes, perforated, moth-eaten; oozing, as water in the sand; seepage.

**nonoi.** Redup. of *noi.*

**no'ono'o.** Thought, reflection, meditation, thinking; to think, reflect; to consider, as a case at law; thoughtful. *No'ono'o hāiki,* narrow-minded; a narrow mind. **ho'ono'ono'o.** To cause to think, reflect; reminiscent.

**nou. 1.** To throw, pelt, pitch, hurl; buffeting, throwing; pitcher. **ho'onou.** To throw, pelt; to put forth physical effort. **2.** For you, yours, in your honor (singular, *o*-class).

**no'u.** For me, mine, in my honor *(o*-class). *No'u kēlā,* give that to me.

**Nowemapa.** November. *Eng.*

**nū. 1.** To cough; to roar, as wind; grunting, as of pigs; cooing, as of doves; patter, as of rain; groaning, deep sighing, moaning; worried, grief-stricken. **ho-'onū.** To moan, groan, sigh, roar, etc. **2.** The letter *n. Eng.* **3.** News. *Eng.* See *nū hou.*

**nuha.** Sulky, sullen; to sulk, balk. Cf. *nunuha.* **ho'onuha.** To cause to sulk; to sulk.

**nuhe.** Same as *'enuhe.*

**nū hou.** News, recent or late news. *Nū hou kūloko,* local news.

**nui.** Big, large, great, important; many, much; size, number, magnitude, quantity, the greater part; enough. Cf. *hapa nui, mea nui. Leo nui,* loud voice. *'Ano nui,* important. *Aloha nui loa,* very much aloha. Before a noun, *nui* may mean "group," as *nui manō,* group of sharks, or *nui manu,* flock of birds. **ho'onui.** To enlarge, increase, multiply, magnify. *Ho'onui leo,* loudspeaker.

**nui kino.** Whole body.

**Nuioka.** New York. *Eng.*

**Nukilani.** New Zealand. *Eng.*

**nuku. 1.** Beak, snout, tip, end; spout, the lip of a pitcher; mouth or entrance, as of a harbor, river, or mountain pass. *Nuku awa,* entrance to a harbor. **2.** Scolding, raving, ranting, grumbling. **3.** Names of birds, legumes, jackfish.

**nukunuku. 1.** Redup. of *nuku, 1, 2;* to scold. **2.** Short, broken off; short, blunt.

**nuku pu'u. 1.** A group of Hawaiian honeycreepers *(Hemignathus lucidus),* now very rare. *Lit.,* hunched beak. **2.** Protruding lips; to pout the lips.

**nuku wai.** Stream mouth.

**numela, numera.** Numeral. *Eng.*

**numi.** To subside gradually, as tears, laughter, emotions.

**numonia.** Pneumonia. *Eng.*

**nūnū. 1.** Moaning, groaning, cooing, grunting. **2.** Trumpet fish *(Aulostomus chinensis).*

**nunuha.** Redup. of *nuha;* sulky, moody.

**nunui.** Plural of *nui.*

**nūpepa.** Newspaper. *Eng.*

**nūpepa puka lā.** Daily newspaper.

**nu'u.** Height, high place; elevation; stratum.

# O

**o. 1.** Of (*o*-class). **2.** Or, lest.

**ō. 1.** To answer, reply yes, agree; yes (in reply). **2.** To remain, endure, survive, continue, go on, exist; continuing. See *oia, oia mau nō.* **3.** Imperative marker.

**'o.** Particle marking the subject, especially common before names of people, the interrogative *wai,* and the pronoun *ia. 'O au nō,* it's I.

**'ō. 1.** Any piercing instrument, fork, pin, sharp-pointed stick, fishing spear; to pierce, prick, stab. **ho'ō.** To cause to enter, put in, thrust in, insert. **2.** There, yonder (very common, often following *ma-, i, mai;* written as one word with *ma-* and always stressed, *ma'ō). Noho ma'ō,* sit over there. **3.** The letter *o. Eng.*

**'ō-.** Similitude prefix.

**o'a. 1.** House rafter. **2.** Fish gill.

**'oā. 1.** Split, cracked, burst; to split, crack. **hō'oā.** To cause to split, crack. **2.** To retch, gag.

**O'ahu.** The most populous Hawaiian island. No accepted meaning.

**'oama.** Young of the *weke* fish.

**'o au.** I.

**'oe.** You (singular).

**'oē.** Murmuring, rustling, soughing, whining, as of surf, leaves, water, wind, a bullet; to sound thus; sound of tearing, as of cloth; buzzing of insects.

**oha.** To greet; affection.

**'ohai.** Monkeypod or rain tree *(Samanea saman).*

**'ohai 'ula.** Royal poinciana or flame tree *(Delonix regia).*

**'ohana. 1.** Family, relative, kin group; related. **2.** To gather for family prayers.

'**ohe.** All kinds of bamboo; reed; flute; pipe, tube; bamboo tube for preserving fish. *Puhi 'ohe,* to play a wind instrument; player of a wind instrument.

'**ōhelo.** A small native shrub *(Vaccinium reticulatum)* in the cranberry family, bearing small, red or yellow edible berries; formerly sacred to the goddess Pele.

'**ōhelohelo.** Pink, rosy, of the color of *'ōhelo* berries. **ho'ōhelohelo.** To color pink.

'**ōhelo papa.** Strawberry.

'**ohe puluka.** Flute. *Lit.,* flute *(Eng.)* bamboo.

'**ohe wai.** Water pipe; bamboo water container.

**ohi.** Young animal, usually female; maiden just entering womanhood; youth; youthful growth. *Ohi moa,* young chicken, pullet.

'**ohi.** To gather, select; to collect, as wages or taxes.

'**ōhi'a.** **1.** Two kinds of trees: see *'ōhi'a 'ai, 'ōhi'a lehua.* **2.** Tomato. See *'ōhi'a lomi.*

'**ōhi'a 'ai.** Mountain apple *(Eugenia malaccensis).* *Lit.,* edible *'ōhi'a.*

'**ōhi'a lehua.** The tree *Metrosideros collina;* see *lehua.*

'**ōhi'a loke.** Rose apple *(Eugenia jambos).* *Lit.,* rose *(Eng.).* *'ōhi'a.*

'**ōhi'a lomi.** The common table tomato, sometimes used for *lomi* salmon.

'**ōhiki.** **1.** To probe, pry, pick out; to prod, as the earth with a digging stick; to shell, as peas; to pick, as the teeth or nose; to clean out, as the ears. **2.** Sand crab, probably *Ocypode ceratophthalma* and *O. laevis.*

'**ōhiki niho.** Toothpick.

'**ohina.** Gathering, collecting; selection. Cf. *'ohi.*

'**ōhinu.** Shiny, greasy; piece of roasted meat; roast; grease.

**ohiohi.** To grow vigorously, flourish, of plants.

**oho.** **1.** Hair of the head; leaves of plants; to leaf out, sprout. Cf. *lauoho.* **2.** To call out, cry; outcry; to leap up, as startled birds. **ho'ōho.** To exclaim, shout, halloo.

**ohohia.** Enthusiasm; enthusiastic, delighted, pleased; enthusiastic acclaim.

**ohoku'i.** Wig, switch. *Lit.,* added hair.

'**ohu.** Mist, fog, vapor. **hō'ohu.** To form mist; misty, etc.

**ōhua.** Retainers, dependents, servants; passengers, as on a vessel.

'**ōhule.** **1.** Bald; bald person. **ho'ōhule.** To cause baldness; to shear the hair completely. **2.** Defeated without getting a single score. **ho'ōhule.** To defeat.

'**ōhulu.** To feather out; to grow, especially of vines growing from discarded or broken bits of sweet potato.

'**ōhuluhula.** Hairy (of body hair), shaggy.

'**ōhumu.** To grumble, complain, find fault, conspire, plot.

'**ōhumuhumu.** Redup. of *'ōhumu;* to relate one's woes, as to a sympathetic friend.

**oi.** To move; to turn sideways, as contemptuously; to slouch along; to pull away, as in anger.

'**oi.** **1.** Sharp; sharpness. **hō'oi.** To sharpen. **2.** Best, superior, exceeding; to exceed, excel; extra, above. *A 'oi, emi mai,* more or less. *Maui nō ka 'oi,* Maui is the very best. **hō'oi.** To excel; best.

'**o'i.** To limp.

**oia.** Same as *ō, 2;* to keep doing, persevere.

'**oia.** **1.** Truth; true. Often used idiomatically to mean this, namely this, namely, thus, that's it, that's right, go ahead. *'Oia nō!* Yes, that's so; that's right! *'Oia paha,* maybe so. **hō'oia.** To confirm, audit. *Luna hō'oia,* auditor. **2.** He, she, it *('o + ia, 1).*

**'oia ana nō.** It's the same result; regardless.

**'oia ho'i hā!** All right, then; so that's it after all.

**'oiai. 1.** While, meanwhile. **2.** Although.

**'oia'i'o.** True, truth; truly, certainly; faithfulness. **hō'oia'i'o.** To verify, prove; to acknowledge, as a title; deed, proof.

**oia mau nō.** Same as ever, continuing the same, just the same (often said in answer to *Pehea 'oe?* How are you?). See *ō, 2; oia, 1.*

**'oia paha.** See *'oia.*

**'oihana.** Occupation, trade, job, industry, business; department, office; Biblical book of Acts; professional. *Noho 'oihana,* office holder, job holder; to stay in an office or job.

**'oihana ho'ona'auao. 1.** Educational system. **2.** *(Cap.)* Department of Instruction. **3.** Profession.

**'oihana kahuna. 1.** Priesthood, office and duties of a priest. **2.** *(Cap.)* Book of Leviticus in the Old Testament.

**'oihana kinai ahi.** Fire department; job of putting out fires. *Lit.,* fire-extinguishing job or department.

**'oihana leka.** Postal department. *Lit.,* letter department.

**'oihana wai. 1.** Water works. **2.** *(Cap.)* Department (or Board) of Water Supply.

**'ō'ili. 1.** To appear, come into view; appearance. *'Ō'ili ka maka,* to come up, as seeds, bulbs; to sprout. **2.** File-fishes, including *(Cantherhines dumerili).*

**'ōilo.** Young eel.

**-'oio. hō'oio.** To show off; to assume an air of superiority, as a child who cuts capers; conceited.

**'oi'o.** Procession of ghosts of a departed chief and his company. More commonly called *huaka'i pō.*

**'ō'io.** Bonefish, ladyfish *(Albula vulpes).*

**'oi'oi.** Redup. of *'oi, 2;* superior person.

**o'io'ina.** Resting place for travelers, such as a shady tree, rock.

**'ōiwi.** Native, native son. **ho'ōiwi.** To pass oneself off as a native son; like a native son.

**oka.** Dregs, crumbs.

**'ōka'a.** To revolve, spin; to roll, as a mat; a top; a roll.

**'Okakopa, Okatopa.** October. *Eng.*

**'ōkala. 1.** Gooseflesh, creepy sensation; to bristle, stand up, as hair. **2.** Rough, coarse, as cloth.

**'okana. 1.** District or subdistrict, usually comprising several *ahupua'a;* portion, as of food (probably a contraction of *'oki 'ana,* cutting). **2.** Organ. *Eng.*

**ōkea.** White sand or gravel (contraction of *one,* sand, and *kea,* white).

**oki.** To stop, finish, end. Cf. *uoki.* **ho'ōki.** To put an end to, finish, stop; end.

**'oki.** To cut, sever, hew, separate, divorce, fell; to cut, as cards; to operate, amputate; a cut, division, operation, amputation. **hō'oki.** To pretend to cut short, to cause to cut, to cut; to divorce.

**'okika.** Orchid. *Eng.*

**'okika honohono.** An orchid *(Dendrobium anosmum).*

**'oki male (mare).** Divorce; to divorce. *Lit.,* cut marriage.

**'oki mau'u.** To mow the grass. *Mīkini 'oki mau'u,* lawn mower.

**'okina. 1.** Cutting off; ending, severance, separation. **2.** Glottal stop.

**'oki'oki.** Redup. of *'oki;* to cut into pieces.

**'oki poepoe.** Circumcision; to circumcise (Biblical; the old Hawaiian term was *kahe*). *Lit.,* round cut.

**'oko'a.** Different, another; whole;

entirety; a whole note in music; entirely, wholly, completely; independently. Cf. *holo'oko'a.* **hō'oko'a.** To make different, to set apart, separate, discriminate.

**'ō koholā.** Whaling; to whale. *Lit.,* pierce whale. Cf. *moku 'ō koholā.*

**'ōkole.** Anus, buttocks.

**'ōkolehao.** Liquor distilled from ti root in a still of the same name; later, a gin as made from rice or pineapple juice. *Lit.,* iron bottom.

**'ōkole 'oi'oi.** Marigolds. *Lit.,* jutting buttocks. Cf. *melekule.*

**'ōkomo.** To insert; to calk, as a ship; to inlay.

**'okomopila.** Automobile. *Eng.*

**'ōku'eku'e.** Knuckles. See *ku'eku'e.*

**ola.** Life, health, well-being, living, salvation; alive, spared; healed; to live; to spare, heal, grant life. *Mālama ola,* financial support, means of livelihood. **ho'ōla.** To save, heal, cure, spare; salvation; healer; savior.

**ola hou.** To revive, resuscitate; resurrected; resurrection. **ho'ōla hou.** To restore to life, revive.

**ōla'i.** Earthquake.

**olakino.** State of health. *Mea olakino,* things necessary for life, as food.

**'ōlali. 1.** To glide smoothly along, as a ship on the sea or as a fish slipping through one's hand. **2.** Bright, shiny, glistening; brightness.

**ola loa.** Long life; completely cured or recovered.

**'ōlani.** To toast over a fire, broil, warm in sunlight.

**'ōlapa. 1.** To flash, as lightning; to blaze suddenly, flare up; to rumble uneasily, as a queasy stomach. **2.** Dancer, as contrasted with the chanter or *ho'opa'a* (memorizer); now, any dance accompanied by chanting and drumming on a gourd drum.

**ola pāna'i.** Redeemed, ransomed, saved; to redeem. **ho'ōla pāna'i.** To redeem, ransom; redeemer.

**'ole. 1.** Not, without, lacking; to deny; zero, nothingness. Cf. *'a'ole, mea 'ole, 'ole loa. Maika'i 'ole,* not good; bad. **hō'ole.** To deny, refuse, contradict; refusal, denial, negative. **2.** *(Cap.)* Seventh, eighth, ninth, tenth, twenty-first, and twenty-second nights of the moon.

**'olē.** Conch shell *(Charonia tritonis).*

**'ōlelo.** Language, speech, word; to speak, say, tell; oral, verbatim, verbal.

**'ole loa.** Not at all, not in the least, none whatsoever; of no value, worthless.

**'ōlelo 'ē.** Foreign language, incomprehensible lingo.

**'ōlelo ha'i mua.** Foreword, preface. *Lit.,* word told first.

**ōlelo hō'ike.** Affidavit, testimony.

**'ōlelo ho'oholo.** Verdict (as of a jury), judgment, decision; resolution; conclusion.

**'ōlelo ho'onalonalo.** Figurative language; obscure speech with puns and poetical references; to speak thus.

**'ōlelo huna.** Secret language, speech with hidden meaning.

**'ōlelo kauoha.** Decree, order, commandment; to order, decree.

**'ōlelokīkē.** Dialogue, repartee; to engage in dialogue. Cf. *kīkē'ōlelo.*

**'ōlelo kūkā.** Consultation, discussion; to discuss, consult.

**'ōlelo maika'i.** Good word, gospel.

**'ōlelo makuahine.** Mother tongue.

**'ōlelo nane.** Riddle, parable, allegory.

**'ōlelo no'eau.** Proverb, wise saying, traditional saying.

**'ōlelo pa'i 'ai.** Pidgin English. *Lit.,* hard-taro speech.

'ōlelo paipai. Word of encouragement, exhortation, commandment.

'ōlelo uea 'ole. Wireless message.

'ōlena. Turmeric *(Curcuma domestica)*, a kind of ginger; used medicinally and as a source of dyes. See *lena, 2.*

'ōlenalena. Yellow. See *lenalena.*

'ōlepe. 1. To turn, as on hinges; to shut and open, as Venetian blinds. ho'ōlepe. To cause to turn, shut. 2. Any kind of bivalve, as a mussel or oyster.

'ōlepolepo. Somewhat dirty, sullied; to sully.

-'Olepope. Hō'olepope. Protestant. *Lit.*, Pope denier.

'ole wale! Not at all! Of no interest, value, use.

oli. Chant that was not danced to. *Mea oli*, chanter.

'oli. Joy, happiness, pleasure; happy, joyful. Cf. *hau'oli.* hō'oli. To give joy, make happy.

'oliana. All kinds of oleander grown in Hawai'i *(Nerium* spp.). *Eng.*

'ōliko. To bud. See *liko.*

'ō lima. Arm vaccination. *Lit.*, arm piercing.

'ōlino. Bright, brilliant, dazzling; brightness. See *lino.*

'ōlinolino. Redup. of *'ōlino.*

olioli. Redup. of *oli;* chanter.

'oli'oli. Redup. of *'oli.*

'oliwa, oliva. Olive tree *(Olea europaea).*

olo. 1. To rub back and forth, grate, saw; a saw. 2. To resound, sound long. 3. Long surfboard. 4. Hill.

'olo. Double chin, sagging skin, jowls, calf of leg; scrotum; to roll with fat; to sag, hang down.

'oloa. Fine white tapa.

olohaka. Empty, sunken, hollow, as eyes or cheeks; emptiness, deficiency.

olohani. To strike, quit work; mutiny, riot (said to be from *Eng.* "all hands"). hō'olohani. To cause or foment a strike or mutiny.

'ōlohe. Bare, naked, barren; hairless, as a dog; bald; destitute, needy.

'ōlohelohe. Redup. of *'ōlohe.*

oloka'a. To roll along, as a wheel; to remove; to transfer, as a debt.

olo kani. To sound.

olokē. Clamorous, incoherent, excited in speech or sound.

'oloke'a. Cross, gibbet, gallows, scaffolding; crisscross. hō'oloke'a. To crisscross; to cross.

'olokele. Bog, swamp.

ololī. Narrow.

olomea. A native shrub or small tree *(Perrottetia sandwicensis).*

olomio. Tapering, narrowing; to start to form a crust, as on a wound; to go quickly, vanish.

olonā. A native shrub *(Touchardia latifolia);* the very strong, durable fiber from the bark was used for fish nets and carrying nets, and as a base for feather capes, etc.

'olo'olo. 1. Redup. of *'olo;* to hang too low, as a petticoat; to hang loose and long. *Waiū 'olo'olo*, sagging breasts. 2. To overflow, flood, as streams.

'olo'olo wāwae. Calf of the leg.

'olopū. Inflated, billowed out, as a sail in the wind; puffed out, as cheeks of a person eating; blistered, as hands from hard work. hō'olopū. To dilate, inflate, blister.

'olu. Cool, refreshing; soft, flexible, elastic; pleasant, comfortable; polite, kind, courteous; coolness; comfort; courtesy, kindness. Cf. *'olu'olu.* hō'olu. To make soft, limber, pleasant, cool, comfortable; to comfort, please.

'olua. You two.

'olu'olu. Redup. of *'olu. E 'olu-'olu 'oe e hele mai,* please come here. hō'olu'olu. Redup. of *hō'olu;* to retire to rest, to seek rest; parade rest, at ease (military commands).

**'oma.** Oven, baking pan; to roast; roasted.

**'ōma'i.** Sickly, weak, ailing, not well. See *ma'i.*

**'ōma'ima'i.** Redup. of *'ōma'i.*

**'ōmaka.** Budding; beginning; source, as of a stream; to leaf out or bud; to nip off. See *maka, 3.*

**'ōmaka wai.** Stream source.

**'ōmali.** Weak, infirm, puny, shriveling.

**'ōmalu.** Cloudy, overcast, shady. **ho'ōmalu.** To cast a heavy shade; overcast. See *malu.*

**'ōma'o.** 1. Green, as plants. 2. Hawaiian thrush *(Phaeornis obscurus)*. Also called *ma'o.*

**'ōma'oma'o.** Redup. of *'ōma'o;* an emerald. **ho'ōma'oma'o.** To make green, paint green.

**'ōmea.** Reddish; murky.

**'ōmilo.** To twist, turn, drill, curl; to taper, as a baby's fingers by rolling the tips between thumb and index finger; to spin, as thread; to produce abortion, destroy. See *milo, 2.*

**'ōmilu.** Same as *ulua.*

**omo.** To suck; suckling; to evaporate, as water; suction tube, rubber nipple. *Keiki omo waiū,* suckling child.

**'omo.** Lid, cover, plug, cork, as of a calabash; lamp chimney.

**'omo ipukukui.** Lamp chimney.

**omo koko.** Bloodsucker, leech; to suck blood.

**'ōmole.** Bottle.

**'omo'omo.** Loaf; any long, oval body. **hō'omo'ono.** To mold, shape.

**'omo'omo palaoa.** Loaf of bread.

**omo waiū.** Nipple for a milk bottle; to suck a nipple.

**'ōmuku.** Stump, projection, pommel of a saddle; to project; to cut off short. See *muku.*

**'ōmu'o.** Bud, budding; to have buds; to nip off, as a leaf bud; to be cut off, stopped. See *mu'o.*

**ona.** 1. Mite, louse. 2. Infatuated, attracted. Cf. *onaona.* 3. His, hers, its (zero-class, *o*-class).

**'ona.** 1. Drunk, dizzy and unsteady; intoxicating; intoxication. *Wai 'ona,* intoxicating liquor. **hō'ona.** Intoxicating. 2. Owner. *Eng.* Cf. *'ona miliona.*

**'ona lama.** Drunk on rum or any alcoholic liquor; drunkenness; alcoholic.

**'ona mau.** Constantly drunk, alcoholic.

**'ona miliona.** Millionaire. *Lit.,* owner [of a] million. *Eng.*

**onaona.** Softly fragrant; soft fragrance or perfume; gentle and sweet, as the eyes or disposition; inviting, attractive. **ho'ōnaona.** To impart fragrance; attractive, sweet.

**one.** Sand; sandy; silt; poetic name for land (cf. *one hānau).* **ho'ōne.** Pumice; to rub and polish with sand.

**one hānau.** Birthplace.

**'one'i.** Here; local. *Kō 'one'i keiki,* the local youngsters.

**'oneki.** Deck. *Eng.*

**oneone.** Sandy, gritty, grainy.

**oni.** To appear, reach out to, jut out.

**'oni.** To move, stir, shift; to take to court, as land matters; movement, motion, moving. *'Oni ā puhi,* to squirm like an eel. **hō-'oni.** To bestir, cause to move, shake, disturb.

**'ōniho.** Toothed, sharp-edged, tooth-edged. See *niho.*

**'ōnini.** A slight breeze, puff of wind; to gasp for breath.

**'oni'oni.** Redup. of *'oni.* See *ki'i 'oni'oni.*

**'onipa'a.** Fixed, immovable, steadfast, firm. *Lit.,* fixed movement. **hō'onipa'a.** To fix, establish firmly.

**ono.** 1. Long, slender mackerel- or tuna-like fish *(Acanthocy-*

*bium solandri);* a fine food fish.
**2.** Six; sixth.

**'ono.** Delicious, tasty, savory; to relish, crave; deliciousness, savor. Cf. *mea'ono.* **hō'ono.** To tempt the appetite; to make tasty.

**'ōnohi.** Eyeball; center; setting, as of a ring.

**'ono'ono.** Redup. of *'ono.* **hō'ono'ono.** To make tasty, create a desire. *Hō'ono'ono 'ai,* appetizer, condiment, dressing, relish.

**'onou.** To shove, push, force into, thrust on; to persuade.

**'onou po'o.** To shove or push into something headlong, regardless of consequences. *Lit.,* shove head.

**'ono wai.** Thirsty; to crave water.

**o'o.** Matured, ripe, as fruit; of mature age; to mature, as fruit; an adult human; to ripen.

**'o'ō.** To crow.

**'ō'ō. 1.** Redup. of *'ō, 1;* to pierce, poke, put in, insert; to hurl, as a spear; to abort. **hō'ō'ō.** To insert, put in, pierce, cause to pierce. **2.** Digging stick, digging implement, spade. **3.** A black honeyeater *(Moho nobilis),* much prized by early Hawaiians for their few yellow feathers, which were used in making feather capes and helmets. A separate species occurred on each of the four islands: Kaua'i, O'ahu, Moloka'i, and Hawai'i; are all now extinct except the very rare Kaua'i species.

**'ō'ō hao.** Iron tool for digging, plow.

**'ō'ō ihe.** To hurl spears; sport of spear throwing.

**'ō'ō kila.** Steel spade.

**'o'ole'a.** Hard, stiff, strong; hardness, strength. **hō'o'ole'a.** To harden, stiffen, resist.

**'o'oma.** Concave; concavity, spout, gouge, flare of a bonnet; oval-shaped chisel; large sharp nose. **hō'o'oma.** To shape con-cavely; to turn down the rim of a hat on both sides of the face so that the front is like the flare of a bonnet.

**'o'opa.** Lame, crippled; a cripple, lame person; to limp, be lame. **hō'o'opa.** To cause lameness, to feign lameness.

**'ō'ō pālahalaha.** Trowel. *Lit.,* flat digging instrument.

**'ō'ō palau.** A plow; to plow. *Lit.,* plow *(Eng.)* digging implement.

**'ō'ōpē.** Spade. *Lit.,* spade *(Eng.)* digging implement.

**'o'opu.** General name for fishes included in the families Eleotridae and Gobiidae (gobies); some live in salt water near the shore, others in fresh water, and still others prefer brackish water.

**'o'opu hue.** Puffers, balloonfishes, globefishes *(Arothron melagris* and other species).

**'ōpā. 1.** To press, squeeze, as in massaging or in working dough. **hō'ōpā.** To cause to squeeze. **2.** To ache, as from sitting in a cramped position. **hō'ōpā.** To cause such aching.

**'ōpae.** General name for shrimps and prawns.

**'ōpae kai.** Any sea shrimp.

**'ōpae kākala.** Spiked shrimp.

**'ōpae-kala-'ole.** Species of freshwater shrimp. Also called *'ōpae kuahiwi,* mountain shrimp, and *'ōpae kolo,* crawling shrimp. *Lit.,* spineless shrimp.

**'ōpae kolo.** See *'ōpae-kala-'ole.*

**'ōpae kuahiwi.** See *'ōpae-kala-'ole.*

**'ōpakapaka.** Blue snapper *(Pristipomoides microlepis),* an important market fish.

**'ōpala.** Trash, rubbish, refuse, litter, garbage. **ho'ōpala.** To litter, make rubbish. See *pala.*

**'ōpalapala.** Redup. of *'ōpala;* bits of trash and rubbish.

**'ope.** Bundle; to tie in a bundle. **hō'ope.** To tie a bundle.

**‘ōpe‘a.** To twist, bind, or cross the hands, as behind the back; to throw over the shoulder, as a shawl; to overturn, overthrow; to evict, as a tenant. **ho‘ōpe‘a.** Treacherous; to cause to twist, cross, etc. See *pe‘a, 1.*

**‘ōpe‘a kua.** To cross the hands behind the back, a gesture considered rude because it was thought to bring bad luck to a fisherman or one beginning a venture.

**‘ōpe‘ape‘a.** 1. General name for starfish. 2. Bat. 3. Window shutters, Venetian blinds.

**‘ōpelu.** Mackerel scad *(Decapterus pinnulatus),* an excellent food fish, also used as bait for tuna and marlin.

**‘ope‘ope.** Redup. of *‘ope;* bundles, baggage; to fold up, as clothes; pillow.

**‘opi.** Fold, crease; to fold, crease.

**‘opihi.** 1. Limpet *(Cellona* spp.). 2. Salted and dried abalone from the mainland.

**‘ōpikikiki.** Anxiety, mental disturbance; agitated, as the sea.

**‘ōpili.** Cramped or numbed, as by cold or sitting long in one position; aching; clamped together, as leaves of a sensitive plant when touched; a cramp. **ho‘ōpili.** To cause a cramp, numbness, etc. See *pili.*

**‘ōpio.** Youth, juvenile; young. *Kale ‘Ōpio,* Charles, Junior. **ho‘ōpio.** To make young, freshen, refresh; to act young.

**‘ōpiopio.** Young, immature, juvenile; unripe; youth, young person. **ho‘ōpiopio.** Redup. of *ho‘ōpio.*

**‘opiuma.** 1. Opium. 2. Manila tamarind *(Pithecellobium dulce).*

**‘ōpū.** Belly, stomach, abdomen, tripe, giblet, gizzard, bladder.

**‘ōpua.** Puffy clouds, as banked up near the horizon.

**‘ōpū ahonui.** Patient; patience; a patient person. *Lit.,* disposition of great breath.

**‘ōpū ‘ai, ‘ōpū ‘ai‘ai.** Stomach, craw, as of a bird.

**‘ōpule.** A common labrid fish or wrasse *(Anampses cuvier, A. godeffroyi).*

**‘ōpulepule.** Somewhat crazy, moronic.

**‘ōpū makani.** Bellows. *Lit.,* wind belly.

**‘ōpū mimi.** Bladder. *Lit.,* urine belly.

**‘ōpū nui.** Corpulent, large-bellied; corpulency; big belly.

**‘ōpū pipi.** Beef tripe.

**‘ōpū pua‘a.** Pig intestine; tripe.

**‘ōpu‘u.** 1. A bud, the budding breasts of a girl; to bud; a child. 2. A whale-tooth pendant, not tongue-shaped like the *lei palaoa.*

**‘ōpu‘u mai‘a.** The root bud and buds of a banana plant, and the sheaths enclosing them.

**‘ōpu‘upu‘u.** 1. Lumpy, bumpy, hilly, rough, as cloth or a road. 2. Knuckle, as on fingers, wrist.

**ou.** Your, yours (singular, zero-class, *o*-class).

**o‘u.** Mine, my, of me (zero-class, *o*-class).

**‘ou.** To protrude, project, puncture.

**‘oukou.** You (plural). *Kō ‘oukou,* your (*o*-class). *Kā ‘oukou,* your (*a*-class).

**‘ōuli.** Sign, omen, portent; nature, symptom, character.

**‘o wai.** See *wai,* who.

**‘owali.** Weak, sickly, puny. Cf. *wali, nāwali.*

**‘o wau, ‘o au.** See *au, I,* and *‘o.*

**‘ōwela.** Hottish, feverish; burned and blistered, as by sun; heat. See *wela.*

**‘ōwili.** Roll, bolt, as of cloth or paper; skein, coil; to roll up, twist; to fold, as the arms. See *wili.*

**‘ōwiliwili.** Redup. of *‘ōwili.* See *wiliwili.*

# P

**pā. 1.** Fence, wall, pen, corral, sty, (house) lot, enclosure, yard; to build a fence or enclosure. **2.** Dish, plate, pan (preceded by *ke*). **3.** Mother-of-pearl shell; pearl-shell lure. **4.** To touch, get, contact, reach, hit, experience, blow (of wind), shine (as moon or sun), drink, hear. **hoʻopā.** To touch. **5.** Barren, as a female.

**pa-.** In the nature of, having the quality of. Also, *pā-.*

**pā-.** At a time, at once, number of times (prefix to numerals).

**paʻa.** Firm, solid, fixed, fast, stuck, secure, closed, busy, steady, steadfast, permanent, finished, completed; learned, memorized, stubborn, determined, solid or fast (of colors), strong, vigorous, learned; to hold, keep, retain, bear; a solid, as in geometry. **hoʻopaʻa.** To make fast, firm, tight, solid; to bind; to learn, memorize, complete, keep, detain, withhold; to subscribe, as to a newspaper; to order, reserve, register, insure, bolt; drummer and hula chanter; insurance. *Hoʻopaʻa manawa,* to make an appointment. *Hoʻopaʻa moʻolelo,* to record a story, keep minutes. *Leka i hoʻopaʻa ʻia,* registered letter. *Hoʻopaʻa hao,* to weld. *Hoʻopaʻa kuleana,* to copyright.

**paʻa ʻāina.** Landholder; to hold land.

**paʻahana.** Busy, industrious, hard-working; laborer, worker.

**paʻahao.** Prisoner, convict. *Lit.,* iron-held. **hoʻopaʻahao.** To jail, imprison.

**pāʻaila.** Castor oil plant *(Ricinus communis).*

**paʻaʻili.** A solid (usually with number of sides given), as *paʻaʻili hā,* four-sided solid.

**paʻa kāhili.** Bearer of the royal feather standard; to carry a *kāhili.*

**paʻakai.** Salt.

**paʻa kāmaʻa.** Pair of shoes.

**paʻakea.** Limestone, coral beds.

**paʻakikī.** Hard, compact, difficult, stubborn, obstinate.

**paʻalima.** Pentagon.

**paʻalole.** Suit of clothes.

**paʻalula.** Formal, according to rules.

**paʻa male.** Married couple.

**paʻa mau.** Regular, customary, usual.

**paʻa moʻolelo.** Versed in lore, legends, history, tradition; one so versed.

**paʻanaʻau.** Memorized, remembered. **hoʻopaʻanaʻau.** To memorize.

**pāʻani.** Play, sport, game, amusement, joke; to play, sport. *Pāʻani kinipōpō,* to play ball; ball player. *Pāʻani pepa,* to play cards. *Mea pāʻani,* plaything, toy.

**paʻapaʻa.** Dispute, argument, quarrel. **hoʻopaʻapaʻa.** To argue, dispute; argument.

**paʻapaʻani.** Playful.

**paʻapū.** Covered with, solid with, as people, fog, clouds.

**paʻa uma.** Hand wrestling.

**-paʻa waiwai. hoʻopaʻa waiwai.** To insure property.

**pae. 1.** Cluster, row, bank. **hoʻopae.** To build up an embankment, row. **2.** To land, as a surf-rider; washed or drifted ashore.

**pae ʻāina.** Group of islands, archipelago.

**pāʻele. 1.** Negroid, dark, black; to blacken. **2.** *(Cap.)* Negro, Black.

**pae moku.** Group of islands, archipelago.

**paepae.** Pavement, support, house platform; to support, hold.

**pae puʻu.** Row or cluster of hills.

**pa'ewa.** Crooked, misshapen, uneven, odd, imperfect, wrong, incorrect; error, mistake.

**paha.** 1. Maybe, perhaps (very common, making speech less blunt; often preceded by *pēlā* or *'a'ole,* and never occurring after a pause). *Ā . . . paha,* or. *'Elua ā 'ekolu paha,* two or three. 2. Chant, especially an improvised or conversation chant; to chant thus.

**pā hale.** House lot, yard, or fence.

**pā halihali.** Tray (preceded by *ke*).

**pāha'oha'o.** Mysterious, puzzling.

**pahē.** Soft-spoken, soft-mannered; soft. See *waipahē.*

**pāheahea.** To call, especially to invite someone to eat.

**pahe'e.** Slippery, smooth, soft, satiny; to slide, slip, skid. **ho'o-pahe'e.** To cause to slip.

**pahe'e 'ulu.** To bowl; bowling.

**pahele.** Snare, noose, trap; to ensnare, trap; deceit, treachery. **ho'opahele.** To ensnare, deceive.

**pāhemahema.** About the same as *hemahema;* awkward, unskilled.

**pāhenehene.** To ridicule, laugh at, make fun of.

**pahi.** Knife.

**pahi kaua.** Sword.

**pahi keke'e.** Sickle.

**pahi koli.** Carving knife.

**pahi 'ō.** Dagger.

**pahi olo.** Saw; to saw.

**pahi pelu.** Jackknife, penknife.

**pahi 'umi'umi.** Razor. *Lit.,* beard knife.

**pāhoa.** Dagger.

**pāhoehoe.** Smooth, unbroken type of lava, contrasting with *'a'ā.*

**pā holoi.** Wash basin.

**pāhono.** To mend, patch, repair.

**pā ho'okani.** Phonograph record.

**pahu.** 1. Box, drum, chest, barrel, ship binnacle, collection box, ark, coffin, cabinet, cask, barrel. 2. Stick, stake, staff, post.

3. To push, shove, thrust. 4. To cut off short. 5. Boxfishes, cowfishes (esp. *Ostracion*). Also *moamoa.*

**pahū.** To explode, burst, blast, thud. **ho'opahū.** To set off, as firecrackers or dynamite.

**pahu aniani.** Glass box, especially a glass-bottomed box for fishing; glass case.

**pahu hao.** Safe.

**pahu hau.** Icebox, refrigerator.

**pahu hope.** Final goal or stake.

**pahu hula.** Hula drum.

**pahu kui.** Hypodermic injection; to be injected. *Lit.,* needle piercing.

**pahu kupapa'u.** Coffin. *Lit.,* corpse box.

**pā hula.** Hula troupe, studio.

**pahulu.** 1. Nightmare. **ho'opa-hulu.** To have a nightmare; to haunt, bring bad luck; unlucky. 2. Exhausted, worn out, of soil.

**pahu manamana.** Crossroads,. intersection.

**pahu meli.** Beehive.

**pahu 'ōlelo.** Phonograph.

**pahu pā.** Cupboard, meat safe.

**pahupahu.** Billiards, pool; to play such.

**pahūpahū.** Redup. of *pahū.*

**pahu pa'i.** Small sharkskin hula drum.

**pahupa'iki'i.** Camera, Kodak. *Lit.,* box for printing pictures.

**pahu pānānā.** Binnacle.

**pahu 'ume.** Drawer, bureau.

**pahu wai.** Water barrel, tank.

**pai.** 1. To urge, encourage, rouse, excite. **ho'opai.** To encourage. 2. To raise, lift up. 3. To laud, praise, exalt. 4. To pamper, spoil, make a pet of.

**pa'i.** 1. To slap, clap, applaud by clapping, print; printing (preceded by *ke*). **ho'opa'i.** To slap, hit, punish, revenge; punishment, revenge, fine, penalty. *'Ōlelo ho'opa'i,* sentence. 2. To tie; a draw, equal. 3. To mix, as ingredients.

**paia.** Wall, side of a house; clearing of trees; walled in. *Paia ʻala i ka hala,* forest bower fragrant with pandanus.

**paʻi ʻai.** Hard, pounded, undiluted taro. See *ʻōlelo paʻi ʻai.*

**paʻi ʻana.** Printing, edition.

**paiʻea.** An edible crab, perhaps one of the grapsids.

**paʻi hakahaka.** Printing; form, questionnaire.

**paʻi hewa.** Misprint, typographical error; to make such.

**paʻihi.** Clear, bright, neat, tidy.

**pai hua.** Custard pie, egg pie, fruit pie.

**paikau.** To march, drill, parade, practice firearms.

**paiki.** Bag, suitcase, pocketbook, purse. *Eng.*

**paʻi kiʻi.** To take pictures, photographs; photographer. *Lit.,* snap picture.

**paikikala.** Bicycle. *Eng.*

**paila.** 1. Pile, heap. *Eng.* 2. Also **baila.** To boil. *Eng.*

**pā ilina.** Cemetery, graveyard.

**pailua.** Nausea; abominable. **hoʻopailua.** To cause nausea; nauseating, disgusting, loathsome.

**paʻimalau.** Portuguese man-of-war *(Physalia).*

**paina.** Pine, all kinds of conifers, ironwood. *Eng.*

**paʻina.** To crackle, snap, click, tick, pop.

**pāʻina.** Dinner, small party with dinner.

**pāʻina male.** Wedding feast or reception.

**paio.** To quarrel, argue, debate, fight; argument, battle, struggle. See *hoa paio.*

**paipai.** Redup. of *pai, 1, 3.* See *noho paipai.*

**paʻipaʻi.** 1. Redup. of *paʻi, 1;* to applaud, clap; applause. 2. Redup. of *paʻi, 3.* See *lama paʻipaʻi ʻia.*

**paʻipaʻi lima.** To clap, applaud; applause.

**Paipala, Baibala.** Bible; Biblical. *Eng.*

**paʻi palapala.** Printing press; to print.

**paipu.** Pipe, faucet. *Eng. Paipu lawe ʻino,* sewage system.

**pā ipu.** Calabash, wooden dish or bowl.

**paʻipunahele.** To fete a favorite.

**paʻi umauma.** Chest-slapping hula.

**paka.** 1. To criticize constructively, as chanting. 2. Raindrops. 3. Curds. *Eng.* 4. Butter. *Eng.* 5. Tobacco. *Eng.*

**pāka.** 1. Park. *Eng.* 2. To park, as a car. *Eng.*

**pākaha.** To cheat, fleece, rob, raid.

**pāka lāhui.** National park.

**pakalaki.** Bad luck, unlucky. *Eng.*

**pakalana.** Chinese violet *(Telosma cordata).* See *miulana.*

**paka lōlō.** Marijuana.

**paka ua.** Raindrops.

**pākaukau.** Table, counter.

**pākaukau ʻaina.** Dining table.

**pākaukau ʻopiʻopi.** Folding table.

**Pākē.** China; Chinese.

**pākela.** Excess; excessive, surpassing; to exceed, surpass, excel.

**pākela ʻai.** To eat to excess; gluttonous; glutton.

**pakele.** To escape, get away. **hoʻopakele.** To rescue.

**pakelo.** To slip, thrust.

**pakeneka.** Percent, percentage. *Eng.*

**pakī.** To splash, spatter, squirt.

**pākiʻi.** Various flatfishes *(Bothus mancus).*

**pakika.** Slippery, smooth.

**pākīkē.** Rude, sarcastic, saucy, impudent.

**Pākīpika.** Pacific. *Eng.*

**Pakoa.** Catholic term for Easter, Passover.

**pākōlī.** Musical scale.

**paku.** To drive or send away, expel.

**pākū.** Curtain, screen, partition, veil.

pāku'i. To splice, add on, annex.

pāku'iku'i. Surgeon fish *(Acanthurus achilles)*.

pala. 1. Ripe, mellow, rotten. ho'opala. To ripen. 2. Daub, smear, smudge, blot, dab of excreta. ho'opala. To daub, besmear. 3. A fern *(Marattia douglasii)*.

pala'ā. Lace fern *(Sphenomeris chinensis,* syn. *chusana)*.

pālaha. Spread out, extended, flattened, wide, broad. See *laha*.

palahī. Diarrhea.

palahū. 1. Rotten. 2. Same as *pelehū*, turkey.

palai. A native fern *(Microlepia setosa)*.

pala'ie. Game of loop and ball (played with a flexible stick made of braided coconut leaflets with a loop at one end and a tapa ball on a string attached below the loop; the object was to catch the ball in the loop).

palaka. 1. Indifferent, inactive, uninterested. 2. Sturdy blue-and-white checked cloth, used originally for work clothing. 3. Block. *Eng.*

palaki. Brush; to brush. *Eng.*

palaki lauoho. Hairbrush.

palaki niho. Toothbrush.

palalā. A rumbling sound.

pālama. Sacred taboo enclosure.

palamimo. To pilfer.

palani. A surgeonfish *(Acanthurus dussumieri)*. 2. *(Cap.)* Also **Farani**. France, Frenchman; French; Frank. *Eng.* 3. Also **barani**. Brandy. *Eng.*

palaoa. 1. Sperm whale, ivory. See *lei palaoa*. 2. Flour, bread, wheat. *Eng.*

palaoa li'ili'i. Roll, biscuit.

palaoa maka. Flour.

palaoa palai. Pancake.

palaoa pāpa'a. Toast. *Lit.,* crisp bread.

palapala. Document of any kind, bill, deed, warrant, certificate, tract, writ, manuscript; former-ly, the Scriptures or book learning in general.

palapala 'ae. Permit, license.

palapala 'aelike. Written contract, as for labor; treaty.

palapala 'ai'ē. Note (to pay money), bond. *Lit.,* debt document.

palapala 'āina. Map.

palapala hānau. Birth certificate.

Palapala Hemolele. Holy Scriptures.

palapala ho'ālohaloha. Written condolence.

palapala ho'āmana. Power of attorney.

palapala ho'āpono. Passport, document granting permission.

palapala hō'ike. Affidavit, report.

palapala hō'ike no ke ola. Bill of health.

palapala hō'ike pilikino. Identification papers.

palapala ho'ohanohano. Honorary diploma or document.

palapala ho'ohiki 'ia. Affidavit.

palapala hō'oia. Certificate.

palapala hō'oia'i'o. Voucher.

palapala hō'oia kulanui. College diploma.

palapala ho'oilina. Last will or testament.

palapala ho'oka'a. Receipt, as for paying a bill.

palapala ho'okō. Award, verdict, written decision, warrant.

palapala ho'okohu. Certificate of appointment, power of attorney.

palapala ho'okuleana. Patent, copyright.

palapala ho'olauna. Letter of introduction.

palapala ho'olimalima. Lease.

palapala ho'omaika'i. Letter of commendation, graduation diploma, certificate of merit.

palapala ho'opa'a. Bond, insurance policy.

palapala hopu. Warrant of arrest.

palapala 'inikua. Insurance policy.

**palapala kāko'o.** Letter of recommendation or support.

**palapala kauoha.** Last will and testament.

**palapala kīko'o.** Check, draft, warrant.

**palapala kila (sila).** Deed, patent.

**palapala kono.** Invitation.

**palapala kū'ai.** Deed or bill of sale.

**palapala kuhikuhi kino.** Certificate or identification, as a passport.

**palapala male.** Marriage license or certificate.

**palapala noi.** Written petition.

**palapala puka.** Graduation diploma.

**palapala waiho 'oihana.** Letter of resignation.

**palau. 1.** Betrothal; engaged to marry. **ho'opalau.** To become engaged. **2.** Plow; to plow. *Eng.*

**pālau. 1.** To tell tall tales, exaggerate. **2.** War club.

**palaualelo.** Lazy, idle, especially of a verbose person; such a person.

**pale. 1.** To ward off, thrust aside, parry; to ignore a command or law, make void, break; protection, defense, guard. **ho'opale.** To fend or ward off. See *'ili pale o kāma'a.* **2.** Canto of a song, division of a hula song. **3.** To deliver, as a child.

**pale ahi.** Fire protection; fireproof.

**pā lehu.** Ash tray (preceded by *ke*).

**pale huila.** Fender, as of a car.

**pale'ili.** Undershirt.

**pale ka'a.** Car bumper.

**pale kai.** Breakwater.

**palekaiko, paredaiso.** Paradise. Probably *Greek.*

**pale kaua.** Shield, war defense.

**paleki.** Brake. *Eng.*

**palekikena, paresidena.** Var. of *pelekikena,* president.

**palekoki.** Petticoat, skirt. *Eng.*

**palema'i.** Underdrawers.

**pale makani.** Windshield.

**palemo.** To sink, drown, vanish.

**palena.** Boundary, limit, border, juncture, separation. See *kaupalena.*

**palena 'āina.** Land boundary.

**palena 'ole.** Boundless, without limit.

**pale pākaukau.** Table cloth.

**palepiwa.** All species of *Eucalyptus* trees. *Lit.,* ward off fever (so called because the leaves were used as medicine for fever and in steam baths).

**pale uhi.** Veil, covering.

**pale uluna.** Pillowcase.

**pale waiū.** Brassiere.

**pale wāwae.** House slippers, sandals.

**pali.** Cliff, precipice, steep hill. *Fig.,* haughty, disdainful, difficult.

**pali ku'i.** Notched cliff.

**palila.** A rare Hawaiian honeycreeper *(Psittirostra bailleui, P. kona),* endemic to the island of Hawai'i.

**Pali-uli.** A legendary land of plenty and joy, said to be on Hawai'i. *Lit.,* green cliff.

**pāloa.** Seine.

**pāloka, balota.** Ballot, vote. *Eng.* See *koho pāloka.*

**pāloio.** Clay, sticky mud, mortar.

**palu.** Relish made of head or stomach of fish, with *kukui* relish, garlic, chili peppers; bait.

**palū.** Flu, influenza. *Eng.*

**pālua.** Two by two, double, twofold, twice.

**palula.** Cooked sweet-potato leaves.

**pālule.** Shirt.

**pālulu.** Screen, shield, protection.

**pālulu kukui.** Lamp shade.

**pālulu makani.** Windbreak.

**pāluna, baluna.** Balloon. *Eng.*

**palupalu.** Weak, soft, limber, flexible, tender.

**pāma.** Palm. *Eng.*

**pāmakani. 1.** A native hibiscus *(Hibiscus arnottianus),* same as *kokiʻo keʻokeʻo.* 2. A native violet *(Viola chamissoniana).*

**pana.** 1. To shoot, as marbles, arrows, a bow; bow and arrows; to snap, as with fingers. 2. Heartbeat, pulse, beat in music; to beat time, pulsate, throb. *Nānā i ka pana,* to take the pulse. 3. Celebrated, noted, or legendary place.

**pānaʻi.** 1. Revenge, reciprocity, reward; to revenge, pay back, reward, reciprocate, replace, substitute. **hoʻopānaʻi.** To seek revenge, reward, etc. 2. To splice, graft, lengthen.

**panakō, banako.** Bank. *Eng.*

**panalāʻau.** Colony, dependency, province; colonist.

**pānānā.** Compass; pilot.

**pana pua.** To shoot with bow and arrow; archer, archery.

**panau.** To move restlessly.

**pane.** 1. Answer, reply; to answer. 2. Hind part of the head; top, summit (preceded by *ke*).

**paneʻe.** 1. To move along, push along a little. *Paneʻe i mua,* to progress. 2. Delayed, postponed; delay, postponement; to do in installments. **hoʻopaneʻe.** To postpone, delay, put off, procrastinate. See *uku hoʻopaneʻe.*

**panepane.** To retort, talk back.

**pani.** To close, shut, substitute, replace; closure, stopper, lid, cover, gate, door, substitute.

**pani hakahaka.** To substitute, fill a vacancy, replace; substitute, replacement, successor, proxy.

**paniinoa.** Pronoun. *Lit.,* name substitute.

**pani kai.** Levee, dike, protection against the sea.

**panina.** End, closing, conclusion, finish.

**pānini.** Prickly pear *(Opuntia megacantha),* the common wild cactus of Hawaiʻi; the fruits are edible. *Lit.,* fence wall.

**pānini-o-Ka-puna-hou.** Night-blooming cereus *(Hylocereus undatus). Lit.,* Ka-puna-hou cactus (for the famous hedge at Punahou School).

**paniolo.** 1. Cowboy. 2. *(Cap.)* Spaniard; Spain; Spanish. (Spanish, *español.*)

**pani ʻōmole.** Bottle stopper, cork.

**pani puka.** Door, gate; beggar sitting near a doorway.

**pani pūpū.** Cat's-eye, operculum or valve that closes a shell.

**pani wai.** Dam, sluice, levee, dike.

**pano.** Dark, as clouds; black.

**pānoʻo.** Same as *pāoʻo.*

**pao.** 1. To scoop out, dub out, chisel out, peck, bore. 2. Cave, pit, cavern.

**paoa.** Strongly odoriferous; a strong odor.

**paoka, paoda.** Powder. *Eng.*

**paona.** Pound, balance, scales, weight. *Eng.* See *kaupaona.*

**paona kaulike.** Balance, scales.

**pāoʻo.** Name for several species of blennies (the fish family Blenniidae).

**pāoʻo kauila.** Blenny *(Exallias brevis).*

**papa.** Flat surface, stratum, layer, level, foundation, reef, board, lumber, story of a building; class, rank, order; flat, level; wooden.

**pāpā.** 1. To forbid, prohibit. 2. To touch. **hoʻopāpā.** To touch repeatedly; contest in wit or strength; repartee.

**papaʻa.** Redup. of *paʻa;* tight, secure.

**pāpaʻa.** Cooked crisp, overdone, burned, parched; scab.

**papa ʻaiana.** Ironing board.

**pāpaʻa lā.** Sunburned, tanned, parched.

**pāpaʻa palaoa.** Slice of bread.

**papa heʻe nalu.** Surfboard. *Lit.,* board [for] sliding waves.

**papahele.** Floor.

**papa helu.** Table, list, enumeration, statistics.

**papa hīmeni.** Choir.

**papa hōʻike.** Program, timetable.

**papa hoʻolaha.** Billboard.

**Papa Hoʻonaʻauao.** Board of Education.

**papa hulei.** Seesaw, teeter.

**pāpaʻi. 1.** General name for crabs. **2.** Temporary hut or shelter.

**papa inoa.** List or catalog of names.

**papakema, bapatema.** Baptism. *Eng.*

**papa kuhikuhi.** Table of contents, index, program, timetable.

**papa kuhikuhi manawa.** Schedule, as of ship arrivals.

**papa kuʻi ʻai.** Poi-pounding board.

**pāpala.** All species of a native genus *(Charpentiera)* of shrubs and small trees.

**papa lāʻau.** Board, plank, large platter.

**pā pālahalaha.** Platter (preceded by *ke*).

**pā palai.** Frying pan (preceded by *ke*).

**papale.** Redup. of *pale,* to ward off.

**pāpale.** Hat; to put on or wear a hat.

**pāpale aliʻi.** Crown.

**pāpale kapu.** Cap.

**papa lele kawa.** Springboard for diving.

**pāpale ʻoʻoma.** Bonnet, sunbonnet.

**pāpālina, papālina.** Cheek, cheeks.

**Papa Luna Kiaʻi.** Board of Supervisors.

**papani.** Redup. of *pani,* to close; interception.

**papa niho.** Row of teeth, set of teeth, jaw.

**papa noho.** Bench.

**Papa Ola.** Board of Health.

**pāpāʻōlelo.** To converse, talk.

**Papa o nā Kahu Kula o ke Kulanui.** Board of Regents of the University.

**pāpapa. 1.** Low, flat. **2.** Beans, peas, lentils.

**papa paʻi.** Printing press.

**papa palapala.** Writing desk, board, flat surface for writing.

**papa puʻukani.** Choir, choral group.

**papau.** Deeply engaged, absorbed, engrossed; united; all together.

**pāpaʻu.** Shallow, shoal.

**papekema, bapetema.** Same as *papakema.*

**Papekike, Bapetite.** Baptist. *Eng.*

**papekiko, bapetiso.** To baptize; baptismal; *(cap.)* Baptist.

**pāpio.** Same as *pāpiopio,* a fish.

**pāpiopio.** Young stage of growth of *ulua,* a fish.

**pāpū. 1.** Fort, fortress. **2.** Clear, unobstructed.

**pāpū lewa.** Flying fortress, battleship.

**pau.** Finished, ended, completed, over, all done, final; entirely, completely, very much; all, to have all; to be completely possessed, consumed, destroyed. *Pau Pele, pau manō,* consumed by Pele, consumed by a shark (an oath meaning "May I be destroyed if I have not spoken truth"). *Pau iā kākou,* we've finished. **hoʻopau.** To put an end to, finish, stop, cancel, revoke, repeal, abolish, consume, discharge. See *hoʻopau manawa.*

**paʻu. 1.** Soot, smudge. **hoʻopaʻu.** To soil, smudge. **2.** Drudgery, slavery, tedious work.

**paʻū.** Moist, damp, moldy.

**pāʻū.** Woman's skirt or sarong, especially as worn by female horseback riders.

**paua.** A clam.

**pau ahi.** Destruction by fire, burned; to put out a fire. See *ʻinikua pau ahi, kāhea pau ahi.*

**pauaho.** Out of breath, panting, discouraged, despairing, weary, exhausted. **hoʻopauaho.** To cause shortness of breath or weariness.

**pau ā pau.** Everyone, all the people.

**pauka, pauda.** Powder. *Eng.*

**paukū.** Section, link, piece, stanza, verse, article (as of law), paragraph; to section off, cut in sections, slice.

**paukū manawa.** Portion of time, era.

**paukū ʻolokaʻa.** Cylinder.

**paula.** Powder. *Eng.*

**paulele.** Faith, confidence, trust; to have faith, confidence.

**pau loa.** All, everything; to have all.

**pāuma.** 1. Large curved needle. 2. Bent, curved. 3. Breastbone.

**pā uma.** Standing wrist wrestling.

**-pau manawa. hoʻopau manawa.** To waste time; not worth doing, waste of effort or time.

**pāʻumeʻume.** 1. Tug-of-war game; to play this. 2. Contentious, quarreling, fighting.

**pāʻū-o-Hiʻiaka.** A native beach vine *(Jacquemontia sandwicensis)* in the morning-glory family.

**-pau pilikia. hoʻopau pilikia.** To attend the calls of nature. *Wahi hoʻopau pilikia,* toilet, outhouse.

**pau pono.** Completely finished.

**pau pū.** All together, including all; completely demolished.

**pawa.** Darkness just before dawn.

**pā waʻa.** Canoe enclosure.

**pāwehe.** Generic name for colored geometric motifs, as on *makaloa* mats made on Niʻihau, bowls, and gourds; to make such.

**pe, pē-.** Thus, so, like. See *pehea, pēia, pēlā, penei.*

**pē.** 1. Crushed, flattened, humble, low. **hoʻopē.** To crush. 2. Perfumed, fragrant. **hoʻopē.** To perfume, anoint. 3. Drenched, soaked. **hoʻopē.** To drench, soak.

**pea.** 1. Also **fea.** Fair, carnival, exhibit. *Eng.* 2. Pear, avocado. *Eng.* 3. Also **bea.** Bear. *Eng.*

**peʻa.** 1. Cross; to cross, turn and go. 2. Kite. 3. Bat. 4. Sail, as of a canoe. 5. See *hale peʻa.*

**peʻahi.** Fan; to fan, brush, signal.

**peʻahi uila.** Electric fan.

**peʻa nui.** Mainsail.

**peʻapeʻahi.** Redup. of *peʻahi.*

**peʻe.** To hide; hiding.

**peʻelua.** Caterpillar.

**peʻepeʻe.** Redup. of *peʻe.*

**pehea.** How? What? How about it? *Pehea ʻoe?* How are you? *Pehea lā!* I don't know how.

**pehi.** To throw, throw at.

**pehu.** Swollen; to swell; dropsy.

**pēia.** Thus, like this, this way; to say.

**pekapeka.** To tattle, tell tales; stool pigeon.

**peke.** Dwarf, brownie.

**peki.** 1. To pace, move along step by step, trudge. *Eng.* 2. To back up. *Eng.* 3. Spade. *Eng.*

**peku.** Kick; to kick.

**pekunia.** Petunia.

**pela.** Fertilizer, decayed flesh.

**pēlā.** In that way, like that, thus, so, that way; to say. *Pēlā paha,* maybe so.

**pela moe.** Mattress.

**pelapela.** Filthy, dirty, nasty, obscene.

**pele.** 1. Lava flow, volcano, eruption. 2. *(Cap.)* The volcano goddess.

**pelehū.** Turkey. *Lit.,* swollen swelling.

**Pelekane.** Britain, British, England, English, Englishman. *Eng.*

**Pelekania, Beretania.** Britain, British. *Eng.*

**peleki.** Brake; to apply brakes. *Eng.*

**pelekikena, peresidena.** President; presidential. *Eng.*

**pelekunu.** Musty, rank, or moldy odor.

**pelena, berena.** Crackers, bread.

**pelu.** To fold, turn over, turn under; hem, tuck; to take a hem or tuck.

**pena.** Paint; to paint. *Eng.*

**penei.** This way, like this, thus, as follows; to be thus.

**peni.** Pen, pencil. *Eng.*

**penikala.** Pencil (sometimes preceded by *ke*).

**penu.** To sop up, as gravy; to dunk, dab.

**pepa.** 1. Paper, card, playing cards; to play cards. *Eng.* 2. Pepper. *Eng.*

**pepa hahau.** Playing cards.

**pepa hale.** Wallpaper.

**pepa hāleu.** Toiletpaper.

**pepa kalakala.** Sandpaper.

**pepa kīkoʻo.** Check, for paying money.

**pepa lahilahi.** Tissue paper, thin paper.

**pepa mānoanoa.** Cardboard.

**pepa poʻoleka.** Postcard.

**pepe.** Flat, as a nose, low, squatty.

**pēpē.** Redup. of *pē, 1. Naʻau pēpē*, modest spirit.

**pepeʻe.** Twisted, crooked, deformed.

**pepehi.** To beat, strike, pound, kill.

**pepehi kanaka.** Murder, murderer, manslaughter; to commit murder.

**pepeiao.** 1. Ear. 2. Chinese cake stuffed with meat.

**pepeiao akua.** Tree fungus, bracket fungus, Jew's-ear *(Auricularia auricula).*

**pepeiao ʻeha.** Earache.

**pepeiaohao.** Horn of an animal.

**pepeiao kuli.** A deaf ear, deafness, disobedience, refusal to listen to advice.

**Pepeluali.** February. *Eng.*

**peu.** To thrust or push up, uproot, prod.

**pewa.** Tail of fish, shrimp, lobster.

**pī.** 1. Stingy (sometimes preceded by *ke*). 2. To sputter, snort. 3. To sprinkle. 4. Peas, beans. *Eng.* 5. The letter *p. Eng.*

**pia.** 1. Polynesian arrowroot *(Tacca leontopetaloides).* 2. Starch. 3. Also **bia.** Beer. *Eng.*

**piʻa.** A kind of yam *(Dioscorea pentaphylla).*

**pīʻalu.** Wrinkled with age.

**pīʻāpā.** Alphabet.

**piapia.** Encrusted white matter in the eyes, as after sleeping or from sore eyes, "sand" in the eyes.

**pīʻena.** Fiery tempered.

**piha.** Full, complete, filled, full-blooded; completion, capacity, fullness; pregnant. **hoʻopiha.** To fill, complete, stuff, eat one's fill; to load, as a gun.

**piha ʻekelo.** Mynah bird *(Acridotheres tristis).*

**piha makahiki.** Yearly anniversary; to have such. *Lā piha makahiki,* birthday.

**pihapiha.** Full, complete, filled. **hoʻopihapiha.** To fill, complete, file (as cards); questionnaire, form to be filled in.

**-pihapiha ʻōlelo. hoʻopihapiha ʻōlelo.** To stir up dislike, gossip.

**piha pono.** Completely full, complete. *Piha pono ka manaʻo,* completely clear and intelligible idea.

**pihe.** Din of voices, crying, shouting; to mourn, shout.

**pihi.** 1. Scab, scar. 2. Button, badge; to button (preceded by *ke*). 3. Blunt, dull.

**pihi pūlima.** Cuff button.

**pīhoihoi.** Disturbed, excited, worried. **hoʻopīhoihoi.** To cause anxiety or worry; to worry, excite, astonish.

**pihole.** To fidget, paw, squirm.

**piholo.** To sink, founder, drown, be swamped.

**pīhopa, bihopa.** Bishop; Episcopalian. *Eng.*

**piʻi.** 1. To go inland (whether uphill or not); to go up, climb, ascend, mount, rise. **hoʻopiʻi.** To cause to rise. 2. To experience, as heat, cold, emotion. *Piʻi ke anu,* to get chills. *Piʻi ka wela,* to get a fever; to feel the heat of anger. **hoʻopiʻi.** To stir up ill feelings.

**-pi'i.** ho'opi'i. To sue, bring suit, accuse in court; lawsuit, court case.

**pi'ikoi.** To claim honors not rightfully due, seek preferment, aspire to the best.

**pi'ina.** Climb, ascent, rise.

**pi'ipi'i.** 1. Redup. of pi'i, 1, 2; bubbling forth, overflowing; to arouse anger, jealousy. 2. Curly, curled, wavy.

**pi'ipi'i 'ōlelo.** Words of anger, emotion, controversy.

**pī kai.** To sprinkle with sea water or salted water, as to remove taboo.

**pīkake.** 1. Arabian jasmine *(Jasminum sambac)*, a shrub with fragrant, small white flowers used for leis. 2. Peafowl *(Pavo cristata)*.

**pīkake hōkū.** Star jasmine *(Jasminum multiflorum)*.

**pika wai.** Water pitcher.

**piki.** 1. Shrunk, shortened, irregular. *Lei piki*, lei made of feathers of uneven length. 2. Peach. *Eng.*

**Pīkī.** Fiji, Fijian. *Eng.*

**pikipiki'ō.** Rough, stormy, choppy, agitated.

**piko.** 1. Navel, navel string, umbilical cord, genitals. *Pehea kō piko?* How is your navel? (a facetious greeting avoided by many because of the double meaning). 2. Summit of a hill or mountain, crown of the head, ear tip, end of a rope.

**pīkoi.** 1. Core, as of breadfruit or pandanus. 2. Tripping club.

**piku, fiku.** Fig *(Ficus carica)*.

**pila.** 1. Any string musical instrument, formerly the fiddle. *Eng. Ho'okani pila*, to play music. 2. Also **bila**. Bill; to make out a bill. *Eng.*

**pila (bila) 'ai'ē.** Voucher.

**pila kīko'o.** Check, draft, bill.

**pila kīko'o hale leka.** Money order.

**pila koi.** Requisition.

**pīlali.** Gum, hardened sap of the *kukui* tree; resin, wax; sticky, gummy.

**pila puhipuhi.** Harmonica, mouth organ.

**pilau.** Rot, stench, rottenness; to stink; putrid, spoiled, rotten, decomposed.

**pila 'ume'ume.** Accordion.

**pilawaiwai.** Account, reckoning.

**pili.** 1. To cling, stick, adhere, touch, join, associate with, be with; clinging, sticking; close relationship. *E pili kāua*, let's be together. See *hoa pili*. ho'opili. To bring together, stick. 2. A grass *(Heteropogon contortus)*, formerly used for house thatch; thatch. See *hale pili*. 3. To refer, concern, relate, apply. ho'opili. To refer. 4. Wager, bet; to bet.

**pilialoha.** Close friendship, beloved companionship; to have such.

**pilikia.** Trouble of any kind, tragedy, nuisance, bother, distress, accident, inconvenience. ho'o-pilikia. To cause trouble, bother.

**piliko'a.** Hawkfishes *(Paracirrhites forsteri, Cirrhitops fasciatus, Amblycirrhites bimacula)*. *Lit.*, coral-clinging.

**pili koko.** Blood relationship or relative.

**pilimua.** Article (the part of speech): *ka, ke, nā, he*.

**pilimua maopopo.** Definite article.

**pilina.** Association, relationship, union; joining.

**pili'ōlelo.** Grammar.

**-pilipili 'ōlelo.** ho'opilipili 'ōlelo. Word play, punning; to illustrate with parable, story, or anecdote.

**Pilipino, Filipino.** Philippines, Filipino. *Eng.*

**pili pono.** Well-suited, well-matched, close-fitting; to refer exactly or concisely.

**pili pū.** To unite, join, cling to.

**piliwaiwai.** Gambling, betting, gambler; to bet, gamble.

**piliwi.** To believe. *Eng.*

**pilo.** Swampy, foul odor; halitosis; polluted.

**pina'i.** Again and again, repeatedly; to come or do repeatedly; close together, crowded.

**pinana.** To climb; a climb.

**pinao.** Dragonfly.

**pine.** Pin, peg, bolt, picket; to pin. *Eng.*

**pineki.** Peanut. *Eng.*

**pinepine.** Frequent, often, frequently.

**pinika.** Vinegar. *Eng.*

**pio.** 1. Captive, prisoner; conquered, captured; game of tag. **ho'opio.** To conquer, make prisoner, capture. 2. Extinguished or out, as a fire or light. **ho'opio.** To put out, extinguish. 3. To peep, chirp.

**pi'o.** Arch, arc; bent, arched, curved; to arch, as the rainbow.

**pi'oe.** General name for barnacles.

**pi'oloke.** Alarmed, startled, confused, agitated.

**pipi.** 1. Pearl oyster *(Pinctada radiata).* 2. Also **bipi.** Beef, cattle. *Eng.*

**pipi.** Redup. of *pī, 2;* squinting, twinkling.

**pipī.** Redup. of *pī, 1, 3;* to urinate *(Eng.) Pīpī holo ka'ao,* sprinkled, the tale runs on (phrase used at the end of tales).

**pipi'i.** 1. Expensive, high-priced. 2. Bubbling, overflowing. *Wai pipi'i,* bubbling water, charged water.

**pipika.** To draw away, shrink away, crinkle up, avoid.

**pipi kāne.** Bull.

**pipi kaula.** Jerked beef (salted and dried) broiled before being eaten. *Lit.,* rope beef.

**pipi keiki.** Calf.

**pipiki.** Shrunk, crinkled, tight, cramped.

**pipine.** Promiscuous; promiscuous person.

**pipine.** Miserly, stingy.

**pipi palai.** Beefsteak.

**pipipi.** General name for small mollusks, including *Theodoxus neglectus.*

**pipipi kōlea.** Periwinkle *(Littorina pintado, L. scabra).*

**pipi po'a.** Steer. *Lit.,* castrated beef.

**pipi pulu.** Bull.

**pipi wahine.** Cow.

**pipi waiū.** Milk cow.

**piula.** 1. Mule, donkey. 2. Tired, exhausted. *Slang.* 3. Pewter, tin, corrugated iron. *Eng.* See *wai piula.*

**piwa.** 1. Also **fiwa.** Fever. *Eng.* 2. Also **biwa.** Beaver. *Eng.*

**piwa ho'onāwaliwali.** Typhoid fever.

**piwa lenalena.** Yellow fever.

**piwa 'ula'ula.** Scarlet fever.

**pō.** Night, darkness; realm of the gods; dark, benighted. *Ua pō,* it's late (not necessarily night). *Ua hana māua ā pō ka lā,* we worked until night (until the day darkened). *Ka pō nei,* last night.

**pōā.** To rob, plunder; robber.

**po'a.** 1. Castrated; eunuch. 2. Sudden sound; to make such. 3. To dig under, undermine.

**pō'ae'ae.** Armpit.

**pō'aha.** Circle, as of flowers; trailing plant.

**Pō'ahā.** Thursday. *Lit.,* fourth day.

**pō'aha mālamalama.** Halo. *Lit.,* light circle.

**poahi.** 1. Dim, obscure. 2. To revolve, spin, rotate.

**pō'ai.** Circle, circuit, hoop, girdle, group (as of friends); to make a circuit, go around, encircle.

**pō'ai hapalua.** Semicircle, half circle.

**pō'ai-waena-honua.** Equator.

**Pō'akahi.** Monday. *Lit.,* first day.

**Pō'akolu.** Wednesday. *Lit.,* third day.

**Pō'akolu Kau Lehu.** Ash Wednesday.

**Pō'alima.** Friday. *Lit.,* fifth day.

**Pō‘alima Hemolele, Pō‘alima Maika‘i.** Good Friday.

**pō‘alo.** To gouge out, scoop out, pluck, extract; to shell, as beans.

**Pō‘alua.** Tuesday. *Lit.*, second day.

**Pō‘aono.** Saturday. *Lit.*, sixth day. *Ho‘omana Pō‘aono,* Seventh Day Adventist religion.

**poe.** Round, rounded. **ho‘opoe.** To round, shape. *Pipi ho‘opoe,* meat ball.

**po‘e.** People, persons, group of people, number of. *Ka po‘e wāhine,* the women. *Po‘e hale,* group of houses.

**poehi.** Dim, obscure.

**poeko.** Fluent, clever in speaking.

**pō‘ele.** Black, dark; dark night; ignorant.

**pō‘ele‘ele.** Redup. of *pō‘ele.*

**poepoe.** Round, rounded; compact, compressed; full, as the moon; globe, sphere.

**poepoe honua.** Globe of the earth.

**pohā.** 1. To burst, crack, break forth. 2. Cape gooseberry *(Physalis peruviana).*

**pōhae.** Torn, fragile.

**pōhāhā ahi.** Fireball.

**pōhāhā wai.** Bubble.

**pōhai.** Circle group; gathering.

**pōhaku.** Rock, stone, mineral, tablet; rocky, stony. See *haku, 3.*

**pōhaku hānau.** Stones at Kū-kaniloko, O‘ahu, and Holoholokū, Kaua‘i, against which chiefesses rested as they gave birth.

**pōhaku ke‘oke‘o.** Marble.

**pōhaku kihi.** Cornerstone.

**pōhaku ku‘i ‘ai, pōhaku ku‘i poi.** Poi pounder.

**pōhaku lepo.** Brick, adobe.

**pōhaku maika‘i.** Precious stone.

**pōhaku ‘ōma‘oma‘o.** Emerald.

**pōhaku pa‘a.** General name for hard rocks, such as those used for adzes.

**pōhaku pele.** Lava rock.

**pohala.** 1. To revive after fainting, recover consciousness; to recover from sickness; relieved of worry; relief, rest. 2. To open, as petals.

**pohāpohā.** 1. Redup. of *pohā, 1.* 2. A kind of passionflower called running pop *(Passiflora foetida).*

**pohe haole.** Nasturtium.

**pōheo.** Knob or knoblike object; penis head.

**pōheoheo.** Knob or knoblike object.

**pohihihi.** Obscure, entangled, intricate, confusing, difficult.

**pōhina.** 1. Gray, misty, foggy, hazy. 2. To topple, fall prone.

**poho.** 1. Hollow or palm of the hand; depression, hollow; container, receptacle. 2. Mortar; to knead. 3. Patch, as in clothes or in a calabash; to patch. 4. To belly out, puff out. 5. Chalk.

**pohō.** 1. Loss, damage; out of luck. See *koi pohō.* **ho‘opohō.** To cause a loss, sell at a loss. 2. Bog, swamp, mire, slough.

**poho ahi.** Matchbox.

**poholalo.** Underhanded, deceitful, dishonest; to burrow, filch, deal dishonestly.

**pohole.** Bruised, skinned, scraped, peeled.

**poho lima.** Palm or hollow of the hand, handful.

**poholo.** To sink, slip into, vanish; to miscarry.

**poholua.** To billow out, as sails.

**poho mea kanu.** Flowerpot.

**poho pa‘akai.** Salt shaker, salt container.

**poho pauka.** Powder container, compact, vanity case.

**pohopoho.** Redup. of *poho, 2, 3;* patched. *Kapa pohopoho,* crazy quilt or patchwork quilt.

**poho wāwae.** Hollow of the foot.

**pohu.** Calm, quiet; calmed, soothed; to calm down.

**pōhue.** 1. General name for gourd plant; potsherd. Also called *ipu.* 2. A climbing legume *(Canavalia sericea).*

pōhuehue. Beach morning-glory *(Ipomoea pes-caprae* subsp. *brasiliensis).*

pōhuku. Swollen, protruding, heaped.

pōhuli. Sucker, sprout; to sprout, as bananas.

poi. Poi, the Hawaiian staff of life, made from cooked taro corms, or rarely breadfruit, pounded until smooth and thinned with water.

po'i. 1. Cover, lid; to cover (preceded by *ke*). 2. Top or crest of a breaking wave; to break, of waves. 3. To pounce, catch between cupped hands, snatch.

poi mai'a. Mashed ripe bananas and water.

po'imalau. Portuguese man-of-war *(Physalia).*

poina. To forget, forgotten. *Mai poina 'oe ia 'u,* don't forget me.

pō'ino. Misfortune, ill luck, distress, misery, damage, injury; unfortunate. ho'opō'ino. To harm, injure, devastate; to cause distress, damage. *Ho'opō'ino malū,* to harm secretly; sabotage.

po'ipū. To cover completely, as with clouds or waves; to attack, overwhelm; attack.

po'i wai holoi. Washbasin, finger bowl.

pōkā. Bullet, cannon ball.

pōka'a. Ball, coil, roll, spool; to wind, roll, coil, revolve.

pōkā lū. Buckshot, grapeshot.

pōka'o. Barren, dry, tasteless, naked, destitute, boring.

pōkā pahū. Bomb, bombardment; to bomb.

pōkā pū. Bullet.

poke. To slice, cut crosswise; section, slice, piece.

pōkē. Bouquet; to make a bouquet. *Eng.*

pōkeokeo. 1. Turkey gobble, turkey. 2. Plump, prosperous.

pōki'i. Younger brother or sister or closely related younger cousin.

pōki'i kaina. Younger sibling of one's own sex.

pokipoki. 1. Box crab *(Calappa hepatica).* 2. Sow bug, pill bug.

poko. Short for *pōkole.*

pōkole. Short; shortage. ho'opōkole. To shorten, abbreviate.

Pokoliko. Puerto Rico. *Eng.*

pola. 1. Flap, as of a loincloth; tail of a kite. 2. Also bola. Bowl, cup (preceded by *ke*). *Eng.*

polapola. 1. Recovered from sickness; well after sickness; sprouting, as a bud. ho'opolapola. To cure; to fill out, as after sickness. 2. *(Cap.)* Tahiti, Borabora; Tahitian.

Polenekia. Polynesia; Polynesian. *Eng.*

poli. Bosom, breast, depression, heart, arms. *Ma ka poli iho nei,* in the arms.

polinahe. Soft and gentle, as a breeze.

poli wāwae. Hollow of the foot, instep.

polohiwa. Dark, glistening black, as clouds.

poloka. Frog, toad. *Eng.*

poloke. Broken; broke (without funds). *Eng.*

pololei. 1. Straight, correct, right, accurate, all right. ho'opololei. To straighten, correct. 2. A land shell *(Lamellaxis).*

pōloli. Hunger; hungry.

pololoi. Var. of *pololei, 1.*

pololū. Long spear.

polopeka. Professor; professorial; to be a professor. *Eng.*

polū. Blue, as clothes. *Eng.*

poluea. Nausea, dizziness, seasickness, hangover; seasick.

pōmaika'i. Good fortune, blessedness, blessing, prosperity; prosperous, fortunate, lucky; benefits and improvements to property. ho'opōmaika'i. To cause good fortune; to bless, say grace.

pona. 1. Socket, eyeball; joint of

sugarcane stalk or bamboo. **2.**
Also **bona.** Bond. *Eng.*

**pōna'ana'a.** Confused, bewildered.

**pōnalo.** Plant louse, gnat, small
fly such as *Drosophila;* blight;
shriveled; swarming.

**pō nei.** Last night.

**poni. 1.** To anoint, consecrate, oil,
crown, ordain, inaugurate,
daub; ointment. **ho'oponi.** To
anoint, crown, ordain, consecrate, inaugurate. **2.** Purple.

**ponimō'ī.** Carnation *(Dianthus
caryophyllus).*

**poni mō'ī.** Coronation; to crown
a king or queen.

**ponimō'īli'ili'i.** Sweet william
*(Dianthus barbatus).*

**poniponi.** Redup. of *poni, 2.*

**pōniu.** Dizzy, giddy; dizziness; to
rotate, whirl, spin.

**pōniuniu.** Redup. of *pōniu.*

**pono. 1.** Goodness, morality,
moral qualities, correct or proper procedure, excellence, well-being, prosperity, welfare, duty;
moral, fitting, proper, right,
just, fair, successful; should,
ought, must, necessary. *Ka pono
kahiko,* the old morality. *Pono i
ke kānāwai,* legal. *Pono 'ole ka
mana'o,* disturbed, worried. *Me
ka pono,* respectfully. *E pono iā
'oe ke hele,* you should go.
**ho'opono.** Righteous, respectable, correct; to behave correctly. **2.** Completely, properly,
carefully, much. *Pau pono,*
completely finished. *Nānā pono,*
look carefully. **3.** Property, gear,
possessions, necessities.

**pono hale.** Furniture, household
goods.

**pono hana.** Tools.

**pono'ī.** Self, own; directly, exactly. *'O wau pono'ī,* I, myself. *Hawai'i pono'ī,* Hawai'i's own
[people].

**pono kīwila.** Civil rights.

**ponokope.** Copyright; to copyright.

**ponopono. 1.** Neat, in order, arranged. **ho'oponopono.** To
correct, revise, edit, put to right;
mental cleansing, as by family
discussion. *Luna ho'oponopono,* editor, adminstrator. See
*hale ho'oponopono.* **2.** Redup.
of *pono, 1;* well off, wealthy.

**pono 'uhane.** Spiritual welfare.

**po'o. 1.** Head, summit, director;
end, as of rope, pole, cane (preceded by *ke*). **2.** Depression,
cavity; to dip, scoop, dub,
erode.

**po'ohiwi.** Shoulder, wing of a
kite.

**po'o kanaka.** Human head, skull.
See *heiau po'o kanaka.*

**po'okela.** Foremost, best, superior; champion; to excel.

**po'olā.** Stevedore.

**po'oleka.** Postage stamp.

**po'o lua.** Child sired by other than
the husband, but accepted by
both husband and sire.

**po'omana'o.** Topic, theme, headline, title.

**po'o'ōlelo.** Title, text.

**po'opa'a.** Hawkfish *(Cirrhites
pinnulatus).* Lit., hard head.

**po'opo'o.** Redup. of *po'o, 2;*
sunken; nook, cranny.

**Pope.** Pope, papist, Catholic.
*Eng.*

**pōpilikia.** Trouble, distress, misfortune. **ho'opōpilikia.** To
cause distress, trouble.

**popo.** Rot.

**pōpō. 1.** Ball, cluster, bunch. **2.**
Short for *'apōpō,* tomorrow.

**pōpōahi.** Fireball.

**pōpōhau.** Hydrangea *(Hydrangea
macrophylla).*

**popohe.** Round, shapely, neat.

**pōpoki.** Cat.

**pōpolo. 1.** Black nightshade *(Solanum nigrum),* herbaceous
plant important in Hawaiian
medicine; bears clusters of
small, black, edible berries. **2.**
Negro. *Slang.* **3.** An endemic
lobelia *(Cyanea solanacea).*

**pōpolohua.** Purplish blue; dark, as a bruise.

**popopo.** Rot, decay; rotten, decayed.

**pou.** 1. Post. 2. Ridge, as of nose.

**pou kihi.** Corner post.

**pouli.** 1. Dark, darkness, ignorance. **ho'opouli.** To darken, mislead. 2. Eclipse.

**pōuliuli.** Redup. of *pouli, 1;* murky, gloomy.

**poupou.** Short and stocky, stout.

**pū.** 1. Large triton conch shell or triton's trumpet *(Charonia tritonis);* wind instrument, as horn, trumpet, cornet. 2. Gun, pistol. 3. General name for pumpkin or squash. 4. Tree with cluster of several stalks, as banana, pandanus, or kava; clump, as of sugarcane. 5. Together, entirely. *Like pū,* just the same. *'O wa pū,* me too. 6. Sluggish, inactive, quiet, bored.

**pua.** 1. Flower, blossom. 2. To appear, come forth, emerge; to smoke, blow, speak, shine. 3. Child, descendant, young fish, fry. 4. Arrow, dart.

**pū'ā.** 1. Flock, herd; to flock. 2. Sheaf, bundle; to tie in bundles.

**pua'a.** 1. Pig, hog, swine, pork. 2. Bank of fog or clouds.

**pū'ā'ā.** Scattered, dispersed; to flee.

**pua'a hame.** Ham.

**pua ahi, puahi.** To glow like fire.

**pua ahiahi.** Same as *nani ahiahi,* four-o'clock flower.

**pua ali'i.** Descendant of a chief.

**pua aloalo.** See *aloalo.*

**puaaneane.** Extreme old age.

**pua'a wahine.** Sow.

**pua hilahila.** Sensitive plant *(Mimosa pudica* var. *unijuga).* Lit., bashful flower.

**pua hipa.** Lamb.

**pū'ā hipa.** Flock of sheep.

**pua hōkū hihi.** Waxflower or wax plant *(Hoya bicarinata).*

**pua'i.** To flow out, as water; to bubble, gurgle, boil, vomit; to utter, as speech.

**pū'ā'ī.** Adam's apple.

**pua kala.** 1. Beach poppy or prickly poppy *(Argemone glauca);* the yellowish juice, which contains a narcotic, was used by Hawaiians to relieve pain. 2. Spear thistle *(Cirsium vulgare).*

**pua kalaunu.** Crown flower *(Calotropis gigantea);* large shrub of the milkweed family, bearing small white crown-shaped flowers often used in leis.

**puakea.** Pale; a tint between white and pink, as sunset clouds. See *'ilipuakea.*

**pua kenikeni.** A shrub or small tree *(Fagraea herteriana),* bearing fragrant yellow flowers used in leis.

**pua kīkā.** Cigar flower *(Cuphea ignea).*

**pua kō.** Stem and tassel of sugarcane.

**pualele.** Sow thistle *(Sonchus oleraceus).*

**pualena.** 1. Yellow. 2. Lazy.

**pū'ali.** 1. Warrior. 2. To gird tightly about the waist; notch, tight belt.

**Pū'ali Ho'ōla.** Salvation Army.

**pū'ali inu wai.** Temperance league. *Lit.,* water-drinking host.

**pū'ali kaua ka'i wāwae.** Infantry. *Lit.,* war army going afoot.

**pū'ali koa.** Armed forces.

**pualoalo.** Same as *pua aloalo,* hibiscus flower.

**pualu, puwalu.** A specis of surgeonfish.

**pū'alu.** Loose, slack, crumpled.

**pua makahiki.** Annual flower.

**puana.** 1. Beginning of a song; to begin a song; summary refrain of a song; theme of a song. *Ha'ina 'ia mai ana ka puana,* tell the summary refrain. 2. Pronunciation.

**pua nānā lā.** Common sunflower.

**puaneane.** Var. of *puaaneane.*

**pūanuanu.** Cold, chilly, damp.

**pū'ao. 1.** Mesh. **2.** Womb.

**pua'ohi.** To chatter, gush, ramble verbally.

**pua pepa.** Same as *nani mau loa. Lit.,* paper flower.

**pua pihi.** All kinds of zinnias, especially *Zinnia elegans.*

**pua pilipili.** Spanish clover *(Desmodium uncinatum).*

**pū'ā pipi.** Herd of cattle.

**puapua. 1.** Tail feathers, streamer. **2.** Redup. of *pua, 2.*

**pua pua'a.** Piglet.

**puapua'i.** Redup. of *pua'i.*

**pue.** To huddle, sit crouched.

**pu'e. 1.** Hill, as of sweet potatoes; dune; to hill up. **2.** To attack, rape.

**pu'e'eke.** To shrink away from, wrinkle up; to shorten, contract.

**puehu.** Scattered, dispersed, routed, gone.

**pūehuehu.** Redup. of *puehu;* tousled.

**pueo.** Hawaiian short-eared owl *(Asio flammeus sandwichensis).*

**pu'e one.** Sand dune or sandbar.

**pu'e wale.** To force, attack, rape.

**pūhā. 1.** Abcess, burst sore, ulcer; to break, burst. **2.** Hollow, as in a tree. **3.** To belch, clear the throat. **4.** To breathe air, as a turtle.

**pūhaka.** Loins.

**pū hala.** Pandanus tree.

**pūhā lā'au.** Hollow in a tree.

**puhalu.** Soft, flabby, loose, sagging, deflated; to loosen, stretch, sag. *Fig.,* relaxed, unenthusiastic.

**pūhau.** Cool spring.

**pūheheo.** Round and swirling, as a full skirt.

**puhemo. 1.** Loose, set free, released. **2.** Weak, listless.

**puhi. 1.** To burn, set on fire, bake. **2.** To blow, puff; to smoke, as tobacco; blowhole. **3.** Eel.

**puhi kō.** To burn cane trash or a cane field.

**puhi 'ohe.** To play a wind instrument; player of a wind instrument; flute. See *hui puhi 'ohe.*

**puhi 'ōni'o.** Whitemouth moray eel *(Lycodontis meleagris). Lit.,* spotted eel.

**puhi paka. 1.** To smoke tobacco; one who smokes; smoking. **2.** Large eel *(Lycodontis flavimarginatus).*

**pūhi'u.** To break wind audibly; considered rude.

**puhi ūhā.** A large eel *(Conger cinereus).*

**pūholo.** To steam, as of pig; to take a sweat bath.

**pū ho'okani.** Conch trumpet, wind instrument.

**pūhuluhulu.** Hairy, shaggy, downy, hirsute.

**puīa.** Sweet-smelling; diffused, as fragrance; permeated with fragrance. **ho'opuīa.** To perfume.

**pū'ili. 1.** Bamboo rattles, as used for dancing. **2.** To clasp, hold firmly in the hand, embrace.

**pu'ipu'i.** Plump, stout, stocky.

**pū'iwa.** Startled, surprised, astonished, frightened; fright, surprise. **ho'opū'iwa.** To startle, astonish, etc.

**pū'iwa'iwa.** Redup. of *pū'iwa.*

**puka. 1.** Hole (perforation; cf. *lua,* pit); door, gate, opening. **ho'opuka.** To make a hole or opening. **2.** To pass through, appear, issue, come into sight; to rise, as the sun. *Puka lā,* daily issue, as of a newspaper. **ho'opuka.** To issue, as a permit; to acquit, as a defendant in court. **3.** To graduate. **ho'opuka.** To graduate. **4.** To say, utter. **ho'opuka.** To proclaim, say, pronounce. *Ho'opuka 'ana,* pronunciation. **5.** To gain, win, profit, draw interest; winnings, gain, profit. **ho'opuka.** To invest, make a profit.

**puka 'ana.** Exodus (in the Bible), exit.

**pukaaniani, pukāniani.** Window.

**puka hale.** Door of a house, window.

**pukana lā.** Sunrise.

**pū kani.** Trumpet.

**puka pihi.** Buttonhole.

**pūkaua.** General, war leader, champion.

**pū kaua.** Artillery.

**puka uahi.** Smokestack, chimney.

**puke, buke.** Book. *Eng.*

**puke heluhelu.** Reader.

**puke hoʻomanaʻo.** Memorandum, memoirs, diary, journal.

**puke kuhikuhi.** Manual, book of instructions.

**puke pakeke.** Pocketbook.

**puke wehewehe ʻōlelo.** Dictionary. *Lit.*, book explaining words.

**pūkiawe. 1.** Black-eyed susan *(Abrus precatorius).* Also called *pūkiawe lei.* **2.** Native shrubs and small trees *(Styphelia [Cyathodes]).*

**pūkiʻi.** To tie.

**Pukikī.** Portuguese. *Palaoa Pukikī,* Portuguese sweetbread. *Eng.*

**pūkipa.** Bookkeeper. *Eng.*

**pū kō.** Clump of sugarcane.

**pūkoʻa.** Coral head.

**pūkolu.** Trio, triplet.

**pūkonakona.** Strong, husky, tough. Cf. *konakona.*

**puku.** To gather together, pucker; shrunken.

**pūkuʻi. 1.** To collect, assemble; council, assembly. **2.** To sit doubled up; to nestle together, hug. **3.** Hub.

**pūkuʻikuʻi.** Redup. of *pūkuʻi, 2.*

**pū kuni ahi.** Cannon. *Lit.*, gun burning fire.

**pukupuku.** Redup. of *puku;* wrinkles, frowns; to wrinkle, frown.

**pula.** Particle, as dust; particle in the eye, mote; to have something in the eye.

**pula lānahu.** Cinder.

**pūlale.** To hurry, rush.

**pūlama. 1.** Torch. **2.** To care for, cherish, save.

**pulapula.** Seedlings, sprouts, cuttings; descendant, offspring.

**hoʻopulapula.** To start seedlings or cuttings; to multiply, rehabilitate; rehabilitation. *Hoʻopulapula lāhui,* rehabilitation of the nation. *ʻĀina hoʻopulapula,* homesteading land.

**pule. 1.** Prayer, church service, grace, blessing; to pray. *Pule a ka Haku,* Lord's prayer. See *kahuna pule, Lāpule.* **2.** Week. *Kēia pule aʻe,* next week. *Kēlā pule aku nei,* last week.

**pule hoʻolaʻa.** Dedicatory prayer.

**pule hoʻomaikaʻi.** Prayer of thanks, benediction, grace; to say grace, offer a prayer of thanks.

**pule hoʻopōmaikaʻi.** Blessing; to ask a blessing.

**pūlehu.** To broil.

**pūlehulehu.** Dusk, twilight.

**pulelehua. 1.** Butterfly, moth, the Kamehameha butterfly *(Vanessa tameamea).* **hoʻopulelehua.** To act the butterfly, talk much but say little; frivolous. **2.** Windblown, as spray.

**pulelo.** To float, wave, as a flag (sometimes in sense of triumph).

**pule ʻohana.** Family prayer; to hold such.

**pulepule. 1.** Crazy. See *pupule.* **2.** Spotted, speckled.

**pūlewa. 1.** To float back and forth; unstable, changeable, unsteady. **2.** Weak, feeble. **3.** Same as *hālili,* sundial shell.

**pūliki. 1.** To embrace, hug, gird on, grip tightly. **2.** Vest.

**pūlima. 1.** Wrist, cuff; to clasp hands. See *pihi pūlima.* **2.** Handwriting, signature.

**pulo, buro.** Bureau, agency. *Eng.*

**Pulo ʻEʻe Moku.** Bureau of Emigration.

**pulo hoʻokō.** Executive board.

**pūloʻu.** Head covering; to cover the head.

**pūloʻuloʻu. 1.** Redup. of *pūloʻu.* **2.** A tapa-covered ball on a stick carried before a chief as insignia of taboo. **3.** Steam bath.

**pulu.** 1. Wet, moist, soaked. **hoʻopulu.** To wet, soak, moisten. 2.. Soft, glossy, yellowish wool on the base of tree-fern leaf stalks, formerly used to stuff mattresses and pillows. 3. Mulch, any greenery or underbrush used as mulch, coconut fiber, cushion, fine linen, tinder, kindling (preceded by *ke*). See *kapa pulu.* **hoʻopulu.** To mulch, fertilize with compost. 4. Also **bulu.** Bull. *Eng. Keoni Pulu,* John Bull. 5. Fool; to fool. *Eng.*

**pūlumi, burumi.** Broom; to sweep. *Eng.*

**pūlumi hale.** To sweep a house; janitor.

**puluna.** One's child's parents-in-law or aunts and uncles by marriage (often followed by *kāne* or *wahine*).

**pulu niu.** Coconut husk or fiber.

**pulu pē.** Thoroughly drenched, soaked; drunk.

**pulupulu.** Redup. of *pulu, 1, 2, 3.* 2. Cotton.

**pulupulu ahi.** Fire kindling; to kindle fire; hot-tempered.

**pulupulu haole.** The cotton plant.

**pū maiʻa.** Banana stalk.

**pumehana.** Warm, warmhearted; warmth, affection. *Me ka aloha pumehana,* with warm affection. **hoʻopumehana.** To warm, heat.

**puna.** 1. Spring (of water). 2. Coral, lime, plaster. 3. Section between joints or nodes, as of bamboo or sugarcane. 4. Spoon. *Eng.*

**punahele.** A favorite; to treat as a favorite.

**punalua.** Formerly, spouses sharing a spouse.

**pūnana.** Nest, hive; to nest.

**pūnana meli.** Beehive.

**pūnanana.** 1. Same as *nananana,* a spider. 2. Spider's web.

**pūnāwai.** Water spring.

**punawelewele.** Cobweb, spider web, spinning spider.

**pūneʻe.** Movable couch. See *hikieʻe.*

**puni.** 1. Surrounded, controlled, overcome; to gain control of. **hoʻopuni.** To surround, get control of. 2. To be fond of, love, covet; favorite thing, delight, love. **hoʻopuni.** To be charmed by, desire greatly. 3. Deceived. **hoʻopuni.** To deceive. 4. Completed.

**puni ʻai.** Fond of eating; glutton.

**punihei.** Ensnared, entangled; gullible; captivating, entrancing. *Moʻolelo punihei,* fascinating tale. **hoʻopunihei.** To fascinate, charm, ensnare, decoy, trap.

**puni hele.** Fond of going about from place to place.

**puni kālā.** Avaricious, mercenary.

**puni koko.** Bloodthirsty.

**puni leʻaleʻa.** Pleasure-loving, fond of fun.

**punipuni.** Redup. of *puni, 3.* **hoʻopunipuni.** To lie; lie, liar.

**pūniu.** 1. Polished coconut shell or bowl. 2. Small knee drum. 3. Human skull. 4. Fontanel of an infant. 5. To spin, as a top.

**puni waiwai.** Avaricious.

**puni wale.** Gullible, easily deceived.

**pūnohu.** To rise, as smoke or mist; to billow or spread.

**pūnono.** Gorgeously red, ever-beautiful, flushed.

**pūnua.** Young bird, fledgling.

**pūnuku.** Muzzle, halter; to muzzle.

**pūʻoʻa.** Tower, steeple, pyramid, peak.

**pūʻoheʻohe.** Job's-tears *(Coix lachryma-jobi).*

**puoho.** Startled; to cry out in fright.

**pū ʻoleʻolē.** Conch horn.

**pūʻolo.** Bundle, bag, container; to tie in a bundle.

**pūpanapana.** Pistol.

**pū poʻohiwi.** Musket.

**pupū.** To stall, move slowly; stuck, blocked.

**pūpū.** 1. General name for sea and land shells; beads. 2. Relish, snack, hors d'oeuvre; formerly, fish, chicken, or banana served with kava. 3. Bunch, bundle, as of grass; bouquet.

**pūpū ʻalā.** Cone shell (*Conus* sp.).

**pūpū ʻawa.** A sea shell *(Drupa ricinas, Purpura aperta)*.

**pupue.** Redup. of *pue*.

**pupuʻe.** Redup. of *puʻe, 2;* to attack, force.

**pupuhi.** Redup. of *puhi, 1, 2;* to spit.

**pū puhi.** Trumpet, horn, conch shell trumpet.

**pupuka.** Ugly, unsightly.

**pupule.** Crazy, insane. **hoʻopupule.** To drive insane.

**pūpū loloa.** Auger shell.

**pūpū momi.** Small mother-of-pearl shell.

**pupuni.** Redup. of *puni, 1-4.*

**pūpū Niʻihau.** A small shell (Columbellidae) found on Niʻihau.

**pūpū ʻōkole ʻoiʻoi.** Trochidae shell.

**pupupu.** 1. Numerous, crowded; congested. 2. Double-flowering.

**pūpū puhi.** Sundial shell *(Solarium* sp.); also called *hālili.*

**pupuʻu.** To double up.

**pūpū weuweu.** Clump of greenery.

**puʻu.** 1. Any kind of protuberance, from a pimple *(puʻu, 2)* to a hill; hill, peak, mound, bulge, heap, quantity, mass, clot, knob; heaped. 2. Any of various round parts or protuberances of the body, as pimple, wart, mole, callus, lump, Adam's apple, throat, larynx, tonsils, fist, knuckle, gizzard.

**puʻu ʻako.** Throat inflammation.

**puʻu ʻeha.** Sore throat.

**puʻuhonua.** Place of refuge, asylum, place of peace and safety.

**puʻu kālā.** Sum of money.

**puʻukani.** Sweet-voiced, sweet-toned; singer.

**puʻukaua.** Fort, fortification.

**pūʻukiʻuki.** Crowded, packed tightly, difficult.

**puʻu koko.** Blood clot, heart, fetus.

**puʻukole.** Mons pubis.

**puʻukū.** Treasurer.

**puʻulele.** Rupture, hernia.

**pūʻulu.** Group, crowd, army, party; to form a group; to crowd, assemble.

**pūʻulu kaua.** Army, fighting band, division.

**puʻumimi.** Bladder.

**puʻumoni, puʻumoniʻai.** Throat.

**puʻunaue, puʻunauwe.** To divide, share; division.

**puʻunaue loa.** Long division.

**puʻunaue pōkole.** Short division.

**puʻuōlaʻi.** Sharp-nosed puffer fish *(Canthigaster rivulatus).*

**puʻuone.** 1. Divination. 2. Pond near the shore.

**puʻu one.** Sand dune or heap.

**puʻupā.** Obstacle, struck object.

**puʻupaʻa.** 1. Virgin, virginity. 2. Kidneys.

**puʻupau.** Sore throat, throat cancer.

**puʻu pele.** Volcanic mound, hill.

**puʻu pepa.** Deck or hand of cards; pile of paper.

**puʻupuʻu.** 1. Redup. of *puʻu, 1;* lumpy, heaped, swollen. 2. Redup. of *puʻu, 2;* knuckles, joints; pimply, full of blotches; scurvy.

**puʻupuʻu liʻiliʻi.** Smallpox.

**puʻupuʻu lima.** Clenched fist, knuckles, blow of the fist.

**puʻupuʻu maneʻo.** Itching skin irritation or eruption.

**puʻupuʻu wāwae.** Ankle, ankle bones.

**puʻuwai.** Heart.

**puʻu welu.** Heap of rags.

**puwalu, puala.** 1. All together, in unison, united, cooperative. 2. Var. spelling of *pualu,* surgeonfish.

**puwŏ, puŏ.** To roar, wail, howl.

# R

All loan words from English sometimes spelled with initial *r* are entered under *l*-. For example: *raisi,* see *laiki,* rice; *ropi,* see *lopi,* rope; *rumi,* see *lumi,* room.

# S

All loan words from English sometimes spelled with initial *s* are entered under *k*-. For example: *Sabati,* see *Kāpaki,* Sabbath; *sopa,* see *kopa,* soap.

# T

All loan words from English sometimes spelled with initial *t* are entered under *k*-. For example: *tausani,* see *kaukani,* thousand; *tiga,* see *kika,* tiger.

# U

**u-.** Prefix to some words to denote plural, as *uhaele, ulawaiʻa, unonoho.*

**-u.** Second person singular possessive.

**-ʻu.** First person singular possessive.

**ū. 1.** Breast, teat, udder. Cf. *waiū.* **2.** Moist; to drip, drizzle; impregnated, as with salt. Cf. *maʻū.*

**ʻū. 1.** To grunt, groan, moan, sigh, mourn, grieve; sorrow; an exclamation of delight or assent. *Noho ʻū,* grief; grief-stricken. **hoʻoʻū, hōʻū.** To grunt and strain, as with physical exertion; to mourn. **2.** The letter *u.*

**ua. 1.** Rain; to rain; rainy. *Ua loa,* long period of rain. **hoʻoua.** To cause rain. **2.** Aforementioned, the one talked of (a demonstrative preceding a noun, which is usually followed by *nei,* here, or *lā,* there). **3.** A very common particle preceding verbs and denoting completed action.

**ʻuā.** To shout, cry out, sound loud.

**uahi.** Smoke; smoked; dustlike; spray, wisps. *Pipi uahi,* smoked beef. **hoʻouahi.** To smoke, emit smoke, cure by smoking.

**uakea. 1.** Mist (famous at Hāna, Maui). *Lit.,* white rain. **2.** White as mist, mist-white, white as breaking surf or snow.

**uaki, uati.** Watch, clock; a watch on shipboard.

**uaki hoʻāla.** Alarm clock.

**uaki pūlima.** Wrist watch.

**ʻuala.** Sweet potato *(Ipomoea batatas).*

**ʻuala kahiki.** White or Irish potato *(Solanum tuberosum). Lit.,* foreign sweet potato.

**ʻuala pilau.** Turnip. *Lit.,* smelly potato.

**ualo.** To call for help.

**ʻuao.** To intercede, arbitrate, reconcile; conciliator, peacemaker.

**uapo.** Wharf, pier, bridge. *Eng.*

**ʻuaʻu.** Dark-rumped petrel *(Pterodroma phaeopygia sandwichensis),* a sea bird.

**uaua.** Tough, glutinous, willful.

**ue.** 1. To jerk, pull, twist, sway. Cf. *naue.* 2. A hula step.

**uē.** To cry, weep, lament, mourn; a cry, lamentation. *Uē wale,* to cry for no reason; cry-baby. **ho-'ouē.** To cause weeping, to make someone cry.

**uea.** Wire. *Eng.*

**uea hakahaka.** Wire screen. *Lit.,* space wire.

**uea kelepona.** Telephone wire.

**uea maka 'upena.** Chicken wire. *Lit.,* net-mesh wire.

**uea moana.** Undersea cable.

**uea 'ole.** Wireless.

**'uehe.** 1. To open, uncover, reveal; to pry open, as a bivalve. Cf. *wehe.* 2. Hula step.

**ueka.** Dirty, bleary, as the eyes. Cf. *weka.*

**ueko.** Bad-smelling, musty.

**uene.** To move back and forth.

**uepa.** 1. Wafer. *Eng.* 2. Whip.

**uēuē.** Redup. of *uē.* To wriggle, squirm.

**'uha.** Wasteful, extravagant; waste, extravagance.

**'ūhā.** Thigh, lap; shoulder, hindquarters, as of a horse or pig. *'Ūhā moa,* drumstick of chicken.

**uhaele.** Plural of *haele,* to go, come.

**'ūhā hame.** Leg of ham.

**'ūhā hipa.** Leg of mutton.

**'ūhā hope.** Hindquarters, as of pig, beef.

**uhai.** Same as *hahai.*

**uha'i.** Same as *uhaki,* to break.

**'uhane.** Soul, spirit, ghost.

**'Uhane Hemolele.** Holy Ghost.

**uhau.** Var. of *hahau.*

**'uhene.** To play a merry tune, converse quietly and romantically; exclamation of exultation, as in songs.

**'uhe'uhene.** Redup. of *'uhene.*

**uhi.** 1. Covering, cover, veil, lid; solid tattoing; to cover, engulf, overwhelm; to don, as a feather cloak. 2. Large bluish-brown birthmark. 3. Yam *(Dioscorea alata).* 4. Mother-of-pearl bivalve, mother-of-pearl shank.

**uhikino.** Body covering, garment, shield.

**uhi moe.** Bedspread.

**uhina.** Covering; throw or cast net.

**'ūhini.** Long-horn grasshopper; cricket; locust.

**'ūhini lele.** Beetle, cricket. *Lit.,* flying grasshopper.

**uhi pākaukau.** Tablecloth.

**uhi pūku'i.** Hubcap.

**uhiuhi.** 1. Redup. of *uhi, 1.* 2. An endemic Hawaiian forest tree *(Mezoneuron kauaiense)* of the legume family, with pink or red flowers.

**uhu.** The parrot fishes, of which *Scarus perspicillatus* is among the most abundant and largest.

**ui.** To ask, question, appeal, turn to for help or advice, query; question, catechism.

**ūi.** Halloo.

**u'i.** Youthful, handsome, pretty, beautiful; youth; youthful vigor and beauty; youthful hero. **ho'ou'i.** To beautify.

**'uī.** 1. To squeak, squeal; to gnash, as teeth. Cf. *wī.* 2. To twist, squeeze, wring; to express, as juice from fruit; to milk, as a cow.

**'uiki, 'uwiki.** 1. To glimmer, especially of a light through a hole, crack, or narrow opening; to twinkle faintly. **hō'uiki.** To open a crack or sliver; to cause to gleam. 2. Piping, as used for dress trimming. 3. Wick.

**uila, uwila.** Lightning, electricity; electric. *Kapuahi uila,* electric stove. **ho'ouila, hō'uila.** To flash, as lightning.

**'u'ina.** 1. Sharp report, as crack of a pistol; to crack, snap, crackle, creak (as joints); to make a splashing sound. 2. Glottal stop.

**'u'inakolo.** Rustle, roar; to rustle *('u'ina* and *nākolo).*

**uka.** Inland, upland, toward the mountain; shore, uplands; shoreward (from at sea) (often preceded by the particles *i, ma-,* or *o* and often written *mauka*). *Kō uka,* those belonging to the uplands; mountain folk.

**-uka. ho'ouka.** To load, as cargo or freight; to put on, as gear on a horse. Cf. *ukana.*

**ukali.** To follow, come after, succeed; follower, attendant. *Lede ukali,* lady in waiting. **ho'oukali.** To cause, pretend, or try to follow, accompany.

**Ukali-ali'i.** The planet Mercury. *Lit.,* following the chief (i.e., the sun).

**ukana.** Baggage, luggage, freight, cargo, supplies. **ho'oukana.** To bundle up, pack up, load, as freight.

**'ūke'e.** Twisted, crooked, as the mouth. **hō'ūke'e.** To screw or twist the mouth to one side, as in disapproval or dislike.

**'ūkēkē.** A variety of musical bow having two or three strings, which were strummed.

**'ūkele.** Muddy; oily.

**'uki.** Coarse native sedges.

**'uki haole.** All cultivated forms of gladiolus.

**ukiuki.** Anger, resentment; angry, annoyed, offended, vexed, irritated. **ho'oukiuki.** To provoke, offend, displease.

**uku.** 1. Pay, wages, fee, fine, tax; to pay, remunerate, compensate, repay. **ho'ouku.** To make someone pay; to levy a tax, fine, assess, charge. 2. Deepsea snapper *(Aprion virescens).*

**'uku.** 1. Louse, flea. 2. Small, tiny (less used than *'u'uku*).

**uku hana.** Wages, salary, pay for work; to pay wages.

**uku hapa.** Installment payment; to pay in part.

**ukuhi.** To pour out, dip, as water; to wean, as a child.

**ukuhina.** A pouring out, dipping, weaning.

**uku ho'opa'i.** A fine.

**uku ho'opane'e.** Interest, usury. *Lit.,* delayed payment.

**uku ka'a.** Carfare.

**'uku kapa.** Body louse. *Lit.,* tapa louse.

**uku komo.** Entrance fee.

**uku kū'ike.** Cash payment.

**uku kula.** School tuition.

**uku leka, uku leta.** Postage.

**'ukulele.** Ukulele. *Lit.,* leaping flea.

**'uku lele.** Flea.

**uku makana.** Tip, gift payment.

**uku male (mare).** Dowry; marriage fee, as to the minister. *Lit.,* marriage payment.

**uku manawa.** Installment payment; to make installment payments.

**uku moku.** Steamship fare.

**ukupau.** Piece labor, pay by the job rather than according to time; used in pidgin for any work that everyone should pitch in gladly to finish. *Lit.,* finished pay.

**uku pohō.** Damages; to pay damages.

**'uku po'o.** Head louse.

**ula.** 1. Hawaiian or spiny lobsters. *(Panulirus marginatus* and *P. pencillatus).* 2. Flame.

**'ula.** 1. Red, scarlet; brown, as skin of Hawaiians; to appear red. *Pi'i ka 'ula,* to blush. **hō'ula.** To redden. 2. Sacred; sacredness; regal.

**ula ahi.** Fire flames.

**'ula ali'i.** Chiefly blood.

**'ulae.** Lizardfish *(Saurida gracilis).*

**'ulāli'i.** Measles; red spots of measles.

**ulana.** To plait, weave, knit, braid; plaiting, weaving.

**ula pāpapa.** A gray crayfish *(Parribacus antarcticus).*

**'ula'ula.** 1. Redup. of *'ula, 1.* **hō'ula'ula.** Same as *hō'ula.* 2.

One of the red snappers *(Etelis marshi,* family Lutjanidae). **3.** The cardinal, Kentucky cardinal *(Cardinalis cardinalis).*

**ulawai'a.** To fish (of many persons or often).

**ule.** Penis.

**ule kahe.** Circumcised or subincised penis.

**ulele. 1.** To leap at, get into action, do quickly. **2.** To set, as type.

**'ūlepe.** Harelip. Also, *kūlepe.*

**ule'ulu.** Male breadfruit flower. *Lit.,* breadfruit penis.

**uli. 1.** Any dark color, including the deep blue of the sea, the ordinary green of vegetation, and the dark of black clouds; the black-and-blue of a bruise. *Kai uli,* the deep blue sea. **ho'ouli.** To darken, to make blue, green, etc.; to make the skin black and blue. **2.** To steer; steersman.

**'ulī.** To rattle. Cf. *'ulī'ulī.*

**ulia.** Accident; sudden; to come upon suddenly. *Ulia ka'a,* auto accident.

**'ūlili.** Wandering tattler *(Heteroscelus incanum);* th cry of the bird; to cry thus. **ho'ūlili.** To act like the tattler bird.

**'ulī'ulī.** A gourd rattle containing seeds and fitted with colored feathers at the top, used in certain hulas; to rattle. **hō'ulī'ulī.** To shake the *'ulī'ulī;* to rattle.

**'ūlōlohi.** Same as *lohi,* slow.

**ulu. 1.** To grow, increase, spread; grove, growth, collection; an increase or rising of the wind. **ho'oulu.** To grow, cause to increase, as the surf. **2.** Possessed by a spirit; inspired by a spirit, god, ideal, person; stirred; to enter in and inspire. **ho'oulu, ho'ūlu.** To stir up, inspire, excite.

**'ulu. 1.** Breadfruit *(Artocarpus altilis).* **2.** Round, smooth stone as used in *'ulu maika* game; bowling ball; bell clapper.

**ulua.** Species of crevalle, jack, or pompano game fishes. Since *ulua* may replace men in human sacrifices, it is used for men and sweethearts.

**uluhe.** All Hawaiian species of false staghorn fern: the genera *Dicranopteris, Hicriopteris, Sticherus.*

**uluhia.** Passive/imperative of *ulu, 1, 2.*

**uluhua.** Vexed, annoyed, discouraged, displeased, harassed. **ho'ouluhua.** To annoy, weary, vex.

**ulu kanu.** Garden patch.

**ulu kukui.** Candlenut grove.

**ulu lā'au.** Forest, grove of trees.

**ulumāhiehie.** Festive, attractively adorned and arrayed; pleasing. **ho'oulumāhiehie.** To adorn, decorate attractively.

**'ulu maika.** Same as *maika;* the stone used in the game; to play the *'ulu maika* game; bowling.

**ulu manu.** Flock of birds.

**ulu moku.** Fleet, collection of ships.

**uluna. 1.** Pillow, cushion, formerly made of pandanus leaves; to use as a pillow. **2.** Upper part of the arm.

**ulunahele.** Wilderness, place of wild growth.

**ulu niu.** Coconut grove.

**ulu pua.** Flower garden, growth of flowers.

**'ulu'ulu.** Collection, gathering, assembly. **hō'ulu'ulu.** To collect, assemble; addition, to add; collection.

**uluwehi.** Lush and beautiful verdure; festively adorned. **ho'o-uluwehi.** To bedeck with plants.

**uluwehiwehi.** Redup. of *uluwehi.*

**uma.** Hand wrestling; to push, grip; to pry, as a lever.

**umauma.** Chest, breast.

**'ume. 1.** To draw, pull, attract; attractive, alluring; attraction. **2.** A sexual game.

**'umeke.** Bowl, calabash, circular vessel, as of wood or gourd.

**'umeke 'ai.** *Poi* bowl. *Fig.,* source

of vegetable food, of the uplands.

**‘umeke lā‘au.** Wooden bowl.

**‘umena.** An attraction, pulling. See *‘ume, 1.*

**‘umi. 1.** To strangle, choke, suffocate, throttle; to repress, as desire. **2.** Ten; tenth.

**‘ūmi‘i.** Clamp, clip, clasp, buckle, vise; to pinch, clip, clasp, clamp, squeeze; sharp body pain or cramp, as in the side. *Makaaniani ‘ūmi‘i,* spectacles held on the nose with clips; pincenez.

**‘ūmi‘i ‘iole.** Rattrap, mousetrap.

**‘ūmi‘i lauoho.** Hair clasp.

**‘ūmi‘i pepa.** Paper clip, clamp, staple.

**‘umi kūmā-.** An element compounded with numbers from one to nine to indicate 11 to 19, as *‘umi kūmāhā,* fourteen.

**‘umi kumamā-.** Same as *‘umi kūmā-.* Numbers one to nine are suffixed to this also. *Biblical.*

**‘umina.** Strangling, choking, etc. See *‘umi, 1.*

**‘umi‘umi. 1.** Whiskers, beard, mustache; tendril; barbel or feelers on lower jaw of a fish. **2.** Redup. of *‘umi, 1.*

**‘umoki.** Cork, stopper, bung; to cork, stop up; wad of a gun.

**umu.** Oven, furnace. More commonly called *imu.* **ho‘oumu.** To make an *umu.*

**-una. ho‘ouna.** To send, transmit, send on an errand, to put to work.

**unahi.** Scales of a fish; scaly; to scale.

**una‘oa.** Same as *kauna‘oa,* a mollusk.

**unauna.** Hermit crabs in general.

**unele.** Honk of a goose; to honk.

**‘ūniki.** Graduation exercises, as for *hula, lua* fighting, and other ancient arts.

**uniona.** Union, labor union. *Eng.*

**unonoho.** Plural and frequentative of *noho.*

**uno‘o.** Scorched, partly consumed by fire, inflamed.

**unu.** Small stone, pebble, stone chip.

**‘unu.** To shorten, hoist, jerk upwards; to pull or draw together, as the hair.

**unuhi.** To take out, withdraw, as money from a bank; to take off, as a ring; to translate, interpret. *Mea unuhi,* translator, interpreter. **ho‘ounuhi.** To have something translated, withdrawn, etc.

**unuhia.** Passive/imperative of *unuhi.*

**unuhina.** Translation.

**unuhi pili.** Close, literal translation.

**unuunu.** To singe, pluck, as the feathers of a chicken before dressing it.

**‘uo.** A group of feathers tied together in a small bunch, to be made into a feather lei or cloak; to tie thus; to string on a needle; to splice, as strands of a rope.

**uoki, uwoki.** Stop it! Quit! Don’t touch!

**‘ūpā.** Any instrument that opens and shuts, as shears, scissors, tongs, bellows, carpenter’s compass; to beat, as the heart; to open and shut, as the mouth champing food.

**‘upa‘i.** To flap, as wings, or clothes in the wind; to bend in the wind, as a branch.

**‘ūpā mau‘u.** Grass shears.

**‘ūpā miki‘ao.** Fingernail scissors.

**‘ūpā nui.** Shears.

**upāpalu.** The larger cardinal fishes (*Apogon* spp.).

**‘ūpā ‘ūmi‘i.** Pliers.

**‘upa‘upā.** Redup. of *‘ūpā;* to rub clothes up and down on a washboard.

**ūpē.** Crushed; humble, bashful. **ho‘oūpē.** To crush, belittle.

**‘ūpē.** Mucus. *Fig.,* tears, grief.

**‘upena.** Fishing net, net, web.

**‘upena kiloi,** **‘upena kiola.** Throwing net.

**'upena lauoho.** Hairnet.

**'upena nananana.** Spider web. Also, *punawelewele*.

**'ūpepe.** Flat-nosed.

**'ūpiki.** Trap, snare, clamp; to snap or clamp together, as a trap, the jaws, or a bivalve; to shut, as a flower.

**'ūpiki 'iole.** Rattrap, mousetrap.

**'ūpiki lima.** Handcuff.

**'ūpo'i.** Same as *po'i, 1–3*.

**'ūpo'i maka.** Eyelid.

**'upu.** Recurring thought, desire, attachment, hope; to desire, long for, covet.

**'u'u.** To strip, as leaves or *maile* bark; to draw in, as a line on a ship; to hoist, as a sail; to pour suddenly, as rain.

**'ū'ū.** 1. Redup. of *'ū, 1;* to stutter, stammer. 2. All soldier fishes of the genus *Myripristis*.

**'u'uku.** Tiny, small; few. **ho'o'u-'uku.** To make small, reduce.

# W

**wā.** 1. Period of time, epoch, era, time, season, age. *Ia wā*, then, at that time. 2. Tense, in grammar. *Wā i hala*, past tense. 3. To make a noise, roar, din; noisy. Cf. *wa-wā*. **ho'owā.** To make a sound, roar; to cause gossip, talk. 4. Space, interval, as between objects; channel. Cf. *kōwā*. 5. Fret of a ukulele, guitar, or similar instrument.

**wa'a.** Canoe. **ho'owa'a.** To make or shape a canoe.

**wa'a kaukahi.** Single canoe. *Lit.*, single-placed canoe.

**wa'a kaulua.** Double canoe. *Lit.*, double-placed canoe.

**wā 'ānō.** Present tense.

**wa'apā.** Skiff, rowboat; ferryboat. *Lit.*, board canoe.

**wae.** To choose, select, sort, separate; to draft, as soldiers; to preen, as of a chicken; finicky. **ho'owae.** To choose, pretend to choose; finicky.

**waele.** To weed.

**waena.** 1. Middle, between, center (often preceded by *i, ma-,* or *mai*); mean, average. 2. Cultivated field, garden, vegetable plot.

**waenakonu.** Center, middle.

**waha.** 1. Mouth; opening; oral; to talk too much. **ho'owaha.** To talk excessively, insult; to make an opening. 2. To carry on the back, as a child.

**wahahe'e.** To lie; lying, deceitful; a lie, liar. *Lit.*, slippery mouth.

**waha nui.** A big mouth; to talk too much, tattle; tattler.

**waha 'ōlelo.** Spokesman; speaking mouth.

**wahapa'a.** To goad, tease; argumentative. *Lit.*, hard mouth.

**wahāwahā. ho'owahāwahā.** To treat with contempt, despise, abhor, ridicule. *Ho'owahāwahā i ka 'aha*, contempt of court.

**wahi.** 1. Place. *(Ka wahi* contracts to *kahi*.) 2. Some, a little, a few, a bit of. 3. To say (usually followed by the possessive *a*, and not preceded by either verb or noun particles). *Wahi a wai?* Who said so?

**wahī.** Wrapper, envelope, covering; to wrap, cover, bundle up; to dress, as a wound.

**wāhi.** To cleave, split, burst through, break through.

**wahie.** Fuel, firewood; to serve as firewood.

**wahī leka.** Envelope.

**wahi moe.** Bed, place to sleep.

**wahine.** Woman, lady, wife; sister-in-law, female cousin-in-law of a man; queen in a deck of cards; womanliness, female, femininity; feminine; Mrs.; to become a woman, as an adolescent. **ho'owahine.** To behave like a woman, to imitate the ways of a woman; to grow into womanhood; to become a wife; to take a wife; feminine.

**wāhine.** Plural of *wahine. Nā wāhine,* the women.

**wahine kāne make.** Widow. *Lit.,* woman with dead husband.

**wahine kāne ʻole.** Spinster, woman without a husband, single woman.

**wahine male (mare).** Married woman, bride.

**wahi noho.** Residence, address.

**waho.** Outside, beyond, out, outer, outward (frequently preceded by *ʻo, ma-,* or *mai*). *Mawaho aku ʻolua!* Go out, you two!

**wai. 1.** Water, liquid of any kind other than sea water, juice, sap, honey; any liquid discharged from the body, as blood, semen; color, dye; to flow like water; fluid. Cf. *hanawai.* **2.** *(Cap.)* Place names beginning with *Wai-,* river, stream. **3.** Who, whom, whose, what (in questions only and referring to persons). *ʻO wai?* Who? *ʻO wai kou inoa?* What is your name? **4.** To leave, place, retain, deposit. See *waiho, waihona, waiwai.*

**wai ʻaleʻale.** Rippling water, artesian water.

**wai anuhea.** Tepid water, neither hot nor cold.

**wai au.** Swirling water of a current.

**wai ʻauʻau.** Bath water; bathing place or pool.

**wai hau.** Ice water.

**waiho.** To leave, lay down, place before, present, deposit; to cease, stop, resign, abandon; a leaving, depository, etc. **hoʻo-waiho.** To leave, abandon, ignore. See *waiwai.*

**wai hoʻāno.** Holy water.

**waiho loa.** To abandon completely, give up.

**waihona.** Depository, place for putting things in safekeeping; funds, treasury; fiscal.

**waihona kālā (dala).** Treasury, money depository. *Lit.,* dollar depository.

**waihona meli.** Honeycomb.

**waihona panakō.** Bank account, depository.

**waihona puke (buke).** Library.

**waihona waiwai.** Treasury, depository for goods, property.

**waihoʻoluʻu.** Dye, water for coloring; color.

**waiho wale.** To leave without reason; to leave carelessly.

**wai inu.** Drinking water, potable water.

**waikahe.** Stream; to flow, overflow, as a stream. *Lit.,* flowing water.

**wai kī.** Water in which tea has been brewed.

**Waikīkī.** Famous beach, Honolulu. *Lit.,* spouting water, named for swamps drained 1919–1928 to form Ala Wai Canal.

**wailele.** Waterfall, cataract. *Lit.,* leaping water.

**wai lemi.** Lemon juice, lemonade, limeade.

**waimaka.** Tears. *Lit.,* eye water.

**wai meli.** Honey. *Lit.,* bee liquor.

**wai momona.** Soda water, sweet water.

**waina.** Wine. *Eng.*

**waina maloʻo.** Raisins. *Lit.,* dry grapes.

**wai nui.** Coconut water or cream.

**waioleka.** Fragrant cultivated violets. *Eng.*

**waiolina.** Violin. *Eng.*

**wai ʻona.** Intoxicating liquor.

**waipaʻa.** Ice. *Lit.,* hard water.

**wai paʻakai.** Salty water, brine.

**waipahē.** Gentlemanly, courteous. See *pahē.*

**waipahū.** Gunpowder. *Lit.,* explosive liquid.

**wai piula.** Water from a faucet.

**wai puhia.** Wind-blown water, especially of a waterfall; name of the "upside-down" waterfall in Nuʻu-anu Valley.

**waipuʻilani.** Waterspout.

**wai puna.** Spring water.

**waiū.** Milk; wet nurse; breast. *Lit.,* breast liquid.

**waiū kini.** Canned milk.

**wai ʻula.** Red liquid, blood, menstrual flow; rain run-off red with soil.

**waiūpaʻa.** Cheese. *Lit.,* solidified milk.

**waiūpaka, waiu bata.** Butter.

**waiwai.** Goods, property; value, worth; estate; rich, costly; financial. *Hoʻoponopono waiwai,* administrator of property or of an estate. **hoʻowaiwai.** To enrich, bring prosperity. See *waiho.*

**waiwai hoʻoilina.** Inherited property.

**waiwai hoʻopaʻa.** Security.

**waiwai kālepa.** Merchandise.

**waiwai kaua.** War goods, spoils.

**wā kamaliʻi.** Childhood. Also called *wā liʻiliʻi.*

**waki.** Var. spelling of *uaki,* watch.

**Wakinekona, Wasinetona.** Washington. *Eng.*

**walaʻau.** To talk, speak; formerly, to talk loudly, shout. **hoʻowalaʻau.** To cause talk, start talk or conversation.

**walakīkē.** To toss, hurl back and forth, as spears in battle.

**walania.** Anguish, burning pain, woe, torment. **hoʻowalania.** To cause pain, wound.

**wale.** 1. Slime, mucus, phlegm; sticky sap, as from cuts in tree ferns and *māmaki* wood. 2. A common particle that follows modified words and has many meanings, as: only, just; very; alone; without pay, cause, reason; easily; gratuitous, free, casual. See *hele wale, hikiwale.*

**walea.** 1. Same as *nanea.* 2. Accustomed; so familiar that one does a thing without effort, as a dance. *Ua hana ā walea,* done until automatic.

**wale nō.** Only, just; all; very. *ʻElua wale nō,* only two.

**walewale.** Redup. of *wale, 1.*

**hoʻowalewale.** To tempt, decoy, lead astray; tempter; temptation.

**wali.** Smooth, thin, as *poi;* fine, mashed, soft; supple, limber, as a dancer's body. **hoʻowali.** To make soft, smooth; to mix, as *poi* or dough. See *nāwali.*

**wā liʻiliʻi.** See *wā kamaliʻi.*

**waliwali.** Redup. of *wali;* gentle, easygoing.

**walo.** Same as *ualo,* to call, resound.

**walohia.** Passive/imperative of *walo;* pathos, touching.

**walu.** 1. To claw, scratch, rub, grate, rasp. 2. Eight, eighth.

**wana.** 1. Sea urchin with long, pointed dangerous spines, especially the species *Diadema paucispinum* and *Echinothrix diadema.* 2. Sharp-pointed, as sea urchin spines. 3. A long spike or ray of light, as at dawn; to appear, as a ray of light. Cf. *wanaʻao.*

**wanaʻao.** Dawn; to dawn.

**wānana.** Prophecy; to prophesy, predict.

**wanawana.** Redup. of *wana, 2;* spiny, thorny, as cactus.

**wanila.** Vanilla. *Eng.*

**wao.** General term for inland region, usually not precipitous and often uninhabited.

**wao kele.** Rain belt.

**wao nahele.** Inland forest region.

**wā ʻōpio.** Youth (time of).

**wau, au.** I (often preceded by *ʻo*).

**waʻu.** To grate, scrape, claw, wear away by friction; grater.

**wā ua.** Rainy season.

**wauke.** Paper mulberry *(Broussonetia papyrifera),* a small tree or shrub the bark of which was used to make tapa.

**waʻu niu.** Coconut grater; to grate coconut.

**wā ʻuʻuku.** Childhood. *Lit.,* small time.

**wawā.** Redup. of *wā, 3;* tumultuous; sound of distant voices, roar; rumored. **hoʻowawā.** To cause a loud shouting.

**wāwae.** Leg, foot.

**wāwae huki.** Cramps in the foot or leg.

**wāwae ʻiole. 1.** Club moss *(Lycopodium cernuum),* a creeping, evergreen, mosslike plant used in Hawaiʻi for Christmas wreaths, etc. **2.** Same as *ʻaʻala ʻula,* a seaweed.

**wāwahi.** Redup. of *wāhi;* to tear down, break into, demolish.

**wāwahi hale.** Burglary, housebreaking; to break and enter.

**wāwahi panakō.** To break the bank, as in *chee-fah* or other games.

**wawe.** Quickly; fast. See *hikiwawe.*

**wē.** The letter *w.*

**wehe.** To open, untie, loosen; to take off, as clothes; to tip, as a hat. **hoʻowehe.** To cause to open, undo, etc.

**wehena.** Opening, unfastening, taking off; solution, as of a problem.

**wehewehe.** To explain. *Wehewehe ʻana,* explanation, definition.

**wehi.** Decoration, adornment; to decorate. **hoʻowehi.** To beautify, decorate, adorn.

**wehiwehi.** Redup. of *wehi.* Cf. *uluwehiwehi.*

**weka. 1.** Ink discharged by squid or octopus. **2.** Also **weta.** Weight. *Eng.*

**weke. 1.** Crack, narrow opening; to open a crack, as a door; to loosen, free. **2.** Certain species of goatfishes, much prized since early times as food fishes.

**weke ʻaʻā.** Samoan goatfish *(Mulloidichthys samoensis). Lit.,* staring goatfish.

**wekekē.** Whiskey. *Eng.*

**weke ʻula.** A *weke* fish *(Mulloidichthys vanicolensis). Lit.,* red *weke* (yellow in water but red when taken out).

**wēkiu.** Tip, top, topmost, summit; of the highest rank or station.

**wela.** Hot, burned; heat, temperature. **hoʻowela.** To heat, burn, arouse passion.

**wēlau.** Tip, top, extremity, end.

**Wēlau ʻĀkau.** North Pole.

**Wēlau Hema.** South Pole.

**wele. 1.** Suspended, hanging; fine, thin, as thread. **2.** To weed.

**weleweka.** Velvet. *Eng.*

**weli. 1.** Fear, terror; fearful, afraid. *Kau ka weli,* full of fear. **hoʻoweli.** To frighten, terrify, arouse fear. **2.** Sea cucumber.

**welina.** A greeting of affection, similar to *aloha.*

**weliweli.** Redup. of *weli, 1;* respectful, as of the word of a chief. **hoʻoweliweli.** Redup. of *hoʻoweli.*

**welo.** To flutter, float, or stream, as in the wind.

**welu.** Rag, ragged fragment; ragged, frayed.

**weluwelu.** Redup. of *welu;* shredded to bits.

**wena.** Glow, as of sunrise or fire. *Wena ʻula,* red glow.

**weuweu.** Herbage, grass; bushy or fuzzy, as a beard.

**wī. 1.** Famine; to suffer a famine. **2.** To squeal, tinkle; the sound of wind, of gnashing teeth; any high shrill sound. **3.** The *wī* tree or Otaheite apple *(Spondias dulcis),* which bears edible apple-flavored fruits. **4.** The tamarind *(Tamarindus indica)* tree; also *wī ʻawaʻawa.*

**wiki, wikiwiki.** To hurry, hasten; quick. *Hele wiki,* quick time; quick step. **hoʻowiki.** To hurry, hasten.

**wiko, vito.** Veto; to veto. *Eng.*

**wili. 1.** To wind, twist, writhe, crank, grind, mix; to dial, as a telephone; to roll up, as a mat; coil, lock, as of hair. **hoʻowili.** To wind, coil, drill; to mill about, as a school of fish. **2.** Mill, drill; bit.

**wilia.** Passive/imperative of *wili, 1.*

**wilikī.** Engineer, turnkey; engineering. *Lit.,* turn key.

**wili kō.** Sugar mill, sugar grinder; to grind sugarcane.

**wili kope.** Coffee mill, coffee grinder.

**wili makani.** Windmill.

**wili oho.** Coil or strand of hair, as in a *lei palaoa* necklace.

**wilipuaʻa.** Corkscrew, hand drill, gimlet, screw auger. *Lit.,* pig twist.

**wiliwili. 1.** Redup. of *wili, 1.* **hoʻowiliwili.** Redup. of *hoʻowili.* **2.** A native Hawaiian leguminous tree *(Erythrina sandwicensis).*

**wiliwili haole.** Tiger's claw or coral tree *(Erythrina variegata* var. *orientalis,* syn. *E. indica),* resembling the *wiliwili,* but having thorned branches and bearing long clusters of scarlet blossoms.

**wīneka, vinega.** Vinegar. *Eng.*

**wini.** Sharp, as a point. **hoʻowini.** To sharpen, make a point.

**wiola, viola.** Viol. *Eng.*

**wīwī.** Thin, slender.

**wiwo. 1.** Fearful, bashful, modest, afraid, timid. **2.** Obedient; to mind, obey.

**wiwoʻole.** Fearless, brave, bold.

**wiwowiwo.** Redup. of *wiwo, 1, 2.*

**wōwō.** To bellow, roar.

# Z

Loan words from English sometimes spelled with initial z are entered under k-. For example: *zebela,* see *kepela,* zebra; *zizania,* see *kīkānia.*

# English-Hawaiian

# A

a. 1. *The letter* 'ā. 2. *Article.* He, kekahi, ho'okahi.

aa. 'A'ā.

abalone. 'Ōpihi malihini.

abandon. Ha'alele, waiho, ho'o-ku'u.

abbreviate. Ho'opōkole.

abbreviation. Hua hō'ailona, ho'opōkole 'ana.

ability. Hiki, mākaukau.

able. Hiki, mākaukau.

abnormal. 'Ano 'ē.

aboard. Maluna.

abolish. Ho'opau.

abominable. Ho'opailua, 'ino loa.

abomination. Mea 'ino, mea haumia.

aboriginal. Maoli, kupa maoli. *Hawaiian aboriginal,* Hawai'i maoli.

abortion. 'Ōmilo, milo, milomilo.

about. 1. *Concerning.* E pili ana no, no, i. 2. *See* almost.

above. Maluna, i luna.

abroad. Ma ka 'āina 'ē *(in foreign lands).*

absence. Hele 'ole mai.

absent. Ma kahi 'ē, ma kahi 'oko'a, 'a'ole i hiki mai.

abundant. Nui, nui 'ino, manoa.

accent. 1. *Speech.* Hopuna. 2. *Stress.* Kaulele, kālele leo. 3. *Diacritical mark.* Kaha, kiko.

accept. 'Āpono, ho'āpono, 'ae, lawe.

accident. Ulia, pilikia.

accompany. Hele pū, ukali, 'alo, hahai.

accumulate. Ho'āhu, hō'ili'ili, ho'ākoakoa.

accurate. Pololei, pono.

accuse. Ho'āhewa, ho'olawehala.

accustomed. Ma'a, ma'ama'a.

ache. 'Eha, hu'i.

acquainted. Kama'āina.

acquire. Loa'a, lawe.

acre. 'Eka.

across. Ma kēlā 'ao'ao.

act. 1. *To do.* Hana. *To act as,* noho. 2. *Theatrical.* Mahele *(of a play).* *To act in a play,* hana keaka. 3. *Law.* Kānāwai. 4. *To pretend.* Ho'omeamea, ho'o-mea.

action. Hana.

active. 'Eleu, miki.

activity. Hana, 'oihana.

actor. Mea hana keaka, kanaka hana keaka.

actress. Wahine hana keaka.

actual. Maoli, 'oia'i'o.

Adam's apple. Pu'u, pū'ā'ī, kani'ā'ī.

add. Hō'ulu'ulu, ho'ohui, pāku'i, ku'i lua, ho'onui; ho'oku'i *(as numbers).*

addition. Hō'ulu'ulu.

address. 1. *Speech.* Ha'i'ōlelo. 2. *Residence.* Wahi noho.

adjacent. Kokoke, pili.

adjourn. Ho'omalolo.

adjust. Ho'oponopono.

administer. Ho'oponopono, ho'ohana, ho'oholo.

administrator. Luna ho'opono-pono, kahu, kahu ho'opono-pono.

admire. Mahalo.

admit 1. *Allow to enter.* Ho'oko-mo, 'ae. 2. *Acknowledge.* 'Ae.

adopt. 1. *As a child.* Hānai, lawe hānai. 2. *To approve.* 'Āpono.

adore. Ho'onani, ho'omana.

adorn. Ho'ohiwahiwa, ho'onani, ho'okāhiko, ho'owehi, ho'oulu-māhiehie.

adult. Makua, kanaka makua, o'o.

advance. Holomua, hele i mua.

advertise. Ho'olaha.

advice. 'Ōlelo a'o. *To give advice,* ha'i a'o.

adze. Ko'i, lipi.

affection. Aloha, aloha pume-hana.

aforementioned. Ua . . . nei, ua . . . lā.

aforesaid. I 'ōlelo 'ia, ua.

**afraid.** Maka'u, weli, weliweli, wiwo.

**after.** Hope, mahope, muli, mamuli, pau.

**afternoon.** 'Auinalā.

**afterward.** Hope, mahope, mahope iho.

**again.** Hou. *To do again,* hana hou.

**against.** Kū'ē.

**age.** 1. *Period.* Au, manawa, wā. 2. *Age of a person.* Kūlana makahiki, heluna makahiki. *What is your age?* 'Ehia ou makahiki? He aha kou heluna makahiki?

**agile.** 'Eleu.

**agitated.** Pīhoihoi, pi'oloke.

**ago.** Mamua aku nei, wā i hala.

**agree.** 'Ae, 'aelike, lōkahi.

**agreement.** 'Aelike, palapala 'aelike, lōkahi.

**agriculture.** 'Oihana mahi 'ai.

**ah!** 'Ā! Kāhāhā! *To oh and ah,* āhē, kāhāhā.

**aha!** Āhā!

**ahead.** I mua, mamua aku.

**aid.** Kōkua, kāko'o.

**ailing.** 'Ōma'ima'i, ma'ima'i, nāwali.

**air.** Ea, eaea, lewa.

**air mail.** Ho'ouna ma ka mokulele.

**airplane.** Mokulele.

**airport.** Kahua ho'olulu mokulele.

**air raid.** Pākaha mai ka lewa.

**alas!** Aloha 'ino! Auē!

**alcoholic.** 'Ona lama, 'ona mau.

**alert.** Maka'ala, miki'ala, 'eleu.

**alga.** Limu.

**algaroba.** Kiawe.

**alike.** Like, like pū, kohu like. *Just alike,* like loa, like 'ālike, kūlike loa. *To make alike,* ho'ohālikelike, kaulike.

**alive.** Ola.

**all.** Āpau, pauloa, pau.

**all right.** Hiki, hiki nō, pololei, maika'i. *All right, then,* 'oia ho'i hā. *It's all right,* 'oia a'e lā nō.

**almost.** Kokoke, 'ane'ane.

**aloha.** Aloha.

**alone.** Ho'okahi wale nō, wale, ho'okahi.

**alphabet.** Pī'āpā.

**already.** 'Ē, pau.

**also.** Ho'i, kekahi, kahi, eia kekahi. *I also,* 'o au pū.

**altar.** Ahu, lele, kuahu, ni'o, unu.

**although.** 'Oiai.

**altogether.** 'Oko'a, holo'oko'a. *All of us together,* kākou pū.

**always.** Mau, nā manawa apau loa, pau 'ole.

**amen.** 'Āmene.

**America.** 'Amelika.

**among.** Mawaena, i waena.

**amuse.** Ho'ole'ale'a, ho'okolohe, ho'ohoihoi.

**amusement.** Ho'ole'ale'a, le'ale'a, pā'ani.

**ancestor.** Kupuna.

**anchor.** Heleuma.

**ancient.** Kahiko.

**and.** Ā *(usually preceding verbs);* ā me *(usually preceding nouns);* eia ho'i.

**angel.** 'Ānela.

**anger.** Huhū, inaina, ukiuki, uluhua. *Very great anger,* huhū wela loa, huhū loa. *Anger without cause,* huhū wale. *To become angry,* pi'i ka huhū.

**animal.** Holoholona.

**anniversary.** Piha makahiki, lā ho'omana'o.

**announce.** Hō'ike, kūkala.

**annoy.** Ho'onaukiuki, ho'okolohe, ho'ouluhua.

**annual.** Makahiki, kūmakahiki, ma ka makahiki. *Annual report,* hō'ike makahiki. *Annual salary,* uku ma ka makahiki.

**anoint.** Poni.

**another.** Kekahi, ha'i, 'oko'a, 'ē a'e. *Another day,* kekahi lā.

**answer.** Pane; ha'ina *(as to a riddle);* hua loa'a, ha'iloa'a *(as to a problem).*

**ant.** Naonao.

**anthem.** Mele, hīmeni. *National anthem,* mele aupuni.

**anthropology.** Huli kanaka.

**anxiety.** Hopohopo, pīhoihoi.

**any.** Kekahi.

**anybody.** *See* **anyone.**

**anyhow.** *See* **however.**

**anyone.** Kekahi, kekahi mea, 'o ka mea nō e.

**anything.** Ka mea e loa'a ana.

**anywhere.** Aia nō i kahi e hele ai; ma nā wahi like 'ole.

**apart.** Ka'awale. *To stand apart,* kū ka'awale. *Placed apart,* kau 'oko'a.

**apartment.** Ke'ena noho. *Apartment building,* hale papa'i.

**apiece.** Pākahi.

**apologize.** Mihi, mimihi, mimimihi.

**apostle.** Luna'ōlelo.

**appear.** Puka, kau, hiki, maka, kū, 'ō'ili; pua'i *(as color);* wana *(as a ray of light).*

**appetite.** 'Ono ka 'ai.

**applause.** Pa'ipa'i lima, pa'ipa'i.

**apple.** 'Āpala, poma.

**apply.** 1. *Adhere.* Pili, ho'opili. 2. *Petition.* Noi.

**appoint.** Ho'onoho, ho'okohu, ho'okoho.

**appointment.** 1. *Engagement.* Ho'opa'a manawa. 2. *Nomination.* Wae, ho'okohu.

**appreciate.** Ho'omaika'i.

**approach.** Ho'okokoke, hiki, hō'ea'ea.

**appropriation.** Ha'awina.

**approval.** Ho'āpono, 'ae.

**approve.** Ho'āpono, 'ae, 'āpono.

**approximately.** Kahi, kokoke.

**April.** 'Apelila.

**arch.** Pi'o, pāpi'o, hoaka. *Arch of a foot,* poho wāwae. *Arch of a rainbow,* pi'o ke ānuenue.

**arena.** Kahua, pā.

**argue.** Ho'opa'apa'a, paio, pāku-'iku'i, kīkē'ōlelo.

**argument.** Paio, pa'apa'a, ho'opa'apa'a.

**argumentative.** Wahapa'a, puni ho'opa'apa'a.

**arithmetic.** Huina helu, helu, 'alimakika.

**arm.** 1. *Anatomy.* Lima; kālele *(as of a chair);* upper part of arm,*

uluna. *Arm below elbow,* kū'aulima. 2. *To supply arms.* Ho'olako i nā mea kaua.

**armed forces.** Pū'ali koa.

**armpit.** Pō'ae'ae, kīpō'ae'ae, napo'o.

**arms.** 1. *Anatomy.* Nā lima. 2. *War.* Lako kaua.

**army.** Pū'ali, kaua, pū'ulu, pū'ulu kaua.

**around.** Puni, kēlā wahi kēia wahi. *To go around,* ka'apuni, pō'ai, kalawai. *"Around the island" hula step,* ka'apuni.

**arrange.** Ho'onoho, ho'onohonoho, ho'onoho papa, ho'oponopono, kūkulu papa, haku.

**arrest.** *Seize.* Hopu, hopuna.

**arrive.** Hō'ea, hiki, kū, kau.

**arrow.** Pua, pua pana.

**arrowroot.** Pia.

**art.** Hana no'eau.

**artery.** A'a.

**article.** 1. *Object.* Mea. 2. *Essay.* Mo'olelo. 3. *Grammatical.* Pilimua.

**artist.** Kaha ki'i.

**as.** 1. *Resembling.* Me, like me. *As though,* mehe. *As follows,* penei, 'oia ho'i. *As if,* mehe mea lā. *As far as,* ā, ā hiki i. 2. *See* **because.**

**ascend.** Pi'i.

**ascent.** Pi'ina, alapi'i.

**ash.** Lehu, pa'u ahi.

**ashamed.** Hilahila.

**ashes.** Lehu, lehu ahi, lehu ane.

**ash tray.** Pā lehu.

**aside.** Ma ka 'ao'ao, ma kahi ka'awale. *To set aside,* ho'oka-'awale.

**ask.** 1. *To question.* Nīnau, ui. *To ask insistently,* koi. 2. *To request.* Noi, nonoi. 3. *To invite.* Kono.

**asleep.** Hiamoe. *Fast asleep,* pa'uhia i ka hiamoe, hiamoe pa'a loa.

**assemble.** 1. *To meet.* Hui pū, anaina, 'ākoakoa, ho'ākoakoa. 2. *To collect.* Hō'ili'ili, hō'ulu-'ulu.

**assets.** Waiwai.

**assist.** Kōkua, kāko'o.

**assistant.** Hope, kōkua.

**association.** Launa 'ana, pilina; 'ahahui; hui.

**asthma.** Hānō.

**astonished.** Pū'iwa, ha'oha'o, kāhāhā.

**at.** Ma, i, iā. *Look at him,* nānā iāia.

**athlete.** Mea i ma'ama'ahia i nā pā'ani ho'oikaika kino.

**athletic.** 'Ālapa.

**athletic contest.** Ho'okūkū ho'o-oikaika kino.

**athletic field.** Kahua pā'ani.

**atmosphere.** Lewa.

**atomic.** 'Akomika.

**attach.** Ho'opili, ho'opa'a.

**attack.** Ho'ouka kaua, pu'e, po'i-pū, po'i pō, lele, ku'ia, limanui.

**attempt.** Ho'ā'o.

**attention.** Nānā, maliu. *To pay attention,* nānā, maliu, ho'oma-opopo.

**attentive.** Ho'olohe, ho'olono, lohe pono.

**attorney.** Loio.

**attract.** 'Ume, ala'ume, hōnēnē, kā'ana.

**attractive.** 1. *As a magnet.* 'Ume. 2. *As a person or scene.* Hie, makahehi, ma'ema'e.

**audience.** Anaina.

**August.** 'Aukake.

**aunt.** Makuahine, makuahine hanauna, 'anakē.

**Australia.** 'Aukekulelia.

**authentic.** 'Oia'i'o.

**author.** Mea kākau, kākau mo'olelo, haku mo'olelo.

**auto license.** Laikini ka'a 'oko-mopila.

**automobile.** Ka'a, ka'a 'okomo-pila, otomobila.

**avenue.** Alanui ākea.

**avoid.** 'Alo, hō'alo, kē, ka'akepea.

**awake.** Ala, makalahia. *To awak-en from sleep,* lana ka hiamoe.

**awaken.** Ala, ho'āla, ho'ālahia.

**away.** Aku, 'ē, ma kahi 'ē, lilo. *Go away!* Hele ma kahi 'ē! Hele pēlā.

**awe.** 'E'ehia, ano, hōano.

**awful.** Weliweli.

**awhile.** Manawa pōkole, li'uli'u iki.

**awkward.** Hemahema, pāhemahe-ma, hāwāwā.

**axe.** See **adze.**

# B

**b.** *No Hawaiian term.*

**baby.** Keiki, pēpē, kama.

**bachelor.** Wahine 'ole, kanaka i male 'ole.

**back.** 1. *Anatomy.* Kua. 2. *Be-hind.* Hope, muli. *At the back,* i hope, mahope.

**backbone.** Iwikuamo'o, kua-mo'o.

**backpack.** 'Awe, 'awe'awe.

**backward.** I hope. *To go back-ward,* emi hope, emi kua, peki.

**bacon.** 'I'o pua'a uahi.

**bad.** Maika'i 'ole, 'ino, kolohe. *Too bad!* Minamina noho'i! Aloha 'ino! Auē! *Bad luck,* pō'ino, pakalaki.

**bag.** 'Eke, 'eke'eke.

**baggage.** Ukana, 'ope'ope.

**bait.** Maunu.

**bake.** Kālua, ho'omo'a, 'oma, ho'o'oma, puhi, ho'olua.

**balance.** 1. *Weigh.* Kaulike, ana paona, paona, paona kaulike. 2. *Remainder.* Koena, koehonua.

**bald.** 'Ōhule.

**ball.** 1. *Sphere.* Kinipōpō, pōpō pōko'a, pōkā. *To play ball,* kini-pōpō, pā'ani kinipōpō: 2. *Dance.* 'Aha hulahula, anaina hulahula.

**balloon.** Pāluna.

**balloon fish.** 'O'opu hue.

**ballot.** Pāloka. *To cast a ballot,* koho pāloka. *To count ballots,* helu pāloka.

**bamboo.** 'Ohe. *Bamboo pipes,* kā'eke'eke, pahūpahū. *Bamboo rattles,* pū'ili.

**banana.** Mai'a. *Banana blossoms and sheath,* pola. *Dry banana leaf,* lauhulu. *Banana bunch,* 'āhui mai'a. *Hand, as of banana,* 'ekā. *Banana stalk,* pū mai'a.

**bandage.** Wahī'eha.

**bang.** Pohā *(as a gun).*

**bank. 1.** *Border.* Kapa, ka'e. **2.** *Finance.* Panakō.

**baptize.** Papekema, papekiko.

**bar. 1.** *Barrier.* Kaola, lā'au kī, lā'au ke'a, paukū, pale. **2.** *As of soap.* 'Aukā kopa. **3.** *For drinking.* Wahi inu lama, pākaukau. **4.** *Music.* Pale.

**barbecue.** Kō'ala.

**barber.** Kanaka 'ako lauoho.

**bare.** Kohana.

**barefoot.** Kāma'a 'ole.

**barely.** Wale nō.

**bargain.** Makepono, ho'ēmiemi i ke kumu kū'ai. *Bad bargain,* makehewa, pohō.

**bark. 1.** *Of a tree.* 'Ili, 'ili lā'au. *Outer bark,* 'ili luna. **2.** *Of an animal.* Hae, 'aoa.

**barracuda.** Kākū.

**barrel.** Pahu, palala, palela. *Water barrel,* pahu wai.

**base.** Kumu, kahua, kū.

**baseball.** Kinipōpō. *To play baseball,* pā'ani kinipōpō.

**bashful.** Hilahila.

**basic.** Kumu, honua. *Basic knowledge,* 'ike kumu.

**basin. 1.** *Container.* Ipu, po'i, ipu holoi, po'i wai, pā holoi, pā kini. **2.** *Land.* Poho 'āina, kīpoho.

**basket.** 'Eke, 'ie, hīna'i, hīna'i poepoe.

**basketball.** Kinipōpō hīna'i.

**bass. 1.** *Music.* Leo kāne, leo uō. **2.** *Fish.* 'O'opu haole *(black bass).*

**bastard.** Keiki manuahi, keiki kāmeha'i.

**baste. 1.** *Sewing.* Ho'oholoholo,

kāholo, 'ōmau. **2.** *Cooking.* Ho'oma'ū.

**bat. 1.** *Mammal.* 'Ōpe'ape'a, pe'a, pe'ape'a. **2.** *To strike.* Hili. **3.** *Bat for ball.* Lā'au kinipōpō, lā'au pa'i kinipōpō.

**bath.** 'Au'au.

**bathhouse.** Hale 'au'au.

**bathing suit.** Lole 'au'au.

**bathroom.** Lumi 'au'au, lua. *See* **toilet.**

**bathtub.** Kapu 'au'au.

**batter. 1.** *As in basball.* Mea hili kinipōpō. **2.** *Cookery.* Mea 'ono mo'a 'ole.

**battery. 1.** *Artillery.* Huina pū kuni ahi. **2.** *Electric.* Pākali, iho uila. **3.** *Assault.* Hō'eha 'ana.

**battle.** Kaua, ho'ouka kaua, paio.

**battleship.** Moku kaua, manuā, pāpū lewa.

**bay.** Kū'ono, kai kū'ono; Hono-, Hana- *(in place names only).*

**be.** *There is no verb "to be" in Hawaiian. The copula is omitted entirely in equational sentences, or may be represented by verb markers* (ua, e . . . ana, ke . . . nei, i, e) *or by the article* he. *I am well, I was well,* ua maika'i au. *I will be well,* e maika'i ana au. *You are happy,* hau'oli 'oe. *This is a box,* he pahu kēia.

**beach.** Kahakai, kahaone, papa kea.

**beacon.** Lama kuhikuhi.

**beak.** Nuku, ihu.

**beam.** *Ray of light.* Kukuna.

**bear. 1.** *Carry.* Hāpai, hi'i, hali, pa'a; hā'awe *(on the back).* **2.** *Reproduce.* Hānau, hāpai, hua, ho'ohua. **3.** *Animal.* Pea.

**beard.** 'Umi'umi.

**beast.** Holoholona.

**beat. 1.** *Strike.* Pepehi, ku'i, pa'i, hahau, uhau, pā. *Beat, as the heart or pulse,* pana, 'api. **2.** *Defeat.* Make, eo, lanakila, pio.

**beautiful.** Nani, u'i, maika'i, makalapua.

**beautify.** Ho'onani, ho'ou'i, ho'ou'iu'i, ho'owehi, ho'ohiehie.

**beauty.** Nani; u‘i *(youthful).*
**because.** No, no ka mea, ma, i, ma o, muli, mamuli.
**beckon.** Ani, pe‘ahi.
**become.** Lilo, hele . . . ā, ua, lawe.
**becoming. 1.** *Befitting.* Kūpono.
**2.** *Attractive.* Kohukohu, hiehie.
**bed.** Moe, moena, wahi moe.
**bedroom.** Lumi moe.
**bed sheet.** Uhi pela.
**bedspread.** Kapa moe *(general name);* hāli‘i moe, uhi moe.
**bedtime.** Wā hiamoe, manawa moe.
**bee.** Meli, nalo meli *(honey bee).*
**beef.** Pipi. *Beef meat,* ‘i‘o pipi.
**beehive.** Pahu meli, pūnana meli.
**beer.** Pia, bia.
**beetle.** Pu‘u, ane.
**before.** Mua, ‘ē, alia, i ka wā mamua.
**beforehand.** Mua, ‘ē.
**befriend.** Ho‘omakamaka, ho‘ohoaloha, ho‘āikāne.
**beg, beggar.** Mākilo.
**begin.** Ho‘omaka, ho‘okumu. *To begin again,* ho‘omaka hou.
**beginner.** Mea ho‘omaka.
**beginning.** Ho‘omaka ‘ana, maka, maka mua, kinohi, kumu.
**behave.** Hana, noho. *Behave well,* noho pono.
**behind.** Hope, muli, ma ke kua; mahope *(referring to both time and place);* i hope *(does not refer to time).*
**being.** Mea *(person, thing);* kanaka *(human).*
**believe.** Mana‘o‘i‘o, hilina‘i.
**bell.** Pele.
**belly.** ‘Ōpū, hakualo.
**belong.** No, na, kuleana. *This belongs to me,* na‘u kēia, no‘u kēia.
**belonging.** Kā, kō, na, no. *Belonging to that place,* no laila.
**beloved.** Aloha ‘ia, mea aloha, milimili.
**below.** Lalo, i lalo, malalo, iho.

**belt.** Kuapo, ‘ili kuapo, kuapo ‘ōpū, kā‘ai.
**bench.** Noho, noho lō‘ihi, papa noho.
**bend.** Pelu, ho‘opi‘o, ho‘oke‘e, ho‘okeke‘e.
**beneath.** Lalo, malalo, i lalo.
**benefit.** Pono, maika‘i.
**Bermuda grass.** Mānienie haole.
**berry.** Hua li‘ili‘i.
**beside.** Ma, ma ka ‘ao‘ao.
**besides.** Koe, ho‘i, kekahi, kahi. *Besides that,* koe kēlā.
**best.** ‘Oi, ‘oi loa, maika‘i a‘e, po‘okela, kilohana. *Maui is the very best,* Maui nō ka ‘oi.
**bet.** Pili, piliwaiwai.
**betray.** Kumakaia.
**better.** Maika‘i a‘e, aho, ahona, ho‘okā‘oi; polapola *(of health). That is better,* e aho ia.
**between.** Waena, mawaena, i waena.
**beverage.** Mea inu. *Cold beverage,* mea inu ho‘ohu‘ihu‘i.
**beware.** Akahele, mālama, ao.
**bewilder.** Ho‘opōhihihi, ho‘opōna‘ana‘a, ho‘opāha‘oha‘o.
**beyond.** Waho, ‘ō. *Far beyond,* ma‘ō loa aku.
**Bible.** Paipala, Baibala. *Holy Bible,* Paipala Hemolele.
**bicycle.** Paikikala, ka‘a paikikala, ka‘a hehi wāwae.
**big.** Nui, nunui.
**bill.** Pila; kāki *(charge);* palapala *(document). Bill of sale,* palapala kū‘ai.
**billiards.** Pahupahu, pilioki.
**billow.** ‘Ale.
**bind.** *See* tie.
**bird.** Manu.
**birdhouse.** Hale manu.
**bird's-nest fern.** ‘Ēkaha.
**birth.** Hānau, hanauna, ho‘ohānau.
**birth certificate.** Palapala hānau.
**birth control.** Kaupalena hānau.
**birthday.** Lā hānau, lā piha makahiki. *Happy birthday,* hau‘oli lā hānau.
**birthmark.** Ila.

**birthplace.** 'Āina hānau, one hānau.

**biscuit.** Pelena.

**bishop.** Pīhopa.

**Bishop Museum.** Hale Hō'ike-'ike o Kamehameha.

**bitch.** 'Īlio wahine.

**bite.** Nahu, nanahu, 'aki, 'a'aki, 'akina.

**bits.** Li'ili'i, oka, hunahuna, hunehune.

**bitter.** 'Awa, 'awa'awa.

**black.** 'Ele'ele, 'ele, pō'ele, pā'ele, uliuli, hiwa, hiwa pa'a.

**blackboard.** Papa 'ele'ele.

**black eye.** Maka uli.

**blame.** 'Āhewa, 'imi hala, ho'āhewa, ho'ohewa, kāpilipili.

**blanket.** Kapa moe, huluhulu, kapa huluhulu.

**bleach.** Ho'oke'oke'o, pūkai, kuakea, ho'okuakea, ho'oheu.

**bleed.** Kahe koko.

**bless.** Ho'omaika'i, ho'opōmaika'i, mōlia.

**blind.** Makapō, maka'alā. *Blind in one eye,* makapa'a.

**blink.** 'I'imo, 'ōnini, ho'olili, ha'alili.

**blister.** Pō'olopū, hō'olopū, 'olopū, 'ōwela.

**block.** 1. *Obstruct.* 'Āke'ake'a, ke'ake'a, ke'a, pa'a. 2. *Piece of wood.* Paukū wahie, palaka.

**blonde.** Oho hākeakea, lauoho melemele.

**blood.** Koko. *Flow of blood,* kahe koko, he'e koko.

**blossom.** Pua.

**blow.** 1. *As air current.* Puhi, pā, papā, pā makani *(wind).* 2. *Strike.* Haua, hāuna, hahau, hauhāuna, uhau.

**blowhole.** Lua puhi, puhi.

**blue.** *No exact equivalent:* uli, uli-uli *(of deep sea);* polū *(as of clothes, eyes). Blue eyes,* maka 'ālohilohi, maka polū.

**blunder.** Lalau, hewa, kīna-'una'u.

**blunt.** Kūmūmū, mūmū.

**blush.** Pi'i ka 'ula.

**board.** 1. *Lumber.* Papa, papa lā'au, laupapa. *Rough, unfinished board,* papa huluhulu. *Ironing board,* papa 'aiana. 2. *To go on board.* Kau e'e. *To board a ship,* e'e moku. 3. *To feed.* Hānai, 'ai. 4. *Council.* Papa, ke'ena.

**boarding school.** Kula hānai, kula noho pa'a.

**Board of Education.** Papa Ho'ona'auao.

**Board of Health.** Papa Ola.

**Board of Supervisors.** Papa Luna Kia'i.

**boast.** Kaena, ha'anui, liki, ha'a-kei.

**boat.** Moku. *Rowboat,* wa'apā. *Steamboat,* mokuahi.

**body.** Kino.

**body hair.** Hulu, huluhulu.

**body surfing.** He'e umauma, kaha nalu.

**boil.** 1. *As water.* Paila, kupa, lapalapa. 2. *Carbuncle.* Ma'i hēhē, makalau; maka pala, palapū *(ready to burst).*

**bold.** Koa, maka koa, wiwo 'ole, 'a'a, maha'oi.

**bomb.** Pōkā pahū.

**bone.** Iwi.

**bonefish.** 'Ō'io.

**bonito.** Kawakawa.

**bonus.** Uku makana, uku keu.

**booby.** *Bird.* 'Ā, 'a'ā.

**book.** Puke.

**bookstore.** Hale kū'ai puke.

**border.** Palena, lihi, nihi, kapa, pe'a, ka'e.

**boring.** *Uninteresting.* Hoihoi 'ole, manakā, ho'omanakā.

**born.** Hānau.

**borrow.** Hō'ai'ē, nonoi no ka manawa.

**boss.** Luna, haku hana, poki. *To boss,* noho haku.

**bossy.** Ho'ohaku, kuhikuhi, kuhilani.

**both.** Lāua 'elua, nā mea 'elua. *Both you and I,* 'o kāua pū.

**bother.** Pilikia, ho'opilikia, hana luhi, ho'oluhi.

**bottle.** 'Ōmole, hue wai. *Nursing bottle,* 'ōmole hānai waiū.

**bottom.** Kumu, mole, kō lalo loa, papakū, kahi malalo.

**"bottoms up."** Huli pau; 'ōkole maluna *(vulgar).*

**boundary.** Palena, mokuna, 'ao-'ao, kapa, lihi. *Land boundary,* palena 'āina.

**bow. 1.** *Obeisance.* Kūlou, kūnou, kimo po'o. **2.** *Forward part of vessel.* Ihu, ihu wa'a. **3.** *Weapon.* Pana, pana 'iole, kīko'o.

**bowels. 1.** *Evacuation.* Ki'o, kākā, pāki'o; hana lepo *(euphemism).* See **excrement. 2.** *Innards.* Na'au, 'ōpū.

**bowl. 1.** *Container.* 'Umeke, ipu, pola. **2.** *Game.* 'Ulu maika, maika, pahe'e 'ulu. *Bowling ball* 'ulu, pu'upā.

**box. 1.** *Receptacle.* Pahu. **2.** *Fight.* Ku'iku'i, ku'iku'i pu'u-pu'u, mokomoko.

**boxfish.** Makukana, pahu.

**boy.** Keiki, keiki kāne, kama kāne. *Oh boy!* Auē!

**bracelet.** Kūpe'e, kūpe'e lima, apo, apo lima.

**brag.** Kaena, akena, ha'akoi, ho'okelakela.

**braid.** Hilo, hili, pahili, ulana.

**brain.** Lolo, lolo po'o.

**branch.** Lālā, mana, 'ohā.

**branches.** Manamana.

**brand.** Kuni, hao.

**brandy.** Palani.

**brass.** Keleawe.

**brave.** Koa, ho'okoa, wiwo 'ole.

**bread.** Palaoa, pelena.

**breadfruit.** 'Ulu.

**break.** *There is no general term; the main usages follow.* **1.** *As a stick or bones broken in two.* Ha'i, haha'i, uha'i, haki, haki-haki, uhaki; *break easily,* ha'i wale. **2.** *As a flat surface split or broken into pieces.* Wāhi, wāwa-hi, wāhia, 'ulupā. **3.** *As a string that is severed.* Moku, momoku, mokumoku. **4.** *As a dish.* Nahā. **5.** *General.* Ho'opilikia *(dam-*age); *break open or burst,* pohā; pakū; *break, as waves,* po'i, ha-ki; *break, as law,* wāwahi, pale, ha'iha'i. *To break and enter a house,* wāwahi hale.

**breakfast.** 'Aina kakahiaka.

**breast.** Ū, waiū.

**breath.** Hanu, aho, ea, eaea.

**breathe.** Hanu, aho.

**breeze.** Ahe, aheahe makani, ani, aniani, makani aniani.

**brick.** Winihapa.

**bride.** Wahine male hou, wahine mare.

**bridegroom.** Kāne male hou, kāne mare.

**bridge.** Uapo.

**brief. 1.** *Short.* Pōkole, muku. **2.** *Summary.* Palapala ho'opōkole 'ia.

**bright.** 'Alohi, 'ālohilohi, kōnane, 'ōlino, la'ela'e, akamai *(smart).*

**bring.** Lawe mai, hō mai.

**brisk.** Maka'ala, 'eleu, māmā.

**Britain.** Pelekane, Pelekania.

**broad.** Laulā, ākea.

**broadcast.** Ho'olele leo, ho'ola-ha.

**broaden.** Ho'olaulā.

**broil.** Pūlehu *(on coals);* lāwalu *(in leaves).*

**broom.** Pūlumi.

**brother.** Kaikua'ana, kua'ana *(older sibling of same sex);* kaikaina, kaina *(younger sibling of same sex);* kaikunāne, kunāne *(of a female).*

**brother-in-law.** Kaiko'eke, ko'eke *(of a male);* kāne.

**brown.** *No exact Hawaiian equivalent;* uliuli, kama'ehu.

**bruise.** Pohole, ho'opohole, māhole, mōhole.

**brush. 1.** *Instrument.* Palaki, hu-lu. *Scrubbing brush,* palaki 'ānai. *Scrubbing or painting brush,* hulu'ānai. *Hairbrush,* palaki lauoho. *To brush,* palaki. **2.** *To brush aside.* Pale, pale-pale.

**bubble.** Hu'a.

**bucket.** Pākeke. See **pail.**

**bud.** Liko, 'ōpu'u. *To bud,* 'ōmamaka.

**buds.** Makamaka; makalau *(fig., many offspring).*

**bug.** Mū, pu'u.

**bugle.** Pū.

**build.** Kūkulū, hana, kāpili.

**building.** Hale.

**bull.** Pipi kāne, pipi laho, pipi pulu, pulu.

**bullet.** Pōkā, pōhaku waikī.

**bump.** Pu'u, 'anapu'u, 'ōhū.

**bunch.** 'Āhui *(as of bananas);* hui, huihui, huhui.

**bundle.** Pū'olo, 'ope, 'ope'ope.

**bur.** Kukū.

**burden.** Luhi; hā'awe, hō'awe, 'awe *(carried on back);* amo, 'auamo *(carried on shoulders).*

**bureau.** 1. *Office.* Ke'ena, 'oihana, mahele, pulo. 2. *Chest of drawers.* Pahu 'ume.

**burglary.** Wāwahi hale, 'aihue.

**burial.** Kanu, kanu 'ana.

**burn.** 'Ā, 'a'ā, hō'ā, puhi, kuni, puhi ahi.

**burned.** Pau ahi, wela, welawela, pāpa'a, kunia.

**burst.** Pahū, pakū, pohā, pūhā.

**bury.** Kanu.

**bus.** Ka'a 'ōhua.

**bush.** 1. *Shrub.* Lā'au li'ili'i, lā'au ha'aha'a. 2. *Vegetation.* Nahele.

**business.** 'Oihana, hana, kuleana. *To transact business,* ho'oholo i ka hana.

**busy.** Pa'ahana, pa'a i ka hana, lilo, limahana.

**but.** Akā, na'e, aia na'e, eia (nō) na'e, koe, koe kēia.

**butter.** Waiūpaka, paka.

**butterfly.** Pulelehua, lepelepe-o-Hina.

**butterfly fish.** Kīkākapu.

**buttocks.** Lemu, 'ōkole, pāpākole, 'elemu, hope.

**button.** Pihi.

**buy.** Kū'ai, kū'ai mai.

**by.** E, na, ma, i. *By me,* na'u. *By him, her, it,* nāna. *By you,* nāu.

**by-and-by.** Mahope, mamuli, auane'i.

# C

**c.** *No Hawaiian term.*

**cabbage.** Kāpiki, kākipi.

**cabinet.** 1. *Furniture.* Waihona, pahu waihona. 2. *Political.* 'Aha kuhina.

**cactus.** Pānini, pāpipi.

**café.** Hale 'aina.

**cage.** Pahu manu, pahu holoholona.

**cake.** Mea 'ono. *Chinese meat cake,* pepeiao. *Chinese pork cake,* mea 'ono pua'a *(today called* manapua). *Flour cake,* pa'i palaoa. *Pound cake,* mea 'ono paona.

**calabash.** 'Umeke, ipu, pā ipu, hōkeo, hue, ōpū hue, ipu pāwehe.

**calendar.** 'Alemanaka, kalenekalio.

**calf.** 1. *Animal.* Pipi keiki. 2.

*Anatomy.* 'Olo, 'olo'olo wāwae, 'olo wae.

**California.** Kaleponi.

**call.** 1. *To speak out.* Hea, kāhea. 2. *To give a name.* Kapa. 3. *To visit.* Kipa.

**calm.** Mālie, la'i, hāla'i, kāla'e, māla'e, malino, manino, linolino.

**calmed.** La'i, mālie, nā.

**camera.** Pahupa'iki'i.

**camp.** Kahua. *To make a camp, to camp,* ho'okahua, ho'omoana.

**campground.** Kahua ho'omoana.

**can.** 1. *Able.* Hiki. 2. *Tin.* Kini.

**Canada.** Kanaka, Kanada.

**canal.** Alawai, 'auwai, 'auwaha, kōwā, kanela.

**cancel.** Ho'opau, kāpae.

**candidate.** Moho.

**candle.** Ihoiho, ihoiho kukui.

**candlenut.** Kukui.

**candy.** Kanakē.

**cane.** 1. *See* **sugarcane.** 2. *Staff.* Koʻokoʻo.

**cannery.** Hale hoʻokomo kini. *Pineapple cannery,* hale hana hala kahiki.

**cannon.** Pū kuni ahi. *Cannon ball,* pōkā pū kuni ahi.

**canoe.** Waʻa.

**canoe bailer.** Kā.

**canoe man.** Mea waʻa.

**canoe paddler.** Hoe waʻa.

**canoe race.** Heihei waʻa.

**can opener.** Mea wehe kini.

**can't.** ʻAʻole hiki, hiki ʻole. *I can't go,* ʻaʻole hiki iaʻu ke hele.

**canvas.** Kapolena.

**cap.** Kapu, pāpale kapu.

**cape.** 1. *Geographical.* Lae, ʻōlae, ʻoiʻoina. 2. *Garment.* Kīhei, ʻahu, kīpuka, koloka. *Feather cape,* ʻahu ʻula.

**cape gooseberry.** Pohā, paʻina.

**capital.** 1. *City.* Kapikala. 2. *Wealth.* Kumu waiwai, kumupaʻa.

**captain.** Kāpena, luna kaua, kāpena aliʻikoa.

**captive.** Pio.

**capture.** Lawe pio, hopu.

**car.** Kaʻa, *To ride in a car,* kau kaʻa, holo kaʻa. *To drive a car,* kalaiwa kaʻa. *To get in a car,* kau i ke kaʻa. *To get out of a car,* lele mai ke kaʻa.

**carbon paper.** Pepa kope.

**card.** Pepa.

**cards.** Nā pepa, pepa hahau *(playing).*

**care.** *To care for.* Mālama, nānā. *Well cared for,* mālama pono ʻia.

**career.** ʻOihana.

**carefree.** ʻAʻohe noʻonoʻo, ʻaʻohe hoʻokaumaha, ʻaʻohe pīhoihoi.

**careful.** Akahele, nānā pono, mālama pono.

**carefully.** Pono, nihi, aka-.

**careless.** Kāpulu, palaka, kīkoʻolā, hoʻoponopono ʻole, hoʻohemahema.

**caretaker.** Kahu.

**carfare.** Uku kaʻa.

**cargo.** Ukana.

**carnation.** Ponimōʻī.

**carpenter.** Kamanā.

**carpet.** Moena weleweka, kāpeka.

**carrot.** Kāloke.

**carry.** Lawe, hāpai, hali.

**cart.** Kaʻa, kaʻa huila lua.

**carve.** Kālai, kalakalai, kuʻikepa *(as wood);* ʻokiʻoki *(as meat).*

**case.** 1. *Container.* Pahu, wahī, poho. 2. *Court case.* Hihia, hihia kalaima, hihia waiwai. 3. *Situation,* Kūlana.

**cash.** Kālā kūʻike.

**cash payment.** Uku kūʻike.

**casket.** Pahu, pahu kupapaʻu.

**cast.** 1. *To throw.* Hoʻolei, nou, kiola. 2. *To cast for fish.* Kākele, kāʻili, hī, hoʻokelekele.

**cat.** Pōpoki, ʻoau.

**catalog.** Puke nānā mea kūʻai, puke hōʻike hana.

**catch.** Hopu *(grab);* ʻapo *(as a ball);* ʻapoʻapo; hei *(in a net);* loaʻa, hoʻopaʻa.

**caterpillar.** Peʻelua, ʻenuhe, nuhe, ʻanuhe, poko.

**Catholic.** Kakōlika, Kakōlika Loma *(Roman). Catholic religion,* Hoʻomana Pope.

**Catholicism.** Kakōlika, Hoʻomana Palani.

**cat's cradle.** Hei.

**cattle.** Pipi; pūʻā pipi, kumu pipi *(herd).*

**Caucasian.** Haole. *See* **white man.**

**caught.** Hopu ʻia, ʻapo ʻia; mau *(snagged, as a fish or hook).*

**cautious.** Akahele, hoʻokanahaʻi.

**cave.** Ana, lua, pao.

**cavity.** Poʻo, napoʻo, ʻāpoʻopoʻo. *Tooth cavity,* puka niho.

**cease.** Pau, hoʻopau, oki, hoʻōki, waiho.

**ceiling.** Kaupaku.

**celebrate.** Hoʻolauleʻa, hauʻoli, hoʻokelakela.

**celebration.** Hoʻolauleʻa; hana hoʻohiwahiwa *(as to honor an individual).*

**cement.** Kameki, kimeki, palaina kimeki. *To smooth fresh cement with a trowel,* palaina.

**cemetery.** Ilina, pā ilina, pā kupapa'u. *Plot in a cemetery,* pā ilina.

**cent.** Keneka. *Ten cents,* kenikeni.

**center.** Waena, waenakonu, konuwaena, kikowaena.

**central.** Waena; kikowaena *(telephone operator).*

**ceremony.** Hana ho'ohanohano. *Religious ceremony,* hana pili haipule.

**cereus.** Pāpipi pua.

**certain.** 1. *Particular.* Kekahi. 2. *Positive.* Maopopo loa.

**certainly.** Hiki, hiki nō, ā 'oia, pēlā nō, 'oia'i'o, pēlā 'i'o nō. *Certainly not!* 'A'ole loa!

**certificate.** Palapala, palapala hō'oia, palapala hō'ike. *Birth certificate,* palapala hānau.

**chain.** Kaula, kaula hao. *Watch chain,* kaula uaki.

**chair.** Noho. *Kinds:* noho ali'i *(throne);* noho huila *(wheel);* noho 'ie *(wicker);* noho kū *(straight);* noho moe *(divan);* noho 'opi'opi *(folding);* noho paipai *(rocking).*

**chairman.** Luna ho'omalu, ali'i ho'omalu.

**chalk.** Poho.

**challenge.** 'A'a.

**champion.** Mea lanakila, po'okela, pūkaua.

**chance.** Manawa *(opportunity). Take a chance,* ho'ā'o.

**change.** 1. *Transformation.* Loli, ho'olilo, ho'ololi, huli. 2. *Money.* Kenikeni; wāhi *(to change a bill).*

**chant.** Oli *(not for dancing);* hula *(for dancing);* mele *(general term).*

**chapter.** Mokuna.

**character.** 1. *Nature.* 'Ano. 2. *Symbol.* Hō'ailona.

**charcoal.** Lānahu, nānahu.

**charge.** 1. *Levy a price.* Ho'ouku, uku. 2. *Defer payment.* Hō'ai'ē,

kāki, 'auhau. 3. *Accusation.* 'Ōlelo ho'āhewa, 'āhewa.

**charity.** Aloha, manawale'a.

**charming.** Māhie, ho'omāhie, ho'opunihei.

**chase.** Alualu, hahai, uhai, 'āha'i.

**chat.** Kama'ilio, keaka.

**cheap.** Emi, makepono.

**cheat.** 'Āpuka, pākaha, kikiki, kolohe, 'aihue, ho'opunipuni.

**check.** 1. *Bank.* Pila kīko'o, pepa kīko'o, palapala kīko'o. 2. *To restrain.* Ke'ake'a, kāohi, ho'ālia. 3. *To mark.* Kaha. 4. *To verify.* Nānā pono i nā hewa, hō'oia'i'o.

**checkerboard.** Papa kōnane, papamū.

**checkers.** Kōnane.

**check mark.** Kaha.

**cheek.** Papālina.

**cheer.** 1. *Encourage.* Ho'olana, ho'opaipai. 2. *Shout.* Ho'ōho.

**cheerful.** Hoihoi, hau'oli mau, ho'olana.

**cheers.** Hipahipa, hulō, ho'ōho hau'oli.

**cheese.** Waiūpa'a, waiūpakapa'a.

**cherish.** Pūlama, ho'oheno; ha'aheo *(with pride).*

**chest.** 1. *Anatomy.* Umauma, houpo, ke'apa'a. 2. *Container.* Pahu, holowa'a.

**chew.** Mama *(without swallowing);* nau *(with closed mouth).*

**chicken.** Moa.

**chicken pox.** Ma'i pu'upu'u li'ili'i.

**chief.** Ali'i, lani.

**chief of police.** Luna māka'i.

**child.** Keiki.

**childbirth.** Hānau, ho'ohānau.

**childhood.** Wā kamali'i, wā li'ili'i, wā 'u'uku.

**childish.** Ho'okamali'i.

**childless.** Kama 'ole, keiki 'ole, lālā 'ole.

**children.** Kamali'i.

**chili pepper.** Nīoi.

**chilly.** Hu'ihu'i, lī, ko'eko'e, make anu, anuanu.

**chin.** 'Auwae.

**China. 1.** *The country.* Pākē, 'Āina Pākē. **2.** *(Not cap.)* *Crockery.* Pā a me nā pola like 'ole *(usually white, hard, sonorous porcelain).*

**Chinese.** Pākē.

**Chinese New Year.** Konohī.

**chisel.** Pao, kila, ko'i pāhoa.

**chocolate.** Kokoleka.

**choice. 1.** *Selection.* Koho, wae 'ana. **2.** *Of high quality.* Laha 'ole, mea laha 'ole, hiwa.

**choir.** Papa hīmeni.

**choke.** 'Umi, laoa, pu'ua, kalea.

**choking.** 'Umina.

**choose.** Koho, ho'okoho, wae, ho'owae, waewae.

**chop.** Kua, kākā, 'oki'oki, 'āpahu, pokepoke.

**chopsticks.** Lā'au 'ai, lā'au lālau mea 'ai.

**chorus.** Hui, mele hui.

**Christ.** Kristo. *Jesus Christ,* Iesu Kristo.

**Christian.** Kalikiano, Kristiano, Kiritiano.

**Christianity.** Ho'omana Kalikiano.

**Christmas.** Kalikimaka, Kalikamaka.

**church.** Hale pule, luakini, pule.

**Church of Jesus Christ of Latter-Day Saints.** Ho'omana o Iesu Kristo o nā Po'e Ho'āno o nā Lā Hope Nei.

**cigar.** Kīkā.

**cigarette.** Kikaliki.

**circle.** Apo, pō'ai, pōhai, ho'owiliwili.

**circuit court.** 'Aha ka'apuni, 'aha ho'okolokolo ka'apuni.

**circular.** Poepoe.

**circulate.** Ho'olaha, ho'olaulaha, wiliau.

**circumcise.** Kahe, kahe ule, 'oki poepoe.

**citizen.** Kupa, maka'āinana.

**city.** Kūlanakauhale. *"City of refuge,"* pu'uhonua.

**claim.** Palapala ho'opi'i; kuleana *(for land).*

**clam.** 'Ōlepe, pāpaua, paua.

**clan.** 'Ohana nui, 'ohana holo'oko'a, 'alaea.

**clap.** Pa'i, pa'ipa'i, pa'ipa'i lima; ku'i *(as of thunder).*

**class.** Papa. *Chiefly class,* papa ali'i.

**classify.** Ho'onohonoho, ho'onohonoho papa, kūkulu papa.

**classmate.** Hoa kula.

**claw.** Miki'ao, mānea, mai'ao, māi'u'u.

**clay.** Pālolo, lepo kāwili, lepo mānoanoa.

**clean.** Ma'ema'e. *To clean,* ho'oma'ema'e, holoi, ho'oholoi.

**clear.** Mōakaaka, akaaka, akāka, māla'e, kāla'e, mālamalama.

**clerk.** Kākau 'ōlelo, kupakako.

**clever.** Akamai, no'eau, loea.

**cliff.** Pali, palipa'a.

**climb.** Pi'i.

**cling.** Pili, pili pū.

**clock.** Uaki. *Alarm clock,* uaki ho'āla.

**close. 1.** *Near.* Kokoke, pili. **2.** *To shut.* Ho'opa'a, pani, panipani, panikū, 'ūpiki. **3.** *To finish.* Ho'opau. *Close-out sale,* kū'ai ho'opau.

**closed.** Pa'a.

**closet.** Waihona, ke'ena waiho.

**cloth.** Lole.

**clothe.** 'A'ahu, hō'a'ahu, ho'okomo lole.

**clothes.** Lole, 'a'ahu, kapa komo, lole komo.

**clothesline.** Kaula kaula'i lole.

**clothing store.** Hale kū'ai lole.

**cloud.** Ao; 'ōpua *(banks, billows).*

**cloudburst.** Ua lanipili.

**cloudless.** Kaula'ela'e, māla'e, pa'ihi.

**cloudy.** 'Ōmalumalu, 'omamalu.

**club. 1.** *Organization.* Hui, 'ahahui. **2.** *Weapon.* Lā'au, lā'au pālau, lā'au māka'i, pālau, newa.

**clumsy.** Hemahema, pepe'ekue, hāwāwā.

**cluster.** 'Āhui, huihui.

**coal.** Lānahu, nānahu pikimana.

**coarse.** Mānoanoa.

**coast.** Kapakai.

**coast guard.** Kiaʻi kai.

**coat.** Kuka, ʻahu.

**cobweb.** Pūnāwelewele.

**cock.** Moa kāne.

**cockfighting.** Hakakā-a-moa, hākā moa, hoʻohākā moa.

**cockroach.** ʻElelū.

**cocktail.** Lama hoʻohuihui ʻia, lama paʻipaʻi.

**cocoa.** Kōkō.

**coconut.** Niu.

**coffee.** Kope.

**coffee grounds.** Oka kope.

**coffin.** Pahu, pahu kupapaʻu.

**cold. 1.** *Not warm.* Anu, anuanu; koʻekoʻe, huʻihuʻi *(chilly).* **2.** *Disease.* Anu. *Head cold,* hanu paʻa, punia. *To have a cold,* anu. *To catch a cold,* loaʻa i ke anu.

**collar.** ʻĀʻīkala, kala.

**collarbone.** Iwilei.

**collect.** ʻOhi, hoʻākoakoa, hoʻāhu, hōʻili, hōʻiliʻili. *To collect taxes,* ʻohi ʻauhau.

**collection.** Hoʻāhu, hōʻiliʻili; lūlū *(church).*

**college.** Kulanui.

**colony.** Panalāʻau.

**color.** Waihoʻoluʻu, kala.

**column.** Kolamu.

**comb.** Kahi.

**combat.** Paio, kaua paio, hakakā.

**come.** Hele mai; mai *(in commands);* hiki mai; haele mai; uhaele mai *(plural).*

**comfort.** ʻOlu, hōʻolu, maha, hoʻonā.

**comfortable.** ʻOluʻolu, hōʻolu, mōhalu, mōhaluhalu.

**comma.** Koma.

**command.** Kauoha, kēnā.

**commandment.** ʻŌlelo kauoha. *Ten Commandments,* nā Kānāwai he ʻUmi.

**commendation.** Hoʻomaikaʻi. *Letter of commendation,* palapala hoʻomaikaʻi.

**commerce.** ʻOihana kālepa.

**commission.** Komikina *(board).*

**commissioner.** Komikina, luna.

**committee.** Kōmike.

**common.** Hana mau, maʻamau, laha, lauākea. *Not common,* laha ʻole.

**commoner.** Makaʻāinana, noa, noanoa.

**communion.** Komunio. *Holy Communion,* ʻAhaʻaina a ka Haku.

**community.** Wahi noho like o ka poʻe, kūlanakauhale.

**companion.** Hoa.

**company.** Hui, ʻahahui.

**compare.** Hoʻohālikelike, hoʻokūkū.

**compass.** Pānānā.

**compete.** Hoʻokūkū.

**complain.** Hoʻohalahala, namunamu, ʻōhumu, ʻōhumuhumu.

**complete.** Piha pono, pau pono, hoʻopau, hoʻopaʻa, hoʻokō pono, holoʻokoʻa.

**compose.** Haku, haku mele *(song or chant);* haku moʻolelo *(story).*

**computer.** Lolo uila, kamepiula.

**conceal.** Hūnā, peʻe, hoʻonalo.

**conceited.** Hoʻokano, hoʻokiʻekiʻe, hōʻoio, hoʻokelakela.

**conch shell.** Pū, ʻolē; ʻolēʻolē *(small).* Conch horn, pūʻolēʻolē.

**condemn.** Hoʻāhewa, hoʻohewa.

**conduct. 1.** *Deportment.* Hana, ʻano o ka hana ʻana, noho ʻana, kūlana. **2.** *To lead.* Alakaʻi, hoʻokele, mālama, lawelawe.

**confess.** Mihi, hōʻike i ka hana i hana ʻia.

**confuse.** Hoʻopohihihi, hoʻohuikau.

**confused.** Huikau, pohihihi, pōnaʻanaʻa.

**confusion.** Huikau, haunaele, pōnaʻanaʻa, piʻoloke.

**congratulate, congratulations.** Hoʻomaikaʻi.

**Congregational.** Kalawina.

**congress.** ʻAhaʻōlelo lāhui *(as of the United States).*

**connect.** Hoʻokuʻi, hoʻohui.

**conquer.** Lanakila, lawe pio, naʻi.

**conqueror.** Naʻi.
**conquest.** Lanakila, lawe pio ʻana.
**consent.** ʻAe, ʻāpono, hoʻāpono.
**consequence.** Hopena, hope.
**consider.** Noʻonoʻo pono, manaʻo.
**constant.** Mau, kūpaʻa.
**constellation.** Huihui.
**constipation.** Kūkae paʻa, lepo paʻa.
**constitution.** *Document.* Kumukānāwai.
**consul.** Kanikela, kanikele.
**consult.** Kūkā, kūkākūkā, ʻōlelo kūkā.
**consume.** ʻAi, hoʻopau, luku, kemu, hamu.
**contagious.** Lele.
**container.** Ipu, pūʻolo, poʻi, kā, poho.
**contempt.** Hoʻowahāwahā.
**contest.** Hoʻokūkū, hoʻopāpā, pāpā; kahului *(athletic).*
**continue.** Hoʻomau.
**contract.** 1. *Agreement.* ʻAelike, kepa, palapala ʻaelike, ukupau, hoʻoholo. 2. *Shrink.* Mimiki, hoʻohāiki.
**contrast.** Hoʻohālike, hoʻohālikelike; ʻokoʻa *(noun).*
**control.** Kāohi.
**convention.** ʻAha, ʻahahui, hōʻike.
**conversation.** Kamaʻilio ʻana, pāpāʻōlelo, kūkaʻi kamaʻilio.
**converse.** Kamaʻilio, walaʻau, kamakamaʻilio, pāpāʻōlelo.
**convict.** 1. *Find guilty.* ʻĀhewa, hoʻāhewa. 2. *Prisoner.* Paʻahao.
**convinced.** Manaʻopaʻa, hoʻokūʻiʻo, hoʻomaopopo.
**cook.** Hoʻomoʻa, kuke, ʻōlala, lala *(over a fire);* kahu, kahuna *(at an oven);* kahu ʻai, kahūmu ʻai *(taro or vegetable food). See* **bake, boil, broil, roast.**
**cooked.** Moʻa; pāpaʻa, pāpaʻapū *(to a crisp);* māhinu *(underdone);* moʻa leʻa *(thoroughly).*
**cookie.** Mea ʻono, mea ʻono kuki.
**cool.** ʻOluʻolu *(pleasantly);* huʻihuʻi *(chilly);* maʻū *(damp).*

**cooled.** Maʻalili; maʻūʻū; kōaniani *(by a breeze).*
**cooperate.** Hoʻolaulima, kōkua, huki like, kākoʻo, alu, alu like, hana like.
**cooperation.** Laulima, kōkua.
**copra.** Niu maloʻo.
**copy.** Hoʻohālike; kope, kopena, mea like, kākau kope, lua, ponokope.
**copyright.** Palapala hoʻokuleana.
**coral.** Puna, koʻa, koʻakoʻa.
**cord.** Aho, kaula; piko *(umbilical).*
**cork.** ʻUmoki, ʻomo, pani, pani ʻōmole *(stopper).*
**corn.** Kūlina; kūlina ʻono *(sweet);* kūlina, mānoanoa ka ʻili *(as on a toe).*
**corner.** Huina; kūʻono *(inside);* kihi *(outside);* kohe *(mat);* huina alanui *(street);* hio.
**cornstarch.** Pia kūlina.
**corpse.** Kupapaʻu, kino wailua, kino make, heana.
**corral.** Pā.
**correct.** Pololei, pono. *To correct,* hoʻopololei, hoʻopono, hoʻoponopono, hoʻomaikaʻi.
**correspond.** *Write letters.* Launa palapala, kūkaʻi leka, hololeka.
**cost.** Kumu kūʻai, kumu lilo.
**costly.** Pipiʻi, nui ka hoʻolilo, waiwai.
**costume.** ʻAʻahu, lole.
**cot.** Moe ʻopiʻopi, moe ʻuʻuku.
**cottage.** Hale ʻuʻuku.
**cotton.** Pulu, pulupulu, maʻo.
**couch.** Hikieʻe *(large);* pūneʻe *(movable);* kokī, noho moe.
**cough.** Kunu, ʻehē, ʻahē, ʻahēʻahē.
**council.** ʻAha kūkā, pūkuʻi.
**count.** 1. *Number.* Helu, heluhelu, heluna. 2. *Title of nobility.* Kauna.
**countrified.** Kuaʻāina, hoʻokuaʻāina, pilikua.
**country.** ʻĀina *(land);* kuaʻāina *(as distinct from the city);* kahiki *(any foreign).*
**county.** Kalana.

**couple.** Lua, pa'a, papa lua.

**courage.** Koa, wiwo 'ole.

**course.** Ala, alanui, kahua. *Of course,* 'oia ho'i.

**court 1.** *Legal.* 'Aha. **2.** *Royal.* Aloali'i. **3.** *To woo.* Ho'oipo, ho'oipoipo. **4.** *See* **courtyard.**

**courthouse.** Hale ho'okolokolo.

**courtship.** Ho'oipoipo 'ana.

**courtyard.** Pā, kahua.

**cousin.** Hoahānau, kaukini.

**cousin-in-law.** Kaiko'eke *(of same sex). Female of a male,* wahine. *Male of a female,* kāne.

**cover.** Uhi, pani, pale, wahī.

**cow.** Pipi wahine, pipi waiū.

**coward.** Hōhē, ho'ohē, maka'u wale.

**cowboy.** Paniolo.

**cowrie shell.** Leho.

**crab.** Pāpa'i *(general name). Common kinds:* 'a'ama, 'elemihi, 'alamihi, 'ōhiki, unauna, 'ala'eke, mo'ala, kūhonu.

**crack. 1.** *Aperture.* Māwae. **2.** *Noise.* 'U'ina *(as a gun);* ko'ele *(as thunder);* kohā, ho'okani *(as a whip);* pāpa'a'ina *(as joints).*

**cracked.** Nahā, naka, makili, 'oā.

**cracker.** Pelena.

**cradle.** Moe luliluli, moe paipai.

**cramp.** Huki, lā'au, 'ūmi'i, wāwae huki.

**cramped.** 'Ōpili, pipiki, muikiiki, pilikia.

**crane. 1.** *Bird.* Manu 'ū. **2.** *Machine.* Kewe, hāpuku.

**crank.** Wili, kū'au wili. *Hand crank,* wili lima.

**cranky.** 'A'aka, kekē, kekē niho, 'eke'eke, ho'oke'eke'e.

**crash. 1.** *Hit.* Ho'oku'i. **2.** *Sound.* Pohā, pahū.

**crater.** Lua, lua pele.

**crawl.** Kolo.

**crazy.** Pupule, hehena, hewahewa.

**cream.** Kalima, kalima waiū; kalima hamo *(face).*

**create.** Hana, ho'okumu.

**creation.** Kumulipo, kumu honua.

**creature.** Mea ola *(living);* holoholona *(animal).*

**credit.** Hō'ai'ē *(debt);* hua, heluna *(as for a university course).*

**creep.** Kolo.

**crevalle.** Ulua.

**crib.** Moe kamali'i.

**crime.** Kalaima, hewa.

**criminal.** Kanaka hana kalaima.

**cripple.** 'O'opa, hapaku'e, kīnā.

**crisscross.** Kaha pe'a, 'oloke'a, hō'oloke'a, kaupe'a, kahahiō *(mark).*

**criticize.** Loiloi, kē *(often constructively);* ho'ohalahala *(fault-finding).*

**crook. 1.** *Bend.* Kīke'e, ke'e, lanahua, ho'okeke'e. **2.** *Cheat.* Kanaka pale kānāwai.

**crooked.** Kapakahi, keke'e, kīke'eke'e, hapaku'e, nanahū, ke'e.

**crop. 1.** *Harvest.* Mea ho'oulu. **2.** *Of a bird.* 'Ōpū.

**cross. 1.** *Of disposition.* 'A'aka, nauki, ka'e, kekē niho, niha. **2.** *Overlap.* Ke'a, pe'a. **3.** *As a street.* Hele ma kēlā 'ao'ao.

**crossroads.** Huina, huina alanui.

**crotch.** Kumuhele, mana; kapakapa *(human).*

**crouch.** 'Ōku'u.

**crow. 1.** *Bird.* 'Alalā. **2.** *Sound.* 'O'ō, kokō, kani.

**crowd.** Lehulehu, pihana kanaka, anaina, pū'ulu.

**crowded.** Pa'apū, pihaku'i, kukū.

**crown.** Kalaunu, kolona, pāpale ali'i, lei ali'i.

**crown flower.** Pua kalaunu.

**crucifix.** Ke'a.

**crucify.** Kaulia i ke ke'a, mākia.

**crude. 1.** *Harsh.* Lula 'ole, ho'oku'iku'i, hanahihi.

**cruel.** Loko 'ino, māino, hana 'ino, ho'omāinoino, hainā.

**crumb.** Huna. *Bread crumb,* huna palaoa.

**crush.** Lomi, ho'oūpē, ho'opē, 'ōpā, pākī, ho'omāui.

**crust.** Pāpa'a.

**crutch.** Koʻokoʻo kālele.

**cry.** Uē *(weep);* kani, oho, ʻuā *(call out);* puoho *(in alarm);* olo pihe, kāhea, pūʻalalā.

**crybaby.** Uē wale.

**cucumber.** Kaʻukama.

**cue.** 1. *Billiards.* Lāʻau pahupahu. 2. *Reminder.* Kumu hoʻomanaʻo, ʻōlelo hoʻomanaʻo.

**cultivate.** Mahi.

**cunning.** Maʻalea, ʻāpiki.

**cup.** Pola, ipu, kīʻaha, kīʻoʻe.

**cupboard.** Pahu pā, waihona pā ipu, waihona ipu.

**cup-of-gold.** Ipu kula.

**curb.** 1. *Street curb.* Kaʻe. 2. *To restrain.* Kāohi.

**cure.** Hoʻōla, lapaʻau, hoʻopolapola.

**cured.** Ola loa *(completely).*

**curiosity.** Nīele.

**curious.** 1. *Strange.* ʻAno ʻē, kupanaha, kupaianaha. 2. *Inquisitive.* Nīele.

**curl.** Milo. *To curl, as hair,* hoʻomimilo.

**curly.** Piʻipiʻi *(as hair).*

**currency.** Kālā, kālā aupuni.

**current.** 1. *Moving matter.* Au *(in the sea);* kai holo, wai kō. 2. *Contemporary.* O kēia au, o kēia manawa.

**curse.** Kūamuamu, amu, ʻānai, ʻōlelo hōʻino.

**curtain.** Pākū, pale, pālulu, pālulu ʻaoʻao. *Window curtain,* pākū pukaaniani.

**curved.** Piʻo, kiwi, pāuma, kākiwi, kihikihi.

**cushion.** Kūkini, uluna.

**customary.** Maʻamau, paʻa mau, kūmau, kuluma, laha.

**customer.** Mea kūʻai mai.

**customs.** Kuke, dute. *Customs duty,* kuke.

**cut.** ʻOki, hōʻoki, moku, mō, mokumoku, momoku, mokuhia, kālai, kaha; kua *(as a tree);* paʻipaʻi *(as a plant or the hair).* *Cut off,* muʻumuʻu, ʻakumu, poʻomuku. *Cut into pieces,* maʻoki, hoʻomākoli, ʻokiʻoki, paukū. *Cut in short pieces,* ʻāpoke, pokepoke. *Cut in half,* pahupū. *To cut cards,* ʻoki puʻu pepa. *To cut stone,* kālai pōhaku.

**cycle.** 1. *Period.* Au, wā. 2. *Wheel.* Huila.

# D

**d.** *No Hawaiian term.*

**dagger.** Pāhoa, pahi ʻō, pīkoi lua.

**daily.** I kēlā me kēia lā; puka lā *(as a newspaper).*

**dairy.** Hale ʻuī waiū, hui ʻuī waiū, wahi mālama pipi waiū.

**dam.** Pani wai, kaupale, māno.

**damage.** Pohō, pōʻino, hōʻinoʻino, hoʻoʻino. *To damage,* hōʻino.

**damages.** Uku pohō.

**damn.** Hōʻino wale, kūamuamu.

**damp.** Maʻū.

**dampen.** Hoʻomaʻū, hoʻomāʻūʻū.

**dance.** Hula; hulahula *(ballroom dance).*

**dancing school.** Kula aʻo hulahula.

**danger.** Mea pōʻino, makaʻu.

**dangerous.** Makaʻu loa, weliweli ʻia, pōʻino.

**dare.** ʻAʻa, hoʻohoa.

**dark.** Pōʻele, pōʻeleʻele, ʻeleʻele, pāʻele, uli, uliuli, āuli, hāuli, hāuliuli, lāuli, māuli, pouli, polohiwa, ʻāhiwa, pōuliuli, pō; mākuʻe *(any dark color).* *Dark-complexioned,* ʻili uliuli, ʻili pala uli, ʻili mākuʻe, ʻili kou, pāʻele; pōpolo *(slang).* *To become dark,* hōʻeleʻele.

**darkness.** Pōʻeleʻele.

**darling.** Makamae, hiwahiwa, milimili, lei.

**dart.** *Spear.* Ihe, ihe ʻō, kao.

**dash.** *Run.* Holo māmā, heihei.

**date.** 1. *Time.* Manawa, lā, makahiki. 2. *Fruit.* Hua pāma. 3. *En-*

*gagement.* Ho‘opa‘a manawa no ka launa pū.

**daughter.** Kaikamahine.

**daughter-in-law.** Hūnōna wahine.

**dawn.** Ao, wana‘ao, kaiao, moku ka pawa.

**day.** Lā, ao. *Weekday,* lā noa. *Day of worship,* lā ho‘āno. *School day,* lā kula. *Workday,* lā hana.

**dead.** Make, make loa, moe lepo. *Dead body,* kino make, kino kupapa‘u.

**deadline.** Kaupalena.

**deadly.** Make.

**deaf.** Kuli, ho‘okuli, pepeiao kuli.

**deaf-mute.** Leo pa‘a, a‘alolo kuli. *Deaf-mutes,* po‘e kuli ā ‘ā‘ā.

**deal. 1.** *Apportion.* Mahele; hā‘awi, ha‘awina *(as cards).* **2.** *Agreement.* ‘Aelike. **3.** *Act.* Hana, ho‘ohana.

**dear. 1.** *Beloved.* Aloha. **2.** *Exclamation.* Auē! **3.** *Costly.* Pipi‘i.

**death.** Make, make loa. *His death,* kona make.

**debit.** Ka ‘ao‘ao ‘ai‘ē *(in bookkeeping);* pōkole ke kālā *(shortage of funds).*

**debt.** ‘Ai‘ē.

**decay.** Palahō, palahū; popopo *(wood).*

**deceitful.** Ho‘opunipuni, ‘āpiki, wahahe‘e, waha wale, haku ‘epa.

**December.** Kēkēmapa, Lēkēmapa, Dekemaba.

**decide.** Ho‘oholo, holo mana‘o, koho.

**decision.** Ho‘oholo, ‘ōlelo ho‘oholo, mana‘o ho‘oholo.

**deck. 1.** *Platform.* ‘Oneki, papahele. **2.** *Of cards.* Pu‘u pepa. **3.** *Adorn.* Ho‘okāhiko, ho‘ohiluhilu, ho‘owehiwehi, ho‘onani.

**declaration.** Kuahaua, ha‘ina.

**declare.** Ha‘i, ho‘olaha, wahi, ‘ī, ‘ōlelo, ho‘ike.

**decline. 1.** *Descending slope.* ‘Aui, ‘auina. **2.** *Refuse.* Hō‘ole.

**decorate.** Wehi, wehewehi, ho‘owehi, ho‘owehiwehi, ho‘ouluwehi, ho‘ouluwehiwehi, ho‘o-

ulumāhiehie, kauluwehi, ho‘ohiwahiwa, ho‘okāhiko, ho‘ohiluhilu, pāpahi, ho‘onani.

**decrease.** Emi, ho‘oli‘ili‘i, koi‘i.

**dedicate.** Ho‘ola‘a, ho‘omāhanahana.

**deed. 1.** *Act.* Hana. **2.** *Document.* Palapala, palapala ho‘olilo, palapala kila, hō‘oia‘i‘o, kila.

**deep.** Hohonu, kūhohonu; kūlipo *(as a cave).*

**defeat.** Make, ho‘opio, holopapa, hō‘auhe‘e, lilo, ha‘ule.

**defect.** Kīnā, kīna‘u.

**defend.** Pale, kūpale, ālai; ‘ōlelo pale, ho‘opale *(in court).*

**define.** Wehewehe ‘ano, wehewehe pono.

**definite.** Pa‘a, maopopo, kā‘oko‘a.

**deformed.** Pepe‘e, kīnā, hapaku‘e, ku‘e.

**degree.** Kekele.

**deify.** Ho‘ākua, ho‘omanamana.

**dejected.** Kaumaha, pilihua, pū, noho pū, kukule.

**delay.** Lohi, kali, ho‘okali, ‘apa. *Without delay,* ‘emo ‘ole.

**delegate.** ‘Elele.

**delicate.** Lahi, lahilahi, lālahi, pīlahi, hunehune, palupalu.

**delicious.** ‘Ono, mikomiko. *Very delicious,* ‘ono loa.

**delight.** Hau‘oli, ‘oli‘oli, hau‘oli‘oli, hoihoi, ho‘ohoihoi, puni.

**delighted.** Ohohia, kamahoi, hia‘ai, hia‘ai‘ono.

**delightful.** Māhie, ho‘omāhie, ho‘ohie, le‘a.

**deliver.** Hā‘awi, lawe. *To deliver a child,* pale, pale keiki, ho‘ohānau.

**demand.** Koi, kauoha.

**democracy.** Aupuni a ka lehulehu.

**Democrat.** Kemokalaka.

**demolish.** Wāwahi, ho‘ohiolo, ku‘i palu, nāhāhā.

**Denmark.** Kenemaka, Denemaka.

**dense.** Pa‘apū, lanipō, pōpō uahi.

**dentist.** Kauka niho.

**deny.** Hōʻole, ʻole, hoʻonele.

**depart.** Hele i kahi ʻē, haʻalele, waiho.

**department.** Mahele, keʻena, ʻoihana.

**Department of Instruction.** ʻOihana Hoʻonaʻauao.

**Department of Water Supply.** ʻOihana Wai.

**depend.** Kaukaʻi, kaukoʻo, kālele. *That depends on you,* aia nō ia iāʻoe.

**deposit.** Hoʻokomo; uku hoʻopaʻa *(as on a purchase). Deposit money in the bank,* hoʻokomo i ke kālā i ka panakō.

**depressed. 1.** *Sad.* Kaumaha, luʻuluʻu. **2.** *See* **sunken.**

**depth.** Hohonu.

**descend.** Iho, hele iho, hele i lalo.

**descendant.** Mamo, pua, moʻopuna, keiki, pulapula.

**descent.** Ihona, hoʻoihona, ʻauina.

**describe.** Hōʻike ʻano, haʻi ʻano, hoʻākaaka.

**desert.** *Abandon.* Haʻalele.

**design.** Lau, ana, kiʻi.

**desire.** Makemake, ʻiʻini, ʻanoʻi, hia, make, ake, puni, ʻupu.

**desk.** Pākaukau, pākaukau hana.

**despair.** Hāʻule ka manaʻolana, kuʻihē ka naʻau.

**despise.** Hoʻokae, hoʻowahāwahā.

**dessert.** Mea ʻai momona.

**destroy.** Luku, hoʻopau, hana make. *Destroy completely,* luku hoʻopau, hoʻopau, kuʻikē. *Destroy by fire or lava,* lauahi, pau ahi, heʻa.

**destruction.** Luku, lukuna, make.

**detective.** Mākaʻikiu, makākiu.

**determine.** Holo manaʻo, holo, hoʻoholo, manaʻo paʻa.

**detour.** Ala kāpae.

**develop.** Hoʻomōhala, hana *(as a photograph);* hoʻokino *(as an infant).*

**developed.** Mōhala, mohahala, mōhalahala, mōhola. *See* **muscular.**

**devil.** Kiapolō, kepolō, akua.

**devoted.** Aloha, laʻa, laʻahia, puni, lilo; pili aloha *(loving);* hoʻopapau.

**dew.** Kēhau, hau.

**diagonal.** Lala, kaʻakepa, hiō.

**diagram.** Kiʻi.

**dial.** Wili *(as on a telephone).*

**diamond.** Kaimana.

**Diamond Head.** Kaimana Hila, Lēʻahi.

**diaper.** Kaiapa.

**diarrhea.** Hī, palahī.

**dictionary.** Puke wehewehe ʻōlelo.

**did.** *See* **do.** *The one who did,* ka mea i, ka i. *He did go,* ua hele nō ʻoia.

**die.** Make, make loa *(contrasted to* make, *which may mean "defeated, faint").*

**diet.** Mea ʻai e pono ai ke kino.

**difference.** Mea ʻokoʻa.

**different.** ʻOkoʻa, ʻē, ʻē aʻe, ʻano ʻē, like ʻole.

**difficult.** Paʻakikī, hana nui.

**difficulties.** He mau pilikia, hihia.

**dig.** ʻEli.

**digging stick.** ʻŌʻō; ʻōʻō hao *(iron).*

**dignified.** Hanohano, kūoʻo, kei, ʻihi, keha.

**dignity.** Hanohano, kapukapu, hie, hiehie, keha.

**diligent.** Huli hana, hana mau, paʻahana.

**dillydally.** Hoʻolohi, loloiāhili, lōiele, hōʻapaʻapa.

**dim.** Poahi, kōliʻuliʻu, palaweka, lipo, ʻāhiahia.

**dime.** Kenikeni.

**diminish.** Emi, hoʻēmi, hoʻoiki.

**dining room.** Lumi ʻaina.

**dining table.** Papa ʻaina.

**dinner.** ʻAina ahiahi, papa ʻaina, pāʻina. *Dinner party,* ʻahaʻaina.

**dip. 1.** *To plunge or immerse.* Kūpenu, hoʻoluʻu, luʻu. **2.** *Depression.* Hālua.

**diploma.** Palapala. *High school*

*diploma,* palapala puka, palapala hoʻomaikaʻi. *University diploma,* palapala hōʻoia kulanui.

**direct.** 1. *Oversee.* Alakaʻi, kuhikuhi, kaʻi. 2. *Straight.* Pololei.

**direction** 1. *Compass direction.* ʻAoʻao. 2. *See* **direct,** 1. *Wrong directions,* kuhi hewa.

**directory.** Papa kuhikuhi, puke inoa.

**dirge.** Kanikau, mele kanikau, hoʻoueuē, ʻuhane.

**dirt.** Lepo, lepo hānai, ʻeka.

**disagree.** Kūʻēʻē, hukihuki, kūlike ʻole, lōkahi ʻole.

**disagreement.** Kūʻēʻē, mokuāhana.

**disappear.** Nalo, nalowale, nalohia, pio.

**disappointment.** Hoka, mokuāhua, homa.

**disapprove.** ʻĀpono ʻole, hoʻāhewa.

**disaster.** Pōpilikia, pōʻino, ulia weliweli.

**disbelieve.** Hilinaʻi ʻole, manaʻoʻiʻo ʻole.

**discard.** Kiloi, kiola, hoʻolei, kāpae, haʻalele.

**discharge.** 1. *Dismiss.* Hoʻokuʻu, noʻopau, kipaku. 2. *See* **unload.** 3. *Flow.* Hoʻokahe, walewale, walewalena; heheʻe *(as of pus).* 4. *Fire, as a gun.* Kī pū.

**discomfort.** ʻOluʻolu ʻole, noʻonoʻo ʻihaʻiha, ʻīnea, ʻihaʻiha.

**disconnect.** Hoʻokaʻawale, hoʻohemo, kala.

**discount.** Uku hoʻēmi, hoʻēmi.

**discouraged.** Pauaho.

**discover.** ʻImi ā loaʻa, ʻike mua, loaʻa, hōʻike.

**discuss.** ʻŌlelo kūkā, kūkā, kūkākūkā, hoʻokamaʻilio.

**disease.** Maʻi.

**disgrace.** Waia, hoʻohilahila, ʻālina.

**disguise.** Hoʻomeamea, hoʻokohukohu, hoʻonalonalo i ke kūlana, hūnā.

**disgusting.** Hoʻopailua, kāpulu, luaʻikū.

**dish.** Pā, ipu. *Glass dish,* pā aniani. *Iron dish or pan,* pā hao. *Paper dish,* pā pepa.

**dishcloth.** Kāwele pā. *To wipe or dry with a dishcloth,* kāwele.

**dishonest.** Hoʻopono ʻole, pono ʻole, ʻāpiki, paukeʻe, ʻapakeʻe.

**dislike.** Makemake ʻole, hoihoi ʻole.

**dismiss.** Hoʻokuʻu, kuʻu, hoʻopau, waiho.

**disobey.** Hoʻolohe ʻole, pale ʻōlelo, hoʻokuli.

**disorder.** Mōkākī, kīpalalē, hōkai.

**display.** Hōʻike, hōʻikeʻike, hoʻokahakaha, hoʻokelakela.

**disposition.** ʻAno, loko, manawa, naʻau, ʻōpū.

**dispute.** Hoʻopaʻapaʻa, hakakā ʻōlelo.

**disregard.** Nānā ʻole.

**dissatisfied.** Kūhalahala, hoʻohalahala, loiloi.

**dissipate.** ʻUhaʻuha.

**dissolve.** Hoʻoheheʻe.

**distance.** Mamao, lōʻihi.

**distant.** Mamao, lilo, loa, haʻalilo.

**distinction.** Kaulana, hanohano, poʻokela.

**distinguished.** Hanohano, kūlana hiehie.

**distress.** Pilikia, pōpilikia, pōʻino, hoʻopōʻino, ʻīnea, hoʻīnea, ʻeha, hōʻehaʻeha.

**distribute.** Hoʻomāhelehele, hoʻolaha.

**district.** ʻĀpana, ʻokana, moku, mokuʻāina.

**disturb.** Hoʻoluhi, hoʻopilikia.

**disturbance.** Haunaele, uluāoʻa.

**disturbed.** Hoʻoluhi ʻia, pono ʻole ka manaʻo, pīhoihoi, piʻoloke.

**ditch.** ʻAuwaha, hā, ʻāwaʻa. *Water ditch,* ʻauwai.

**dive.** Luʻu.

**divide.** Mahele, puʻunaue, ʻokiʻoki, helehele, kaʻana. *To divide equally,* kaʻi like; hoʻokaʻana.

**divination.** Hailona, puʻuone.

**divine.** Akua, hoʻākua, ʻano akua, hoʻāno.

**diving board.** Papa lele kawa.

**division. 1.** *Section.* Mahele, pale, mokuna. **2.** *Arithmetic.* Puʻunaue.

**divorce.** ʻOki, hōʻoki, ʻoki male.

**dizzy.** Pōniu, pōniuniu, niniu, niua.

**do.** Hana, lawelawe; hoʻokō *(complete). There is no Hawaiian equivalent for the English auxiliary. Do you like this?* Makemake anei ʻoe i kēia? *Yes, I do,* ʻAe, makemake nō. *See* **done.**

**dock.** Uapo.

**doctor.** Kauka.

**document.** Palapala.

**dodge.** ʻAlo, ʻaloʻalo, hōʻalo, hoʻohala.

**dog.** ʻĪlio.

**doll.** Kiʻi, kiʻi pēpē.

**dollar.** Kālā.

**dolphin. 1.** *Fish.* Mahimahi. **2.** *See* **porpoise.**

**donate.** Hāʻawi wale, makana, hāʻawi manawaleʻa.

**donation.** Lūlū, haʻawina, makana.

**done.** Hana ʻia, pau. *See* **do.**

**donkey.** Kēkake, ʻēkake.

**do-nothing.** Palaualelo, kūhana ʻole, lemukū.

**don't. 1.** *Negative command.* Mai, uoki. **2.** *Negative.* ʻAʻole.

**door.** Puka, puka hale, puka komo, ʻīpuka.

**doorway.** Puka komo.

**dormitory.** Hale moe.

**dot.** Kiko, pōhaka.

**dotted.** Kikokiko.

**double.** Pālua, pāpālua, hoʻopālua, lua like, lua, kaulua.

**doubt.** Kānalua.

**dough.** Palaoa hoʻowali ʻia, pelena moʻa ʻole.

**dove.** Manu kū, manu nūnū, nūnū, kuhukukū.

**down. 1.** *Below.* Lalo, i lalo, iho. *See* **fall. 2.** *Feathers.* Heu, heuheu, ʻae, ʻae moa, hulu weuweu.

**down payment.** Uku hoʻopaʻa.

**downpour.** Loku, ua lanipili, hoʻolokuloku, haʻalokuloku.

**doze.** Moe hoʻolana.

**dozen.** Kākini, ʻumi kūmālua, ʻumi kumamālua.

**draft. 1.** *Current of air.* Hihio, mōhio. *See* **gust. 2.** *Money order.* Palapala kīkoʻo, pepa kīkoʻo, pila kīkoʻo.

**drag.** Kauō, alakō.

**dragged.** Kō.

**dragonfly.** Pinao. *Larvae of dragonfly,* lohelohe.

**draw. 1.** *Sketch.* Kaha. **2.** *Pull, extract.* ʻUme, huki, ʻuʻu. **3.** *Tie.* Paʻi, paʻi wale, paʻi ā paʻi.

**drawer.** Pahu ʻume.

**drawing. 1.** *Picture.* Kiʻi, kiʻi i kaha ʻia, kahana. **2.** *Pulling.* ʻUme ʻana, kō.

**dreadful.** Weliweli, mānaʻonaʻo.

**dream.** Moeʻuhane.

**dregs.** Oka, koʻana, kiʻo, mākū.

**drenched.** Pulu pē, pē.

**dress. 1.** *Garment.* Lole, ʻaʻahu. *To dress,* komo, komo lole. **2.** *To wrap a wound.* Wahī. **3.** *As a fowl.* Unuunu *(pluck);* kuaʻi *(disembowel).*

**dried.** Maloʻo.

**drift.** Lana wale, lana hele.

**drill. 1.** *Tool.* Nao wili, wili, kāhei, ʻōmilo. **2.** *Military.* Paikau. **3.** *Practice.* Hoʻomaʻamaʻa.

**drink. 1.** *Verb.* Inu, inumia, pā. **2.** *Noun.* Mea inu.

**drip.** Kulu, kulukulu.

**drive. 1.** *As cattle.* Hoʻohuli, hōʻā. **2.** *To drive away.* Kipaku, hoʻokuke. **3.** *As a car.* Kalaiwa, hoʻokele. **4.** *As nails.* Kākia, mākia, kīpou.

**driver.** Kalaiwa, hoʻokele kaʻa.

**drool.** Hāʻae, kahe ka hāʻae.

**droop.** Luhe, loha, hoʻoloʻu.

**drop. 1.** *Trickle.* Kulu, kahe, mākili. **2.** *Let fall.* Hāʻule, hāʻuleʻule, hāʻulehia, hoʻohāʻule.

**drought.** Wā maloʻo.

**drown.** Piholo, hoʻopiholo, hoʻopalemo.

**drowsy.** Maka hiamoe, kulu, kulu hiamoe.

**drug.** Lāʻau ʻona, lāʻau hoʻomalule kino, lāʻau hoʻonoenoe, lāʻau hoʻohiamoe, lāʻau moe, mea ʻona. *See* **medicine.**

**drum.** Pahu, ipu.

**drunk.** ʻOna.

**dry.** Maloʻo.

**dual.** Pālua.

**duck.** 1. *Bird.* Kakā *(domesticated),* koloa *(Hawaiian).* 2. *To plunge or bow.* ʻAlu, lumaʻi, luʻu.

**dues.** Uku kūmau.

**dull.** 1. *Not sharp.* Kūmūmū, mūmū. 2. *Stupid.* Lolohi, leʻaleʻa ʻole, hoihoi ʻole, maluhi.

**dumb.** Leo paʻa, mūmule, ʻāʻā. *Struck dumb,* hakanū.

**dust.** Ehu lepo, kuehu, ehu, ʻehu, uahi, lelehuna, lepo ʻaeʻae.

**dusty.** Ehu, ehu lepo, ʻeʻa.

**duty.** 1. *Obligation.* Pono, hana, mahele hana. 2. *Customs.* Kuke.

**dwelling.** Nohona, noho ʻana. *Dwelling house,* hale noho. *Dwelling place,* wahi noho, kahi noho.

**dye.** Wai, waihoʻoluʻu, wai ʻele, wai ʻeleʻele.

**dynamite.** Kianapauka.

**dysentery.** Hī, kulu.

# E

**e.** ʻĒ.

**each.** Kēlā mea kēia mea, pākahi.

**ear.** Pepeiao.

**early.** Koke, mua, hiki mua, mikiʻala.

**earn.** Loaʻa.

**earring.** Kulapepeiao.

**earth.** 1. *World.* Ao, honua, ʻāina. 2. *Dirt.* Lepo.

**earthquake.** ʻŌlaʻi, nāueue.

**ease.** Maha, nanea, puʻuhoʻomaha.

**easily.** Hikiwale, wale, maʻalahi.

**east.** Hikina.

**Easter.** Ka lā i ala hou ai ka Haku *(Protestant); Pakoa (Catholic).*

**easy.** Hikiwale, maʻalahi.

**eat.** ʻAi, ʻai iho, amu.

**eavesdrop.** Hoʻolohelohe ʻōlelo, hoʻolono.

**ebb.** Emi.

**eccentric.** ʻAno ʻē.

**echo.** Kūpinaʻi, nakulu, papā, hākuʻi.

**eclipse.** Pouli.

**economical.** Makauliʻi, minamina, pākiko.

**Eden.** ʻĒkena, Edena. *Garden of Eden,* Kīhāpai o ʻĒkena, mahina ʻai ma ʻĒkena.

**edge.** Kaʻe, kapa, kihi, lihi, nihi, nīao, maka, kūkulu, huʻa, peʻa.

**edit.** Hoʻoponopono.

**edition.** Paʻi ʻana, hoʻopuka ʻana.

**editor.** Luna hoʻoponopono.

**educate.** Hoʻonaʻauao.

**education.** Aʻo palapala, hoʻonaʻauao.

**eel.** Puhi, kuna.

**effort.** Hoʻāʻo, hoʻāho, hoʻoikaika.

**egg.** Hua, hua moa *(chicken).*

**eggplant.** Lahopipi.

**eight.** ʻEwalu, walu, ʻawalu.

**eighteen.** ʻUmi kūmāwalu, ʻumi kumamāwalu.

**eighty.** Kanawalu.

**eighty-one.** Kanawalu kūmākahi, kanawalu kumamākahi.

**either.** Kekahi.

**elbow.** Kuʻekuʻe, kuʻekuʻe lima, kuʻe lima.

**elder.** Kahiko aʻe; kaikuaʻana *(sibling of the same sex);* lunakahiko *(church).*

**elderly.** ʻĀoʻo, oʻo, makule.

**elect.** Koho, hoʻokoho, wae.

**election.** Koho, koho pāloka.

**electric, electricity.** Uila.

**elephant.** ʻElepane, ʻelepani.

elevate. Hāpai, hoʻokiʻekiʻe, hōʻiu.

elevator. ʻEleweka.

eleven. ʻUmi kūmākahi, ʻumi kumamākahi.

else. ʻĒ aʻe.

elsewhere. Ma kahi ʻē, ʻē.

embarrass. Hoʻohilahila.

embarrassed. Hilahila.

embassy. Nohona kuhina.

emblem. Hōʻailona.

embrace. Pūʻili, pūliki, ʻāpona, kūwili, apo.

embroider. Humulau, ʻōniʻoniʻo.

emerge. Puka, pua.

emergency. Ulia pōpilikia, pilikia kūhewa.

emotion. *No general term, but emotions may be described by descriptive words following* puʻuwai, naʻau, *or* piʻi ka, *as* puʻuwai hauʻoli, *happiness,* piʻi ka huhū, *to be angry.*

emphasize. Hoʻokoʻikoʻi, kālele leo, kālele manaʻo.

employ. Hoʻohana.

employed. Paʻa i ka hana.

employee. Poʻe hana, limahana.

employer. Haku, haku hana.

employment. Hana, ʻoihana.

empty. Haka, hakahaka, ʻolohaka, ukana ʻole.

encircle. Pōʻai, anapuni, ʻaipuni, kaʻapuni.

enclose. Puni, kaʻapuni, hoʻokomo.

enclosure. Pā.

encourage. Hoʻopaipai, hoʻoikaika, hōʻikaika, hoʻolana, hōʻeu.

end. Pau ʻana, panina, hope. *To end,* hoʻopau, hoʻōki.

endearing. Hoʻālohaloha.

ending. Hopena, ʻokina, panina.

endless. Pau ʻole, mau loa.

endure. Hoʻomanawanui, mau, ʻalo, ō.

enemy. Hoa paio, hoa kaua, ʻenemi.

energetic. ʻEleu, mikimiki, hōʻeleʻeleu.

enforce. Hoʻokō, hoʻoneʻe ikaika, hoʻoholo.

engaged. 1. *Occupied.* Paʻa, lilo. 2. *Betrothed.* Palau, hoʻopalau.

engine. ʻEnikini, mīkini.

engineer. Wilikī.

England. Pelekane, ʻEnelani.

English. Pelekane. *English language,* ʻōlelo Pelekane, ʻōlelo haole.

engrave. Kaha, kālai.

enjoy. Luana, walea, nanea, hoihoi, ʻoliʻoli, leʻa.

enjoyment. ʻOliʻoli, hauʻoli, hoihoi.

enlarge. Hoʻonui, hoʻomāhua, hoʻomāhuahua; hoʻolele *(as a picture).*

enough. Lawa, nui, lawa puni.

ensnare. Hoʻopunihei, hei, hoʻoheihei.

entangled. Hihia, kāhihi, hihipeʻa, hakakē.

enter. Komo, hoʻokomo.

entertain. Hoʻokipa, hoʻohale kipa, hoʻoleʻaleʻa, hoʻohauʻoli.

entertaining. Hoihoi.

entertainment. Mea hoʻohauʻoli, hōʻikeʻike hoʻohauʻoli.

enthusiasm. ʻOliʻoli nui, ohohia.

entire. Holoʻokoʻa, kāʻokoʻa.

entirely. Holoʻokoʻa, apau, pū, ʻokoʻa, pau.

entrance. *Opening.* Komo ʻana, puka, ʻīpuka, nuku.

envelope. Wahī, wahī leka.

envy. Lili, huā.

epidemic. Maʻi laulā, maʻi ahulau, maʻi pālahalaha.

Episcopalian. ʻEpekopala, hoʻomana Pīhopa.

equal. Like, like ʻā like, lua, kau like, paʻi.

equator. Pōʻai-waena-honua, ke alanui a ke kuʻukuʻu.

equip. Hoʻolako, hoʻolawa.

-er *(Agent).* 1. *Agent in Hawaiian same as act performed. See* driver, leader, paddler. 2. Mea, kanaka. *See* actor, rider, translator.

era. Wā, paukū manawa, au.

erase. Holoi.

erect. Kū, kūkulu.

**error.** Hewa, hala, pa'ewa.
**eruption.** Lua'i pele, hū ka pele.
**escape.** Pakele.
**escort.** Hele pū, 'alo, ukali, ho'oholoholo.
**establish.** Ho'okahua, ho'okumu, ho'okū.
**establishment.** Hale 'oihana *(business);* kūkulu 'ana; ka po'e e loa'a 'o ka mana *(those with power).*
**estate.** 1. *Property.* Waiwai, kuleana, ho'olina. 2. *Position.* Kūlana.
**eternal.** Mau loa, i ka wā pau 'ole, manawakolu.
**eucalyptus.** Palepiwa.
**Europe.** 'Eulopa, Europa.
**Europeanized.** Ho'ohaole 'ia.
**evening.** Ahiahi. *Good evening,* aloha ahiahi.
**ever.** Mau. *Forever and ever,* ā mau loa aku.
**every.** Kēlā . . . kēia, āpau.
**everyone.** Ka po'e āpau, pau āpau.
**everything.** Nā mea āpau, pau loa, kēlā mea kēia mea.
**everywhere.** Ma nā wahi āpau, mai 'ō ā 'ō, holopuni.
**evidence.** 'Ōlelo hō'ike, 'ōlelo a nā hō'ike.
**evil.** Loko 'ino, lawehala, 'ino.
**exactly.** Pono, pono'ī.
**exaggerate.** Ho'onui, ho'onuinui, ho'onui 'ōlelo.
**examination.** Ha'awina hō'ike, nīnau hō'ike.
**example.** Mea ho'ohālikelike, hō'ike, 'ano, kumu ho'ohālike.
**excel.** Kela, ho'okela, po'okela, 'oi, hō'oi, pākela.
**excellence.** Maika'i loa, pono loa, kūpono.
**excellent.** Kilohana, maika'i.
**except.** Koe.
**excess.** Pākela, koe, kaulele.
**exchange.** Kūka'i, ku'aku'ai, pāna'i, ku'ololi.
**excite.** Ho'opīhoihoi, hō'eu'eu, ho'olalelale.
**exclaim.** Ho'ōho, 'ū, āhē.

**excrement.** Kūkae, kae; lepo, hana lepo *(euphemisms).*
**excuse.** 1. *Pretext.* 'Ōlelo hō'alo-'alo. 2. *Pardon.* Kala, huikala, mihi, ho'oku'u. *Excuse me,* kala mai ia'u.
**exercise.** Ho'oikaika kino *(bodily);* ha'awina ho'oma'ama'a *(lesson).*
**exhale.** Hanu, hanu i waho, hā.
**exhausted.** Paupauaho, mālo'elo'e; piula *(slang).*
**exhibit.** Hō'ike, hō'ike'ike.
**exist.** Kū, ō, ola.
**exit.** Puka 'ana, pukana, 'īpuka.
**expand.** Ho'onui, ho'omāhua, ho'omāhuahua.
**expect.** Mahu'i, kuhi, mana'olana.
**expel.** Kipaku, ho'okuke, paku, lua'i.
**expense.** Ho'olilo, lilo.
**expensive.** Pipi'i, pi'i, nui ka ho'olilo.
**experience.** 'Ike.
**expert.** Kahuna; akamai, 'ailolo, lolo, no'eau, loea, mākaukau.
**explain.** Wehewehe, ho'ākaaka, hō'ike; ho'omōakaaka, ho'omāla'e *(clearly).*
**explode.** Ho'opahū, pahū.
**explore.** 'Imi loa, huli.
**expose.** Hō'ike ākea, ho'owaiho, waiho wale.
**express.** 1. *To state.* Ho'opuka, ha'i, ho'ākaaka, hō'ike. 2. *To extract.* 'Uī, 'ūpī *(by squeezing).*
**expression.** Māpuna leo, māpuna 'ōlelo.
**extend.** Ho'oloa, ho'olō'ihi, kīko'o.
**exterior.** Waho.
**extinguish.** Ho'omake, ho'opio, kinai *(as a fire).*
**extra.** Keu, 'oi, kaulele.
**extraordinary.** Kupaianaha, kupanaha, mea 'ē.
**extravagant.** 'Uha'uha, 'uha, 'uha 'ai, māunauna.
**extreme.** Wēlau, 'ēlau, welelau, palena, 'oi loa aku.
**eye.** Maka.

**eyeball.** 'Ōnohi, haku 'ōnohi, pona.

**eyebrow.** Ku'emaka, ku'eku'emaka, hulu ku'emaka.

**eyeglasses.** Makaaniani.

**eyelashes.** Lihilihi.

**eyelid.** 'Ūpo'i maka, kuapo'imaka, lihilihi.

**eyesight.** 'Ike maka.

**eye socket.** Pona, naho, lua maka.

# F

**f.** *No Hawaiian term.*

**face.** Maka, helehelena, alo. *To face,* huli. *Face to face,* he alo ā he alo.

**fact.** Mea kū'i'o, mea 'oia'i'o.

**factory.** Hale hana.

**faculty.** *Academic.* 'Āuna kumu kula, pū'ulu kumu kula.

**fade.** Mae, ho'omae *(as flowers);* hehe'e *(as clothes);* hākea, hākeakea, kuakea, ākeakea *(as in the sun).*

**fail.** Pohō; holo le'a 'ole *(as in business);* hā'ule *(as in school);* emi mau ke olakino *(in health).*

**faint.** 1. *Lose consciousness.* Ma'ule, ho'oma'ule, make. 2. *Weak, dizzy.* Makapōuli, maka pōniuniu, 'ona'ona. 3. *Difficult to see.* Aneane, 'āwe'awe'a, 'ehu, pōehiehi.

**fair.** 1. *Just.* Kūpono, pono, kaulike. 2. *Complexion.* 'Ili kea, 'ili mā'ila. 3. *Exhibit.* Pea hō'ike-'ike. 4. *Somewhat good.* 'Ano maika'i.

**faith.** Mana'o'i'o, paulele.

**fall** 1. *From a height.* Hā'ule *(a solid object);* helelei, helele'i, ho'ohelele'i *(as leaves, rain).* 2. *Topple.* Hina. 3. *Autumn. No Hawaiian word; terms sometimes used:* hā'ule lau, la'a make, la'a 'ula.

**false.** Ho'opunipuni, wahahe'e.

**familiar.** Kama'āina, walea, ma'a, ma'ama'ahia, 'ike.

**family.** 'Ohana.

**famine.** Wī, pōloli.

**famous.** Kaulana.

**fan.** Pe'ahi.

**fancy.** Mana'o ulu wale, moemoeā.

**far.** Mamao, lilo loa.

**fare.** 1. *Pay.* Uku. 2. *Happen.* 'Ano, holo 'ana. 3. *Food.* 'Ai.

**farewell.** Aloha.

**farm.** Mahi 'ai, mahi, mahina 'ai.

**farmer.** Mahi 'ai.

**farther.** Mamao a'e, mamao aku, mamao mai, ma'ō aku.

**fascinate.** Ho'opunihei, ho'oheihei, punihei.

**fast.** 1. *Quick.* 'Āwīwī, wikiwiki, māmā, holo, ala-, alamimo, alapine, alawiki. 2. *Fixed.* Pa'a. 3. *Not eat.* Ho'okē 'ai.

**fasten.** Ho'opa'a, hana pa'a.

**fat.** 1. *As a human.* Momona. 2. *Animal fat, food.* Momona *(uncooked);* kelekele *(cooked).*

**father.** Makua kāne, makua.

**father-in-law.** Makuahūnōai kāne.

**fatherland.** 'Āina makua.

**fathom.** Anana.

**fatigue.** Māluhiluhi, luhi.

**fault.** Hewa, hala, ke'e, kīnā.

**favor.** Hana lokomaika'i; kāko'o, makemake *(prefer).*

**favorite.** Punahele, milimili.

**fear.** Maka'u, weli, weliweli, 'e'ehia.

**fearless.** Maka'u 'ole, wiwo 'ole, koa.

**feast.** 'Aha'aina, lū'au.

**feather.** Hulu.

**feather cloak.** 'Ahu 'ula.

**feather helmet.** Mahiole.

**feather standard.** Kāhili.

**features.** Hi'ohi'ona, helehelena *(human).*

**February.** Pepeluali, Feberuari.

**fee.** Uku.

**feeble.** Nāwaliwali, hāpauea, nāwali, palupalu.

**feed.** Hānai, hānai 'ai, hō'ai, ho'omā'ona.

**feel. 1.** *Grope, touch.* Hāhā, hāhā hele, hāpapa, ho'opāpā, pā. **2.** *As emotion.* 'Ike, lohe, komo. *Feel angry,* pi'i ka huhū, pi'i ka 'ena.

**feelings.** Na'au, loko. .

**feet.** *See* **foot.**

**fellow.** Hoa, kōko'olua.

**fellow worker.** Hoa hana, hoa pa'ahana.

**female.** Wahine.

**fence. 1.** *Barrier.* Pā. *Wooden fence,* pā lā'au. **2.** *With swords or sticks.* Kākā pahi, kākā lā'au.

**fern.** Kupukupu. *Common kinds include:* 'ama'u, 'āma'uma'u; hāpu'u *(tree fern).*

**ferry.** Moku halihali, wa'apā.

**fertile.** Momona; hānau, hānau kama *(person).*

**fertilize.** Ho'opulu, ho'omomona, kīpulu.

**festival.** Ho'olaule'a, manawa ho'olaule'a.

**festive.** Hiwahiwa, ulumāhiehie, ho'owehiwehi.

**fetch.** Ki'i, lawe.

**fetus.** 'Alu'alu.

**fever.** Piwa.

**few.** Kaka'ikahi, wahi, kekahi, 'u'uku, li'ili'i.

**fiddle.** Pila.

**field.** Kīhāpai, kula.

**fierce.** Hae, ho'oweliweli.

**fiery.** 'Ā, ahi.

**fifteen.** 'Umi kūmālima, 'umi kumamālima.

**fifth.** Lima, hapalima.

**fifty.** Kanalima.

**fifty-one.** Kanalima kūmākahi, kanalima kumamākahi.

**fig.** Piku.

**fight.** Hakakā, paio, kaua; mokomoko *(general hand-to-hand, including wrestling and boxing);* pā'ume'ume.

**fighter.** Pūkaua, koa.

**figure. 1.** *Number.* Huahelu, helu, hua. **2.** *Human figure.* Kino.

**Fiji.** Pīkī.

**file. 1.** *Rasp.* Apuapu, waiehu, waiahu. **2.** *Row.* Lālani. **3.** *Collection.* Waihona (palapala).

**Filipino.** Pilipino.

**fill.** Ho'opiha.

**film.** Pepa pa'i ki'i *(photographic).*

**filth.** Lepo, pelapela, 'eka, 'eka-'eka, mea 'ino, moka, hauka'e.

**fin.** Lā.

**final.** Hope, hope loa, pau, panina.

**finance.** 'Oihana kālā, 'oihana 'imi kālā.

**find.** Loa'a.

**fine. 1.** *Minute.* Hune, hunehune; makali'i *(as mats, mesh);* nāwele, māhune, 'ae'ae, puehu, li-li'i. **2.** *Excellent.* Maika'i nō, maika'i loa, pono. **3.** *Penalty.* Uku ho'opa'i, uku.

**finger.** Manamana lima.

**fingernail.** Miki'ao, mai'ao.

**finish.** Ho'opau, oki, ho'ōki; panina *(noun);* kaekae *(rub smooth).*

**finished.** Pau, pa'a, kūpau.

**fire.** Ahi; pau ahi *(incendiary).*

**firecracker.** Pahūpahū.

**fire department.** 'Oihana kinai ahi.

**fire engine.** Ka'a kinai ahi, ka'a pau ahi, ka'a wai.

**fireplace.** Kapuahi.

**fire-plow.** 'Aunaki.

**fireproof.** Pale ahi.

**fire station.** Hale kinai ahi.

**firewood.** Wahie.

**firm 1.** *Solid.* Pa'a, kūpa'a, 'onipa'a. **2.** *See* **company.**

**first.** Mua, mua loa, 'akahi . . . ā. *First time,* maka mua, malihini, 'akahi nō . . . ā. *First child,* hiapo.

**fish.** I'a. *To fish,* lawai'a.

**fisherman.** Lawai'a.

**fishhook.** Makau; lou *(any kind of a hook).*

**fishing grounds.** Ko'a, kai lawai'a, ka'aka'a.

**fishing pole.** Mākoi, koi, mōkoi.

**fishline.** Aho.

**fish net.** 'Upena.

**fishpond.** Loko i'a, loko kuapā.

**fist.** Pu'upu'u lima, pu'u, pu'u lima, pu'upu'u.

**fit. 1.** *Suitable.* Kohu, kū, kūpono; komo *(as a garment).* **2.** *Seizure.* Huki, ma'i huki, 'apo'apo. **3.** *To join.* Ho'oku'i, pāna'i.

**five.** Lima, 'elima, 'alima.

**five cents.** 'Elima keneka, hapa-'umi.

**fix.** Ho'opa'a, kāpili hou, hana ā maika'i, hō'onipa'a.

**flabby.** 'Alu'alu, nenelu.

**flag.** Hae, lepa.

**flagpole.** Pahu hae, kia hae.

**flame.** Ula ahi, ula, lapa ahi.

**flap. 1.** *Motion.* 'Upa'i, 'ōpa'i-ipa'i, kūlepe, hulei. **2.** *End.* Pola *(as of a* malo*).*

**flash.** 'Ōlapa, lapa.

**flashlight.** Kukui pa'a lima.

**flat.** Pālahalaha.

**flatter.** Ho'omalimali.

**flavor.** 'Ono, hō'ono'ono.

**flea.** 'Uku lele.

**flee.** He'e, 'auhe'e, mahuka.

**fleet.** *Naval.* 'Au moku, 'au wa'a, ulu moku, ulu wa'a.

**flesh.** 'I'o.

**flesh food.** I'a.

**flight.** Lele.

**fling.** Kā, hiu, ho'olei. *See* throw.

**flirt.** Ho'oha'i, ho'oha'i wale, ho'oha'ilua.

**float. 1.** *Not sink.* Lana. **2.** *Of a net.* Mouo, pīkoi, ou. **3.** *Of a fishhook.* Kōheoheo. **4.** *See* **outrigger float.**

**flock.** Pū'ā, 'āuna, ho'āuna, ulu.

**flood.** Wai hālana, wai pi'i.

**floor.** Papahele, papa ke'ehina, papa.

**flounder.** *The fish.* Pāki'i, moe-one.

**flour.** Palaoa maka.

**flow.** Kahe. *Flow swiftly,* kikī, kīpalalē.

**flower.** Pua.

**flu.** Palū.

**fluent.** Poeko, mākaukau i ka 'ōlelo, 'ōlelo pahe'e.

**fluid.** Wai, hehe'e.

**flush. 1.** *Show red.* Pi'i ka 'ula, nono'ula, 'āpane. **2.** *To wash out.* Ho'oholo i ka wai. **3.** *In poker.* Palaki.

**flute.** 'Ohe kani, puhi 'ohe, 'ohe puluka, puluka.

**flutter.** Kōwelo, kapalili, kolili, welo, konikoni.

**fly. 1.** *As a bird.* Lele. **2.** *Insect.* Nalo.

**flycatcher.** 'Elepaio.

**flying fish.** Mālolo.

**foam.** Hu'a, 'ehu.

**fog.** 'Ohu, noe, ua noe, uhiwai.

**fold.** 'Opi, pelu, 'opi'opi, pelupe-lu, 'ōwili.

**folding chair.** Noho 'opi'opi.

**follow.** Hahai, ukali, alualu, ma'awe, kaukolu. *As follows,* penei.

**fond.** Puni, laka, aloha.

**fontanel.** Manawa.

**food.** 'Ai, mea 'ai.

**fool. 1.** *Simpleton.* Hūpō, wa'a-wa'a; pulu *(Eng.).* **2.** *To deceive.* Ho'opuni wale, ho'owalewale.

**foot. 1.** *Anatomical.* Wāwae. **2.** *Twelve inches.* Kapua'i.

**football.** Kinipōpō peku.

**for.** No, na, i, iā. *For me,* no'u, na'u.

**forbid.** Pāpā, ho'okapu, hō'ole.

**force. 1.** *Strength.* Ikaika. **2.** *To use force.* Ha'akoi, pu'e, pu'e wale, hao, hu'e.

**forecast.** Wānana.

**forehead.** Lae.

**foreign.** Mai ka 'āina 'ē mai, 'ē, haole.

**foreigner.** Kanaka 'ē, haole, mea mai ka 'āina 'ē.

**foreman.** Luna, luna hana, luna nui.

**foremost.** Mua loa, po'okela.

**forest.** Ulu lā'au, nahele.

**forever.** Mau loa, i ka wā pau 'ole, kau ā kau.

**forget.** Poina.

**forgive.** Kala, huikala.

**forgotten.** Nalo, nalowale, nalo-hia, poina, poina 'ia.

**fork.** Mana *(branch);* 'ō *(for eating).*

**form.** Kino *(figure);* kaila *(style).*

**former.** Mua, kēlā.

**fort.** Pāpū, hale pūkaua, pu'ukaua, hale kaua.

**forth.** I mua, aku. *And so forth,* ā pēlā aku, ā pēlā wale aku.

**fortress.** Pāpū.

**fortunate.** Pōmaika'i, ahona.

**forty.** Kanahā.

**forty-one.** Kanahā kūmākahi, kanahā kumamākahi.

**forty thousand.** Kanahā kaukani, kini.

**forward.** Mua, i mua.

**foster.** Hānai, ho'omakua, hi'i, mālama, kōkua.

**foul.** 1. *Filthy.* 'Eka, kelo, 'ino-'ino. 2. *In sports.* Pā'ani hewa.

**found.** Ho'okahua *(establish);* kū-kulu *(as a society);* ho'okumu. *See* **find.**

**foundation.** Kahua, kumu, papa, mole, kumupa'a. *House foundation,* kahua hale.

**four.** 'Ehā, hā, 'ahā, kāuna.

**four hundred.** 'Ehā haneli, lau.

**four o'clock.** Hola 'ehā; nani ahiahi, pua ahiahi *(the flower).*

**fourteen.** 'Umi kūmāhā, 'umi kumamāhā.

**fourth.** Hā, hapahā.

**Fourth of July.** Lā 'Ehā o Iulai, Pokiulai.

**four thousand.** 'Ehā kaukani, mano.

**fowl.** Moa, manu.

**fraction.** Hakina; 'ano pili, hapa.

**fracture.** Ha'i.

**fragile.** Haki wale, palupalu, 'ūpalu, palahē.

**fragrance.** 'A'ala, onaona, paoa, kūpaoa, māpu, moani.

**frail.** Nāwaliwali, palupalu.

**frame.** Haka kaula'i, hakakū *(for drying);* lā'au *(picture frame);* kū *(of a bed).*

**France.** Palani, Farani.

**free.** 1. *State, condition.* Kū'o-ko'a, kuakahi; manuahi, mana-wale'a *(gratis);* ka'awale *(as*

*time).* 2. *To free.* Ho'oku'u, ho'oku'u la'ela'e, kala, weke, ho'ohemo.

**freedom.** Kū'oko'a.

**freight.** Ukana.

**freighter.** Moku lawe ukana.

**frequent.** Mau, pinepine, mau-mau, alapine.

**fresh.** Hou; maka, makamaka hou *(as fish).*

**freshman.** Haumāna komo hou.

**fret.** 1. *Complain.* Nē, ho'onē. 2. *Of ukulele.* Wā.

**friction.** 1. *Rubbing.* 'Ānai. 2. *Disagreement.* Hukihuki, kū'ē.

**Friday.** Pō'alima.

**fried.** Palai.

**friend.** Hoaloha, makamaka (o-*class);* aikāne (a-*class);* hoa.

**friendly.** Ho'ālohaloha, ho'oho-aloha, laulauna, maka launa.

**friendship.** Pilialoha, makamaka ola, laule'a.

**frigate bird.** 'Iwa.

**fright.** Pū'iwa, hopohopo, maka'u, puoho, hikilele.

**frighten.** Ho'omaka'u, ho'oweli.

**frog.** Poloka, lana.

**from.** Mai, mai . . . mai, no. *From Honolulu,* mai Honolulu, mai Honolulu mai; no Honolulu *(in sense of "native of").*

**front.** Alo, mua.

**frown.** Ho'oku'emaka, pupuku, ho'oku'eku'emaka.

**fruit.** Hua, hua 'ai.

**fruitful.** Hua nui, huahua, momona.

**fry.** 1. *Cook.* Palai. 2. *Small fish.* Pua, pua 'i'i.

**frying pan.** Pā palai.

**fuel.** Wahie.

**full.** Piha; poepoe *(as the moon);* mā'ona, piha ka 'ōpū *(from eating). Completely full,* piha pono. *Fullblooded,* piha.

**full-grown.** Makua.

**fun.** Le'ale'a, ho'ole'ale'a.

**funds.** Kālā. *Out of funds,* 'a'ohe kālā; puki, poloke *(slang).*

**funeral.** Ho'olewa.

**funny.** Hoʻomākeʻaka, kū i ka ʻaka, hoʻokolohe.

**fur.** Hulu, huluhulu, huhulu, hulu kupu, ʻili holoholona.

**furious.** Hae, piʻi ka huhū wela loa.

**furnish.** Hoʻolako. *Well-furnished,* lako.

**furniture.** Lako hale, pono hale.

**furthermore.** Koe kēia, eia hou hoʻi, eia nō naʻe, aia naʻe.

**future.** Mua, ka wā mahope.

# G

**g.** *No Hawaiian term.*

**gain.** Loaʻa, puka.

**gale.** Makani nui, kelawini.

**gallon.** Kālani.

**gamble.** Piliwaiwai.

**game.** Paʻani, mea paʻani, kemu, hoʻokūkū. *See* **baseball, basketball, checkers, football, hide-and-seek, jacks, marbles, swing, top, tug-of-war, wrestling.**

**gannet.** Kaʻupu.

**garage.** Hale kaʻa.

**garbage.** ʻŌpala.

**garden.** Māla, māla pua, māla ʻai, mahi, mahina ʻai, kīhāpai, pā kanu, ulu kanu, ulu pua, waena.

**gardenia.** Kiele, nāʻū, nānū.

**garlic.** ʻAkaʻakai pilau, ʻakaʻakai pūpū, kālika.

**garment.** ʻAʻahu, lole komo.

**gas.** 1. *A fluid, vapor.* Ea, eaʻaʻā. 2. *Of the stomach.* ʻŌpihapiha.

**gasoline.** Kakalina, ʻailaea, ʻailea.

**gasp.** Paʻa ka hanu, hanu paʻa, pauaho, paupauaho.

**gate.** Puka, puka pā, ʻīpuka, pani, pani puka.

**gather.** 1. *Collect.* ʻOhi *(pick);* hoʻāhu, hōʻiliʻili *(collect);* ʻako *(as papayas, seaweed).* 2. *Assemble.* Hoʻākoakoa.

**gay.** Hauʻoli, oliʻoli, leʻaleʻa.

**gem.** Pōhaku makamae.

**genealogy.** Kūʻauhau, moʻo kūʻauhau, moʻo aliʻi, moʻo kupuna.

**general.** 1. *Army.* ʻAlihikaua, pūkaua, kenelala. 2. *Widespread.* Laulaha, laulā, laha.

**generation.** Hanauna.

**generous.** Manawaleʻa, puʻuwai aloha, lokomaikaʻi.

**genital.** Maʻi, piko.

**genital chant.** Mele maʻi.

**gentle.** Akahai, mālie, laka, waipahē.

**gentleman.** Keonimana.

**genuine.** Maoli, ʻiʻo.

**geography.** Hōʻike honua.

**germ.** Mū, ʻeleao, ʻanoʻano.

**Germany.** Kelemānia.

**gesture.** Kuhi, ani ka lima.

**get.** Loaʻa, kiʻi, hoʻokiʻikiʻi, pā.

**ghost.** Lapu, akua lapu, akua, ʻuhane.

**giant.** Pilikua.

**gift.** Makana, haʻawina.

**gin.** Kini.

**ginger.** ʻAwapuhi.

**girdle.** Kāʻai.

**girl.** Kaikamahine.

**give.** Hāʻawi, hō.

**glad.** Hauʻoli, lauleʻa.

**glance.** ʻAlawa, ʻalaʻalawa, kilohi, leha, maka leha, maka lena, kokoe maka.

**glare.** Maka weli, ʻaʻā maka.

**glass.** Aniani; kīʻaha *(for drinking).*

**glasses.** *Spectacles.* Makaaniani.

**gleam.** ʻAnapa, ʻōlino, huali.

**glide.** Kīkaha.

**glimpse.** ʻIke mahuʻi, ʻike lihi, ʻaweʻaweʻa.

**glitter.** ʻĀlohi, ʻālohilohi, ʻanapa.

**globe.** Paʻa poepoe, poepoe, hulipoepoe, poepoe honua.

**gloom.** Pōuliuli, pouli, ʻomamalu.

**glorify.** Hoʻonani, hoʻohanohano, hoʻokapukapū.

**glory.** Hanohano, nani, kei.

**glottal stop.** 'Okina, 'u'ina.

**glove.** Mīkini lima, mikilima.

**glow.** 'Ena, 'ena'ena, 'a'ā.

**glue.** Kolū, mea ho'opipili.

**go.** Hele, hele aku, haele, uhaele, uhele. *Go down,* iho, hele iho; napo'o *(as the sun).* *Go up,* pi'i, pi'i aku.

**goal.** Pahu; kumu *(objective).*

**goat.** Kao.

**goatfish.** Weke, kūmū, moano.

**goby.** 'O'opu.

**god.** Akua; Makua *(in Christian prayers).* *Stone fishing god,* kū'ula. *Family or personal god,* 'aumakua.

**gold.** Kula, gula.

**goldfish.** I'a 'ula'ula.

**golf.** Kolepa, golepa.

**gone.** Nalowale, lilo, hele i kahi 'ē.

**good.** Maika'i.

**good-bye.** Aloha; ā hui hou aku *(lit, until meet again).*

**good evening.** Aloha ahiahi.

**good-for-nothing.** Lapuwale, mea waiwai 'ole.

**Good Friday.** Pō'alima Hemolele, Pō'alima Maika'i.

**good-looking.** Maika'i, maika'i ke nānā aku; kūmū *(slang).*

**good morning.** Aloha kakahiaka.

**good-natured.** Waipahē, 'olu-'olu.

**goodness.** Pono, maika'i, hemolele; kā, auē *(exclamations).*

**goods.** Waiwai, pono, mea.

**good will.** Lokomaika'i.

**goose.** Nēnē.

**gooseberry.** Pohā, pa'ina.

**gooseflesh.** 'Ōkala, 'ōkakala, lī ka 'ili, lī ka 'i'o.

**gospel.** 'Euanelio.

**gossip.** Holoholo 'ōlelo, lawe 'ōlelo, 'imi 'ōlelo, ho'owā, hauwala'au.

**got.** Loa'a.

**gourd.** Ipu, hue, pōhue, 'umeke pōhue.

**govern.** Ho'omalu, noho aupuni, noho ali'i.

**government.** Aupuni.

**governor.** Kia'āina.

**grab.** Kā'ili, 'apo.

**grace.** Aloha *(mercy, compassion);* lokomaika'i *(kindness);* pule ho'omaika'i i ka papa'aina *(before a meal);* kalakia *(Catholic).* *To ask grace,* pule ho'omaika'i.

**grade. 1.** *Rank, class.* Kūlana, papa, 'ano. *Sixth grade,* papa 'eono. **2.** *Evaluation.* Heluna, kaha. **3.** *To level.* Hō'iliwai.

**graduate.** Puka, ho'opuka.

**graft.** *Verb.* Pāku'i, pāna'i, ho'o-pili.

**grain. 1.** *Small particle.* Huna. **2.** *In wood, stone.* 'I'o, wai, nao.

**grammar.** Pili'ōlelo, hō'ike 'ōlelo.

**grand.** Maika'i loa *(fine);* hanohano *(glorious);* nui *(large, important).*

**grandchild.** Mo'opuna.

**grandfather.** Kupuna kāne, tūtū, kūkū, kūkū kāne.

**grandmother.** Kupuna wahine, tūtū, kūkū, kūkū wahine.

**grandparent.** Kupuna.

**granny.** Tūtū, kūkū.

**grasp.** Hopu, 'apo, hao, lālau.

**grass.** Mau'u, weuweu.

**grasshopper.** 'Ūhini, 'ūhini akelika.

**grateful.** Ho'omaika'i.

**gratitude.** Ho'omaika'i, mahalo.

**grave. 1.** *Burial.* Hē, lua kupapa'u. **2.** *Serious.* Ko'iko'i.

**gravel.** 'Ili'ili makali'i.

**gravestone.** Kia ho'omana'o.

**graveyard.** Pā ilina, pā kupapa'u.

**gravy.** Kai, kai penu, kai likoliko.

**gray.** 'Āhinahina, hinahina; hina, po'o hina *(of hair).*

**grease.** 'Aila, 'aila hamo, hinu, 'ōhinu.

**great.** Nui, nunui. *Very great,* nui loa, 'oi aku ka nui.

**greatest.** Nui, po'okela, heke, hapa nui, hapa loa.

**Greece.** Helene.

**greed.** 'Ālunu, 'ānunu, nunu.

**green.** 'Ōma'oma'o, 'ōma'o, ma-'oma'o, ma'o, uliuli *(vegetation);* maka *(as fruit).*

**greenery.** Lau nahele; iau hoʻohiwahiwa *(for decorations).*

**green rose.** Loke lau.

**greens.** Lau; lau ʻai ʻia *(edible).*

**greet.** Aloha, aloha aku. *Old forms:* weli, welina, ʻanoʻai.

**greeting.** Aloha.

**grief.** Kaumaha, kaniʻuhū, kūmakena, ʻū.

**grill.** Hao manamana, hao hakahaka.

**grin.** ʻŌlēʻolē *(widemouthed, as of an image).* See **smile.**

**grind.** Wili, ʻuwī, hoʻokala, ʻānai.

**groan.** Nā, ʻū, uhū, kaniʻū.

**groceries.** Mea ʻai.

**grocery store.** Hale kūʻai mea ʻai.

**groin.** Kumu ʻūhā; pani kai *(sea wall).*

**grope.** Hāhā.

**ground 1.** *Earth.* Lepo, honua. **2.** See **grind.**

**group.** Pūʻulu, ʻaoʻao.

**grove.** Ulu, ulu lāʻau, maha lāʻau, moku lāʻau, nahele. *Coconut grove,* ulu niu.

**grow.** Ulu, hoʻoulu, kupu.

**growl.** Nunulu, hae.

**grudge.** Mauhala, ʻauʻa. *To bear a grudge,* hoʻomauhala, manawahuā.

**grumble.** ʻŌhumu, ʻōhumuhumu, namunamu, kunukunu, ʻōhalahala.

**grunt.** Hū.

**guard.** Kiaʻi, mea kiaʻi, mākaʻi, makaʻina, pale.

**guardian.** Kahu.

**guava.** Kuawa.

**guess.** Koho, koho wale, mahuʻi.

**guest.** Malihini kipa, mea i kono ʻia. *My guest,* kaʻu malihini.

**guide.** Alakaʻi, hōʻike.

**guilty.** Hewa. *To find guilty,* hoʻāhewa.

**guitar.** Kīkā. *To play the guitar,* hoʻokani kīkā.

**gulch.** Awāwa, kahawai, ʻoawa.

**gulp.** Ale, alapoho, moni.

**gum.** Kamu *(for chewing);* pīlali *(from kukui tree).*

**gums.** ʻIʻo pale niho.

**gun.** Pū.

**gunpowder.** Pauka kī pū.

**gush. 1.** *Of water.* Huahuaʻi, huaʻina, hū, hūlani. **2.** *Of speech.* Puaʻohi, waha kale, ʻohi.

**gust.** Kokololio, makani pūkīkī.

**guts.** Naʻau.

**gutter.** ʻAuwaha *(ditch);* ʻalu *(ravine);* pulumi *(as on a house).*

# H

**h.** Hē.

**habit.** Hana maʻa, ʻaoʻao.

**habitual.** Maʻamau.

**hag.** Luahine pīʻalu, luahine ʻāluʻa.

**hair.** Lauoho, oho *(head);* hulu, huluhulu, huhulu *(body).*

**hairbrush.** Palaki lauoho.

**haircut.** ʻOki (ʻako) i ka lauoho.

**hairy.** Huluhulu, ʻōhuluhulu.

**half.** Hapalua. *Half dollar,* hapalua.

**hall.** Holo, hale. *Meeting hall,* hālau, keʻena hālāwai.

**halloo.** ʻŌ, hoʻōho; ūi, hūi *(modern).*

**halt.** Kū.

**ham.** Puaʻa hame, ʻūhā puaʻa, hame, ʻūhā hame.

**hamburger.** ʻIʻo pipi i wili ʻia.

**hammer.** Hāmale. *To hammer,* kuʻi, hāmale.

**hammerhead shark.** Manō kihikihi.

**hand.** Lima; manamana, lima kuhikuhi *(of a clock);* ʻekā, keʻa *(of bananas);* haʻawina *(of cards).* To hand, hāʻawi, hō mai *(toward speaker).*

**handbag.** ʻEkeʻeke paʻa lima, ʻeke paʻa lima.

**handbook.** Puke lawe lima.

**handful.** Piha lima, poho lima, haona lima.

**handkerchief.** Hainakā, hinakā. *Paper handkerchief,* hainakā pepa.

**handle. 1.** *Verb.* Lawelawe, limalima, lole, lapulapu, mili. **2.** *Noun.* 'Au, kū'au, pa'a lima, kano, kau; kākai *(as of a bucket).* *Axe handle,* 'au ko'i.

**handmade.** Hana lima.

**handshake.** Lūlū lima.

**handsome.** U'i, nohea, maika'i.

**hand wrestling.** Uma, pā uma, huinalima.

**handwriting.** Kākau lima, lima kākau, pūlima kākau, pūlima.

**handy.** Mākaukau, loea, no'eau.

**hang.** Ho'olewalewa, lewalewa, lewa, kau.

**hanging.** Kālewa, kūlewa, kaulia, kauna, uleule.

**happen. 1.** *Occur.* Hana, lo'ohia. *What happened?* He aha ka mea i hana 'ia? I aha 'ia? **2.** *By chance.* Kupu wale, hiki honua.

**happiness.** Hau'oli, 'oli'oli, laule'a, hoihoi. *To cause happiness,* ho'ohau'oli.

**happy.** *See* **happiness.** *Happy birthday,* hau'oli lā hānau; hānau *(in toasts).* *Happy New Year,* Hau'oli Makahiki Hou, Hapenuia.

**harbor.** Awa, awa kū moku.

**hard. 1.** *Not soft.* 'O'ole'a, pa'a. **2.** *Difficult.* Pa'akikī, hana nui.

**hardhearted.** Loko 'ino, mākonā, laukōnā.

**hardly.** 'Ane'ane, kokoke.

**hardship.** Pōpilikia, 'īnea, ho'īnea.

**harelip.** 'Ūlepe.

**harm.** Ho'opōpilikia, ho'opō'ino, ho'opilikia, ho'o'ino, 'ino, pō'ino.

**harmony. 1.** *Agreement.* Lōkahi, like ka nohona. **2.** *Musical.* Ka hui maika'i ana o nā leo mele.

**harp.** Hāpa.

**harpoon.** 'Ō; 'ō koholā *(for whales);* hāpuna.

**harsh.** 'O'ole'a, kakana'i.

**harvest.** Loa'a, wā 'ohi *(season).* *To harvest,* 'ohi.

**hasten.** Ho'ohikiwawe, 'āwīwī, māmā, wiki, wikiwiki.

**hat.** Pāpale.

**hatch.** Kiko, ho'okiko, kiko ka hua.

**hate.** 'Ino, mana'o 'ino, pu'uwai 'ele'ele, inaina. *Full of hate,* makawela.

**haul.** Kauō, huki, lawe.

**haughty.** Ho'okano, hukikū, ha'akei, ha'aheo.

**have. 1.** *To possess.* No word in Hawaiian; commonly expressed by he followed by a possessive: *I have a car, I had a car,* he ka'a ko'u. **2.** *Necessity.* Pono. *I have to go,* pono au e hele. **3.** *Verb auxiliary.* Ua *or* unexpressed. *I have gone,* ua hele au; hele au.

**Hawaiian.** Hawai'i. *Hawaiian person,* Hawai'i, kanaka Hawai'i.

**Hawaiian Islands.** Kō Hawai'i Pae 'Āina.

**hawk.** 'Io.

**he.** 'Oia, ia, 'oia nei, 'oia ala.

**head.** Po'o. *Human head,* po'o kanaka.

**headache.** 'Eha ke po'o, nahoa; nalulu *(dull);* po'o hua'i *(splitting).*

**headman.** Ali'i, po'o, luna; konohiki *(of an* ahupua'a).

**headquarters.** Kikowaena.

**headstrong.** Po'o pa'akikī, uhu, ho'ohuki, ho'ohuhuki, hukihuki.

**heal.** Lapa'au, ola, ho'ōla; kōhi *(as a wound);* pāla'au *(as with herbs).*

**health.** Olakino, ola pono, ola. *Good health,* olakino maika'i.

**health certificate.** Palapala hō'ike olakino.

**heap.** Pu'u, ahu, kūāhua, 'āhua, kuapapa, anu'a, nu'a, ho'onu'a.

**hear.** Lohe, ho'olono.

**heart.** Pu'uwai; iho *(as of celery, core);* 'i'o *(as of wood, central part);* haka *(in deck of cards).* *Generous heart,* manawale'a, lokomaika'i.

**heart attack.** Ma'i hohola, houpo 'ume pau, ma'i 'uhola; kauhola *(fatal)*.

**heartbreaking.** Hō'eha'eha i ka na'au.

**heartless.** Laukōnā, loko 'ino, mākonā.

**heartsick.** Māna'ona'o, hō'eha-'eha i ka pu'uwai.

**heat.** Wela, hahana, ikiiki, wela-wela, wewela, wāwena, 'āwela, 'ōwela. *In heat (of a bitch)*, kahe.

**heathen.** Pekana.

**heave.** Ho'olei.

**heaven.** Lani, papa lani, lewa, aouli.

**heavenly.** Lani.

**heavy.** Kaumaha, ko'iko'i.

**hedge.** Pā lā'au, pā la'alā'au, pālulu lā'au.

**heed.** Maliu, ho'omaliu, ho'olohe, mālama.

**heedless.** Nānā 'ole, ho'olohe 'ole.

**heel.** Ku'eku'e wāwae *(human)*; hila *(of a shoe)*.

**heiau.** Heiau.

**height.** Ki'eki'e, ki'eki'ena, loa, lō'ihi, nu'u.

**heir.** Ho'oilina, ho'īlina.

**hell.** Kehena, lua ahi, ki'o ahi, pō.

**Hello!** Aloha! *See* **halloo.**

**helmet.** Mahiole; 'a'ahu a po'o.

**help.** Kōkua, lawelawe lima.

**helpless.** Nāwaliwali, kūnānā.

**hem.** Pelu.

**hen.** Moa wahine.

**her.** 1. *Possessive. Same as* **his.** 2. *Pronoun. Same as* **him.**

**herb.** Lau nahele, lā'au palupalu, la'alā'au, mau'u.

**herd.** Pū'ā, kumu. *Herd of cattle,* pū'ā pipi.

**here.** Ma'ane'i, eia nei, i ne'i, ne'i, 'o ne'i, 'ane'i. *Here!* Eia! 'Ei'a!

**hereditary.** Mai nā kūpuna mai, welo.

**hermit crab.** Unauna, pāpa'i iwi pūpū.

**hernia.** Laho he'e.

**hero.** Me'e, koa. *Youthful hero,* u'i.

**heron.** 'Auku'u.

**hers.** *Same as* **his.**

**herself.** *Same as* **himself.**

**hesitate.** Kali, kūnānā, kānalua, ho'ohākālia, ka'ulua.

**hibiscus.** Aloalo, koki'o. *Hibiscus tiliaceus.* Hau.

**hiccough.** Mauli'awa.

**hidden.** Huna, nalowale, nalona-lo, nalohia. *Hidden meaning, see* **meaning.**

**hide.** Hūnā, ho'ohūnā *(transi-tive); pe'e (oneself, intransitive).*

**hide-and-seek.** Pe'epe'e kua, pe'epe'e akua, haupe'epe'e.

**high.** Ki'eki'e.

**higher.** Ho'okela, 'oi aku ke ki'e-ki'e.

**highest.** Ki'eki'e loa.

**high school.** Kula ki'eki'e.

**highway.** Alanui, alaloa, ala hele.

**hike.** Hele wāwae mamao.

**hill.** Pu'u, kuahiwi *(high);* pu'e *(as of sweet potatoes).*

**hilly.** 'Ōpalipali.

**him.** Ia. *To him,* iāia. *For him,* nona, nāna.

**himself.** 'Oia iho, 'oia pono'ī *(subject);* iāia iho *(object). For himself,* nona iho. *By himself,* nāna iho, 'oia ho'okahi.

**hinder.** Ālai, ke'a, ke'ake'a, ho'oke'a.

**hinge.** 'Ami; pu'u *(of pearl oy-ster). Door hinge,* 'ami puka.

**hint.** Ho'ohelehele 'ōlelo, ho'o-hele 'ōlelo.

**hip.** Kīkala, pāpākole.

**hire.** Limalima, ho'olimalima, hai.

**his.** 1. *Singular possessed object.* Kona (o-*class);* kāna (a-*class).* 2. *Plural possessed objects.* Ona (o-*class);* āna (a-*class*).

**history.** Mo'olelo, kuamo'o 'ōle-lo.

**hit.** Ku'i, ho'oku'i, pa'i, ho'opa'i, hahau, kū, ku'ia, kā, pā.

**hive.** Pūnana meli, pahu meli.

**hoard.** Ho'āhu; ho'olaholaho *(as a miser).*

**hoarse.** Hā, leo hā, hano, hanopilo.

**hobby.** Hana punahele, hana ho'onanea, hana ho'ohala manawa.

**hog.** Pua'a.

**hoist.** Hāpai, huki i luna.

**hold.** 1. *Grip.* Pa'a, ho'opa'a. *Hold a note,* kō. 2. *Of a ship.* O lalo.

**hole.** Puka *(usually of a perforation);* lua *(with a bottom);* haka *(breach). Full of holes,* pukapuka, haka, ho'ohaka, lualua, hālua.

**holiday.** Lānui.

**hollow.** Pūhā *(as a log);* hakahaka, 'olohaka *(as a surfboard);* po'opo'o, 'āpo'opo'o, hālua, napo'o, kānoa *(as in earth);* poho, pāiki, ka'ele, kāwaha, homa *(as of the hand or of a bowl).*

**holy.** Hemolele, ho'āno, kapu, la'a, la'ahia, 'ihi'ihi, Kaneka, Saneta. *Holy day,* lā ho'āno.

**Holy Communion.** 'Aha'aina a ka Haku, 'Aha'aina Pelena.

**Holy Ghost.** 'Uhane Hemolele.

**Holy Trinity.** Akua Kahikolu, Kolukahi Hemolele.

**home.** Home, kauhale.

**homeland.** One hānau, 'āina hānau, kulaiwi.

**homeless.** Kuewa, lewa, home 'ole.

**homely.** Pupuka.

**homesick.** Aloha kaumaha i ka home.

**homestead.** 'Āina ho'okū'ono-'ono, home ho'okū'ono'ono. *To homestead,* ho'okahua i ka 'āina ho'okū'ono'ono.

**homosexual.** Māhū.

**honest.** Kūpono, pono.

**honey.** Meli, wai meli, wai pua, hone, pīlali.

**honey bee.** Nalo meli.

**honeycomb.** Waihona meli.

**honeycreeper.** 'I'iwi, mamo, 'ō'ū, 'akeke'e, 'apapane, 'amakihi.

**honey eater.** 'Ō'ō, 'ā'ā.

**honeymoon.** Mahina meli.

**honk.** Ho'okani i ka 'olē; unele *(of goose).*

**Honolulu.** Honolulu *(lit., sheltered bay).*

**honor.** Ho'ohanohano, ho'onani, ho'ohiwahiwa.

**hoof.** Mai'ao holoholona, mānea, māi'u'u.

**hook.** Lou, loulou, kīlou *(as on a door);* kēlou, huka.

**hoop.** Apo, kuapo, hupa.

**hoot.** Ke'u, he'u *(as owl).*

**hop.** Lele, lelele.

**hope.** Mana'olana, 'upu, lana ka mana'o.

**horizon.** Hālāwai, pō'ailani, kumulani, 'alihi, 'alihi lani.

**horizontal.** 'Iliwai, moe.

**horn.** 1. *On animal.* Kiwi, hao, pepeiaohao; kākala *(as of fish or caterpillar).* 2. *Wind instrument.* Pū, pū puhi.

**hornet.** Hope'ō, kopena, nalo 'aki, nalo hope 'eha.

**horrible.** Weliweli, māna'ona'o, 'ino loa.

**hors d'oeuvre.** Pūpū, hō'ono'ono 'ai.

**horse.** Lio. *Race horse,* lio heihei, *Pack horse,* lio lawe ukana.

**horseback.** Kau lio. *To ride horseback,* kau lio, holo lio.

**horseshoe.** Kāma'a hao, kapua'ihao lio. *Horseshoe pitching,* kīolaola hao lio.

**hose.** 1. *See* stocking. 2. *Conveyor.* 'Ili. *Water hose,* 'iliwai. *To hose,* kikī wai.

**hospitable.** Ho'okipa aloha, ho'ohale kipa, heahea, makamaka nui.

**hospital.** Hale ma'i, haukapila.

**hospitality.** Ho'okipa.

**host.** 1. *As at a party.* Haku hale, mea ho'okipa, ka mea nāna ka 'aha'aina, ka mea nona ka hale. 2. *Crowd.* Lehulehu.

**hostess.** Haku hale wahine.

**hostile.** Kū'ē, paio, kamaniha, ho'okamaniha, 'āniha, loko 'ino.

**hot.** Wela, hahana; ikiiki *(stifling);* wewela, welawela, ʻāwela.

**hotel.** Hōkele.

**hour.** Hola.

**house.** Hale, kauhale.

**housefly.** Nalo.

**household.** ʻOhana *(family);* kauhale *(houses occupied by a family).*

**housekeeper.** Mālama hale, kahu mālama hale.

**House of Representatives.** Hale o nā Lunamakaʻāinana.

**housewife.** Wahine o ka hale.

**how.** Pehea, pehea lā. *How?* Pehea? *How are you?* Pehea ʻoe?

**however.** Akā, koe kēia, eia naʻe.

**hug.** Apo, pūliki.

**huge.** Nui loa, nui hewahewa.

**hula.** Hula. *Kinds:* ʻōlapa, ʻulīʻulī, paʻi umauma, ʻiliʻili, ʻauana, kahiko. *See* **studio.**

**human.** Kanaka.

**humane.** Lokomaikaʻi, kūʻē i ka hoʻomāinoino.

**humanity.** Lāhui kānaka.

**humble.** Haʻahaʻa, hoʻohaʻahaʻa, pē, pēpē, ūpē. *See* **modest.**

**humid.** Kawaū, maʻū; ikiiki *(and hot).*

**humiliate.** Hoʻohilahila, hoʻohaʻahaʻa.

**humility.** Haʻahaʻa. *See* **humble.**

**humor.** Hoʻomākeʻaka, piha ʻeu.

**hunchback.** Kuapuʻu.

**hundred.** Hanele, haneri.

**hungry.** Pōloli, make ʻai.

**hunt.** Hahai, ʻimi, hahai holoholona.

**hurricane.** Makani pāhili, makani uluulu, makani hele uluulu.

**hurry.** ʻĀwīwī, ʻāwiki, wiki, hoʻowiki, wikiwiki, alawiki, elewiki.

**hurt.** ʻEha, hōʻeha, ʻino, māino.

**husband.** Kāne, pilikua.

**husk.** Pulu. *To husk,* wehe i ka pulu.

**hut.** Pupupu hale, pāpaʻi, hale kāpiʻo ʻili lāʻau.

**hymn.** Hīmeni, leo hoʻonani, mele haipule, mele hoʻomaikaʻi.

**hyphen.** Kiko moe, kahamoe.

**hypocrite.** Hoʻokamani, kanaleʻo, hūpō kaliko.

# I

**i. 1.** *The letter.* ʻĪ. **2.** *(Cap.) Pronoun.* Au, wau, ʻo wau, ʻo au.

**ice.** Hau.

**icebox.** Pahu hau.

**ice cream.** Haukalima, ʻaikalima.

**iced.** Hau. *Iced beverage,* mea inu hoʻohuʻihuʻi.

**ice water.** Wai hau.

**idea.** Manaʻo; manaʻo ʻino *(evil);* manaʻo nui *(important).*

**ideal.** Kūpono ma nā ʻano apau *(perfect);* mea i kuko ʻia, mea i manaʻo nui ʻia *(thing desired).*

**identical.** Like loa, kūlike.

**identify.** Hōʻoia, hoʻomaopopo.

**idiom.** ʻIkeoma.

**idiot.** Lōlō, hūpō, hepa.

**idol.** Kiʻi akua.

**if.** Inā, aia nō, i, ke.

**ignite.** Hoʻā, hōʻaʻā.

**ignorance.** Naʻaupō; pō, pouli.

**ignore.** Nānā ʻole, kāpae ʻōlelo, huli kua.

**ill.** Maʻi, ʻōmaʻimaʻi.

**illegal.** Kū ʻole i ke kānāwai, mawaho o ke kānāwai.

**illegitimate.** Manuahi, poʻo ʻole, mawaho o ke kānāwai.

**ill-feeling.** Manaʻo ʻino, ʻōpū kopekope.

**illness.** Maʻi, nāwaliwali.

**illustrate.** Kaha kiʻi; hoʻohālikelike *(exemplify).*

**image.** Kiʻi, akua, kiʻi akua.

**imagination.** Noʻonoʻo ulu wale, manaʻo ulu wale.

**imitate.** Hoʻopili.

**immediate.** Koke, hikiwawe, wawe.

**immediately.** Koke, manawa ʻole, ʻemo ʻole, ʻānō.

**immense.** Nui loa, nui hewahe-wa.

**immigrant.** E'e moku.

**immortal.** Ola mau, make 'ole.

**immovable.** Kūpa'a, 'onipa'a.

**impatient.** Nauki, kū'aki, pauaho wale, ahonui 'ole.

**imperfect.** Kīnā, hemahema, 'a'ole i ponopono loa, pa'ewa, 'ewa.

**impertinent.** Maha'oi, ho'oma-'oi, kīko'olā.

**import. 1.** *Bring in.* Ho'okomo. *See* **imports. 2.** *Meaning.* Mana'o nui.

**importance.** Waiwai, 'ano nui.

**important.** Nui, 'ano nui.

**imports.** Waiwai ho'opae mai, waiwai komo.

**impossible.** Hiki 'ole.

**impression.** 'Ikena, pa'i 'ana, mō'ali.

**imprison.** Ho'opa'ahao.

**improper.** Kohu 'ole, kūpono 'ole.

**improve.** Holomua, ho'omaika'i, ho'onui aku ka maika'i.

**impulse.** Mana'o ulu wale, no'ono'o ulu wale.

**impure.** Paumā'ele, haumia, kele.

**in.** I, ma, i loko, maloko, i luna, maluna.

**in-.** 'Ole.

**inability.** Hiki 'ole.

**inaccurate.** Hewa, 'apake'e, hape.

**inactive.** Noho wale, noho hana 'ole.

**inaugurate.** Poni, ho'oponi, ho'okumu.

**incapable.** Mākaukau 'ole, hemahema.

**incest.** Moe 'ohana pili pono'ī.

**inch.** 'Īniha.

**incident.** Hanana, mea hiki wale mai, hana.

**incline.** Pi'ina, ihona, hiō.

**include.** Helu, ho'okomo pū, ho'ohui pū, pau pū, ā me.

**income.** Kālā loa'a mai.

**income tax.** 'Auhau maluna o ka loa'a.

**incoming.** Komo mai ana.

**incompetent.** Mākaukau 'ole, hemahema, hāwāwā.

**incomplete.** 'A'ole piha pono, hapapū, kīhapa.

**incorrect.** Pololei 'ole, pa'ewa, hewa, hape, 'ewa, kuhihewa.

**increase.** Ho'onui, ho'omāhua-hua, ulu, ho'olaha.

**indeed.** Pēlā, nō, pēlā 'i'o, ho'i, noho'i.

**indefinite.** Maopopo 'ole, akaaka 'ole.

**independence.** Kū'oko'a, ea.

**index.** Papa kuhikuhi, papa hō'ike.

**indicate.** Kuhikuhi, hō'ike.

**indifference.** Ho'omaopopo 'ole, palaka, nānā 'ole.

**indirect.** Hiliau, lauwili.

**indistinct. 1.** *Of vision.* Pāpala-weka, palaweka, poehi, pōwehi-wehi. **2.** *Of speech.* Akaaka 'ole, huikau ka leo, 'olē, nei, hepa.

**individual.** *See* **person, personal.**

**industrious.** Pa'ahana, lawe-hana, limahana.

**inexperienced.** 'Akahi akahi, hemahema, ma'a 'ole, hāwāwā.

**infancy.** Wā li'ili'i, wā 'u'uku, manawaea.

**infant.** Pēpē, keiki, kamali'i.

**infanticide.** 'Umi keiki.

**infantry.** Pū'ali kaua ka'i wāwae, koa hele wāwae.

**infection.** Ma'i lele, ma'i laha, 'a'ai.

**inferior.** 'A'ohe maika'i loa, ha'a-ha'a, emi iho.

**inflate.** Ho'ohū, hō'olopū, ho'o-pūhalalu.

**influence.** Ho'ohuli mana'o, ho'ololi.

**influenza.** Palū.

**inform.** Hō'ike, ha'i, ho'omaopo-po.

**information.** 'Ike, hō'ike.

**infrequent.** Kaka'ikahi, no ka manawa.

**-ing.** Ana, 'ana. *His going,* kāna

hele 'ana. *He is going,* e hele ana
'oia.

**ingratitude.** 'Awahua, hoʻomaikaʻi 'ole.

**inhabit.** Noho.

**inhale.** Hanu, hanu i loko.

**inherit.** Ili.

**inheritance.** Hoʻoilina, hoʻīlina,
waiwai hoʻoilina, ili.

**initiate.** Hoʻomaka, hoʻokumu;
hoʻolilo i lālā *(to membership).*

**injection.** Hoene, pahu kui *(hypodermic).*

**injure.** 'Ino, hoʻoʻino, hana 'ino,
hoʻopōʻino.

**injustice.** Kaulike 'ole, pololei
'ole, hana pono 'ole.

**ink.** 'Īnika.

**inland.** Uka, mauka, i uka; wao.

**in-laws.** 'Ohana pili ma ka male
'ana.

**inn.** Hōkele, hale kipa, hale hoʻokipa.

**innocent.** Hala 'ole, hewa 'ole.

**innumerable.** Hiki 'ole ke helu,
nui hewahewa, lehulehu, kinikini, kini lau ā mano.

**in order to.** E, i, no, i hiki ai ke.

**inquire.** Nīnau.

**inquisitive.** Nīele.

**insane.** Pupule, ulala, hehena,
lōlō.

**insect.** Mea kolo, holoholona
lele; mū *(destructive);* huhu
*(wood-boring).*

**insecure.** Paʻa 'ole ke kahua.

**insert.** Hoʻokomo, hoʻō, 'ōʻō,
hōʻōʻō.

**inside.** Loko, i.

**insignificant.** Mea 'ole.

**insist.** Koi, hoʻolāʻau, hoʻopaʻa,
haʻakoi.

**inspect.** Nānā, mākaʻi.

**inspire.** Ulu, hoʻoulu, hoʻolale-
lale.

**installment 1.** *Payment.* Uku mahele. **2.** *Portion.* Mahele, hapa,
'āpana.

**instance.** Mea hoʻohālike. *For
instance,* penei; e laʻa me kēia.

**instant.** Manawa pōkole loa.
*Instant coffee,* kope hikiwawe.

**instead.** Ma kahi o.

**instinct.** 'Ike hānau.

**institution.** Hui hoʻohana 'imi
naʻauao *(scholarly);* hui, hale.

**instruction.** Aʻo, 'ōlelo aʻo, aʻo
palapala, kuhikuhina.

**instrument.** Mea paʻahana; pila
*(musical).*

**insult.** Hōʻino, kūamuamu.

**insurance.** Hoʻopaʻa, 'inikua.

**intelligent.** Naʻauao.

**intercourse.** Launa 'ana. *See*
**sexual intercourse.**

**interest 1.** *Concern.* Hoihoi, ku-
leanā, pili laulā *(broad, general).*
**2.** *On principal.* Kuwala, puka,
puka o ke kālā, uku paneʻe.

**interfere.** 'Akeʻakeʻa, kakekake,
komo kuleana 'ole, hōkake.

**interior.** Loko, wālua.

**interisland.** Pili 'āina.

**intermarry.** Male 'ohana, male nō
iā loko iho.

**intermediate.** Mawaena.

**internal.** Kō loko.

**international.** O nā 'āina 'ē, kō nā
'āina like 'ole.

**interpret.** Unuhi, unuhi 'ōlelo,
hoʻomahele, mahele 'ōlelo.

**interrupt.** Kahamaha.

**intersection.** Huina.

**interview.** Kūkā kamaʻilio.

**intestines.** Naʻau; naʻanaʻau
*(small);* uha *(large).*

**intimate.** Pili koke.

**into.** I loko, i loko o.

**intoxicated.** 'Ona.

**introduce.** Hoʻohui, hoʻolauna
*(as people);* hoʻokomo.

**intrude.** Komo wale, komo hewa,
kipa wale.

**invalid. 1.** *Ill.* Mea nāwaliwali,
mea 'ōmaʻimaʻi. **2.** *Not valid.*
Mana 'ole, waiwai 'ole.

**invent.** Haku wale.

**inventory.** Helu, helu waiwai.

**investigate.** Kolokolo, hoʻokolo-
kolo, noiʻi.

**investment.** Waiwai no ka hoʻo-
pukapuka 'ana.

**invisible.** 'Ike maka 'ole 'ia, poʻo
huna.

**invitation.** Kono, palapala kono
*(written).*

**invite.** Kono.
**involuntary.** Me ka 'ae 'ole.
**involve.** Hihia, kūhihi, kāwili kā'ekā.
**Irish potato.** 'Uala kahiki.
**iron.** Hao; pāpa'a hao *(scrap)*; 'aiana *(for pressing clothes).*
**irregular.** E like 'ole me ka mea mau, 'ewa'ewa, loli ke kūlana.
**irrigate.** Ho'okahekahe wai, kau wai, ho'oma'ū, hanawai.
**irritable.** Nauki, 'a'aka, huhū koke.
**irritate.** Ho'oukiuki, ho'ouluhua.
**is.** *See* **be.**
**island.** Moku, mokupuni, moku-'āina, 'ailana.
**islands.** Pae 'āina. *Hawaiian Islands,* kō Hawai'i pae 'āina.

**isn't.** 'A'ole. *Isn't it?* 'A'ole anei?
**isolate.** Ho'oka'awale.
**issue. 1.** *Offspring.* Pua, keiki. **2.** *Put or come out.* Puka, ho'opuka, pukana.
**it.** Ia, 'oia, kēlā; akua *(in game of tag). This word is frequently omitted. It is said,* ua 'ōlelo 'ia.
**itch.** Mane'o.
**item.** 'Ikamu.
**its.** *Same as* **his.**
**itself.** 'Oia nō, 'oia iho, 'oia pono'ī.
**ivory.** Palaoa *(whale tooth);* niho 'elepani.

# J

**j.** *No Hawaiian term.*
**jack. 1.** *A fish.* Ulua. **2.** *(Cap.) In deck of cards.* Keaka.
**jackass.** *Same as* **donkey.**
**jacket.** Lakeke.
**jackknife.** Pahi pelu.
**jacks.** Kimo *(game).*
**jagged.** Nihoniho, nihoa.
**jail.** Hale pa'ahao. *To jail,* ho'opa-'ahao.
**jam.** Kele *(jelly).*
**janitor.** Kahu mālama ā ho'oma'e-ma'e hale.
**January.** 'Ianuali, Ianuari.
**Japan.** Iāpana, 'Āina Kepanī.
**jar.** *Noun.* 'Ōmole waha nui; poho aniani *(glass).*
**jasmine.** Pīkake.
**jaw.** Ā, papa niho; papa 'auwae *(lower jaw).*
**jealous.** Lili, nini, 'ōpū nini, manawa huā.
**Jehovah.** Iēhowa, Iehova.
**jelly.** Kele.
**jerk.** Huki 'ino.
**Jesus.** Iesū.
**jet.** Kī.
**Jew.** Kiu, Iukaio.
**jewelry.** Lako kula, mea ho'onani kino.

**jiggle.** Hō'oni'oni, 'oni'oni.
**jingle.** Kanikani. *Jingle bells,* kani nā pele.
**job.** 'Oihana, hana.
**join.** Pili, pili pū, hui, ku'i, kāpili.
**joined.** Ku'i, hui 'ia, huihui.
**joint. 1.** *Anatomical.* Ku'eku'e, 'ami ho'oku'i, 'ami, ha'i. **2.** *United.* Hui 'ia.
**joke.** 'Ōlelo pā'ani, ho'opā'ani.
**jolly.** Le'ale'a, laupa'apa'ani.
**journal.** Mo'olelo, puke ho'omana'o.
**journey.** Huaka'i.
**joy.** Hau'oli, 'oli, le'a.
**judge.** Luna kānāwai *(noun);* ho'okolokolo *(verb).*
**judgment.** 'Ōleloho'oholo, 'ōleloho'okō, 'ōlelo kūpa'a, ho'oholo.
**juice.** Wai.
**July.** Iulai.
**jump.** Lele, lelele.
**June.** Iune.
**jungle.** Wao nahele, uluāo'a.
**junior.** 'Ōpio. *Charles, junior,* Kale, 'ōpio.
**jury.** Kiule, kiure. *Grand jury,* kiule nui.
**just. 1.** *Fair.* Pono, kūpono,

kaulike, na'au pono. 2. *Recent-ly*. 'Akahi, 'ānō iho nei. 3. *See* almost.

**justice.** Kaulike.
**juvenile.** 'Ōpio, 'ōpiopio.

# K

**k.** Kē.
**kava.** 'Awa.
**keep.** Mālama, pa'a. *To keep still,* noho mālie.
**keepsake.** Mea ho'omana'o.
**kerosene.** 'Ailahonua, 'aila māhu.
**kettle.** Ipu hao, kikila.
**key.** Kī.
**kick.** Peku, pekuna.
**kidneys.** Pu'upa'a, kōnāhua.
**kill.** Pepehi ā make, ho'omake, make, hana make.
**kin.** 'Ohana, pili koko, pilikana.
**kind.** 1. *Sort.* 'Ano, kaina. 2. *Not cruel.* 'Olu'olu, lokomaika'i, aloha, na'au ali'i.
**kindergarten.** Kula kamali'i.
**kindling.** Pulu, pulupulu ahi, pula, mea hō'a'ā ahi.
**king.** Mō'ī, ali'i kāne, kini.
**kinship.** Pili 'ohana.
**kiss.** Honi.

**kitchen.** Lumi kuke.
**kite.** Lupe, pe'a.
**knapsack.** 'Eke lawe ukana, 'eke hā'awe.
**knead.** Kūpele, ho'opele, pele, poho, 'ōpā, ka'awili.
**knee.** Kuli.
**kneel.** Kukuli.
**knife.** Pahi.
**knit.** Kā, ulana.
**knob.** Pōheo, pōheoheo, heo, heoheo, pu'u, 'āpua.
**knock.** Kīkēkē.
**knot.** 1. *Tied.* Hīpu'u, kīpu'u, nīpu'u. 2. *In a tree.* Kīnā o ka lā'au. 3. *Nautical.* Mile loa.
**know.** 'Ike.
**knowledge.** 'Ike, na'auao.
**knuckle.** Ku'eku'e, 'ōku'eku'e, pu'upu'u, pu'u, 'ōpu'upu'u; pu'upu'u lima *(of hands).*
**Korea.** Kōlea, Korea.

# L

**l.** Lā.
**labor.** Hana, limahana, lawehana, luhi.
**laboratory.** Ke'ena hana, ke'ena 'imi na'auao.
**Labor Day.** Lānui o nā Limahana.
**laborer.** Limahana, lawehana. *Fellow laborer,* hoa lawehana.
**labor pains.** Nahu kuakoko, nahunahu, hō'i'ī, kōhi.
**lace.** 1. *Needlework.* Lihilihi, lihilihi hana lima. 2. *Cord.* Lī. *Shoelace,* lī kāma'a.
**lacking.** Nele, 'ole, hemahema.
**lad.** Keiki, keiki kāne.
**ladder.** Alapi'i, alahaka, haka.
**lady.** Wahine, haku wahine.
**ladyfish.** 'Ō'io.

**lagoon.** Kai kohola, loko kai, kua'au.
**lake.** Loko, loko wai. *Salt lake,* loko pa'akai.
**lamb.** Keiki hipa, hipa keiki, pua hipa.
**lame.** 'O'opa, kī'opa, mā'ulu'ulu.
**lament.** Uē, uē helu, makena, kanikau, kūmākena.
**lamp.** Kukui, ipukukui, kukui pōhaku.
**lance.** 1. *Spear.* Ihe pakelo. 2. *Surgical instrument.* Ā, ā 'ō'ō, koholua.
**land.** 1. *Ground.* 'Āina, honua, one. 2. *Debark.* Pae, lele, hō'ili, ho'oili.
**landholder.** Pa'a 'āina.

**landing.** Paena, kāhonua.

**landlady.** Haku hale wahine.

**landlord.** Haku ʻāina, haku hale.

**landmark.** Hōʻailona ʻāina.

**landscape.** Hiʻohiʻona ʻāina, waihona ʻāina, ka moena ʻana o ka ʻāina.

**land shell.** Pūpū kuahiwi, hinihini, kāhuli.

**landslide.** Hāneʻe ka mauna, heheʻe, hiolo, holo, ʻaholo.

**lane.** Ala ʻololī.

**language.** ʻŌlelo.

**lantana.** Lākana.

**lantern.** Ipukukui hele pō, kukui hele pō, lamakū.

**lap.** **1.** *Noun.* ʻŪhā. **2.** *Verb.* Mē, palu, paluhia.

**lard.** ʻAila puaʻa.

**large.** Nui, nunui.

**larger.** Nui loa.

**lash.** *Tie.* Hāwele, hauhana, hauhoa.

**lashing.** Aho, aho kā, luʻukia.

**last.** **1.** *Most recent.* Hope, muli, nei, aku nei. *Very last,* hope loa, muli hope; hopena, panina. **2.** *To continue.* Kāmau, hoʻomau, mau.

**late.** Lohi, hope, mahope. *Late at night,* aumoe.

**lately.** Aʻe nei, ʻānō iho nei, ʻānō wale iho nei nō.

**later.** Mahope aku.

**Latter-Day Saints.** Poʻe Hoʻāno o nā Lā Hope Nei.

**laugh.** ʻAka, ʻakaʻaka.

**laundry.** Lole lepo, lole holoi, lole pia *(with starch),* lole wai *(without starch). Laundry room,* lumi holoi.

**lava.** ʻĀ, ʻaʻā, ʻā pele *(rough lava);* pāhoehoe *(smooth lava);* ʻalā *(water-worn).*

**law.** Kānāwai. *Code of law,* kumukānāwai. *Lawmaking body,* ʻahaʻōlelo kau kānāwai.

**lawn.** Pā mauʻu.

**lawsuit.** Hoʻopiʻi, hihia ma ke kānāwai.

**lawyer.** Loio.

**lay.** Waiho, moe, hoʻomoe. *To lay*

*eggs,* hānau i ka hua, hāʻule hua.

**lazy.** Moloā; palaualelo *(and verbose).*

**lead.** **1.** *Mineral.* Kēpau, kēpau pōkā. **2.** *To guide.* Alakaʻi, kaʻi, kaʻikaʻi.

**leader.** Alakaʻi, mua, aliʻi, luna.

**leaf.** Lau; lā- *(in contractions, as* lāʻalo, *taro leaf;* lāʻī, *ti leaf;* lāʻie ʻie, *leaf;* lāʻō, *sugarcane leaf).*

**leak.** Kulu, kulukulu, liu, nō.

**lean.** **1.** *Thin.* Wīwī, ʻōlala, ʻāʻaua, ʻaua. **2.** *As meat.* Pākā, pākaʻa, kōkaʻa. *Lean beef,* ʻiʻo pipi momona ʻole. **3.** *Incline.* Hiō, hiōhiō, pahiō, kahiō.

**leap.** Lele.

**learn.** Aʻo, hoʻopaʻa, ʻimi naʻauao.

**lease.** Hoʻolimalima, palapala hoʻolimalima.

**leash.** Kaula paʻa lima.

**leather.** ʻIli holoholona, lapaʻau ʻia.

**leave.** *Verb.* Hoʻi, haʻalele, waiho.

**lecture.** Haʻiʻōlelo, haʻi aʻo.

**ledge.** Kaulu, kaulu ʻanuʻu, ʻanuʻu, kaola, lihi kaola, niao.

**lee.** Lulu. *Lee side of the island,* ʻaoʻao Kona o ka moku, lalo.

**leeward.** Lalo. *See* **lee.**

**left.** **1.** *Direction.* Hema. **2.** *Remaining.* Koe. **3.** *Departed.* Haʻalele.

**leg.** Wāwae.

**legal.** Kū i ke kānāwai, pono i ke kānāwai, kau kānāwai, kānāwai.

**legend.** Moʻolelo, kaʻao, mai ka wā kahiko.

**legislature.** ʻAhaʻōlelo, ʻahaʻōlelo kau kānāwai, ʻaha kau kānāwai. *Session of the legislature,* ʻaha kau kānāwai, kau ʻahaʻōlelo.

**legitimate.** Kū i ke kānāwai.

**lei.** Lei.

**leisure.** Manawa nanea, manawa walea, wā kaʻawale.

**lemon.** Lemi, kukane, lemona.

**lemonade.** Wai lemi.

**lend.** Hāʻawi no ka manawa.

**length.** Lōʻihi, loa, loloa, lau loa.

**Lent.** Kalema, Karema.

**leprosy.** Maʻi lēpela, lēpela, maʻi Pākē, maʻi aliʻi, maʻi hoʻokaʻawale.

**less.** Hapa iki, hapa ʻuʻuku, emi iho, hapa.

**lesson.** Haʻawina.

**lest.** O.

**let.** ʻAe, hoʻokuʻu, e.

**letter.** 1. *Missive.* Leka. 2. *Character.* Hua palapala, hua, hua nui, hua iki, hua liʻi.

**lettuce.** Lekuke.

**level.** ʻIliwai, ʻiliwai like, pālahalaha. *Carpenter's level,* ʻiliwai.

**lever.** Une.

**levy.** Kau, hoʻouku, ʻauhau.

**liar.** Wahaheʻe, hoʻopunipuni.

**libel.** Laipila.

**liberal.** Ākea, laulā, lipelala.

**liberty.** Kūʻokoʻa.

**librarian.** Kahu puke, mea mālama puke, mea mālama waihona puke.

**library.** Hale waihona puke, waihona puke.

**lice.** ʻUku, ona.

**license.** Laikini, palapala ʻae.

**lick.** Palu.

**lid.** Pani, poʻi, uhi, ʻomo.

**lie.** 1. *Recline.* Moe, hina moe. 2. *Falsify.* Hoʻopunipuni, wahaheʻe, waha wale.

**lieutenant.** Lukānela.

**life.** Ola *(as opposed to death)*; nohona, noho ʻana *(way of life).*

**lifeguard.** Kiaʻi ola.

**life insurance.** ʻInikua ola.

**lifesaving.** Hoʻopakele ola.

**lifetime.** Ka wā e ola ana.

**lift.** *Verb.* Hāpai.

**light.** 1. *Illumination.* Ao, lama, malama, kukui. 2. *Ignite.* Hōʻā, hōʻaʻā. 3. *Not heavy.* Māmā.

**lighthouse.** Hale ipukukui.

**lightning.** Uila. *Flash of lightning,* lapa uila.

**like.** 1. *As.* Ā, me, like me, kū, kohu, mehe, mehe mea, pe, hele ā,

laʻa. *Like this,* penei, pe kēia, pēia, ʻano like me kēia, e laʻa me kēia. 2. *Wish, to be fond of.* Makemake, mamake, puni, ʻiʻini; ʻono *(food).*

**likeness.** Kohu, kohu like, ʻano, kiʻi, aka, lua.

**lily.** Lilia.

**limb.** Lālā, mana.

**lime.** 1. *Fruit.* Lemi. 2. *Calcium oxide.* Puna.

**limestone.** Hauone, paʻakea, pāpaʻakea, pōhā kea.

**limit.** Palena, kaupale. *To limit,* kaupalena.

**limp.** 1. *Verb.* ʻOʻopa, ʻopa, māʻopaʻopa, hakiʻopa, kīʻopa, ʻoʻi. 2. *Adjective.* Malule, nāwali, nāwaliwali.

**limpet.** ʻOpihi.

**line.** 1. *Cordage.* Kaula, aho. 2. *Geometric.* Lālani, laina, kaha. 3. *To cover.* Pale.

**lineage.** Lālani ʻohana, kūʻauhau, welo, ēwe.

**linen.** Lilina, pulu, pulupulu, olonā.

**linger.** Kali, ʻapa.

**link.** Paukū, loulou, hoʻohui, hoʻokuʻi. *Link of chain,* paukū kaula hao.

**lion.** Liona.

**lip.** Lehe, lehelehe.

**liquid.** Wai, ʻae.

**liquor.** Wai; wai ʻona *(intoxicating).*

**list.** Helu, papa helu. *List of names,* papa inoa.

**listen.** Lohe, hoʻolohe, hoʻolono.

**literature.** Moʻolelo; palapala *(written only).*

**litter.** 1. *Trash.* ʻŌpala, mōkākī, hoʻoʻōpala. 2. *Stretcher.* Mānele.

**little.** Iki, liʻi, liliʻi, liʻiliʻi.

**live.** 1. *Exist.* Ola. 2. *Dwell.* Noho.

**livelihood.** Ola, pono.

**lively.** ʻEleu, ʻeuʻeu.

**liver.** Ake, akepaʻa. *Raw liver,* ake maka.

**livestock.** Holoholona hānai (i ka mahina ʻai).

**living.** Nohona, 'ao'ao *(way of life);* ola *(life).*

**living room.** Lumi ho'okipa.

**lizard.** Mo'o, mo'o kiha.

**load.** Hā'awe. *To load,* ho'okaumaha, ho'īli, ho'oili, ho'ouka, ho'oukana.

**loaf.** 1. *Noun.* 'Omo'omo. *Loaf of bread,* 'omo'omo palaoa, pa'i pelena. 2. *Verb.* Noho hana 'ole, ho'ohala manawa, ho'onanea.

**loafer.** Palaualelo, moloā.

**loan.** Hā'awi no ka manawa, hō'ai'ē.

**lobby.** 1. *Foyer.* Lumi ho'okipa. 2. *Political.* Hana ho'opaipai, paipai.

**lobster.** Ula.

**local.** Kūloko, kō laila, ne'i, 'one'i. *Local people,* kō 'one'i po'e.

**location.** Kahua, wahi, kahi.

**lock.** Kī, laka.

**locomotive.** Ka'aahi.

**locust.** 'Ūhini.

**lodge.** 1. *House.* Hale, ho'ouka. 2. *Fraternal or secret society.* Hui malū.

**log.** 1. *As of wood.* Paukū kumulā'au, kua lā'au. 2. *Ship's record.* Mo'olelo.

**loincloth.** Malo.

**loiter.** Kali, 'apa.

**lone.** Ho'okahi, kaukahi, noho ho'okahi.

**loneliness.** Mehameha.

**long.** Loa, loloa *(usually spatially);* lō'ihi; kō *(as a sound).*

**long for.** *See* **want.**

**long rice.** Laiki loloa.

**look.** Nānā, kilo.

**lookout.** Wahi nānā, wahi kia'i, 'ale'o.

**loose.** Hemo, puhemo, 'alu'alu, hō'alu'alu, pū'alu.

**lopsided.** Kapakahi.

**lord.** Haku.

**lose.** Nalo, nalowale, ho'olilo.

**loss.** Pohō; pohō ma'ū *(complete);* emi.

**lost.** Lilo; lilo loa *(permanently);* nalo, nalowale, nalohia.

**lot.** 1. *Quantity.* Nui, nui 'ino, nui loa. 2. *Land.* Pā, pā hale. 3. *Chance.* Hailona.

**loud.** Wā, hana kuli, kulikuli *(too loud).*

**loudspeaker.** Ho'onui leo, ho'onui i ka leo.

**lounge.** 1. *See* **couch.** 2. *Parlor.* Lumi ho'oluana, lumi ho'okipa. 3. *Relax.* Ho'onanea, hō'olu-'olu i ke kino.

**louse.** 'Uku, 'uku li'i, ona; 'uku po'o *(head louse);* 'uku kapa *(body louse).*

**love.** Aloha, 'ano'i, nipo, kaunu, ho'oipoipo, ho'oheno, puni.

**love affair.** Pili ho'oipoipo.

**lovely.** Nohea, onaona.

**lover.** Ipo.

**low.** Lalo, ha'a, ha'aha'a, pē, pēpē, emi; pāpapa *(as a reef).*

**lower.** Lalo, lalo iho, emi, ho'oha-'aha'a; ku'u *(as a net);* ho'ēmi, emiemi, ho'ēmiemi *(price).*

**loyal.** Kūpa'a, ho'okūpa'a.

**luck.** Pōmaika'i, laki. *Bad luck,* pō'ino, pakalaki, moe wa'a. *Out of luck,* pohō.

**lucky.** Laki, pōmaika'i.

**luggage.** Ukana, ukana pilikino.

**lukewarm.** Mūhea, 'ala'alae, 'ano 'ōwelawela.

**lullaby.** Mele ho'ohiamoe keiki, mele ho'onānā keiki, mele ho'oluluhi.

**lumber.** Papa, papa lā'au, laupapa.

**lump.** Pu'u, haku, huku.

**lunatic.** Hehena.

**lunch.** 'Aina awakea.

**lung.** Akemāmā, akemakani.

**lure.** 1. *Attract.* 'Ume, makaki'i *(with the eyes);* ho'ōnaona. 2. *See* **fishhook.**

**luscious.** 'Ono.

**lush.** Uluwehi, uluwehiwehi, ulu nui.

**lust.** Kuko, 'a'ako, 'ako.

**Lutheran.** Lukelano.

**luxury.** Mea e ho'ohiwahiwa ai ka noho 'ana, lako loa.

# M

**m.** Mū.

**machine.** Mīkini.

**mad.** 1. *Insane.* Hehena, pupule. 2. *Angry.* Huhū.

**madam.** Makame.

**magazine.** *No special term. See* **book.**

**maggot.** Ilo.

**magic.** Hoʻokalakupua.

**magnet.** Mākēneki, hao mākēneki.

**magnificent.** Hanohano, nani loa, hīhīmanu.

**magnify.** Hoʻonui.

**maid.** Wahine lawelawe, kauā wahine.

**maidenhair fern.** ʻIwaʻiwa.

**mail.** Leka.

**maile.** Maile.

**main.** ʻAno nui, hapa nui.

**mainland.** ʻĀina makua, ʻāina nui, loko. *To go to the mainland,* hele i loko.

**majestic.** Kilakila.

**majority.** Hapa nui, hapa loa.

**make.** Hana.

**male.** Kāne.

**mama.** Māmā. *See* **mother.**

**man.** Kanaka, kāne.

**manage.** Hoʻoponopono, hoʻoholo, hoʻohele, hoʻohana.

**manager.** Haku nui, luna hoʻohana.

**mango.** Manakō.

**mangrove.** Kukuna-o-ka-lā.

**manioc.** Manioka.

**mankind.** Lāhui kanaka.

**manners.** Lula, loina, ʻano launa.

**man-of-war.** Manuwā. *See* **Portuguese man-of-war.**

**manta ray.** Hāhālua.

**manual.** 1. *Directory.* Kumu, aʻo, manuale. 2. *By hand.* Hana lima.

**manure.** Kūkae.

**many.** Nui, nunui, lau, mano, manomano, lehu, lehulehu, kini.

**map.** Palapala ʻāina.

**marbles.** Kinikini. *To shoot, as marbles,* pana.

**march.** 1. *Action.* Naue, kaʻi huakaʻi. 2. *Month. (Cap.)* Malaki.

**marigold.** ʻŌkoleʻoiʻoi.

**marijuana.** Paka lōlō.

**marine.** 1. *Of the sea.* Kai. 2. *Military.* Koa malina.

**mark.** Kaha, kahakaha, kiko, kākau, kākau kaha.

**market.** Mākeke.

**marlin.** Aʻu.

**marriage.** Male ʻana, moe, noho pū ʻana, hoʻāo.

**marry.** Male, moe, hoʻāo, noho.

**marvelous.** Kupaianaha, kupanaha, kamahaʻo.

**masculine.** Kāne, hoʻokāne.

**mask.** Makakiʻi, poʻokiʻi, uhi maka.

**mass.** 1. *Quantity.* Puʻu, nuʻa, anuʻa, ahu. 2. *Ritual.* Meka, pule meka.

**massacre.** Luku.

**massage.** Lomi, lomilomi, kōkō, kaomi, kōmi.

**master.** Haku, kahu.

**masterbate.** ʻUʻu, puaʻuʻu.

**mat.** Moena.

**match.** 1. *Contest.* Hoʻokūkū. 2. *Equal.* Lua, kohu like. 3. *For starting fire.* Kūkaepele.

**mate.** 1. *Companion.* Hoa, kōkoʻolua. 2. *Of ships.* Mālama moku.

**mathematics.** Makemakikia.

**matter.** 1. *Thing.* Mea; kumuhana *(topic).* 2. *To be important.* ʻAno nui, manaʻo nui.

**mattress.** Pela, pela moe.

**mature.** Makua, oʻo.

**may** 1. *See* **can.** 2. *See* **maybe.** 3. *Month. (Cap.)* Mei.

**maybe.** Paha; pēlā paha, malia paha.

**mayor.** Meia.

**me.** Aʻu, iaʻu, i oʻu. *To me,* iaʻu, i oʻu.

**meal.** ʻAina, pāʻina.

**mean.** 1. *Cruel.* Mākonā. 2. *Average.* Waena. 3. *Signify.* Manaʻo.

**meaning.** Mana'o, mana'o nui.

**meantime.** Ia wā nō, ia manawa.

**measles.** 'Ulāli'i.

**measure.** Ana, ho'āna.

**meat.** 'I'o, 'i'o holoholona, i'a.

**medal.** Mekala.

**medical.** Lā'au, kauka.

**medicine.** Lā'au, lā'au lapa'au, wai lā'au.

**medium. 1.** *Intermediate.* Waena. **2.** *Spiritualist.* Haka.

**meek.** Akahai, ha'aha'a.

**meet.** Hui, hālāwai.

**meeting.** 'Aha, hālāwai.

**melody.** Leo, melokia.

**melon.** Ipu.

**melt.** Hehe'e, kahe.

**member.** Lālā *(as of a society).*

**memorize.** Ho'opa'ana'au, ho'opa'a.

**memory.** Ho'omana'o 'ana.

**men.** Kānaka, nā kāne.

**mend.** Hono, pāhonohono, poho, hana hou, kāpili.

**menstruate.** Hanawai, kahe, pe'a.

**mentality.** Waihona no'ono'o.

**mention.** Ha'i, 'ōlelo, ho'opuka.

**menu.** Papa kuhikuhi mea 'ai.

**merchant.** Kālepa.

**mercy.** Aloha.

**merry.** Le'ale'a, 'oli'oli, 'aka'aka; mele *(as in Merry Christmas).*

**merry-go-round.** Lio lā'au.

**mesh.** Maka, maka 'upena.

**mess.** Mōkākī.

**message.** 'Ōlelo ho'ouna 'ia.

**messenger.** 'Elele.

**meteor.** Hōkū lele.

**meter. 1.** *Distance.* Mika, mekele. **2.** *For measuring.* Ana.

**method.** 'Ano hana, papa hana.

**Mexico.** Mekiko.

**microphone.** Mea ho'olele leo.

**microscope.** 'Ohe nānā, 'ohe ho'onui 'ike.

**midday.** Awakea.

**middle.** Waena, waenakonu.

**midnight.** Aumoe.

**midrib.** Nī'au *(coconut frond).*

**midway.** Mawaena, waenakonu.

**might.** Ikaika loa, mana loa. *See* **maybe.**

**mildew.** Auloli, kūkaeloli.

**mile.** Mile *(statute);* mile loa *(nautical).*

**military forces.** 'Oihana koa.

**milk.** Waiū.

**milkfish.** Awa.

**milk shake.** Waiū luliluli.

**Milky Way.** Hōkū-noho-aupuni, I'a.

**mill.** Wili, hale wili. *Sugar mill,* wili kō.

**million.** Miliona.

**mimic.** Ho'opili.

**mind. 1.** *Intellect.* Mana'o, waihona no'ono'o, na'au. **2.** *Obey.* Lohe. **3.** *Heed.* Mālama, maliu.

**mine. 1.** *Possessive.* Ko'u, ka'u, ku'u, o'u, a'u, no'u, na'u. *See* **my. 2.** *Pit.* Lua, lua 'eli waiwai. **3.** *Military.* Pōkā pahū kai.

**minimum.** Hapa 'u'uku loa.

**minister. 1.** *Priest.* Kahuna, kahuna pule, kahu. **2.** *Statesman.* Kuhina.

**minor. 1.** *Small.* 'U'uku iho. **2.** *Underage.* O'o 'ole.

**minority.** Hapa iki, hapa 'u'uku.

**minute.** Minuke.

**miraculous.** Mana, ho'okalakupua, kupaianaha.

**mirror.** Aniani, aniani kilohi; aniani pa'a lima *(hand).*

**miscarriage.** He'e wale, poholo.

**mischief.** Kolohe, 'eu.

**miser.** Pī, puni kālā.

**misery.** Pō'ino oki loa.

**misfortune.** Pō'ino, pōpilikia.

**misprint.** Pa'i hewa.

**mispronounce.** Hewa ka hopuna, pa'ewa ka hopuna.

**miss. 1.** *Fail to hit.* Hala, hewa. **2.** *Perceive absence.* Ha'o. **3.** *Nostalgia.* Ha'o wale, minamina. **4.** *Unmarried woman.* Wahine male 'ole. *No equivalent to the title.*

**missing.** Nalowale, nalo.

**missionary.** Mikanele, mikionele.

**mist.** Uhiwai, noe, 'ohu, 'ehu *(in approximate order of decreasing denseness).*

**mistake.** Hewa, kuhi hewa, pa‘ewa, lalau; kīna‘u *(flaw).*

**mister.** *See* **Mr.**

**mite.** Ona, ane.

**mix.** Ho‘ohui, ho‘owali *(as poi, dough).*

**mix up, mix-up.** Huikau, ho‘ohuikau.

**moan.** ‘Ū, ‘uhū, ‘uhū‘uhū, kani‘ū.

**mob.** Uluāo‘a, po‘e ho‘ohaunaele.

**model.** Ana, ana ho‘ohālike.

**modern.** No kēia au.

**modest.** Akahai, ha‘aha‘a, pē, na‘au pē. *See* **humble.**

**moist.** Ma‘ū, mā‘ū‘ū, ko‘ū, pa‘ū, līhau.

**molasses.** Malakeke.

**moment.** Manawa iki. *Wait a moment,* kali iki, eia iho.

**Monday.** Pō‘akahi.

**money.** Kālā, moni.

**mongoose.** ‘Iole manakuke, manakuke.

**monkey.** Keko, mākinikā.

**monkeypod.** ‘Ōhai.

**mons pubis.** Hene, hena, pu‘ukole.

**month.** Mahina, malama.

**monthly.** Kēlā mahina, kēia mahina, puka mahina.

**moon.** Mahina, malama.

**moonlight.** Mālamalama o ka mahina.

**mop.** Lā‘au holoi papahele, kāwele wai.

**moral.** Pono.

**more.** Hou, keu.

**moreover.** Kekahi, eia kekahi, eia hou, koe kēia.

***Morinda citrifolia.*** Noni.

**Mormon.** Molemona.

**morning.** Kakahiaka. *See* **good morning.**

**morning-glory.** Koali.

**Morning Star.** Hōkūao, Hōkūloa.

**mortgage.** Molaki.

**mosquito.** Makika.

**mosquito net.** Pākū makika.

**moss.** Limu.

**most.** Hapa nui, nui, hapa loa, loa.

**moth.** Pulelehua; mū *(clothes moth).*

**mother.** Makuahine, māmā.

**mother-in-law.** Makuahūnōai wahine.

**Mother's Day.** Lā o nā mākuahine.

**Mother Hubbard.** Holokū.

**mother tongue.** ‘Ōlelo makua.

**motion. 1.** *Movement.* ‘Oni, au, ne‘e mōkio. **2.** *Parliamentary.* Noi. *to second a motion,* kōkua.

**motor.** Mīkini.

**motorcycle.** Mokokaikala, ka‘a mokokaikala.

**motto.** Mākia.

**mound.** Ahu, āhua, pu‘u.

**mount.** Pi‘i, e‘e, hō‘e‘e, kau.

**mountain.** Mauna, kuahiwi.

**mountain apple.** ‘Ōhi‘a ‘ai.

**mourn.** Kanikau, uē, ‘ū.

**mouse.** ‘Iole.

**mousetrap.** ‘Ūmi‘i ‘iole.

**mouth.** Waha.

**move.** Ne‘e, ho‘one‘e, naue; ka‘i hele *(in line or succession, or as in checkers).*

**movement.** Au, ‘oni, ne‘ena.

**movie.** Ki‘i ‘oni‘oni.

**mow.** ‘Oki.

**Mr.** *No term today; formerly, but not used commonly:* Mī, Mika.

**Mrs.** *No term today; formerly, but not used commonly:* wahine.

**much.** Nui. *Very much,* nui ‘ino, nui hewahewa, nui loa, kai! *How much?* ‘Ehia?

**mucus.** Hūpē, ‘ūpē, hākelo, wale.

**mud.** Kelekele, pālolo, lepo ‘ūkele.

**mudhen.** ‘Alae, nūkea, koki.

**mulberry.** Wauke.

**mule.** Hoki, miula, piula.

**mullet.** ‘Ama‘ama.

**multiplication.** Ho‘onui.

**multiply.** Ho‘omāhuahua, ho‘onui.

**mumble.** Namunamu.

**mumps.** ‘Auwaepahāha, ‘ā‘īpahāha.

**murder.** Pepehi kanaka.

**murmur.** Nē, hamumu, hē.

**muscle.** 'I'o, 'i'o huki, olonā.
**muscular.** 'Awa'awa'a.
**museum.** Hale hō'ike'ike.
**mushroom.** Kūkaelio, māmalu.
**mushroom coral.** Ko'a kohe, 'āko'ako'a kohe.
**music.** Mele *(vocal);* pila ho'okani *(instrumental).*
**musician.** Mea ho'okani pila *(player);* mea hīmeni, pu'ukani *(singer);* haku mele *(composer).*
**must.** Pono.
**mustache.** 'Umi'umi.
**mute.** Mumule. *Deaf mute,* kanaka kuli ā 'ā'ā.

**mutiny.** 'Olohani, mokuāhana, kipi i luna o ka moku.
**mutter.** Namunamu.
**mutton.** 'I'o hipa. *Leg of mutton,* 'ūhā hipa.
**mutual.** Like, kaulike, pāna'i like.
**my.** 1. *Singular possessed object.* Ko'u, ka'u, ku'u. 2. *Plural possessed object.* O'u, a'u.
**mynah.** Piha'ekelo.
**myself.** 'O wau nō, 'o wau pono'ī, 'o wau iho nō.
**mystery.** Pohihihi, kumulipo, mikelio.
**myth.** Mo'olelo o ka wā kahiko.

# N

**n.** Nū.
**nail.** 1. *Carpenter's.* Kui, kui nao, kui hao. 2. *Human.* Mai'ao, miki'ao.
**naked.** Kohana.
**name.** 1. *Noun.* Inoa. 2. *Verb.* Hea, hea inoa, kapa, kāhea.
**name chant.** Inoa, mele inoa.
**namely.** 'Oia ho'i.
**nap.** Hiamoe iki.
**napkin.** Kāwele. *Paper napkin,* Kāwele pepa. *Sanitary napkin,* mea hume.
**narcotic.** Lā'au ho'ohiamoe, lā-'au moe, lā'au ho'omalule kino.
**narrow.** Lā'iki, hāiki, ho'ohāiki.
**nasty.** Pelapela, hauka'e.
**nation, national.** Aupuni, lāhui.
**native.** Kama'āina, maoli, 'ōiwi, kupa, keiki papa.
**natural.** Kūpono.
**nature.** 'Ano *(kind). There is no single Hawaiian word for the physical universe.*
**naughty.** Kolohe, 'eu, 'āpiki.
**nausea.** Pailua, papailua, liliha.
**nauseating.** Ho'opailua.
**navel.** Piko.
**navy.** 'Oihana moku.
**near.** Kokoke.
**neat.** Maiau, 'auli'i; mikioi *(in craftsmanship).*
**necessary.** Pono, kūpono.

**neck.** 'Ā'ī; waha *(of a dress).*
**necklace.** Lei.
**necktie.** Lei 'ā'ī.
**need.** 1. *Necessity.* Pono. 2. *To lack.* Nele, hemahema.
**needle.** Kui, kui kele, kui humuhumu, mānai.
**needlefish.** 'Aha, 'aha mele, 'aha'aha.
**negative.** 1. *Negate.* 'Ole, hō'ole. 2. *Of a picture.* Aka ki'i.
**neglect.** Mālama 'ole, waiho wale, ho'opalaleha, ho'ohemahema.
**Negro.** Pā'ele; pōpolo *(slang);* nekelo.
**neighbor.** Hoa noho, hoalauna.
**neither.** 'A'ole, 'a'ole ho'i.
**nephew.** Keiki (ke keiki kāne a ke kaikua'ana, ke kaikaina, ke kaikunāne, ke kaikuahine), ke keiki hanauna.
**nerve.** A'a, a'alolo, a'alolo lohe.
**nervous.** Pīhoihoi wale, ha'alulu o loko.
**nest.** Pūnana.
**net.** 'Upena; kōkō; 'a'aha *(carrying net).*
**neutral.** Kā'oko'a.
**never.** 'A'ole, 'a'ole loa.
**nevertheless.** Akā, akā ho'i, na'e.
**new.** Hou, mea hou, 'ano hou, malihini.

**newcomer.** Malihini.
**news.** Mea hou, nū hou, nū, lono.
**newspaper.** Nūpepa.
**New Testament.** Kauoha Hou.
**New York.** Nuioka.
**New Zealand.** Nukīlani.
**next.** A'e, hope, hiki. *Next week*, kēia pule a'e.
**nibble.** Nalinali, 'a'aki, nome.
**nice.** 'Auli'i; 'olu'olu *(pleasant)*; maika'i.
**nickel.** Hapa'umi.
**nickname.** Inoa kapakapa.
**niece.** Kaikamahine.
**night.** Pō. *Last night*, i ka pō nei.
**night-blooming cereus.** Pānini-o-Ka-puna-hou.
**nightgown.** Mu'umu'u moe pō, lole moe pō.
**nightmare.** Moehewa, moe 'ino.
**nimble.** 'Eleu, miki, māmā.
**nine.** Iwa, 'eiwa, 'aiwa.
**nineteen.** 'Umi kūmāiwa, 'umi kumamāiwa.
**ninety.** Kanaiwa.
**ninety-one.** Kanaiwa kūmākahi, kanaiwa kumamākahi.
**nipple.** Maka waiū, maka.
**nit.** Liha, lia.
**no.** 'A'ole, 'a'ohe.
**nobody.** 'A'ohe mea, 'a'ohe kanaka.
**noddy tern.** Noio kōhā.
**noise.** Hana kuli, kulikuli, wā, wawā, kani.
**nominate.** Koho, wae, waiho inoa.
**none.** 'A'ohe mea, 'a'ohe, 'a'ole.
**nonsense.** 'Ano 'ole, kohu 'ole.
**noon.** Awakea, kau ka lā i ka lolo.
**normal.** Kūlike me ke 'ano mau, 'ano mau.

**north.** 'Ākau.
**North America.** 'Amelika 'Ākau.
**northeast.** Hikina 'ākau.
**North Pole.** Wēlau 'Ākau.
**North Star.** Kio-pa'a, Hōkūpa'a.
**northwest.** Komohana 'ākau, noweke.
**nose.** Ihu.
**nose flute.** Hano, kōheoheo.
**nostril.** Pukaihu.
**not.** 'A'ole, 'ole, 'a'ohe.
**notched.** Nihoniho, nihoa, pū'ali.
**note. 1.** *Letter.* Leka pōkole, 'ōlelo ho'omana'o. **2.** *Financial.* Palapala 'ai'ē, pila hō'ai'ē. **3.** *Musical.* Leo mele, hua, hua mele.
**notebook.** Kālana kākau.
**nothing.** 'Ole, mea 'ole, 'a'ohe mea, nele.
**notice.** Hō'ike. *To notice*, nānā.
**notify.** Hō'ike.
**nourish.** Hānai.
**novel. 1.** *Story.* Ka'ao. **2.** *Strange, new.* 'Ano 'ē.
**November.** Nowemapa.
**novice.** 'Akahi akahi, ma'a 'ole.
**now.** I kēia manawa, 'ānō.
**nuisance.** Pilikia, mea ho'opilikia wale, ho'oluhi.
**numb.** Lōlō, mā'e'ele.
**number.** Helu, heluna, nui *(quantity)*; hua helu *(numeral)*.
**numerous.** Lau, ho'olau, mano, manoa, lehu, lehulehu, kinikini, kini lau.
**nun.** Wilikina, nuna.
**nurse.** Kahu ma'i, kahu mālama ma'i.
**nut.** Kukui haole.

# O

**o.** 'Ō.
**oar.** Hoe.
**oarsman.** Mea hoe wa'a, hoe wa'a.
**oath. 1.** *In court.* Ho'ohiki, 'ōlelo ho'ohiki, 'ōlelo pa'a. **2.** *See* swear.

**obedient, obey.** Ho'olono, ho'olohe.
**obituary.** Mo'olelo o ka mea 'akahi nō ā make.
**object. 1.** *Thing.* Mea. **2.** *Purpose.* Kumu, mea. **3.** *See* oppose.

**obligation.** 'Ai'ē *(debt)*.

**obscene.** Pelapela, haumia, ho'o-hilahila.

**obscure.** Poahi, poehi, pohihihi.

**observe.** Nānā, nānā pono, hāki-lo, haka pono.

**obstacle.** Ālaina, mea ala'alai, mea ke'ake'a.

**obstetrician.** Kauka ho'ohānau.

**obstinate.** Pa'akikī, 'o'ole'a, pa'a loa, po'o pa'a.

**obstruct.** Ālai, ke'a, ho'oke'a, ho'okāpae.

**obtain.** Loa'a.

**obvious.** Maopopo le'a, aniani, mōakaaka.

**occasion.** Wā, hanana.

**occupation.** 'Oihana, hana.

**occupy.** Noho *(as a house)*.

**occur.** Kupu, hiki mai.

**ocean.** Moana, kai.

**o'clock.** Hola.

**October.** 'Okakopa.

**octopus.** He'e.

**odd.** 'Ano 'ē *(unusual);* pa'ewa *(uneven)*.

**odor.** *See* **smell.**

**of.** O, a, kō, kā.

**off.** Mai *(from);* 'ē *(away)*.

**offend.** Ho'ohuhū, ho'onāukiuki.

**offense.** Hewa, hala, lawehala.

**offer.** Hā'awi, hō.

**offering.** Mōhai. *Church offering,* lūlū, ho'okupu, mahina hou.

**office. 1.** *Position.* 'Oihana, hana. **2.** *Room.* Ke'ena, ke'ena hana.

**officer.** Ali'i, luna.

**offspring.** Keiki, hānau, pua, hua.

**often.** Pinepine.

**oh.** Auē, kā, 'ā.

**oil.** 'Aila, hinu.

**oilfish.** Walu.

**oily.** Hinuhinu, kūhinu, kelekele, 'ūkele, liliha.

**ointment.** Mea hamo, 'aila hamo, lā'au hamo, hinu.

**O.K.** Hiki, hiki nō, pololei.

**old.** Kahiko *(usually not of people);* o'o, 'elemakule, luahine.

**old age.** Wā 'elemakule, wā lua-hine.

**older.** Mua, hiapo *(of children in a family),* makua.

**old-fashioned.** Ho'okahiko, mamua, 'ano o ke au kahiko.

**old man.** 'Elemakule.

**Old Testament.** Kauoha Kahiko.

**old woman.** Luahine.

**oleander.** 'Oliana, 'oliwa, noho-mālie.

**olive.** 'Oliwa.

**omelet.** Hua pākā, hua palai i ka'awili 'ia.

**omen.** 'Ōuli, hō'ailona.

**omit.** Waiho, kāpae, holoi.

**on.** I, ma, maluna o.

**once.** Ho'okahi wā, kekahi wā, pākahi, 'ekahi, 'akahi, kuakahi.

**one.** 'Ekahi, 'akahi *(counting in a series);* ho'okahi, kahi, kekahi; hapa- *(in fractions: one-eighth,* hapawalu).

**onion.** 'Aka'akai.

**only.** Wale nō, wale.

**onward.** I mua.

**open. 1.** *State of being open, as a door.* Hāmama, makili, mikili, nakili, ho'omakili *(as a crack).* **2.** *As a flower.* Mōhala, mōhalu. **3.** *Verb, transitive (as a door, package).* Wehe, weke, 'uwehe.

**openhearted.** Pu'uwai hāmama.

**opening.** Puka, wehena, wehe 'ana, waha, ho'owaha, mōhala, 'īpuka.

**opera.** Keaka mele.

**operate.** 'Oki, kaha *(surgically)*.

**opinion.** Mana'o.

**opium.** 'Opiuma.

**opponent.** Hoa paio, mea kūē, 'ao'ao kū'ē.

**opportunity.** Manawa kūpono.

**oppose.** Kū'ē, ālai, ke'ake'a, pāku'i, kē.

**opposite.** Kū'ē, 'ē'ē.

**oppress.** Ho'olu'ulu'u, ho'oluhi hewa, ho'okaumaha, ho'oko'i-ko'i.

**optimism.** Hoihoi mau, ho'ohoihoi mau.

**or.** A i 'ole, ā . . . paha.

**oral.** Ha'i waha, waha, 'ōlelo.

**orange.** *The fruit or tree.* 'Alani.

**orchard.** Māla lā'au hua 'ai, kīhāpai.

**orchestra.** Hui ho'okani pila.

**orchid.** 'Okika.

**order.** 1. *Command.* Kauoha, kēnā. 2. *Arrangement.* Ho'onohonoho 'ana, papa, noho papa.

**ordinary.** Ma'amau, laha, mea loa'a wale, a'e nei.

**organ.** 1. *Musical instrument.* 'Okana. 2. *Part of body.* Mahele. *Internal organs,* loko.

**organization.** Hui, 'ahahui.

**origin.** Kinohi, ho'omaka 'ana, kumu.

**ornament.** Wehi, kāhiko, kīnohi, ho'okāhiko.

**orphan.** Keiki makua 'ole.

**other.** Kekahi, 'ē a'e, 'ē.

**otherwise.** Akā na'e, ma kekahi 'ano 'ē a'e.

**ouch.** Auē, auī.

**ought.** Pono.

**ounce.** 'Aunaki.

**our.** Kō kāua, kā kāua, kō māua, kā māua, kō kākou, kā kākou, kō mākou, kā mākou, o kāua, a kāua, o māua, a māua, o kākou, a kākou, o mākou, a mākou.

**ours.** No kāua, no māua, no kākou, no mākou, na kāua, na māua, na kākou, na mākou.

**out.** Waho, i waho, mawaho; pio *(extinguished).*

**outcast.** Kauā.

**outcry.** Oho.

**outdoors.** O waho.

**outhouse.** Wahi ho'opau pilikia, hale li'ili'i, lua li'ili'i, lua, hale lua.

**outrigger boom.** 'Iako.

**outrigger canoe.** Wa'a.

**outrigger float.** Ama.

**outside.** Waho, i waho, mawaho, kō waho, kūwaho.

**outsider.** Kanaka 'ē, kanaka o waho.

**outstanding.** Po'okela, kau i ka wēkiu, kūlana ki'eki'e.

**oven.** Imu, umu, 'oma.

**over.** 1. *Above.* Luna, i luna, maluna. 2. *Completed.* Pau. 3. *Again.* Hou.

**overcast.** 'Ōmalumalu, 'omamalu, ho'ōmalumalu.

**overcome.** 1. *To defeat.* Lanakila, ho'opio. 2. *Defeated.* Pio, puni. 3. *Possessed, as by fear, passion, joy, or grief.* Lo'ohia, ilihia.

**overcooked.** Mo'a loa.

**overeat.** Pākela 'ai.

**overflow.** Hū, hālana, hanini, ho'ohanini, pi'ipi'i.

**overload.** Ho'ouka nui, ho'olu'ulu'u loa.

**overseer.** Luna, luna hana, luna kia'i, haku, haku hana.

**overshadow.** Ho'omalumalu, ho'oūmalu.

**oversized.** Nui loa, nui maluna o ka mea ma'amau.

**oversleep.** Hiamoe loa, moe loa.

**overthrow.** Kahuli, ho'okahuli, hiolo, ho'ohiolo.

**overtime pay.** Uku kaulele.

**overwhelm.** Po'ipū, popo'i, uhi.

**owe.** 'Ai'ē.

**owl.** Pueo.

**own.** Pono'ī *(self);* kuleana *(ownership).*

**owner.** Haku, mea, 'ona.

**oyster.** 'Ōlepe.

# P

**p.** Pī.

**Pacific.** Pākīpika, Moana Pākīpika.

**pack.** Ho'okomo *(as a trunk);* 'awe, hā'awe *(carry).*

**package.** Pū'olo.

**paddle.** Hoe.

**paddler.** Hoe wa'a.

**page.** 'Ao'ao.

**paid.** Ka'a.

**pail.** Pela, kini, kini pela, pākeke.

**pain.** 'Eha; hu'i *(in tooth, bones);*

nalulu *(dull, in stomach, head)*;
'ūmi'i *(side)*.

**paint.** Pena.

**painter.** Kaha ki'i *(artist)*; mea
pena *(as of houses)*.

**pair.** Pa'a, kaulua.

**pajamas.** Lole wāwae moe pō.

**palace.** Hale ali'i.

**pale.** Hākea.

**pali.** *See* **cliff.**

**palm.** 1. *Tree.* Pāmá, pālama; niu
*(coconut)*. **2.** *Of hand.* Poho,
poho lima.

**pan.** Pā.

**pancake.** Palaoa palai.

**pandanus.** Hala.

**panic.** Maka'u kūhewa, haunaele.

**pansy.** Po'okanaka, pāneki.

**pantry.** Lumi waiho pā.

**pants.** Lole wāwae.

**papa.** Pāpā.

**papaya.** Mīkana, hē'ī, papaia.

**paper.** Pepa.

**parade.** Huaka'i, ka'i huaka'i;
paikau *(as of military)*.

**paradise.** Palekaiko.

**paragraph.** Paukū, palekalapa.

**parallel.** Kaulike, moe like, 'iliwai
like.

**paralysis.** Lōlō, ma'i lōlō.

**parasite.** 1. *Plant.* Lā'au kumu
'ole. **2.** *Person.* Kū 'īpuka hale,
kūkake, lelewa, ho'opilimea'ai.

**parched.** Malo'o loa.

**pardon.** Kala, huikala.

**parent.** Makua.

**Paris.** Palika, Parisa.

**park.** 1. *Recreation area.* Pāka. **2.**
*To station.* Ho'okū, kūkulu.

**parlor.** Lumi ho'okipa.

**parrot.** Manu aloha.

**parrot fish.** Uhu.

**part.** *Portion.* Mahele, mokuna,
hapa, 'āpana.

**particle.** Hunahuna 'ōlelo *(part of
speech)*.

**particular.** 1. *Special.* Nō. **2.**
*Fussy.* 'Ano waewae, 'eke'eke,
kamalani.

**partition.** Pale, kau pale, pākū.

**partner.** Hoa, hoa hana, kōko'o,
pakanā.

**party.** 1. *Group.* 'Aha, pū'ulu,
'ao'ao *(political)*. **2.** *Festivity.*
Ho'olaule'a *(large)*, pā'ina *(dinner or supper)*. **3.** *Person.* Kanaka, mea, po'e.

**pass.** 1. *Movement.* Mā'alo, kā-
'alo, 'aui, kaha *(pass by)*, holo.
**2.** *Permission.* Palapala ho'o-
ku'u.

**passenger.** 'Ōhua.

**passion.** Konikoni, kaunu. *The
Passion of Christ,* ka 'Eha'eha o
ka Haku.

**passion fruit.** Liliko'i, lemi wai,
lemona, pohāpohā.

**passover.** Pakoa, mōliaola.

**passport.** Palapala ho'āpono, palapala kuhikuhi, palapala 'ae e
holo.

**past.** Hala, ka'a i hope.

**paste.** Ho'opipili, mea ho'opipili.

**pastime.** Ho'ohala manawa, hana
ho'ohala manawa.

**pastor.** Kahuna pule, kahu.

**pastry.** Mea 'ono.

**pasture.** Kula, pā holoholona,
kula holoholona.

**patch.** 1. *On clothes.* Poho. **2.**
*Garden.* Mahi, māla.

**paternal.** Makua kāne, ma ka
'ao'ao o ka makua kāne.

**path.** Ala.

**patience.** Ahonui, 'ōpū ahonui,
ho'omanawanui.

**patient.** Ma'i, mea ma'i.

**patriotism.** Aloha 'āina.

**pattern.** Ana, ana ho'ohālike.

**pause.** Ho'omaha.

**pavement.** Kīpapa, paepae.

**paw.** Wāwae, kapua'i.

**pawnshop.** Hale hō'ai'ē.

**pay.** Uku, ho'oka'a.

**pea.** Pī, pāpapa.

**peace.** Malu, maluhia, la'i.

**peach.** Piki.

**peacock.** Pīkake.

**peak.** Pu'u 'oi'oi, pu'u, wēkiu,
'oi'oina.

**peanut.** Pineki.

**pear.** Pea.

**pearl.** Momi.

**pearl shell.** Pā, uhi, kea.

**pebble.** 'Ili'ili.
**pebble hula.** Hula 'ili'ili.
**peculiar.** *Unusual.* 'Ē, 'ē'ē, 'ano
  'ē, 'e'epa.
**pedal.** Hehi wāwae.
**pedestrian.** Kanaka hele wāwae.
**peel.** Mā'ihi; koli *(pare).*
**peeved.** Ukiuki, nuha.
**Pele's hair.** Lauoho-o-Pele.
**Pele's tears.** Waimaka-o-Pele.
**pelt. 1.** *Skin.* 'Ili. **2.** *To throw, hit.*
  Pehi, pehia, nou.
**pen. 1.** *Enclosure.* Pā. **2.** *Writing
  instrument.* Peni kila.
**penalty.** Ho'opa'i, uku hala.
**pencil.** Penikala, peni.
**penetrate.** Komo.
**penis.** Ule.
**penknife.** Pahi pelu.
**pen name.** Inoa kapakapa.
**penny.** Keneka, keneta.
**pension.** Uku ho'omau, ha'awina
  ho'omau.
**people.** Po'e, lāhui, lāhui kanaka,
  kānaka. *See do.*
**pepper.** Pepa, nīoi.
**percent.** Pakeneka.
**perch.** Haka kau.
**perfect.** Hemolele, kīnā 'ole,
  pono loa.
**perform.** Lawelawe, hana, ho'o-
  kō. *See do.*
**perfume.** Lūkini, wai lūkini, wai
  'ala, wai hō'a'ala.
**perhaps.** Paha, pēlā paha, malia,
  malia paha.
**period. 1.** *Punctuation.* Kiko. **2.**
  *Time.* Wā, manawa, au.
**permanent.** Pa'a, loa, mau, mau
  loa.
**permission.** 'Ae.
**persecute.** Ho'omāino, ho'omāinoino, māino, hō'ino.
**persevere.** Noke, ho'omanawanui, ho'omau.
**persist.** Ho'omau, ho'opa'a,
  noke.
**person.** Kanaka, mea, kama.
**personal.** Pilikino, kino, pono'ī.
**perspiration.** Hou.
**persuade.** Koi, mali.
**pessimist.** Kūlana hoihoi'ole.

**pet. 1.** *Favorite.* Punahele, milimili. **2.** *To caress.* Hamohamo.
**petal.** Lihilihi.
**petition.** Palapala noi, palapala
  ho'opi'i.
**petrel.** 'Ua'u, 'ou, 'ou'ou, 'akē-
  'akē, lupe'akeke.
**petroglyph.** Ki'i pōhaku.
**petticoat.** Palekoki.
**pharmacy.** Hale kū'ai lā'au.
**Philippines.** 'Āina Pilipino.
**phonograph.** Pahu 'ōlelo, pono-
  karapa. *Phonograph record,* pā,
  pā ho'okani.
**photograph.** Ki'i. *To photograph,*
  pa'i ki'i.
**physical.** Kino, pilikino.
**physician.** Kauka, kauka lapa'au,
  kahuna lapa'au.
**piano.** Piano.
**pick.** 'Ohi, 'ako *(gather);* wae,
  koho *(select).*
**pickaxe.** Kipikua.
**pickle.** Pīkala.
**picnic.** Pikiniki.
**picture.** Ki'i.
**pidgin English.** 'Ōlelo pa'i 'ai,
  namu pa'i 'ai.
**pie.** Pai. *Apple pie,* pai 'āpala.
**piece.** 'Āpana, paukū, māmala,
  mahele, poke.
**pieces.** Okaoka *(small, as broken
  glass);* 'āpa'apana *(larger);* momoku *(severed objects);* mahele.
**pier.** Uapo.
**pierce.** 'Ō, hou, pahu, 'ō'ō.
**pig.** Pua'a.
**pigeon.** Nūnū, manu kū.
**pile.** Ahu, pu'u, āhua.
**pill.** Huaale.
**pillow.** Uluna, 'aki, 'ope'ope.
**pilot.** Pailaka.
**pimple.** Pu'u. *Pimples,* huehue.
  *Pimpled,* hāpu'upu'u, kukuku,
  pu'upu'u.
**pin.** Kui, pine, mākia, hākia,
  kākia, 'ō. *Safety pin,* pine kaiapa.
**pinch.** 'Iniki, 'ūmi'i, 'ini'iniki.
**pineapple.** Hala kahiki, hala 'ai.
  *Pineapple cannery,* hale hana
  hala kahiki.

**pine tree.** Lāʻau paina, paina.
**pink.** *Color.* ʻĀkala.
**pinkeye.** Maka ʻulaʻula.
**pint.** Paina.
**pipe.** ʻOhe, paipu. *Tobacco pipe,* ipu paka. *Water pipe,* hā wai, ʻohe wai.
*Piper methysticum.* See **kava.**
**pistol.** Pū, pūpanapana.
**pit.** Lua.
**pitch.** 1. *Throw.* Nou, hoʻolei. 2. *Motion of a vessel.* Luli, kulana. 3. *Resin.* Hū lāʻau, kēpau. 4. *Music.* Kī, kiʻina o ka leo, kani.
**pitcher.** 1. *Vessel.* Pika, kīʻaha, kīʻaha ʻoʻoma. 2. *Thrower.* Nou, mea nou.
**pity.** Aloha, aloha menemene, mokuāhua.
**place.** 1. *Locality.* Wahi, kahi, kaha, kauwahi. 2. *To put.* Kau.
**plain.** 1. *Level land.* ʻĀina pālahalaha, kula, ʻāina pāpū. 2. *Clear.* Mōakaaka. 3. *Simple.* ʻAʻohe i hoʻonani ʻia *(unadorned);* uʻi ʻole *(not beautiful).*
**plait.** Ulana.
**plan.** Hoʻolālā, kālai, ana. *To draw plans,* kaha kiʻi.
**planet.** Hōkū hele, hōkū ʻaeʻa, hōkū lewa.
**plant.** Lāʻau, mea ulu, lau nahele. *To plant,* kanu.
**plantain.** Maiʻa.
**plantation.** Mahi, māla, māla ʻai. *Sugar plantation,* mahi kō.
**plaster.** Puna, hamo puna.
**plastic.** *Malleable.* ʻŪlina.
**plate.** Pā. *Paper plate,* pā pepa.
**platform.** Kahua, haka, paepae.
**platter.** Pā pālahalaha.
**play.** 1. *Recreation.* Pāʻani. 2. *Play music.* Hoʻokani, hoʻokani pila. 3. *Drama.* Hana keaka.
**playful.** Piha ʻeu.
**playground.** Kahua, kahua pāʻani.
**playing cards.** Pepa, pepa pāʻani, pepa hahau.
**playmate.** Hoa pāʻani.
**pleasant.** ʻOluʻolu, waiʻolu.
**please.** Hōʻolu, hōʻoluʻolu, hoʻo-

leʻa, hoʻohoihoi; ʻoluʻolu *(command).* *Please come,* e ʻoluʻolu ʻoe, e hele mai.
**pleasing.** Hiaʻai, leʻa, waiʻolu.
**pleasure.** Leʻaleʻa, ʻoliʻoli, hoihoi.
**Pleiades.** Makaliʻi, Nā-huihui.
**plenty.** Lawa pono, nui, lako.
**pliers.** ʻŪpā ʻūmiʻi.
**plot.** 1. *Conspiracy.* Kipi, ʻōhumu, ʻōhumu kipi. 2. *Plot of story.* Kahua o ka moʻolelo. 3. *See* **lot,** 2.
**plover.** Kōlea.
**plow.** ʻŌʻō hao, ʻōʻō palau, ʻōʻō hou, palau.
**pluck.** Unuunu *(as fowl),* ʻako *(as flowers).*
**plug.** Pani, ʻumoki.
**plumber.** Palama.
**plumeria.** Melia.
**plump.** Puʻipuʻi, nepunepu.
**plunder.** Waiwai pio, waiwai hoa. *To plunder,* hao, pōā.
**plunge.** Luʻu.
**plural.** Helu nui.
**plus.** Ā me.
**P.M.** ʻAuinalā *(afternoon);* ahiahi *(evening);* pō *(night).*
**pneumonia.** Numonia.
**pocket.** Pākeke, paʻeke, ʻekeʻeke, ʻeke.
**poem.** Mele.
**poet.** Haku mele.
**poi.** Poi, ʻai.
**poinciana.** ʻOhai ʻula.
**point.** Kiko *(dot);* lae *(of land);* wēlau, ʻēlau, welelau *(tip);* maka, ʻoiʻoina.
**poison.** Lāʻau make.
**poke.** ʻŌʻō, hou, ʻoʻe.
**poker.** 1. *Implement.* Ulu ahi, ʻōʻōahi. 2. *Card game.* Konoki.
**pole.** Pou, lāʻau.
**police.** Mākaʻi. *Chief of police,* luna mākaʻi.
**policy.** 1. *Plan.* Manaʻo hoʻokō, kahua, papa hana. 2. *Document.* Palapala.
**polish.** ʻĀnai, hoʻohinuhinu.
**polite.** ʻOluʻolu, waipahē, waipehē.

**politician.** Loea kālai'āina.
**politics.** Kālai'āina, polokika.
**pollute.** Ho'ohaumia, ho'opaumā'ele, ho'opelapela.
**polluted.** Pilopilo.
**Polynesia.** Polenekia.
**pond.** Loko. *Freshwater pond,* loko wai.
**pony.** Pone, lio 'u'uku.
**pool. 1.** *Pond.* Ki'o wai. **2.** *The game.* Pahupahu.
**poor. 1.** *Impoverished.* 'Ilihune. **2.** *Quality.* 'Ino'ino, pono 'ole.
**popcorn.** Kūlina pohāpohā.
**pope.** Pope.
**popular.** Makemake nui 'ia, nui nā makamaka.
**population.** Heluna kānaka, po'e, lehulehu, kānaka.
**porch.** Lānai.
**pork.** Pua'a, 'i'o pua'a.
**porpoise.** Nai'a, nu'ao.
**port.** Awa.
**porter.** Hali ukana, kanaka hali ukana.
**portion.** 'Āpana, mahele, kuleana, ha'awina.
**Portuguese.** Pukikī.
**Portuguese man-of-war.** Pa'imalau.
**position.** Kūlana.
**possible.** Hiki.
**post. 1.** *Pole.* Pou, kia. **2.** *To deposit.* Ho'ouna; ho'okomo *(as mail);* kū *(as a bond).* **3.** *Military.* See **fort.**
**postage.** Uku leka. *Postage stamp,* po'oleka.
**postcard.** Pepa po'oleka.
**postman.** Lawe leka.
**postmaster.** Luna leka.
**post office.** Hale leka.
**postpone.** Ho'opane'e.
**pot.** Ipu.
**potato.** 'Uala kahiki *(Irish).* See **sweet potato.**
**poultry.** Nā manu laka 'ai 'ia e like me ka moa.
**pound. 1.** *With hammer.* Ku'i. **2.** *Unit of weight or currency.* Paona.

**pounder.** Mea ku'i. *Poi pounder,* pōhaku ku'i 'ai.
**pour.** Ninini.
**powder.** Pauka, paoka, pouka, paula.
**power.** Mana, lima ikaika.
**practice. 1.** *Train.* Ho'oma'ama'a. **2.** See **procedure.**
**praise.** Mahalo, ho'omaika'i, ho'onani.
**pray, prayer.** Pule.
**preach.** Ha'i'ōlelo, ha'i 'euanelio.
**preacher.** Kahuna pule, kahu.
**precaution.** Hana ho'omākaukau mamua o ka pōpilikia.
**precede.** Hele mamua.
**precious.** Makamae, hiwahiwa.
**precise.** Kūlike loa.
**predict.** Wānana.
**pregnant.** Hāpai.
**prejudice.** Mana'o kū'ē, ho'okae. See **race prejudice.**
**premature.** 'Ē, mamua o ka wā kūpono.
**preparation.** Mākaukau, ho'omākaukau 'ana.
**prescription.** Kuhikuhi.
**present. 1.** *Now.* 'Ānō, kēia manawa. **2.** *At hand.* Ma'ane'i; eia *(as response to roll call).* **3.** *Gift.* Makana. **4.** *To present.* Hā'awi, waiho.
**president.** Pelekikena.
**press. 1.** *Exert pressure.* Kaomi; 'aiana *(as clothes).* **2.** *Printing press.* Pa'i palapala, papa pa'i.
**pretend.** Ho'omeamea, ho'okohukohu, ho'okamani.
**pretty. 1.** *Attractive.* Nani, maika'i, u'i, nohea. **2.** *Somewhat.* 'Ano.
**prevent.** Kāohi, pale, ke'ake'a.
**previous.** Mua, mamua a'e.
**price.** Kumu kū'ai, kālā.
**pride.** Ha'aheo.
**priest.** Kahuna.
**prime minister.** Kuhina nui.
**prince.** Keiki ali'i, kamāli'i kāne.
**princess.** Kamāli'i wahine.
**principal. 1.** *Main, head.* Nui, mua, po'o. *School principal,*

po'o kumu. **2.** *Capital sum.* Kumupa'a.

**print.** Pa'i, kākau, kākau kaha.

**print shop.** Hale pa'i.

**prison.** Hale pa'ahao.

**private.** Pilikino, pono'ī.

**prize.** Makana, uku.

**prized.** Makamae.

**probably.** Paha, pēlā paha, malia.

**problem.** Pilikia, hihia.

**procedure.** Hana 'ana, lawelawe 'ana.

**proceed.** Hele mua, holo mua.

**procession.** Huaka'i, ka'i huaka'i.

**proclaim.** Kūkala.

**profession.** 'Oihana, ho'ona-'auao.

**professor.** Polopeka.

**profit.** Loa'a, puka, waiwai ho'opuka.

**profound.** Hohonu, kūli'u.

**program.** Papa kuhikuhi.

**progress.** Holomua, holo i mua.

**prohibit.** Pāpā, ho'okapu.

**project.** *Plan.* Papa hana.

**prominent.** 'Oi, ki'eki'e.

**promise.** 'Ōlelo pa'a, 'ōlelo ho'ohiki.

**promote.** Ho'opi'i.

**prompt.** Hikiwawe.

**pronounce.** Ho'opuka.

**pronunciation.** Hopuna, hopuna 'ōlelo.

**proof.** Hō'oia'i'o.

**proofread.** Heluhelu ho'oponopono.

**propaganda.** Ho'olaha mana'o.

**proper.** Kūpono, kū, pono.

**property.** Waiwai, pono, kuleana.

**prophecy.** Wānana.

**prophet.** Kāula, makāula.

**propose.** Ho'olale, noi.

**prosecute.** Ho'opi'i.

**prostitute.** Wahine ho'okamakama, wahine laikini.

**protect.** Ho'omalu, ho'omāmalu, ho'omaluhia.

**protest.** Kū'ē, ho'ohalahala.

**Protestant.** Hō'ole Pope.

**proud.** Ho'okano, ha'aheo, ha'akei.

**prove.** Hō'oia'i'o.

**proverb.** 'Ōlelo no'eau, 'ōlelo akamai.

**provide.** Ho'olako, ho'onoho.

**provoke.** Ho'oukiuki, ho'onāukiuki, ho'ohae.

**prune.** Puluna.

**psalm.** Halelū.

**public.** Lehulehu, ākea.

**publicity.** Ho'olaha, ho'olaulaha.

**publish.** Pa'i, ho'olaha.

**pudding.** Pūkini.

**puddle.** Ki'o wai.

**Puerto Rican.** Pokoliko.

**pull.** Huki.

**pulse.** Pana.

**pumice.** 'Ana, 'ana ōla'i.

**pump.** Pauma.

**pumpkin.** Pala'ai, ipu pū.

**punch. 1.** *Strike.* Ku'i. **2.** *Beverage.* Mea inu ho'ohuihui, wai hua'ai.

**punctuation.** Kiko.

**puncture.** Puka.

**punish.** Ho'opa'i.

**pupil. 1.** *Scholar.* Haumāna. **2.** *Of eye.* 'Ōnohi maka.

**purchase.** Mea kū'ai. *To purchase,* kū'ai mai.

**pure.** Ma'ema'e, hemolele.

**purify.** Ho'oma'ema'e.

**purple.** Poni, māku'e.

**purpose.** Kumu.

**purse.** 'Eke'eke, 'eke'eke pa'a lima.

**push.** Pahu. *Push along,* ne'e, pane'e.

**put.** Kau.

**puzzled.** Kāhāhā, kūnānā, ha'oha'o.

# Q

**q.** *No Hawaiian term.*

**quail.** Manu kapalulu.

**quake.** Ha'alulu, naue. *See* **earthquake.**

**qualified.** Mākaukau, kūpono.
**quality.** ʻAno, kūlana.
**quantity.** Nui.
**quarantine.** Hoʻomalu maʻi.
**quarrel.** Hoʻopaʻapaʻa, paio.
**quarry.** Lua ʻeli pōhaku.
**quart.** Kuaka.
**quarter.** Hapahā.
**queen.** Mōʻī wahine, aliʻi wahine, kuini.
**queer.** ʻAno ʻē.
**question.** Nīnau, ui.
**question mark.** Kiko nīnau.
**questionnaire.** Palapala ninani-nau, mea hoʻopihapiha, paʻi hakahaka.
**quick.** ʻĀwīwī, koke, māmā, wiki, wikiwiki, wawe, hikiwawe, ʻeleu, ʻemo ʻole, alawiki.
**quiet.** Mālie, hoʻomālie, hilu, wailana, malu, maluhia, hoʻomalu, hoʻolaʻi, laʻi. *Be quiet!* Kulikuli! Hāmau *(polite)!*
**quilt.** Kapa kuiki.
**quit.** Haʻalele, waiho.
**quite.** ʻAno, wale, nō.
**quiz.** Hōʻike pōkole.
**quota.** Mahele.

# R

**r.** *No Hawaiian term.*
**rabbit.** Lāpaki, ʻiole lāpaki.
**race.** 1. *People.* Lāhui. 2. *Contest.* Heihei.
**race prejudice.** Hoʻokae ʻili.
**radiant.** Mālamalama, ʻālohilohi, ʻōlinolino.
**radio.** Radio, lekiō.
**radio broadcast.** Hoʻolele leo.
**rafter.** Kua, oʻa.
**rag.** Welu.
**rage.** Huhū loa, piʻi ka huhū wela loa, inaina.
**raid.** Pākaha.
**railing.** Pale.
**railroad.** Alahao, kaʻaahi.
**rain.** Ua.
**rainbow.** Ānuenue.
**raincoat.** Kuka ua, kukaweke, kuka ʻaila.
**raindrops.** Paka ua.
**raise.** 1. *Lift.* Hāpai, pai. 2. *Bring up a child.* Hānai, luhi.
**raisin.** Hua waina maloʻo.
**rake.** Kope, ʻōʻō kope.
**ram.** 1. *Sheep.* Hipa kāne. 2. *Shove.* Hou, pahu.
**ramble.** ʻAuana, ʻaeʻa.
**ranch.** Wahi hānai holoholona, kuleana.
**rancher.** Kahu pipi *(cattle).*
**randy.** Kuko ʻino, kuko hewa.
**rank.** Kūlana, papa.
**ransom.** Hoʻōla pānaʻi, uku pānaʻi, kūʻai hoʻōla.
**rape.** Puʻe, puʻe wale.
**rare.** 1. *Infrequent.* Kakaʻikahi. 2. *Underdone.* Moʻa iki, moʻa kolekole *(as of meats).*
**rascal.** Kolohe, kupuʻeu, ʻāpiki.
**rash.** 1. *Bold.* ʻAʻa makehewa. 2. *Of sin.* ʻŌhune.
**raspberry.** ʻĀkala, kala.
**rat.** ʻIole.
**rather.** 1. *Somewhat.* ʻAno. 2. *Prefer.* ʻOi aku ka makemake.
**ration.** Hāʻawi kaupalena.
**rattle.** Koʻele, nakeke.
**rattles.** Pūʻili *(bamboo);* ʻulīʻulī *(gourd).*
**ravine.** Kahawai, awaawa, awāwa.
**raw.** Maka, makamaka; kolekole *(as meat or a wound).*
**ray.** 1. *As of the sun, or spoke.* Kukuna, wana. 2. *Fish.* Hīhīmanu, hailepo, hāhālua. *See* **sting ray.**
**razor.** Pahi ʻumiʻumi.
**reach.** *Arrive at.* Hiki, kū, loaʻa.
**read.** Heluhelu.
**ready.** Mākaukau.
**real.** Maoli, ʻoiaʻiʻo, ponoʻī.
**real estate.** Waiwai paʻa.
**realize.** Hoʻomaopopo.
**really.** ʻĀ ʻoia, ʻoia, ʻiʻo.
**rear.** 1. *Back.* Hope. 2. *Raise, as a child.* Hānai. 3. *As a horse.* ʻOwala.
**reason.** Kumu, mea, kuleana.

**reasonable. 1.** *Sensible.* Kaulike ka noʻonoʻo. **2.** *Not expensive.* Makepono.
**rebel.** Kipi.
**recede.** Emi, hoʻi i hope.
**receipt.** Palapala hoʻokaʻa.
**receive.** Loaʻa mai.
**recent.** Hou.
**receptacle.** Waihona.
**reception.** Kipa ʻana.
**receptionist.** Mea kiaʻi keʻena hana *(office)*.
**recess.** Hoʻomalolo.
**recipe.** Lula no ke kuke ʻana.
**recite.** Haʻi walewaha mai.
**reckless.** Nānā ʻole i ka pono, hoʻoponopono ʻole.
**recline.** Kāmoe, momoe.
**recognize.** Hoʻomaopopo, ʻike.
**recommendation.** Kākoʻo *(support)*.
**record. 1.** *Account.* Moʻolelo. **2.** *Phonograph.* Pā, pā hoʻokani.
**recorder.** Mīkini ʻapo leo, kākau moʻolelo, kākau hana.
**recover.** Ola, ola hou, ola loa.
**recreation.** Mea hoʻonanea, mea leʻaleʻa. *Board of Parks and Recreation,* Papa o nā Pāka a me nā Hana Hoʻonanea.
**rectum.** ʻŌkole, ʻamo, ʻamo hulu.
**red.** ʻUla, ʻulaʻula, wena.
**Red Cross.** Hui Keʻa ʻUlaʻula, Keʻa ʻUlaʻula.
**redeem.** Uku pānaʻi.
**red-eyed.** Mākole.
**red-hot.** ʻEna, ʻenaʻena.
**red pepper.** Nīoi.
**red snapper.** ʻUlaʻula, koʻi.
**reduce.** Hoʻēmi, hoʻoʻuʻuku.
**reef.** Kohola.
**reel. 1.** *Whirl.* Kunewa, newa, kāhulihuli. **2.** *Spool.* Pōkaʻa; mīkini hoʻowili lawaiʻa *(fishing)*.
**refer.** Pili, waiho.
**referee.** ʻUao.
**reflection.** Aka, wai aka, noʻonoʻo.
**reform.** Hoʻopololei, hoʻohuli.
**refrain. 1.** *Abstain.* Hoʻōki. **2.** *Song.* Puana.
**refreshment.** Mea ʻai māmā.
**refrigerator.** Pahu hau.

**refuge.** Puʻuhonua.
**refund.** Uku pānaʻi.
**refuse. 1.** *Deny.* Hōʻole, kē. **2.** *See* **rubbish.**
**regain.** Loaʻa hou.
**regal.** Aliʻi, hoʻāliʻi, lani, ʻihiʻihi.
**regards.** Aloha, mahalo.
**register.** Kākau hoʻopaʻa, kākau inoa, papa inoa.
**regret.** Mihi.
**regular.** Maʻamau.
**regulation.** Lula, kānāwai.
**rehearsal.** Hoʻomaʻamaʻa.
**reign.** Noho aliʻi, noho aupuni, noho, ʻai, kū, hoʻomalu.
**reins.** Kaula waha, laina kaula waha, ʻili.
**reject.** Hōʻole, haʻalele.
**rejoice.** ʻOli, hauʻoli, ʻoliʻoli.
**related.** Pili ʻohana.
**relationship.** Pili, pilina, pilikana.
**relative.** ʻOhana, pili koko.
**relax.** Kuʻu aku, hoʻonanea, luana.
**release.** Kala, kuʻu, hoʻokuʻu.
**relief.** Kōkua, kanaaho.
**religion.** Hoʻomana.
**religious.** Haipule.
**relish.** Pūpū, mea hōʻonoʻono. *To relish,* ʻono.
**rely.** Paulele, hilinaʻi.
**remain.** Koe, noho loa, waiho.
**remarkable.** Kamahaʻo, kupaianaha, kupanaha.
**remedy.** Lāʻau *(medicine)*.
**remember.** Hoʻomanaʻo, hoʻomaopopo.
**remind.** Hoʻomanaʻo mai, hoʻomaopopo, hoʻāla manaʻo.
**remnant.** Koena.
**remote.** Mamao.
**remove.** Lawe i kahi ʻē, lawe aku, kāpae.
**renew.** Hana hou, hoʻomau hou, hoʻomaka hou.
**rent.** Hoʻolimalima.
**reorganize.** Hoʻonohonoho hou, hoʻoponopono hou.
**repair.** Pāhonohono, kāpili, hana hou.
**repeat.** ʻŌlelo hou, hana hou.
**repent.** Mihi.

**replace.** Pani, pani hakahaka.
**report.** Hōʻike, palapala hōʻike; lono *(news)*.
**reporter.** Kākau nūpepa, ʻahaʻilono.
**representative.** Lunamakaʻāinana.
**reptile.** Moʻo. *See* snake.
**republic.** Lepupalika. *See* democracy.
**Republican.** Lepupalika, Repubalika.
**reputation.** Kūlana.
**request.** Noi, nonoi.
**requirement.** Koi.
**rescue.** Hoʻopakele, hoʻopalekana.
**research.** ʻImi i ke kumu; huli puke *(literary)*.
**resemble.** Kohu like, kohu, like, kū, kūlike, hoʻohālikelike.
**resent.** Ukiuki, mauhala.
**reserve.** Hoʻokaʻawale, hoʻopaʻa, mālama.
**reservoir.** Luawai, luawai hoʻokiʻo.
**residence.** Hale noho, kahi noho, nohona.
**resign.** Haʻalele, waiho.
**resist.** Kūʻē, pale, kipi, ʻalo, hōʻoleʻa.
**resolution.** ʻŌlelo hoʻoholo.
**resources.** Kumu waiwai.
**respect.** Mahalo, ʻihi, hōʻihi.
**respectfully.** Me ka mahalo, me ka pono.
**responsibility.** Kuleana, kuleana hana, koʻikoʻi.
**rest.** 1. *Stop work.* Maha, hoʻomaha, mahana. 2. *Remainder.* Koe, koena.
**restaurant.** Hale ʻaina.
**resting place.** Oʻioʻina, puʻuhoʻomaha, moena.
**restless.** Pīhole, hīʻō, ulukū.
**restrain.** Kāohi.
**rest room.** Lumi hoʻomaha.
**result.** Hopena, hope, hua.
**resurrection.** Ola hou, ala hou, kū hou ʻana.
**retail.** Kūʻai liʻiliʻi.
**retarded.** Lohi, lohiʻau.

**retire.** Hoʻomaha loa.
**retreat.** Neʻe hope, hoʻi hope.
**return.** Hoʻi hou, hoʻihoʻi.
**reveal.** Hōʻike, hōʻike ā maka.
**Revelations.** Hōʻike ʻAna *(Biblical)*.
**revenge.** Hoʻopaʻi, pānaʻi, hoʻopānaʻi, uku.
**reverend.** Kahu.
**reverent.** Haipule, manaʻo haipule, manaʻo hoʻoʻihiʻihi.
**reverse.** Huli, lole, hoʻi i hope.
**review.** Hoʻomaʻamaʻa hou.
**revise.** Hoʻoponopono hou, hoʻololi hou.
**revive.** Ola hou, hoʻōla hou, hoʻāla hou, hoʻūlu hou.
**revolt.** Kipi, hoʻokipi.
**revolting.** Hoʻopailua, liliha.
**revolution.** Hōʻauhuli ʻana, kipi ʻana.
**revolve.** Kaʻa, kaʻapuni, kakaʻa.
**revolver.** Pūpanapana.
**reward.** Makana, uku, uku pānaʻi.
**rheumatism.** Lumakika.
**rhythm.** Pana o ka mele, pā.
**rib.** Iwi ʻaoʻao *(human); nīʻau (of coconut leaf or umbrella)*.
**ribbon.** Lipine. *Typewriter ribbon,* lipine kikokiko.
**rice.** Laiki.
**rich.** 1. *Wealthy.* Waiwai, lako, kūʻonoʻono. 2. *Of food.* Liliha, momona, kelekele.
**rid.** Hoʻokaʻawale aku, kipaku, hoʻopau.
**riddle.** Nane, ʻōlelo nane, nane huna.
**ride.** Holo, holoholo; kau *(as on a horse)*.
**rider.** Holo lio, kau lio *(horseback)*.
**ridge.** Kualapa, kualono, lapa.
**ridgepole.** Kaupoku, kauhuhu.
**ridicule.** Hoʻohenehene, henehene, hoʻowahāwahā, pāhenehene, hōʻakaʻaka.
**ridiculous.** Kohu ʻole, kū i ka pāhenehene.
**rifle.** Pū laipala, pū laipela.
**right.** 1. *Direction,* ʻĀkau. 2.

*Correct.* Pololei, pono. **3.** *Privilege.* Kuleana. *Right-of-way,* pono ala hele.

**righteous.** Pono.

**rim.** Lihi, nihi, kaʻe, huʻa.

**rind.** ʻIli, ʻaluʻalu.

**ring. 1.** *Jewelry.* Komo, apo. **2.** *Circle.* Pōʻai, pōʻaha, lina. **3.** *To sound.* Kani, hoʻokani, kakani.

**rinse.** Mūmū *(mouth);* kaka *(fish, clothing).*

**riot.** Haunaele, anaina hoʻohaunaele.

**rip.** Nahae, nohae.

**ripe.** Pala.

**ripple.** ʻAle, ʻaleʻale, holu, lapalapa.

**rise. 1.** *To rise up.* Ala, piʻi, aea, ea, kau, hoʻāla. **2.** *An incline.* Piʻina, alana, kiʻekiʻena.

**risk.** Makaʻu, ʻaʻa, hoʻāʻo me ka nānā ʻole.

**ritual.** *See* ceremony.

**rival.** Hoa paio, hoa pāonioni.

**river.** Kahawai, muliwai, wai.

**roach.** ʻElelū.

**road.** Ala, alanui, ala hele.

**roar.** Wawā, wā, hoʻowā, uō, halulu, nākolokolo.

**roast.** ʻOma, loke, ʻōhinu.

**rob.** ʻAihue, pōā.

**robe.** ʻAʻahu, lole hoʻoluʻeluʻe.

**rock. 1.** *Stone.* Pōhaku, ʻā, ʻalā. **2.** *Motion.* Kulana, hoʻoluli, naue, hoʻonaue, kāhulihuli, paipai.

**rocket.** Kao lele.

**rocking chair.** Noho paipai.

**rocky.** Nui ka pōhaku, pōhaku.

**roll. 1.** *Turn.* Kakaʻa, kaʻa. **2.** *Bundle.* Lola, ʻōwili, ʻāpā, pōkaʻa. **3.** *Bread.* Palaoa liʻiliʻi.

**roll call.** Hea inoa.

**Roman Catholic.** Kakōlika Loma.

**romance. 1.** *Novel.* Kaʻao. **2.** *Love affair.* Pili hoʻoipoipo.

**roof.** Kaupoku, kaupaku.

**roofing.** Pili.

**room. 1.** *Part of a house.* Lumi, keʻena. **2.** *Space.* Hakahaka.

**roommate.** Hoa lumi.

**rooster.** Moa kāne.

**root. 1.** *Of plant.* Aʻa, mole, weli. **2.** *Source.* Kumu, mole. **3.** *Dig.* ʻEku, naku, haunaku, peu.

**rope.** Kaula.

**rosary.** Lōkālio, kolona, lei kolona.

**rose.** Loke, loke lani; roselani *(a red rose).*

**rotate.** Kaʻapuni, kaʻa, pōniu.

**rotten.** Pilau, palahū, ʻinoʻino, palahō, popopo.

**rough. 1.** *As terrain.* Hoʻolua, ʻālualua, mālualua, lualua. **2.** *As cloth or skin.* ʻŌkala, kala, kākala, pākala. **3.** *As sea or wind.* Pikipikiʻō, ʻaloʻaloʻa, loʻaloʻa. **4.** *Manner.* ʻŌkalakala, kākala, kalakala.

**round.** Poepoe, popohe, kūpoepoe.

**roundabout.** Hoʻolalau, lauwili.

**roundup.** Hoʻohuli pipi, hoʻā pipi.

**route.** Ala hele.

**row. 1.** *Paddle.* Hoe. **2.** *Line.* Pae, lālani, laina. **3.** *See* riot.

**rowboat.** Waʻapā.

**royal.** Aliʻi, lani.

**rub. 1.** *Friction.* ʻĀnai, kuai, kuolo, hoana. **2.** *Massage.* Lomi, kōmi, kaomi.

**rubber.** Laholio.

**rubbish.** ʻŌpala.

**rudder.** Hoe uli.

**rudder fish, needle fish.** Nenue.

**rude.** Kīkoʻolā.

**rug.** *See* carpet.

**ruin.** ʻInoʻino, pilikia, hōʻino, māʻinoʻino. *Hawaiian* heiau *ruins,* koena heiau.

**rule 1.** *A regulation.* Lula, loina, kānāwai. **2.** *To govern.* Noho aliʻi, kū, ʻai, noho aupuni.

**ruler. 1.** *Leader.* Aliʻi. **2.** *Measuring stick.* Lula.

**rum.** Lama, rama.

**rumble.** Halalū, nākuʻi, nākolo, kamumu, kani.

**rumor.** Lono wale.

**run. 1.** *Move swiftly.* Holo, hoho-

lo, hoʻoholo, kaʻaholo. 2. *Manage*. Hoʻoholo, kaʻa.
**runner.** 1. *Messenger.* Kūkini. 2. *Of a vine.* ʻAweʻawe, hāʻaweʻawe; kāili, kālī.
**rupture.** Laho heʻe.
**rural.** Kuaʻāina.

**rush.** Holo ʻino, holo ʻāwīwī, leleʻino, auau, pūlale.
**Russia.** Lukia, Rusia.
**rust.** Kūkaehao, lepohao.
**rustic.** Kuaʻāina.
**rye.** Lai, rai.

# S

**s.** *No Hawaiian term.*
**-s.** *The plural is shown in Hawaiian by the particles* nā, mau, wahi, kau, poʻe *before nouns, or by the zero-class possessives.*
**-ʼs.** *Same as* **of.**
**Sabbath.** Kāpaki, Sabati.
**sabotage.** Hoʻopōʻino malū.
**sack.** ʻEke, ʻekeʻeke.
**sacrament.** Kakelema, kakelemeneka *(Catholic);* kino o ka Haku *(other churches).*
**sacred.** Kapu, laʻa, ano, ʻihi.
**sacrifice.** Mōhai, kaumaha, hai.
**sad.** Kaumaha, luʻuluʻu.
**safe.** 1. *Not in danger.* Palekana, malu. 2. *Depository.* Pahu hao, pahu kālā.
**sail.** 1. *Verb.* Holo, hoʻoholo, kele, hoʻokele, holomoku. 2. *Noun.* Lā, peʻa.
**sailfish.** Aʻu.
**sailing vessel.** Moku peʻa.
**sailor.** Kelamoku, kela, holomoku, luina, ʻaukai.
**saint.** Kaneka, Saneta, Kāna.
**salad.** Lau ʻai.
**salary.** Uku hana.
**sale.** Kūʻai aku, kūʻai hoʻolilo, kūʻai hoʻēmi.
**salesman.** Kanaka kūʻai aku, kālepa.
**saliva.** Kuha, hāʻae, ʻae.
**salivate.** Kahe ka hāʻae.
**salmon.** Kāmano.
**salt.** Paʻakai. *To salt,* kāpī, kōpī, hoʻomiko. *Ocherous earth used to color and flavor salt,* ʻalaea. *Salt thus treated,* paʻakai ʻulaʻula.

**salutation.** Aloha, welina, weli, ʻanoʻai.
**salvation.** Ola, ola mau loa.
**Salvation Army.** Pūʻali Hoʻōla.
**same.** Like, like pū, kohu like, hoʻokahi. *Same as ever,* ʻoia mau nō. *The same father,* hoʻokahi nō makua kāne.
**Samoa.** Kāmoa.
**sanctuary.** Wahi hoʻāno.
**sand.** One.
**sandal.** Kāmaʻa hāwele, kāmaʻa hakahaka, pale wāwae.
**sandalwood.** ʻIliahi.
**sandbar.** Puʻe one.
**sand crab.** ʻŌhiki.
**sandpaper.** Pepa kalakala.
**sandpiper.** Upupā, ʻūlili.
**sandwich.** Nā palaoa me nā mea hōʻonoʻono i waena.
**sandy.** Oneone.
**San Francisco.** Kapalakiko.
**sap.** Kohu, wai, wale, wale hau, wai lāʻau.
**sarcastic.** Kīkoʻolā, pākīkē.
**sardine.** Makalē.
**sarong.** Pāʻū, kīkepa.
**sash.** Kāʻai, kāʻei.
**Satan.** Kākana, Satana.
**satin.** Pāhoehoe.
**satisfactory.** Pono, kūpono.
**Saturday.** Pōʻaono.
**sauce.** Kai.
**saucepan.** Pā hoʻolapalapa, ipu hao.
**saucer.** Pā liʻiliʻi.
**sausage.** Naʻaukake.
**savage.** Hihiu loa, mākaha.
**save.** 1. *As a life.* Ola, hoʻōla, hoʻopakele. *God save the king,* ola ka mōʻī i ke Akua.

2. *Keep.* Mālama, pūlama, ho'oili.

**saving.** *Thrifty.* Makauli'i, minamina.

**savings bank.** Panakō ho'āhu.

**savior.** Ho'ōla, palekana.

**saw. 1.** *Tool.* Pahi olo, olo. **2.** *Same as* **see.** *I saw,* ua 'ike au.

**say.** 'Ōlelo, ha'i, 'ī, wahi a, pēlā, mea mai.

**saying.** 'Ōlelo no'eau.

*Scaevola* **sp.** Naupaka.

**scale. 1.** *Measure.* Alapi'i. **2.** *Fish.* Unahi. *To scale,* unaunahi.

**scales.** *Balance.* Kaupaona, paona, ana paona.

**scalp.** 'Ili po'o. *To scalp,* lole.

**scandal.** Hana i wā 'ia.

**scar.** 'Ālina, linalina.

**scarce.** Kaka'ikahi, pānoanoa.

**scarf.** Lei 'ā'ī.

**scarlet fever.** Piwa 'ula'ula.

**scatter.** Ho'opuehu, lū, lūlū.

**sceptical.** Hilina'i 'ole, ho'omahuakala.

**schedule.** Papa kuhikuhi, papa hō'ike.

**scholarship. 1.** *Pursuit of knowledge.* Hana 'imi na'auao. **2.** *Student aid.* Waihona kōkua ho'ona'auao.

**school. 1.** *Educational.* Kula. **2.** *Of fish.* I'a kū, kū.

**schoolhouse.** Hale kula.

**schooner.** Moku, moku kia lua, kuna.

**science.** Akeakamai, hana 'imi na'auao, huli kanaka.

**scissors.** 'Ūpā.

**scold.** Nuku, ke'u, ho'okekē niho, huhū.

**scorch.** Kuni, pāpa'a wela, eina, pāwela.

**score.** Helu, 'ai.

**scorpion.** Mo'o-niho-'awa.

**Scotch.** Kekokia.

**scoundrel.** Lapuwale, pu'uwai 'ele'ele.

**scour.** Kuai, 'ānai, kuolo.

**scowl.** Ho'oku'eku'emaka.

**scramble.** Ho'ohuikau. *Scrambled eggs,* hua kai, hua pākā.

**scrap.** Huna, hakina, hunahuna, 'āpana li'ili'i.

**scrape.** Wa'u, wawa'u, wa'uwa'u, koe, kuai, kahi.

**scratch.** Walu, wawalu; helu *(as a hen).*

**scream.** 'Alalā, pū'alalā.

**screen.** Pākū, pālulu, ālai, ānai.

**screw.** Kui nao.

**screwdriver.** Kuikala, kala.

**Scriptures.** Palapala Hemolele.

**scrotum.** Laho.

**scum.** Hu'a, hu'ahu'a.

**sea.** Kai, moana.

**sea area.** Kai.

**seacoast.** Kahakai.

**sea cucumber.** Loli.

**sea gull.** Nēnē 'au kai *(poetic).*

**seal. 1.** *Emblem.* Kila. **2.** *Mammal.* 'Īlio-holo-i-ka-uaua.

**seam.** Ku'ina, ku'i, humu, humuna.

**search.** 'Imi, huli, 'imina, hulina.

**seashell.** Pūpū.

**seashore.** Kahakai, kapa kai.

**seasick.** Poluea, luea, ho'opapailua, 'ōlanalana.

**season. 1.** *Time.* Kau, wā, manawa. **2.** *Impart taste.* Hō'ono, ho'omiko.

**seat.** Noho, nohona, ho'onoho.

**sea urchin.** Wana, 'ina, hā'uke.

**seaward.** Makai, i kai, o kai.

**seaweed.** Limu. *Kinds:* kala, kohu, līpoa, 'a'ala'ula, 'ele'ele, līpe'e, līpe'epe'e, manauea, līpa'akai, pakele-a-wa'a.

**second.** Lua, kualua; kekona *(time unit).*

**secret.** Mea huna, huna, malū.

**secretary. 1.** *Clerical aid.* Kākau 'ōlelo. **2.** *High official.* Kuhina.

**secretary of interior.** Kuhina kālai'āina.

**secretary of state.** Kuhina moku-'āina.

**secret service.** 'Oihana kiu.

**section.** Paukū, moku, mokuna, 'āpana, mahele.

**secure.** Pa'a.

**seduce.** Ho'owalewale hewa, alaka'i hewa.

see. 'Ike, nānā.

seed. 'Ano'ano, hua.

seek. 'Imi, huli.

seen. 'Ike 'ia, kūmaka.

seer. Kāula, kilo, kuhikuhipu-
'uone, nānā ao, 'imi loa.

segregate. Ho'oka'awale.

seine. Hukilau, lau, 'upena kō
lau.

seize. Hopu, 'apo, lālau, kā'ili.

seldom. Kaka'ikahi.

select. Koho, wae, 'ohi.

self. Iho, kino, pono'ī, 'ōiwi.

selfish. 'Au'a, no'ono'o iāia wale
iho nō.

sell. Kū'ai aku, kālepa, ho'olilo.

semen. Keakea.

semester. Kau.

senate. 'Aha kenekoa.

senator. Kenekoa.

send. Ho'ouna, kēnā, ki'i,
kauoha.

senior. Mua, makua, hele mua,
hānau mua.

sennit. 'Aha.

sense. 1. *Faculty.* 'Ike. *Sense of
taste,* 'ike i ka 'ono. 2. *Meaning.*
Mana'o nui.

sensitive 1. *Perceptive.* 'Ike
ho'omaopopo. 2. *As to criticism.* 'Eha wale, ku'ia wale.

sensitive plant. Pua hilahila.

sentence. Māmala'ōlelo *(words),*
'ōlelo ho'opa'i *(penalty).*

separate. 1. *Adjective.* Ka'awale,
kau 'oko'a. 2. *Verb.* Ho'oka'a-
wale.

September. Kepakemapa.

sergeant. Kakiana.

series. Mahele, mo'o.

serious. Kūo'o.

sermon. Ha'i'ōlelo, ha'i a'o.

servant. Kanaka hana, kanaka
lawelawe, wahine hana.

serve. Lawelawe.

service. Lawelawe. *Church service,* hālāwai haipule. *Military
service,* 'oihana koa.

session. Kau.

set. Kau, ho'onoho, ho'omoe,
ku'u.

settle. Kau, mākū, ko'ana.

settlement. Kauhale.

seven. Hiku, 'ehiku, 'ahiku.

seventeen. 'Umi kūmāhiku, 'umi
kumamāhiku.

Seventh-day Adventist. Ho'o-
mana Pō'aono.

seventy. Kanahiku.

seventy-one. Kanahiku kūmākahi, kanahiku kumamākahi.

sever. 'Oki, moku.

several. Kekahi, kekahi mau.

severe. 'O'ole'a, 'a'aka.

sew. Humuhumu, hono, ku'i.

sewer. 'Auwai, kua, hā wai.

sewing machine. Mīkini humuhumu.

sex. *No Hawaiian term. Masculine sex,* keka kāne. *Feminine
sex,* keka wahine.

sexual intercourse. Ai, ei, hana
ma'i, moe, pi'i, panipani, aina.

shade. Malu, māmalu.

shadow. Aka, huaka, 'ūmalu.

shady. Malumalu.

shake. Naue, nāueue, lūlū, hō'o-
ni, ho'olulululi.

shall. E . . . ana, e.

shallow. Pāpa'u, hāpapa.

shame. Hilahila, waia.

shampoo. Holoi lauoho.

shape. 'Ano; hō'omo'omo *(verb).*

share. Mahele, pu'u; kea *(stocks).*

shark. Manō, lālākea, niuhi.

sharp. 'Oi, 'āwini, 'oi'oi.

sharpen. Ho'okala.

shatter. Wāwahi, nahā, nāhāhā,
kā.

shave. Kahi.

shawl. Kīhei.

she. *Same as* he.

shearwater. 'Ua'u kani, hō'io.

shed. 1. *Building.* Hale ho'āhu,
hale pupupu, hale kāmala. 2.
*Throw off.* Helele'i, ho'omalule.

sheep. Hipa.

sheet. Lau, papa. *Sheet of paper,*
'āpana pepa. *Bed sheet,* uhi
pela, hāli'i moe.

shelf. Haka, haka kau, papa.

shell. Pūpū, iwi.

shelter. Wahi lulu, wahi ho'omalu, hale pupupu.

**shepherd.** Kahu hipa.

**sheriff.** Mākaʻi nui, ilāmuku.

**shield.** Pālulu, pale.

**shiftless.** ʻAeʻa.

**shin.** Lapawāwae.

**shine.** Hulali, liko, ʻānapanapa, ʻalohi.

**ship.** Moku.

**shipmate.** Hoa waʻa, hoa holomoku.

**shipwreck.** Ili *(go aground)*, nāhāhā *(broken to bits)*.

**shirt.** Pālule, ʻahu.

**shiver.** Haʻukeke, naka, hulilī.

**shoal.** Hāpapa.

**shock.** Puoho, hikilele, hoʻolele hauli; loaʻa i ka uila *(electric)*.

**shoe.** Kāmaʻa. *Pair of shoes,* paʻa kāmaʻa.

**shoelace.** Lī kāmaʻa.

**shoot.** **1.** *Discharge.* Pana, kī. *Shoot with bow and arrow,* pana pua, pāpua. **2.** *Sprout.* Keiki, ʻao, ʻohā.

**shooting star.** Hōkū lele.

**shop.** Hale kūʻai *(store);* hale ʻoihana *(workshop).*

**shopping.** Kūʻai hele, mākaʻikaʻi hale kūʻai.

**shore.** Kahakai, kapa kai, kai, ʻae kai.

**short.** Pōkole, ʻekekeʻi, mūʻekekeʻi.

**shorten.** Hoʻopōkole.

**shorthand.** Kākau hua liʻiliʻi.

**shorts.** Lole wāwae ʻekekeʻi.

**shot.** Pōkā.

**shotgun.** Pū kī lū.

**shot-put.** Maika.

**should.** Pono e, pono ke.

**shoulder.** Poʻohiwi, hokua.

**shoulder blade.** Hoehoe, iwi hoehoe.

**shout.** ʻUā, hoʻōho, kani ka pihe.

**shove.** Pahu, kē, hou, kulaʻi.

**shovel.** Kopalā.

**show.** **1.** *Demonstrate.* Hōʻike, kuhikuhi. **2.** *Performance.* Hana keaka.

**shower.** Kuāua, ua nāulu, nāulu, kualau.

**shriek.** Pūʻalalā, alawī.

**shrimp.** ʻŌpae.

**shrine.** Heiau, haiau, ahu, koʻa, kūʻula.

**shrink.** Miki, hoʻohāiki.

**shudder.** Mania, manene, liha, liliha.

**shut.** Pani.

**shutter.** ʻŌlepelepe, ʻōpeʻapeʻa.

**shy.** Hilahila, ʻena.

**sick.** Maʻi.

**sickle.** Pahi kākiwi, pahi kekeʻe.

**sickly.** ʻŌmaʻimaʻi, maʻimaʻi.

**side.** ʻAoʻao, kūkulu, paia, kapa.

**sideburns.** ʻUmiʻumi pēheuheu.

**sidewalk.** Ala hele wāwae.

**sieve.** Kānana, kālana.

**sigh.** Nui ka hanu, nū, nāʻū, ʻū, ʻuhū.

**sight.** Nānaina, maka, hiʻohiʻona.

**sign.** Hōʻailona, ʻōuli; papa hōʻike *(as for a store).*

**signal.** Hōʻailona, peʻahi.

**signature.** Kākau inoa, pūlima.

**signboard.** Papa hōʻike.

**silent.** Hāmau, leo ʻole.

**silk.** Kilika, kalika.

**silly.** Kohu ʻole, ʻūlala.

**silver.** Kālā keʻokeʻo, kālā.

**silversword.** Hinahina, ʻāhinahina.

**similar.** Kohu like, ʻano like, like pū.

**simple.** Maʻalahi.

**sin.** Lawehala, hala, hewa.

**since.** **1.** *After.* Mahope mai. **2.** *Because.* No ka mea.

**sincere.** ʻOiaʻiʻo. *I am, yours sincerely,* ʻo au nō me ka ʻoiaʻiʻo.

**sing.** Mele, hīmeni, kani.

**singer.** Puʻukani, mea mele.

**single.** **1.** *One only.* Hoʻokahi, kahi. **2.** *Unmarried.* Male ʻole.

**sink.** **1.** *Descend.* Palemo, piholo. **2.** *Basin.* Kahi holoi pā.

**sinker.** Kēpau.

**sip.** Mūkī, mūkīkī.

**sir.** *No modern word; in old days as term of address:* ē kuʻu haku, ē kuʻu lani, *O my lord, O my royal one. Dear Sir (in letters),* aloha kāua.

**Sirius.** Hōkū-hoʻokele-waʻa, ʻAʻā.

**sisal.** Malina.

**sister.** **1.** *Sibling.* Kaikuaʻana *(older, of a female);* kaikaina *(younger, of a female);* kaikuahine *(of a male);* tita *(slang). Terms of address are frequently* kuaʻana, kaina, kuahine. **2.** *Nun.* Nuna, wilikina.

**sister-in-law.** Wahine, wahine makua, wahine ʻōpio *(of a male);* kaikoʻeke *(of a female);* punalua.

**sit.** Noho.

**site.** Kahua, wahi, kūlana.

**sitting hula.** Hula noho.

**situation.** Kūlana.

**six.** Ono, ʻeono, ʻaono.

**sixteen.** ʻUmi kūmāono, ʻumi kumamāono.

**sixty.** Kanaono.

**sixty-one.** Kanaono kūmākahi, kanaono kumamākahi.

**size.** Nui.

**skate.** Holo paheʻe.

**skeleton.** Kino iwi, iwi kanaka.

**sketch.** Kiʻi, kaha.

**skid.** Paheʻe.

**skilled.** Noʻeau, loea, mākaukau, akamai, ʻailolo, lolo, ʻōlohe. *Skilled labor,* hana lima ʻike.

**skin.** ʻIli.

**skip.** Lelele, lele.

**skipjack.** Aku.

**skirt.** Palekoki.

**skull.** Iwi poʻo, poʻo kanaka, pūniu.

**skunk.** ʻĪlio hohono.

**sky.** Lani.

**slack.** ʻAluʻalu.

**slack key.** Kī hōʻalu.

**slacks.** Lole wāwae.

**slander.** Holoholoʻōlelo, ʻaki, hoʻomāʻinoʻino.

**slang.** ʻŌlelo ʻeu hoʻohaku wale.

**slant.** Hiō. *"Slant" eyes,* maka lilio.

**slap.** Paʻi, hoʻopaʻi.

**slave.** Kauā.

**sled.** Hōlua, papa hōlua, kaʻa holo hau.

**sleep.** Moe, hiamoe.

**sleepless.** Hiaʻā, makahia, makalahia.

**sleepy.** Maka hiamoe.

**sleeve.** Lima.

**slender.** Wīwī.

**slice.** Poke, ʻāpana, kaha, pāpaʻa.

**slide.** Heʻe, paheʻe, holo.

**slime.** Wale, walewale.

**sling.** Maʻa.

**slip.** **1.** *Slide.* Heʻe, paheʻe, pakika, poholo. **2.** *Scion.* Lālā hoʻoulu. **3.** *Garment.* Muʻumuʻu.

**slipknot.** Pikoholo.

**slipper.** Kāmaʻa pale wāwae, pale wāwae.

**slippery.** Palaha, pakika, pakelo.

**slope.** Ihona, lapa, papali.

**slow.** Lohi.

**sly.** Maʻalea.

**small.** Iki, liʻi, liʻiliʻi, ʻuku, ʻuʻuku.

**smallpox.** Maʻi puʻupuʻu liʻiliʻi.

**smart.** **1.** *Intelligent.* Akamai. **2.** *Pain.* Liliʻu, welawela.

**smash.** Nahā, hoʻonahā, palahē.

**smell.** *Transitive verb.* Honi, honihoni. *See* **fragrant, stench.**

**smile.** Minoʻaka.

**smoke.** Uahi. *To smoke tobacco,* puhi paka.

**smooth.** Malino, paheʻe.

**smuggle.** Hoʻopae malū.

**snack.** ʻAi māmā, pūpū.

**snail.** Kamaloli, hīhīwai, wī, pūpū.

**snake.** Naheka, nahesa.

**snap.** **1.** *Break.* Haʻi, haki, uhaki, kepa. **2.** *Bite.* ʻAki, hae.

**snapper.** ʻUlaʻula, ʻōpakapaka.

**snare.** Hei, ʻahele, pahele, ʻūpiki, hihi.

**snarl.** **1.** *Growl, snap.* Nunulu, nanā, kekē niho. **2.** *Tangle.* Hihia.

**snatch.** Kāʻili, kāʻiliʻili, poʻi.

**sneeze.** Kihe.

**snore.** Nonō, hohō, ʻōlāʻolā ka ihu.

**snow.** Hau, hau kea.

**so.** **1.** *Similar.* Penei, pēlā. *That's so,* pēlā nō; ʻoiaʻiʻo kā hoʻi. *So* *do I,* 'o au pū. *Maybe so,* pēlā paha. **2.** *Therefore.* No laila.

**soak.** Ho'oma'ū, ho'opa'ū.

**soap.** Kopa; kopa pauka *(powdered soap),* kopa holoi *(wash soap).*

**soar.** Kīkaha, lele ho'olahalaha.

**society. 1.** *Club.* 'Ahahui, hui, hui malū, kalapu. **2.** *Companionship.* Launa 'ana.

**soft.** Palupalu, palu, nahe, nahenahe, hone.

**soil. 1.** *Noun.* Lepo. **2.** *Verb.* Ho'olepo.

**soldier.** Koa, pū'ali.

**solid.** Pa'a, pa'apū.

**solitary.** Mehameha, kakahi.

**solution. 1.** *Explanation.* Ha'ina, wehewehe 'ana, wehena, loa'a. **2.** *Liquid.* Wai pa'ipa'i.

**some.** Kekahi, wahi.

**someone.** Kekahi kanaka. *Someone else,* ha'i.

**somersault.** Kuwala, 'owala.

**something.** Kekahi mea.

**sometime.** Kekahi manawa.

**somewhat.** 'Ano, 'ō-.

**son.** Keiki kāne.

**song.** Mele, hīmeni.

**son-in-law.** Hūnōna kāne.

**soon.** Koke, auane'i, koe, eia aku.

**soothsayer.** Kilo lani, kuhikuhipu'uone, ha'i 'ōuli.

**sorcerer.** Kahuna, kahuna 'anā-'anā, kahuna ho'opi'opi'o.

**sorcery.** Hana kahuna, 'anā'anā, ho'ounauna, ho'opi'opi'o, kuni, hana aloha, kala aloha.

**sore.** 'Eha.

**sorrow.** Kaumaha.

**sorry.** Kaumaha, minamina. *I'm sorry,* kala mai ia'u.

**sort. 1.** *Kind.* 'Ano. **2.** *Select.* Wae, māwae, ho'oka'awale.

**soul.** 'Uhane.

**sound.** Leo, kani, pā, papā, wawā, 'uā, walo, puō.

**soup.** Kai, kupa.

**sour.** 'Awa, 'awa'awa, mala, malaia, mulemule, 'ī'ī.

**source.** Kumu, mole.

**south.** Hema.

**South America.** 'Amelika Hema.

**southeast.** Hikina hema.

**Southern Cross.** Hōkū-ke'a, Newa.

**South Pole.** Wēlau Hema.

**southwest.** Komohana hema.

**souvenir.** Mea ho'omana'o.

**space.** Lewa, haka.

**spade.** 'Ō'ō, peki.

**Spain.** Kepania, Sepania.

**Spaniard.** Paniolo.

**spare. 1.** *Save.* Ola, ho'ōla, kāpae. **2.** *Extra.* Keu, koe.

**spareribs.** Iwi 'ao'ao.

**spark.** Hunaahi.

**sparkle.** 'Ā, hulali, hulili.

**sparrow.** Manu li'ili'i.

**speak.** 'Ōlelo, wala'au.

**speaker.** Ha'i'ōlelo, luna ho'omalu.

**spear.** Ihe, ihe pahe'e, pololū.

**special.** Mea i wae 'ia, kūikawā.

**species.** Lāhui.

**speckled.** Kikokiko, pulepule.

**spectacles.** Makaaniani.

**speech.** 'Ōlelo, ha'i'ōlelo.

**speed.** 'Āwīwī, māmā, wikiwiki.

**spell.** Pela, kepela.

**spend.** Ho'olilo, ho'omauna.

**spider.** Lanalana, nananana, ku'uku'u, pūnāwelewele.

**spider web.** Hihi pūnāwelewele, 'upena nananana.

**spill.** Hanini, nini.

**spin.** Niniu, ho'oniniu.

**spine.** Iwikuamo'o, kuamo'o.

**spirit.** 'Uhane, wailua, akua.

**spirits.** Wai 'ona.

**spiritual.** Pili 'uhane, mana, lani.

**spit.** *Expectorate.* Kuha, pupuhi.

**spite.** Na'au kopekope, mauhala. *In spite of,* i loko o.

**splash.** Pakī.

**splendor.** Nani, nani kamaha'o, hinuhinu.

**splinter.** Māmala.

**split.** Wāhi.

**spoil. 1.** *Decay.* Pilau, pilapilau, 'ino, mā'ino'ino. **2.** *Pamper.* Pai, mailani, pailani, ho'okamalani. **3.** *Booty.* Waiwai kaua, loa'a.

spool. Pōka'a.

spoon. Puna.

sport. Mea pā'ani ho'oikaika kino.

spot. Kiko.

spotted. Kikokiko, pākikokiko, panini'o, kīnohi, pulepule.

sprain. Māui, 'anu'u.

spray. 'Ehu, ehu, 'ehu kai, huna kai, hune kai.

spread. Hāli'i, laha.

spring. 1. *Water source.* Puna, kumu wai, māpuna. 2. *Season. No Hawaiian word; terms sometimes used:* kupulau, la'a ulu. 3. *Coil.* Pilina.

sprinkle. 1. *Scatter.* Pīpī, kāpīpī, kūpīpī. 2. *Rain.* Ua kilikili, ua kilikilihune.

sprout. Kupu.

spry. 'Eleu.

spy. Kiu.

squander. 'Uha'uha, ho'omāunauna, lū.

square. Huinahā, huinahā kaulike, kuea.

squash. Pū, ipu pū, pala'ai.

squat. 'Ōku'u.

squeak. 'Uī'uī, kakani.

squeeze. 'Uī, 'ōpā, kaomi, lomi, 'ūmi'i.

squid. Mūhe'e. *See* octopus.

squint. Pipī, pipipi, maka pili.

squirm. Pīhole, hole, laumilo.

squirrel fish. 'Ū'ū, 'ala'ihi.

squirt. Pakī, 'ūpī, kī.

stab. Hou, 'ō.

stadium. Kahua pā'ani.

stage. Kahua.

stagger. Kunewa, kūnewanewa.

staghorn fern. Uluhe.

stain. Kohu, kāpala, hauka'e, kīkohu, palahe'a.

stairs. Alapi'i, 'anu'u.

stake. 1. *Staff.* Pahu. 2. *Wager.* Pili.

stalk. 1. *Stem.* Hā, 'au, kū'au, ko'o. 2. *See* follow.

stamp. 1. *Postage.* Po'oleka. 2. *Imprint.* Hō'ailona pa'i.

stand. 1. *Upright position.* Kū, kukū, kūlia. 2. *Table.* Pākaukau.

stanza. Paukū.

star. Hōkū.

starboard. 'Ao'ao 'ākau.

starch. Pia.

stare. Nānā pono, haka pono, hō'a'ā maka.

starfish. Pe'a, pe'ape'a, 'ōpe'ape'a, hōkū kai.

start. Ho'omaka, maka hou.

startle. Ho'opū'iwa.

starve. Make pōloli, ho'ōki 'ai.

state. 1. *Condition.* 'Ano, kūlana, kū. 2. *Political unit.* Moku'āina. 3. *To say.* Ha'i, ha'i mana'o.

statement. 'Ōlelo, ha'ina. *Bank statement,* hō'ike panakō.

station. Hale ho'olulu. *Stations of the cross,* alanui o ke ke'a.

stationary. Pa'a, mau.

stationery. Kālana, kānana.

statue. Ki'i, ki'i kālai 'ia.

stay. Noho, kū.

steadfast. Kūpa'a, 'onipa'a, pa'a.

steak. Pipi kō'ala, pipi palai.

steal. 'Aihue.

steam. Māhu.

steam bath. Pūlo'ulo'u.

steamship. Mokuahi, mokumāhu.

steel. Kila.

steep. Kūnihinihi, kūnihi, kū, laumania.

steeple. Pū'o'a.

steer. 1. *To direct.* Uli, ho'okele, kia, 2. *Male bovine.* Pipi po'a.

stem. *Same as* stalk.

stench. Pilau, pilapilau, 'ōhonohono, hohono, 'ōpilopilo, hauna, maea.

stenographer. Kākau hua li'ili'i.

step. 1. *Foot movement.* Ke'ehi, ka'i, ne'e. 2. *On stairway.* Alapi'i, 'anu'u.

stepfather. Makua kāne kōlea.

stepmother. Makuahine kōlea.

sterile. Pā, hua 'ole.

stevedore. Po'olā.

stew. Kupa, kū.

steward. Kuene, 'ā'īpu'upu'u, pu'ukū, kanaka lawelawe.

**stewardess.** Wahine lawelawe, kuene wahine.

**stick. 1.** *Wood.* Lā'au. *See* **digging stick. 2.** *To adhere.* Pili.

**sticky.** Pipili, ho'opili.

**stiff.** 'O'ole'a, mālo'elo'e, 'ainā, mākū.

**stiff neck.** 'Ā'īkū, 'ā'ī 'o'ole'a, 'ā'ī uaua.

**stifle.** 'Umi, 'u'umi.

**still. 1.** *Motionless, silent.* Mālie, lana, wailana, ho'omalu. **2.** *Yet.* Na'e, koe, ā hiki i kēia wā. **3.** *Distilling apparatus.* Ipu hao puhi 'ōkolehao.

**stilts, stilt** *(bird).* Kukuluae'o, ae'o.

**stimulant.** Mea ho'oikaika, mea ho'opaipai.

**stimulate.** Ho'oulu, ho'oikaika, hō'eu'eu, ho'opaipai, ho'olalelale.

**sting.** Kiki, kui, 'ō, 'o'oi.

**sting ray.** Hīhīmanu, lupe.

**stingy.** Pī, 'au'a.

**stir.** 'Oni, kāwili.

**stirrup.** Ke'ehi, 'ili ke'ehi, hao ke'ehi.

**stitch.** Humu, ku'i, hono.

**stocking.** Kākini.

**stomach.** 'Ōpū.

**stone.** Pōhaku, 'ili'ili, 'alā, 'a'ā, pāhoehoe. *Precious stone,* pōhaku makamae.

**stool.** Noho li'ili'i, paepae.

**stoop.** Kūlou, kūnou.

**stop.** *Cease.* Ho'opau; ho'oku'u *(disperse);* waiho *(leave off);* kū *(as a car).* Stop it! Uoki! *Stop the car,* ho'okū i ke ka'a.

**stopper.** 'Umoki, popo'i, mea ho'opa'a, pani.

**store. 1.** *Noun.* Hale kū'ai. **2.** *Verb.* Hō'ili'ili, ho'āhu.

**storehouse.** Hale ho'āhu, hale ahu waiwai, hale ukana.

**stork.** Kikonia, pia.

**storm.** 'Ino.

**story. 1.** *Narrative.* Mo'olelo, ka'ao. **2.** *See* **lie, 2. 3.** *Floor.* Papahele, papa.

**stout.** Pu'ipu'i, poupou.

**stove.** Kapuahi.

**straight.** Pololei; kālole *(as hair).*

**straighten.** Ho'opololei.

**strain. 1.** *Filter.* Kānana, kālana. **2.** *Exert.* Ho'oikaika, kōhi.

**strait.** Kōwā, kaikōwā.

**strand.** *Fiber.* Ma'awe, awe, mō'ali.

**stranded.** Ili.

**strange.** 'Ē, 'ano 'ē, mea 'ē, kupaianaha, kupanaha, ha'oha'o.

**stranger.** Malihini, kanaka 'ē, mea 'ē.

**strangle.** 'Umi, 'u'umi, kā'awe.

**strap.** Kaula 'ili.

**straw.** Mau'u malo'o.

**strawberry.** 'Ōhelo papa.

**stray.** 'Auana, 'ae'a, holoholo.

**streak.** Wana, no'a.

**streaked.** Mā'oki'oki, ni'o, kāni'o, 'awe'awe'a.

**stream.** *Same as* **river.**

**street.** Alanui.

**strength.** Ikaika.

**stress.** Ko'iko'i, ho'okālele; kālele mana'o; kālele leo *(diacritical mark).*

**stretch.** Kīko'oko'o.

**stretcher.** Mānele, moe ho'olewa.

**strike. 1.** *Hit.* Ku'i, pepehi, hau, hahau, uhau, kā. **2.** *Work stoppage.* 'Olohani.

**string.** Kaula, aho, 'aha.

**string figure.** Hei.

**stripe.** Kaha.

**striped.** 'Ōni'oni'o, kahakaha.

**stroke. 1.** *Blow.* Hāuna, pā. *Breast stroke in swimming,* 'au umauma. **2.** *To touch lightly.* Kahi, hamo. **3.** *Sudden attack.* Huki, kūhewa, ulupō.

**strong.** Ikaika, mahi, wīkani, lawakua, ho'olehua.

**struggle.** Paio, 'ā'ume'ume.

**stubborn.** Pa'akikī, po'o pa'a, lae pa'a, kananuha.

**stuck.** Pa'a.

**student.** Haumāna.

**studio.** Hālau, pā hula, ke'ena.

**studious.** Ho'opa'a ha'awina, puni ho'opa'a ha'awina.

**study.** Ho'opa'a ha'awina.

**stumble.** Ku'ia ka wāwae, 'ōku-pe.

**stump.** 'Ōmuku.

**stupid.** Hūpō, wa'awa'a.

**stutter.** 'Ū'ū, mā'ū'ū, 'ā'ā.

**stylish.** Kū i ke kaila, kū i ke paikini.

**subject. 1.** *Citizen.* Maka'āinana, kanaka. **2.** *Topic.* Kumuhana, kumumana'o.

**subscribe.** Kākau inoa.

**subtract.** Ho'olawe.

**suburb.** Hu'a.

**succeed. 1.** *Accomplish.* Holo-mua, holopono, kō, loa'a. **2.** *Follow.* Ukali, pani, hahai.

**such.** Like.

**suck.** Omo, omomo, mūkī.

**suddenly.** 'Emo 'ole, hikiwawe.

**sue.** Ho'opi'i.

**suffer.** 'Eha'eha.

**sugar.** Kōpa'a.

**sugarcane.** Kō.

**sugar mill.** Wili kō, hale wili kō.

**sugar plantation.** Mahi kō.

**suggest.** Ho'opuka mana'o, ho'olale.

**suit. 1.** *Clothing.* Pa'alole. **2.** *Court action.* Ho'opi'i, hihia.

**suitable.** Kūpono, kū, kohu.

**suitcase.** Paiki.

**summer.** Kau, kau wela.

**summit.** Wēkiu, piko, po'o.

**summon.** Ki'i, kēnā, kāhea, kauoha.

**sun.** Lā.

**sunburned.** Pāpa'a lā.

**Sunday.** Lāpule.

**Sunday school.** Kula Kāpaki.

**sunken.** Po'opo'o, napo'o.

**sunrise.** Pukana lā, puka 'ana o ka lā.

**sunset.** Napo'o 'ana o ka lā.

**sunshine.** Pā 'ana a ka lā.

**superintendent.** Haku hana, luna nui. *School superintendent,* kahu kula nui.

**supermarket.** Mākeke nui.

**supervisor.** Luna, luna ho'opo-nopono, luna kia'i.

**supper.** 'Aina ahiahi, pā'ina ahi-ahi.

**supplies.** Lako, ukana, pono.

**support.** Kāko'o, kōkua.

**suppose.** Mahu'i, kuhi, mana'o.

**suppress.** Kaomi.

**Supreme Court.** 'Aha Ho'okolo-kolo Ki'eki'e.

**sure.** 'Oia'i'o. *See also* **certain, 2.**

**surf.** Nalu. *To surf,* he'e nalu.

**surface.** 'Ili, 'iliwai, papa.

**surfboard.** Papa he'e nalu.

**surgeon.** Kauka kaha.

**surgeonfish.** Kala, 'api, kole, palani, manini.

**surprise.** Pū'iwa, ho'opū'iwa, ho'oha'oha'o.

**surrender.** Hā'awipio, hā'ulepio.

**surround.** Ka'apuni, ho'opuni.

**survey.** Ana.

**suspect.** Ho'ohuoi, mahu'i.

**swallow. 1.** *Ingest.* Ale, moni. **2.** *Bird.* Manu 'io'io, kualo.

**swamp.** Pohō, naele, kele.

**swear. 1.** *Vow.* Ho'ohiki. **2.** *See* **curse.**

**sweat.** Hou.

**sweater.** Kueka.

**sweep.** Pūlumi, kāhili.

**sweet.** Momona.

**sweetheart.** Ipo, aloha, huapala, hoa.

**sweet potato.** 'Uala.

**swelling.** Pehu, hū.

**swift.** *Same as* **fast, 1.**

**swim.** 'Au.

**swing.** Lele, lele koali, kālewa.

**sword.** Pahi kaua.

**swordfish.** A'u.

**symbol.** Hō'ailona.

**sympathy.** Aloha menemene.

**syphilis.** Kaokao.

# T

**t.** *No Hawaiian term.*
**table.** Pākaukau.
**tablecloth.** Uhi pākaukau, pale pākaukau.
**tablet.** Kālana kākau.
**taboo.** Kapu.
**tag. 1.** *Game.* 'Io, pio. **2.** *Symbol, label.* Hō'ailona, mekala *(as for a dog).*
**Tahiti.** Kahiki.
**tail.** Huelo *(of animal);* hi'u *(of fish and other sealife);* puapua, pupua *(of birds);* pola *(of a kite).*
**tailor.** Kela, kela lole.
**take.** Lawe, lawe aku, hopu, loa'a. *Take off,* kala, wehe, unuhi, ho'ohemo.
**tale.** Mo'olelo, ka'ao.
**talk.** 'Ōlelo, kama'ilio; wala'au *(colloquial).*
**talkative.** Wala'au wale, 'ama.
**tall.** Loa, loloa *(as a person);* ki'eki'e *(as a hill).*
**tame.** Laka, ho'olaka.
**tangle.** Hihia, ho'ohei, kāhihi.
**tank.** Pahu.
**tanned.** Pāpa'a lā.
**tapa.** Kapa.
**tapioca.** Kapioka.
**tar.** Kā, kēpau.
**tardy.** Lohi, li'u.
**target.** Māka, hō'ailona.
**taro.** Kalo.
**tart. 1.** *Pie.* Pai. **2.** *Sour.* 'Awa-'awa.
**taste.** *Verb.* Ho'ā'o.
**tasteless.** Ko'eko'e, hūkākai.
**tasty.** 'Ono.
**tattler.** 'Ūlili.
**tattoo.** Kākau.
**tavern.** Hale inu lama, hale 'aina.
**tax.** 'Auhau.
**taxi.** Ka'a ho'olimalima, ka'a 'ōhua.
**tea.** Kī.
**teach.** A'o, kula.
**teacher.** Kumu, kumu a'o, kumu kula.
**teacup.** Kī'aha kī, pola kī.

**teahouse.** Hale inu kī.
**teakettle.** Ipu kī *(common term),* kikila kī.
**team.** Hui, 'ao'ao.
**teapot.** Ipu kī, kikila kī.
**tear. 1.** *Weeping.* Waimaka. **2.** *Sunder.* Hae, nahae, haehae.
**tease.** Ho'ohenehene, ho'ohene, ho'ohaehae.
**teeth.** Niho.
**teetotaler.** Hō'ole lama.
**telegram.** Kelekalama.
**telephone.** Kelepona. *To telephone,* kelepona, kāhea.
**telescope.** 'Ohe nānā, aniani ho'onui 'ike.
**tell.** Ha'i, ha'ina, hō'ike, 'ōlelo.
**temper.** Na'au, 'ano, 'ano o ka na'au.
**temperature.** Anu, wela.
**temple. 1.** *Edifice.* Luakini, heiau. **2.** *Anatomical.* Maha.
**temporary.** Kūikawā, no ka manawa pōkole.
**tempt.** Ho'owalewale.
**ten.** 'Umi.
**tenant.** Hoa'āina, mea ho'olimalima.
**tender.** Palupalu *(as meat).*
**tennis.** Kenika.
**tent.** Hale lole, hale pe'a.
**tentacle.** 'Awe.
**tenure.** Kuleana.
**term. 1.** *Period of time.* Kau, mahele manawa, wā. **2.** *Expression.* Inoa, hua 'ōlelo.
**terminal.** *Station.* Hale ho'olulu.
**terminate.** Ho'opau, ho'ōki.
**termite.** Naonao lele, huhu.
**tern.** Noio, 'eki'eki.
**terrible.** Weliweli, kau ka weli.
**terrify.** Ho'oweli, ho'oweliweli, ho'omaka'u.
**territory.** Kelikoli.
**test.** Hō'ike.
**testament.** Kauoha. *Last will and testament,* palapala kauoha, palapala ho'oilina. *Old Testament,* Kauoha Kahiko. *New Testament,* Kauoha Hou.

**testicles.** Hua, huahua.
**testify.** Hōʻike, haʻi manaʻo.
**than.** Mamua o.
**thank.** Mahalo, hoʻomaikaʻi.
**Thanksgiving Day.** Lā Hoʻomaikaʻi.
**that.** Kēlā, lā *(at a distance);* kēnā, nā *(near the person addressed);* ia, ua . . . lā. *That way,* pēlā. *Is that so?* Pēlā anei?
**thatch.** Ako, pili.
**the.** Ka, ke *(singular);* nā *(plural).*
**theater.** Keaka.
**their.** Kō lāua, kā lāua, kō lākou, kā lākou, o lāua, a lāua, o lākou, a lākou.
**theirs.** No lāua, no lākou, na lāua, na lākou.
**them.** Iā lāua, iā lākou.
**then.** Ā laila, malaila, i laila.
**therefore.** No laila, no ia mea.
**thermometer.** Kelemomeka, ana wela, mea ana wela.
**these.** Kēia mau, ua . . . nei.
**they.** Lāua, lākou.
**thick.** Mānoanoa.
**thicket.** Ōpū nāhelehele.
**thief.** ʻAihue.
**thigh.** ʻŪhā.
**thighbone.** Iwi hilo.
**thimble.** Komo, komo humuhumu.
**thimbleberries.** ʻĀkala.
**thin.** 1. *As the body.* Wīwī, emi. 2. *As cloth, paper.* Lahi, lahilahi.
**thing.** Mea.
**think.** Manaʻo, noʻonoʻo.
**third.** Hapakolu, kolu.
**thirst.** Make wai.
**thirteen.** ʻUmi kūmākolu, ʻumi kumamākolu.
**thirtieth.** Kanakolu.
**thirty-one.** Kanakolu kūmākahi.
**this.** Kēia, ia, ʻoia, nei.
**thorn.** Kukū, ʻoiʻoi, kākala.
**thorough.** Pau pono, pila pono.
**those.** Kēlā mau, ua . . . lā.
**thou.** ʻOe.
**though.** I loko o. *As though,* mehe.
**thought.** Manaʻo, noʻonoʻo.
**thousand.** Kaukani.

**thread.** Lopi.
**threadfish.** Moi.
**threat.** ʻŌlelo hoʻoweliweli.
**three.** Kolu, ʻekolu, ʻakolu.
**three-fourths.** ʻEkolu hapahā.
**thrifty.** Makauliʻi.
**thrill.** Kapalili ka houpo.
**throat.** Puʻu, puʻumoni.
**throb.** Koni, konikoni, kapalili.
**throne.** Noho aliʻi.
**through.** 1. *Finished.* Pau. 2. *In.* Ma, ma loko o.
**throw.** Nou, hoʻolei, pehi, lū.
**thrush.** Kāmaʻo, ʻōmaʻo, ʻāmaui.
**thumb.** Manamana lima nui.
**thunder.** Hekili.
**Thursday.** Pōʻahā.
**thus.** Pēlā, pēia, pe, penei.
**ti.** Kī.
**ticket.** Kikiki, likiki.
**tickle.** Hoʻomāneʻoneʻo.
**ticklish.** Maneʻo.
**tidal wave.** Kai eʻe.
**tide.** Au, kai. *Low tide,* kai make, kai maloʻo. *Rising tide,* kai piʻi, kai ea. *High tide,* kai nui, kai piha.
**tie.** 1. *To bind.* Hīkiʻi, nīkiʻi, hākiʻi, nākiʻi, mūkiʻi, lawa, hele, hoʻopaʻa, hoa, lī, paʻi, hīpuʻu. 2. *A draw.* Paʻi, paʻi wale, paʻi ā paʻi.
**tight.** Pili pono, likiliki.
**till.** *See* until.
**time.** Wā, manawa, au; hola *(o'clock).*
**timekeeper.** Kikolā.
**timetable.** Papa kuhikihi, papa helu kaʻaahi.
**timid.** Makaʻu, hilahila, hoʻopē.
**tin.** Kini, keleawe, piula.
**tinkle.** Kani, wī, ō.
**tiny.** ʻUʻuku, ʻuku liʻi.
**tip.** 1. *Top.* Wēkiu, wēlau, ʻēlau. 2. *To tilt.* Kāhulihuli. 3. *Gratuity.* Uku lawelawe.
**tired.** Luhi, māluhiluhi.
**title.** 1. *Rank.* Kūlana. 2. *Right.* Kuleana. 3. *Heading.* ʻInoa, poʻo.
**to.** I, iā, iō; ā, ā hiki i.
**toad.** Poloka.

**toast. 1.** *Bread.* Palaoa ho'opā-pa'a. **2.** *Drinking.* Inu ho'omai-ka'i.

**tobacco.** Paka.

**today.** Kēia lā.

**toe.** Manamana wāwae.

**toenail.** Mai'ao, mānea o ka manamana wāwae.

**together.** Pū.

**toilet.** Lua, wahi ho'opau pili-kia.

**toilet paper.** Pepa hāleu.

**tolerant.** Mana'o laulā.

**tomato.** 'Ōhi'a, 'ōhi'a haole, kamako.

**tomb.** Hale kupapa'u, lua kupapa'u, ilina.

**tomorrow.** 'Apōpō.

**ton.** Kana, kona.

**tone.** Leo, kani o ka leo.

**tongue.** Alelo, elelo.

**tonight.** Kēia pō.

**too. 1.** *Also.* Kekahi, ho'i. *Me too,* 'o au pū. **2.** *Excessive.* Loa, nui loa, keu.

**tool.** Mea hana, mea pa'ahana.

**tooth.** Niho.

**toothache.** Niho hu'i.

**toothbrush.** Palaki niho.

**toothpick.** Lā'au 'ōhikihiki niho.

**top. 1.** *Uppermost.* Wēkiu, wēlau. **2.** *Toy.* Hū, 'ōniu, 'ōka'a.

**topic.** *See* **subject, 2.**

**torch.** Lama, lamakū.

**torment.** Hō'eha'eha.

**torture.** Ho'omāinoino.

**toss.** Ho'olei, kiola.

**total.** Huina, huina helu, heluna.

**touch.** Pā, ho'opā, pili.

**tough.** Pa'akikī, māuaua, uaua.

**tour.** Ka'apuni, ka'ahele. *Tour group,* po'e māka'ika'i like.

**tourists.** Po'e māka'ika'i, mali-hini māka'ika'i, malihini.

**towel.** Kāwele.

**tower.** 'Ale'o, pū'o'a.

**town.** Kūlanakauhale, kaona.

**toy.** Mea pā'ani, milimili.

**track.** Meheu, kapua'i, mō'ali.

**trade. 1.** *Barter.* Kālepa. **2.** *Occupation.* 'Oihana, 'oihana hana lima.

**tradition.** Nā hana a ka wā kahi-ko.

**traffic.** Ne'e 'ana i ke alahele.

**tragic.** Kaumaha loa.

**trail.** Ala, ala hele.

**train. 1.** *Teach.* A'o, ho'oma'a-ma'a. **2.** *See* **railroad.**

**trait.** Welo, ēwe.

**traitor.** Kumakaia.

**transfer.** Ho'olilo, ho'īli.

**transform.** Loli.

**translate.** Unuhi, unihi 'ōlelo.

**translator.** Mea unuhi, unuhi 'ōle-lo.

**transport.** Halihali, lawe.

**trap.** 'Ūmi'i, 'ūpiki, pahele.

**trash.** 'Ōpala.

**travel.** Ka'ahele, ka'apuni, hua-ka'i hele, huaka'i.

**tray.** Pā halihali.

**treachery.** Kumakaia, 'āpiki, 'ūpiki.

**tread.** Hehi, hehihehi, ke'ehi.

**treason.** Kipi.

**treasure.** Mea makamae.

**treasurer.** Pu'ukū.

**treasury.** Waihona, waihona wai-wai.

**treat. 1.** *Attend to.* Lapa'au, hana. **2.** *Pleasure.* Mea e hoihoi ai, mea ho'ohau'oli. *My treat,* na'u e uku.

**treaty.** Palapala 'aelike.

**tree.** Lā'au, kumulā'au, kumu.

**tremble.** Ha'alulu, kapalili.

**trepang.** Loli.

**trespass.** Komohewa, komo wale, 'ae'a, kahakū, 'a'e kū.

**trial.** Ho'okolokolo.

**triangle.** Huinakolu.

**tribe.** Lāhui.

**tribute.** Ho'okupu, uku, 'auhau.

**trick.** Hana ma'alea, 'āpiki, hana kolohe.

**trickle.** Kahe, kulu.

*Tridacna.* 'Ōlepe nui.

**trifle.** Mea 'ole, mea iki.

**triggerfish.** Humuhumu.

**trinity.** Kahikolu.

**trio.** Pūkolu.

**trip. 1.** *Voyage.* Huaka'i. **2.** *Stumble.* 'Ōkupe.

**triple.** Kaukolu.
**trite.** Pākūwā.
**triumph.** Lanakila.
**troll.** *Verb.* Hī. *To troll for bonito,* hī aku.
**troops.** Pū'ali koa.
**trophy.** Hō'ailona lanakila.
**tropicbird.** Koa'e.
**trouble.** Pilikia, pōpilikia.
**trough.** Holowa'a.
**troupe.** Hui. *Hula troupe,* pā hula.
**trousers.** Lole wāwae.
**truck.** Kalaka.
**true.** 'Oia'i'o.
**trumpet.** Pū, pū ho'okani.
**trumpet fish.** Nūnū, nuhu.
**trunkfish.** Pahu, moa, moamoa.
**trust.** Hilina'i, kālele, paulele.
**trustee.** Kahu waiwai.
**truth.** 'Oia'i'o.
**try.** Ho'ā'o.
**tub.** Kapu.
**tuber.** Hua.
**tuberculosis.** Ma'i-'ai-ake, akepau, hōki'i.
**tuberose.** Kupaloke.
**Tuesday.** Pō'alua.
**tug-of-war.** Hukihuki, pā'ume-'ume.

**tuna.** 'Ahi, aku, kawakawa, hi'uwīwī.
**tune.** Leo, leo mele.
**tunnel.** Ana puka, lua pao, alapao.
**turn.** 1. *Move.* Huli; kā *(to turn a jump rope).* 2. *Time.* Manawa. *My turn,* ko'u manawa.
**turtle.** Honu.
**turtledove.** Kuhukukū.
**tusk.** Niho, ku'i.
**twelve.** 'Umi kūmālua, 'umi kumamālua.
**twenty.** Iwakālua.
**twenty-one.** Iwakālua kūmākahi, iwakālua kumamākahi.
**twice.** Pālua, lua, 'elua, 'alua, 'elua manawa.
**twilight.** Mōlehu.
**twin.** Māhoe, māhana.
**twinkle.** 'Imo, 'amo.
**twist.** Wili, ka'awili, lauwili, milo.
**two.** Lua, 'elua, 'alua.
**type.** 1. *Kind.* 'Ano. 2. *Print.* Hua, hua ho'onoho. *To type,* kikokiko.
**typewriter.** Mīkini kikokiko hua.
**typhoid.** Piwa ho'onāwaliwali.
**typist.** Kikokiko hua.

# U

**u.** 'Ū.
**ugly.** Pupuka.
**ukulele.** 'Ukulele.
**ulcer.** Pūhā, pūhō, hēhē. *Stomach ulcer,* 'ōpū pūhā.
**umbilical cord.** Piko.
**umbrella.** Māmalu, loulu.
**umpire.** 'Uao.
**un-.** 'Ole, hiki 'ole.
**unanimous.** Mana'o lōkahi.
**unbelieving.** Hilina'i 'ole, maloka.
**uncertain.** Kānalua, kūlanalana, kūnānā.
**uncle.** Makua kāne, 'anakala.
**unclean.** Ma'ema'e 'ole, haumia, kāpulu, hawa, pe'a.
**uncomfortable.** 'Olu'olu 'ole, ho'o'iha'iha.

**uncomplaining.** Leo 'ole, ho'ohalahala 'ole.
**unconditional.** Kaupalena 'ole 'ia.
**unconscious.** Pau ka 'ike, pau ka lohe.
**unconstitutional.** Kū'ē kumukānāwai.
**under.** Lalo, malalo, i lalo.
**underdrawers.** Palema'i.
**underline.** Kaha lalo.
**underneath.** Malalo iho.
**undershirt.** Pale'ili.
**understand.** Maopopo, ho'omaopopo. *I understand,* maopopo ia'u; ho'omaopopo au.
**undertaker.** Kanaka ho'olewa.
**undress.** Wehe i ka 'a'ahu.

**unethical.** Kū ʻole i nā lula maikaʻi.

**unfaithful.** Kūpaʻa ʻole, moekolohe, ʻauana.

**unfasten.** Wehe, hoʻohemo.

**unfold.** Lole.

**unfortunate.** Pōʻino, pōpilikia.

**unfriendly.** Laulauna ʻole.

**unhappy.** Kaumaha.

**uniform.** 1. *Dress.* Makalike, paʻalole makalike. 2. *Similar.* Kohu like, like.

**unimportant.** Mea ʻole.

**union.** Hui, pilina; uniona *(labor).*

**unique.** Lua ʻole, laha ʻole.

**unite.** Hui, hui pū, pili pū, kāpili, hoʻohui.

**united.** Hui pū ʻia, huihui, hui kahi.

**United Nations.** Nā Lāhui Huipū.

**United States of America.** ʻAmelika Hui, ʻAmelika Huipū.

**unity.** Lōkahi, kuʻikahi.

**universe.** Ao holoʻokoʻa.

**university.** Kulanui.

**unless.** Ke ʻole, inā ʻaʻole.

**unlimited.** Palena ʻole, kaupalena ʻole ʻia.

**unload.** Wehewehe i ka ukana.

**unlock.** Wehe me ke kī.

**unlucky.** Pakalaki, pōmaikaʻi ʻole.

**unnecessary.** Hoʻopaumanawa, waiwai ʻole, makehewa.

**unpleasant.** Hoihoi ʻole.

**unprepared.** Mākaukau ʻole, hemahema.

**unskilled.** Pāhemahema, hemahema.

**unsteady.** Luliluli, kāhulihuli, kūlanalana.

**unsuccessful.** Pohō, holo pono ʻole.

**unsuitable.** Kohu ʻole, kūpono ʻole.

**untidy.** Mōkākī, kāpulu.

**untie.** Wehe, ʻuehe, kala.

**until.** Ā, ā hiki i.

**unusual.** Mea ʻē, ʻano ʻē, ʻē, ʻike nui ʻole ʻia.

**up.** Luna, i luna, maluna.

**upland.** Uka.

**upper.** Luna, maluna aʻe.

**upright.** 1. *Erect.* Kū, kūpono. 2. *Moral.* Naʻau pono.

**upset.** 1. *Capsize.* Hoʻokahuli, kahuli. 2. *Worried.* Pīhoihoi ka manaʻo.

**upside down.** Hulihia.

**upstairs.** Papahele o luna.

**urge.** Koi, haʻakoi, pai, hoʻopai, lale.

**urgent.** Koʻikoʻi, hiki ʻole ke kāpae.

**urinate.** Mimi.

**us.** Iā kāua, iā māua *(dual);* iā kākou, iā mākou *(plural).*

**use.** 1. *Value.* Waiwai, pono. 2. *Utilize.* Hoʻohana.

**used to.** Maʻa, maʻamaʻa, maʻamaʻahia.

**useful.** Waiwai, mea kōkua.

**useless.** Waiwai ʻole, makehewa, ʻole wale.

**usual.** Maʻamau, mea mau.

# V

**v.** *No Hawaiian term.*

**vacant.** Haka, hakahaka.

**vacation.** Wā hoʻomaha, hoʻomahana.

**vaccinate.** ʻŌ.

**vacuum cleaner.** Mīkini hoʻomaʻemaʻe hale.

**vagabond.** Kanaka ʻaeʻa, kuewa, lewa.

**vagina.** Kohe, peo.

**vain.** 1. *Proud.* Hoʻokano, hoʻokela, hoʻokiʻekiʻe. 2. *Without results.* Pohō, makehewa.

**valley.** Awaawa.

**valuable.** Waiwai, makamae.

**"vamp" hula step.** Kāholo. *See* flirt.

**vanish.** Nalowale.

**variety.** ʻAno.

**vast.** Nui ʻino, nui loa.

**vault.** Waihona, keʻena.

**veal.** ʻIʻo pipi.

**vegetable.** *No Hawaiian equivalent; early Hawaiians distinguished* poi ('ai, poi) *and accompaniments to* poi (i'a, 'īna'i). *Nearest equivalents to English term:* mea ulu, mea kanu, mea 'ai launahele.

**vehicle.** Ka'a, wa'a.

**vein.** A'a koko, a'a.

**velvet.** Weleweka.

**Venus.** Hōkū-ao, Hōkū-loa, Mānalo.

**verb.** Ha'ina.

**verify.** Hō'oia, hō'oia'i'o.

**verse.** Laina, lālani *(line);* paukū, 'oki *(stanza).*

**very.** Loa, nō, wale, maoli, 'ino.

**vessel.** **1.** *Container.* Ipu, 'umeke, hue. **2.** *Ship.* Moku.

**veteran.** Koa mua.

**veterinary.** Kauka holoholona.

**veto.** Hō'ole, wiko.

**vice.** Hewa, hala, 'ino, hana haumia.

**vice-.** Hope, pani. *Vice-president,* hope pelekikena.

**victim.** Luaahi, pio, heana.

**victory.** Lanakila, eo.

**view.** 'Ikena, nānaina.

**village.** Kūlanakauhale, kauhale.

**vine.** Lā'au hihi.

**vinegar.** Pinika, wīneka.

**violet.** Waioleka.

**violin.** Pila, waiolina.

**virgin.** Pu'upa'a *(female);* ulepa'a *(male).*

**virile.** Ke'a, pūkonakona.

**virtue.** Hemolele, pono.

**vision.** Haili moe, hihi'o, 'ike, akakū.

**visit.** Māka'ika'i, kipa, launa.

**visitor.** Mea māka'ika'i, mea kipa.

**visitors' bureau.** Pulo ho'okipa malihini.

**vocabulary.** Papa 'ōlelo *(list);* huina 'ōlelo *(word totality).*

**voice.** Leo.

**volcanic.** Pele, 'a'ā pele.

**volcano.** Lua pele, pele, ahi 'ai honua.

**volume.** **1.** *Quantity.* Nui. **2.** *Book.* Puke, helu.

**volunteer.** 'A'a.

**vomit.** Lua'i, pua'i.

**vote.** Koho pāloka.

**vowel.** Hua palapala leokani.

**voyage.** Huaka'i, holokai.

# W

**w.** Wē.

**wages.** Uku, uku hana.

**wagon.** Ka'a.

**wail.** Uē, uē helu, 'alalā, kanikau.

**wait.** Kali, alia. *Wait on tables,* lawelawe.

**waiter.** Kuene.

**wake.** *Awaken.* Ala, ho'āla.

**walk.** Hele wāwae, hele.

**wall.** Pā; paia *(of houses).*

**wallpaper.** Pepa hale.

**wander.** 'Auana, ki'ihele, lalau, 'ae'a, kuewa.

**want.** **1.** *Desire.* Makemake; mamake *(colloquial).* **2.** *Lack.* Nele, hemahema.

**war.** Kaua. *Civil war,* kaua kūloko. *Revolutionary war,* kaua hulihia.

**wardrobe.** Nā 'a'ahu apau *(clothes);* ke'ena waihona 'a'ahu *(clothes closet).*

**warehouse.** Hale ukana, hale ho'āhu.

**warm.** Mahana, pumehana.

**warning.** Hō'ike pilikia.

**warrant.** Palapala.

**warrior.** Koa, pū'ali.

**warship.** Moku kaua, manuā.

**was.** *No equivalent; see* be, ua.

**wash.** Holoi.

**washcloth.** Kāwele holoi.

**washing machine.** Mīkini holoi.

**Washington.** Wakinekona, Wasinetona.

**wasp.** Hope'ō, kopena.

**waste.** Ho'omāunauna, 'uha'uha.

**wastebasket.** 'Ie 'ōpala.

**watch. 1.** *Observe.* Kia'i, nānā pono, kilo. **2.** *Timepiece.* Uaki. *Wrist watch,* uaki pūlima.

**watchful.** Maka'ala, miki.

**watchman.** Kia'i, kū uaki.

**water.** Wai *(fresh). To water,* ninini wai, ho'okahe wai, hanawai. *Spring water,* wai puna, wai māpuna.

**water bottle.** Hue wai, ipu wai, 'ōmole wai.

**watercress.** Lēkō.

**waterfall.** Wailele.

**water hole.** Lua wai, ki'o wai.

**watermelon.** Ipu, ipu haole.

**waterproof.** Komo 'ole ka wai.

**waterspout.** Waipu'ilani.

**wave. 1.** *Of the ocean.* Nalu, 'ale. **2.** *Motion.* Ani, pe'ahi, welo, kālepa.

**way. 1.** *Route.* Ala, ala hele, alanui. **2.** *Manner, custom.* 'Ano. *That way,* pēlā. *This way,* penei.

**we.** Kāua *(dual, inclusive),* kākou *(plural, inclusive),* māua *(dual exclusive),* mākou *(plural, exclusive).*

**weak.** Nāwaliwali; lahilahi *(as coffee).*

**wealth.** Waiwai, lako, loa'a.

**weapon.** Mea kaua, mea make, mea pepehi kanaka.

**wear.** Komo, 'a'ahu.

**weary.** Luhi, māluhiluhi, pa'a luhi, pauaho.

**weather.** *No equivalent. Good weather,* mālie. *Bad weather,* 'ino'ino.

**wedding.** Male 'ana. *Wedding feast,* 'aha'aina male.

**Wednesday.** Pō'akolu.

**weed.** Nahele, nāhelehele. *To weed,* waele.

**week.** Pule. *Next week,* kēia pule a'e. *Last week,* kēlā pule aku nei.

**weekday.** Lā noa.

**weekly.** I kēlā me kēia pule.

**weep.** Uē.

**weigh.** Kaupaona, ana kaumaha.

**weight.** Kaumaha, ana kaumaha, paona.

**weird.** Āiwaiwa.

**welcome.** Heahea. *There is no equivalent to the English. One may say* komo mai. *You are welcome,* he mea 'ole, he mea iki *(modern).*

**welfare.** Pono, pōmaika'i. *Public welfare,* pono o ka lehulehu. *Spiritual welfare,* pono 'uhane.

**well. 1.** *Good.* Maika'i, pono. **2.** *Source of water.* Luawai, wai 'eli. *Artesian well,* luawai aniani.

**well-being.** Ola kino, pono.

**were.** *No equivalent; see* be.

**west.** Komohana.

**wet.** Pulu, pulu pē, ma'ū, 'elo.

**whale.** Koholā, palaoa.

**whale tooth.** Niho palaoa.

**whaling.** 'Ō koholā.

**wharf.** Uapo.

**what. 1.** *Interrogative.* Aha. *What is that?* He aha kēlā? **2.** *Relative pronoun.* Mea.

**whatsoever.** Nā mea like 'ole.

**wheat.** Huika, hua palaoa.

**wheel.** Huila.

**when. 1.** *Declarative past.* I ka manawa . . . i, i ka wā . . . i. **2.** *Declarative future.* I ka manawa . . . e, i ka wā . . . e, ke. **3.** *Interrogative future.* Āhea? I ka manawa hea . . . e? **4.** *Interrogative past.* Ināhea? I ka manawa hea . . . i? I ka wā hea . . . i?

**where. 1.** *Declarative.* Kahi. **2.** *Interrogative.* Ai hea? I hea? Aia i hea? 'Auhea?

**whether.** Inā.

**whetstone.** Hoana.

**which. 1.** *Declarative.* Ka mea i, ka i *(past);* ka mea e, ke *(future).* **2.** *Interrogative.* Hea? Ka mea hea?

**while.** 'Oiai, 'oi, i ka manawa, i ka wā, i.

**whip.** Hahau, hau, uhau.

**whirlpool.** Wiliwai, mimilo.

**whiskers.** 'Umi'umi.

**whiskey.** Wekekē, waikekē.

**whisper.** Hāwanawana.

**whistle.** Hōkio, hōkiokio, pio.

**white.** Ke'oke'o, kea; hina *(of hair).*

**white man.** Haole, 'ilipuakea.

**whitewash.** Pa'i puna, puna, hamo puna.

**whitish.** Ha'akea.

**whittle.** Kalakalai, kolikoli.

**who. 1.** *Declarative.* I, e, nāna. **2.** *Interrogative.* Wai? 'O wai? Iā wai?

**whole.** Holo'oko'a, oko'a, pa'a.

**wholesale.** Kū'ai nui, kūka'a.

**whom.** Iā wai.

**whose. 1.** *Declarative.* Nona, nāna. **2.** *Interrogative.* Na wai? No wai?

**why. 1.** *Declarative.* Ke kumu, ka mea. **2.** *Interrogative.* Aha? Hea?; no ke aha?

**wick.** 'Uiki.

**wicked.** 'Ino, hana 'ino, 'aiā.

**wide.** Laulā, ākea.

**widow.** Wahine kāne make.

**widower.** Kāne wahine make.

**wife.** Wahine, wahine male.

**wig.** Lauoho ku'i.

**wiggle.** 'Oni'oni.

**wild.** 'Āhiu, hihiu, hae.

**wilderness.** Wao akua, wao nahele.

**will. 1.** *Testament.* Kauoha, palapala ho'oilina. **2.** *Desire.* Makemake, mana'o. **3.** *Verb markers.* E . . . ana.

**wilt.** Mae.

**win.** Lanakila, eo, loa'a, puka.

**wind. 1.** *Air movement.* Makani. **2.** *To twist.* Wili, wini, pōka'a, ka'a.

**windbreak.** Kūmakani, pālulu.

**windmill.** Wili makani.

**window.** Pukaaniani, puka hale.

**windshield.** Pale makani, pālulu.

**windward.** 'Ao'ao Ko'olau, 'ao'ao makani, na'e.

**wine.** Waina.

**wing.** 'Ēheu.

**wink.** 'Imo, 'amo.

**winter.** Ho'oilo.

**wipe.** Kāwele, holoi, hāleu.

**wire.** Uea.

**wisdom.** Na'auao, akamai.

**wish.** Makemake, ake, 'i'ini.

**witchcraft.** Hana mana, ho'okalakupua.

**with.** Me.

**withdraw.** Emi hope, ho'i, unuhi.

**withhold.** 'Au'a, lau'au'a.

**without.** Nele, 'ole.

**witness.** Hō'ike.

**woe.** Pōpilikia nui, kaumaha nui.

**wolf.** 'Īlio hae, lupo.

**woman.** Wahine.

**womb.** Pū'ao, 'ōpū.

**women.** Wāhine.

**wonder.** Kāhāhā, pāha'oha'o.

**wonderful.** Kupaianaha, kupanaha, kamaha'o, makahehi.

**woo.** Ho'oipo, ho'onipo.

**wood.** Lā'au.

**wood borer.** Huhu-pao-lā'au.

**wool.** Hulu, pili.

**woolen.** Huluhulu.

**word.** 'Ōlelo, hua 'ōlelo, hua.

**work.** Hana.

**worker.** Kanaka hana, limahana, pa'ahana.

**workshop.** Ke'ena hana, hale hana.

**world.** Ao, honua.

**world war.** Kaua honua.

**worm.** Ko'e, ilo.

**wormy.** Iloilo, huhuhu.

**worried.** Pīhoihoi, pono 'ole ka mana'o.

**worry.** Ho'opīhoihoi, pīhoihoi o i ka na'au.

**worse.** 'Oi aku ka 'ino.

**worship.** Ho'omana, haipule, pule.

**worth.** Waiwai, waiwai 'i'o.

**worthless.** Lapuwale.

**worthy.** Kūpono, pono.

**wound.** Palapū, 'eha.

**wrap. 1.** *Bind.* Wahī. **2.** *Garment.* 'A'ahu, kuka.

**wrasses.** Hīnālea, 'a'awa, 'ōpule.

**wrath.** Inaina.

**wreath.** Lei.

**wreck.** Wāwahi, ho'opō'ino. *See* shipwreck.

**wrench.** *Tool.* Wili, hao wili.

**wrestling.** Hākōkō, uma.

**wretch.** Lapuwale.

**wretched.** Kaumaha, luʻuluʻu.
**wrinkle.** Minomino, ʻaluʻalu.
**wrist.** Pūlima.
**write.** Kākau, kākau lima.

**writer.** Mea kākau.
**writing.** Palapala, kākau.
**wrong.** Hewa, pono ʻole, ʻolalau.

# Y

**y.** *No Hawaiian term.*
**yacht.** Moku peʻa.
**yam.** Uhi.
**yard.** 1. *Unit of measure.* Iā, iwilei. 2. *Enclosure.* Pā.
**year.** Makahiki. *New Year,* Makahiki Hou. *Happy New Year.* Hauʻoli Makahiki Hou.
**yellow.** Melemele, ʻōlenalena.
**yes.** ʻAe, ʻē, ō, eō.
**yesterday.** Nehinei, i nehinei.
**yet.** 1. *Still.* Koe, naʻe. 2. *See* **but.**
**you.** ʻOe *(singular),* ʻolua *(dual),* ʻoukou *(plural).*

**young.** ʻŌpio, ʻōpiopio.
**your.** 1. *Singular possessed object, singular.* Kou (o-*class*); kāu (a-*class*); kō *(neutral class).* 2. *Singular possessed object, dual.* Kō ʻolua (o-*class*), kā ʻolua (a-*class*).* 3. *Singular possessed object, plural.* Kō ʻoukou (o-*class*); kā ʻoukou (a-*class*). To show plural possessed objects, delete k- *in all except the neutral class.*
**yours.** Nou, no ʻolua, no ʻoukou, nāu, na ʻolua, na ʻoukou.

# Z

**z.** *No Hawaiian term.*
**zero.** ʻOle.
**zigzag.** Kīkeʻekeʻe, kihikihi.

**zoo.** Kahua hōʻikeʻike holoholona laka ʻole.

# Grammar

## 1. OVERALL VIEW

Hawaiian grammar is complex and imperfectly studied; only salient features are discussed here.

The inventory of significant sounds in the language includes only eight consonants, five short vowels, and five long vowels. Certainly few other languages in the world have so meager a list.

Words in Hawaiian are of two main types, content words and particles. Content words may occur alone and usually have dictionary glosses. Many particles are short *(ka, ke, na, nā, ua, e, i, iā, 'o, no, nō),* but the functions are manifold. They are important, as they may indicate whether the nearby content words are nouns or verbs, whether action is completed or going on, whether a noun is subject, object, agent, possessor, or locative— the sort of grammatical information that in Latin and Greek is often given by inflectional endings. Hawaiian, in contrast, has no inflections.

If this be thought simple, one should examine Hawaiian pronouns, possessives, and demonstratives. They are more numerous than their English counterparts and have very explicit meanings that make the English ones seem crudely vague.

Another feature surprising to those whose linguistic sophistication is confined to European languages is that the Hawaiian language contains no verbs corresponding to English 'to be' and 'to have'. And no Hawaiian terms exist for sex or weather. The large dictionary, however, has names for more than 130 types of rain and 160 types of winds.

The common order of content words in sentences is:

Verb ± subject ± object or other prepositional phrase

Each of these slots may begin and close with particles, and be followed by qualifying content words. There are no words that serve only as qualifiers, in the manner of English adjectives and adverbs.

Another common type of sentence contains no verb at all: "I am a man" is *he kāne au,* literally, 'a man I'.

## 2. PRONUNCIATION
### AMPLIFICATION AND COMMENTARY

For the list of sounds in the Hawaiian language, and comments on stress, see the table on page xi.

By the term *aspiration* of *p* and *k* is meant that a puff of breath accompanies the release of these sounds, as occurs in initial *p* and *k* in English. In speaking Hawaiian one attempts to reduce the strength of the aspiration and to achieve the *p* in *spit* and the *k* in *skit.*

In the Niʻihau dialect of Hawaiian and occasionally in chants, *k* is irregularly replaced by *t.*

Hawaiian diphthongs and long vowels need to be distinguished: *ē* and *ei: kē* 'protest', *kei* 'proud'; *ō* and *ou: nō* 'very', *nou* 'for you'. (The English speaker tends to say *kei* for *kē* and *nou* for *nō.*)

Similarly, the speaker of English must learn to distinguish *-ae* and *-ai,* and *-ao* and *-au.* The following pairs are troublesome: *pae* 'row', *pai* 'to urge'; *mae* 'to wilt', *mai* 'hither'; *kao* 'dart', *kau* 'to place'; *pao* 'to scoop', *pau* 'finished'.

Diphthongs are *always* stressed on the first vowel, whether it is short or long (*ʻáina* 'meal', *ʻáina* 'land').

The presence or absence of glottal stops and macrons changes both pronunciation and meaning, as shown by the following groups of words conventionally spelled *pau, kau,* and *koi:*

| | | |
|---|---|---|
| *pau* 'finished' | *kau* 'to place' | *koi* 'to urge' |
| *paʻu* 'soot' | *kaʻu* 'mine' | *koʻi* 'adze' |
| *paʻū* 'moist' | *Kaʻū,* a place name | *kōī* 'shrill' |
| *pāʻū* 'sarong' | | |

The glottal stop also occurs nonsignificantly before vowels preceded by silence. A Hawaiian will greet a friend with the single word *Aloha!* (pronounced with a glottal stop at the beginning). The same word *within* an utterance will have no glottal stop: *ua aloha mai* 'did send greeting'. Such utterance-initial glottal stops do not influence meaning and are not written.

Other utterance-initial glottal stops persist in noninitial position and their occurrence does change meanings, as evidenced by the following pairs:

| | | |
|---|---|---|
| *ai* 'sexual intercourse' | *ili* 'to inherit' | *ulu* 'to grow' |
| *'ai* 'to eat' | *'ili* 'skin' | *'ulu* 'breadfruit' |
| | | |
| *ea* 'life' | *oli* 'chant' | |
| *'ea,* turtle species | *'oli* 'joy' | |

All monosyllabic content words bear macrons. Vowels marked with macrons are stressed regardless of position: *kū* 'standing', *wāhíne* 'women', *mò'ī* 'king', *hòlokū* 'dress with a train'.

Spaces between words indicate boundaries of particles or content words, but do not necessarily mark pauses in pronunciation. The phrase *ka imu kī* 'the ti oven' is composed of three words, but in normal speech is pronounced as a single word (kàimukī).

## GLIDES

A glide is a sound made by a gliding movement of the tongue toward a high front position (*y*-glide) or a high back position (*w*-glide); *w*-glides are frequently not "significant" in Hawaiian (Elbert and Pukui 1979:180). This means that such sounds are predictable, do not distinguish meaning, and ought not to be written. They are not phonemic. Here are some examples:

au$^W$ē = auē 'oh'  kau$^W$ā = kauā 'outcast person'
u$^W$ē = uē 'to weep'  'au$^W$ana = 'auana 'wander'
u$^W$aki = uaki 'watch'

*y*-glides also occur, but as there is no *y*-phoneme, they are never written.

## COLLOQUIAL SPEECH

The orthography used in the New Pocket Dictionary represents the slow speech of careful speakers. Normal fast speech differs in several ways. Some of them are:

(a) *Ai* assimilates to *ei,* and, less commonly, *au* to *ou: ikaika* 'strong' is usually *ikeika; kēlā mau mea* 'those things' is sometimes *kēlā mou mea.*

(b) Like vowels separated by a glottal stop reduce to glottal stop plus vowel: Hawai'i becomes Hawa'i; *pua'a* 'pig' becomes *pu'a.*

(c) *-aCo* (C = consonant) assimilates to *-a'a*: *'a'ole* 'not' becomes *'a'ale; ma'ona* 'full' becomes *ma'ana; mahope* 'afterwards' becomes *mahape.*

(d) Vowels before silence may be whispered or dropped; thus *Punalu'u,* a place name, becomes *Punalu'* (not *Punaluw); hele akula* 'went away' becomes *hele akul* or even *hele kū.*

## 3. HYPHENS AND NO HYPHENS

To designate genus and species of plants and animals, the editors decided to adopt the hyphenless system used by natural scientists: thus *'ōhi'a, 'ōhi'a 'ai, 'ōhi'a lehua* for types of *'ōhi'a* trees. The same rule applies to sociological series: *anaina, anaina ho'olewa,* and *anaina ho'omana* for types of meetings.

Components of long names are separated by hyphens: Kau-i-ke-ao-uli ('placed in the dark blue sky', a name for Kamehameha II), Ka-wena-'ula-a-Hi'iaka-i-ka-poli-o-Pele-ka-wahine-'ai-ho-nua ('the red glow of the sky made by Hi'iaka in the bosom of Pele the earth-eating woman'), Ke-one-poko ('the short sand').

The *Hawaiian Dictionary* also separates by hyphens parts of names of winds, rains, stars, *lua* fighting holds, and tapa and mat designs (see examples in Elbert and Pukui 1979:37).

Many long names are poetic and are unwieldy in colloquial conversation. The hyphens make it possible to understand the meaning of the component parts.

## 4. VERBS AND VERB PHRASES

Verbs may be defined as content words that may be preceded by *verb-marking particles.* The most common of these particles are:

*ua* (verb), perfective aspect (completed action)
*e* (verb) *ana,* imperfective aspect (incomplete action)
*ke* (verb) *nei,* present
*e* (verb), imperative
*mai*₁ (verb), negative imperative

*Ua* indicates that the following verb represents a completed action, state of being, or newly arrived state ("inceptive"). The verb following *ua* is usually translated in English by present or past tense: *ua maika'i 'oia* 'he is well'; *ua hele 'oia* 'he went'.

*E* (verb) *ana* is incomplete action. *E hele ana au* may be translated, according to context, 'I was going, I am going, I will go', but never 'I went'. *Ke* (verb) *nei* indicates present continuing action, as the lover says in the famous love song, *Ke kali nei au* 'I am waiting'. The imperative is *e: E hele!* 'Go ahead!' The negative imperative is *mai: Mai hele!* 'Don't go!'

*Ua* and the imperative *e* are frequently omitted in colloquial speech if the context is clear.

The verb phrase is diagrammed in the lower portion of figure 1.

Most verbs may function also in other capacities. Very commonly they are used as nouns; that is, they follow noun markers such as articles *(ka, ke, he, nā)* and possessives. The situation is something like that of English 'love' and 'hope':

Verb:    *Ua aloha au iāia* 'I *love* her'
Noun:   *Ko'u aloha* 'my *love*'

Verb:    *Ua mana'olana lākou* 'they *hope*'
Noun:   *Kō lākou mana'olana* 'their *hope*'

Such words in Hawaiian are extremely numerous and impart great flexibility to the language. Besides functioning as both noun and verb, they may also qualify nouns and verbs:

Verb: *Ua maika'i lākou* 'they [are] *well*'
Verb qualifier: *Ua hana maika'i lākou* 'they work *well*'

Noun: *Ka maika'i o ka 'āina* 'the *goodness* of the land'
Noun qualifier: *He 'āina maika'i* 'a *good* land'

Most verbs may be followed by the particle *'ia,* which usually passivizes the verb, but sometimes marks the imperative. Thus *'ai 'ia ka poi* is usually 'the poi was eaten' but could also mean 'eat the poi!' There is a very restricted list of verbs that take also certain closely bound suffixes with the same dual roles *(-a, -hia, -lia, -mia, -nia, -na).*

Some verbs, called *loa'a*-type or stative, do not take *'ia* or the suffixes just mentioned; they seem to be inherently passive, as in the sentence *loa'a ka i'a iā Pua* 'the fish was obtained by Pua'. But once a stative, not always a stative. Statives, like most verbs, may take causative prefixes *(ho'o-, hō'-, ho-, hō-);* they are then transitives rather than statives.

Stative: *Pau ka hana iāia* 'the work was finished by him'
Transitive: *Ho'opau 'oia i ka hana* 'he finished the work'

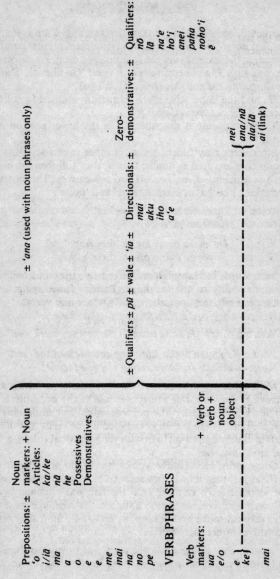

Figure 1. Hawaiian phrases.

**NOUN PHRASES**

Prepositions: ± + Noun markers: + Noun Articles: *ka/ke*, *nā*, *he*, Possessives, Demonstratives

'*o*
*i / iā*
*ma*
*a*
*o*
*e*
*me*
*mai*
*na*
*no*
*pe*

± Qualifiers ± *pū* ± *wale* ± '*ia* ± Directionals: ± *mai*, *aku*, *iho*, *a'e* Zero-demonstratives: ± Qualifiers: *nō*, *lā*, *na'e*, *ho'i*, *anei*, *paha*, *noho'i*, *ē*

± '*ana* (used with noun phrases only)

**VERB PHRASES**

Verb markers: *ua*, *e/o*

+ Verb or verb + noun object

*e*
*ke*}

*nei*
*ana/nā*
*ala/lā*
*ai* (link)

*mai*

In the stative sentence the agent is marked by *iā;* in the transitive sentence by *'o.* Some persons today rarely use the stative construction. They might translate the stative sentence above as *pau 'oia ka hana.*

Repetition of an entire base or part of a base is common. Such reduplication indicates repetition or frequency of action, and in some instances, a diminutive. Examples are *hoe* 'paddle', *hoehoe* 'paddling on and on, several persons paddling'; *puhi* 'to blow', *pupuhi* 'blowing frequently or for a long time, several persons blowing'; *āhole,* adult stage of a fish, *āholehole,* young stage of the same fish.

Verbs are commonly followed by particles termed directionals. They are *mai₂,* toward the speaker; *aku,* away from the speaker; *iho* 'down'; and *a'e* 'up, adjacent'. They are usually separated from the preceding verb by a slight pause: thus, *manà'o ího* 'think', not *màna'óiho.*

Use of directionals is complicated. *Mai* may be used as a complete sentence meaning 'come'; however, it never follows verb markers. On the other hand, *iho* may be used as a verb 'to go down' and follows all the verb markers; it is also used reflexively, as in the preceding paragraph. *A'e* expresses comparative and superlative degrees: *maika'i* 'good', *maika'i a'e* 'better, best'.

For use of directionals after nouns, see section 5.

## 5. NOUNS AND NOUN PHRASES

Nouns are content words that may occur in noun phrases consisting of optional preposition plus optional noun marker plus noun. The noun markers include articles (section 5), possessives (section 6), and demonstratives (section 6). The noun phrase is diagrammed in the upper part of figure 1.

### PREPOSITIONS INTRODUCE NOUN PHRASES

The important prepositions, with examples, follow:

*'o,* subject marker: *Ua hele 'o Pua. Ua hele 'oia.* 'Pua went. She went.' (*'O* is used most commonly before names of persons and before the third person singular pronoun *ia* used as subject. Otherwise, the subject is commonly unmarked.)

*i/iā,* object marker, 'at (general locative)': *Ua nānā 'o Pua i ka hale* 'Pua looked at the house'. *Ua nānā 'o Pua iā Kimo* 'Pua looked at James'. *Ua nānā 'o Pua iāia* 'Pua looked at him'. *Ua noho i Maui* 'living at Maui'. (*Iā* precedes pronouns and names of people; otherwise *i* is used; occasionally *iā* precedes place names. In fast speech *i* is sometimes omitted.)

*ma* 'at, in (specific locative)': *Noho ma Kahuku i O'ahu* 'living at Kahuku on O'ahu'. (Note the contrast between *ma* and *i*.)

*a* 'of, acquired by': *Hale-a-ka-lā,* place name, literally 'house acquired by the sun'.

*o* 'of (inherited, spatial), in honor of': *Nā-iwi-o-Pele,* place name, literally 'the bones of Pele'. (The *a-o* distinction is discussed in section 6.)

*e₁* 'by': *'Ai 'ia e Pua* 'eaten by Pua'.

*e₂*, vocative: *E Pua, hele mai!* 'Pua, come here!'

*me* 'with, and, like, by means of': *Noho 'oia me Pua* 'he lived with Pua'. *Hele mai lāua, Pua me Kimo* 'the two came, Pua and Jim'. *Holo mehe lio* 'run like a horse'. *Kākau me kēia penikala* 'write with this pencil'.

*mai₃* 'from': *Mai Maui* 'from Maui'. *Mai Maui mai* 'here from Maui'. (The second *mai* is the directional particle.)

*na* 'for, by': *Na Pua ka puke* 'the book is by Pua'.

*no* 'for': *No Pua ka puke* 'the book is for (or about) Pua'. (*-a* and *-o* in these prepositions are similar to the *a* and *o* possessives. See section 6.)

*pe* 'like': *Pe kēia* 'like this'.

The prepositions *a, o, ma, na,* and *no* are usually short, but are automatically lengthened before long vowels and diphthongs: *nā lei a Lani* 'the leis (made) by Lani' and *nā lei ā Kū* 'the leis (made) by Kū'; *nā hale o ke ali'i* 'the houses of the chief' and *nā hale ō Maui* 'the houses of Maui'; *ma ka hale* 'at the house' and *mā laila* 'there'; *na Kimo* 'by James' and *nā lākou* 'by them'; *no Pua* 'for Pua' and *nō mākou* 'for us'. This lengthening is predictable and hence is not indicated in the spelling nor in the entries in the New Pocket Dictionary.

## Articles Mark Nouns

*Ka* and its variant *ke* are usually called singular definite articles, commonly translated 'the'. *Ke* precedes nouns beginning with *a-, e-, o-,* and *k-,* and before some nouns beginning with the glottal stop and *p-; ka* occurs elsewhere (*ke aloha* 'the love', *ke ea* 'the life', *ke oho* 'the hair', *ke kanaka* 'the person', *ka hale* 'the house'; *ke 'ala,* 'the fragrance' but *ka 'alā* 'the stone', *ke pā* 'the dish' but *ka pā* 'the fence'). The plural definite article is *nā* (*nā pua* 'the flowers'). In contrast to English usage, the articles precede abstract nouns (*maika'i ke aloha* 'love is good'). *He* is a singular indefinite article (*he pepa kēia* 'this is a paper'). *He* does *not* follow prepositions other than *me* (see the New Pocket Dictionary for *mehe*). *He* coalesces with the negative *'a'ole* to *'a'ohe* 'to be or have none': *'a'ohe āna puke* 'he has no books', literally, 'to-be-none his (plural) book'.

The articles are omitted if the meaning is 'any, any whatsoever': *Lawe mai he puke* 'bring a book'. *Lawe mai i puke* 'bring any book'. *Hele mai nā kānaka* 'the people came'. *Hele mai kānaka* 'some people (any at all) came'.

Nouns classed as locatives (place words) occur most commonly without articles, as in noun phrases that may be schematized as follows:

$$
\left.\begin{matrix} i \\ ma\text{-} \end{matrix}\right\} + \left\{\begin{matrix} luna \text{ 'over, on top'} \\ lalo \text{ 'under'} \\ mua \text{ 'first, front'} \\ waena \text{ 'middle'} \\ hope \text{ 'after, last'} \\ loko \text{ 'in, inside'} \\ waho \text{ 'out, outside'} \\ kai \text{ 'seaward'} \\ uka \text{ 'inland'} \end{matrix}\right\} + o + \left\{\begin{matrix} ka \\ ke \\ k\text{-word} \end{matrix}\right\} + \text{noun}
$$

Examples: *i luna o ka mauna* 'on top of the mountain', *maloko o ka hale* 'inside the house'.

*Laila* 'there' and names of people and places also occur without articles.

*Ma-* is written, by convention, joined to the locative (*i lalo o ka hale, malalo o ka hale* 'under the house').

Following articles, the locatives have somewhat different meanings:

*ka luna* 'the foreman'
*ka lalo* 'the bottom'

*ka mua* 'the firstborn, first'
*ka waena* 'the middle'
*ka hope* 'the youngest, last'

> *ka loko* 'the inside, lake'
> *ka waho* 'the outside'
>
> *ke kai* 'the sea'
> *ka uka* 'the uplands'

The locatives are characterized by metonymy, that is, the use of one term to mean another—in this case the term for the container to mean the thing contained; for example, *waho* 'outside' also means 'the people who are outside'. Other nouns may also be personalized. *Wa'a* means both 'canoe' and 'people in the canoe, crew'.

## COMPOUNDS

Compounds are indivisible sequences of content words whose total meaning is not readily apparent. *Na'auao* 'intelligent' is composed of the sequence *na'au* 'intestines' and *ao* 'daylight' and thus meets the test. It is a compound. *Kanaka akamai* 'smart man', however, is not. Another compound noun is *'ōkole'oi'oi* 'marigold' (literally 'jutting buttocks'). *Uluwehi* 'to be lush and beautiful, verdure' (literally 'decorative growth') is a compound verb-noun, but less obviously a compound. Compound verbs seem to be lacking, although verb + noun object is a common sequence that behaves like a single verb (*hoe wa'a mai!* 'canoe-paddle here!')

## NOMINALIZATIONS

Some verbs are made into nouns by the addition of the particle *'ana* or the suffix *-na*. *'Ana* is probably productive (that is, it occurs with nearly any verb), but *-na* occurs only with a restricted list, as *kālai* 'to carve' and *kalaina* 'carved object' (the long vowel is shortened). Compare *ua maika'i kāna kālai 'ana* 'his carving (the act rather than the object) is good'.

## DIRECTIONALS AFTER NOUNS

Use of the four directionals after verbs or as verbs was described in section 4.

Directionals also follow nouns. *Mai* and *iho* used alone have direction meanings similar to those when following verbs: *mai*

*Maui mai* 'from Maui this way, from Maui'; *maluna iho* 'not quite on top, a little below the top'.

*Aku* and *a'e* also follow time words; *aku* expresses past or future time and *a'e* future time, the *aku* time being perhaps more distant than the *a'e* time. *Kēia* and *ia* meaning 'this' refer to the future; *kēlā* 'that' refers to the past.

| | | |
|---|---|---|
| this, future | *kēia*<br>*ia* } *pule aku nei*<br>'week after this' | *kēia pule a'e*<br>'next week (imminent)' |
| | *'apōpō ā ia lā aku*<br>'day after tomorrow' | |
| that, past | *kēlā pule aku nei*<br>'last week' | |

## 6. PERSON WORDS

Person words differ from other content words such as *hale* 'house' in that all of them (except the singular pronouns and the zero-demonstratives) are made up of at least two elements that cannot be used alone; that is, they do not contain bases. The three types of person words are pronouns, possessives, and demonstratives. In the following treatment of each of these types, identifiable elements are set off by hyphens.

### PRONOUNS

The pronouns in Hawaiian may be tabulated as follows:

| Person | | Singular | Dual | Plural |
|---|---|---|---|---|
| 1 | inclusive<br>exclusive | *au* 'I', *a'u* 'me' | *kā-ua* 'we'<br>*mā-ua* 'we' | *kā-kou* 'we'<br>*mā-kou* 'we' |
| 2 | | *'oe* 'you' | *'o-lua* 'you' | *'ou-kou* 'you' |
| 3 | | *ia* 'he, she, it' | *lā-ua* 'they' | *lā-kou* 'they' |

The elements set off by hyphens are easily labeled: *kā-*, inclusive; *mā-*, exclusive; *-ua/-lua*, dual; *-kou*, plural; *'o-/'ou-*, second person; *lā-*, third person.

With the inclusive pronouns, the person addressed is included. He is unequivocably excluded by the exclusive pronouns. The use of inclusive pronouns imparts a nuance of cozy intimacy that is completely lacking with the exclusive pronouns.

>*Aloha kā-ua* 'may there be love between you and me'
>*Aloha kā-kou* 'may there be love among all of us'

>*Hele kā-ua i Honolulu* 'you and I are going to Honolulu'
>*Hele mā-ua i Honolulu* 'someone else and I are going to Honolulu'

In English, 'we're going to the hula' is ambiguous. The addressee can't be sure that she's invited. Perhaps the speaker is going with someone else. But if the Hawaiian is used, *hele kā-kou i ka hula,* the addressee knows she is included because of the inclusive *kā-kou.*

The third person singular form when used as the subject is usually preceded by the subject marker *'o,* the sequence being written *'oia;* similarly, *ia* when preceded by the object marker *iā* is usually written *iāia.*

A few speakers pronounced the duals *kā-'ua mā-'ua, lā-'ua,* that is, with glottal stops.

### POSSESSIVES

Possessives are of two types: *k*-possessives (those beginning with *k*-) and zero-possessives (without *k*-). The *k*- possessives are listed below.

| Person | Singular | Dual | Plural |
|--------|----------|------|--------|
| 1   inclusive | | $k$-$\frac{a}{o}$ *kā-ua* 'our' | $k$-$\frac{a}{o}$ *kā-kou* 'our' |
|     exclusive | $k$-$\frac{a}{o}$-*'u* 'my' <br> $k$-*u*-*'u* 'my' | $k$-$\frac{a}{o}$ *mā-ua* 'our' | $k$-$\frac{a}{o}$ *mā-kou* 'our' |
| 2 | $k$-$\frac{a}{o}$-*u* 'your' <br> $k$-*o* 'your' | $k$-$\frac{a}{o}$ *'o-lua* 'your' | $k$-$\frac{a}{o}$ *'oukou* 'your' |
| 3 | $k$-$\frac{a}{o}$-*na* 'his' <br> her, its' | $k$-$\frac{a}{o}$ *lā-ua* 'their' | $k$-$\frac{a}{o}$ *lā-kou* 'their' |

The English glosses do not indicate that the possessives are translated by English possessive pronouns as well as by English possessive adjectives: *k-o-'u hale* '*my* house' and *k-o-'u kēlā* 'that is mine'.

The table becomes less formidable when it is noted that the dual and plural forms consist of *k-ā* or *k-ō* plus the standard pronoun forms.

The most salient feature shown in the table is that in nearly every position at least two forms occur: one with *ā* (or *a*) and another with *ō* (or *o*). This important distinction is discussed below.

The *a-* (or *ā-*) in the possessives is equatable with the possessive preposition *a* (section 5). Similarly, *-o* (or *-ō*) is equatable with the possessive prepositions treated in the same section. They will be referred to henceforth as *a-* and *o-*forms.

As suggested by Albert J. Schütz and William H. Wilson, the use of *a* or *o* depends less on the nature of the possessed object than on the *relationship* of possessed and possessor. For example, in *k-o-'u lima* 'my hand', the relationship between the possessor and the possessed can be neither begun nor ended by the possessor.

A change of possessive marker may change the meaning: *k-ā-na lei* 'lei made by her (or him)', *k-o-na lei* 'lei given to her (or him)'; *k-ā-na mele* 'song composed by him (or her)', *k-o-na mele* 'song in his (or her) honor'; *k-ā-u ali'i* 'your (subordinate) chief', *k-o-u ali'i* 'your (inherited) chief'.

Some words nearly always take a single form. Small possessions, as book, pencil, breadfruit, take *a*. Body parts take *o* (one does not set out to acquire them). Certain important objects in the old culture ordinarily take *o:* land, house, canoe, superior chief, ancestors, gods. These are "wished" on one; everyone has an inalienable right to them.

Words indicating spatial relation commonly take *o: i loko o ka hale* 'inside of the house'. Clothing that one wears takes *o;* one is inside them. Similarly, a chair, horse, or automobile one sits on or in takes *o*.

For interesting discussions of *a* and *o* see Alexander's Hawaiian grammar (1968:9–11), Biggs' treatment of Māori (1969:43–49), and a paper by William H. Wilson. (See References.)

Two forms in the table of possessives are without *ā/a* and *ō/o*. They are alternate forms, sometimes called neutral, in the first and second persons singular. The *a/o* distinction is not involved in these forms. *K-u-'u* usually contains a nuance of affection.

Thus, *k-u-ʻu ipo* 'my sweetheart', but not *k-u-ʻu pākaukau* 'my table'. *K-o,* second person singular, is likewise neutral, but without any particular connotation. It is perhaps most common in highly colloquial speech.

The prepositions *na* and *no* contain the same *a* and *o.* Both mean 'for', but *na* is also agentive.

*K-ā* and *k-ō* also directly precede proper nouns, locatives, and article or possessive + noun sequences. *Ke keiki a Lani* 'Lani's child'. *K-ā Lani keiki* '*Lani's* child'. Note that the focus is on the first noun.

Other examples: *Ka poʻe o uka* 'the *people* of the uplands'. *K-ō uka poʻe* 'the *upland* people'. *Ka ʻāina o ke aliʻi* 'the *land* of the chief'. *K-ō ke aliʻi ʻāina* 'the *chief's* land'. *Ka ʻāina o k-o-na aliʻi* 'the *land* of his chief'. *K-ō k-o-na aliʻi āina* 'his *chief's* land'.

The zero-possessives are used as indication of plural possessed objects, especially after numerals and the negative *ʻaʻohe* 'to have none': *ʻElua a-ʻu puke* 'I have two books'. *ʻEhia ā-u puke?* 'how many books have you?' *ʻAʻohe ā-na puke* 'he has no books'. (In sentences bereft of numerals or negatives, the *k*-possessives are used, and the plural is shown by *mau: k-a-ʻu mau puke* 'my books'.)

## DEMONSTRATIVES

The three types of demonstratives are listed below.

|  | Near speaker | Near addressee | Far | Inter-rogative |
|---|---|---|---|---|
| *kē-* demonstratives | *kē-ia* 'this' | *kē-nā* 'that' | *kē-lā* 'that' |  |
| *pē-* demonstratives | *pe-nei, pē-ia* 'like this' | *pē-nā* 'like that' | *pē-lā* 'like that' | *pe-hea* 'how?' |
| zero- demonstratives | *ia* 'this' *nei* 'this, here, now' | *nā* 'that, there' | *lā, ala* 'there' *-lā* 'then' |  |

The *kē*-demonstratives, as well as the *k*-possessives and the articles *ka/ke*, may be called *k*-words. They fill the same positions in the noun phrase. All contain the same *k*-.

$$i \left\{ \begin{array}{l} ka \\ k\text{-}o\text{-}'u \\ k\bar{e}\text{-}ia \end{array} \right\} hale \qquad 'in \left\{ \begin{array}{l} the \\ my \\ this \end{array} \right\} house'$$

The *kē*-demonstratives have a link, not indicated by the translations in the table, with pronouns in that they often substitute for pronouns.

*Maikaʻi ʻoia* 'he is well'

*Maikaʻi kē-ia* 'this person is well; he (whom we have been discussing and who is nearby) is well'

The *pē*-demonstratives most commonly function as unmarked verbs: *pē-ia nō* 'just like this', *pe-hea ʻoe?* 'how are you?'

Note that the glosses of the difficult zero-demonstratives are demonstrative, locative, and (except for *nā*) temporal ('now, then'). *Ia* seems to be in a class by itself in that its only meaning is demonstrative and that it commonly *precedes* nouns and may substitute for nouns: *Maikaʻi ia mea* 'this thing is good'. *He maikaʻi ia* 'this is good'. *Ia* seems less specifically near the speaker than *nei*. *Nei*, extremely common, has the three types of meanings, and after nouns often carries a nuance of affection: *Hawaiʻi nei* 'this (beloved) Hawaiʻi'. Its temporal meaning is fairly common but comes near the end of verb phrases; note the famous lover's *ke kali nei au* 'I am now waiting here'. *Lā/ala* occurs in positions similar to those of *nei* but becomes a clitic *-la* in its temporal role: *ʻAi iho-la ʻoia* 'he then ate'. *Nā* seems not to have temporal functions and usually follows nouns. Both *nei* and *nā* (but not *lā/ala*) occasionally precede nouns.

Another demonstrative, *ua*$_2$, is pedantically translated 'aforementioned' but merely indicates that the noun head has already been mentioned. The noun is nearly always followed by the zero-demonstratives *nei, nā,* or *la: ua kanaka nei* 'this person (we've been talking about)'.

## 7. TRANSFORMATIONS

The manipulations that a native speaker unconsciously performs in his language may be termed transformations. This is a vast

subject. A Hawaiian transformational grammar is yet to be written. Only two types of transformations will be mentioned here:
concatenations (combining of more than one sentence into a single sentence) and fronting. The processes include substitution,
deletion, and transposition.

CONCATENATIONS

(a)     Replacement of *ua* by *i* (verb) *ai*.

> { *'Oia ka manawa* 'that's the time'
> { *Ua hele mai ke ali'i* 'the chief came'

> *'Oia ka manawa i hele mai ai ke ali'i* 'that's the time the
> chief came'.

The *ai* at the end of the final verb phrase refers to the previous
noun *manawa* 'time'. It is called by various writers relative, link-
ing, resultative, and anaphoric, and somewhat corresponds to
perhaps nonstandard English prepositions at the end of sentences such as "That's where it's at" or "Where are you going
to?"

(b)     Deletion of *mea* and replacement of *ua* by *i* and deletion
of the subject in the combined sentence.

> { *'O wau ka mea* 'I'm the person'
> { *Ua hele mai au* 'I came'

> *'O wau ka i hele mai* 'I'm the one who came'

(c)     Replacement of *ua* by *i* and transposition of a pronoun
(but rarely if ever a noun) subject.

> { *Ua hele au* 'I went'
> { *'A'ole* 'no'

> *'A'ole au i hele* 'I didn't go'

> { *Ua hele ke kanaka* 'the man went'
> { *'A'ole* 'no'

> *'A'ole i hele ke kanaka* 'the man didn't go'

FRONTING

A rule of Hawaiian syntax is that important things come first.
Nouns, for example, are followed by qualifiers, not preceded by

them, as in English. Alexander (1968:28) lists five ways to translate the English sentence "I give this to you," by fronting the phrase in focus.

One example will be given here.

Usual order: *Ua makemake nui au i kēlā mea* 'I liked that thing very much'.

To emphasize the object: *Kēlā oʻu mea i makemake nui ʻia* '*that's* what I liked very much'.

Another example of fronting is given at the end of the discussion of *k*-possessives in section 6.

## 8. NUMERALS

The cardinal numbers below 10 are as follows: 1 *kahi*, 2 *lua*, 3 *kolu*, 4 *hā*, 5 *lima*, 6 *ono*, 7 *hiku*, 8 *walu*, 9 *iwa*. These may be preceded by the general classifier *ʻe-* (or rarely *ʻa-*), usually separated by a slight pause (*ʻe íwa*, not *ʻéiwa).* *Kahi* 'one' is usually preceded by *hoʻo-.* Numbers above 9 have no classifying particles: 10 *ʻumi*, 11 *ʻumi-kūmā-kahi*, 12 *ʻumi-kūmā-lua*, 20 *ʻiwakā-lua*, 21 *ʻiwakālua-kūmā-kahi*, 30 *kana-kolu*, 40 *kana-hā*, 50 *kana-lima*, 60 *kana-ono*, 70 *kana-hiku*, 80 *kana-walu*, 90 *kana-iwa*. In Biblical usage *-kūmā-* is replaced by *-kumamā-*.

Formerly the vague numbers *lau, mano, kini,* and *lehu* were used for large numbers, or for 400, 4,000, 40,000, and 400,000, respectively. Missionaries introduced the terms *hanele* 'hundred', *kaukani* 'thousand', and *miliona* 'million', all from English.

The numeral interrogative *-hia* is usually preceded by *ʻe-.* *ʻE-hia āu puke?* 'How many books have you?' *ʻE-lua aʻu puke* 'I have two books'.

## 9. QUALIFYING PARTICLES

The qualifying particles may be listed in order of occurrence within the phrase. Those in group (a) below may precede *ʻia,* the passive/imperative marker. Those in group (b) end the phrase; several of them may occur in the same phrase but in the sequence indicated in the list. This is shown in figure 1.

(a)    *pū* 'together'
       *wale* 'so much, very, for no reason'

(b)   *nō*, intensifier
      *lā*₂, dubitative
      *na'e* 'yet'
      *ho'i*, intensifier
      *anei*, interrogative
      *paha* 'maybe, perhaps'
      *noho'i*, mild intensifier
      *ē*, intensifier

*Pū* in group (a) may precede *wale*. Most of the particles in group (b) may follow *wale* or *nō*. Common sequences are *wale nō* 'only' (*'elua wale nō* 'just two'), *nō na'e* (*mai-ka'i nō na'e* 'still pretty good'), *noho'i ē* (*aue noho'i ē!* 'Oh my!').

## 10. CONJUNCTIONS

Particles called conjunctions sometimes introduce simple sentences that have only one verb, and sometimes connect two simple sentences into a sentence with more than one verb. A few are listed here.

*ā* 'and, until, similar unto, like'
*āhea* 'when (interrogative future)'
*akā* 'but'
*i/iā/iō* 'when, at the time that, while'
*inā, i* 'if'
*ināhea* 'when (interrogative past)'
*kē* 'when (future)'
*'oiai, 'oi* 'while, at the time that'

## 11. LOANWORDS

Most of the hundreds of loanwords in Hawaiian are from English. The replacement of English phonemes by Hawaiian ones is in the main regular.

| English | Hawaiian |
|---------|----------|
| p, b, f | p |
| v, w | w |
| hw | hu |
| s, h, š | h |
| l, r | l |
| m | m |

| | |
|---|---|
| n, ŋ | n |
| t, d, θ, đ, s, z,<br> ž, tš, dž, k, g | k |
| y, i, ɪ | i |
| e, ɛ | e |
| æ, a, ɚ, ə, ʌ | a |
| ɔ, o, ɝ | o |
| ʊ, u | u |

As there are no consonant clusters in Hawaiian, English adjoining consonants are separated in Hawaiian by a vowel (*pūlumi* 'broom', *palaki* 'brush'), or one of the English consonants is deleted (*kila* 'steel', *Kapalakiko* 'San Francisco'). A vowel is added in Hawaiian to every word taken from English ending in a consonant (*poloka* 'frog'). Similarly, an initial glottal stop is added to every English word beginning with a vowel (*'alimakika* 'arithmetic' and *'īnika* 'ink'). Some loanwords follow English spelling rather than English sounds (*koma* 'comma', *hīmeni* 'hymn', *liona* 'lion').

Bible translators introduced words from Hebrew (*mula* 'myrrh'), Greek (*hepekoma* 'week'), and Latin (*Kaikala* 'Caesar'). Words from Chinese include *Pākē* 'Chinese' (*pai-kei),* and *pakalana* 'Chinese violet' (*pak-lan).* From Portuguese is *pakaliao* 'codfish' (*bacalhau).* From Tahitian are *mano'i* 'perfume' and *Lalako'a* 'Rarotonga' (*Raroto'a).*

SAMUEL H. ELBERT

# Given Names in Hawaiian

Before the arrival of the American missionaries in the early 1820s, the Hawaiians had no family names, and there was no difference in male and female names. The Hawaiians were required to adopt one of their father's names as a family name. This is why so many names in the telephone directory begin with K-, as in the articles *ka* and *ke*.

Today glottal stops precede initial vowels in Hawaiian entries, but these have been eliminated below so as to conform with established usage.

A few names from English have variant spellings: note Derryl (Darryl) in the list of names of males. Biblical names were popular in the revival days of Christianity, and the preferred spelling follows the new orthography.

## NAMES OF MALES

**Aaron.** Āʻālona, Aarona.
**Abel.** Apela, Abela.
**Abelard.** Apelaka, Abelada.
**Abiah.** Apia, Abia.
**Abiathar.** Apiakala, Apiekela, Abiatara.
**Abihu.** Apihu, Abihu.
**Abijah.** Apiʻia, Abiia.
**Abinadab.** Apinakapa, Abinadaba.
**Abiram.** Apilama, Abirama.
**Abishai.** Apikai, Abisai.
**Abner.** Apenela, Abenera.
**Abraham.** Apelahama, Aberahama.

**Abram.** Apelama, Aberama.
**Absalom.** Apekaloma, Abesaloma.
**Adam.** Akamu, Adamu.
**Adonijah.** Akoniʻia, Adoniia.
**Adoniram.** Akonilama, Adonirama.
**Adrian.** Akiliano, Adiriano.
**Adriel.** Akeliela, Aderiela.
**Agrippa.** Akelipa, Ageripa.
**Ahab.** Ahapa, Ahaba.
**Ahasuerus.** Ahakuelo, Ahasuero.
**Ahaz.** Ahaka, Ahaza.
**Ahaziah.** Ahakia, Ahazia.
**Ahiah.** Ahia.

**Ahimelech.** Ahimeleka.

**Aladdin.** Alakana, Aladana.

**Alan.** *Same as* **Allen.**

**Alban.** Alepana, Alebana.

**Albert.** Alapaki, Alabati.

**Alberto.** Alepako, Alebato.

**Alex.** Alika.

**Alexander.** Alekanekelo, Alekanedero.

**Alexis.** Aleki.

**Alfred.** Alepeleke, Aleferede, Alapai.

**Allen.** Alena.

**Aloysius.** Aloiki, Aloisi.

**Alton.** Alekona, Aletona.

**Alvin.** Alewina, Alevina.

**Ambrose.** Amapolokio, Amaborosio.

**Amos.** Amoka, Amosa.

**Ananias.** Anania.

**Anastasius.** Anakakio, Anatasio.

**Andre.** Anakalē, Anadare.

**Andrew.** Analū *(not Biblical);* Anekelea, Anederea *(Biblical).*

**Andros.** Anekaloka, Anedarosa.

**Anselm.** Anakelemo, Anaselemo.

**Anthony.** Akoni, Atoni; Anakoni, Anatoni *(Catholic).*

**Antone.** Akoni, Atoni.

**Apollo.** Apolo.

**Appolyon.** Apoluona.

**Archibald.** Ake.

**Archie.** Ake.

**Ariel.** Aliela, Ariela.

**Armand.** Amana; Alemana, Aremana.

**Artemas.** Alekema, Aretema.

**Arthur.** Aka, Ata.

**Asa.** Aka, Asa.

**Aser.** Akela, Asera.

**Ashur.** Akela, Asera.

**Aubert.** Aupeleke, Auberete.

**Aubrey.** Aupele, Aubere.

**August.** Aukake, Augate.

**Augustine.** Aukukino, Augutino.

**Augustus.** Aukukeko, Auguseto.

**Aurelius.** Aulelio, Aurelio.

**Aymar.** Aima.

**Azariah.** Akalia, Azaria.

**Ballam.** Pala'ama, Balaama.

**Barnabas.** Palenapa, Barenaba.

**Barsabbas.** Palekapa, Baresaba.

**Bartholomew.** Palekolomaio, Baretolomaio.

**Bartimaeus.** Pakimea, Batimea.

**Basil.** Pakile, Basile.

**Belshazzar.** Pelehakala, Belehazara.

**Ben.** Peni, Beni.

**Benedict.** Penekiko, Benedito.

**Benjamin.** Peni'amina, Beniamina.

**Bernard.** Pelenalako, Berenarado *(Catholic);* Pelenako *(not Catholic).*

**Bethuel.** Pekuela, Betuela.

**Bill.** Pila.

**Bob.** *Same as* **Robert.**

**Bonaventure.** Ponawenekula, Bonavenetura.

**Boniface.** Ponipake, Bonifake.

**Boyd.** Poe.

**Bruce.** Puluke, Buruse.

**Bruno.** Puluno, Buruno.

**Caesar.** Kaikala, Kaisara.

**Caiaphas.** Kai'apa.

**Cain.** Kaina.

**Caius.** Kaio.

**Caleb.** Kalepa, Kaleba.

**Calvin.** Kalawina, Kalavina.

**Carrolus.** Kalolo.

**Casimir.** Kasimilo.

**Casper.** Kakapa, Kasapa.
**Cecil.** Kekila, Kikila.
**Cedric.** Kekelika, Kederika.
**Celestino.** Kelekino, Keletino.
**Cephas.** Kepa.
**Charles.** Kale; Kalolo, Karolo
  *(Catholic)*.
**Christopher.** Kilikikopa,
  Kirisitopa.
**Chrysostom.** Kalekokome,
  Karesotome.
**Cicero.** Kikelo, Sisero.
**Clarence.** Kalalena, Kalarena.
**Claude.** Kalauka, Kalauda.
**Claudius.** Kelaukio, Kelaudio.
**Claus.** Kalauka, Kalausa.
**Clement.** Kelemeneke,
  Kelemenete.
**Clifton.** Kalipekona, Kalifetona.
**Clyde.** Kalaila, Kalaida.
**Constantine.** Konekākino,
  Konesatino.
**Cornelius.** Kolenelio, Korenelio.
**Crispus.** Kelikepo, Kerisepo.
**Cyprinus.** Kipiliano, Kipiriano.
**Cyril.** Kilila, Kirila.
**Cyrus.** Kulo, Kuro.
**Damasius.** Kamakio, Damasio.
**Dan.** Kana, Dana.
**Dana.** Kana, Dana.
**Daniel.** Kaniela, Daniela.
**Darius.** Kāliu, Dariu.
**David.** Kāwika, Davida; Kewiki.
**Demitrius.** Kemikilio, Demitirio.
**Dennis.** Kenika, Denisa.
**Derryl, Darryl.** Keli.
**Dick.** *Same as* **Richard.**
**Dionisius.** Kionikio, Dionisio.
**Domingo.** Kominiko, Dominigo.
**Dominik.** Kominiko, Dominiko.
**Don.** Kona, Dona.

**Douglas.** Koukakala, Dougalasa.
**Dwight.** Kuaika, Duaita.
**Eben.** Epena, Ebena.
**Ebenezer.** Epenekela, Ebenezera.
**Edgar.** Ekeka, Edega.
**Edmond.** Ekemona, Edemona;
  Ekumena, Edumena.
**Edward.** Ekewaka, Edewada;
  Ekualo, Eduaro *(Catholic)*.
**Edwin.** Eluene, Ailuene.
**Eleazar.** Eleakala, Eleazara.
**Eli.** Eli.
**Eliezer.** Eliekera, Eliezera.
**Elihu.** Elihū.
**Elijah.** Elia.
**Elisha.** Elikai, Elisai.
**Elmer.** Elema.
**Elroy.** Eleloe, Eleroe.
**Elton.** Elekona, Eletona.
**Emmanuel.** Emanuela.
**Enoch.** Enoka.
**Enos.** Enoka, Enosa.
**Ephraim.** Epelaima, Eperaima.
**Erasmus.** Elamo, Eramo.
**Erastus.** Elakeko, Eraseto.
**Eric.** Elika, Erika.
**Ernest.** Eleneki, Ereneti; Eneki,
  Eneti.
**Esau.** Ekau, Esau.
**Ethan.** Ekana, Etana.
**Eugene.** Iukini, Iugini.
**Eusebius.** Eukepio, Eusebio.
**Eustace.** Eukakio, Eutakio.
**Evaristus.** Ewaliko, Evarito.
**Ezekiel.** Ekekiela, Ezekiela.
**Ezra.** Ekela, Ezera.
**Fabian.** Papiano, Fabiano.
**Faustinus.** Paukekino, Fausetino.
**Felix.** Pelike, Felike.
**Ferdinand.** Pelekinako,
  Feredinado.

**Floyd.** Poloika, Foloida.
**Francis.** Palakiko, Farakiko.
**Francisco.** *Same as* **Francis.**
**Frank.** Palani, Farani.
**Franklin.** Pelanekelina,
Feranekelina.
**Fred.** Peleke, Ferede.
**Frederick.** *Same as* **Fred.**
**Gabriel.** Kapeliela, Gaberiela.
**Gamaliel.** Kamaliela, Gamaliela.
**Gelasius.** Kelakio, Gelasio.
**Geoffrey.** Keopele, Geofere.
**George.** Keoki, Geogi.
**Gerald.** Kelala, Gerala.
**Gideon.** Kileona, Kikeona,
Gideona.
**Gilbert.** Kilipaki, Gilibati;
Kilipeka, Gilibeta.
**Gilmore.** Kilemoa, Gilemoa.
**Goliath.** Kolia, Golia.
**Gordon.** Kolekona, Goredona.
**Greg.** Keli.
**Gregory.** Kelekolio, Geregorio.
**Gustav.** Kukakawe, Gusatave.
**Habakkuk.** Hapakuka, Habakuka.
**Haggai.** Hakai, Hagai.
**Ham.** Hama.
**Haman.** Hamana.
**Hannibal.** Hanipala, Hanibala.
**Hans.** Haneke, Hanese.
**Haran.** Halana, Harana.
**Harold.** Halola, Harola.
**Harry.** Hale, Hare.
**Hector.** Hekekā, Heketa.
**Henry.** Henelē, Hanalē; Heneli,
Heneri.
**Herbert.** Hapaki, Habati.
**Herman.** Helemano, Heremano.
**Herod.** Heloke, Herode.
**Hezekiah.** Hekekia, Hezekia;
Hezekea.

**Hilary.** Hilalio, Hilario.
**Hiram.** Hailama, Hairama;
Hilama; Hirama.
**Homer.** Hōmela, Homera.
**Honorius.** Honolio, Honorio.
**Horace.** Holeka, Horesa.
**Horatio.** Holakio.
**Hosea.** Hokea, Hosea.
**Howard.** Haoa.
**Hubert.** Hupeka, Hubeta.
**Hugh.** Hiu, Hiuwe.
**Hugo.** Huko, Hugo.
**Humbert.** Humepaka, Humebata;
Humepeleka, Humebereta.
**Ichabod.** Ikapoka, Ikaboda.
**Ignatius.** Iʻkenaki, Igenati.
**Innocent.** Inokene.
**Irving.** *Same as* **Irwin.**
**Irwin.** Iʻwini, Ivini.
**Isaac.** Ikaʻaka, Isaaka *(Biblical);*
Aikake *(not Biblical).*
**Isaiah.** Ikaia, Isaia.
**Ishmael.** Ikemaʻela, Isemaela.
**Isidore.** Ikikolo, Isidoro.
**Israel.** Ikelaʻela, Iseraela.
**Ivan.** Iwana, Ivana.
**Ivanhoe.** Iwanahō, Ivanaho.
**Jack.** Keaka.
**Jacob.** Iakopa, Iakoba.
**Jael.** Iaʻela.
**James.** Kimo; Iakopo, Iakobo.
**Japheth.** Iapeka, Iapeta.
**Jason.** Iakona, Iasona.
**Jared.** Ialeka, Iareda.
**Jasper.** Iakepa, Iasepa.
**Jehu.** Iehu.
**Jephthah.** Iepeka, Iepeta.
**Jeremiah.** Ielemia, Ieremia.
**Jerome.** Ielome, Ierome;
Hieronimo *(Catholic).*
**Jesse.** Ieke, Iese.

**Jesus.** Ieku, Iesu.
**Jethro.** Iekelo, Ietero.
**Jim.** Kimo.
**Joaquin.** Iōkina; Wākina.
**Job.** Iopa, Ioba.
**Joe.** Keō.
**Joel.** Io'ela.
**John.** Keoni *(not Biblical);* Ioane *(Biblical).*
**Jonah.** Iona.
**Jonathan.** Ionakana, Ionatana.
**Jose.** Hokē, Hose.
**Joseph.** Iokepa, Iosepa; Iokewe, Ioseve *(Catholic).*
**Joshua.** Iokua, Iosua.
**Josiah.** Iokia, Iosia.
**Jotham.** Iokama.
**Juan.** Huanu.
**Judah.** Iuka, Iuda.
**Jules.** Kiule.
**Julian.** Kuliano.
**Julius.** Iulio.
**Jupiter.** Iupika, Iupita.
**Justin.** Iukekini, Iusetini.
**Justinian.** Kukiniano, Iutiniano.
**Kelvin.** Kelewina, Kelevina.
**Kenneth.** Keneke, Kenete; Keneki, Keneti.
**Kevin.** Kewini.
**Laban.** Lapana, Labana.
**Lamech.** Lameka.
**Lawrence.** Lauleneke, Laurenete; Lowene.
**Lazarus.** Lakalo, Lazaro.
**Lemuel.** Lemuela.
**Leo.** Leone.
**Leonard.** Leonaka, Leonada.
**Leopold.** Leopolo.
**Levi.** Lewi, Liwai.
**Liberius.** Lipelio, Liberio.
**Libert.** Lipeleko, Libereto.

**Linus.** Lino.
**Lionel.** Laionela.
**Lloyd.** Loeka, Loeda.
**Lorenzo.** Loleneko, Lorenezo.
**Lorin.** Lolina.
**Lot.** Loka, Lota.
**Louis.** Lui.
**Lucifer.** Lukipela, Lukipera.
**Lucius.** Lukio.
**Luke.** Luka.
**Luther.** Lukela, Lutera.
**Mahlon.** Mahelona.
**Malachi.** Malaki.
**Malcolm.** Malakoma.
**Manasseh.** Manake, Manase.
**Manoah.** Manoa.
**Manuel.** Manuela.
**Marcellus.** Malakelo.
**Marion.** Maliona, Mariona.
**Mark.** Maleko, Mareko.
**Matthew.** Makaio, Mataio.
**Matthias.** Makia, Matia.
**Maximus.** Makimo.
**Melchizedek.** Melekikekeka, Melekizedeka.
**Melvin.** Melewina, Melevina.
**Mephibosheth.** Mepipokeka, Mepiboseta.
**Methuselah.** Mekukala, Metusala.
**Micah.** Mika.
**Michael.** Mika'ele, Mikala.
**Michal.** Mikala.
**Michel.** Mikala.
**Miguel.** Mikuela, Miguela.
**Mike.** *Same as* **Michael.**
**Mohammed.** Mohameka, Mohameda.
**Mordecai.** Molekekai, Moredekai.
**Moses.** Moke, Mose.

**Naaman.** Naʻamana.
**Nabal.** Napala, Nabala.
**Nahor.** Nahola, Nahora.
**Napoleon.** Napoliana,
Napoliona.
**Nathan.** Nakana, Natana.
**Nathaniel.** Nakanaʻela.
**Nebuchadnezzar.** Nepukaneka,
Nebukaneza; Nebukadeneza.
**Ned.** Neki, Nedi.
**Nehemiah.** Nehemia.
**Nero.** Nelo, Nero.
**Nicholas.** Nikolao; Nikolo.
**Nicodemus.** Nikokemo,
Nikodemo.
**Noah.** Noa.
**Noel.** Noela.
**Norbert.** Nolepeleko, Norebereto.
**Norman.** Nolemana, Noremana;
Nōmana.
**Obadiah.** Opakia, Obadia.
**Obed.** Opeka, Obeda.
**Oliver.** Oliwa, Oliva.
**Oscar.** Oka.
**Oswald.** Okewoleka, Osewoleda.
**Patrick.** Pakelika, Paterika.
**Paul.** Paulo.
**Pedro.** Pekelo, Petero.
**Percy.** Peleki, Peresi.
**Peter.** Pekelo, Petero; Pika *(not
Biblical)*.
**Philemon.** Pilemona, Filemona.
**Phillip.** Pilipo.
**Phineas.** Pinehaka, Pinehasa.
**Pilate.** Pilako, Pilato.
**Pius.** Pio.
**Polycarp.** Polikape.
**Pomponius.** Pomeponio.
**Potiphar.** Pokipala, Potipara.
**Ptolemy.** Petolomai.
**Quentin.** Kuenekina, Kuenetina.

**Ralph.** Lalepa, Ralepa.
**Raphael.** Lapaʻela, Rafaela;
Lapaʻele, Rafaele.
**Ray.** Lei, Rei.
**Raymond.** Leimana; Remone.
**Rechab.** Lekapa, Rekaba.
**Reginald.** Lekinala, Reginala.
**Rehoboam.** Lehopoama,
Rehoboama.
**Reuben.** Leʻupena, Reubena.
**Reuel.** Leuela, Reuela.
**Richard.** Likeke, Rikeke.
**Robert.** Lopaka, Robata.
**Robin.** Lopine, Robine.
**Rodney.** Lokenē, Rodene.
**Roger.** Lōkela, Rogera.
**Roland.** Lolana, Rolana.
**Rolin.** Lolina, Rolina.
**Romeo.** Lomiō, Romio.
**Romulus.** Lomulu, Romulu.
**Rufus.** Lupe, Rufe; Rupo.
**Rupert.** Lupeko, Rupeto.
**Salathiel.** Kalakiela, Salatiela.
**Samson.** Kamekona, Samesona.
**Samuel.** Kamuela, Samuela.
**Saul.** Kaulo, Saulo.
**Sebastian.** Kepakiano,
Sebatiano; Pakiana.
**Sergius.** Kelekio, Seregio.
**Seth.** Keka, Seta.
**Shadrach.** Kakelaka, Saderaka.
**Shem.** Kema, Sema.
**Sidney.** Kikinē; Kikanē.
**Silas.** Kila, Sila.
**Simeon.** Kimeona, Simeona.
**Simon.** Kimona, Simona.
**Simplicius.** Kimipilikio,
Simipilikio.
**Socrates.** Kokalakē, Sokarate.
**Solomon.** Kolomona, Solomona.
**Stanislaus.** Kanilao, Tanilao.

**Stanley.** Kanalē, Sanale.

**Stephen.** Kepano, Tepano
*(Catholic);* Kekepana, Setepana
*(Protestant).*

**Steven.** Kiwini, Tivini.

**Tarzan.** Kakana.

**Ted.** *Same as* **Theodore.**

**Tertius.** Kelekio, Teretio.

**Thaddeus.** Kakaio, Tadaio.

**Theodore.** Keokolo, Teodoro
*(Catholic);* Keokoa, Teodoa.

**Theophilus.** Keopilo, Teopilo.

**Thomas.** Koma, Toma; Kamaki.

**Timothy.** Kimokeo, Timoteo.

**Titus.** Kiko, Tito.

**Tobias.** Kopia, Tobia.

**Tom.** Koma, Toma. *Tom Thumb,*
Koma Kamu.

**Ulrich.** Ulaliko, Ulariko.

**Ulysses.** Uleki, Ulesi.

**Uriah.** Ulia, Uria.

**Uriel.** Uliela, Uriela.

**Valentine.** Walenekino, Valene-
tino; Walekino, Walakino.

**Valerian.** Waleliano, Valeriano.

**Vernon.** Wenona, Venona.

**Victor.** Wikoli, Vitori.

**Victorinus.** Wikolino, Vitorino.

**Vincent.** Winikeneke,
Vinikeneke.

**Virgil.** Wilikilia, Virigilia.

**Waldemar.** Waledema.

**Walter.** Walaka, Walata.

**Warren.** Walena, Warena.

**Wilbert.** Wilipaki, Wilibati.

**Wilford.** Wilepoka, Wilefoda.

**Wilfred.** Wilipeleke, Wileferede.

**Wilhelm.** Wilehailama.

**Willard.** Wilika, Wilida.

**William.** Wiliama, Uilama.

**Willie.** Wile.

**Wilmore.** Wilemoa.

**Winfred.** Winipeleke, Winiferede.

**Zacchaeus.** Kakaio, Zakaio.

**Zacharias.** Kakalia, Zakaria.

**Zadok.** Kakoka, Zadoka.

**Zebedee.** Kepekaio, Zebedaio.

**Zebulun.** Kepuluna, Zebuluna.

**Zedekiah.** Kekekia, Zedekia.

**Zepherin.** Kepelino, Zeferino;
Kepilino.

**Zerubabel.** Kelupapela,
Zerubabela.

**Zorobabel.** Kolopapela,
Zorobabela.

# NAMES OF FEMALES

**Abbie.** Apī.

**Abigail.** Apika'ila, Abigaila.

**Abishag.** Apikaka, Abisaga.

**Ada.** Aka.

**Adelaide.** Akelaika, Adelaida.

**Adeline.** Akelina, Adelina.

**Adella.** Akela, Adela.

**Agatha.** Akaka, Agata.

**Agnes.** Akeneki, Ageneti.

**Ahinoam.** Ahinoama.

**Ailene.** Ailina.

**Alberta.** Alepeka, Alebeta.

**Alethia.** Alekia, Aletia.

**Alexandria.** Alekanekalia,
Alekanedaria.

**Alexandrina.** Alekanekelina,
Alekanederina.

**Alice.** Aleka, Alesa.

**Alma.** Alema.

**Almira.** Alamila, Alamira.

**Alvina.** Alawina, Alavina.
**Amanda.** Amanaka, Amanada.
**Amelia.** Amelia.
**Amy.** Eme.
**Anastasia.** Anakakia, Anatasia.
**Andrea.** Anakalia, Anadaria.
**Angela.** Ānela.
**Anita.** Anika, Anita.
**Anitra.** Anikala, Anitara.
**Ann.** Ana.
**Anna.** Ana.
**Annabelle.** Anapela, Anabela.
**Annette.** Aneka, Aneta.
**Annie.** Ane.
**Antoinette.** Anakonia, Anatonia.
**Antonia.** *Same as* **Antoinette.**
**Arabella.** Alapela, Arabela.
**Asenath.** Akenaka, Asenata.
**Athalia.** Akalia, Atalia.
**Audrey.** Aukele, Audere.
**Augusta.** Aukaka, Augata.
**Aurelia.** Aulelia, Aurelia.
**Aurora.** Alola, Arora.
**Barbara.** Palapala, Barabára.
**Bathsheba.** Pakekepa, Bateseba.
**Beatrice.** Peakalika, Beatarisa;
  Piakilika, Biatirisa.
**Becky.** Peke.
**Bella.** Pela, Bela.
**Belle.** *Same as* **Bella.**
**Bernadette.** Pelenakeka,
  Berenadeta.
**Bernadine.** Pelenakino,
  Berenadino.
**Bernice.** Berenike.
**Bertha.** Peleka, Bereta.
**Beryl.** Pelulo, Berulo.
**Beth.** *Same as* **Elizabeth.**
**Betty.** Peke.
**Beulah.** Peula, Beula.
**Bilhah.** Pileha, Bileha.

**Bonnie.** Poni.
**Bridget.** Pilikika, Birigita.
**Carlotta.** Kaloka, Kalota.
**Carmelia.** Kamelia; Komela,
  Pua-komela.
**Carmen.** Kalamela.
**Carmilla.** Kamila.
**Carol.** Kālola, Karola.
**Caroline.** Kalolaina, Karolaina;
  Kalalaina, Karalaina;
  Kealalaina.
**Catherine.** Kakalina, Katarina.
**Cecelia.** Kikilia, Sisilia; Kekilia,
  Sesilia.
**Celestine.** Kelekina, Keletina.
**Celia.** Kilia.
**Charlotte.** Halaki, Harati;
  Kaloke, Kalote.
**Cheryl (Sheryl).** Kelia.
**Chloe.** Koloe.
**Christina.** Kilikina, Kiritina.
**Christine.** *Same as* **Christina.**
**Christophine.** Kilikipine,
  Kirisipine.
**Cinderella.** Kinikalela, Kinidarela.
**Clara.** Kalala, Kalara.
**Clarice.** Kalalika, Kalarisa.
**Claudia.** Kalaukia, Kalaudia;
  Kelaukia, Kelaudia.
**Claudine.** Kalaukina, Kalaudina.
**Cleopatra.** Kaleopakala,
  Kaleopatara.
**Clotilda.** Kelokilaka, Kelotilada.
**Cobina.** Kopina, Kobina.
**Consuelo.** Konokuelo,
  Konosuelo.
**Cordelia.** Kokelia, Kodelia.
**Corinne.** Kolina, Korina.
**Cornelia.** Kolenelia, Korenelia.
**Cynthia.** Kinikia, Kinitia, Sinitia.
**Dagmar.** Kakamā, Dagama.

**Dawn.** Wana'ao.
**Deborah.** Kepola, Debora.
**Delia.** Kelia, Delia.
**Deliah.** *Same as* **Delia.**
**Della.** Kela, Dela.
**Delphine.** Kelepine, Delepine.
**Denise.** Kenike, Denise.
**Diana.** Kiana, Diana.
**Dinah.** Kina, Dina.
**Dolores.** Kololeke, Dolorese.
**Dora.** Kola.
**Dorcas.** Koleka, Doreka.
**Doreen.** Kōlina, Dorina.
**Doris.** Kolika, Dorisa.
**Dorothy.** Kolokea, Dorotea, Kōleka.
**Drusilla.** Kelaukila, Derausila.
**Edith.** Ekika, Edita.
**Edna.** Ekena, Edena.
**Edwina.** Eluina, Eluena.
**Eilene.** Ailina.
**Elaine.** Ileina.
**Elberta.** Elepeka, Elebeta.
**Eleanor.** Elenola, Elenora; Elenoa.
**Eliza.** Laika.
**Elizabeth.** Elikapeka, Elisabeta; Kapeka.
**Ella.** Ela.
**Ellen.** Elena.
**Elmira.** Elemila, Elemira.
**Eloise.** Eloika, Eloisa.
**Elsie.** Eleki, Elesi.
**Elvira.** Elewila, Elewira, Elevira.
**Emelia.** Emelia, Emalia.
**Emily.** Emelē.
**Emma.** Ema.
**Emmaline.** Emalaina.
**Erica.** Elika, Erika.
**Ernestine.** Elenekina, Erenetina.
**Estelle.** Ekekela, Esetela.

**Esther.** Ekekela, Esetera.
**Ethel.** Ekela, Etela.
**Eugenia.** Iukinia, Iuginia; Iukina, Iugina.
**Eulalie.** Ulalia; Iulalia.
**Eunice.** Eunike; Iunia.
**Euphemia.** Eupemia.
**Eva.** Īwa.
**Evangeline.** Ewanekelina, Evanegelina.
**Eve.** Ewa.
**Evelyn.** Ewalina, Evalina.
**Faith.** Mana'o'i'o.
**Fanny.** Pane, Fane.
**Faustina.** Paukekina, Fausetina.
**Fidelia.** Pikelia, Fidelia.
**Flora.** Polola, Folora.
**Florence.** Pololena, Folorena.
**Florinda.** Pelolina, Felorina.
**Frances.** Palakika, Farakika.
**Freda.** Pelika, Ferida.
**Georgiana.** Keokiana, Geogiana.
**Georgina.** Keokina, Geogina.
**Gertrude.** Kekaluka, Getaruda; Kelekuluke, Gereturude *(Catholic).*
**Gloria.** Kololia, Goloria.
**Hagar.** Hakala, Haraga.
**Hannah.** Hana.
**Harriet.** Haliaka, Hariata.
**Hazel.** Hakela, Hazela.
**Heidi.** Heiki.
**Helen.** Helena, Helene, Helina.
**Helena.** Helena.
**Henrietta.** Heneliaka, Heneriata.
**Hepzibah.** Hepeziba.
**Herodias.** Helokia, Herodia.
**Hester.** Hekekela, Hesetera; Hekeka, Heseta.
**Hettie.** Heke, Hete; Heki, Heti.
**Hilaria.** Hilalia.

**Hilda.** Hileka, Hileda.
**Hope.** Mana'olana.
**Hortense.** Holekeneke, Horetenese.
**Hulda.** Huleka, Huleda.
**Ida.** Aika, Aida.
**Ina.** Aina.
**Inez.** Aineki, Ainesi.
**Irene.** Ailina, Airina.
**Isabelle.** Ikapela, Isabela.
**Jane.** Kini.
**Janet.** Ianeke, Ianete.
**Jean.** Kini.
**Jennie.** Kini.
**Jennifer.** Ienipa.
**Jerusha.** Keluka, Kerusa.
**Jezebel.** Iezebela.
**Joan, Joann, Jo Ann.** Iō'ana, Koana.
**Johanna.** Iō'ana, Koana.
**Josephine.** Iokepine, Iosepine.
**Joyce.** Ioke.
**Juanita.** Wanika, Wanita.
**Judith.** Iukika, Iudita.
**Julia.** Iulia, Kulia.
**Julianna.** Kuliana.
**Juliette.** Kuliana.
**June.** Iune.
**Juno.** Iuno.
**Justina.** Iukikina, Iusitina.
**Karen.** Kalini.
**Kate.** Keke.
**Katherine.** *See* **Catherine.**
**Kathleen.** Kakalina, Katalina.
**Katie.** Keke, Kete.
**Keturah.** Kekula, Ketura.
**Kim (Kym).** Kimi.
**Laura.** Lala, Lara.
**Leah.** Lea.
**Lena.** Lina.
**Leonora.** Leonola, Leonora.

**Letitia.** Lekikia, Letitia.
**Libbie.** Lipe, Libe.
**Liberta.** Lipeka, Libeta.
**Lillian.** Liliana.
**Lily.** Lilia.
**Linda.** Lika.
**Lois.** Loika, Loisa.
**Lolita.** Lolika, Lolita.
**Loretta.** Loleka, Loreta.
**Lorraine.** Loleina, Loreina.
**Louisa.** Luika, Luisa.
**Louise.** *See* **Louisa.**
**Lucia.** Lukia, Lusia.
**Lucille.** Lukila, Lusila.
**Lucinda.** Lukina, Lusina.
**Lucy.** Luke, Luse; Lukia.
**Lydia.** Lukia, Ludia; Lulia.
**Mabel.** Meipala, Meibala.
**Madeline.** Makelina, Madelina.
**Malvina.** Malawina, Malavina.
**Mamie.** Mame.
**Marcella.** Mākela, Masela.
**Margaret.** Makaleka, Magareta.
**Marguerite.** Makalika, Magarita.
**Maria.** Malaea, Maraea.
**Marian.** Maliana, Mariana.
**Marianne.** *Same as* **Maryann.**
**Marie.** Malia, Maria.
**Marietta.** Meliaka, Meriata; Maliaka, Mariata.
**Marilda.** Malilaka, Marilada.
**Marilyn.** Melelina, Merelina.
**Marlene.** Malina.
**Martha.** Maleka, Mareta *(Biblical);* Malaka, Marata *(Catholic).*
**Martina.** Malakina, Maratina.
**Mary.** Malia, Maria *(Biblical);* Mele, Mere.
**Maryann.** Meleana, Mereana.
**May.** Mei.
**Maybelle.** Meipela, Meibela.

**Melissa.** Melika, Melisa.
**Mercedes.** Mekeke, Mesede.
**Michelle.** Mikala.
**Milcah.** Mileka.
**Mildred.** Milikeleka, Milidereda.
**Millicent.** Milikena, Milisena.
**Millie.** Mile.
**Minerva.** Minewa, Mineva.
**Minnie.** Mine.
**Miriam.** Miliama, Miriama.
**Mona.** Mona.
**Monica.** Monika.
**Muriel.** Miuliela, Miuriela.
**Myra.** Maila, Maira.
**Myrna.** Milena, Mirena.
**Myrtle.** Makala, Matala.
**Nancy.** Naneki.
**Nanette.** Naneka, Naneta.
**Naomi.** Naomi.
**Nathalie.** Nakeli, Nateli.
**Nell.** *Same as* **Nellie.**
**Nellie.** Nele.
**Nettie.** Neki, Neti.
**Nina.** Nina.
**Nora.** Nola, Nora.
**Noreen.** Nolina, Norina.
**Norma.** Noma.
**Olga.** Oleka, Olega.
**Olive.** Oliwa, Oliva.
**Olivia.** Oliwia, Olivia.
**Olympia.** Olumepia.
**Orpah.** Orepa.
**Orpha.** Olepa, Orepa.
**Pamela.** Pamila.
**Pansy.** Pāneki.
**Patience.** Ahonui.
**Patricia.** Pakelekia, Paterekia.
**Paulette.** Poleke, Polete.
**Pauline.** Polina.
**Pearl.** Momi.
**Persis.** Peleki, Peresi.

**Phillipa.** Pilipa.
**Philomena.** Pilomena, Pilomina.
**Phoebe.** Pō'ipe.
**Phyllis.** Piliki.
**Polly.** Pole.
**Portia.** Polekia, Poretia.
**Priscilla.** Pelekila, Peresila;
  Peresekila.
**Prudence.** Pelukena, Perudena.
**Rachel.** Lāhela, Rahela.
**Rahab.** Lahapa, Rahaba.
**Rebecca.** Lepeka, Rebeka.
**Reina.** Leina.
**Rena.** Lina, Rina.
**Rhoda.** Loke, Rode.
**Roberta.** Lopeka, Robeta.
**Romelia.** Lomelia, Romelia.
**Rosa.** Loka, Rosa.
**Rosabelle.** Lokapela, Rosabela.
**Rosalie.** Lōkālia, Rosalia.
**Rosamond.** Lokamona,
  Rosamona.
**Rose.** Loke, Rose.
**Roselind.** Lokelina, Roselina.
**Rosemary.** Lokemele, Rosemere.
**Rosina.** Lokina.
**Rowena.** Lowena, Rowena.
**Ruby.** Lupe, Rube.
**Ruth.** Luka, Ruta.
**Sally.** Kāle, Sale.
**Salome.** Kalome, Salome.
**Sandra.** Kala.
**Sarah.** Kala, Sara; Kela, Sera.
**Sarai.** Kalai.
**Selina.** Kelina.
**Serah.** Sera.
**Sharon.** Kalana.
**Sibyl.** Kipila, Sibila.
**Sonya.** Kōnia, Sonia.
**Sophia.** Kopia, Sofia; Kopaea,
  Sofaea.

**Stephanie.** Kekepania, Setepania.

**Susan.** Kukana, Susana.

**Susannah.** *Same as* **Susan.**

**Susie.** Kuke, Suse.

**Sybil.** Kepila, Sebila.

**Sylvia.** Kiliwia, Silivia.

**Tabitha.** Kapika, Tabita.

**Tallulah.** Kalula, Talula.

**Tamar.** Kamala, Tamara.

**Theresa.** Keleka, Teresa.

**Therese.** Kelekia, Teresia.

**Thomasine.** Komakina, Tomasina.

**Toy.** Milimili.

**Tryphena.** Kelupaina, Terupaina.

**Ulrica.** Ulalika, Ularika.

**Ursula.** Ulukula, Urusula.

**Valeria.** Walelia, Valeria.

**Vera.** Wila, Vira.

**Verna.** Welena, Verena.

**Veronika.** Walonika, Varonika, Walanika, Welonika.

**Victoria.** Wikolia, Vitoria.

**Viola.** Waiola.

**Violet.** Waioleka, Vaioleta.

**Virginia.** Wilikinia, Virginia.

**Vivian.** Wiwiana, Viviana.

**Wanda.** Wanaka.

**Wilhelmina.** Wilemina.

**Willa.** Wīla.

**Winifred.** Winipeleke, Winiferede.

**Yolanda.** Iolana.

**Yvonne.** Iwone, Ivone.

**Zenobia.** Kenopia, Zenobia.

**Zilpah.** Kilepa, Zilepa.

**Ziporah.** Kipola, Zipora.

Hawaiian names popular with women: Noelani (heavenly mist),
Pua (flower) (also used by males), Pualani (royal flower,
heavenly flower), Puanani (beautiful flower).

# References

Alexander, W. D. *A Short Synopsis of the Most Essential Points in Hawaiian Grammar.* Rutland, Vt.: Charles E. Tuttle Co., 1968. (First published in 1864).

Biggs, Bruce. *Let's Learn Maori, a Guide to the Study of the Maori Language.* Wellington: A. H. and A. W. Reed, 1969.

Elbert, Samuel H., and Mary Kawena Pukui. *Hawaiian Grammar.* Honolulu: The University Press of Hawaii, 1979.

Nishizawa, Yu Mapuana. *Hawaiian-Japanese Dictionary.* Translation of the Hawaiian-English section of *The Pocket Hawaiian Dictionary* by Mary Kawena Pukui, Samuel H. Elbert, and Esther T. Mookini. Tokyo: Chikura Shobo, 1990.

Pukui, Mary Kawena. *'Ōlelo No'eau: Hawaiian Sayings and Poetical Sayings.* Honolulu: Bernice P. Bishop Museum Special Publication 71, 1983.

Pukui, Mary Kawena, and Samuel H. Elbert. *Hawaiian Dictionary: Hawaiian-English, English-Hawaiian.* Honolulu: University of Hawaii Press, 1986.

Pukui, Mary Kawena, Samuel H. Elbert, and Esther T. Mookini. *The Pocket Hawaiian Dictionary, with a Concise Hawaiian Grammar.* Honolulu: The University Press of Hawaii, 1975.

————. *Pocket Place Names of Hawai'i.* Honolulu: University of Hawaii Press, 1989.

Wagner, Warren L., Derral R. Herbst, and S. H. Sohmer. *Manual of the Flowering Plants of Hawai'i.* 2 vols. Honolulu: University of Hawaii Press and Bishop Museum Press.

Wilson, William H. "The *o/a* Distinction in Hawaiian Possessives." *Oceanic Linguistics* 15:39–50.